Handbook of Research on the Global Empowerment of Educators and Student Learning Through Action Research

Alina Slapac
University of Missouri-St. Louis, USA

Phyllis Balcerzak
University of Missouri-St.Louis, USA

Kathryn O'Brien
University of Missouri-St.Louis, USA

A volume in the Advances in Educational Technologies and Instructional Design (AETID) Book Series

Published in the United States of America by
IGI Global
Information Science Reference (an imprint of IGI Global)
701 E. Chocolate Avenue
Hershey PA, USA 17033
Tel: 717-533-8845
Fax: 717-533-8661
E-mail: cust@igi-global.com
Web site: http://www.igi-global.com

Copyright © 2021 by IGI Global. All rights reserved. No part of this publication may be reproduced, stored or distributed in any form or by any means, electronic or mechanical, including photocopying, without written permission from the publisher. Product or company names used in this set are for identification purposes only. Inclusion of the names of the products or companies does not indicate a claim of ownership by IGI Global of the trademark or registered trademark.

Library of Congress Cataloging-in-Publication Data

Names: Slapac, Alina, 1973- editor. | Balcerzak, Phyllis, 1954- editor. |
   O'Brien, Kathryn G., 1952- editor.
Title: Handbook of research on the global empowerment of educators and student
   learning through action research / Alina Slapac, Phyllis Balcerzak, Kathryn
   G. O'Brien, editors.
Description: Hershey, PA : Information Science Reference, [2021] | Includes
   bibliographical references and index. | Summary: "This book provides
   teachers, faculty and educational leaders with an opportunity to share
   their recent research with focus on best teaching practices through the
   use of online platforms"-- Provided by publisher.
Identifiers: LCCN 2021009741 (print) | LCCN 2021009742 (ebook) | ISBN
   9781799869221 (hardcover) | ISBN 9781799869245 (ebook)
Subjects: LCSH: Action research in education. | Effective
   teaching--Research. | Computer-assisted instruction.
Classification: LCC LB1028.24 .A262 2021 (print) | LCC LB1028.24 (ebook)
   | DDC 370.72--dc23
LC record available at https://lccn.loc.gov/2021009741
LC ebook record available at https://lccn.loc.gov/2021009742

This book is published in the IGI Global book series Advances in Educational Technologies and Instructional Design (AETID) (ISSN: 2326-8905; eISSN: 2326-8913)

British Cataloguing in Publication Data
A Cataloguing in Publication record for this book is available from the British Library.

All work contributed to this book is new, previously-unpublished material. The views expressed in this book are those of the authors, but not necessarily of the publisher.

For electronic access to this publication, please contact: eresources@igi-global.com.

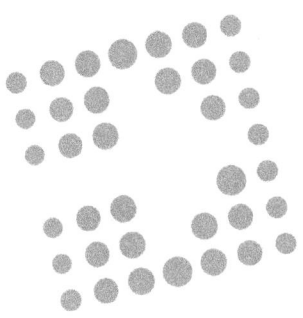

Advances in Educational Technologies and Instructional Design (AETID) Book Series

Lawrence A. Tomei
Robert Morris University, USA

ISSN:2326-8905
EISSN:2326-8913

Mission

Education has undergone, and continues to undergo, immense changes in the way it is enacted and distributed to both child and adult learners. In modern education, the traditional classroom learning experience has evolved to include technological resources and to provide online classroom opportunities to students of all ages regardless of their geographical locations. From distance education, Massive-Open-Online-Courses (MOOCs), and electronic tablets in the classroom, technology is now an integral part of learning and is also affecting the way educators communicate information to students.

The **Advances in Educational Technologies & Instructional Design (AETID) Book Series** explores new research and theories for facilitating learning and improving educational performance utilizing technological processes and resources. The series examines technologies that can be integrated into K-12 classrooms to improve skills and learning abilities in all subjects including STEM education and language learning. Additionally, it studies the emergence of fully online classrooms for young and adult learners alike, and the communication and accountability challenges that can arise. Trending topics that are covered include adaptive learning, game-based learning, virtual school environments, and social media effects. School administrators, educators, academicians, researchers, and students will find this series to be an excellent resource for the effective design and implementation of learning technologies in their classes.

Coverage

- Digital Divide in Education
- K-12 Educational Technologies
- Adaptive Learning
- Hybrid Learning
- Collaboration Tools
- Web 2.0 and Education
- Virtual School Environments
- Curriculum Development
- Higher Education Technologies
- Educational Telecommunications

IGI Global is currently accepting manuscripts for publication within this series. To submit a proposal for a volume in this series, please contact our Acquisition Editors at Acquisitions@igi-global.com or visit: http://www.igi-global.com/publish/.

The Advances in Educational Technologies and Instructional Design (AETID) Book Series (ISSN 2326-8905) is published by IGI Global, 701 E. Chocolate Avenue, Hershey, PA 17033-1240, USA, www.igi-global.com. This series is composed of titles available for purchase individually; each title is edited to be contextually exclusive from any other title within the series. For pricing and ordering information please visit http://www.igi-global.com/book-series/advances-educational-technologies-instructional-design/73678. Postmaster: Send all address changes to above address. Copyright © 2021 IGI Global. All rights, including translation in other languages reserved by the publisher. No part of this series may be reproduced or used in any form or by any means – graphics, electronic, or mechanical, including photocopying, recording, taping, or information and retrieval systems – without written permission from the publisher, except for non commercial, educational use, including classroom teaching purposes. The views expressed in this series are those of the authors, but not necessarily of IGI Global.

Titles in this Series

For a list of additional titles in this series, please visit: www.igi-global.com/book-series/advances-educational-technologies-instructional-design/73678

Acquiring Learning Skills With Digital Technology
Charles Westerberg (Beloit College, USA) and Tom McBride (Beloit College, USA)
Information Science Reference • © 2021 • 148pp • H/C (ISBN: 9781799844266) • US $175.00

Emerging Realities and the Future of Technology in the Classroom
Inaya Jaafar (The Chicago School of Professional Psychology, USA) and James M. Pedersen (Delaware Valley University, USA)
Information Science Reference • © 2021 • 338pp • H/C (ISBN: 9781799864806) • US $195.00

Leading Schools With Social, Emotional, and Academic Development (SEAD)
Tara Madden-Dent (Sierra Nevada University, USA) and Deborah Oliver (National University, USA & Mindful SEAD, USA)
Information Science Reference • © 2021 • 336pp • H/C (ISBN: 9781799867289) • US $195.00

Simulation and Game-Based Learning in Emergency and Disaster Management
Nicole K. Drumhiller (American Public University System, USA) Terri L. Wilkin (American Public University System, USA) and Karen V. Srba (Saint Francis University, USA)
Information Science Reference • © 2021 • 290pp • H/C (ISBN: 9781799840879) • US $195.00

Applications of Work Integrated Learning Among Gen Z and Y Students
Trevor Gerhardt (University of West London, UK) and Paulette J. Annon (London School of Economics, UK)
Business Science Reference • © 2021 • 345pp • H/C (ISBN: 9781799864400) • US $215.00

Career Ready Education Through Experiential Learning
Karen Rasmussen (University of West Florida, USA) Pamela Northrup (University of West Florida, USA) and Robin Colson (University of West Florida, USA)
Information Science Reference • © 2021 • 305pp • H/C (ISBN: 9781799819288) • US $195.00

Advancing the Power of Learning Analytics and Big Data in Education
Ana Azevedo (CEOS:PP, ISCAP, Polytechnic of Porto, Portugal) José Manuel Azevedo (CEOS:PP, ISCAP, Polytechnic of Porto, Portugal) James Onohuome Uhomoibhi (Ulster University, UK) and Ebba Ossiannilsson (International Council for Open and Distance Education (ICDE), Norway & European Distance and e-Learning Network (EDEN), UK & Swedish Association for Distance Education (SADE), Sweden)
Information Science Reference • © 2021 • 296pp • H/C (ISBN: 9781799871033) • US $195.00

701 East Chocolate Avenue, Hershey, PA 17033, USA
Tel: 717-533-8845 x100 • Fax: 717-533-8661
E-Mail: cust@igi-global.com • www.igi-global.com

Editorial Advisory Board

Sally Durand, *Augsburg University, USA*
Margaret Finders, *Augsburg University, USA*
Nicole M. Houser, *Rutgers University, USA*
Virginia Navarro, *University of Missouri-St. Louis, USA*
Lina Trigos-Carrillo, *Universidad de La Sabana, Colombia*
Andrea Gay Van Duzor, *Chicago State University, USA*
Erin I. Whitteck, *University of Missouri-St. Louis, USA*
Laura Wood, *Lesley University, USA*

List of Reviewers

Stephanie L. Anderson, *University of Arizona Global Campus, USA*
Diana-Elena Banu, *Colegiul National "Andrei Şaguna," Romania*
Alpana Bhattacharya, *Queens College, City University of New York, USA*
Constanta Bordea, *Colegiul National "Andrei Şaguna," Romania*
Anne Carr, *Universidad del Azuay, Ecuador*
Sarah A. Coppersmith, *University of Missouri-St. Louis, USA*
Tiffany Cunningham, *University of San Diego, USA*
Kristin E. Harbour, *University of South Carolina, USA*
Sherri Lyn Horner, *Bowling Green State University, USA*
Nurdan Kavakli, *Izmir University of Democracy, Turkey*
Shea N. Kerkhoff, *University of Missouri-St. Louis, USA*
Ruhi Khan, *Arizona State University, USA*
Monica Martinez-Sojos, *Universidad del Azuay, Ecuador*
Christy McMahon, *University of Arizona Global Campus, USA*
Svetlana Nikic, *St. Louis Public Schools, USA*
Patricia Ortega-Chasi, *Universidad del Azuay, Ecuador*
Francisco Javier Palacios-Hidalgo, *Universidad de Córdoba, Spain*
Michelle L. Rosser-Majors, *University of Arizona Global Campus, USA*
Madalina F. Tanase, *University of North Florida, USA*
Rachel E. Terlop, *George Mason University, USA*

List of Contributors

Anderson, Stephanie L. / *University of Arizona Global Campus, USA* 170
Aydarova, Elena / *Auburn University, USA* 49
Balcerzak, Phyllis / *University of Missouri-St.Louis, USA* 23
Banu, Diana Elena / *Colegiul Național "Andrei Șaguna", Romania* 316
Bell, Andreea Roxana / *Colegiul Național "Andrei Șaguna", Romania* 316
Bhattacharya, Alpana / *Queens College and Graduate Center, CUNY, USA* 91
Bordea, Constanța / *Colegiul Național "Andrei Șaguna", Romania* 316
Bularca, Elena Corina / *Colegiul Național "Andrei Șaguna", Romania* 316
Carr, Anne / *Universidad del Azuay, Ecuador* 144
Chesser, Svetlana / *Auburn University, USA* 49
Coppersmith, Sarah A. / *University of Missouri-St.Louis, USA* 23
Cunningham, Tiffany / *University of San Diego, USA* 397
Durham, Kate / *Auburn University, USA* 49
Enriquez Gates, Alejandra / *Arizona State University, USA* 289
Fonseca, Laura / *Universidad de La Sabana, Colombia* 199
Grijalva, Rebecca / *Arizona State University, USA* 289
Hammack, Shae / *University of North Florida, USA* 121
Harbour, Kristin E. / *University of South Carolina, USA* 343
Horner, Sherri L. / *Bowling Green State University, USA* 1
Huertas-Abril, Cristina A. / *University of Córdoba, Spain* 68
Kerkhoff, Shea N. / *University of Missouri-St. Louis, USA* 264
Khan, Ruhi / *Arizona State University, USA* 289
Lazăr, Elena Diana / *Colegiul Național "Andrei Șaguna", Romania* 316
Manfra, Meghan McGlinn / *North Carolina State University, USA* 245
Mardi, Fatemeh / *University of Missouri-St. Louis, USA* 264
Martin, Christie Lynn / *University of South Carolina, USA* 343
Martinez-Sojos, Monica / *Universidad del Azuay, Ecuador* 144
McMahon, Christine / *University of Arizona Global Campus, USA* 170
Mereoiu, Mariana / *Bowling Green State University, USA* 1
Mrachko, Alicia A. / *Bowling Green State University, USA* 1
Nielsen, Ann / *Arizona State University, USA* 289
Nikic, Svetlana / *Busch Middle School of Character, USA* 366
O'Brien, Kathryn G. / *University of Missouri-St. Louis, USA* 23, 219
Ortega-Chasi, Patricia / *Universidad del Azuay, Ecuador* 144
Palacios-Hidalgo, Francisco Javier / *University of Córdoba, Spain* 68

Polly, Drew / *University of North Carolina at Charlotte, USA* 343
Rebeor, Sandra / *University of Arizona Global Campus, USA* 170
Rong, Han / *University of Missouri-St. Louis, USA* 264
Rosser-Majors, Michelle L. / *University of Arizona Global Campus, USA* 170
Slapac, Alina / *University of Missouri-St.Louis, USA* 23
Spuderca, Lorena Mirela / *Colegiul Național "Andrei Șaguna", Romania* 316
Tanase, Madalina F. / *University of North Florida, USA* 121
Trigos-Carrillo, Lina / *Universidad de La Sabana, Colombia* 199
Wafa, Nada Zaki / *North Carolina State University, USA* 245

Table of Contents

Foreword xviii

Preface xx

Acknowledgment xxx

Section 1

Chapter 1
Fostering Student Engagement Through Showing Empathy and Caring in an Online College Course: An Action Research Project for COVID-19 and Beyond 1
    Sherri L. Horner, Bowling Green State University, USA
    Mariana Mereoiu, Bowling Green State University, USA
    Alicia A. Mrachko, Bowling Green State University, USA

Chapter 2
Resilience in Crisis: Developing Community Through Action Research 23
    Alina Slapac, University of Missouri-St.Louis, USA
    Sarah A. Coppersmith, University of Missouri-St.Louis, USA
    Kathryn G. O'Brien, University of Missouri-St. Louis, USA
    Phyllis Balcerzak, University of Missouri-St.Louis, USA

Chapter 3
Using Action Research to Promote Meaningful E-Service-Learning Experience for Preservice Teachers 49
    Svetlana Chesser, Auburn University, USA
    Kate Durham, Auburn University, USA
    Elena Aydarova, Auburn University, USA

Chapter 4
The Potential of English for Social Purposes and Cooperation for Emergency Remote Language Teaching: Action Research Based on Future Teachers' Opinions 68
    Francisco Javier Palacios-Hidalgo, University of Córdoba, Spain
    Cristina A. Huertas-Abril, University of Córdoba, Spain

Chapter 5
Assessment of Case-Based Instruction in a Graduate Educational Psychology Course: Preparing
P-12 Teachers for Classroom Management 91
    Alpana Bhattacharya, Queens College and Graduate Center, CUNY, USA

Chapter 6
The Challenges and Benefits of Online Instruction: Navigating the Rough Waters of Teaching
College Classes During the COVID-19 Pandemic 121
    Madalina F. Tanase, University of North Florida, USA
    Shae Hammack, University of North Florida, USA

Chapter 7
Online Teaching: Taking Advantage of Complexity to See What We Did Not Notice Before 144
    Anne Carr, Universidad del Azuay, Ecuador
    Patricia Ortega-Chasi, Universidad del Azuay, Ecuador
    Monica Martinez-Sojos, Universidad del Azuay, Ecuador

Chapter 8
Applying Online Instructor Presence Amidst Changing Times.. 170
    Michelle L. Rosser-Majors, University of Arizona Global Campus, USA
    Sandra Rebeor, University of Arizona Global Campus, USA
    Christine McMahon, University of Arizona Global Campus, USA
    Stephanie L. Anderson, University of Arizona Global Campus, USA

Chapter 9
Critical Participatory Action Research in a Rural Community Committed to Peacebuilding in
Times of Crisis.. 199
    Lina Trigos-Carrillo, Universidad de La Sabana, Colombia
    Laura Fonseca, Universidad de La Sabana, Colombia

Chapter 10
Between Two Crises: Identity Reconstruction Through Critical Action Research Self-Study 219
    Kathryn G. O'Brien, University of Missouri-St. Louis, USA

Chapter 11
Investigating Inquiry-Based, Technology-Rich Global Education Through Action Research 245
    Nada Zaki Wafa, North Carolina State University, USA
    Meghan McGlinn Manfra, North Carolina State University, USA

Chapter 12
An Action Research Study on Globally Competent Teaching in Online Spaces................................ 264
    Shea N. Kerkhoff, University of Missouri-St. Louis, USA
    Fatemeh Mardi, University of Missouri-St. Louis, USA
    Han Rong, University of Missouri-St. Louis, USA

Chapter 13
Teaching Action Research to International Educators: Transitioning Professional Development Online.. 289
    Ruhi Khan, Arizona State University, USA
    Alejandra Enriquez Gates, Arizona State University, USA
    Rebecca Grijalva, Arizona State University, USA
    Ann Nielsen, Arizona State University, USA

Section 2

Chapter 14
Reflecting on Self-Reflection: Overcoming the Challenges of Online Teaching in a Romanian School Through Action Research 316
    Andreea Roxana Bell, Colegiul Național "Andrei Șaguna", Romania
    Diana Elena Banu, Colegiul Național "Andrei Șaguna", Romania
    Constanța Bordea, Colegiul Național "Andrei Șaguna", Romania
    Elena Corina Bularca, Colegiul Național "Andrei Șaguna", Romania
    Elena Diana Lazăr, Colegiul Național "Andrei Șaguna", Romania
    Lorena Mirela Spuderca, Colegiul Național "Andrei Șaguna", Romania

Chapter 15
Transitioning the Elementary Mathematics Classroom to Virtual Learning: Exploring the Perspectives and Experiences of Teachers... 343
    Christie Lynn Martin, University of South Carolina, USA
    Kristin E. Harbour, University of South Carolina, USA
    Drew Polly, University of North Carolina at Charlotte, USA

Chapter 16
Ready to Engage? Urban Middle School Teachers' Responsiveness to Virtual Engagement Interventions on Their Instructional Practices 366
    Svetlana Nikic, Busch Middle School of Character, USA

Chapter 17
Action Research Is Cyclical: A Study in 9th Grade Conceptual Physics 397
    Tiffany Cunningham, University of San Diego, USA

Compilation of References 415

About the Contributors 456

Index 465

Detailed Table of Contents

Foreword xviii

Preface xx

Acknowledgment xxx

Section 1

Chapter 1
Fostering Student Engagement Through Showing Empathy and Caring in an Online College
Course: An Action Research Project for COVID-19 and Beyond 1
Sherri L. Horner, Bowling Green State University, USA
Mariana Mereoiu, Bowling Green State University, USA
Alicia A. Mrachko, Bowling Green State University, USA

This chapter describes a collaborative action research project in which one post-secondary instructor used the experiences in her undergraduate teacher education course to learn how to best support students and peers in a health crisis and social justice uncertainty climate. The authors used empathy and care theories and universal design for learning (UDL) to plan, implement, and reflect on ways to empathize and show care for students in a course that was online due to COVID-19. Using the action research processes, the authors found five themes related to using UDL practices and showing empathy and caring. They conclude with recommendations for other instructors interested in supporting their students in online classes and in times of crisis.

Chapter 2
Resilience in Crisis: Developing Community Through Action Research.. 23
Alina Slapac, University of Missouri-St.Louis, USA
Sarah A. Coppersmith, University of Missouri-St.Louis, USA
Kathryn G. O'Brien, University of Missouri-St. Louis, USA
Phyllis Balcerzak, University of Missouri-St.Louis, USA

Teacher action research serves as a framework that can transform practice while supporting inquiry, investigation, and problem-solving. This chapter provides a research report on the challenges experienced, strategies used, and lessons learned from 41 graduate education teacher-researchers who designed and implemented their own educational research during the COVID-19 crisis as part of their Action Research Capstone course before graduation. Graduate students were enrolled in three sections of the

Action Research course in a Midwestern university. Methodology included a qualitative approach to data collection and analysis. Findings from discussion board posts, reflections, and research papers captured challenges in facing COVID-19, yet participants' engagement in the community of learners within the course ameliorated and buffered stress, trauma, and compassion fatigue felt due to the pandemic's impact on these frontline workers.

Chapter 3
Using Action Research to Promote Meaningful E-Service-Learning Experience for Preservice Teachers 49
Svetlana Chesser, Auburn University, USA
Kate Durham, Auburn University, USA
Elena Aydarova, Auburn University, USA

Research on service-learning has documented the importance of relationships and meaningful community connections for preservice teachers' development. What remains less explored is the opportunities and challenges provided by e-service learning integrated into teacher preparation coursework. In this study, the authors utilize action research methodology to explore how preservice teachers engaged in e-service learning during the move towards remote instruction in the summer of 2020. Drawing on the analysis of students' weekly journals, final reflections, and the survey of stakeholders, they examine how e-service-learning created opportunities for students to feel connected to the community during the time of social isolation and be motivated by their ability to make an impact on children's interest in learning STEM content. The challenges emerged out of a disconnect between course content and some of the e-service learning assignments. This study's implications include better integration of e-service learning into teacher education courses.

Chapter 4
The Potential of English for Social Purposes and Cooperation for Emergency Remote Language Teaching: Action Research Based on Future Teachers' Opinions 68
Francisco Javier Palacios-Hidalgo, University of Córdoba, Spain
Cristina A. Huertas-Abril, University of Córdoba, Spain

Due to the COVID-19 pandemic, it is necessary to explore new practices in language teacher education. English for Social Purposes and Cooperation, a socially-responsive and technology-friendly approach to English language learning, may help students around the world continue learning from home. This chapter analyzes the perceptions of a group of pre-service teachers after designing socially responsive materials specially created for the COVID-19 crisis. Action research is employed to improve teacher educators' activity and pre-service teachers' training, and a mixed-method approach based on grounded theory and content analysis is performed. Findings show that the experience has provided participants with meaningful examples of material design. This encourages teacher educators to include the proposed approach in their teaching and reveals the need for specific training in material design. Results may help prove the potential of action research for improving the teaching practice.

Chapter 5
Assessment of Case-Based Instruction in a Graduate Educational Psychology Course: Preparing P-12 Teachers for Classroom Management 91
Alpana Bhattacharya, Queens College and Graduate Center, CUNY, USA

This chapter showcases a teacher educator's assessment of case-based instruction in an advanced level educational psychology course. First, action research, self-study, and reflective practice are explained as constructs of practitioner inquiry. Then, case-based instructional models related to teacher candidates' classroom management proficiencies are reviewed. Next, the teacher educator's examination of own teacher preparation practice is described to highlight development, implementation, and improvement of the target educational psychology course geared towards advancement of teacher candidates' classroom management capacities. Thereafter, solutions and recommendations for promoting teacher candidates' P-12 grades classroom management expertise are discussed. Finally, future research directions are proposed for ascertaining effectiveness of case-based instruction as evidence-based pedagogical approach for strengthening teacher candidates' P-12 grades classroom management aptitudes.

Chapter 6
The Challenges and Benefits of Online Instruction: Navigating the Rough Waters of Teaching College Classes During the COVID-19 Pandemic 121
Madalina F. Tanase, University of North Florida, USA
Shae Hammack, University of North Florida, USA

Because of the COVID-19 pandemic, educators everywhere transitioned to an online environment. This abrupt transition brought about some challenges: educators shifted their content and activities online, while their students attended classes and completed assignments online. This action research study analyzed the challenges experienced by an educator and her students during the summer and Fall 2020 semesters at a mid-size university. The researchers collected student surveys about their experiences with online learning. Results highlight the educator's struggle to make learning more interactive, as well as students' challenges with navigating the online platform and maintaining focus in class. Conversely, the online experience provided the following benefits: flexibility (logging in from different locations), comfort (joining class from home), and convenience (recorded class sessions). In alignment with the action research, the educator will continue to reflect on her practice in an attempt to make changes to the instruction and content of her classes.

Chapter 7
Online Teaching: Taking Advantage of Complexity to See What We Did Not Notice Before 144
Anne Carr, Universidad del Azuay, Ecuador
Patricia Ortega-Chasi, Universidad del Azuay, Ecuador
Monica Martinez-Sojos, Universidad del Azuay, Ecuador

The purpose of this participatory action research study was to investigate if teaching in virtual spaces could offer the opportunity to exercise reflexivity and transform pedagogy by including new roles, modes of interaction, and authentic practice to increase connectivity with students. The study was conducted with a small convenience group of university teachers in a private university in the south of Ecuador. Data was triangulated through individual and group interviews, a specifically designed blog, and participation in three learning-teaching modules. Certain dialogic characteristics in the data demonstrate epistemological and pedagogical transformations. Short-term results show that the complexity of teaching in virtual spaces indicates more research is necessary on the role of professional development that focuses on both pedagogy, effective communication, and technical abilities with discipline content.

Chapter 8
Applying Online Instructor Presence Amidst Changing Times.. 170
    Michelle L. Rosser-Majors, University of Arizona Global Campus, USA
    Sandra Rebeor, University of Arizona Global Campus, USA
    Christine McMahon, University of Arizona Global Campus, USA
    Stephanie L. Anderson, University of Arizona Global Campus, USA

Online learning can be challenging for both the students and instructors. Students can feel isolated or intimidated by the asynchronous environment, and instructors may find it difficult to connect with students as well as encourage active learning and critical thinking. Instructor presence (IP), as presented by the community of inquiry model (CoI), suggests that there are three areas of presence that must be applied cohesively to create an environment that is satisfying to students and the instructor: teaching, social, and cognitive. In this chapter, the authors report their findings of applied IP on student pass rates, drop rates, and satisfaction after exposing online instructors to IP training that provided immediate application examples. The findings suggested that when IP is applied effectively, student outcomes are significantly improved and are sustainable. This chapter will also share specific strategies, based on this model, that were utilized in the authors' research protocol.

Chapter 9
Critical Participatory Action Research in a Rural Community Committed to Peacebuilding in
Times of Crisis.. 199
    Lina Trigos-Carrillo, Universidad de La Sabana, Colombia
    Laura Fonseca, Universidad de La Sabana, Colombia

Conducting critical community research during the COVID-19 pandemic has brought unexpected challenges to academic communities. In this chapter, the authors analyze the obstacles faced in a Critical Participatory Action Research (CPAR) education project with a rural community of former guerrilla members in the Amazon piedmont in Colombia. After this analysis, the authors present four CPAR principles to support critical community work during difficult times. The authors argue that communicative action, horizontal community participation in all the stages of the research process, time commitment, and the leverage of other competing needs should be guaranteed and maintained during times of crisis. CPAR offers opportunities to advocate better conditions for the most affected communities in moments of increasing inequality.

Chapter 10
Between Two Crises: Identity Reconstruction Through Critical Action Research Self-Study 219
    Kathryn G. O'Brien, University of Missouri-St. Louis, USA

The purpose of this chapter was to critically examine the reconstruction of professional identity between two crises: The Great Recession of 2008 and the COVID-19 pandemic of 2020. Using a critical participatory action research self-study design, the author deconstructs the transition from for-profit behavioral health care business leadership to adjunct professor. Data sources include U.S. government job classification profiles, syllabi from courses taught, and the university's corresponding student surveys to answer the primary research question: How can teaching action research contribute to the reshaping of professional identity? Data analysis revealed that iterative cycles of reflection and action in teaching action research supported the development of identity as an academic across time. The knowledge, skills, and abilities required for a career in business supported, and also interfered with, career transition. Lastly, the author understood that the problem of practice stemmed from lack of recognition of her own privilege.

Chapter 11
Investigating Inquiry-Based, Technology-Rich Global Education Through Action Research 245
    Nada Zaki Wafa, North Carolina State University, USA
    Meghan McGlinn Manfra, North Carolina State University, USA

As teachers increasingly face new challenges related to the COVID-19 pandemic and instructional adjustments related to digital and online learning, action research may provide a more effective approach for bringing about change. In this chapter, the authors provide an example of an innovative project in which a university-based researcher worked alongside an elementary school teacher to implement and assess a technology rich, global education program. The case followed the global education teacher from the initial stages of the curriculum implementation through teaching a complete unit. Using a collaborative inquiry model, the authors merged action research with qualitative case study methodology to develop a rich description of instruction. The aim was to understand teacher and student outcomes, while also exploring the benefit of engaging practitioners as co-researchers. The authors offer this project as a representative example of the myriad ways educators can leverage action research to develop innovative approaches to teaching and learning global education.

Chapter 12
An Action Research Study on Globally Competent Teaching in Online Spaces 264
    Shea N. Kerkhoff, University of Missouri-St. Louis, USA
    Fatemeh Mardi, University of Missouri-St. Louis, USA
    Han Rong, University of Missouri-St. Louis, USA

Research shows that teachers understand why global competence is important but do not necessarily know how to implement global teaching. One way to address this problem of practice is integrating global competence with teacher education. Education abroad is an effective method to internationalize teaching, but travel is suspended due to the global pandemic. At the same time, the pandemic also highlights how global cooperation and global competence are vital in mitigating the effects of the virus. The purpose of this action research study was to investigate the impact of infusing global learning in an online education methods course. Data sources included products of learning and reflections from 24 master's students. Findings include five themes (multilingual communication, current event awareness, content-aligned integration, utilizing students' identities, and practicing local-global inquiry) that describe the prerequisites, barriers, challenges, and successes as teachers develop global competence and implement globally competent teaching in their K-12 classrooms.

Chapter 13
Teaching Action Research to International Educators: Transitioning Professional Development Online 289
    Ruhi Khan, Arizona State University, USA
    Alejandra Enriquez Gates, Arizona State University, USA
    Rebecca Grijalva, Arizona State University, USA
    Ann Nielsen, Arizona State University, USA

This chapter examines how a team of university experts within the field of education adjusted the focus of a professional development (PD) model to teach action research to 60 international educators. Three key educational elements were used to create the PD model: 1) transformational learning theory, 2) language acquisition and learning methodologies, and 3) a personalized system of instruction (PSI). When the unexpected worldwide pandemic caused a shift to remote learning, the team was tasked with adjusting the original face-to-face model. Evidence from meeting agendas, action plan tracking spreadsheets, and personal communication were analyzed as the program moved to an online learning environment. Based on this data, the team recognized that the theoretical principles and conceptual framework did not change but were refocused and emphasized a more human-centered approach. Future research should explore continued long-term professional development after action research has been implemented to support reflective practice and inquiry.

Section 2

Chapter 14
Reflecting on Self-Reflection: Overcoming the Challenges of Online Teaching in a Romanian School Through Action Research 316

Andreea Roxana Bell, Colegiul Național "Andrei Șaguna", Romania
Diana Elena Banu, Colegiul Național "Andrei Șaguna", Romania
Constanța Bordea, Colegiul Național "Andrei Șaguna", Romania
Elena Corina Bularca, Colegiul Național "Andrei Șaguna", Romania
Elena Diana Lazăr, Colegiul Național "Andrei Șaguna", Romania
Lorena Mirela Spuderca, Colegiul Național "Andrei Șaguna", Romania

This chapter discusses the challenges of online teaching faced by six English teachers in a state school in Romania in the context of the COVID-19 pandemic. As first-time action researchers, these teachers self-reflected on their challenges to make sense of their experiences as they transitioned from face-to-face to online teaching in a collaborative research self-study. Reflective practice is the conceptual framework within which the complexities and tensions of online teaching will be explored, as well as the process by which the authors have responded to the social and technological changes caused by the pandemic. Excerpts from the authors' voices highlight their personal views and experiences as online teachers. It is hoped that not only will this self-study reflection-in-action research provide some useful lessons regarding online teaching, but it will also showcase the benefits of collaboration and reflective practice and the action it led to.

Chapter 15
Transitioning the Elementary Mathematics Classroom to Virtual Learning: Exploring the Perspectives and Experiences of Teachers 343

Christie Lynn Martin, University of South Carolina, USA
Kristin E. Harbour, University of South Carolina, USA
Drew Polly, University of North Carolina at Charlotte, USA

In this chapter, the authors explore the experiences of K-12 teachers as they navigated an abrupt transition from a traditional face-to-face mathematics classroom to virtual learning. The authors used a survey to ask teachers to explain what effective mathematics instruction meant for their classroom. Their responses most closely aligned with four of the National Council of Teachers of Mathematics (NCTM) effective practices. The survey continued to prompt teachers to share their concerns for the transition, the most effective virtual tools they implemented, support they received, how their virtual classrooms would influence their return to face, and where they needed more support. The authors offer recommendations for supporting teachers as the virtual classroom currently remains in place for many and for transitioning back to the traditional face-to-face classroom. Technology use and digital competence continues to expand in K-12 education.

Chapter 16
Ready to Engage? Urban Middle School Teachers' Responsiveness to Virtual Engagement
Interventions on Their Instructional Practices 366
    Svetlana Nikic, Busch Middle School of Character, USA

This chapter examined teachers' responsiveness to targeted engagement interventions in their instructional practices in an urban middle school during virtual learning. These interventions were addressed through action research and consisted of professional development, coaching, and instructional feedback. Data collected in this eight-week study contained observational field notes, coaching plans, frequency charts, coaching questions, professional development constructs, surveys, artifacts, and interviews with six participant teachers. Findings show 1) positive responsiveness to teachers' engagement interventions, 2) increase in teachers' perceptions about instructional feedback and professional development, 3) coaching surfaced as most impactful intervention, 4) socio-emotional and behavioral engagement practices were least responsive to change, and 5) teachers' beliefs and growth mindset drove the need in practice change. Future recommendations consist of exploration into virtual practices.

Chapter 17
Action Research Is Cyclical: A Study in 9th Grade Conceptual Physics 397
    Tiffany Cunningham, University of San Diego, USA

Due to the global pandemic, teachers have had to find and implement effective instructional strategies through distance learning. Current research surrounding "flipped learning" indicates this may be a viable option during distance learning. This study takes place in a 9th grade conceptual physics course taught entirely online. It focuses upon the cyclical nature of action research using four curricular units, concluding that the process of continual reflection, modifications, and improvements made as a result of data analysis contributes to student engagement and academic achievement. Finally, it brings to light the importance in guiding students to understand that teachers are always learning, modifying, and adapting, and that learning is a lifelong process. This transparency is crucial when developing rapport with students, especially during a global pandemic that we are all working through together.

Compilation of References 415

About the Contributors 456

Index 465

Foreword

A global pandemic this past year and counting has thrust all of us into uncertainty and has required a quick pivot from our usual teaching and learning practices *to what*? This book addresses the puzzles offered to many of us as we functioned primarily in cyberspace with little notice or guidance. The overall task for all of us was one of holding fast to valued concepts and practices as educators while trying to re-create them in new contexts. This edited book brings to life how a range of educators across the spectrum from teacher-educators, in-service teachers, graduate and pre-service students as well as community members, were well-served by practices of action research in its many forms.

This collection, co-edited by Alina Slapac, Phyllis Balcerzak, and Kathryn G. O'Brien, has any number of offerings to commend it to readers, but we'd like to highlight a few areas that particularly struck us. This volume is boundary spanning in several ways. It gathers authors globally to offer insights into common struggles during what truly has been a global pandemic. As COVID-19 has so aptly illustrated, national borders are a fiction of sorts when it comes to a rapidly spreading virus. This collection illustrates that hard-won knowledge also has no boundaries and this shared knowledge can inform us all, no matter where we each are located. This sense of being interdependent in creating shared knowledge and practices necessary for these times seems an apt model for making our way through a pandemic.

Handbook of Research on the Global Empowerment of Educators and Student Learning Through Action Research also pushes boundaries in the genres of action research that are included in this book. Action research is a big umbrella and the co-authors have gathered into one volume a wide range of the possibilities of this approach. A reader of this volume will be exposed to the breadth of action research and its many possibilities. This collection of studies represents an example of how action research can both respond to immediate concerns on the ground, such as the struggle to teach online in a time of COVID, as well as build substantive knowledge and insights into the methodological dilemmas that every action researcher encounters. The studies also include a range of stances toward the change process as well as methodological approaches, including those situated on the more critical end of the continuum.

And finally, while we know that a lot of action research takes place in schools, universities and communities, we may or may not have access to it. Because action research is local – that is, researchers do this work to solve particular problems of practice or gain insight in how change might occur in a local context – it may or may not ultimately be written for publication. We also know action research can include various actors – students, teachers, university instructors, community members – in various forms of collaboration with one another but who sometimes remain invisible to us. While the action research spiral of knowledge building is invaluable in specific contexts and to various actors, this volume illustrates that a broader audience benefits from this knowledge as well. It is valuable for the local but also for the broader field of education.

Foreword

Co-editors Slapac, Balcerzak and O'Brien have managed to produce an incredibly timely volume for these times, and we appreciate their vision in shepherding it to publication.

Kathryn Herr
Montclair State University, USA

Gary L. Anderson
New York University, USA

Authors of *The Action Research Dissertation: A Guide for Students and Faculty* (2014; 2015) and *Studying Your Own School: An Educator's Guide to Qualitative Practitioner Research* (with Ann Sigrid Nihlen) (1994; 2007)

Preface

The year 2020 brought an unprecedented worldwide health crisis through the COVID-19 pandemic that has been affecting all sectors, including education. There were questions surrounding the effectiveness of online trainings for teachers, online teaching practices, the motivation and engagement of students, and the quality of learning and education in these times. Action research emerged to address these concerns, being a systematic process of inquiry using reflection within a cyclical model of planning, acting, implementing, evaluating, and continuous reflection. While the world was dealing with the COVID-19 pandemic, many educators across the globe were advancing their online teaching practices through action research. This method of research was employed with the expertise and passion from educators to better enhance online practices and education while using authentic learning and experiences. Using collaboration, social advocacy, and community within action research methodology, educators sought opportunities to advance teaching for students, families, and communities without a physical or with a very limited physical context involved.

Action Research is a method for everyday people to systematically discover solutions for problems of everyday life (Hendricks, 2017), represented by a cycle of reflection, action, and evaluation, followed by reflection, action, and evaluation, and so forth. In this way, Action Research might also be viewed as a forward-moving spiral, as reflection leads to adjustment of the action, and as evaluation guides the individual to reflect on the next action. The method is particularly suited to teachers, who constantly seek solutions for classroom quandaries. Equal emphasis on each phase of the cycle places the researcher at the center, rather than as a scientist observing some external phenomenon (Zeni, 1996). Action Research is personal. External threat from the pandemic prompted educators to work harder than ever to create new methods for student engagement and achievement, and for a sense of organization in the midst of the chaos caused by lockdowns, sudden shifts to virtual-only teaching and learning, and then back to the classroom. While extraordinary flexibility and planning were required for a pandemic circumstance, action research is a longstanding method for an educator to advance self-knowledge and teaching practice to better meet the needs of students, colleagues, or the individual's sense of accomplishment.

This book explores successful teaching and learning skills through the method of action research, and intersects it with online learning in order to uncover best teaching practices in online platforms. This book showcases educational professionals' action research for solutions in advancing teaching and learning, the practical benefits of action research, recommendations for improving online teaching and learning, and a focus on professional growth as well as social justice advocacy. It highlights important topics including student learning, teacher collaboration, authentic learning, advocacy, and action research in both K-12 and higher education settings.

Preface

TARGET AUDIENCE

This book is ideal for in-service and pre-service teachers, administrators, teacher educators, practitioners, researchers, academicians, and students interested in how action research is improving and advancing knowledge on the best teaching practices for online education.

This co-edited book could be used as the primary book for a graduate course in Action Research, or as a supplemental text for other undergraduate or graduate-level courses not necessarily focusing on research methods but on the action/interventions instead (e.g., curriculum and instruction, counseling, and/or administration). This book features empirical research findings within the (teacher) action research methodology, resources and recommendations from experienced teacher educators and teachers from Ecuador, Colombia, Romania, Spain, and the United States.

ORGANIZATION OF THE BOOK

The book is organized into two sections and 17 chapters. Section 1, which contains Chapters 1 to 13, focuses on different types of action research (such as, classroom, collaborative, self-study and critical participatory action research) in teacher education programs. Section 2, which contains Chapters 14 to 17, focuses on action research in school settings. A brief description of each chapter in this book highlights ideas, concepts, research, and suggestions as follows:

Chapter 1 describes a collaborative action research study using Empathy and Care theories (Trout, 2012), and Universal Design for Learning (UDL) (Meyer et al., 2014) as overlapping guiding theoretical perspectives. The three authors, who normally teach undergraduates majoring in early childhood education courses, and who developed specific techniques to foster student engagement and learning in their courses, including showing empathy and caring to their students, continued to use the same techniques while having to teach their courses online during COVID-19 pandemic. Their collaboration prompted an action research project, to plan, implement, evaluate and reflect on their teaching strategies, student activities, and how to effectively use the various online functions to foster student engagement and learning. Recognizing that the online formats could be impersonal with students having multiple issues going on in their lives (e.g., anxiety, social isolation due to the pandemic), the faculty-researchers implemented strategies of empathy and caring while modeling those themselves for their students and collecting data from their online courses, based on teacher-student and student-student interactions. In their chapter and based on the study findings, the authors made recommendations for other teacher educators to enhance student engagement, show empathy and caring to their students through using UDL guidelines, and help them learn how to show empathy and caring to their future students in both virtual and face-to-face venues.

Chapter 2 provides an analysis of the challenges experienced, strategies used, and lessons learned from 41 teacher-researchers who designed and implemented their own educational research during the COVID-19 crisis. The teacher-researchers were graduate students who were enrolled in three sections, each with a different instructor, of the capstone action research course in a Midwestern university. For over 20 years, this Master's program has promoted action research as an effective strategy to reflectively improve practice while enacting innovations (Slapac & Navarro, 2011; Zeni, 2001). The program's focus on teachers as agents of change has resulted in an accumulation of reports documenting the power of action research to build confidence and competence for both new and experienced teachers in order to meet the daily rigor of the profession. Compared to prior research and experience, the authors note significant increases in the anxiety and distress in teachers' communications. These findings were derived from discussion board posts, reflections, and research papers that captured challenges they encountered in teaching during the pandemic, providing a view of the teacher-student interface during this unique time. The authors discuss the themes that emerged from participants' engagement in the community of learners within the course with special attention to the representation of teacher voice. The collaborative practices that were routine aspects in the course design prior to the pandemic assumed heightened importance as evidence emerged about how they buffered stress, trauma, and compassion fatigue felt due to the pandemic's impact on these front-line workers. The authors conclude with a discussion of the value of action research as a resource to be considered in times of crisis when immediate action is required.

Chapter 3 showcases an action research study designed to promote meaningful e-service learning experience in an online class for preservice teachers through community-based participation. Arguing that e-service-learning is a helpful approach to create a bridge between academic learning and community service in online classes, while still being a rare component in online courses (Waldner et al., 2012), the three authors explored the benefits of e-service learning at a 4-year university in the Southeast of the United States. Their students enrolled in 10-week foundations of education class and had to complete 25 hours of service learning to satisfy the requirements of the course. The students helped to create social media presence for a newly founded non-profit hands-on children science center community organization, assisted with grant writing, and organized fundraising while networking with local businesses. Findings indicated that the preservice teachers' engagement with their service-learning tasks enhanced their understanding of science teaching and equipped them with the skills of preparing grant applications to support STEM learning. Participating in community life through social media campaigns allowed preservice teachers to feel productive and motivated during otherwise challenging time of a lockdown and limited contact with others. The synergy between students' contributions and the center's offerings met community needs for STEM learning for preschoolers and kindergarteners during the time when other educational opportunities were limited. The empirical insights and the identified successful practices point out the importance of implementing e-service learning projects in online courses to serve the community and grow personally and professionally.

Chapter 4 examines the English language learning process in the context of the global COVID-19 pandemic, in particular English for Social Purposes and Cooperation (ESoPC), which aims at providing learners with effective learning of English paying special attention to 21st-century social issues and cultural values (Huertas-Abril & Gómez-Parra, 2018). While ESoPC targets language proficiency development, cultural awareness raising, and social responsibility consciousness including technology-based teaching strategies, the authors also used Emergency Remote Language Teaching (ERLT) (Hodges et al., 2020) as an additional framework encompassing those language teaching processes developed during crises and emergencies, such as the current pandemic. The chapter presents the results of an exploratory action research study in which pre-service bilingual primary teachers of the University of Córdoba (Spain) designed ESoPC materials in a real ERLT setting. To do so, their perceptions about the experience are examined using qualitative analysis based on a grounded-theory scheme and content analysis techniques. The participants of this study consist of students of the course 'English as a Foreign Language for Primary Education Teachers', bilingual itinerary, of the University of Córdoba (Spain), in the 2019-2020 academic year. Within this population, three different groups of participants can be found: (i) Year 3 students of the BA in Primary Education; (ii) Year 3 students of the Double BA in Primary Education and English Studies; and (iii) international students from Poland, Austria, Finland,

Preface

and Turkey. Recommendations are made to aid teacher trainers design ESoPC materials and improve future ESoPC formative experiences.

Chapter 5 showcases the author's self-assessment and evidence-based analysis of teaching practices and teacher preparation measures, as a teacher educator, from an advanced-level educational psychology course, Classroom Management, completed by P-12 teachers during spring 2016, 2017, 2018, 2019, and 2020 semesters. Due to increasing scrutiny and expectations of accountability from teacher preparation programs as producers of competent and caring P-12 teachers, professional development of teacher educators is crucial. Reflections and analysis of two proficiency measures, case-based simulations and field-based research are discussed by way of addressing the challenges of aligning elements of instructional models, teaching and learning practices, and teachers' knowledge, skills, and dispositions related to professional proficiencies. Research on a case-based approach for problem solving such as the Hybrid Case-Learning Model (HCL) developed by Strangeways and Papatraianou (2016), and the Conceptual Framework of Teaching Case (CFTC) developed by Kim and her colleagues (2006) are reviewed. In addition, the author conceptualized her theoretical framework based on Choi and Lee (2009), Piwowar, Thiel, and Ophardt (2013), and Simonsen et al. (2014)'s evidence-based models of classroom management proficiencies. The findings of this action research self-study pinpoint the effectiveness and the limitations of case-based simulations and field-based research as measures of teachers' knowledge, skills, and dispositions as related to their professional specialty.

Chapter 6 is another action research self-study of a teacher educator discussing the challenges and successes with transitioning from face-to-face instruction to online teaching over the course of the summer and fall 2020 semesters, as well as the changes she made while teaching remote instruction in the fall in order to improve the online learning experience of her students. In their literature review, the authors focused on challenges of online teaching and learning, inequities issues related to technology access, and stress caused by the pandemic (Assunção & Gago, 2020; Bakker & Wagner, 2020; Wang, Pan et al., 2020). The first author taught a section of a Classroom Management and Communications course, in the distance learning format, due to the pandemic safety measures. While the instructor struggled at times along with the students with the new online format of the course, such as lack of communication, and overall student poor attendance, through reflective practice and the action research process, including data gathered from students, the instructor was able to overcome the challenges and made changes in the fall semester that ultimately created a better online learning environment and a community of learners. The recommendations made are valuable for other faculty and students in teacher education programs.

Chapter 7 also describes the shift in instruction due to the COVID-19 pandemic that prompted faculty/ university instructors to develop their ideas about teaching and learning online instead of the traditional in-person classes (Sorcinelli, 2006) and to restructure traditional classroom roles and relationships individually and collectively. Using a participatory action research (PAR) model, and its four essential elements (participation, action, research, and social change for social justice), the authors bring attention to the fact that all these elements require equal and critical consideration in the ways they are planned and implemented in their projects. The authors examined if learning educational technologies for teaching online can be a catalyst for faculty and teachers to reflect on and evaluate their current teaching practice in a private university in the south of Ecuador. In order to document the process of transformative learning, a 'community of learners' of six teachers participated through three cycles of continuous planning, acting, observing and reflecting. These teachers were prompted to reflect on the aspects of the professional development activities they perceived as being most effective in helping them to reflect on and question their previously held assumptions and beliefs about teaching (Samuelowicz & Bain, 2001). The authors argue for continuous reflexivity in teaching in virtual spaces, and invite us to consider engaging in action research studies that create opportunities for social advocacy and community participation.

Chapter 8 focuses on pertinent action research developed to support student and instructor success in the online classroom through the use of instructor presence applications, based on the Community of Inquiry (CoI) model (e.g., Castellanos-Reyes, 2020; Flock, 2020; Garrison et al., 2000, 2001, 2010;), adapted for differing education levels and applicable to a wide range of content areas. Instructors will find useful strategies covering social, cognitive, and teaching presence as they embark on this new challenge of teaching and learning online. Lastly, based on the increased challenges that instructors can experience when teaching in this environment (Hodges et al., 2020), recommendations are discussed on how the application of the CoI strategies may be useful to improve educators' effectiveness and satisfaction in the online classroom resulting in an enhanced work-life balance, feelings of competence, and autonomy (Korthagena & Evelein, 2016). Findings also suggest improved student retention and success.

Chapter 9, grounded in the tenets of Critical Participatory Action Research (CPAR), examines the partnership between researchers from a private university in Colombia and a small town named Centro Poblado Héctor Ramírez (CP-HR), located in the Caquetá Department near the Amazon piedmont. This community, organized by former FARC-EP guerrilla members and their families, expressed their desire to collaborate with the university in the co-construction of an educative model for this rural community committed to the peacebuilding process in Colombia. CPAR is oriented towards making social change with the different members of the communities, which implies taking decisions collectively and following the model of a self-reflective spiral (Kemmis et al., 2014). The chapter explored the reflections of the different project members, particularly undergraduate students, university researchers and the education committee members from the CP-HR about the challenges, opportunities and advances of each stage in the consolidation of a rural educative project for children and youth in the context of peacebuilding. Focusing on the deconstruction of hegemonic ways of understanding education and the incorporation of local understandings of development, the authors reflect on the challenges and opportunities of building research-practice partnerships in a peacebuilding context. The authors also emphasize the role of academia that must involve a critical analysis of the opportunities of social transformation, and the promotion of social justice, as recognition and involvement of the diverse social actors that are part of a peacebuilding context.

Chapter 10 details a critical action research self-study, the purpose of which was to examine and understand the transition of the author's professional identity between The Great Recession of 2008 through the end of 2020 during the COVID-19 pandemic. Much has been written about career transitions, but little research is available from the insider perspective of a transition from business operations to teacher educator. The transition from corporate leadership to adjunct professor was anything but easy, involving job loss at a critical time of life, return to graduate school as a student, and starting over as a beginner after achieving profession expertise and recognition. The author deconstructs the transition from for-profit behavioral health care business leadership to adjunct professor through lenses of discourse and identity, career derailment, and critical action research self-study. Data sources include U.S. government job classification profiles, syllabi from courses taught, and the university's corresponding student surveys to answer the primary research question: How can teaching action research contribute to the reshaping of professional identity? Data analysis revealed that iterative cycles of reflection and action in teaching action research supported the development of identity as an academic across time. The knowledge, skills, and abilities required for a career in business supported, and also interfered

Preface

with, career transition. Lastly, the author understood that the problem of practice stemmed from lack of recognition of her own privilege.

Chapter 11 provides an example of an innovative collaborative-research model, in which a university-based researcher worked alongside with an elementary school teacher to implement and assess a technology-rich, global education program while exploring the benefit of engaging practitioners as co-researchers. The study focused on the implementation of an inquiry-based model, technology-rich, global education curriculum in a first-grade classroom. Working with the classroom teacher as a practitioner researcher, the authors examined classroom instruction and student outcomes. The authors focused specifically on a global education class, taught as an elective class once or twice a week. The results of the study provide insights about the integration of technology and inquiry into global education. The authors hope that others will use their action research study as a model for developing innovative approaches to teaching and learning global education in the midst of a changing world.

Chapter 12 explores the growing area on integrating global learning and teacher education curricula, in the context of online teacher education. Research shows that teachers understand why global competence is important for their students, but that they do not necessarily know how to implement global teaching in their classrooms (Kerkhoff et al., 2019; Kerkhoff & Cloud, 2020; Slapac, 2021). The authors chose to focus on the importance of global competence while addressing the problem of practice through integrating globally competent teaching with formal teacher education. The researchers investigate the impact of a masters-level online education methods course infused with global learning, in a time when global travel is prohibited while global cooperation and global competence are vital in mitigating the effects of the COVID-19 virus. The researchers collected products of learning from the online course that related to global teaching. Primary data sources included assessments that were intentionally added to the course to integrate globally competent teaching throughout the courses as well as assessments of the Global Teaching Module. The results of this action research study describe the prerequisites, barriers, challenges, and successes as teachers develop global competence and implement globally competent teaching in their K-12 classrooms.

Chapter 13 describes how a team of university experts taught action research to sixty international educators and focuses on the process of transitioning this professional development (PD) online during the COVID-19 pandemic. The university team, comprised of English instructors, content area experts and leadership team members, developed the PD by drawing upon three key elements: (a) Transformational Learning Theory (b) Language Acquisition and Learning Methodologies, and a (c) Personalized System of Instruction (PSI). Considering the needs of the international educators, the team refined the approaches to second language development and made strategic programmatic adjustments. The authors provide in-depth examples of the strategic shifts made to refocus elements of conceptual framework, the impact on the educators' learning experiences and the way the program design was strengthened. Shifts in implementation involved drawing upon the successes of the face-to-face training and reinforcing those elements to make them much more forthcoming in an online environment. Recommendations are provided regarding key transition elements from face-to-face to online learning environments.

Chapter 14 presents an action research study conducted by six teachers in the English department, in a high school in Romania. The study aimed to highlight the challenges of online teaching at the start of the pandemic (spring 2020) compared to the second wave of online teaching, the challenges of the hybrid teaching format at the start of the new school year (fall 2020), and the changes that the English-as-a foreign language teachers adopted in order to be better prepared for both hybrid and online teaching and to enhance student learning during the new school year. Besides the lack of technology supports and other resources, the teachers-researchers focused on other questions to inform their study: Have face-to-face teachers suddenly become online teachers as a result of the experience gained during the lockdown? Have online training courses truly equipped teachers with the necessary skills to adapt to the hybrid teaching format? Or should we envisage a new approach to teaching, devise new methodologies in order to make teaching effective in such trying circumstances? Results from the self-reflections, instructional changes and meeting notes addressed such questions. Solutions and recommendations for other educators facing similar challenges are provided.

Chapter 15 explores the transition of elementary mathematics teachers to virtual learning, by acknowledging the concerns related to the long-term school closure exacerbating issues of equality, equity, and access (Van Lancker & Parolin, 2020). The authors provide an overview of the literature of effective practices pertaining to discourse, questioning, high-level tasks, formative assessment, manipulatives, and equity. Using survey and interview data, the authors share the findings of their action research study, in particular, teachers' identified concerns, strategies used for support during the transition from in-person to virtual learning, teachers' tools and practices they were found most effective than others, and the pedagogical shifts in practice that had long-lasting effects.

Chapter 16 investigates six urban middle school teachers' responsiveness to targeted engagement intervention (such as, coaching cycles, instructional feedback and professional development) through an action research study. The author, who is also the instructional coach at the respective school and a collaborative-participant in the study, provided useful learning opportunities for the teachers' virtual instructional practices. This study uses insights from the 2019 findings of Garret, Citkowitz, and Williams' meta-analysis of research relevant to teachers' responsiveness to intervention in classroom practice. The results point to the complexities of teachers' professional needs, in particular, to positive responsiveness to teachers' engagement interventions evidenced by an increase in engagement practices; increase in teachers' perceptions about instructional feedback and professional development. Coaching surfaced as the most impactful intervention. Socio-emotional and behavioral engagement practices were least responsive to change while teachers' beliefs and growth mindset drove the need in practice change. Further recommendations are discussed relevant to teachers, coaches and policy makers.

The last chapter, Chapter 17, focuses on an action research study and flipped classroom pedagogy as optimizing time in class with students. Specifically, the study describes the instructional strategies used from a flipped classroom in a distance learning conceptual physics class for 9th graders during the current global pandemic. The flipped classroom instructional strategies used were: providing traditional classwork as homework while focusing on more student-led activities during class time. The author describes the several cycles that teachers implement in order to find the most effective instructional strategies encourages educators. It also brings to light the importance in guiding students to understand that teachers are always learning, modifying, and adapting and that learning is not only done in school, but continues for their entire lives. The study adds to the growing literature on teaching during a global pandemic: the unknown territory that comes with teaching K-12 online, or virtually, and the need for action research as a foundation to implement instructional strategies, using data to guide any modifications needed. It concludes by emphasizing the need for compassion and empathy during this global pandemic, a reminder that relationships with students are needed before learning can take place.

Preface

CONCLUSION

Since its introduction into the field of education, action research has become an effective way to capture and communicate the knowledge of the practitioner, both experimental and cumulative. The proximity of the researcher to the processes being studied often provides important insights into both data and interpretations, insights often invisible to researchers whose positionality is more distant in time and space. Additionally, the iterative cycle of improvement organizes evidence-based changes in practice so they can be implemented in short time intervals. This feature became an important asset during the pandemic, when dramatic changes in practice were mandated by the global lockdown and subsequent move to remote teaching. Frontline workers who respond to urgent situations often employ solutions with a knowledge base rich in experience yet difficult to record. The collected stories of rapid responses presented in this book highlight the value of a research methodology that was able to inform practice during a time of urgent need and offer collaborative support during a time of social isolation. Each chapter is unique in its study population, location on the globe, strategies employed, and data collected, yet tell a story of their response to the same intense social challenge-at the same time. The commitment of these educators to study their practice while confronted with the constraints of the global pandemic, have given us a picture defined by the themes that emerged from the responses of professionals in this single field of study. The intellectual space that opened for these authors is represented in the narratives that follow. The collective insights that emerge across sites will be determined by the reader.

Alina Slapac
University of Missouri-St. Louis, USA

Phyllis Balcerzak
University of Missouri-St. Louis, USA

Kathryn O'Brien
University of Missouri-St. Louis, USA

REFERENCES

Assunção Flores, M., & Gago, M. (2020). Teacher education in times of COVID-19 pandemic in Portugal: National, institutional and pedagogical responses. *Journal of Education for Teaching*, *46*(4), 507–516. doi:10.1080/02607476.2020.1799709

Bakker, A., & Wagner, D. (2020). Pandemic: Lessons for today and tomorrow? *Educational Studies in Mathematics*, *104*(1), 1–4. doi:10.100710649-020-09946-3

Castellanos-Reyes, D. (2020). 20 Years of the Community of Inquiry Framework. *TechTrends*, *1–4*(4), 557–560. Advance online publication. doi:10.100711528-020-00491-7

Choi, I., & Lee, K. (2009). Designing and implementing a case-based learning environment for enhancing ill-structured problem solving: Classroom management problems for prospective teachers. *Educational Technology Research and Development*, *57*(1), 99–129. doi:10.100711423-008-9089-2

Flock, H. (2020). Designing a community of inquiry in online courses. *The International Review of Research in Open and Distributed Learning, 21*(1), 134–152. doi:10.19173/irrodl.v20i5.3985

Garret, R., Citkowicz, M., & Williams, R. (2019). How responsive is a teacher's classroom practice to intervention? A meta-analysis of randomized field studies. *Review of Research in Education, 43*(1), 106–109. doi:10.3102/0091732X19830634

Garrison, D. R., Anderson, T., & Archer, W. (2000). Critical inquiry in a text-based environment: Computer conferencing in higher education model. *The Internet and Higher Education, 2*(2-3), 87–105. doi:10.1016/S1096-7516(00)00016-6

Garrison, D. R., Anderson, T., & Archer, W. (2001). Critical thinking, cognitive presence, and computer conferencing in distance education. *American Journal of Distance Education, 15*(1), 7–23. doi:10.1080/08923640109527071

Garrison, D. R., Anderson, T., & Archer, W. (2010). The first decade of the community of inquiry framework: A retrospective. *The Internet and Higher Education, 13*(1–2), 5–9. doi:10.1016/j.iheduc.2009.10.003

Hendricks, C. (2017). *Improving schools through action research: A reflective practice approach* (4th ed.). Pearson.

Hodges, C., Moore, S., Lockee, B., Trust, T., & Bond, A. (2020, March 7). The difference between emergency remote teaching and online learning. *EDUCAUSE Review*. https://bit.ly/2DwKOYM

Huertas-Abril, C. A., & Gómez-Parra, M. E. (2018). English for social purposes: A new approach to language learning. In M. I. Amor, M. Osuna, & E. Pérez (Eds.), *Fundamentos de enseñanza y aprendizaje para una educación universal, intercultural y bilingüe* (pp. 73–78). Octaedro.

Kemmis, S., & McTaggart, R. (2005). Participatory action research: Communicative action and the public sphere. In N. Denzin & Y. Lincoln (Eds.), Handbook of qualitative research (3rd ed., pp. 559-604). Sage.

Kerkhoff, S. N., & Cloud, M. (2020). Global teacher education: A mixed methods self-study. *International Journal of Educational Research, 103*. Advance online publication. doi:10.1016/j.ijer.2020.101629 PMID:32834467

Kerkhoff, S. N., Dimitrieska, V., Woerner, J., & Alsup, J. (2019). Global teaching in Indiana: A quantitative case study of K-12 public school teachers. *Journal of Comparative Studies and International Education, 1*(1), 5–31. https//www.jcsie.com/ojs/dir/index.php/JCSIE/article/view/14

Korthagena, F. A. J., & Evelein, F. G. (2016). Relations between student teachers' basic needs fulfillment and their teaching behavior. *Teaching and Teacher Education, 60*, 234–244. doi:10.1016/j.tate.2016.08.021

Meyer, A., Rose, D. H., & Gordon, D. (2014). *Universal design for learning: Theory and practice*. CAST.

Piwowar, V., Thiel, F., & Ophardt, D. (2013). Training inservice teachers' competencies in classroom management. A quasi-experimental study with teachers of secondary schools. *Teaching and Teacher Education, 30*, 1–12. doi:10.1016/j.tate.2012.09.007

Preface

Rosser-Majors, M., Rebeor, S., McMahon, C., & Anderson, S. (2020). *Instructor presence training: Sustainable practices supporting student retention and success.* Teaching and Learning Conference, University of Arizona Global Campus (virtual). https://www.youtube.com/watch?v=4zrFNOtp198

Samuelowicz, K., & Bain, J. D. (2001). Revisiting academics' beliefs about teaching and learning. *Higher Education, 41*(3), 299–325. doi:10.1023/A:1004130031247

Simonsen, B., MacSuga-Gage, A. S., Briere, D. E. III, Freeman, J., Myers, D., Scott, T. M., & Sugai, G. (2014). Multitiered support framework for teachers' classroom-management practices: Overview and case study of building the triangle for teachers. *Journal of Positive Behavior Interventions, 16*(3), 179–190. doi:10.1177/1098300713484062

Slapac, A. (2021). Advancing students' global competency through English language learning in Romania: An exploratory qualitative case study of four English language teachers. *Journal of Research in Childhood Education, 35*(2), 1–17. doi:10.1080/02568543.2021.1880993

Slapac, A., & Navarro, V. (2011). Shaping action researchers through a Master's capstone experience. *Teacher Education and Practice, 24*(4), 405–426.

Strangeways, A., & Papatraianou, L. H. (2016). Case-based learning for classroom ready teachers: Addressing the theory practice disjunction through narrative pedagogy. *The Australian Journal of Teacher Education, 41*(9), 117–134. doi:10.14221/ajte.2016v41n9.7

Trout, M. (2012). *Making the moment matter: Care theory for teacher learning.* Sense Publishers. doi:10.1007/978-94-6209-110-8

Van Lancker, W., & Parolin, Z. (2020). COVID-19, school closures, and child poverty: A social crisis in the making. *The Lancet. Public Health, 5*(5), e243–e244. doi:10.1016/S2468-2667(20)30084-0 PMID:32275858

Waldner, L. S., Widener, M. C., & McGorry, S. Y. (2012). E-service learning: The evolution of service-learning to engage a growing online student population. *Journal of Higher Education Outreach & Engagement, 16*(2), 123–150.

Wang, G., Zhang, Y., Zhao, J., Zhang, J., & Jiang, F. (2020). Mitigate the effects of home confinement on children during the COVID-19 outbreak. *Lancet, 395*(10228), 945–947. doi:10.1016/S0140-6736(20)30547-X PMID:32145186

Zeni, J. (1996). A picaresque tale from the land of kidwatching: Teacher research and ethical dilemmas. *The Quarterly, 18*(1), 30–35.

Zeni, J. (2001). A guide to ethical decision making for insider research. In J. Zeni (Ed.), *Ethical issues in practitioner research* (pp. 153–165). Teachers College Press.

Acknowledgment

This co-edited book would have not existed without the amazing effort of all the authors, unified through the action research methodology, although geographically apart. We are extremely excited to have authors from Ecuador, Colombia, Romania, Spain, and the United States. Their studies, journeys and commitment to the field of education in K-12 classrooms and in teacher education programs are remarkable. We hope that this book will engage us all in future local and international collaborations with each other.

We are very grateful to our Editorial Advisory Board for their diligent work and support throughout the process of this book; specifically, many thanks to Sally Durand, Margaret Finders, Nicole M. Houser, Virginia Navarro, Lina Trigos-Carrillo, Andrea Gay Van Duzor, Erin I. Whitteck, and Laura Wood, for their valuable editing and feedback on the chapters submitted.

We would also like to thank all the Chapter Reviewers for without their attention to detail, expertise, and thoughtful care for topics, this project would have not been complete. Despite their hard work on their own chapters, these authors took the extra time to review the assigned chapters, with extreme care for quality. Many thanks to: Stephanie L. Anderson, Diana-Elena Banu, Alpana Bhattacharya, Constanta Bordea, Anne Carr, Sarah A. Coppersmith, Tiffany Cunningham, Kristin E. Harbour, Sherri Lyn Horner, Nurdan Kavakli, Shea N. Kerkhoff, Ruhi Khan, Monica Martinez-Sojos, Christy McMahon, Svetlana Nikic, Patricia Ortega-Chasi, Francisco Javier Palacios-Hidalgo, Michelle L. Rosser-Majors, Madalina F. Tanase, and Rachel E. Terlop.

We extend a special thank you to Kathryn Herr and Gary L. Anderson for supporting our effort through their writing of the Foreword to this book and for their relentless advocacy in the uses of the action research methodology in the scholarly traditions embedded in higher education graduate programs.

We are deeply touched by the IGI Global commitment to both local and international endeavors and inquiries. Special thanks to the supportive staff at IGI Global, in particular, to Jan Travers, Maria Rhode, and Lindsay Wertman, among others on the Development and Marketing Teams.

Acknowledgment

We would also like to thank our families, partners and friends for their love, support and understanding throughout this project.

Alina Slapac
University of Missouri-St. Louis, USA

Phyllis Balcerzak
University of Missouri-St. Louis, USA

Kathryn O'Brien
University of Missouri-St. Louis, USA

Section 1

Chapter 1
Fostering Student Engagement Through Showing Empathy and Caring in an Online College Course:
An Action Research Project for COVID-19 and Beyond

Sherri L. Horner
Bowling Green State University, USA

Mariana Mereoiu
Bowling Green State University, USA

Alicia A. Mrachko
Bowling Green State University, USA

ABSTRACT

This chapter describes a collaborative action research project in which one post-secondary instructor used the experiences in her undergraduate teacher education course to learn how to best support students and peers in a health crisis and social justice uncertainty climate. The authors used empathy and care theories and universal design for learning (UDL) to plan, implement, and reflect on ways to empathize and show care for students in a course that was online due to COVID-19. Using the action research processes, the authors found five themes related to using UDL practices and showing empathy and caring. They conclude with recommendations for other instructors interested in supporting their students in online classes and in times of crisis.

DOI: 10.4018/978-1-7998-6922-1.ch001

At its heart, action research is a process of interrupting habitual practice by exploring and inspiring innovative alternatives with others most impacted by the choices being made and actions being taken (Bradbury et al., 2019).

INTRODUCTION

In their editorial, Embury et al. (2020) call on action researchers to "… share the messy details of their often imperfect learning process so that others may see themselves in the processes" (p. 127). In this chapter, we describe the beginnings of our collaborative action research (AR) project, with all its messiness and imperfections, relating to how we collaborated to show empathy and caring, and use Universal Design Principles (UDL) within one virtual class during a global pandemic. The first element of imperfection was that we had envisioned this chapter to be about the undergraduate teacher education courses that all three of us were teaching; however, after receiving Institutional Review Board (IRB) approval for this research project, the number of students who submitted a consent form to participate was not as high as we hoped. Therefore, we decided to focus on the course that had the most students consenting.

We used the steps of the two cycles of AR model (Ventura, 2018) as the framework for our project. One cycle in this model is related to *problem-solving* while the other concomitant cycle is *research*. The first steps in the *problem-solving* cycle are: (a) identifying the problem, (b) gathering information, and (c) planning interventions. Similarly, the first steps in the *research* cycle are: (a) selecting the research topics, (b) conducting a literature review, and (c) planning the research. The final steps for both cycles entail: (d) taking action, (e) implementing the action, (f) monitoring the problem-solving efficacy and the research interests, (g) evaluating, and (h) exiting if the problem and research goal are solved or amending the plan if it is not, then repeating parts of the cycle. Although these cycles are explained here as steps, which could imply a sequential process we, like other action researchers (Calhoun, 2019), frequently moved back to a previous step or forward to a later step as we went through the semester and this project. Due to the urgency of converting university courses from face-to-face (F2F) instruction to virtual to reduce the risks involved with COVID-19 and to our desire to "do what is right" by our students, especially in this stressful time, we operated within a very compressed timeline and might have overlapped and cycled back and forth through these steps more quickly or differently than might be done during a typical AR project.

Although there are a number of AR studies (Casselman, 2019; Enerio, 2020; Hendricks, 2009; Slapac & Navarro, 2011; Trout & Basford, 2016) on college classes, we focused this project on teaching and learning in virtual classes in a climate of uncertainty. In describing our AR, we embedded the theoretical frameworks, literature review, our teaching and research activities, methodology and research findings within the various steps of the AR cycles (Ventura, 2018). Then, we concluded with some recommendations for other instructors teaching virtually during the COVID-19 pandemic and afterwards. This book chapter is part of the last step in our current research cycle. Although the problem-solving and research goals have not been completely met because we are continuing this project this semester, we are reporting our preliminary findings from one semester.

BACKGROUND

Authors' Positionality

All three authors are middle-class, able-bodied, white, cis-gendered heterosexual females in their 40s or 50s. The first two authors, Sherri and Mariana (we will refer to ourselves by first names throughout this chapter) are associate professors and the third, Alicia, is an assistant professor. Sherri is in the School of Educational Foundations, Leadership, and Inquiry, Mariana and Alicia are in the School of Counseling and Special Education, and all are members of the Inclusive Early Childhood Program. Below we briefly identify some background information about us that influences our perspectives, teaching, and research.

Sherri's life experiences include living in various places in the United States (U.S.), Europe, and Africa and teaching in a middle-class, predominantly White preschool in the Midwest U.S. She has researched emergent literacy in Head Start and other daycare settings and has taught Educational Psychology at the post-secondary level for twenty-plus years. Some current personal life factors are her father's diagnosis of cancer in May 2020, and helping him and her mother throughout the COVID-19 pandemic and cancer treatments. These personal and professional experiences have influenced her beliefs about importance of social justice, culturally relevant practices, and being a caring teacher and person.

Mariana comes from a working-class family with one of her parents a first-generation college student and an individual with a disability. Her lived and cultural experiences are rooted in Eastern European, Eastern Asian and Western heritages and continue to influence her life and work. Her personal and professional experiences working, teaching, and researching topics that focus on cultural and collaborative issues for children with disabilities and their families have shaped her views on the importance of using another's lenses when attempting to understand them.

Alicia comes from a working-class family and her father and mother were first-generation college students. She encountered significant gender-bias in her first career as an engineer. For more than 20 years in the white female-dominated profession of early childhood special education and applied behavior analysis, she has come to recognize how privilege affects child outcomes and professionals' attitudes. She teaches applied behavior analysis and inclusion practices to both undergraduate and graduate students.

Setting the Stage for our Work on Empathy

In March 2020, we, like many university instructors world-wide, had to pivot quickly from our F2F teaching to a completely virtual platform. Because we were already friends, we often talked about our classes, how our students were dealing with learning virtually, and how we could support them and each other. These discussions were focused on our students, courses, and ourselves, without any thought of research or documenting what we were doing.

During the late spring and early summer, the ongoing social (in)justice issues in the U.S. were spotlighted through George Floyd's and Brionna Taylor's murders and the ensuing protests, the election in the U.S. was heating up, and it became apparent that COVID-19 was going to continue to be a world-wide crisis. Then, on June 22, 2020, our university administration officially announced that there would be three types of class formats for the Fall semester: online (OL), which is virtual asynchronously (through the OL learning platform Canvas); remote, which is virtual synchronously (through Zoom, a video conferencing platform, and Canvas); and hybrid, which is a mixture of F2F and Remote formats. Due to her father's health and potentially exposing him and her mother to COVID-19, Sherri's courses were

OL. Mariana's courses were remote, and Alicia's courses were hybrid at first but switched to remote in early August. We knew the global and national current events and the changes in our own courses would affect how we would teach and interact with our students. Therefore, what started out as friends helping each other turned into a formal collaboration to plan for our courses, especially relating to supporting our students in this uncertain time, and to document how we did this.

In this way, we officially started both the problem-solving and research cycles. We started with the second step of the problem-solving cycle (Ventura, 2018) by gathering information about our particular situations. Next, we cycled back to the first step of identifying the problem in the problem-solving cycle and our research interests in the research cycle. We then moved to the second step in both cycles again by gathering information from previous research.

Gathering Information about our Particular Situations

To gather information for our problem-solving cycle (Ventura, 2018), we reflected on and discussed our own courses. We had learned from the spring semester that most students didn't want to take courses in a virtual format. We also realized that we preferred to teach these courses F2F. Although all of us have taught other OL courses successfully, we believed that these undergraduate courses are most effective with high-impact classroom experiences delivered through in-class activities and personal interactions. Plus, we knew redeveloping effective courses in a virtual format, which would hopefully only be short term, would take a great deal of work.

We also discussed our students, their lives, and the current situations. We were aware of individual and socio-cultural factors that were likely to create challenges for some of our students. Many of our students had personal circumstances, such as food insecurity, financial hardships, mental health issues, and social isolation, that could be exacerbated by the COVID-19 pandemic. Other issues were directly related to the COVID-19 pandemic, such as changed living arrangements (e.g., many students had to go back to living with parents; restrictions on living in dorms), and different responsibilities (e.g., helping younger siblings with OL school). Finally, students could be experiencing increased stress due to the ongoing anger and anxiety over multiple racist crimes that resulted in the deaths of Black individuals, attempts for dialogue and a variety of public reactions.

Identifying the Problem and Selecting the Research Topics

After thinking about our and our students' current situations, we moved back to the first steps of Ventura's (2018) AR models of identifying the problem in the problem-solving cycle and selecting the research topics in the research cycle. We identified the problem as: how can we support our students and each other through this health crisis and the current social (in)justice and political uncertainty in ways that would (a) keep the students engaged and learning in their (now) virtual courses and (b) account for their whole person and lived experiences. The concomitant research goals were to document: (1) how we reflected on our current instructional practices; (2) how we could change and strengthen them to support our students; and 3) whether these changes were effective in keeping students engaged, learning, and feeling like we were supporting them both as learners and as human beings.

Gathering Information about Theories and Previous Research

After identifying the problem and our research goals, we moved to the next step in both the problem-solving and research cycles (Ventura, 2018) where we gathered information beyond our personal experiences. We (re)read articles and books on empathy and care theories and UDL practices, including how to apply them to teacher preparation settings, especially in virtual formats.

Empathy Theory Relating to Teacher Preparation

In broad terms, Davis (2006) defined empathy as "a set of constructs that connects the responses of one individual to the experiences of another" (p.443). They explained that there are four constructs leading to an empathy episode: (a) *antecedents*, or the characteristics of the observer and the situation/target they observe; (b) *processes*, or the mechanisms producing empathetic outcomes (e.g., tendencies to automatically and unconsciously mirror the target, classical conditioning, language-based cognitive associations with the observer's own experiences or feelings); (c) *intrapersonal outcomes*, or the cognitive, emotional and motivational responses of the observer (e.g., estimation of the targets thoughts and feelings, attributional judgments on the target's behaviors, reproducing the target's emotions, affectively reacting to the target's emotions through empathetic concern, personal distress, motivational states); and (d) *interpersonal outcomes*, or behaviors directed towards the target as a result of exposure to the target and their situation (e.g., help-giving behaviors, reduced aggressive behaviors on the observer's part as a result of estimating the target's feelings and behaviors) (Davis, 2006).

Applying this theory to educational settings, when educators show empathy, they become aware of their own and their students' lenses, they attempt to imagine what their students are thinking and feeling, they feel "for" the students and engage in help-giving practices or decrease their tendencies to react negatively to the students' situations. As a result, students should feel understood, validated and supported (Meyers et al., 2019). Considered an important component of teacher preparation and professional disposition, empathy is likely to increase educator effectiveness and should be modeled by teacher educators (Dance, 2002; Pajak, 2001; Warren, 2014). Warren (2018) noted that empathizing starts with the observer and their exposure to the target, but it ends with the target's confirmation that the observer's actions helped reduce their distress. Therefore, empathy is the component that connects the teachers' knowledge about students and families with responses that effectively address student needs.

Perspective taking is considered to be the "anchoring dimension" for empathy (Warren, 2018, p. 171), a prerequisite for empathetic concern (Warren, 2014; Warren, 2018) and to help induce empathy (Batson et al., 1997; Todd et al., 2012; Whitford & Emerson, 2019). Batson et al. (1997) described two ways in which observers engage in estimating what others are feeling and thinking. Imagine Other (IO) is when observers imagine how others perceive the situation they experienced and how they feel as a result of this situation and Imagine Self (IS) is when observers imagine how they would think or feel if they were in the situation of the other person. Batson et al. (1997) cautioned that while IO may lead to authentic empathetic emotions and potential altruistic behaviors, IS leads to a combination of empathetic emotions and self-oriented personal distress, which in turn may lead to self-centered motivation or false empathy. To avoid false empathy, or the assumption that one applied more empathy than can be validated by the target person or subsequent positive outcomes, one should be able to tell the difference between the two ways (IO and IS) to engage in estimating other's perceptions, thinking and feelings (Decety & Lamm, 2006; Warren & Hotchkins, 2015). Similarly, Warren (2018) explains that when educators engage in an

IS perspective-taking process, they use their own experiences, affects and lenses, whereas engaging in IO perspective taking allows educators to acknowledge "the range of external social and cultural variables that may be determining the student's academic performance" (p. 174). More specifically, when educators engage in IO perspective taking, they are more likely to avoid blaming students, examine their own and institutional contributions to the students' educational vulnerabilities, and to identify pedagogical practices (e.g., critical reflection on background knowledge based on experiences with others or with students) that would support positive outcomes (Gehlbach & Brinkworth, 2012; Warren, 2018).

Care Theory

Trout (2012) stated that care theory "focuses on the inner workings of relationships between people and argues that relationships harbor a locale rich with moral action" (p. 5). The ethics of caring embodies a relational view of caring (Noddings, 2002). A caring relation consists of two people – a carer and someone who is cared-for – in some type of an encounter (Noddings, 2002). For a caring relation to exist, at least three things must occur. Using a teacher and student as an example: (a) teacher cares for student through attention and motivational displacement, (b) teacher does something showing caring, and (c) student recognizes that teacher cares for student (Noddings, 1995). These can be brief encounters or long-term relationships. Caring relationships are then made up of multiple encounters where the people may exchange places when needed; that is, sometimes one person is the carer and other times they are the cared-for. (Noddings, 2002).

Showing caring for students in OL courses includes timely feedback and positive, personal comments (Rose & Adams, 2014). Rose and Adams (2014) cautioned that "the experience of feeling cared for, or not, is unique for each student" (p. 7) depending on the instructor's and each student's expectations and interpretations of each other's words, especially in a disembodied OL format. Another critical aspect for students' sense of connection is for the instructor to "develop and maintain a strong online presence. Facilitating timely, supportive responses to students using a range of online communication approaches conveys a sense of individuals being valuable members of the learning community" (Burke & Larmar, 2020, p. 7).

Critical care theory "provides insight to the potential complexities and contradictions inherent within caring interactions, interpretations, expressions, and contexts" (Antrop-Gonzales & de Jesus, 2006, p. 413). An ethic of critical care includes "hard caring," (p. 413) which is building supportive relationships while maintaining high academic expectations.

Universal Design for Learning (UDL)

When planning to engage and create a positive learning environment for all students, UDL provides a strong framework for teaching in a diverse classroom (Meyer, et al., 2014). UDL is a framework of guiding principles that allows the instructor to intentionally plan to meet the needs of all students in the room, including those with disabilities, English language learners, gifted learners, and those from diverse cultural and socio-economic backgrounds (Israel et al., 2014). The three basic principles of access to curriculum are student engagement, representation of materials, and student expression of learning (CAST, 2018). By intentionally designing lesson plans with multiple means of engaging students, presenting content, and providing multiple ways for students to express what they have learned, instructors embrace all learners and encourage a higher level of learning and creativity (Raymond, 2003). When instructors design OL classes using UDL principles, they can increase student engagement and demonstrate empathy and caring by recognizing and utilizing the unique learning needs of each student.

Flexibility is the critical element in all planning using UDL principles (Orkwis, 2003). Flexible means of engaging with the content and expressing what they have learned demonstrates to the students that all are welcome in the class and supported in their work (Orkwis, 2003). When instructors present material in multiple ways (e.g., written text, PowerPoint presentations with audio narration, videos of relevant content), then a learner who struggles with written text can more fully comprehend the information and is more likely to feel a valuable part of the class (Smith, 2012). When students can choose to express their learning through various means, such as a PowerPoint, audio, video, or written formats, all students can tell their own stories.

MAIN FOCUS OF THE CHAPTER

Planning Our Courses

After gathering information, identifying the problem, and selecting the research topics, we then moved into the next step in Ventura's (2018) AR cycles where we used the knowledge we had gained to plan how to adapt our courses (part of the problem-solving cycle), and how we could document that process (part of the research cycle). Perhaps due to the delay in obtaining IRB approval, we were able to obtain consent from a sufficient number of student participants only in Sherri's course. Therefore, although each of us did all the following steps in our courses, we will only describe these steps as related to Sherri's course. We briefly describe Sherri's course, including the typical F2F elements and the changes due to the COVID-19 restrictions. Because the planning on how to adapt the course overlaps conceptually with actual taking action to adapt the course, we don't specifically explain our planning but how we implemented them in the next step, taking and implementing action.

Educational Psychology is a sophomore-level three-credit course, which is required for all teaching and communication disorders majors. There are approximately 30 students in each of the 10 sections, with Sherri typically teaching two sections per semester. Students learn about developmental, motivational, and learning theories through lecture, question and answer sessions, and group activities applying this information to classroom and other settings. However, due to the COVID-19 pandemic, much of this changed. For Fall 2020, Sherri's sections were in an online, asynchronous format. In describing how Sherri went through the rest of these steps, we use the first person, I, to emphasize her lived experience of teaching and interacting with her students; however, when we discuss the research and collaboration part we use the plural verb form.

Data Collection: Planning Our Research

Related to the research cycle (Ventura, 2018), we planned how we would collect data, monitor, and evaluate our AR project to document our goals of reflecting on our instructional practices and developing strategies to strengthen these practices. We also discussed our data collection methods related to our specific research question of whether these practices helped our students keep engaged, learning, and feeling supported as learners and human beings. Specific to this book chapter, we identified the type of data we wanted to collect and the main methods to collect it as based on journaling, instructor-designed well-being weekly surveys, and student course assignments. Subsequently, we wrote a proposal for IRB approval.

Taking Action and Implementing the Plan: Teaching the Course and Documenting the Process

We did the next steps in Ventura's (2018) problem-solving and research cycles of taking action and implementing the plan simultaneously. One of my major goals for my teaching in Fall 2020 was to consciously attempt to increase my caring of and for my students, through empathetic concern, IO perspective-taking, and using UDL practices. Meyers et al. (2019) stated three broad recommendations for instructors to increase their teacher empathy: (1) develop a deep understanding of students' social contexts, (2) make time to learn more about their students' personal contexts, and (3) design course policies that reflect this deep understanding of their students' personal and social situations. They also gave some specific suggestions for how instructors could use these recommendations to inform their teaching and class policies. We briefly describe the ones I used in adapting my course. Instead of focusing on student characteristics (e.g., laziness, unmotivated), instructors should focus on students' social situations, such as time issues (e.g., working, parenting) and fear of failure (e.g., stereotype threat, belonging uncertainty) to help develop non-pejorative explanations for undesirable student behaviors (Meyers et al., 2019). Surveying students, including on relevant academic risk factors, at the beginning and through the semester can help the instructor learn about their students' social and personal situations. Rather than force students to take the initiative and disclose potentially unflattering personal information (e.g., reasons for missing an assignment) to allow for exceptions to course policies, instructors can change the policies to allow for some flexibility on late work and redoing assignments for all students.

We agreed with these ideas and thought they would enhance positive student-teacher relationships, increase student engagement with the course content, and show not only empathy but also caring and use of UDL principles. However, I, the first author, was concerned about whether I could manage the increased workload implementing this AR project could entail, especially when I would also be helping my parents during my Dad's cancer treatments and their self-imposed long-term quarantine. This concern relates to what Noddings (1984) calls a conflict where "we become overburdened and our caring turns into 'cares and burdens' (p. 18)." Another concern was related to how I could maintain the high rigor and academic expectations of my F2F courses in an OL setting. Finally, I also grappled with how to design a course to reflect students' personal and social situations when I needed to develop much of the course before knowing anything about my students as individuals. Similar to how we developed this AR project, I decided to start with what I knew about our student population in general, my students in previous semesters, including Spring 2020, and myself. Then, I designed my course policies, format, and requirements using some from previous semesters, adapting some, and adding some. Finally, as the course progressed, I continued to adapt these based on my own and current students' social and personal situations. In the following paragraphs, I briefly explain my course policies, format, and requirements that I used in a (hopefully) empathetic and caring way to increase positive student-teacher relationships and enhance their engagement in the content even within a disembodied, physically and socially distanced, pandemic-induced online course.

Early/Re-submissions and Tokens

For years, I have had policies relating to early and re-submissions. For instance, I have allowed students to redo three questions on their mid-term exams to both relearn the material and increase their grade. Also, if students submitted assignments early, they could resubmit them after they received feedback from me. However, after reading the literature and discussing social justice issues with my colleagues, I realized this early submission policy might not be equally helpful for students from all personal and social contexts (e.g., time constraints for working, parenting and/or fear of failure). Therefore, I kept the early submission policy but also added tokens (Meyers et al., 2019). Starting with 10 tokens, every student was encouraged to use a token to (a) submit any weekly assignment late; (b) redo an exam question, with a maximum of three; and (c) extend the due date of their major paper by one school day with a maximum of one week.

Quizzes

For the weekly quizzes, I used the same format that I have used successfully for years in my OL graduate classes. The description in the syllabus read, "Because this is mostly used as a formative assessment to help you evaluate your knowledge and for me to evaluate your knowledge as well, students can take these quizzes two times (with the highest score counting)".

Voluntary Zoom Meetings

The university-wide policy for OL courses was that there could not be any mandatory synchronous activities. However, to allow for different ways of learning and a more personal connection, I had voluntary Zoom meetings on Sunday and Thursday evenings, which could substitute for the discussion boards that were also due on those days. I also held voluntary Zoom office hours and study sessions.

Additional Content on Empathy Theory and Current Events

I also adapted some of the course content and assignment topics to include empathy and current issues. I added in a module on empathy theory. Many quizzes and discussions included questions where they could apply the theory to current events. Sample discussion questions are:

1. How could understanding and applying Bronfenbrenner's (1994) Ecological theory help you to be more empathetic, a) in your career, b) related to current events, and/or c) your personal relationships, life, etc.
2. How does empathy relate to the current world events, (COVID-19, social justice, etc.)? That is, what can you and others do to be empathetic in 'modern times'?
3. What you do think are some of the 'dangers' or 'cautions' regarding using behaviorism concepts? For instance, how could someone's explicit and implicit biases regarding race/ethnicity, gender, gender identity, etc. come into play negatively?

First-Day Questionnaire

I adapted my typical F2F "getting to know you" questionnaire, to allow students to reveal a broader range of information about themselves. For instance, they could answer questions related to where they were living; responsibilities beyond this course they might have; potential internet/computer issues; their anxiety level about tests, papers, and other assignments; how they were dealing with the pandemic; and anything else they wanted me to know.

Weekly Surveys

I also instituted weekly surveys that had four well-being questions plus some course-specific questions that varied depending on the feedback I needed. The well-being questions were three forced-choice questions assessing their current feelings about handling: (a) this class, (b) all classes, and (c) everything non-class-related with options of highly positive, somewhat positive, somewhat anxious, and highly anxious and an open-ended "Please let me know anything you would like about this course, your courses in general, and/or your life." Some examples of course-specific questions were: (a) do you find the audio PowerPoints helpful? Please explain; (b) Do you have any suggestions for how I could improve the course?; and (c) What aspects of the modules do you think are least helpful for your learning?

Emails and Announcements

I attempted to interact with them through weekly announcements and emails to the whole class; emails to individual students responding to their surveys and assignments; and encouraging all students to email me when they had questions about anything course-related, school-related, or just life in general.

Monitoring the Implementation and Effectiveness of the Course

The next step in both the problem-solving and research cycles (Ventura, 2018) is to monitor the problem-solving efficacy and the research interests. In regards to Sherri's attempts to be empathic and caring and use UDL practices, this step is embedded within the structure of the course itself. She monitored and adapted her practices through communicating with her students and self-reflection. To monitor our research interests, we continued to journal and to meet virtually to discuss our courses and this project.

Data Analysis: Evaluating the Effectiveness of the Course

For this AR project, the evaluation step in the problem-solving cycle (Ventura, 2018) was using the evaluation step of the research cycle. That is, we analyzed the data we collected to evaluate the effectiveness of the course related to (a) keeping the students engaged and learning in their (now) virtual courses and (b) accounting for their whole person and lived experiences. We chose to use thematic analysis (Braun & Clarke, 2006; 2012) because of its flexibility through theoretical freedom and different ways of identifying themes or patterns (i.e., inductive, deductive; Nowell et al, 2017). We started with a priori, deductive themes based on our interest in showing empathy and caring through UDL practices. Finally, the data set we included was the items from the data corpus that pertained to the research questions of how Sherri, as the instructor, showed empathy and caring and used UDL practices and how that affected her students. The instructor-related item is Sherri's journals. We obtained IRB approval for the use of class artifacts from students who consented to participate in this project. The student-related items are the 18 participants' responses on the 14 well-being surveys plus the anonymous course evaluations from all students who did them (n = 47; 81%). Please see Table 1 for information about the participants.

Table 1. Demographic information for participants

Participant Demographics	n	Percent
Gender		
Female	17	94.4
Male	1	05.6
Age		
18-24 years old	18	100
Race/ethnicity		
White/ Caucasian	17	94.4
Asian/ Pacific Islander	1	05.6
Program level		
Sophomore	15	83.3
Junior	3	16.7
Major		
Adolescence/ Young Adult	2	11.1
Communication Sciences and Disorders	2	11.1
Inclusive Early Childhood	9	50.0
Intervention Specialist	3	16.7
Middle Childhood	2	11.1

In analyzing the data, we went through Braun and Clarke's (2006) six phases of thematic analysis. To increase trustworthiness, Sherri and Mariana reviewed the survey responses while Sherri and Alicia reviewed the course evaluations. First, we familiarized ourselves with the data by reading all the surveys and the course evaluations. Second, keeping the research questions and aim of our teaching related to empathy, caring, and UDL practices in mind, each of us independently coded the data extracts. We discussed and refined our coding, then recoded the data. In phase three, we searched for themes beyond the three deductive ones, developing sub-themes. In phase four and five, we reviewed the potential themes to refine them then we defined and named them. Finally, this book chapter is phase six: producing the report. Although we did find themes beyond our research for this book chapter, we explain only those related to empathy, caring, and UDL practices.

Findings

As mentioned above, we used the three theoretical underpinnings for the changes to our courses – empathy, caring, and UDL practices – to frame our beginning coding. However, through the coding and ongoing discussions, we determined that empathy and caring were overlapping in many of their theoretical constructs, actual practices, and student reactions that we could not completely separate them out in our data. Therefore, we have merged them together and refer to them together as empathy/caring. We could distinguish between UDL practices and empathy/caring

We found five themes – structure of the course, feedback, flexibility, high expectations, and relationships -- that related to Sherri showing empathy, caring, and using UDL practices. See Table 2 for the themes and how they relate to UDL and empathy/caring. In the following paragraphs, we briefly explain each of them and give examples of how students recognized these practices in their evaluations and surveys. In reporting their comments, we have used 'a student' for any of the anonymous comments from the course evaluations and pseudonyms for comments from participants.

Table 2. Relation between themes and UDL and empathy/caring on the evaluations and surveys

	UDL		Empathy/Caring	
Themes	evaluations	surveys	evaluations	surveys
Structure of course	x	x		x
Feedback	x	x	x	x
Flexibility	x	x	x	x
High Expectations	x		x	x
Relationships			x	x

Structure of the Course

Because this was an OL course, this theme deals with the design and organization of the course through Canvas and the course materials, such as readings, videos, and PowerPoints. On the surveys, participants mentioned their own personal learning and how different aspects of the course enhanced their understanding, that it was easy to navigate, the structure was clear, and the information was well organized. More specifically, students expressed, on both the surveys and evaluations, their appreciation for making the class manageable, the consistency of the due dates, and the regular updates and reminders through announcements and emails. For instance, Rebecca writes on Sept 20th survey,

I really like the way that you have this class structured and think that it is very beneficial to my being able to take the time to understand the information that you are presenting to us. I really like the audio powerpoints because I can hear you explaining things while also seeing exactly what you are talking about and they help me understand certain aspects I may not have fully grasped in the readings and viewings alone.

Therefore, the organization of the Canvas site and the frequent emails and announcements seemed to help students deal with the amount of work they had in all their classes and perhaps lessen their feelings of being overwhelmed. These comments highlight instances of hard caring through keeping the rigor of the course but helping all students to strive for success. However, several students when asked on the course evaluation for feedback on how to improve the course, had specific advice related to posting modules earlier and not rushing through the content.

Feedback

This theme dealt both with student feedback about the course and my feedback to them. Several students thanked me for asking them for feedback. On the December 10th (final) survey, Audrey stated, "Thank you for a great semester and being so open about student feedback!" and one student wrote on the evaluation, "I also like that Dr. Horner asks for student feedback (I wish they were anonymous though) regularly and is willing to try new things…" Students also specifically mentioned the relation between my feedback and their own learning. On the December 10th (final) survey, Kayley stated, "You also always gave good feedback which helped with my understanding of each theory and how I could improve for other assignments." Many also mentioned the timeliness of the feedback. For instance, a student wrote on the evaluation, "Dr. Horner's feedback has been extremely helpful and thoughtful. She always does her best to give feedback as soon as she can and let's us know when and why it might take her awhile on certain assignments." Through student feedback, I was able to adapt the course as needed, showing UDL practices. Also, through my feedback, they were able to learn to the best of their abilities, showing hard caring.

Flexibility

Because students mentioned various elements of the course, which I intentionally included and we detail above, we have divided this theme into sub-themes relating to different policies, assignments, and activities. We also include my perspective based on my journaling and personal impressions.

Token System

Tokens were mentioned several times on the evaluation as a strength of the course. When asked specifically about the token system on the final survey, 16 (89%) participants, responded positively whereas the other two replied that they had never used a token. Two quotes from students exemplify their comments. On the evaluation, one student wrote "I really enjoyed our token system throughout this crazy semester, and it was really helpful for me! I am not sure if this system was used in previous courses taught, but I would continue to do it!" And Alaina wrote on the December 10th (final) survey:

The token system was the most helpful thing that I learned about. …Knowing that you can leave an assignment until the next day without repercussions relieved me of so much unneeded stress this semester. Thank you for this system!

Quizzes

On the November 8th survey, Belinda responded to the question, "Please let me know anything you would like…" with, "I'm feeling pretty good about this course and I really like the Sunday quizzes and how we are allowed to have two tries because then it forces me to go back and relook at the readings instead of saying oh well and moving on." On the final survey on December 10th, 12 (66%) participants mentioned the quizzes specifically when asked to briefly explain what elements of the course helped them learn. For example, Alaina stated, "I feel like the quizzes really helped introduce the topics every week. It helps you dive into the details and then the questions that had you apply the theory helped you begin to think about the AA's [application assignment]." No one mentioned the quizzes in response to the question about what did not help them learn. We think this is particularly striking because students traditionally hate quizzes!

Zoom or OL Discussion Board

The choice between doing the online discussion board and attending a Zoom session was a mixed success, with student feedback being consistently positive but the instructor feeling over-burdened. Multiple students who attended the Zoom sessions thanked me regularly on Zoom and in the surveys for holding them. For instance, on the September 20th survey, Ally mentioned, "Also, being able to talk about the theory and application on Zoom afterward always really helps reinforce ideas for me so thank you for hosting those!" She emphasized this again on the final December 10th survey, "Even though this was an online class, I didn't feel so alone in learning this material because I knew I could go to the Zoom meetings and ask you questions, have discussions, and hear other people's perspectives." Plus multiple students, even one who never attended, mentioned them as a strength on the evaluation. For me, it was a balancing act between helping students learn the best they could and the time commitment. The maximum number of students who attended any Zoom was 10 (out of 62) and many times there were only two. Therefore, my vision of less online Discussion posts to read, grade, and give feedback on did not come to fruition and by the end of the semester this act of caring sometimes seemed like a burden as well (Noddings, 1984).

High Expectations

This theme related to the hard caring (Antrop-Gonzales & de Jesus, 2006) of maintaining the rigor of the course, even while adapting it, and expecting students to succeed. On both the evaluations and surveys, multiple students linked how much they learned in the course to both my expectations and help. For instance, on the September 13th survey, Sammi wrote, "I've mentioned this before, … The lay out is really easy to follow, which helps me not only complete what is expected, but learn the material as well." one student wrote on the evaluation, "She always gave us great resources to look over to succeed in this course." And another stated, "We could work at our own pace but still had guidance from the professor as to what we were to be completing."

Relationships

Many students expressed on the evaluations and surveys that they appreciated that I checked in regularly with their lives, was generous and cared about students, was culturally and racially sensitive, and was understanding and helpful. Plus, throughout the semester, students felt free to share both personal challenges and triumphs. For instance, Maggie disclosed on the introductory survey, on Aug 27th, that she was a primary caregiver for her ailing grandparents. She continued to update me on her grandparents throughout the semester through the surveys, emails, and Zooms (attending one in a hospital parking lot). I would email her about her situation as well. Some students seemed to like letting me know positive things, such as "I had a good day today," and "I got a puppy... and it's interesting to see the positive reinforcement they are using in her training."

However, a few students had more negative experiences. As Rose and Adams (2014) mentioned, the experience of feeling cared for is unique and therefore some of my attempts were not true caring. For instance, one student wrote, "Anytime that I fill it [the survey] out she emails me like she is angry at me for saying I have concerns."

Although I believe that building and maintaining relationships through the weekly surveys and the follow-up emails was important for students' engagement and learning in the course, it personally took up a lot of time and energy. Over the course of the 15-week semester, I sent and received close to 700 emails! Also, being aware of the difficulties some students were facing in their personal lives, both past and present, could be heart-breaking, especially when I could not help them. On the other hand, this interaction was key in helping me adapt the course. They also helped me feel connected to students and gave me validation for the amount of time and effort I was spending on this course.

Evaluating the Implementation through Empathy/Caring and UDL

Sherri used UDL principles throughout her lesson-planning to ensure her students felt engaged, and that they could access the content and express their learning (CAST, 2018). While this is important for the academic outcomes of the students, it also created an environment of caring and demonstrated empathy for the individual situations and collective health and social stresses of 2020 (Orkwis, 2003). Through the course structure, Sherri provided multiple means of representation, in audio PowerPoints, written assignments, announcements and emails. This structure and her feedback provided the students the ability to learn the material in the way that worked best for them. By showing flexibility, through the early submission, tokens, and optional Zoom meetings or discussion posts, she provided multiple times to submit an assignment. Her relationship-building activities of the weekly surveys, emails, and optional Zooms kept the students engaged with her and the content.

Sherri engaged in empathy through IO perspective-taking by her relationship-building activities, which allowed her to recognize students' individual circumstances. This then helped her to be flexible and create opportunities for all her students to be successful. This resulted in lower anxiety for the students, as described in their survey and evaluation comments, and to feel understood and supported (Meyers et al., 2019). She provided convincing evidence that she cared about her students and heard their voices. For a caring relationship to occur, the instructor needs to care for student through attention and motivational displacement and do something that shows that caring, and the student must recognize that the instructor cares for student (Noddings, 1995). Using Amy, who was a primary caregiver for her grandparents, as an example, Sherri cared for her, both as a student and a person, by truly listening to her in Zooms, surveys, and emails and through IO perspective taking. She emailed and talked with her about her grandparents and encouraged her through the same methods and in her feedback on assignments. She also maintained her high expectations and hard caring through holding Amy to the same standards while being flexible. Finally, at numerous times, Amy expressed her thanks and gratitude for Sherri. All these strategies created a welcoming "classroom" even though it was not in person.

SOLUTIONS AND RECOMMENDATIONS

Amending the Plan and Recycling through the Steps of the Problem-Solving Cycle

By analyzing the data, writing this chapter, and reflecting on the Fall semester, we have moved into the final step of Ventura's problem-solving cycle of amending the plan, which also becomes the first step of the next cycle that continues as we write this. Because how we are planning to amend our classes is also what we hope other instructors would do in their own courses, we have written this as recommendations for how to teach in a caring and empathic ways, through UDL practices, in virtual courses to foster student engagement through the COVID-19 pandemic and beyond.

Below are some strategies we are planning to implement in Spring 2021 and beyond, and that we consider recommendations based on our experience in fall 2020.

1. Practice empathy through the IO experience of *imagining other perspective taking* to learn more about students' lives and situations (Meyers et al., 2019; Warren, 2018).
    a. Offer virtual "office hours" that are convenient for students. For example, in spring, Alicia made her Zoom office hours in the evening because her students are at their placement during the day.
    b. Be intentional during conversations with students by using their frames of references, sociocultural individual contexts and lived experiences, rather than our own lenses (Warren & Hotchkins, 2014). Listen to what the students are sharing and respond with empathetic statements based on understanding of their needs to effectively provide supports.
2. Practice *empathic concern* by exercising self-awareness and self-monitoring to avoid engaging in self-oriented affects as a result of learning about the students' situations *(personal distress)*. Instead, exercise feeling "for" the student, or engage in "the other-oriented emotional response of compassion" (Davis, 2006, p. 453) for the students. In other words, when we learn about students' circumstances or observe behaviors that are indicative of students' challenges, we orient our emotional reactions towards the experience of the students, and not on how we feel about the situation (e.g., feeling compassion for a student who feels highly anxious vs. feeling surprised, frustrated, anxious ourselves knowing how the student feels).
3. Practice caring for students both as students and people (Meyers et al., 2019). The students should know there is someone who honestly cares about them and is available to listen.
    a. Use informal assessment (e.g., surveys, exit questions in F2F classes, discussion posts) to gauge how students are feeling and coping with their semester. Then respond with empathy.
    b. Take the time to use perspective-taking and empathetic concern for deeper conversations.
    c. Act on the results of the assessment; make changes within the semester if needed.
    d. Recognize that flexibility is the hallmark of good UDL practice and clearly demonstrates empathy without words.
4. Reflect on your instructional practices to improve empathy and caring (Meyers et al., 2019). We recognize that developing and implementing effective empathetic strategies requires ongoing efforts to understand our social justice climate and willingness to confront our own challenges in understanding our contributions to this climate.
5. Incorporate UDL practices within the course structure (CAST, 2018).

Fostering Student Engagement Through Showing Empathy and Caring in an Online College Course

      a. Provide multiple means of presenting content (e.g., video, audio PowerPoints, written text) so all students can access the information easily.
      b. Include multiple means of expression with the learning goal in mind, such as flexible grading practices of allowing late submission by using the token system, allowing resubmission or retaking quizzes, and options for written work such as videos or PowerPoints.
      c. Engage students through email, Canvas, and Zoom.
6. Be sincere. We honestly care about our students, and since you are reading this chapter, we assume you really care about your students too and want to increase your use of real empathy and caring to increase their success. If you are having a rough day, it is ok to let the students know this and reschedule if needed.
7. Be aware of the possible over-burden of empathy and caring (Noddings, 1984; Rose & Adams, 2014). Your ability to provide empathy and caring is dependent on your own health and honesty. Practicing self-care (e.g., meeting with those you care about, journaling, physical exercise, meditation or prayer, etc.) may give you that emotional strength to practice empathy and caring.

These recommendations are particularly pertinent when teaching virtually since the casual, informal showing of empathy and caring that occurs before and after class in F2F settings is not as readily available.

FUTURE RESEARCH DIRECTIONS

Amending the Plan and Recycling through the Steps of the Research Cycle

By analyzing the data, writing this chapter, and reflecting on the Fall 2020 semester, we have also moved into the final step of Ventura's (2018) research cycle of amending the plan, which also becomes the first step of the next cycle that continues as we write this. In the next paragraph, we briefly explain the next steps in our AR project then we advise on what others could do in future research as well.

We are continuing to meet as a support and research group to discuss and reflect on how we can show empathy and caring and use UDL practices in our courses. We are also expanding our group to include other colleagues who are interested in social justice and culturally-relevant ways of teaching, learning, and supporting students. We will continue to investigate our own teaching techniques and how they impact our students directly and also whether they become more empathetic and caring themselves. With this AR project having IRB approval, we will have enough students consent from all our courses to analysis the impact of these practices on students in multiple courses. We also plan to continue to collect data when we go back to F2F classes.

Beyond our own courses, we recommend that other instructors use the AR cycles (Ventura, 2018) and Braun and Clarke's (2006) thematic analysis to investigate their own teaching techniques and how they could increase their empathy and caring for their students. They could use Meyer et al.'s (2019) suggestions or replicate and extend our research. Documenting different ways of structuring courses, giving feedback, being flexible, maintaining high expectations, and building positive relationships could broaden the research and teaching communities' knowledge of good college teaching techniques.

CONCLUSION

Based on the findings of this AR project, we believe that demonstration of empathy through attention to the design of the class structure, timely feedback, and flexibility, hard caring, and building and maintaining positive relationships are critical elements for student engagement in post-secondary courses, especially in a virtual setting and during a global pandemic. Embedding empathetic and caring elements within a course helps create a better climate for students to thrive and feel empowered and understood. Finding a colleague to collaborate with or discuss plans provides support for us when engaged in a potentially emotionally draining endeavor of embedding empathetic practices in our courses. Demonstrating empathy takes intentional effort but potentially reaps large rewards for the students and us as instructors.

REFERENCES

Antrop-Gonzales, R., & de Jesus, A. (2006). Toward a theory of critical care in urban small school reform: Examining structures and pedagogies of caring in two Latino community-based schools. *International Journal of Qualitative Studies in Education: QSE, 19*(4), 409–433. doi:10.1080/09518390600773148

Batson, C., Early, S., & Salvarani, G. (1997). Perspective taking: Imagining how another feels versus imagining how you would feel. *Personality and Social Psychology Bulletin, 23*(7), 751–758. doi:10.1177/0146167297237008

Bradbury, H., Lewis, R., & Embury, D. C. (2019). Education action research. In C. A. Mertler (Ed.), *The Wiley handbook of action research in education* (pp. 7–28). John Wiley & Sons. doi:10.1002/9781119399490.ch1

Braun, V., & Clarke, V. (2006). Using thematic *analysis in psychology. Qualitative Research in Psychology, 3*(2), 77–101. doi:10.1191/1478088706qp063oa

Braun, V., & Clarke, V. (2012). Thematic analysis. In H. Cooper, P. M. Camic, D. L. Long, A. T. Panter, D. Rindskopf, & K. J. Sher (Eds.), APA handbooks in psychology®. APA handbook of research methods in psychology, Vol. 2. Research designs: Quantitative, qualitative, neuropsychological, and biological (p. 57–71). American Psychological Association. doi:10.1037/13620-004

Bronfenbrenner, U. (1994). Ecological models of human development. In T. Husen & T. N. Postlethwaite (Eds.), *International encyclopedia of education* (2nd ed., Vol. 3, pp. 1643–1647). Elsevier.

Burke, K., & Larmar, S. (2020). Acknowledging another face in the virtual crowd: Reimagining the online experience in higher education through an online pedagogy of care. *Journal of Further and Higher Education*, 1–15. Advance online publication. doi:10.1080/0309877X.2020.1804536

Calhoun, E. F. (2019). Action research for systemic change in education. In C. A. Mertler (Ed.), *The Wiley handbook of action research* (pp. 415–438). John Wiley & Sons. doi:10.1002/9781119399490.ch19

Casselman, P. (2019). The experience of students and faculty when elements of Bloom's mastery learning are used in an online statistics course: A participatory action research study. In C. A. Mertler (Ed.), *The Wiley handbook of action research* (pp. 463–480). John Wiley & Sons. doi:10.1002/9781119399490.ch21

CAST. (2018). *Universal Design for Learning Guidelines version 2.2.* http://udlguidelines.cast.org

Dance, L. J. (2002). *Tough fronts: The impact of street culture on schooling*. Routledge.

Davis, M. H. (2006). Empathy. In J. E. Stets & J. H. Turner (Eds.), *Handbook of the sociology of emotions* (pp. 443–466). Springer. doi:10.1007/978-0-387-30715-2_20

Decety, J., & Lamm, C. (2006). Human empathy through the lens of social neuroscience. *TheScientificWorldJournal*, *6*, 1146–1163. doi:10.1100/tsw.2006.221 PMID:16998603

Embury, D. C., Parenti, M., & Childers-McKee, C. (2020). Editorial: A charge to educational action researchers. *Action Research*, *18*(2), 127–135. doi:10.1177/1476750320919189

Enerio, A. T. Jr. (2020). Master teachers' challenges in doing action research: A case study. *Universal Journal of Educational Research*, *8*(7), 2990–2995. doi:10.13189/ujer.2020.080727

Gehlbach, H., & Brinkworth, M. E. (2012). The social perspective taking process: Strategies and sources of evidence in taking another's perspective. *Teachers College Record*, *114*(1), 1–29.

Hendricks, C. (2009). Using modeling and creating a research discourse community to teach a doctoral action research course. *International Journal for the Scholarship of Teaching and Learning*, *3*(1), 1–14. doi:10.20429/ijsotl.2009.030125

Israel, M., Ribuffo, C., & Smith, S. (2014). *Universal Design for Learning: Recommendations for teacher preparation and professional development* (Document No. IC-7). http://ceedar.education.efl.edu/tools/innovation-configurations

Meyer, A., Rose, D. H., & Gordon, D. (2014). *Universal design for learning: Theory and practice*. CAST.

Meyers, S., Rowell, K., Wells, M., & Smith, B. C. (2019). Teacher empathy: A model of empathy for teaching for student success. *College Teaching*, *67*(3), 160–168. doi:10.1080/87567555.2019.1579699

Noddings, N. (1984). *Caring: A feminine approach to ethics and moral education*. University of California Press.

Noddings, N. (1995). A morally defensible mission for schools in the 21st century. *Phi Delta Kappan*, *76*, 365–369.

Noddings, N. (2002). *Starting at home: Caring and social policy*. University of California Press.

Nowell, L. S., Norris, J. M., White, D. E., & Moules, N. J. (2017). Thematic analysis: Striving to meet the trustworthiness criteria. *International Journal of Qualitative Methods*, *16*(1), 1–13. doi:10.1177/1609406917733847

Orkwis, R. (2003). *Universally Designed Instruction*. Council for Exceptional Children. (ERIC number: ED475386). www.eric.ed.gov

Palacios-Hidalgo, F. J. (2020a). An approach for providing LGBTI+ education and bridging the language gap: Integrating ESoPC into EFL teacher training. In C. A. Huertas-Abril & M. E. Gómez-Parra (Eds.), *International approaches to bridging the language gap* (pp. 195–213). IGI Global., doi:10.4018/978-1-7998-1219-7.ch012

Pajak, E. (2001). Clinical supervision in a standards-based environment: Opportunities and challenges. *Journal of Teacher Education, 52*(3), 233–243. doi:10.1177/0022487101052003006

Raymond, O. (2003). *Universally designed instruction.* ERIC/OSEP digest, (ED475386). ERIC. https://files.eric.ed.gov/fulltext/ED475386.pdf

Rose, E., & Adams, C. (2014). "Will I ever connect with the students?": Online teaching and the pedagogy of care. *Phenomenology & Practice, 7*(2), 5–16.

Slapac, A., & Navarro, V. (2011). Shaping action researchers through a Master's capstone experience. *Teacher Education & Practice: The Journal of the Texas Association of Colleges for Teacher Education, 24*(4), 405–426.

Smith, F. G. (2012). Analyzing a college course that adheres to the Universal Design for Learning framework. *The Journal of Scholarship of Teaching and Learning, 12*(3), 31–61.

Todd, A. R., Bodenhausen, G. V., & Galinsky, A. D. (2012). Perspective taking combats the denial of intergroup discrimination. *Journal of Experimental Social Psychology, 48*(3), 738–745. doi:10.1016/j.jesp.2011.12.011

Trout, M. (2012). *Making the moment matter: Care theory for teacher learning.* Sense Publishers. doi:10.1007/978-94-6209-110-8

Trout, M., & Basford, L. (2016). Preventing the shut-down: Embodied critical care in a teacher educator's practice. *Action in Teacher Education, 38*(4), 358–370. doi:10.1080/01626620.2016.1226204

Ventura, A. (2018). Action research to improve higher education. In J. Calder & J. Foletta (Eds.), *Participatory) action research: Principles, approaches, and applications* (pp. 197–213). Nova Science.

Warren, C. A. (2014). Towards a pedagogy for the application of empathy in culturally diverse classrooms. *The Urban Review, 46*(3), 395–419. doi:10.100711256-013-0262-5

Warren, C. A. (2018). Empathy, teacher dispositions, and preparation for culturally responsive pedagogy. *Journal of Teacher Education, 69*(2), 169–183. doi:10.1177/0022487117712487

Warren, C. A., & Hotchkins, B. K. (2015). Teacher education and the enduring significance of "False empathy". *The Urban Review, 47*(2), 266–292. doi:10.100711256-014-0292-7

Whitford, D. K., & Emerson, A. M. (2019). Empathy intervention to reduce implicit bias in pre-service teachers. *Psychological Reports, 122*(2), 670–688. doi:10.1177/0033294118767435 PMID:29621945

ADDITIONAL READING

Collier, M. D. (2005). An ethic of caring: The fuel for high teacher efficacy. *The Urban Review*, *37*(4), 351–359. doi:10.100711256-005-0012-4

Decety, J., & Batson, C. D. (2009). Empathy and morality: Integrating social and neuroscience approaches. In J. Verplaetse, J. Schrijver, S. Vanneste, & J. Braeckman (Eds.), *The moral brain* (pp. 109–127). Springer. doi:10.1007/978-1-4020-6287-2_5

Delgado, R., & Stefancic, J. (2001). *Critical race theory: An introduction*. New York University Press.

Kasl, E., & York, L. (2016). Do I really know you? Do you really know me? Empathy amid diversity in differing learning contexts. *Adult Education Quarterly*, *66*(1), 3–20. doi:10.1177/0741713615606965

Konrath, S. H., Brien, E. H., & Hsing, C. (2011). Changes in dispositional empathy in American college students over time: A meta-analysis. *Personality and Social Psychology Review*, *15*(2), 180–198. doi:10.1177/1088868310377395 PMID:20688954

McCormick, K. I. (2018). Mosaic of care: Preschool children's caring expressions and enactments. *Journal of Early Childhood Research*, *16*(4), 378–392. doi:10.1177/1476718X18809388

Mertler, C. A. (2019). *The Wiley handbook of action research in education*. John Wiley & Sons. doi:10.1002/9781119399490

Rector-Aranda, A. (2019). Critically compassionate intellectualism in teacher education: The contributions of Relational-Cultural Theory. *Journal of Teacher Education*, *70*(4), 388–400. doi:10.1177/0022487118786714

Trivette, C. M., Dunst, C. J., Hamby, D. W., & O'Herin, C. E. (2009). Characteristics and consequences of adult learning methods and strategies. *Research Brief*, *3*(1), 1-33. http://tnt.asu.edu

KEY TERMS AND DEFINITIONS

Care Theory:: A feminist-based theory about the ethics of caring, which takes a relational view of caring for others and teaching them to care.

Caring Relation: A three-part relation where someone cares for someone else, shows that caring through an action, and the cared-for recognizes the caring.

:

Empathy: The ability to understand what others are feeling and thinking by attempting to imagine their perceptions and experiences, feel for others in these situations, and effectively express this understanding.

Imagine Other (IO): Observers imagine how others perceive the situation they experienced and how they feel as a result of this situation. IO may lead to authentic empathetic emotions and potential altruistic behaviors.

Imagine Self (IS): Observers imagine how they would think or feel if they were in the situation of others. IS leads to a combination of empathetic emotions and self-oriented personal distress, which in turn may lead to self-centered motivation or false empathy.

Perspective Taking: Attempting to see things from other's point of view by imagining others' perspectives, thinking or feelings that are different from one's own.

Universal Design for Learning (UDL): A framework of principles for creating lesson plans and curriculum that meets the needs of all learners. Like universal design in architecture, using UDL principles produces a flexible learning environment that helps everyone through three basic guidelines: providing multiple means of representing the content, providing multiple means for students to express what they learn, and focus on student engagement.

Chapter 2
Resilience in Crisis:
Developing Community Through Action Research

Alina Slapac
https://orcid.org/0000-0002-2210-1959
University of Missouri-St.Louis, USA

Sarah A. Coppersmith
https://orcid.org/0000-0001-6275-4711
University of Missouri-St.Louis, USA

Kathryn G. O'Brien
University of Missouri-St. Louis, USA

Phyllis Balcerzak
University of Missouri-St.Louis, USA

ABSTRACT

Teacher action research serves as a framework that can transform practice while supporting inquiry, investigation, and problem-solving. This chapter provides a research report on the challenges experienced, strategies used, and lessons learned from 41 graduate education teacher-researchers who designed and implemented their own educational research during the COVID-19 crisis as part of their Action Research Capstone course before graduation. Graduate students were enrolled in three sections of the Action Research course in a Midwestern university. Methodology included a qualitative approach to data collection and analysis. Findings from discussion board posts, reflections, and research papers captured challenges in facing COVID-19, yet participants' engagement in the community of learners within the course ameliorated and buffered stress, trauma, and compassion fatigue felt due to the pandemic's impact on these frontline workers.

DOI: 10.4018/978-1-7998-6922-1.ch002

INTRODUCTION

Teachers, parents, administrators, and children in schools were caught off-guard and were unprepared for the immediate transitions required during the 2020 COVID-19 pandemic (Duncan, 2020). Challenges included a lack of resources such as professional development, technology, connectivity, and "digital skills training" for the families and educators working to ensure engaging online learning opportunities for all (Duncan, 2020, p. A11). As a result of these and other severe adjustments required during the crisis, "the level of stress for educators rose exponentially" (Fasanella, 2020, p. 191). The impacts of the pandemic occurred in schools from the United States to China (Wong & Moorhouse, 2020; Yang, et al., 2020), where teachers and students experienced physical and mental stress together and researchers worked to examine the phenomena. Resources then quickly emerged to help the over 90 percent of educators reporting high levels of stress and sacrifice during the crisis (Carello, 2019; Fasanella, 2020).

Four instructors, who taught an online graduate action research course during the pandemic, where most of the graduate students were classroom teachers by day and were also working toward their Master's in Education, decided to study their graduate teacher-researchers' daily challenges caused by the pandemic, the ways that they overcame those challenges, and what they took away from this unique experience as teacher action researchers. The focus of this study centers on the challenges faced by the graduate researchers in their classroom settings while accomplishing the required action research projects.

For over 20 years, the master's degree program in this midwestern university's College of Education has promoted action research as a strategy to reflectively improve teaching practice while enacting innovations (Herr & Anderson, 2014; Slapac & Navarro, 2011; Zeni, 2001). The program's focus on teachers as agents of change has resulted in an accumulation of reports documenting the power of action research to build confidence and competence for both new and experienced teachers in order to meet the daily rigor of the profession. Recently, the topics upon which some teachers focused began to shift from issues around traditional pedagogical practices to the mental health of students and, subsequently, to their own personal struggles and challenges. In one author's courses, from 2016-2018, for example, 35 percent of the report topics were focused on how to improve responses to student behavior caused by histories of trauma. During these same years there was only one study that addressed a teacher's socio-emotional health. During 2019, three of 30 teachers addressed the topic of what they called, 'teacher burn-out' and 'socio-emotional health of teachers. As with all other stressors on our institutions, the pandemic amplified this parallel dilemma of the teachers' experiences of secondary trauma and their capacity to meet increasing challenges to students' emotional health. During 2020 and under the influence of the pandemic, the number of teachers who identified their personal mental health as a priority tripled.

Building on the tradition of encouraging the study of issues present and important to our graduate students, we intentionally designed and taught our courses to provide a situated, supportive environment where they could inquire, reflect, learn, and adopt action research projects to benefit their learners and themselves during one of the most challenging times in global history. While we made some assumptions about the power of inquiry to solve problems, the evidence in this study illuminates concrete affordances and challenges faced by these practitioners in their own unique settings as they engaged in action research projects to improve their practice. To focus our inquiry, we collaboratively developed the following research questions:

1. What were the main challenges teachers/educators encountered while doing action research during the COVID-19 pandemic?

2. What were the strategies used by teachers/educators to overcome those challenges?
3. How have the pandemic times influenced teachers/educators' resilience and growth?
4. What were the most relevant lessons teachers/educators learned from the action research experience for their professional career?

Evidence collected from teacher participants situated within an action research course shed light on how teachers navigated service to their students while providing insights into their own self-resiliency.

To avoid confusion on the meaning of the word 'students', we use the terms "graduate students", "teacher-researchers", "course or class members", or "participants" when referring to our students who participated in the study and reserve the term "students" to refer to our teacher-researchers' K-12 students. Additionally, the word "resilience" in this study refers to our definition, as the ability to devise creative strategies for moving forward in adverse circumstances.

LITERATURE REVIEW

In the decade prior to the pandemic, research on teaching and learning processes revealed emerging challenges to educators, beginning and experienced alike. Action Research provides a powerful tool to address embedded problems, especially those without traditional solutions found in the teacher education literature (Herr & Anderson, 2014; Slapac & Navarro, 2011). One of the most challenging of these emerging issues was the impact of socio-emotional distress brought by students into classrooms in increasing numbers (Spinazzola et. al., 2005). At the onset of the pandemic, teachers who were managing these novel problems were confronted with the need to deliver lessons on a remote, digital platform. The need for supports became evident, such as the ones suggested in the framework on trauma-informed teaching with online learning adapted from Carello (2019). This framework names ways to help "acknowledge, normalize and discuss difficult topics"; gives suggestions for strategies such as the following: "create routines/rituals"; "conduct check-ins"; work for "collaboration and mutuality"; give "empowerment, voice and choice"; respect "experiences and identities"; and recognize "our individual and collective strength and resilience" (Carello, 2019, n.p.). The tools made available including such trauma-informed approaches, ("A Trauma-Informed Approach", 2020, n.p.) brought awareness to teachers about how to overcome the ever-insidious compassion fatigue (Teater & Ludgate, 2014).

However helpful such strategies were in engaging students in online learning, they could not remedy the fundamental feature that distanced educators from their students' emotional needs, engendering feelings of helplessness and inadequacy in otherwise highly competent teachers. The gap between a caregiver's awareness of clients' needs and her ability to make a difference is one of the main causes of secondary trauma (Ludick & Figley, 2017), a phenomenon identified in front-line health-care workers and service providers who work with trauma-impacted individuals (Sprang et. al., 2019). The tendency for teachers to feel overwhelmed were amplified by the pandemic and challenged their typical coping strategies, often called self-care (Skovholt & Trotter-Mathison, 2014), which were not able to keep pace with the stressors. In light of this, leaders and advocates suggested taking a realistic examination of the risks and impacts of the caring profession on educators, such as burnout, exhaustion, and potential mental health issues during the crisis (Carello, 2019; Teater & Ludgate, 2014).

While educators were considered front-line workers and schools were often in the news media, questions developed on whether and how schools, teachers, and students were adjusting and surviving in the worsening crisis. Schools closed, re-opened, went online, or were hybrid in efforts to serve diverse student learners with and without the means to achieve (Duncan, 2020). Educators urgently needed to find ways to adopt for all to stay safe, to keep communicating and connecting, while simultaneously predicting 'potential trauma' such as helping students self-regulate ("A Trauma-Informed Approach", 2020, n.p.), yet questions remained on whether the resources were utilized, how teachers adapted, at what cost, and what new supports may be needed going forward. Brown, Freedle, Hurless, Miller, Martin, and Paul (2020) studied the effects of trauma training for teacher candidates. Their findings "suggest positive changes in teacher candidates' attitudes, knowledge, and skills following trauma training" (Brown, et al., 2020, p. 16). A key finding of this work was related to the degree of support from district leadership, which provided a foundation that increased teachers' confidence in implementing trauma-informed practices (Brown, et al., 2020).

Psychological research has presented basic indicators of secondary trauma stress effects (Ludick & Figley, 2017) and document support structures that contradict the stress effects. According to Kapoulitsas and Corcoran (2015), social support, promotion of well-being and self-care represent appreciation that resilience building is a complex process that happens within its own systemic context. The context that will promote and cultivate 'compassion fatigue' resilience is largely dependent upon optimization and nurturance of the positive pathways of self-care, detachment, sense of satisfaction, and social support. Research has shown that the context and environment in which educators work often has more influence on their resilience than teachers' personal attributes (Ainsworth & Oldfield, 2019). Action research is conducted in relevant situated contexts with social supports and stressors within and outside of the researchers' classrooms, and, therefore, can offer supports for resilience and a potential remedy to the forced isolation and social distancing of the pandemic. The university online classroom became a place to find community with other struggling teachers and a place that could model effective online learning pedagogy.

In a longitudinal study examining whether teacher education can make a difference, researchers (Brouwer & Korthagen, 2005) explored educator competence as it evolved from university teacher training to school environments. The authors were interested in influences that changed or eradicated practitioners' prior university learning of best practices and teaching competence. Teachers' "discrepancy experiences" (Brouwer & Korthagen, 2005, p. 213) refers to the disconnect between course learned best teaching practices and the contextual school culture that often contradicts best practice research. The authors indicate that teachers may indeed take up best-practices later on as they adapt to "occupational socialization" (p. 213). Teachers traditionally experience discrepancies between theory and practice, from university to classroom settings, which led to our questions on how teachers adopted strategies while practicing action research in the demanding timeframe of the COVID-19 pandemic. However, this study addresses a gap in research on teacher action research during times of crisis by providing data situated both within the university and the classroom setting.

For this study, the participants were enrolled in a graduate education program studying and utilizing action research, moving from theory to practice in a supportive, situated learning community. Slapac and Navarro (2011) promoted connecting "educational research with teachers' workplace reality" (p. 408) while examining a graduate action research program, thus showing the importance of this close association. While much has been written about teacher induction (Algozzine, et. al, 2007; Hudson, 2012; Killeavy, 2006), it is important to consider the situated nature of learning established within socio-cultural processes (Korthagen, 2010) where "critical understanding can only develop through active dialogue within a community" (Freire, 1972; as cited in Korthagen, 2010, p. 104). Action research by nature is

Resilience in Crisis

"collaborative research" (Stringer, 1999, p. 145), where ideas and actions can develop and grow via group inquiry processes. Strengths of the action research approach include formulating problems and actions within the community (Stringer, 1999), working from inquiry toward social change (Masters, 1995), and working together to refine each researcher-practitioner's reflective strategies. This community of learners' perspective, based on a "theory of participation," is where adults "came to understand it [a phenomenon] through their transforming participation as they engage/d in shared endeavors with other people" (Rogoff et al., 1998, p. 411). When doing action research, it is "essential to have the perspectives of others", as the action research journey "has to do with listening to those around you in seeking different perspectives and kinds of information (data) and supports (collaboration)" (Holly et al., 2009, p. 43). Figuratively, action research has been portrayed as a series of cycles consisting of delineating the problem, observing, planning, reflecting, acting, and then acting again to repeat the cycles to solve problem/s (Hendricks, 2017; Piggot-Irvine, 2002; Wadsworth, 1998). This was made evident in this study as participants worked through changing cycles as they addressed demanding professional transitions together in a community of learners.

MAIN FOCUS OF THE CHAPTER

Research Context and Participants

This study was conducted at a Midwestern university where three sections of a Capstone Action Research course were taught online by three different instructors (also, the researchers) in the M.Ed. program in the fall 2020 during the COVID-19 pandemic. The fourth researcher is also a regular instructor of this course but was teaching a sixteen-week prerequisite course that semester and was not part of the data collection. Each section of the Action Research Capstone course lasted eight weeks, to be taken after eight weeks of a prerequisite course on action research where the graduate students practiced research skills, decided on their research topics, started implementation of interventions and data collection. These two courses are the last required courses in the M.Ed. program, and most students graduate at the end of this Capstone course.

Since all of the graduate students started data collection in the prerequisite course, the Capstone course focused on having them demonstrate their knowledge and ability to use the action research process through implementation of interventions, data gathering and analysis, and continuous reflection on their practice. Our graduate students were encouraged to continue being reflective practitioners and use critical thinking and logical argumentation. A main focus of the course was to create a community of learners through constant collaboration. For example, graduate students and instructors were actively engaged in peer/instructor feedback in different stages of their studies, including instructor and peer feedback on the final PowerPoint or on the online video presentations. Three of the main final assignments of the course were: the final paper of the individual action research studies, the ePortfolio of documentation supporting each participant's research process from start to finish, and the final PowerPoint/video presentation of the study reviewed by external evaluators (faculty, doctoral candidates, former students and other practitioners in different school districts). The final paper had to include the following sections: Introduction, Literature Review, Purpose of the Study, Context and Participants, Interventions (if any), Data Sources, Findings, Implications and Recommendations, References and Appendices. The graduate students' online ePortfolios represented their work as researchers, including their audit trail, articles read and reviewed, samples of materials for their interventions, instruments of data collection, raw data, coding book, and their journals and student work samples/artifacts. While most graduate students worked with the entire class, some chose to use case-study approaches, with only a few students as participants in their study (in particular, with students who were qualified for special services and/or who needed additional supports in social skills and/or in content-knowledge).

The variety and depth of participants' ideas were exemplified in their action research project plans and final Capstone papers and presentations. Evidence from their work revealed the significance of their learning, from initial research inquiries, concerns for their own students' learning, to their growth as teacher researchers and reflective practitioners. The graduate students chose either "What is?" or "What works?" -type of projects, depending on their goals, context and their roles within that context. "What is?"- type of research studies focused on attitudes, perceptions, and/or perspectives, with no interventions used, and with data sources gathered mainly from interviews, surveys or questionnaires, artifacts and observations. For example, some topics focused on teacher collaborations, the importance of culturally responsive advising for minority students, understanding colleagues' stress and trauma related to the pandemic and racial tensions during 2020, and increased access to library books for inmates in a maximum-security prison.

In "What works?" -type of studies the graduate students developed and implemented interventions evaluated for effectiveness to meet their study goals (Hendricks, 2017). Examples of participants' inquiries ranged from interventions in early childhood special education classrooms, math proficiency supports for at-risk youth or students with disabilities, effects of the American Sign Language and translanguaging, cooperative learning or vocabulary instruction on reading comprehension and confidence, comic book writing as a tool of learning English to the power of peer feedback on the quality of writing, impact of positive behavior supports on social skills to the impact of distance learning, digital tools or trauma-informed learning on engagement and/or achievement.

The College of Education offers these action research courses in the M.Ed. program via in-person and online formats. Fortunately, the online versions were developed and taught several times before the pandemic. When the COVID-19 pandemic started, it was decided by the university officials that most courses should be taught online for safety precautions. One section of the course was listed as meeting in a "hybrid" format once per month in person, but the final consensus was to meet online virtually through the semester. Data were collected from three sections of the Capstone course. Most graduate students enrolled in the action research sequence of two eight-week classes so that they remained with the same instructor for the introduction and capstone sections. This meant that each instructor could facilitate development of a robust community of learners across the entire 16 weeks, and also gain a clear understanding of needs, skills and study processes of each graduate student in each course section.

Section 001 of the Capstone course had 16 graduate students at the outset, but one individual withdrew from active class participation for personal reasons. This left 15 students, 10 female-identified and 5 male-identified, as determined by students' designation of preferred personal pronouns at the start of the course. Of the 15, 14 were continuing on immediately after the eight-week prerequisite course and one student was new to the group. Ten students pursued the Masters in Secondary Education, three earned a Masters in Elementary Education, and three focused on a Master's in Special Education. Ten students worked full-time in school settings as teachers, nine in the US, and one in Asia. One student was unemployed, one worked in a maximum-security prison setting, one worked as a supervisor of teachers in a school for children with language-based learning disabilities, and one worked for an education non-profit supporting first-generation college students.

Section 002 started with 17 female-identified graduate students, with 16 students continuing from the previous prerequisite section and one student, new to the group. Another student from this section was not able to finish the final paper and did not present her study so she was not counted as a participant. Twelve students were in the Secondary Education program, with four of them with concentration in TESOL (Teaching English to Speakers of other Languages) and one with concentration in Social Justice, three students were in the Elementary Education program and two in the Special Education Program. Of all seventeen students, 13 were employed as full-time teachers, one as a paraprofessional, two were finishing their student teaching in schools, and one had a staff position in a non-profit organization. Data were collected only from 16 students in this section.

Section 003 had 10 graduate students, with two male-identified and eight female-identified participants. Three were in the Secondary Education program, two were in the Special Education concentration, and five were in the Elementary Education program. One graduate student in Section 003 dropped the course due to an emergency, leaving nine. These elementary, secondary, and elementary educators served in schools as teachers, one participant served in a mental healthcare special education setting, and all were in the prior research 1 class together with this same instructor.

Data Sources and Analysis

A passive consent approach was used with participants and none of the potential participants declined, so 41 graduate students were included in the study. While taking our course, some participants taught entirely virtually, while others taught in-person, hybrid or what we refer to as "in/out," whereby they taught in classrooms when no quarantine was in effect and virtually during quarantine. The main data sources collected from all three sections were: the graduate students' action plans, discussion board postings, and their final action research papers, in particular the Implications and Recommendations section. In addition, data from VoiceThread and Zoom virtual comments were included.

Each of the three researchers initially analyzed their own data sets from their sections using open and axial-coding for pattern finding through connections of developed categories and subcategories (Charmaz, 2006). We coded the discussion board postings that were the most relevant to our research questions (see Table 1):

Table 1 shows initial coding from the instructor of section 001. Discussion Board 7 (DB#7) is the document, followed by the page number, salient text from a participant, an initial note about the topic, a preliminary category, and a final category. (Note: these "final" categories were later merged into broader, overarching categories across data from all sections, as explained below.) Next, we coded additional work, including participants' final action research papers. The action plans allowed for a quick reminder of the individual action research studies.

A constant-comparative approach among all three sections of data sets was then used to refine final themes, while continuing to add evidence for our claims through data triangulation. As the data analysis process evolved, the themes were then compared, contrasted, and correlated systematically, and evidence from the three sessions began to coalesce around concepts which directly related to the research questions.

Table 1. Example of one instructor's initial discussion board coding

Document	Page	Text	Note/Topic	Preliminary Category	Final Category (Sec. 001)
DB#7	18	Sometimes I can make plans but things happen	Planning	Adaptability	Life strategies
DB#7	17	Find focus on your motivation ...If you can find what drives you, adapt and overcome	Adaptability	Motivation	Life strategies
DB#7	22	Most important lesson I learned is accountability and planning. With the pandemic, working as a teacher, dealing with my daughter and unfortunately sick family members made it very difficult but I feel I gave my very best effort even in a pandemic and my daughter being home with me 24/7.	Accountability and planning	Organization	Life strategies
DB#7	17	Take time to celebrate the things that bring you joy; you will be able to handle any situation that life throws at you.	Celebration	Resilience	Life strategies
DB#7	18	I cannot control everything	Locus of control	Self compassion	Life strategies

Main Themes

The research analysis initially proceeded where themes from each section were identified through the data, and then connected directly to the research questions through a structural coding approach (Saldaña, 2012). Structural coding (Saldaña, 2012) allows a way to "categorize the data corpus into segments by similarities, differences, relationships, by using conceptual phrases" (Onwuegbuzie, et al., 2016, p. 135). The conceptual phrases were categorized into these main themes related to the research questions:

- Challenges (Challenges with implementing interventions and data gathering challenges and struggles with participation and engagement; challenges with teaching limitations; and stress and socio-emotional impacts)
- Lessons Learned: Resilience, Personal and Professional Growth, and the Power of Community as an Action Researcher (resilience and personal growth; resilience and professional growth; resilience and growth as an action researcher; *constant support, collaboration and the power of community*.).
- The theme of "strategies" was common, thus is found within each section, including in relation to "growth and lessons learned".

In the same vein, many lessons learned were about resilience, personal and professional growth, support, collaboration and the power of community as an action researcher. These themes revealed the dynamic nature of learning and practicing action research during the global pandemic. Thus, some themes are connected and may overlap in each subsequent section of the findings.

Findings

Challenges

Our teacher-researchers shared common challenges during their teaching while the entire world was devastated by the pandemic. Sub-themes of challenges were related in particular to the implementation of interventions and data gathering, poor student participation and engagement, teaching limitations, such as time and technology issues; and stress, struggles and socio-emotional impacts.

Challenges with Implementing Interventions and Data Gathering

One of the most common challenges encountered by our graduate students during their action research was the difficulty in being consistent with the implementation of interventions or with data collection, which, in turn, led to having to use multiple strategies to increase the validity of the study and trustworthiness of the data sources. For example, one graduate student stated:

My initial plan was to conduct regular conferences with each student, which would have been in person, but became really unmanageable during distance learning. I was still able to hold conferences, but they were not as regular as I had planned. (DB#6_ 002)

Interventions implemented via Zoom conferences or those that required the use of technology, brought challenges. Another teacher recalls: "I've encountered some frustrations implementing my interventions because I had to keep switching breakout rooms and reminding students to stay on task." (DB#6, _002)

Action research processes included data, design, scaling back on projects, and time issues. Data concerns related to wondering about whether data collected during the COVID-19 pandemic might have produced different outcomes than if comparable data were obtained under more normal circumstances. Design had to do with restrictions due to the pandemic that caused one participant, for example, to consider selecting a different problem of practice, or for others, different set of interventions. "The pandemic…completely shaped the way I created my intervention. I wanted to be able to create something that I could continue in the event of my school closing" (DB#7_001). Missing information was a consequence of weeks that schools closed, and one student commented about missing questions and data points that would have been valuable.

Due to the changes from in-person to virtual settings or due to the safety procedures put into place by school districts, collecting data accurately became a difficult task, as some recognized. For example, one teacher recalls having issues tracking the group-work time:

One of the main challenges I had during the pandemic was the times that I was allowed to have groups of students. Our district placed the policy that students from different classes could only be around one another for a maximum of 15 minutes. It was difficult keeping track of how many minutes students were around one another. (DB#6_ 002)

Another special education teacher shared her challenge in regards to being able to conduct regular observations of her colleague, a general education teacher:

It was difficult to get in there to observe the other weeks because the building was closed or the students weren't there or the teacher wasn't there or the paperwork that was needed for virtual took up too much time to get in there. The flip flop back and forth was very difficult. We are 100% virtual until after the New Year right now, and we did come back for 3 days after Thanksgiving. (DB#6_ 002)

Some teachers discussed *"time"* as being one of the encountered challenges, in the sense that they needed more time to be able to fully evaluate the effects of their interventions. While reflecting on the challenges of teaching through an action research lens, one participant noted: "I wanted to gather more types of data than I did, but it was not manageable to teach and also do the data collection that I had planned" (DB#5_003). Changes in scheduling and extra time required for everyone to gain competency in the virtual classroom "limited the time I had to dedicate towards my intervention which took place after a lesson" (DB#7_001). The switch to virtual teaching was completely new for some teachers as virtual lessons ended up lasting longer than expected.

Challenges and Struggles with Participation and Engagement

Health and safety measures comprised school districts' implementation of the Center of Disease and Control (CDC) Guidelines and access to research participants. As school districts sought to implement protections for students and teachers, frequent change ensued. Social distancing, masking, and other means of limiting COVID-19 transmission meant that schools shut down, reopened, implemented virtual learning or hybrid approaches to onsite and/or virtual learning. The chaos experienced by teacher-researchers was evident in their comments. Access to research participants shifted almost daily, as participation throughout the semester waxed and waned due to increased absences, COVID-19 lockdowns and quarantines, student turnover, changes in onsite versus virtual learning, and technology.

For example, teachers dealt with students' lack of consistent attendance and participation. Class members also commented on the decreased parental engagement, which they thought contributed to diminished student engagement and motivation. The teacher-researchers' students were challenged in motivation, engagement, and resistance. Class members described student motivation as lower than expected in the virtual environment, while others complained about technology issues and "instability" that impeded the student learning experiences (see Table 2 below).

Another common challenge for some of our graduate students, especially for the ones who were conducting "What is"- type of studies, was finding enough adult participants to agree to be in their study due to the stress caused by the pandemic: "The pandemic has placed a great deal of extra work and stress on teachers on top of the basic fear and stress that comes with living in pandemic conditions" (DB#6_002). Thus, participants were faced with the dual challenges of teaching during the pandemic while accomplishing their action research goals:

The main challenges I had during my action research study were getting individuals to participate in the survey. I sent my questionnaire out to 43 educators and received 0 responses over a one-week time span. I received many excuses, but the most common was 'I just don't have time to take the survey.' (DB#5_003)

The Covid-19 pandemic also impacted the collaborative aspect of the research:

Table 2. Examples of graduate students' comments regarding issues in virtual learning

"The number of participants I was able to use shrank dramatically." (DB#7_001)
"Students were not consistent in coming to virtual school." (DB#7_001)
"I had to quarantine towards the end of my data collection period. This made my observations less frequent and meant I had less data to work with when drawing my conclusions." (DB#7_001)
"Since I work with EL students, it was very difficult to communicate and reach parents at the beginning of the school year and making sure that they are up to date with the constant changes that were being made to the schedule. My study started out virtual for the first two weeks and then switched to a blended model. I was very concerned if my kids were going to show up to class, so that I could implement the interventions and strategies I had planned. " (DB#5_002)
"We also had a huge issue with participation this year. This seemed to be true across all classrooms in the school. Some students felt overwhelmed and fell into a slump. Other students simply did not try from the beginning because they assumed this semester would run like the end of last year and they would not be penalized or held accountable. " (DB#6_ 002)
"decreased student engagement and participation, and decrease in on-time assignment submissions." (DB#7_001)
"I found the most focused and well-behaved students in person became nightmares online!" (DB#7_001)
"being aware of the social-emotional needs students may have been going through." (DB#7_001)
"Two other students were struggling with engagement because they are naturally shy and were not comfortable showing themselves on camera. Students also encountered internet connection or ZOOM problems." (DB#6_ 002)
"The main challenges I encountered due to the pandemic were the instability of the learning environment, the instability of students' form of participation, online engagement, and logistical issues with a hybrid model." (DB#5_003)

During this study one of the biggest limitations was COVID. COVID caused our building to be shut down for multiple weeks and had the general education teacher out. This caused a break in the interventions and data collection. (Final Paper=FP_002)

Challenges with Teaching Limitations

Inevitably, the teacher-researchers struggled with teaching limitations. Teaching limitations included shifting responsibilities and changing instructional requirements, access to research participants and or technology issues. One class member noted that responsibilities shifted as "day-to-day procedures and teaching were affected dramatically, bringing increased duties every day to keep cohorts separate and managing classes with teachers and students in and out of quarantine". (DB#7_001)

Another factor contributing to shifting responsibilities was classroom management with teachers and students in and out of quarantine. Teaching limitations resulted in access to research participants and ultimately, intervention redesign, because of the difficulty in implementing interventions in a way that permitted students to interact with one another. Low student engagement appeared in this category, along with technology issues. One participant wrote,

Being a one-to-one school with laptops was brand new this year, and video cameras during Zoom calls did not have to be on at any time. As a result, it is insanely hard to judge when a group of students understood a concept since I could not read their body language or see what they were or were not writing. (FP_001)

Furthermore,

I did not get to walk around the room, answer questions in a more private setting (which caused many quieter students to not say anything about the confusion), or check work as we went. Basically, lessons were not as interactive. (FP_001)

A significant challenge and limitation to this study involved knowing if students were truly engaged, and being able to quickly get them on track.

I had utilized the breakout room with some students to check in with them, but a continuous problem that I would run into involved inviting a student to a breakout room and the student not accepting the invitation because they were presumably away from their computer or engaged in something else. I did attempt to call parents/guardians when this occurred, but did not always get an answer due to parents being at work. (FP_002)

Luckily, for some, technology issues were eventually solved:

After a couple of weeks students were more comfortable with being on camera and talking to their classmates. Internet problems were solved by the school district because they provided students with "hotspots." Implementing websites that allowed teachers to monitor student websites was a great help for staying on task because students were aware that their teachers could see what they were doing. (DB#6_ 002)

We tried to overcome these by staying present with our students. We sent out email reminders about homework assignment due dates and upcoming tests. We emailed their parents to keep them in the loop and hoped that they would help to motivate and remind their students about their schoolwork. We changed the way we handed out assignments. (DB#6_002)

A significant challenge for participants involved knowing if their students were truly engaged and being able to quickly get them on track.

Stress and Socio-Emotional Impacts

Teacher-researchers also spoke about personal experiences of the pandemic in terms of fear, guilt, personal loss, and stress. They feared a COVID-19 diagnosis and possible death. Knowing that their colleagues were as overwhelmed as they were, they felt guilty for asking others for help and for asking others to participate in their research. One class member, who was teaching in another country while taking the course experienced the personal loss of a dear colleague due to COVID-19. Participants described stress as "feeling like a caged-in chicken" (DB#7_001), and as "mental fatigue of being in lockdown for so long". (DB#7_001)

Implementing the interventions while some students were virtual and others in-person added to teachers' stress:

My co-teacher and I had originally planned to try a variety of different interventions for our students. However, when our time with them on a live meet was limited to 15 minutes, it had put a strain on interventions. Usually, we have our students for 30 minutes for math where we could spend 15 minutes introducing the chapter lessons and then the last 15 minutes would be split into small groups where we can then focus either extending the strategies introduced from the lessons, work on individual student goals from their IEPs, or build foundation skills they struggle based on their monthly reports. However, with two of our students learning virtually, it was very difficult to build more foundational skills or extend the strategies introduced or even try a different strategy if the first one was not working. (DB#6_002)

One of our findings was a consequence of the pandemic changes in routines, and in our graduate students' personal and professional lives. Although most of them were staying on track, some were dealing with obvious stress throughout the class, and their study: "It has been very difficult to focus and think clearly and while we carry on and adjust to the circumstances, I feel that was a significant challenge" (DB#5_ 002). One participant working in special education noted:

The primary challenge I faced while doing research during the pandemic is that I am exhausted all of the time. There were many times when trying to find the energy to take one more step forward on this research seemed nearly impossible to do. (DB#5_003)

From these comments to conversations during virtual synchronous meetings, where course participants proclaimed, "We are just numb", and we are "putting one foot in front of the other" to get through day by day, we saw and immediately felt the impacts on these front-line workers. (Conversations_ 003)

Lessons Learned: Resilience, Personal and Professional Growth, and the Power of Community as an Action Researcher

Moving beyond the challenges, participants reflected on gains in their own learning, resilience, development of community, and success.

Resilience and Personal Growth

Personal growth comprised accomplishment and a sense of new competence for a lot of our graduate students. Participants reported ways they addressed or overcame challenges, relating to the theme of resilience and growth. *Survival strategies* encompassed engagement with and deepening of personal strengths, new openness to support others, and tolerance of the unthinkable (See Table 3 below):

Table 3. Graduate students' answers regarding their resilience

"the ability to think and to adapt quickly". (DB#7_001)
"having the ability to see the challenge ahead and developing a way to overcome that challenge". (DB#7_001)
"I learned to be more strategic with my time". (DB#7_001)
"If we can make it through this, we can make it through anything". (DB#7_001)
[The pandemic is] "the biggest challenge I will likely face in my entire life, not just in my professional career". (DB#7_001)
"I had to breathe and understand I am only one person and am doing my all". (DB#7_001)
"I just had to keep reminding myself that this will pass and I will eventually be back in person with my students" (DB#7_001)
[I tried] "to survive one day to the next" (DB#7_001)

The concept of 'control' and being 'perfect' were common in discussions, as noted here:

I have definitely grown in my ability to accept that things do not always have to be perfect! I learned that I am more than capable of rolling with the punches, adjusting my methods, and accepting that I cannot have control over every little thing. The most important lesson that I've learned is that it is okay if things do not go as planned. One misstep will not ruin my research or the learning experiences of my students. I can be flexible, I can adapt, and I can, eventually, overcome. (DB#5_003)

Resilience and Professional Growth

Professional growth encompassed both the practical and the human. Practical aspects included "holes in programming" (DB#7_001) and students' losses due to the pandemic, creativity (learning to think outside the box), developing a focus that allows the teacher to identify the essentials of what students need to learn, putting students first, an increased proficiency with technology, learning to adapt. Human aspects were missing the presence of colleagues and support for students. See Table 4:

Table 4. Examples of practical human aspects

"The pandemic has taught me how to give grace during such tough times. We are all struggling and it is important to be human around the students". (DB#7_001)
"This pandemic has forced me … to think about what a student may be going through before I immediately think poorly of their effort or disdain for a…topic". (DB#7_001)
"More often than not, it just came down to putting one foot in front of the other and drinking too much caffeine." (DB#7_001)
"Perfect doesn't actually happen. You can try as hard as possible, and it is still not going to be perfect. This is even more true in a virtual setting, and during a pandemic." (DB#5_003)
"One of the most important lessons I learned throughout this semester is the idea that life is not always perfect. "It is what it is" and I truly live by this saying everyday now. I can't let things outside of my circle of control stress me out or affect my ability to teach my students. I have learned to focus on things that are in my control." (DB#5_003)

Several teachers emphasized *being creative* with the way they approached the materials and interventions, the participants, the new technology, or the communication with students and parents. The creativity involved better organization, better communication with students, with families, with co-workers and/or administration, and providing better accommodations (either for content, grouping strategies or assessment). One kindergarten teacher recalls:

We do a lot of hands-on activity learning in our class. For example, for our in-person kindergarten students, we recently made a little alphabet obstacle course. Using dry-erase markers on the floor, we create a course for our students. When they got to an obstacle, they had to tell us what letter was shown on the course if they got it right, they got to hop the course and go to the next one. However, with our virtual students, we could not do that, so we felt we were unable to be as creative as we could with our virtual students. However, this did help me grow in finding alternative ways to be creative using technology. My co-teacher and I tried to create virtual activities or engaging activities students could do at home, such as going on a scavenger hunt to find things in their house that started with the letter they were learned that day. (DB#6_002)

Resilience in Crisis

Another teacher pointed out: "One big take away I had this year is that I allowed myself to look more in depth at my own teaching practice and how I needed to change in order to accommodate for my virtual learners." (DB#5_002)

Teaching strategies involved the community of practice among teachers and working with students. One class member in a leadership position took on extra duties, such as lunchroom duty, in order to give back as teachers were giving to help her complete her action research project. Relationship-building with students held importance; also, keeping students engaged. Concern for students' welfare and for learning appears to have been paramount for class members (see Table 5):

Table 5. Practicing new and creative strategies

"I felt like I was constantly bartering with colleagues to get things done more efficiently and to do the normal day-to-day tasks". (DB#7_001)
"found engaging reading pieces and changed my strategies to better fit the online environment. I listened to my students the most I ever have, constantly doing wellness checks and asking what they needed from me". (DB#7_001)
"I kept a close eye on students who rarely showed and I advocated for them. I called parents explaining the importance and let students know also how important it was. Students showed more participation when you show you care for them and their success in school". (DB#7_001)

Other graduate students commented on growing as professionals by learning how to be flexible and adapt to changing teaching conditions. See Table 6:

Table 6. Examples of adaptability and flexibility

"The loss of control that was so pervasive made it so that I had to be more flexible than I have ever been" (DB#5_003)
"It encouraged me to be more adaptable and understanding of factors that go into a student's life...you always have to be willing and ready for things to not go as planned." (DB#5_003)
"Flexibility was key this semester. I had to embrace the chaos. For most of these challenges I just had to accept that I had very little control of the situation and adjust my methods, analysis, etc." (DB#5_003)
"The pandemic has also made me more flexible with my teaching plans. I have slowed the pace of the course and been flexible with deadlines. I'm trying to remove as much stress as possible from the learning environment. There's enough stress in every other part of life." (DB#6_002)
"We have to be extremely flexible due to student needs, schedule changes, ever changing curriculum, etc. Especially during a pandemic, I have found that it is/was necessarily to be flexible in every aspect of my day. I coach two sports during the school year and even then, I found myself having to change schedules and the way I hold practices due to the pandemic. Moving forward in this year and my career I will continue to remind myself that I need to stay flexible and go with the flow." (DB#6_002)

Resilience and Growth as an Action Researcher

The strength as a teacher-researcher was about the action research process. Participants mentioned elements such as creativity, learning to be organized, and collecting data accurately, while being engaged in constant "what if" planning. See some examples in Table 7 below:

Table 7. New identities as action researchers

being "more precise and focused on data collection". (DB#7_001)
"As an action researcher I really got a close look at how different teaching methods impact student learning, with the most effective methods pushing students to engage in the actual [subject] instead of passively listening to me." (DB#7_001)
"As an action researcher, it has taught me that research is never ending. There was no research on how to adapt to a pandemic. Just like when the next new issue to affect education comes to light, there will be no research." (DB#7_001)
"These challenging times helped me lean on the data and keep researching. Although the pandemic was a factor, it did not stop the action." (DB#7_001)
"This paper really helped me understand how to gather and analyze data accurately". (DB#5_002)
"I am able to use these research methods I learned going forward to improve the quality of my teaching and share information with my peers." (DB#5_002)

Challenged to reflect upon the takeaways from the unique experience of conducting action research during a pandemic, our graduate students realized that, even if some final results were not as positive as hoped for, the journey and the process of conducting action research seemed to have been more valuable. The chaos of the pandemic required **constant engagement with the action research cycle,** which was foregrounded through a graduate Capstone course, and was also necessary for grounding in everyday teaching (see Table 8 below):

Table 8. Ongoing learning as an action researcher

"The biggest thing I learned from action research is that I can try new interventions throughout my career as a teacher. I don't need a class or some professional development activity to tell me to do something. I can try new things and see what works best as I go." (DB#7_001)
"I learned the extreme importance of being in the work together…This focus helped us feel a sense of mutual accountability and helped me support my coaches in small moments." (DB#7_001)
"I could spend more time consistently reinforcing best practices and trying strategies along the way." (DB#7_001)

Action research strategies included revision of strategies designed in class members' plans of action. One teacher, whose project focused on student participation in Individualized Educational Plan (IEP) meetings, learned that parents would not be allowed into the school building due to COVID-19 restrictions; meetings would have to be conducted telephonically. He revised his approach by using every opportunity to practice "telephone-style IEP meetings as often as possible" (DB#7_001). He also made his personal cell phone visible in the classroom so that students would begin to attach the object to him in their thinking. Another class member reduced the participant pool for the project. "I overcame these challenges by adapting my timeline. Instead of four observations of each intervention, I did three of each" (DB#7_001). Finally, "I had to turn off email and notifications". (DB#7_001)

Reaching out to participants and communicating often to ensure student success was another tool used by teachers, demonstrating again they were also addressing issues 'in action' as reflective practitioners. One teacher stated: "I overcame the challenges of student engagement by reaching out to students and parents. Student engagement was a difficulty all teachers were having, so their conversations with the students helped as well" (DB#6_002). Another teacher maintained students' engagement and participation in-class through social distancing by providing clear expectations and developing routines for her preschool children:

I tried very hard to decrease stress among my students by establishing a clear routine in which they had some freedoms and choices without getting too close to one another. I also tried to establish social distancing as the "new normal." This is easier in preschool because my students are still learning about the world and do not have another school experience to compare this year. (DB#6_002)

Growth as a teacher-researcher was also influenced by allowing students to have a voice and express themselves. This finding correlates with the previous findings in Slapac and Navarro (2011).

One big take away that I had this year is allowing students to express their feelings and really diving deep into their emotions. I think it is so important for students to be able to recognize their emotions and be able to explain themselves. I was trying out different strategies for kids to use when they are frustrated [which] is so important because what works for one student might not work for another. Giving them options and time to try things allows them to be successful. (DB#5_002)

The graduate students also experienced the strength of continuous reflection on teaching practices and what the never-ending cycle of action research meant (Hendricks, 2017). Several students emphasized the importance and impact of constant reflection per examples in Table 9:

Table 9. Action research: Moving from reflecting to acting

"I think one of the most important lessons that I can take away from these two classes is that the key to discovery and growth as a practitioner has nothing to do with 'being right' and everything to do with failing, reflection, gathering new information, and being open to discovery through purposeful, strategic framing, research, and experimentation. I think it was difficult for me to let go of eight students not having shown 100% growth. I was so determined to see growth from every student, but in not seeing growth from each student I can assess what practices should be tweaked based on feedback and reflection within my practitioner journal. It's exciting knowing that five students made growth based on my careful research and strategic implementation of lessons. This isn't an end but a beginning of a new phase to explore how those other three students can grow." (DB#6_002)
"I took away that regular reflection is a key path toward that goal. I continually have to discipline myself in order to practice that reflection but I feel like the only way to move forward in my practice is to be willing to let go of dominant cultural norms that have guided my thinking my entire life." (DB#6_002)
"I learned a lot about the way action research can be used to improve teaching practice and that is something I would like to continue to use. I also learned a lot about resources and ways to keep tracking and improving my global competence. I think the research and reflection will be very helpful in making sure that I am always improving and learning." (DB#5_002)
"I tried out different strategies before and was not very successful. I believe part of that was that I was not consistent and didn't reflect enough to make the necessary changes for improvement." (DB#5_002)

Teaching and engagement with action research impacted members' decisions about their futures as well. One teacher commented, "I ... learned a lot about doing research, how to create and complete an action research project, and the great impact this can have on my career." (DB#7_001). Another wrote, "Seeing the end result of this project has pushed me at least in the short-term to do more action research" (DB#7_001). Two class members indicated a strong inclination to continue applying action research in their work. One wrote:

Surprisingly, despite my setbacks, the pandemic steeled my resolve to continue more in a research capacity, as it fascinated me to watch student progress as well as read up on what potential action research could be done to fix common problems in class. Now I seek to obtain a Ph.D. in Educational Psychology in order to do more substantial research in this area. This is to say that the biggest lesson that I learned from the pandemic was that I really enjoyed research and wanted to pursue this long-term. (DB#7_001)

Constant Support, Collaboration, and the Power of Community

The theme of *learning and being a teacher in a/the community* arose from participants with some poignant stories. Seeking support from others who are going through the same experience, also brought further introspections. The teacher-researchers consoled and supported one another as they developed a community of learners, finding support as they each adjusted to multiple stressors and changes. From each other, participants learned to examine and release tightly-held ideas and practices related to perfectionism and control, an apparent new coping mechanism. For example, when one stated, "Perfect doesn't actually happen", others began to agree and adjusted perceptions and practices by determining ways to move forward through a very dark time - together (DB & Virtual meeting; Section 003). Peer supports and constant collaboration with peers, parents and co-workers was noticed by most as being very meaningful per Table 10 below:

Table 10. New awareness: Collaboration as support via action research

Learning in Community	*Seeking Support from /and Connecting with Others*
"I was able to overcome these challenges with the support of Dr. E, and my colleagues." (DB#5_002)	"The most important lesson I learned from the pandemic was that everyone was struggling and being conscious of this fact I feel like I have become a kinder teacher." (DB#7_001)
"teaching is a very collaborative and community-based career." (DB#5_002).	"Collaboration with your peers will help you view another perspective on a topic." (DB#5_002)
"The most important lesson in my career is that you cannot do this alone (and) I can do this when I'm in a healthy group setting; I didn't know this...until this class." (VoiceThread, Section 003).	"One of the most important aspects in successfully working with others to achieve a goal is focusing on the common ground that brings us all together in the first place. In a team environment, everyone's voice plays a part in the goal you wish to achieve, so listen well." (DB#5_002)
"Community is key. Without a strong classroom community, students are unwilling to take risks, which limits learning; more than anything, I learned to reach out to my peers and colleagues for support...this year has really taught me to go out of my way to strengthen my bonds with my peers. I have learned an incredible amount from my peers and colleagues this semester and I am excited to continue growing". (DB#5_003).	"With parental support, we felt more assured knowing that our students would not fall further behind than their in-person peers because they were there supporting the students from home making sure they attended our live meets and completed the work." (FP_002)

Participants wrote about *learning in terms of life strategies, teaching practice, and constant support from school-peers, class instructors, and colleagues.* Life strategies included planning, flexibility, and acceptance, while overcoming challenges and celebrating every joyful moment as the examples in Table 11 below:

Table 11. Action research as cradle for inquiry and collaboration

"Sometimes I can make plans, but things happen." (DB#7_001)
"If you can find what drives you, adapt and overcome, and take time to celebrate the things that bring you joy, you will be able to handle any situation that life throws at you." (DB#7_001)
"Learning to accept the reality around you and changing to make it work for you is extremely important." (DB#7_001)
"If something is not working, I can make changes to the process or format to make it better for myself and my students." (DB#7_001)
"Inquiry is ever evolving, but it is important to record and celebrate the wisdom won while learning, and it is so important to have accountability in inquiry, some kind of contact or support, partners in goals." (DB#5_002)
"Some days will go great, and other days students may take two steps back in their ability to process their emotions, and that is okay." (DB#7_001)

During virtual Zoom meetings, after getting to know the professors and other graduate students in the context of the course sections and feeling safe, some expressed extreme levels of stress. The instructors referred the course participants to the campus support, including online counseling sessions and community resources when needed. Those resources, and ongoing affirmation of the support to be found in the action research learning community itself, were a couple of ways participants reached out and found "some stability" as one colleague suggested for them during this time.

Another example of constant support is exemplified by participants from Section 003 who supported two class members having challenges with their respective topics and papers. Peers delved into their colleagues' research topics, from culturally responsive teaching related to African American teachers, to impacts of the pandemic and racial unrest for teachers of color. The class members dialoged, shared suggestions, and searched together for inquiry questions and ideas while cheering these teachers on who had difficulty engaging with their own students. The final papers showed that this ongoing support from the learning community, switching up research samples a few times, changing interview questions and processes, was just what was needed to help these two participants succeed at their action research capstone projects. (Zoom conversations, FP, Section 003)

One of the most important lessons I've learned that are most relevant to the next level of my professional journey is the importance of professional relationships. Professional relationships are important because they provide support, encouragement, critical feedback and even job opportunities. (DB#5_003)

That participant's classmate said, "Talking to the other researchers in this class that were as stressed due to COVID-19's impact on our daily lives also helped to alleviate some of the stress" (DB#5_ 003). These comments exemplify the *situated nature of learning within community* (Korthagen, 2010) during this action research process, where "critical understanding can only develop through active dialogue within a community" (Freire, 1972; as cited in Korthagen, 2010, p. 104). This community evolved as the graduate students communicated during and outside of class to complete assignments and make sense and meaning of their action research projects together.

However, one of the main lessons learned was the realization that *learning never stops;* that's when growth and impact happens, as this teacher writes:

There are always things that can be improved within the education system, and a teacher should never stop learning and researching throughout their career. Although there have been improvements made in the education world, there are still so many things that can be improved to reach every student where they are at, emotionally and academically. As a teacher, even though I may not continue on with my education by getting a doctorate, I can, and should, still do my own types of research within my classroom in order to learn more from my students. If at any point I find myself not trying new things, or just teaching the same lessons each year, I know I have stopped doing my job as a teacher. (DB#6_002)

SOLUTIONS AND RECOMMENDATIONS

Adapting to New Teaching Challenges

In line with the idea of adapting to new teaching challenges while becoming an action researcher and tending to their action research which was progressing in cycles (Piggot-Irvine, 2002; Wadsworth, 1998), we saw the instantiation of this process during this study, where participants cycled through attempts to complete their action research plan, only to have to make adjustments all along the way due to the pandemic stressors experienced. The results of the pandemic stress experienced by participants - as they designed and conducted action research - continually emerged as an important condition during the study and became a salient construct as illustrated in Figure 1:

Figure 1.

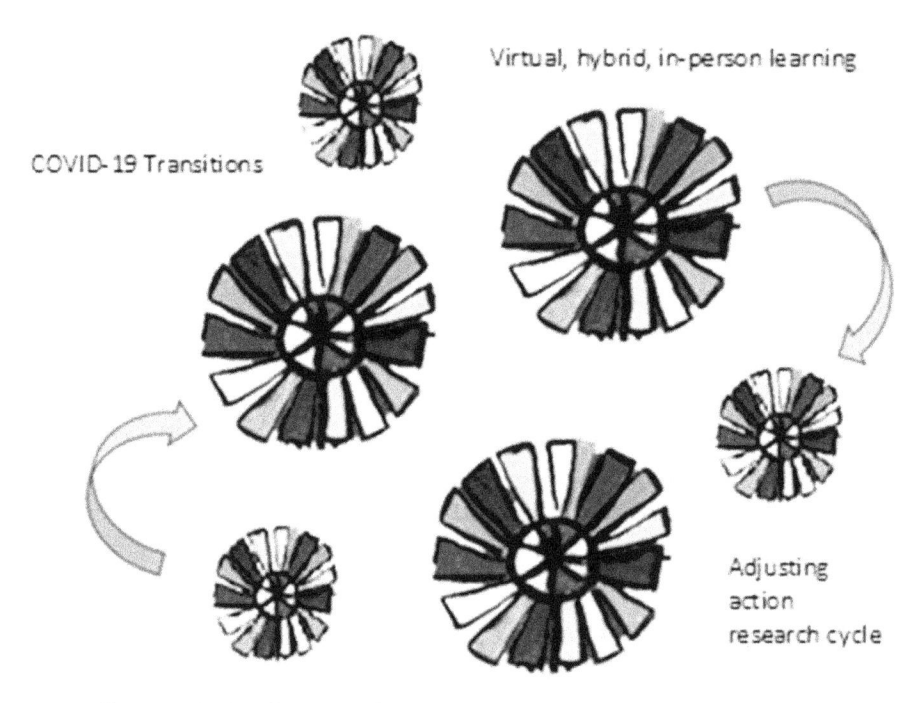

A remarkable result from this study was the observed compassion fatigue resilience, strength, and courage exhibited by all participants as they continually worked to adjust and find solutions to achieve their action research goals within demanding structures of teaching during a pandemic. Thus, one recommendation from these results is for all to be aware that during times of global or national crisis, or disaster (Yang et al., 2020), steps should be taken to consider the impacts that the crisis can have on learners' and educators' mental and physical health, and to adjust expectations. Furthermore, steps should be taken to look for ways to quickly restructure learning environments to allow a learning community to develop in new ways through a trauma-informed approach.

The Power of Community of Practice

Another recommendation from the data is to intentionally design and allow a learner-centered environment to develop, where honest communication can support reflective practice in an action research learning community. This may mean 'over communicating' as one of the instructors learned, which involves ensuring that every single student understands assignments and is checking in, communicating, finding peer supports, and is sharing feedback with the class on a regular basis. Students reported being able to overcome challenges with the support of the instructor and classmates, thus, the recommendation involves being intentional and offering an explicitly-designed process for this communication, a critical component during times of crisis. This gives evidence to the community of learners via a "theory of participation" (Rogoff et al., 1998, p. 409) framework in this study.

Flexibility

To achieve both their teaching and action research goals, the teacher-researchers used strategies like flexibility along with survival techniques such as openness. Equally important were support from others and tolerance of the unthinkable. Participants reported adapting by giving up control and perfection, for their own and for their students' learning, in order to put one foot in front of the other to keep going forward, even while numb from the relentless stressors. Flexibility included continually finding new ways to support their students in virtual, hybrid, and in-person learning settings. Thus, recommendations include the necessity of putting aside regular teaching modes and learning new strategies to connect everyone, and to "journey with students through hardship" as discovered also in China during this time (Wong & Moorhouse, 2020, p. 1).

FUTURE RESEARCH DIRECTIONS

Action research is a powerful tool for connecting teacher education programs directly to school settings and is a proven way to address problems which seemingly have no solutions (Slapac & Navarro, 2011). For example, research on secondary trauma (Ludick & Figley, 2017) prioritizes the social connections of teachers along with collaborative problem-solving as healthy strategies for teachers who work in a trauma rich environment. The same literature specifically discourages go-it-alone strategies. Action research, in the context of this Capstone course provides both social connection and a focus on collaborative problem solving. This chapter highlighted our students' awareness of the positive impact the discussions played during the initial stages of pandemic teaching. In addition to framing the social connections among teachers, the process of action research conveys a sense of professional agency to the individual teachers who use it. The increase in self-confidence that accompanies this increase in agency and the shared group experience about classroom problem-solving were key supports cited by teachers during the 2020 challenges and provides a convincing rationale to encourage the use of action research in teacher education courses.

Suggestions for future directions in research thus include further examining the strengths offered by designing action research programs within higher education as a tool to develop and build community, especially during challenging times such as disaster or global crisis. Further research into action research within an intentional trauma-informed framework in PreK-16 hybrid settings would extend this study to examine future potential for this important resource where community can develop and thrive to help ameliorate the extreme effects of stress on educators, our front-line workers worldwide.

CONCLUSION

Just because everyone else thinks that teachers are expendable, it doesn't mean that we are. We are important. We are frontline workers. Regardless of the outside perception of teachers, we basically allow society to function. (DB5_ 003)

From the quote above, we are reminded of the courageous acts performed by educators worldwide during 2020-2021, and the importance of finding ways to support these everyday heroes. This study was fashioned in order to examine these phenomena at the end of 2020. Evidence from the study answered the research questions about the main challenges experienced by participants during the pandemic, strategies used, resilience and growth and lessons learned while learning and practicing action research.

The analyses and insights from this research offer us new ways to look at a few old issues in the teaching profession. Teaching is a high stress career, evident in the shortages that often emerge during times when alternative career opportunities are high. During the pandemic, this chronic stress became acute; the challenge to the socio-emotional health of teachers became visible while few mitigation mechanisms were in sight. For the teachers who were in these capstone sessions, the Action Research project became an important vehicle for maintaining connection to a collective reality that could ground them and offer guidance through the limitations of pandemic teaching.

Comparatively, it would be interesting to understand how other teachers coped with new expectations amid social isolation. As we track the impact of COVID-19 on education enterprise in a post pandemic time, this study amplifies the importance of including impacts on 1) teachers, 2) their expanded practices amid the rapid acquisition of new technologies, and 3) their choice to stay in the system of education. Will teachers sustain the positive teaching strategies, the flexibility, the attention to student engagement that distance learning necessitated? Will the teaching profession experience a COVID-19 increase in resignations and early retirement of experienced teachers due to the unmitigated stressors on their physical and mental health? Might Action Research be viewed as a support process for teachers in times of collective tragedy? These are questions for future studies, as researchers explore the short- and long-term changes of this time.

ACKNOWLEDGMENT

Special thanks to all our graduate students as participants in our study who worked hard to empower themselves and their student learning through action research, and to ensure their learning environments provided meaningful experiences in challenging times. Many thanks to our friends, Professor Emeritus Virginia Navarro and Mrs. Andreea Bell for their feedback and edits on our final chapter draft. This research received no specific grant from any funding agency in the public, commercial, or not-for-profit sectors.

REFERENCES

A trauma-informed approach to teaching through coronavirus (2020). *Teaching Tolerance*. https://www.tolerance.org/magazine/a-trauma-informed-approach-to-teaching-through-coronavirus

Ainsworth, S., & Oldfield, J. (2019). Quantifying teacher resilience: Context matters. *Teaching and Teacher Education*, *82*, 117–128. doi:10.1016/j.tate.2019.03.012

Algozzine, B., Gretes, J., Queen, A. J., & Cowan-Hathcock, M. (2007). Beginning teachers' perceptions of their induction program experiences. *The Clearing House: A Journal of Educational Strategies, Issues and Ideas*, *80*(3), 137–143. doi:10.3200/TCHS.80.3.137-143

Brouwer, N., & Korthagen, F. (2005). Can teacher education make a difference? *American Educational Research Journal*, *42*(1), 153–244. doi:10.3102/00028312042001153

Brown, E. C., Freedle, A., Hurless, N. L., Miller, R. D., Martin, C., & Paul, Z. A. (2020). Preparing teacher candidates for trauma-informed practices. *Urban Education*, 1–24.

Carello, J. (2019). Trauma-informed teaching and learning online: Principles & practices during a global health crisis. *Examples of trauma-informed teaching and learning in college classrooms*. https://traumainformedteaching.blog/resources

Charmaz, K. (2006). *Constructing grounded theory*. SAGE Publications.

Duncan, A. (2020, December 21). Pandemic has highlighted America's educational gaps: Connectivity has yet to catch up with demand for online, in-home learning. *St. Louis Post Dispatch*, p. A11.

Fasanella, K. P. (2020, October-December). 180 Days of Self-Care for Busy Educators. *Kappa Delta Pi Record*, *56*(4), 191. doi:10.1080/00228958.2020.1813523

Freire, P. (1972). *Pedagogy of the oppressed*. Herder & Herder.

Hendricks, C. (2017). *Improving schools through action research: A comprehensive guide for educators* (4th ed.). Pearson.

Herr, K., & Anderson, G. L. (2014). *The action research dissertation: A guide for students and faculty*. SAGE.

Holly, M. L., Arhar, J. M., & Kasten, W. C. (2009). *Action research for teachers: Traveling the yellow brick road* (3rd ed.). Pearson.

Hudson, P. (2012). How can schools support beginning teachers? A call for timely induction and mentoring for effective teaching. *The Australian Journal of Teacher Education*, *37*(7), 71–84. doi:10.14221/ajte.2012v37n7.1

Kapoulitsas, M., & Corcoran, T. (2015). Compassion fatigue and resilience: A qualitative analysis of social work practice. *Qualitative Social Work: Research and Practice*, *14*(1), 86–101. doi:10.1177/1473325014528526

Killeavy, M. (2006). Induction: A collective endeavor of learning, teaching, and leading. *Theory into Practice*, *45*(2), 168–176. doi:10.120715430421tip4502_9

Korthagen, F. (2010). Situated learning theory and the pedagogy of teacher education: Towards an integrative view of teacher behavior and teacher learning. *Teaching and Teacher Education*, *26*(1), 98–106. doi:10.1016/j.tate.2009.05.001

Ludick, M., & Figley, C. R. (2017). Toward a mechanism for secondary trauma induction and reduction: Reimagining a theory of secondary traumatic stress. *Traumatology*, *23*(1), 112–123. doi:10.1037/trm0000096

Masters, J. (1995). *The history of action research*. Ian Hughes Action Research Electronic Reader, University of Sydney. http://www.aral.com.au/arow/rmasters.html

Onwuegbuzie, A. J., Frels, R. K., & Hwang, E. (2016). Mapping Saldaña coding methods onto the literature review process. *Journal of Educational Issues*, *2*(1), 130–149. doi:10.5296/jei.v2i1.8931

Piggot-Irvine, E. (2002). *Rhetoric and practice in action research*. Paper presented at the annual conference of the British Educational Research Association, University of Exeter.

Rogoff, B., Matusov, E., & White, C. (1998). Models of teaching and learning: Participation in a Community of Learners. In D. R. Olson & N. Torrance (Eds.), The handbook of education and human development: New models of learning, teaching and schooling (pp. 388-414). Blackwell.

Saldaña, J. (2012). *The coding manual for qualitative researchers* (2nd ed.). SAGE.

Skovholt, T. M., & Trotter-Mathison, M. (2014). *The resilient practitioner: Burnout prevention and self-care strategies for counselors, therapists, teachers, and health professionals*. Routledge. doi:10.4324/9780203893326

Slapac, A., & Navarro, V. (2011). Shaping action researchers through a Master's capstone experience. *Teacher Education and Practice*, *24*(4), 405–426.

Spinazzola, J., Ford, J. D., Zucker, M., van der Kolk, B. A., Silva, S., Smith, S. F., & Blaustein, M. (2005). Survey Evaluates Complex Trauma Exposure, Outcome and Intervention Among Children and Adolescents. *Psychiatric Annals*, *35*(5), 433–439. doi:10.3928/00485713-20050501-09

Sprang, G., Ford, J., Kerig, P., & Bride, B. (2019). Defining secondary traumatic stress and developing targeted assessments and interventions: Lessons learned from research and leading experts. *Traumatology*, *25*(2), 72–81. doi:10.1037/trm0000180

Stringer, E. (2007). *Action research in education* (3rd ed.). SAGE. http://repository.umpwr.ac.id:8080/bitstream/handle/123456789/3706/Action%20Research.pdf?sequence=1&isAllowed=y

Teater, M., & Ludgate, J. (2014). *Overcoming compassion fatigue: A practical resilience workbook.* PESI Publishing and Media.

Wadsworth, Y. (1998). What is participatory action research? *Action Research International.* Paper 2. http://www.aral.com.au/ari/p-ywadsworth98.html

Wong, K. M., & Moorhouse, B. L. (2020). The impact of social uncertainty, protests, and COVID-19 on Hong Kong teachers. *Journal of Loss and Trauma, 25*(3), 649–655. doi:10.1080/15325024.2020.1776523

Yang, D., Tu, C., & Dai, X. (2020). The effect of the 2019 novel coronavirus pandemic on college students in Wuhan. *Psychological Trauma: Theory, Research, Practice, and Policy, 12*(S1), S6–S14. doi:10.1037/tra0000930 PMID:32551764

Zeni, J. (2001). A guide to ethical decision making for insider research. In J. Zeni (Ed.), *Ethical issues in practitioner research* (pp. 153–165). Teachers College Press.

ADDITIONAL READING

Aguilar, E. (2018). *Onward: Cultivating emotional resilience in educators* (1st ed.). Jossey-Bass. doi:10.1002/9781119441731

Bruce, C. D., Flynn, T., & Stagg-Peterson, S. (2011). Examining what we mean by collaboration in collaborative action research: A cross-case analysis. *Educational Action Research, 19*(4), 433–452. doi:10.1080/09650792.2011.625667

Foster, K. M. (2006). Bridging Troubled Waters: Principles for Teaching in Times of Crisis. *Penn GSE Perspectives on Urban Education, 4*(2), n2.

Lattimer, H., & Caillier, S. (2015). (Eds.). Surviving and thriving with teacher action research: Reflections and advice from the field. Peter Lang Publishing.

Mertler, C. A. (2019). *Action research: Improving schools and empowering educators* (6th ed.). SAGE.

Nieto, S. (2015). *Why we teach now.* Teachers College Press.

Salgor, R. D., & Williams, C. D. V. (2016). *The action research guidebook: A process of pursuing equity and excellence in education.* Corwin.

Self-Care-Tips-by-Psychologist. (2020). *University of Florida Graduate School.* http://graduateschool.ufl.edu/media/graduate-school/pdf-files/Self-Care-Tips-by-Psychologist-for-COVID-19.pdf

KEY TERMS AND DEFINITIONS

Classroom Action Research: Teachers inquire into their own practice, reflect on classroom challenges, and choose a structured course of action to solve a problem using a process of data collection, analysis, and action.

Community of Learners: Individuals working together toward similar goals, who collaboratively engage in mutual support, critique, problem posing, and solution finding.

Digital Skills Training: Organized instruction providing competency in digital literacy for communicating, interacting, teaching, and networking using a variety of devices and platforms in the classroom and online.

Discussion Board: Online learning management system platform allowing a framework for communication between class participants within a course.

Hybrid Teaching: Weekly classes in-person and online, state-wide and school-district-wide, for K-12 (kindergarten - Grade 12) grades. In the United States, hybrid teaching was introduced during the pandemic for safety purposes.

IEP (Individualized Educational Plan): The IEP is a written plan created by a school district and parents containing goals and services for individual students who receive special education in the United States.

In/Out Teaching: In person, classroom learning that alternates with virtual school during quarantine, a "one or the other" approach.

Resilience: The ability to devise creative strategies for moving forward in adverse circumstances.

Resilient Teaching Techniques: Adaptations applied to instructional processes, expectations, and learning environments including strategies to support learners at all levels during times of stress, crisis, or disruption.

Situated Learning: Learning that is positioned within a context featuring participation and interaction with others.

Student Engagement: The degree to which a student demonstrates interest, initiative, curiosity, and attention in a learning setting. This may be in a brick-and-mortar or virtual classroom, and may occur in a synchronous or asynchronous environment.

Trauma-Informed Teaching Approach: Awareness, knowledge, and skills for educators of the need for specific approaches to fostering safe, supportive learning environments for students who may have experienced prior trauma.

VoiceThread: Tool within an online course allowing video, audio, and text-based interactions as a platform for collaborative learning.

ZOOM: Online video conferencing tool supporting communication via virtual interactions.

Chapter 3
Using Action Research to Promote Meaningful E-Service-Learning Experience for Preservice Teachers

Svetlana Chesser
Auburn University, USA

Kate Durham
Auburn University, USA

Elena Aydarova
Auburn University, USA

ABSTRACT

Research on service-learning has documented the importance of relationships and meaningful community connections for preservice teachers' development. What remains less explored is the opportunities and challenges provided by e-service learning integrated into teacher preparation coursework. In this study, the authors utilize action research methodology to explore how preservice teachers engaged in e-service learning during the move towards remote instruction in the summer of 2020. Drawing on the analysis of students' weekly journals, final reflections, and the survey of stakeholders, they examine how e-service-learning created opportunities for students to feel connected to the community during the time of social isolation and be motivated by their ability to make an impact on children's interest in learning STEM content. The challenges emerged out of a disconnect between course content and some of the e-service learning assignments. This study's implications include better integration of e-service learning into teacher education courses.

DOI: 10.4018/978-1-7998-6922-1.ch003

INTRODUCTION

The term action research was introduced by Kurt Lewin (1946) as a research approach in which the researcher intervenes during the investigation with the purpose of generating knowledge and bringing about positive change. There are two traditions of conceptualizing action research. The first one is linked to education and views action research as an exploration oriented toward the improvement of direct practice (Carr & Kemmis,1986). The second tradition perceives action research as "the systematic collection of information that is designed to bring about social change" by exposing unjust practices or environmental dangers and recommending action for change (Bogdan & Biklen,1992, p.223). In this chapter, the term action research is used to describe a form of instructional practice intended to improve college instructors' skills, techniques, and strategies of online teaching.

The shift away from the classrooms and communities during the COVID-19 pandemic forced many university instructors to reconsider how they conduct their courses while adhering to the rules of lockdown and social distancing, including courses with a service-learning component. The implications from this situation highlight the need to consider the best practices as many educators are wondering whether this shift will persist post-pandemic. While online learning has grown significantly in the last decade (Seaman et al., 2018), online courses with a service-learning component remain rare (Waldner et al., 2012). Typically, service-learning is organized in a local community and close to the higher education institution where students are enrolled. Students who take online courses are often based in their own communities, which might be different from the higher education institution location. The challenge then is how to provide a meaningful learning experience for these students while meeting the needs and serving host institution communities. Electronic service-learning (e-service-learning) is uniquely positioned to free service-learning from these geographical constraints.

The main objective of this chapter is to present an integrative framework that draws on previous e-service-learning research, arguing that e-service-learning is a helpful approach to create a bridge between academic learning and community service in online classes, and action research is a useful methodology that can help educators do it better.

BACKGROUND

In the last few decades, institutions of higher education embraced a form of experiential learning called service-learning, a reflective relational pedagogy that combines community or public service with structured opportunities for learning that allows learning by doing, and connects theory with practice (Heffernan, 2001). Based on John Dewey's (1938) notion of experiential education, service-learning engages students in events that address human and community needs. It also provides them with opportunities to participate in activities designed to promote their learning and development (Strait & Sauer, 2004). What distinguishes service-learning from other approaches to experiential education is its focus on both the service being provided and the learning that is occurring. Typically, service-learning integrates service into the course and is supposed to ensure that the service enhances the learning, and the learning enhances the service (Furco, 2003). For example, students in teacher preparation programs in courses such as Adolescents or Child Development were expected to apply the theories and skills learned in these courses while working with children and teenagers in various educational settings. While the service-learning is intended to provide a much-needed service to children and adolescents, it is also intended to help preservice teachers better understand how development affects learning and provides an opportunity to put into practice theoretical ideas learned in class.

The positive impact of service-learning on students, faculty, and community partners is well documented. Research on service-learning (Celio et al., 2011; Eyler et al., 2001) has shown that it improves students' efficacy, personal identity, spiritual growth, and moral development, their leadership and communication skills, as well as ability to work well with others. Service-learning also has a positive effect on reducing stereotypes and facilitating cultural and racial understanding. Students and faculty report that service-learning improves students' ability to apply what they have learned in "the real world" (Balazadeh, 1996; Eyler & Giles Jr, 1999; O'Donnell et al., 1999; Voss et al., 2015). In addition, service-learning presents many professional and personal opportunities for faculty, including stronger faculty-student relationships (Eyler et al., 2000) and the ability to apply their expertise to serve the community (Boyer, 1990). Likewise, community partners are motivated to participate in service-learning because service-learning students help them enhance organizational capacity, advance an organization's mission, positively impact client outcomes while serving as mentors, tutors, or companions, and gain access to information and academic research to enhance their operations (Geller et al., 2016; Karasik, 2020; Sandy & Holland, 2006;).

E-service-learning occurs when the instructional component of the course, the service component, or both are conducted online. As the number of students pursuing their education online increases, e-service-learning holds the tremendous transformative potential to both service-learning and online learning by freeing service-learning from geographical constraints (Waldner et al., 2012). Just like traditional service-learning, e-service-learning delivers much-needed help to the community organizations and allows students to gain real-life experience while building long-lasting beneficial partnerships with their communities (Strait & Sauer, 2004). What is more, e-service-learning promotes students' innovative thinking and explores new ways of problem-solving.

As a relatively new pedagogical practice, e-service-learning has not been extensively studied and evaluated. Data about e-service-learning is largely qualitative and mainly consists of the description of e-service-learning delivery strategies (Farina, 2018; Hervani et al., 2015; Waldner & Hunter, 2008). One study (Figuccio, 2020) compared experiences of traditional students who had in-person service-learning with online students who had e-service-learning. Two groups did not significantly differ on any of the measures related to the student engagement or understanding of course content, but both sections reported that service-learning helped them relate the subject matter to everyday life, positively impacted their future academic and career choices, and overall resulted in a positive experience. Intriguingly, when compared to the traditional service-learning condition, students in the distance learning section reported that e-service-learning was more relevant to the course, more useful in learning the course material, and more enjoyable. They also indicated that e-service-learning experience reduced their levels of anxiety and reported greater overall satisfaction than did the in-person service-learning students.

While e-service-learning can be a powerful tool to promote student engagement, some practitioners view the online environment as a barrier to service-learning. Undoubtedly, e-service-learning instructors are facing a number of challenges because there is no physical face-to-face interaction with the community partner. Nevertheless, several studies demonstrate that the online environment for service-learning is adequate and works well (Farina, 2018; Figuccio, 2020; Waldner et al., 2010).

This qualitative study was designed to answer the following question: How service-learning can be organized and conducted in an entirely remote environment to provide meaningful experiences for preservice teachers and to effectively serve the community? The purpose of the study was to contribute to the knowledge base regarding the use of e-service-learning and identify what works and what does not in the efforts to improve our e-service-learning practices and the lives of community members with whom we work.

USING ACTION RESEARCH TO PROMOTE E-SERVICE LEARNING EXPERIENCE

Expanded during COVID-19, online teaching and learning introduced new issues and challenges related to the quality of online instruction, including opportunities for and quality of service-learning for teacher education students. Without knowing how long this pandemic will continue and wondering whether this big shift to online teaching and e-service-learning will persist post-pandemic, it is necessary to systematically collect and analyze data to reflect on and adjust online teaching and service-learning delivery. An action research approach offers tools for a disciplined inquiry to inform practice (Ferrance, 2000). In preparation to teach a ten-week course with a service-learning component, we used an action research approach that allowed us to collect and analyze data to improve the delivery of e-service-learning and better meet the needs of the students and the community in our future online courses. The identification of the common issues related to e-service-learning and our efforts to address these issues will be the main focus of this chapter. To conduct this study, we followed the general four-stage action research procedure (planning, acting, developing, and reflecting) with the nine specific steps, outlined by Mertler (2019).

The Planning Stage

Mertler (2019) included the following steps in the planning stage: identifying and limiting the topic, gathering information, reviewing the related literature, and developing a research plan.

When the COVID-19 pandemic forced all university faculty and students to convert to online teaching and learning, service-learning was cut short or substituted for an alternative to service-learning projects. For the university instructors who were scheduled to teach courses with a service-learning component in the upcoming semester in the context of the global pandemic, it was apparent that traditional face-to-face service-learning activities are out of reach and must be reconsidered in order to adhere to the rules of lockdown and social distancing. One of the authors had to teach a ten-week Foundations of Education class with 25 hours of a service-learning component at a 4-year university in the southeast of the United States. Nine students were enrolled in the class, all were secondary education majors - agriscience, English, or social science education, and all had previous service or service-learning experience - volunteering in the community or participating in service-learning for another class in a previous semester.

Methods

Reflecting on the existing situation, we reviewed literature about effective e-service-learning practices. In the traditional service-learning literature, the areas identified as essential to service-learning effectiveness included stakeholders' attitudes, benefits such as real-world projects, improved academic learning, a sense of community, the application of practical skills, and critical analysis (Elyer & Giles 1999; Hagenbuch, 2006). Based on those dimensions, we decided to focus on the following: skill-building, community partner and student satisfaction, and community partner and student interaction. The effectiveness of students' e-service-learning experience largely depends on an organized and attentive community partner. While planning for this e-service-learning, we decided to partner with a newly founded non-profit hands-on children's science center. Before the beginning of the semester, the center's administrator communicated to the course instructor the needs of their organization and how the e-service learning student could be most supportive. A list of possible online tasks to serve this organization was outlined. It was planned that during the course of the semester, service-learning students will help create social media presence for this new community organization, assist with grant writing, and organize fundraising while networking with local businesses.

One of the key components of service-learning is a reflection, the intentional consideration of the service experience in light of particular learning objectives. Reflection, in fact, links the service and the learning providing the bridge between the community service activities and the academic content of the course. Reflection activities direct the student's attention to new interpretations of events and provide a means through which the community service can be understood (Jacoby, 2015; Pigza, 2010). To track the progress of service-learning, the instructor prepared a list of queries for students' weekly reflection journals to document time spent on the project, a list of activities worked on and how these activities relate to the course content, the impact of the weekly activities on the community, as well as problems encountered and planned service-learning activities for the following week. Students completed reflection journals in Canvas learning management platform every week for ten weeks. In addition, at the end of the semester, students and stakeholders anonymously reflected on their experiences and the impact of the e-service-learning in the final reflection survey administered in Qualtrics. This ten-week study was approved by the Institutional Review Board and all participants provided their informed consent prior to using their journal entries and the final reflection surveys for data analysis. Students' weekly reflection journals were uploaded from Canvas into Dedoose and analyzed using the techniques of thematic data analysis (Ryan & Bernard, 2003). The reflection journal data was anonymized during analysis, and pseudonyms were used to present this data. To ensure the trustworthiness of our study (Lincoln & Guba, 1986), we developed a codebook for the qualitative data analysis moving iteratively between the conceptual framework and our data (LeCompte & Schensul, 2013). One researcher applied the codes, while another researcher conducted periodic checks to ensure the credibility of data analysis. We held several meetings to share observations, compare notes on emergent themes, and reconstruct students' experiences with e-service-learning. Overall, three passes at data analysis allowed us to refine the analysis and develop analytic memos that captured the main themes in the data. In what follows, we provide a more detailed description of students' tasks, experiences, and observations drawing on the data we collected throughout the project and the memos we wrote as we engaged in data analysis.

The Acting Stage

According to Mertler (2019), the acting stage consists of implementing the plan, collecting and analyzing the data. This stage of our project started with the director of the children's science center attending class orientation to set general expectations for e-service-learning, express the goals/ mission of the organization, and outline projects that would be available for students to complete. To define specific expectations for each e-service-learning project, a personal conversation between each student and a member of the community partner team was scheduled via the phone, Zoom, or email. Prior to this conversation, students had an opportunity to choose a project they were interested in from the list of projects prepared by the instructor in cooperation with the center's director. The organization we worked with during this e-service-learning was still in its infancy and needed to explore effective practices from similar institutions and how to best serve the local community. Therefore, research was one of the major tasks at the beginning of the semester for most students. Some students were tasked to research children's museums and the services and activities they provide to their communities. One student wrote how this research led to a feeling of impacting the community:

This week showed me more of how this project can have an impact on the community. Some children's museums are extremely successful and helpful to kids. Kids go for field trips, summer camps, and other various events that help them in their learning outside of school. By collecting good data about how these museums operate will hopefully provide (the organization) with the proper knowledge of how to be successful. (Eric, Journal 2, June 2020)

As students got involved in real initiatives, such as Camp-In-A-Box, their positive feelings about impacting the community grew:

I really felt like I was connecting to the community this week, as the boxes were now being sent into the homes for people to use. (The community partner) would send me a lot of pictures I could post of kids using their boxes and it just made me feel really happy. (Kerry, Journal 4, July 2020)

At the end of the semester, the same student commented:

This week (the organization) had so many people registered for their school and it is just so cool to see a small community forming that I will get to interact with. I'm going to miss this summer opportunity, but I am excited to begin working with them in late August. (Kerry, Journal 9, August 2020)

In the final reflection, one student wrote:

I think that this service-learning was one of the most hands-on" that I had experienced. In other education classes that required service-learning, I felt that I was just sitting a lot or just observing. During my time with [the organization) and working under (the community partner), I actually felt like I was doing something beneficial to the community. (Anonymous, Final Reflection, August 2020)

Three students decided to work on developing social media posts. These students worked closely with the community partner team members to learn new software, create posts, and distribute them through various social media platforms. These posts (Figure 1) promoted the socially distanced STEM-themed activities (Camp-In-A-Box) and competitions that the organization developed over the summer, as well as advertisements for upcoming fall events.

Figure 1. Social media posts developed by preservice teachers for their e-service-learning

Students who chose to work on creating social media presence for the community partner worked on creating content throughout the semester. Each week the students communicated with the organization's team members to learn which information needed to be shared and how many posts they needed to create. At the beginning of the semester, in their weekly reflection journals, the students wrote that they often had trouble creating different posts for the same information. They reported that making 5-10 posts around a specific service or event was difficult but forced them to think outside the box and take creative risks. Over time, they learned how to use new software that assisted with the creativity and distribution of their posts. One student noted how creating social media content increased her motivation and productivity:

This week I feel like I was impacting the community by reaching out to it and encouraging learning for the summer. I understand that with the time we live in sometimes it is hard to find fun things to keep us interested and motivated. I felt like getting to make content posts supporting local businesses and a local school, in general, was very fun for me and it just felt like I was encouraging productivity this summer. I believe productivity can keep people motivated in this time, therefore, bettering the community. (Kerry, Journal 2, June 2020)

Two students worked with the organizations' grant coordinator to assist in the process of applying for grants. This process took researching what grants the organization was eligible for, learning how to communicate the organizations' needs and potential, and writing up and submitting the grant. Students who chose to work on grant writing continually worked on this project throughout the semester, documenting their progress and their thoughts on how their work would make an impact in providing financial support to the organization. Three students began the semester organizing a fundraiser for the science center. However, because of the rules of lockdown and social distancing, planned events were canceled and they had to switch projects. Two of these students then transitioned into helping to organize the local virtual Future Farmers of America (FFA) convention. The students communicated with the state staff members of the FFA to see what assistance was needed. They helped to organize the first virtual FFA convention by making presentations, writing speeches, and working with high school students to assure a smooth transition to a virtual state convention. In their weekly reflection journal posts, e-service-learning students reported a lack of motivation among the high schoolers they were working with. One student suggested:

High schoolers are hard to motivate to get items turned in or completed in a timely manner. Most of these students have a severe lack of care about the virtual convention due to the sadness of not being able to have a normal live convention. (Chris, Journal 7, July 2020)

The focal areas during data collection and analysis were skill-building, community partner and student interaction, and community partner and student satisfaction. We present our findings about each of the focal areas.

Findings

Skill Building

Through the e-service learning experience, students had the opportunity to build new skills. This was the first time the students on the grant writing project were attempting to apply for grants. They learned how to identify grants that would pertain to the organization, as well as write up and submit a grant proposal. Students who worked on social media content learned new software systems to create and share content with the community, "I had to figure out how to properly use the social media design website, Canva, as well as get some feedback on the posts" (Jim, Journal 3, June 2020). Students who learned new skills or software wrote their weekly entries with excitement:

This week was a lot of fun! I spent 4 hours making posts this week for [the organization]. It was for the Camp-in-a-Box, construction updates, and registration… This week was really cool as I was just combining a lot of posts from past weeks and revamping them to be something new and different (Kerry, Journal 8, August 2020)

While completing their projects, some students had to interact with local businesses in multiple ways. They emailed and called to gain support for making a coupon book that would help raise funds for the organization, created social media posts to advertise business/ community partner's relations, and thanked businesses for their donations. Cold-calling and communication with local businesses was a novel experience for the students, requiring them to step outside of their comfort zone and speak publicly about the goals and mission of the organization. These people skills could be helpful in creating partnerships with potential supporters of any non-profit organization. One student wrote:

When talking to individuals that I believe would be a great asset to the (organization's) event, I used my knowledge from my research on (the organization) to share what their mission is and impact (on the community). (Chris, Journal 3, July 2020)

Community Partner and Student Interaction

Consistent dialog between the community partner and students was pivotal to the success of this e-service-learning. Starting with an individual orientation with each student, team members of our community partner were always available to answer students' questions and conduct timely changes to the assigned projects. Students were able to perform project progress check-ins and received helpful feedback showing how their work was impacting the organization and the community. Student feedback included comments such as, "(The community partner) was very helpful in offering advice on what to make the post look like" (Samantha, Journal 1, June 2020). Another student wrote:

(This week) I worked on posts as well as talked to the (community partner) for two and half hours. She walked me through what was expected and what type of posts, content, etc. I would be handling it. Last night, I designed a post that would be used as part of (the organization's) local campaign. (Jim, Journal 3, June 2020)

Community partner's team members consistently provided feedback and showed e-service-learning students how their work was impacting the organization and its surrounding community. This attentiveness was instrumental in creating an effective e-service learning experience for the students. One student wrote in his weekly reflection journal:

Speaking with my supervisor allowed me to have an even deeper understanding of the vital impact this fundraiser will have on the organization's mission. (Chris, Journal 2, June 2020)

While some instructors discount the potential for e-service-learning because students are not able to meet the community partner face-to-face, our experience shows that a dynamic work environment can be achieved through adequate communication with community partners via the phone, Zoom, and emails. Some students reported that collaborating and communicating with other students in the course was helpful, especially at the beginning of the semester. One student reported: "I reached out to classmates to ask what some of these new tasks would be and how I would go about this" (Eric, Journal 3, June 2020). Being able to communicate with peers improved some students' understanding of what their goals are and what steps they need to take to meet those goals. Reaching out to more experienced peers is a helpful skill for preservice teachers to practice. When they become teachers, it will be important for them to collaborate with and learn from more experienced colleagues.

Community Partner and Student Satisfaction

Several factors that affected the students' satisfaction with the e-service-learning experience emerged during data analysis. Students reported feeling appreciated by the organization and the community and felt like they were making a difference when they received positive feedback from the community partner. Students who were learning new skills and software wrote their weekly entries with excitement. Finally, e-service-learning students reported feeling very positive when they felt that their work impacted the community.

I really enjoyed working with (the service site) ... I think partnerships with them in the future would be beneficial because I feel like I actually had meaningful work to do rather than sitting and observing. I had a great experience with virtual service learning! (George, Journal 7, July 2020)

Another student wrote reflecting on e-service-learning experience at the end of the semester:

My service learning helped me to want to serve my community more now. This opportunity showed me that there is a lot of work that can be done in our community to help others, and it has made me want to pursue that. (Anonymous, Final Reflection, August 2020)

One student commented on how this e-service-learning experience would influence his future interactions with students:

One take-away I got from this was a connection I could make in my future class. When students ask why they need to be able to dig and find credible sources and things such as that rather than the first thing that pops up, I can state that doing a thorough search is a valuable skill that a bunch of employers would appreciate, seeing as even with grants all of the information is not always just given to you, you have to look for it. (Jim, Journal 7, July 2020)

Two team members completed a community partner satisfaction survey, and both strongly agreed that the quality of work contributed by students was high, communication with the course instructor was adequate to coordinate the partnership, and that e-service-learning students played an integral role in the organization's projects. One community partner team member commented: "I enjoyed working with my two interns! They were diligent and performed excellent work." Recognizing one student, the director of the science center wrote:

She tackled our assignment of managing social media with gusto! She never made any excuses, and she was hardworking, polite, reliable, and extremely competent! We were so impressed with her that we hired her as a part-time employee for the fall! (Stakeholder Survey, August 2020)

Analysis of our data also showed that students who worked continuously on the same project throughout the semester tended to be more goal oriented. For instance, a student who worked on creating social media content throughout the semester wrote:

The goal is to continue to post more and more content to bring awareness to (the organization). My goal next week is to work on content for at least an hour each day. By doing that, it will ensure that there is a steady stream of content going out on all platforms and spreading the good word of (the organization). (Samantha, Journal 3, June 2020)

This suggests that continuous projects with tangible outcomes could lead to higher student satisfaction and more efficient e-service-learning experiences. Participating in community life through social media campaigns allowed students to feel productive and motivated during the otherwise challenging time of a lockdown and limited contact with others. The synergy between students' contributions, the center's offerings, and people/businesses in the community met community needs for children's STEM learning when other educational opportunities were limited. Students' evaluation of their e-service-learning experience in the final reflection was overwhelmingly positive. Most respondents felt they learn something new about the community, provided a needed service, and plan to continue serving in the community.

Figure 2. The percent of students who "Strongly Agree" or " Agree" with the statements related to the efficacy of this e-service-learning

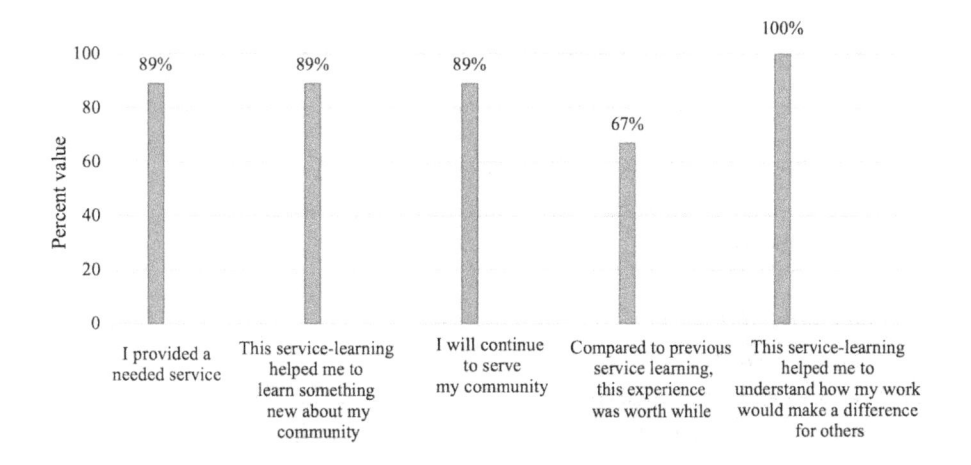

Statement	Percent
I provided a needed service	89%
This service-learning helped me to learn something new about my community	89%
I will continue to serve my community	89%
Compared to previous service learning, this experience was worth while	67%
This service-learning helped me to understand how my work would make a difference for others	100%

Challenges

While executed e-service-learning can be described as successful overall, it was not without pitfalls. One student did not have a tangible finished project at the end of the semester due to interruptions caused by the pandemic. The student continued to make contributions that would help the organization in the future, but the project was still ongoing at the end of the service period. Some other issues encountered by students during their e-service-learning experience included difficulty in accessing needed information or navigating websites:

The hardest part this week was trying to find all of the contact information for the different organizations. Some of them hide the info very well and you have to do a lot of digging to find a simple phone number or email address. (Jim, Journal 7, July 2020)

Students would often wait for the next time they were meeting with the community partner to ask about access to needed information, instead of reaching out immediately, "I mentioned to ((the community partner) that I did not have access to a particular document, and I am waiting to hear back from her" (George, Journal 1, June 2020). Timely communication is critical for the successful completion of the project in a virtual environment. An additional challenge that emerged was a perceived disconnect between course content and some of the e-service learning tasks:

Information from this course did not really have an impact on my service learning this week. Since I was mainly trying to get in contact with businesses it was mostly basic communication skills. (Eric, Journal 5, July 2020)

A few course topics were seen as useful during e-service-learning (i.e., strategies on engagement and holding attention while developing social media content):

My tasks did not directly align with course material, however, I continued to remember how students learn and what they consider rewarding experiences. Through this, I tried to craft my posts to engage students (even through a screen)! (George, Journal 7, July 2020)

While some students wrote in their reflection journals that the course information was not particularly connected to their service-learning projects, they found the overall service-learning experience helpful in tuning their professional skills:

Information from the course did not have an impact on my service learning this week. I did use some past information regarding teachers and unplanned events this week. Teachers have to be flexible and ready for anything. This week I was not prepared to change responsibilities, but I had to be flexible and adapt to this change. That is what I will be doing going forward. (Eric, Journal 3, June 2020)

The Developing Stage

This is the "action" part of the research that consists of developing an action plan, a strategy for implementing the results of the action research project (Mertler, 2019). There is no one size fits all solution on instituting meaningful e-service-learning: decisions on the way service can be adapted to an online environment are local and context-based. While developing and conducting e-service-learning with preservice teachers, we learned that spending some time to understand community partners, their goals and availability is really important for developing reciprocal relations between students, community partners, and faculty. We are going to continue our collaboration with this newly founded non-profit hands-on children's science center and organize e-service-learning activities for students in both online and face-to-face courses to serve our community and work toward the public good. In addition to the successfully executed activities (i.e., creating and maintaining an online presence for the newly founded organization and grant writing), we are planning to develop activities for students that could allow them to work on the same task continuously. For example, e-service-learning students can prepare workshops/webinars that could be offered to the organization members, or organization users, or to reach and enlarge the organization's targets. Analysis of our data indicates that students who worked continuously on the same project throughout the semester tended to be more goal-oriented and motivated.

We are also going to ask for the contribution of projects' ideas from students. Students can be very creative, and their contribution to the tasks' development will serve the organization well. Students know what their counterparts could do, which competencies they can bring to the project, and what could motivate and engage them.

To prevent communication lapses and promote timely task completion, we will encourage each group of students to have a leader who will guide the work and serve as a key contact person with the community partner. Additionally, groups can provide a peer review mechanism as the frequent peer review of each other's projects has been central to the projects' success (Lazar & Preece, 1999).

Constructive communication and establishing clear channels of communication between students and the instructor is vital for the success of e-service-learning and preventing disengagement and confusion. The instructors must remain actively engaged from the beginning to the end of the e-service-learning, giving continuous feedback and offering space for reflection (Hunter, 2007; Tabor, 2007). We will continue to offer weekly reflection journals for students and implement weekly feedback from the instructor either via a comment in the journal, email, or Zoom. In the online environment, students need even more feedback since they lack the immediate response of a traditional classroom environment. Clear and frequent communication between students and the instructor helps make a course and e-service-learning successful and make students feel like the instructor is present, connected, and invested in their success.

Progress check-ins are instrumental in assuring students have meaningful e-service learning experiences. Instructors and community stakeholders should have weekly or bi-weekly check-ins with students on the progress towards project completion. If a student's project cannot be completed within the allotted time of service, it could be helpful for the student to reflect on this in their final reflection. Students could outline the steps they would hypothetically take to complete the project. Not only this information could be helpful for students to comprehend their service-learning experience, but it could be shared with the community partner to assure that the planned future projects can be completed within the semester.

Finally, connecting service experiences to the content learned in the course is a longstanding component of service-learning. In the traditional face-to-face environment, instructors have an opportunity to spontaneously connect course content to shared service experiences during the lecture or class discussion. When both instructions and service-learning are moved online, these "aha" moments need to be intentionally prepared. In the future, we are planning to make connections between course service and course materials clear in online assignments and lectures, being explicit about the course's service-learning purpose and its relevance to the students' lives and careers, or the wellbeing of the community. Specifically, we will invite the community partner to suggest what course readings/activities/materials they could recommend that would help students understand the work they are doing better or see stronger connections between the course and the service-learning assignments. Also, for students to experience integration of course content and the e-service-learning experience, we will include these experiences into course discussions and assignments. When students are explicitly asked to make connections between classroom learning and the service experience, their learning is enhanced. Class discussions focused on students connecting their service-learning experiences to course content are an excellent way to achieve this integration.

The Reflecting Stage

The final stage of the action research includes sharing and communicating the results of action research and reflecting on the process (Mertler, 2019). Reflection is a crucial step in the process of action research and something that must be done continuously during the process of instructional activity, as well as at the end of every action cycle. Perpetual reflection enables instructor-researcher to adapt their procedures if the situation warrants; making reflection is not a final step but part of each step of the action research (Mertler, 2019). For example, when some of our students had their fundraising e-service learning projects collapsed due to the lockdown restrictions, we had to reflect on the situation and promptly find another activity for them to complete by the end of the semester.

We are now in the process of implementing an action plan and revising our e-service-learning strategies for the delivery in the upcoming semester. Informally, we shared the results of our study with our colleagues in individual dialogues.

Discussion of E-Service-learning best practices, Recommendations

A fundamental function of education is the holistic development of an individual, including personal growth and civic engagement. Service-learning is a collaborative teaching and learning strategy that fosters these developmental domains (Miller, 2020). This aspect of education has been challenged by the social distancing imposed by the COVID-19 pandemic and the consequent move to online instruction. To overcome these challenges, teachers, students, and communities can join forces to produce new transformative practices suitable for this novel social reality. At this time, when many institutions require all teaching and learning activities to occur virtually and traditional service-learning is restricted, e-service-learning becomes increasingly relevant. The findings of our study may be particularly interesting for the faculty developing e-service-learning courses.

The best practices to create a quality e-service-learning experience are largely the same as for traditional service-learning. E-service-learning activities have to be meaningful and relevant to the students and offer opportunities to learn and increase understanding for students, faculty, and community partners. Specific e-service-learning projects must have clear reachable and measurable goals and meet the needs of community partners. Ideally, e-service-learning activities should be designed and planned by students actively collaborating with community partners and be linked to the course content explicitly. E-service-learning should include support and coaching for students from both instructor and the community partner and should offer adequate time to complete the real tangible projects. To create effective service-learning experiences, systematic reflection on the learning processes and outcomes for all participants should be encouraged and the final outcome should be assessed by the community partner and the university (Furco, 2002; Hart & Northmore, 2010; NCCPE, 2012). Also, the best practices related to technology and communication should be incorporated (Waldner et al., 2012). Evidently, technology plays a very important role in e-service-learning. In order to maximize its success, students, instructors, and community partners should have the necessary skills and technological resources to perform online activities. Ideally, a successful e-service-learning program should include a digital expert that can help teachers and students to use technological potential according to their goals (Seifer & Mihalynuk, 2005). While technology, the internet, and devices allow the development of a wide range of services without direct contact among people, e-service-learning cannot be efficient without fostering interpersonal relationships. Our findings indicate that planning and implementing relationship-focused events, such as introductory Zoom meetings with the community partner, or allowing students to devise service-learning assignments in cooperation with the community partner can help to ensure meaningful e-service-learning. In addition, active and constructive communication between students, instructors, and the community partner is the key to the success of e-service-learning. The instructor must remain a central figure and coordinate the active engagement of e-service-learning students with the community partner from the beginning to the end of the project. Lastly, faculty and community partners should select short-term rather than long-term projects. When students can view their accomplishments, the impact their service has on the community, they gain greater satisfaction from their e-service-learning experiences.

FUTURE RESEARCH DIRECTIONS

There are many well-done aspects of service-learning research, including documentation of students' experiences with this pedagogy and perceptions of its effectiveness (Roodin et al., 2013). However, there are many ways in which this area of study could be improved by future researchers. For example, the findings of our study show that through their e-service-learning experience students had the opportunity to build new skills. Using a longitudinal design, future studies could examine how these skills evolve over time. Secondly, the field could benefit from more comparative studies that assess the efficacy of traditional and e-service-learning experiences in training preservice teachers. Improved research designs and the use of standardized measurement instruments could enable more robust comparisons of outcomes across different studies. Also, a more effective methodology for assessing costs and benefits for community partners with regard to service-learning programming needs to be planned and developed. Finally, while sharing the results of their studies, researchers could include a table or chart, perhaps in the form of a checklist, that one could use when attempting to implement e-service-learning in the future.

CONCLUSION

According to Ferrance (2000):

Action research is not about learning why we do certain things, but rather how we can do things better. It is about how we can change our instruction to impact students. It involves people working to improve their skills, techniques, and strategies. (p.3)

Action research provides us with a methodology we can use to improve our teaching practices while performing our regular duties. It allows us to blend research and practice since the researchers draw their findings and conclusions predominantly on their own experiences and observations from their practices. Action research can contribute to instructors' own and other instructors' practices, it can help them make the whole educational process more meaningful for themselves, students, and the community. This chapter provides a step-by-step description of action research conducted to promote a meaningful e-service-learning experience in an online class for preservice teachers. Such an integrative framework is timely because, in this unprecedented time brought by COVID-19, educators have to advance best online practices, improving their own teaching and students' learning. Analyzing data from the online course with the e-service-learning component, we presented empirical insights and identified successful practices and those that need to be perfected. To improve our e-service-learning practices and the lives of community members with whom we work, we used an action research methodology that is uniquely positioned to assist with making these advancements.

REFERENCES

Balazadeh, N. (1996, October 10-13). *Service-learning and the sociological imagination: Approach and assessment.* Presentation at the National Historically Black Colleges and Universities Faculty Development Symposium, Memphis, TN. https://files.eric.ed.gov/fulltext/ED402854.pdf

Bogdan, R. C., & Biklen, S. K. (1992). *Qualitative research for education: An introduction to theory and methods* (2nd ed.). Allyn & Bacon.

Carr, W., & Kemmis, S. (1986). Becoming critical: Education, knowledge and action research. Falmer.

Celio, C. I., Durlak, J., & Dymnicki, A. (2011). A meta-analysis of the impact of service-learning on students. *Journal of Experiential Education*, *34*(2), 164–181. doi:10.1177/105382591103400205

Dewey, J. (1986). Experience and education. *The Educational Forum*, *50*(3), 241–252. doi:10.1080/00131728609335764

Eyler, J., & Giles, D. E. Jr. (1999). *Where's the learning in service-learning?* Jossey-Bass.

Eyler, J., Giles, D. E. Jr, Stenson, C. M., & Gray, C. J. (2001). *At a glance: What we know about the effects of service-learning on college students, faculty, institutions and communities, 1993–2000* (3rd ed.). Vanderbilt University.

Farina, M. A. (2018, January 24-25). *E-service-learning and teacher education: A case study of experimental education*. International Congress of Creative Cities, Orlando, FL. 10.7195/piccc.00011

Ferrance, E. (2000). *Action research*. Northeast and Islands Regional Educational Laboratory, Brown University. https://www.brown.edu/academics/education-alliance/sites/brown.edu.academics.education-alliance/files/publications/act_research.pdf

Figuccio, M. J. (2020). Examining the efficacy of e-service-learning. *Frontiers in Education*, *5*, 606451. Advance online publication. doi:10.3389/feduc.2020.606451

Furco, A. (2002). *Self-assessment rubric for the institutionalization of service-learning in higher education* (Unpublished manuscript). University of California, Berkley, CA.

Furco, A. (2003). *Service-learning: A balanced approach to experiential learning. Introduction to service learning toolkit* (2nd ed.). Campus Compact.

Geller, J. D., Zuckerman, N., & Seidel, A. (2016). Service-learning as a catalyst for community development: How do community partners benefit from service-learning? *Education and Urban Society*, *48*(2), 151–175. doi:10.1177/0013124513514773

Hagenbuch, D. J. (2006). Service-learning inputs and outcomes in a personal selling course. *Journal of Marketing Education*, *28*(1), 26–34. doi:10.1177/0273475305280882

Hart, A., & Northmore, S. (2011). Auditing and evaluating university–community engagement: Lessons from a UK case study. *Higher Education Quarterly*, *65*(1), 34–58. doi:10.1111/j.1468-2273.2010.00466.x

Heffernan, K. (2001). *Fundamentals of service-learning course construction*. Campus Compact.

Hervani, A. A., Helms, M. M., Rutti, R. M., LaBonte, J., & Sarkarat, S. (2015). Service learning projects in online courses: Delivery strategies. *The Journal of Learning in Higher Education*, *11*(1), 35–41.

Hunter, D. (2007). The virtual student/client experience. *The Journal of American Academy of Business, Cambridge*, *12*(1), 88–92.

Jacoby, B. (2015). *Service-learning essentials: questions, answers, and lessons learned*. Jossey-Bass.

Karasik, R. J. (2020). Community partners' perspectives and the faculty role in community-based learning. *Journal of Experiential Education*, *43*(2), 113–135. doi:10.1177/1053825919892994

Kemmis, S., & McTaggart, R. (2007). Communicative action and the public sphere. In N. K. Denzin & Y. S. Lincoln (Eds.), *The SAGE handbook of qualitative research* (pp. 559–603). SAGE.

Lazar, J., & Preece, J. (1999, December 22-27). *Implementing service learning in an online communities course* (Paper Presentation). 14th Annual Conference, International Academy of Information Management, Charlotte, NC, United States.

LeCompte, M. D., & Schensul, J. J. (2012). *Analysis and interpretation of ethnographic data: A mixed methods approach.* Rowman Altamira.Lewin, K. (1946). Action research and minority problems. *The Journal of Social Issues*, 2(4), 34–46. doi:10.1111/j.1540-4560.1946.tb02295.x

Lincoln, Y. S., & Guba, E. G. (1986). But is it rigorous? Trustworthiness and authenticity in naturalistic evaluation. *New Directions for Program Evaluation*, 30(30), 73–84. doi:10.1002/ev.1427

Mertler, C. A. (2019). Action research: Improving schools and empowering educators. *Sage (Atlanta, Ga.)*.

Miller, R. L. (2020). Service learning: A review of best practices. In A. Schwartz & R. L. Miller (Eds.), *High impact educational practices: A review of best practices with illustrative examples* (pp. 570–583). http://teachpsych.org/ebooks/highimpacted

O'Donnell, L., Stueve, A., San Doval, A., Duran, R., Haber, D., Atnafou, R., & Piessens, P. (1999). The effectiveness of the "Reach for Health" community youth service learning program in reducing early and unprotected sex among urban middle school students. *American Journal of Public Health*, 89(2), 176–181. doi:10.2105/AJPH.89.2.176 PMID:9949745

Pigza, J. M. (2010). Developing your ability to foster student learning and development through reflection. In B. Jacoby & P. Mutascio (Eds.), *Looking in, reaching out: A reflective guide for community service-learning professionals* (pp. 73–94). Campus Compact.

Roodin, P., Brown, L. H., & Shedlock, D. (2013). Intergenerational service-learning: A review of recent literature and directions for the future. *Gerontology & Geriatrics Education*, 34(1), 3–25. doi:10.1080/02701960.2012.755624 PMID:23362852

Ryan, G. W., & Bernard, H. R. (2003). Techniques to identify themes. *Field Methods*, 15(1), 85–109. doi:10.1177/1525822X02239569

Sandy, M., & Holland, B. A. (2006). Different worlds and common ground: Community partner perspectives on campus-community partnerships. *Michigan Journal of Community Service Learning*, 13(1), 30–43.

Seaman, J. E., Allen, I. E., & Seaman, J. (2018). *Grade increase: Tracking distance education in the United States.* Babson Survey Research Group. https://onlinelearningsurvey.com/reports/gradeincrease.pdf

Seifer, S. D., & Mihalynuk, T. V. (2005). *The use of technology in higher education service-learning.* http://www.servicelearning.org/ instant_info/fact_sheets/he_facts/use_of_tech/

Strait, J., & Sauer, T. (2004). Constructing experiential learning for online courses: The birth of e-service. *EDUCAUSE Quarterly*, 27(1), 62–65.

Tabor, S. W. (2007). Narrowing the distance: Implementing a hybrid learning model for information security education. *Quarterly Review of Distance Education*, 8(1), 47–57.

Voss, H. C., Mathews, L. R., Fossen, T., Scott, G., & Schaefer, M. (2015). Community–academic partnerships: Developing a service–learning framework. *Journal of Professional Nursing*, *31*(5), 395–401. doi:10.1016/j.profnurs.2015.03.008 PMID:26428344

Waldner, L. S., & Hunter, D. (2008). Client-based courses: Variations in service learning. *Journal of Public Affairs Education*, *14*(2), 219–239. doi:10.1080/15236803.2008.12001521

Waldner, L. S., McGorry, S. Y., & Widener, M. C. (2010). Extreme e-service learning (XE-SL): E-service learning in the 100% online course. *Journal of Online Learning and Teaching*, *6*(4), 839–851.

Waldner, L. S., McGorry, S. Y., & Widener, M. C. (2012). E-service-learning: The evolution of service-learning to engage a growing online student population. *Journal of Higher Education Outreach & Engagement*, *16*(2), 123–150. https://files.eric.ed.gov/fulltext/EJ975813.pdf

ADDITIONAL READING

Duesbery, L., & Twyman, T. (2019). 100 questions (and answers) about action research. *Sage (Atlanta, Ga.)*.

Garner, L. C. (2011). Meeting learning objectives through service-learning: A pomology case study. *HortTechnology*, *21*(1), 119–125. doi:10.21273/HORTTECH.21.1.119

Goertzen, B. J., & Greenleaf, J. (2016). A student-led approach to eservice-learning: A case study on service project effectiveness within a fieldwork in leadership studies course. *The International Journal of Research on Service-Learning and Community Engagement*, *4*(1), 1–18.

Ivankova, N., & Wingo, N. (2018). Applying mixed methods in action research: Methodological potentials and advantages. *The American Behavioral Scientist*, *62*(7), 978–997. doi:10.1177/0002764218772673

Ivankova, N. V. (2014). Mixed methods applications in action research. *Sage (Atlanta, Ga.)*.

Malvey, D. M., Hamby, E. F., & Fottler, M. D. (2006). E-service learning: A pedagogic innovation for healthcare management education. *The Journal of Health Administration Education*, *23*(2), 181–198. PMID:16700443

McGorry, S. Y. (2012). No significant difference in service learning online. *Journal of Asynchronous Learning Networks*, *16*(4), 45–54.

Ropers-Huilman, B., Carwile, L., & Lima, M. (2005). Service-learning in engineering: A valuable pedagogy for meeting learning objectives. *European Journal of Engineering Education*, *30*(2), 155–165. doi:10.1080/03043790410001664363

Stefaniak, J. (2020). A systems view of supporting the transfer of learning through e-service-learning experiences in real-world contexts. *TechTrends*, *64*(4), 561–569. doi:10.100711528-020-00487-3

KEY TERMS AND DEFINITIONS

Action Research: A disciplined process of inquiry conducted by and for those taking the action in order to assist the "actor" in improving and/or refining his or her actions.

Community Partner: A nonprofit organization, public agency, government office, school, and certain private business where students provide community service as an integral part of their academic courses.

Community-Based Participation: An involvement of people in the community to get the maximum benefit for the whole society.

E-Service Learning: Occurs when the instructional component of the course, the service component, or both are conducted online.

Experiential Education: A student-focused approach that engages learner in the application of theory and academic content to real-world experiences, either within the classroom, within the community, or within the workplace.

Online Learning: An acquisition of knowledge which takes place through electronic technologies and media.

Preservice Teacher: A college student who is enrolled in a teacher preparation program and working toward teacher certification.

Reflection: A key component of service-learning; the intentional consideration of an experience in light of particular learning objectives.

Service-Learning: A flexible pedagogy organized around learning goals that provides meaningful service activities that address real community needs.

Teacher Education: Any formal program that have been established for the preparation of teachers at the elementary and secondary-school levels.

Chapter 4
The Potential of English for Social Purposes and Cooperation for Emergency Remote Language Teaching:
Action Research Based on Future Teachers' Opinions

Francisco Javier Palacios-Hidalgo
https://orcid.org/0000-0002-4326-209X
University of Córdoba, Spain

Cristina A. Huertas-Abril
https://orcid.org/0000-0002-9057-5224
University of Córdoba, Spain

ABSTRACT

Due to the COVID-19 pandemic, it is necessary to explore new practices in language teacher education. English for Social Purposes and Cooperation, a socially-responsive and technology-friendly approach to English language learning, may help students around the world continue learning from home. This chapter analyzes the perceptions of a group of pre-service teachers after designing socially responsive materials specially created for the COVID-19 crisis. Action research is employed to improve teacher educators' activity and pre-service teachers' training, and a mixed-method approach based on grounded theory and content analysis is performed. Findings show that the experience has provided participants with meaningful examples of material design. This encourages teacher educators to include the proposed approach in their teaching and reveals the need for specific training in material design. Results may help prove the potential of action research for improving the teaching practice.

DOI: 10.4018/978-1-7998-6922-1.ch004

The Potential of English for Social Purposes and Cooperation for Emergency Remote Language Teaching

INTRODUCTION

Although distance education has existed for nearly three centuries (Clark, 2020), it has rapidly grown in the last decades (Richards & Guzman, 2016; Simonson et al., 2019) due to the increasing number of digital technologies that are taking over the world at different scales. In simple words, Milman (2015) defines distance education as "the practice of delivering education and instruction to students not physically present but interacting with the instructor and the educational process remotely (usually by computers and the Internet these days)" (p. 567). In the same way, the author points out at the very fact that this type of learning and teaching allows increasing flexibility of the learning process (for instance, students can decide to what extent they are going to participate according to their own learning schedule and not the teacher's) and entails the opportunity to make education available and accessible to those who cannot physically participate in it for any reason. At this juncture, e-learning education has become the most extended way of distance education (Negash & Wilcox, 2008).

In addition to these decades of rapid technological development, distance learning is filling a new gap in today's education. The widespread concern about the pandemic caused by COVID-19 and the consequent state of alarm and lockdown established by governments from every country is affecting all educational stages. With most of the world's schools closed, educational administrations are facing unprecedented challenges and, in turn, taking measures to ensure learning continuity and guarantee that the learning process of millions of students is minimally affected. In this light, Chang and Yano (2020) developed an overview of nations' policy actions since early March 2020 in an attempt to build a worldwide community of practice; this monitoring has revealed how all countries are employing their already existing technology-enhanced distance education modalities. However, the report also highlights that one of the governments' major concerns is to secure equity when accessing this technology-based learning environment. Despite the attempts of many countries to provide families from low-SES backgrounds with devices and mobile data packages to face these new learning solutions, the digital gap is yet to be bridged, and guaranteeing equity still requires efforts from stakeholders (Giannini, 2020).

Likewise, there is no doubt that language learning, and more specifically learning English, has become essential in the 21st-century society (European Commission, 1995) and in educational systems around the world, acquiring great relevance both in international organizations and in the labor market (Madani, 2017). In this line, new methodologies and approaches to English teaching and learning have been developed in the last years with the premise to guaranteeing meaningful interaction environments and real-world-based contexts for students to become highly competent in the respective language (e.g., Huertas-Abril & Gómez-Parra, 2018b; Slapac & Coppersmith, 2019). Nevertheless, in the context of the aforementioned COVID-19 situation, it is necessary to seek new, motivating practices that not only allow a flexible language learning process but also make education available and accessible to those who cannot physically participate in it for any reason (Milman, 2015). In this light, English for Social Purposes and Cooperation (ESoPC) seems worth considering, a technology-friendly approach aiming at providing learners with effective learning of English paying special attention to 21st-century social issues and cultural values (climate change, immigration and refugees, and health emergencies, among others; Huertas-Abril, 2018). This approach, coined by Huertas and Gómez in 2018, is based upon "encouraging learners to think critically and challenge common assumptions in order to develop their English language level while increasing their social awareness", considering "both local and global issues from a social perspective" (Huertas-Abril & Gómez-Parra, 2018, p. 76).

Additionally, the concept of Emergency Remote Language Teaching (ERLT) has arisen in the literature, comprising language teaching methods used during social crises or health emergencies that combine features of distance and online education (Huertas-Abril, 2020b). Considering the characteristics of both approaches, combining ESoPC and ERLT appears to be a good strategy to address the challenges that education is facing as a result of the COVID-19 pandemic.

Among all the actors involved in education and language teaching, teachers are in charge of ensuring the quality of students' learning process (both onsite and online) and, ultimately, exploiting the potential of learning resources including digital technologies (Redecker & Punie, 2017). But in the context of a pandemic, their role in the design and provision of learning opportunities is of paramount importance and considering the importance of learning languages in the 21st century, there is an urgent need for developing materials that students all across the world can use from their homes. Furthermore, the COVID-19 outbreak requires teachers and parents to educate children on preventive measures to fight the virus.

However, it is necessary to reflect on whether technology implementation is leading to the expected results in the learning process of students and, ultimately, examine if the modalities of distance education implemented around the world's educational systems constitute good alternatives to onsite teaching. To this purpose, action research, which refers to the iterative process of reflection on one's own teaching practice in order to learn about its strengths and limitations and, in turn, to include modifications to improve it (Hendricks, 2017), can provide a sound framework for identifying possible practices and testing their learning potential for these unprecedented times.

This chapter presents the results of an exploratory action research study in which pre-service bilingual primary teachers at the University of Córdoba (Spain) designed ESoPC materials in a real ERLT setting. To do so, their perceptions about the experience are examined using qualitative analysis based on a grounded-theory scheme and content analysis techniques. Action research is used as the base of the study since its ultimate goal is to improve language teaching and future ESoPC training experiences during the COVID-19 health emergency. Results may be of interest to teacher educators and teachers of English. Furthermore, it may contribute to the scientific literature specialized and, eventually, prove the potential of action research as a tool for improving the teaching practice.

BACKGROUND: TEACHING ENGLISH DURING A PANDEMIC

Since the beginning of the century, language teaching has shifted from traditional methodologies, where the teaching process was reduced to magistral lectures aimed at improving young generations' linguistic knowledge, to new technology- and communication-based models (Mishra, 2016). Almost one decade ago, Ulbrich et al. (2011) already advised that "the teaching techniques that have worked for decades do not work anymore because new students learn differently too" (p. i). In this light, the scientific literature has been exploring the potential of a wide array of technologies both for onsite and online language learning and teaching, ranging from blogs, wikis and podcasts, to online courses, social networks, and augmented and virtual realities (e.g., Huertas-Abril, 2020a; Lan, 2020; Reinhardt, 2019). All of these technological responses can be grouped under the broad terms Technology-Enhanced Language Learning (TELL) and Computer-Assisted Language Learning (CALL), which essentially entail the use of computers as complements to language teaching. In the same line, new approaches to English teaching and learning, like ESoPC, are being developed in an attempt to provide learners with meaningful interaction environments and real-world-based contexts that help them become highly competent in the language and, in turn, socially aware of local and global issues affecting the world; likewise, ideas such as ERLT have been developed, too, as ways to guarantee the continuity of students' language learning process during the current health emergency state. In this sense, the following sections explore the potential of both ESoPC as a 21st-century English teaching approach and the power of TELL and CALL to face the COVID-19 pandemic.

TELL and CALL: Bringing Technology into the Language Classroom

As already mentioned, language education today is experiencing an enormous improvement thanks to technology. Many different ways of applying it in language classrooms have resulted in the coining of two broad terms that refer to the enhancement of language learning and teaching by means of technology-based methodologies: TELL and CALL. More as an approach than a teaching method, Patel (2017) defines TELL as the use of technological devices as a complement to the language teacher's instruction. Very similarly, Palacios-Hidalgo (2020) explains how CALL promotes the use of computers as a support for the learning process of the language while creating a digital environment in which the language is presented in a natural way. Both have been proved to be beneficial in the language classroom. For instance, Krystalli et al. (2020) have discussed how TELL allows accessing authentic language and provides real communication environments where the language transcends the classroom. Likewise, Ghanizadeh et al. (2018) have revealed how students show better attitudes and proficiency and less anxiety when using TELL to learn languages. As for CALL, studies have also reported how beneficial it is for students' motivation and communicative competence for languages such as English (Lee et al., 2016; Tafazoli et al., 2019).

By definition, TELL and CALL allow distance education and appear to be virtually the only feasible means to ensure learning continuity during the COVID-19 outbreak. According to Dina and Ciornei (2013) and Patel (2017), these present a more flexible way of learning, since students can organise their learning deciding the path to follow, and they are compatible with a variety of learning styles as opposed to more traditional methodologies, also providing an individualized process for each of the students. TELL and CALL give learners the opportunity to connect with the world and create their own authentic student-centred environment. Users of these approaches also gain independence and increase their motivation and, at the same time, experience a reduction of their stress and anxiety, since lessons and content can be repeated and/or re-accessed as many times as needed. TELL and CALL can be used together with textbooks or other onsite materials, thus guaranteeing the acquisition of contents set in classroom plans and syllabi. Additionally, considering that every human activity is influenced to a greater or lesser extent by technology (Castells, 2010), these approaches can help the learning of linguistic and non-linguistic contents from multiple disciplines at the same time. Similarly, they can also provide learners with immediate feedback on their activities, which is sometimes difficult in an onsite classroom as teachers may need to support many students at the same time. Ultimately, educators in technology-enhanced environments become guides and facilitators of the learning process rather than those in control of it.

TELL and CALL have some disadvantages too, such as the inevitable technical problems, both students' and teachers' lack of training in how to use technology for educational purposes, the difficulty (or impossibility) to access the Internet, and the obvious extra efforts that teachers are required to make when planning ICT-based activities. Educators may even encounter the problem that they are not digitally competent enough (Beatty, 2010; Dina & Ciornei, 2013; Patel, 2017; Tafazoli et al., 2017). Likewise, Tafazoli and Golshan (2014) highlight financial limitations, students' problems when adapting to a new teaching model, and also teachers' uneasiness with using technology as specific barriers of CALL. On their part, Asrifan et al. (2020) point at traditional negative attitudes toward the use of computers in the classroom, such as the idea that "the computer is a just a tool without any inborn wisdom or a mind of its own" or that these can only be used to "augment human capabilities" but not teach students in the same way a real teacher would (p. 96). Nevertheless, teachers seem to be the sole way to guarantee a quality language learning process for students all around the world during these times, and making use of technology might help them significantly in such a task.

English for Social Purposes and Cooperation: A 21st-Century Approach to Language Teaching

The importance of focusing language education on pragmatic meaning, communication and interaction is long accepted today (Ellis, 2005; Ellis & Shintani, 2014). In this line, new approaches to English teaching and learning have been developed in recent years with the premise to guarantee meaningful interplay among students when learning English. One of them is ESoPC, which besides attempting to provide learners with real-world-based contexts for their language learning process, has a fundamental focus on 21st-century social issues and cultural values (Huertas-Abril, 2018).

Based on the English for Specific Purposes model, ESoPC is an approach to English learning that explores social and cultural topics while the language is being learnt with a triple aim: language proficiency development, cultural awareness raising, and social responsibility consciousness. Issues such as gender equality, fair trade, food production policies, environmental problems, immigration and refugees, and cooperation are the main interests of ESoCP which, according to Huertas (2018), make the learning process meaningful.

In this light, the pillars of ESoPC (see Table 1) make this approach the perfect framework to introduce subjects like pandemics and health measures during the COVID-19 outbreak in the English classroom. Furthermore, ESoPC grants a perfect integration of technology into the learning process.

In light of this, ESoCP can be a good solution not only for providing students with quality e-learning through using TELL and CALL methodologies but also to guarantee the continuity of them learning English. Furthermore, considering the necessity to ensure social responsibility in times of a pandemic, the approach's commitment to social issues makes it the perfect framework to develop children's social responsibility towards the issue in hand since, certainly, civil awareness is as imperative as healthcare and governmental measures to fight the COVID-19.

Unfortunately, although the basics of ESoPC are theoretically clear, no examples of implementation can be found in the scientific literature that allow proving its benefits for language learning. In this sense, it is necessary to start using the approach in language classrooms, to train future teachers, and to develop a profound reflection on it so as to improve students' learning and motivation and educators' practice. Action research may help to that purpose (Hendricks, 2017; Slapac & Navarro, 2011).

Emergency Remote Language Teaching in Times of Covid-19

At this new, complex juncture provoked by the COVID-19 pandemic, the concept of Emergency Remote Teaching has been coined (Hodges et al., 2020) to refer to the specific type of teaching that is being implemented during the health crisis, which is neither distance nor online teaching properly:

Table 1. Pillars of ESoPC and suitability of TELL and CALL integration during the Covid-19 outbreak

ESoPC pillars (from Huertas-Abril, 2018b)	Description and suitability to address COVID-19
Authentic language use	ESoPC allows learners to access a native-like in real communicative situations. Learners are exposed to social issues and their global implications (such as the COVID-19 pandemic), and their cultural awareness and social responsibility towards them are raised. The approach also promotes the use of technology-based resources, thus TELL and CALL can be integrated into it.
Meaningful learning	In ESoPC, contents are, by definition, connected to real-life situations. In this light, the current pandemic can be directly addressed meanwhile the language is being taught and learnt. Furthermore, it supports a progressive content organization and eases the students' understanding.
"Learn to learn" competence and autonomous learning	ESoPC allows students' self-management of the learning process. They are taught to find and select accurate information and apply it to real-life sources. In this sense, teachers are in charge of promoting students' competences by, among other things supporting them individually and collectively. In this sense, CALL and TELL can help educators booth their students' work, and provide learners with a quality environment for information access and use.
Cooperative learning	ESoPC fosters cooperative work and enables students to share ideas, take decisions and interact with each other. In this light, the approach creates an ideal environment for learners to work cooperatively on ways to face the current health situation and reflect on forms to encourage social responsibility.
Critical thinking	ESoPC enables learners to analyze and understand the social matters addressed. It, therefore, allows them to be critical of certain people's behaviors during the present situation.
Revised Bloom's taxonomy	ESoPC helps develop diverse mental processes necessary for meaningful learning to happen in the learning of English. In this light, not only the language is acquired, but students also become more cognitively competent when reflecting on the present circumstances or applying what they have learnt to help improve society's circumstances during COVID-19.
Use of Learning and Knowledge Technologies and Technologies for Empowerment and Participation	ESoPC is likely to include multiple technologies in the learning process of a language. Learning and Knowledge Technologies and Technologies for Empowerment and Participation allow students to become active citizens of the 21st century. In this light, since ESoPC is a technology-friendly approach to language learning, it seems reasonable to believe that it can be interwoven with TELL and CALL.
Multiple assessment techniques	ESoPC gives special attention to formative assessment when evaluating students' outcomes' achievement. In this light, TELL and CALL techniques seem to offer many possibilities to carry out this assessment process. Additionally, in ESoPC, both social/cultural issues and the language are important, so this type of assessment is a suitable option to evaluate students' language learning process and social responsibility.

Source: Adapted from Palacios (2020a, p. 202)

In contrast to experiences that are planned from the beginning and designed to be online, emergency remote teaching (ERT) is a temporary shift of instructional delivery to an alternate delivery mode due to crisis circumstances. It involves the use of fully remote teaching solutions for instruction or education that would otherwise be delivered face-to-face or as blended or hybrid courses and that will return to that format once the crisis or emergency has abated (para. 18).

Based on this, the idea of ERLT has also been developed. This encompasses those teaching processes developed during crises and emergencies in the language classroom to enhance students' learning process of contents and skills that would be taught face-to-face in a normal situation. ERLT entails the use of interactive and individualized resources and tasks that students can do autonomously from their homes but in which the role of the teachers is still highly essential during the instruction. Similarly, it has some requirements too, such as enough digital skills of both teachers and learners, technology infrastructure, teacher training to properly design activities, and family support, among others. In this light, and since technology integration is one of the pillars of ESoPC, it seems reasonable to believe that a combination of ERLT and ESoPC can offer effective language education during the COVID-19 pandemic.

METHOD

Objective of the Study

This study aims at analyzing the perceptions and attitudes of pre-service bilingual primary teachers at the University of Córdoba (Spain) designing ESoPC materials in a real ERLT setting, derived from the outbreak of the COVID-19 health emergency. Action research is used as the base of the study since its ultimate goal is to improve language teaching and future ESoPC training experiences during the COVID-19 health emergency. Two research questions are proposed: (RQ1) What are the positive and negative aspects of designing ESoPC materials in ERLT settings according to pre-service bilingual primary teachers? and (RQ2) What are the most important social concerns that pre-service bilingual primary teachers face when designing ESoPC materials in ERLT settings?

Context and Participants

As a result of the state of alarm derived from the outbreak of the COVID-19 pandemic, education in Spanish universities had to be delivered online in the Spring semester of 2020 (February-July 2020). In this light, this study was developed as part of the course 'English as a Foreign Language for Primary Education Teachers', of the bilingual itinerary, of the University of Córdoba (located in the south of Spain). This is a compulsory course part of the third year of the bachelor's degree in Primary Education aimed at strengthening students' level of knowledge of English. Although the course is not intended to train future teachers for material design, the generally high level of English of participants encouraged educators to develop teacher education experiences in which they were asked to use the language while acting as real teachers and then reflecting on what they had done.

In this light, and before the experience, the teacher educators presented the steps to follow to the participants (based on Hendricks' recommendations; 2017, p. 56): first, they had to decide the objectives and contents they wanted to address in their online activities and resources to learn English and preventive measures to fight COVID-19 for Primary Education (6 to 11 years old); second, they had to create the resources either individually, in pairs or groups of three; third, they had to share the resources with their course mates via Zoom, identifying strengths and potential weaknesses of the resources; fourth, they were asked to reflect on the experience and the potential of ESoPC for ERLT situations (using three open-ended questions proposed by the teacher educators; see 'Instrument and Data Gathering'); fifth, they had to introduce modifications (if considered appropriate) in their designed resources considering their course mates' suggestions and their own reflection on the experience; sixth, the resources were gathered and published together[1] (after participants' written consent) so that teachers, students and families from other contexts could use them freely. Table 2 provides an overview of some of the materials designed:

Table 2. Overview of the materials designed

Students' age	Objectives	Description
6-7	- To raise awareness about what to do to stop COVID-19 - To learn basic vocabulary related to the situation	Quizlet with flashcards including vocabulary related to the pandemic and useful actions to stop COVID-19
6-7	- To understand diverse texts related to experiences and interests - To extract general and specific information from them	An audio story related to the pandemic is provided, together with some flashcards with pictures and fragments of the story. Some activities are presented which involve the flashcards.
8-9	- To become aware of COVID-19 - To create a handmade face mask	Students are encouraged to create a face mask with home objects. The use of technology is also encouraged to share their experience and practice their writing skills.
8-9	- To learn daily routines - To practice grammar tenses already studied	In this listening comprehension activity, a song describing the new routine of students during the lockdown period is provided. Students must identify the activities described in the song.
10-11	- To acquire information about COVID-19 - To improve reading and comprehension skills	An online comprehensive reading activity is presented in which students must answer guided questions about a text about COVID-19.
10-11	- To write texts aiming at helping in the pandemic - To promote empathy and solidarity toward others	Students are encouraged to write including possible activities to do during the lockdown period and motivational/supportive messages for others.

Source: Own elaboration

A non-probabilistic sample based on convenience was used for the selection of the participants. Eligibility criteria were based on participation in a training experience based on the design of ESoPC materials for an ERLT situation developed prior to the study[2]. A total of 61 participants took part in the study, all of the students of the aforementioned course, in the 2019-2020 academic year. Within the population, three groups can be identified: (i) Year 3 students of the Degree in Primary Education (37 participants – 60.66%); (ii) Year 3 students of the Double Degree in Primary Education and English Studies (19 participants – 31.15%); and (iii) international students (5 participants – 8.20%). Regarding nationality, 56 participants (91.80%) were from Spain, 2 participants (3.28%) were from Poland, 1 participant (1.64%) was from Austria, 1 participant (1.64%) was from Finland, and 1 participant (1.64%) was from Turkey. According to their gender, 49 participants (80.33%) were female, and 12 (19.67%) were male, and regarding their age, the mean was 21.25 years (range = 20–27; SD = 1.545).

Research Design

Action research was used twice in the study, first for pre-service bilingual primary teachers (see 'Context and Participants') to improve their abilities to design ESoPC materials, and second, for teacher educators (i.e., the researchers) to improve future teacher education experiences. In the case of the latter, five stages were established (following Hendricks, 2017): (i) creating a timeline for the study; (ii) identifying the participants; (iii) establishing ethical guidelines (participants submitted their responses anonymously to guarantee confidentiality and these were analyzed once the course had finished); (iv) developing the analysis; and (v) using member checks "to reduce bias and increase credibility" (Hendricks, 2017, p. 65).

For the analysis of participants' responses, an exploratory mixed-method approach (qualitative and quantitative) was performed. Firstly, a qualitative analysis following the Qualitative Evaluation Checklist (Patton, 2003) was carried out. Qualitative analysis strategies involve "working out how the things that people do make sense from their perspective" (Ezzy, 2002, p. xii) and "study[ing] things in their natural settings, attempting to make sense of, or interpret, phenomena in terms of the meanings people bring to them" (Denzin & Lincoln, 2017, p. 3). To this purpose, the methodological procedure of Grounded Theory (Glaser & Strauss, 1967) was used to make a first approach to the phenomenon, as its main aim is to discover or produce a theory from the collected data (Pidgeon & Henwood, 1997). After this, content analysis was carried out, which allows the study of the internal structure of the information, either in its composition, in its form of organization or structure, or its dynamics (López-Noguero, 2002, p. 173); in this way, we can make replications and inferences from the data obtained from a specific context in order to advance knowledge and develop new approaches, as well as represent the facts and draw up guidelines for action (Krippendorff, 2004). To perform the content analysis, the stages proposed by Arbeláez and Onrubia (2014) were followed, namely: (1) Theoretical phase: the information is initially and superficially organized, thus allowing a first approach to the work; (2) Descriptive phase: description and analysis of the data; and (3) Interpretative phase: the content analysis is interpreted according to the emerging categories.

For the analysis of the data, NVivo Plus version 12 for Windows (QSR International, 2021) was used. This software allows operating with several categories and subcategories that can be compared with each other thanks to the intersection matrices (Valdemoros-San-Emeterio et al., 2011). For this, the quality criteria established by Palacios et al. (2013) have been followed.

Finally, the results were used to improve ESoPC training experiences, identifying the benefits and constraints of ESoPC as a tool for ERLT situations and determining important aspects to consider when designing future teacher education experiences for pre-service teachers.

Instrument and Data Gathering

The instrument used for data gathering consisted of three open-ended questions, which, according to Patton, offer relevant data on people's experiences, perceptions and feelings, and knowledge (2003). The three structured study questions with identical terminology were given to all the pre-service teachers, which guarantees that all results were comparable (Bogdan & Taylor, 1975). The study questions were:

Q1: What are the positive aspects of designing ESoPC materials in a real ERLT setting?
Q2: What are the negative aspects and main challenges of designing ESoPC materials in a real ERLT setting?
Q3: What are the most important social concerns that you have found when designing ESoPC materials in a real ERLT setting to help children, families, and teachers regarding English language learning and teaching?

The instrument was administered at the end of the course after the design experience previously mentioned, and participants responded voluntarily. Their answers had to be submitted written (in order not to interfere with their responses) in English via the official Moodle platform of the University of Córdoba (Spain), and the response rate was extremely high as 100% of the participants submitted their responses, which were anonymized after the written consent to be used for research.

RESULTS

The following sections present the results of the analysis of participants' responses to the three open-ended questions described above.

Results Coded According to the Grounded Theory

Following the procedure of the Grounded Theory (Glaser & Strauss, 1967), a concept map was made derived from the results obtained after the codification and categorization process. Likewise, a process of explanation of the codification was carried out according to the topics and contents gathered in the concept map, together with their corresponding interrelations and definitions. Figure 1 shows the final categorization with respect to the design of ESoPC materials in a real ERLT setting.

Figure 1. Concept map derived from the codification process based on the Grounded Theory
Source: Own elaboration

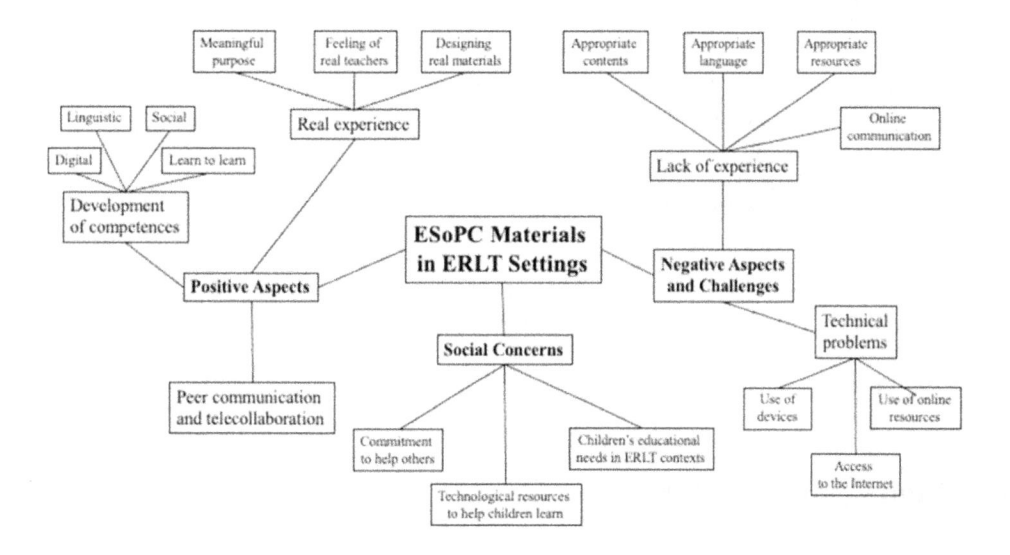

Results of the Semantic Analysis

For the semantic analysis, the 100 most frequent words used by the participants were selected, represented by means of a word cloud (Figure 2); it should be taken into account that the greater the frequency, the larger the representation.

The words most frequently used by participants (equal to or more than 50 entries) were: activities (109), children (97), pandemic (80), designing (74), resources (71), experience (70), English (64), teachers (64), situation (63), global (59), resource (50).

Figure 2. Word frequency represented as a word cloud – 100 words
Source: Own elaboration

Results of the Content Analysis

As shown in Table 3 below, three main categories were identified regarding the design of ESoPC materials in ERLT contexts following data analysis: (i) positive aspects, (ii) negative aspects and challenges, and (iii) social concerns.

Moreover, the number of references (according to both frequencies and percentages) by category was extracted, and the hierarchy is shown below:

- Positive aspects of designing ESoPC materials in ERLT contexts
    - Real experience: 78.69% (229)
        - Meaningful purpose: 30.58% (89)
        - Designing real materials: 24.05% (70)
        - Feeling of real teachers: 20.96% (61)
    - Peer communication and telecollaboration: 13.06% (38)
    - Development of competences: 11.34% (33)

- Digital competence: 7.56% (22)
- Linguistic competence: 2.41% (7)
- Social competence: 1.03% (3)
- Learn to learn competence: 0.34% (1)
- Negative aspects and challenges of designing ESoPC materials in ERLT contexts
  - Lack of experience: 84.47% (98)
    - Online communication: 38.79% (45)
    - Appropriate resources: 21.55% (25)
    - Appropriate contents: 13.79% (16)
    - Appropriate language: 10.34% (12)
  - Technical problems: 15.52% (18)
    - Access to the Internet: 7.76% (9)
    - Use of devices: 6.90% (8)
    - Use of online resources: 0.86% (1)
- Social concerns of designing ESoPC materials in ERLT contexts
  - Commitment to help others: 40.43% (19)
  - Children's educational needs in ERLT contexts: 36.17% (17)
  - Technological resources to help children learn: 23.40% (11)

Table 3. Categorization after data analysis

Category	No. of resources coded	No. of references coded	Percentage
Positive aspects	61	291	64.10%
Negative aspects and challenges	61	116	25.55%
Social concerns	61	47	10.35%
Total	61	454	100%

Source: Own elaboration

Perceived Positive Aspects of Designing ESoPC Materials in ERLT Contexts

The number of references coded in this category was 291. Of these, 78.69% (229) corresponded to a positive attitude derived from a real experience in teaching, 13.06% (38) to the importance of peer communication and telecollaboration, and 11.34% (33) to the development of teachers' competences useful for the labor market.

The subcategory "real experience" was then subdivided into three subsections: (i) meaningful purpose: 30.58% (89); (ii) designing real materials: 24.05% (70); and (iii) feeling of real teachers: 20.96% (61). The subsection "meaningful purpose" was composed of five elements: enriching experience, creativity and innovation, use of technological resources to help children, adaptation to a new experience, and inspiring project. In this light, it is interesting the importance participants give to adapt themselves to new situations and think differently.

Although this situation is a difficult one, it is the perfect time to create new and more attractive content, to discover new resources and to open our minds to different and innovative educational trends. (Student 12)

Similarly, participants appreciated that adaptation to new experiences and innovation are useful skills to their future performance as teachers.

This experience has helped us to innovate as future teachers to think about how to overcome adverse situations that may occur in our classes. (Student 18)

Related to the aforementioned subcategory, we identified the second subsection: "designing real materials", which is composed of four elements: (i) development of resources, (ii) enjoyable project, (iii) motivation, and (iv) creation of activities for real contexts. Participants highlighted the real component of the project as it deals with a real problem (the situation derived from the COVID-19 pandemic) in a real context (teaching English as a Foreign Language to Primary Education students).

Designing real materials that may be useful makes me feel very rewarded. It feels good to see that your materials can be used in a real English class, because designing activities that nobody, except our classmates, will be able to see is not as motivating as that. (Student 20)

The third subsection of "real experience" is "feeling of real teachers", which was composed of three elements: (i) feeling as real teachers, (ii) commitment and responsibility as teachers, and (iii) development and acquisition of new teaching strategies.

Designing resources is always useful, as it gives you the opportunity to create materials or activities that we could use in the future with our students. Sometimes, at university, we are more focused on theory than on practice. (Student 45)

Regarding my experience designing a resource during a global pandemic, I feel very pleased. I have put myself in the position of a real teacher and this has been very gratifying. Moreover, I have developed my creativity... (Student 27)

The subcategory related to the importance of peer communication and telecollaboration (13.06%, 38 references) is divided into two elements: (i) telecollaboration and (ii) learning from others. It must be borne in mind that "telecollaboration for emergency remote language learning and teaching (ERLT) is an interesting opportunity, as it does not only involve virtual exchanges, but also mutual reflection settings within digital learning environments" (Huertas-Abril, 2020b, para. 3).

...when designing the activities at home I have felt calm and sure of what I was doing, I had no doubts, and best of all I have worked with my colleagues through video calls to help each other, talk between us and do it more entertaining than if you were working alone. (Student 03)

Together with telecollaboration, knowing how their classmates have worked and developed their own ESoPC materials has helped the participants in this teaching experience, as they could also discover new resources and strategies that can be useful for their future development as teachers.

During this activity, we have learned some tools and materials to create resources for children. Also, we have learned the resources that our classmates have invented through the presentation. Another good point is the fact that we have had to work with partners via online, something that we almost never do because we prefer to do it face to face. (Student 09)

The third subcategory is the development of competences applicable to teachers' performance (11.34%, 33 references). Due to the context in which the teaching experience was carried out, the most recurrent competence identified by the participants was teachers' digital competence (7.56%, 22 references).

With this task I have improved my digital competences related to teaching, getting to know lots of resources that I am confident with will be of huge help in my professional future. (Student 42)

Moreover, the participants also stated that they had been able to improve their linguistic competence (2.41%, 7 references), their social competence (especially interpersonal skills) (1.03%, 3 references), and learn to learn competence (0.34%, 1 reference).

Perceived Negative Aspects and Challenges of Designing ESoPC Materials in ERLT Contexts

The number of references coded in this category was 116. Of these, 84,47% (98) corresponded to the participants' lack of experience in designing materials, while 15.52% (18) mentioned technical problems.

The subcategory "lack of experience" was then subdivided into four subsections: (i) online communication (38.79%, 45 references), (2) appropriate resources (21.55%, 25 references), (3) appropriate contents (13.79%, 16 references), and (4) appropriate language (10.34%, 12 references).

The negative aspects that participants found regarding online communication are related to exclusively online peer-communication, without face-to-face interaction. Online presentations were via Zoom, and the stress felt by the participants when communicating via the Internet resulted in the comments below.

...the most difficult thing for me has been the communication between colleagues to carry out the work because it is difficult to agree all through social networks to know what to do, when and how to do it. (Student 03)

As I see it, one of the biggest drawbacks of this experience has been having to get out of my comfort zone. Not being able to have a face-to-face conversation with my partner, as we usually do, has increased the difficulty of the project. Neither could we expose our proposal in person with the rest of our classmates, a situation completely new for both of us. We had to get used to this different way of communication, and that was challenging. (Student 07)

The other three subsections are difficulties and challenges directly related to the development of the ESoPC resources as such, as the type of resource that can be better for the target students, the contents that can better suit students' needs, and the level and type of language to be used in the teaching resources.

One of the main challenges was to use an appropriate language that kids can easily understand because the activities that I designed had to be suitable for kids aged 6 or 7 years old. I wanted to be understood by my students. (Student 23)

...when you first face creating a resource, you find [it] difficult to adjust it to the age of the students, choose a topic and focus it correctly. (Student 58)

The second subcategory, "technical problems", was subdivided into three subsections: (1) access to the Internet (7.76%, 9 references); (2) use of devices (6.90%, 8 references), and (3) use of online resources (0.86%, 1 reference).

Unfortunately, there is no rose without a thorn; that is why, if I had to point out some negative aspects or challenges we have had, we would definitely claim that the internet connection and reception was one of the most problematic parts of our online project. (Student 29)

On the other hand, technologies are not always perfect, and we could find some difficulties to work in group due to WiFi failures. It is important to take into account that not everyone has access to the Internet or technologies, and we cannot forget about those families with less resources. (Student 46)

Perceived Social Concerns of Designing ESoPC Materials in ERLT Contexts

The last category addresses participants' social concerns of designing ESoPC materials in ERLT contexts. The first subsection is directly connected with the general commitment to help others in difficult situations (40.43%, 19 references).

… designing this kind of materials has positive aspects such as the feeling of doing something productive and necessary for the society and, at the same time, as a future teacher it is a way to put into practice our own elaboration of materials. (Student 37)

Moreover, the second subsection highlights the concern related to children's educational needs in ERLT contexts (36.17%, 17 references), while the third subsection is about technological resources to help children learn (23.40%, 11 references).

All things considered, I tend to believe that this (sic.) kind of activities are very helpful to teach English since studying a language is not only about learning grammar and vocabulary without establishing a connection to their culture or country, but also about being conscious of current problems that affect society. (Student 08)

Regarding these concerns in light of the social value of action research (Banegas & Consoli, 2020), participants' responses prove that ESoPC can be effective not only for guaranteeing the continuity of the learning process during a pandemic but also for emphasizing the social and cultural dimensions of language. In any case, these assertions link with two important aspects of the training of future teachers: the necessity to demonstrate their competence to integrate technology in their teaching (Sert & Li,

2017) and the need to adapt to the specific requirements of the context in order "to make students' needs central to the educational process" (Díaz-Larenas et al., 2015, p. 177).

SOLUTIONS AND RECOMMENDATIONS

Teachers' attitudes and beliefs are critical for every teaching and learning situation and are a particularly influential factor in implementing new approaches (Ferreira-Barcelos & Kalaja, 2012) in their lessons.

From a general perspective, this study has intended to provide pre-service teachers with an opportunity to act as real teachers, and to experience the importance of being active researchers in their own teaching practice so as to identify effective methods and approaches to integrate into their lessons and the potential limitations and challenges they will have to face. Ultimately, it has allowed them to develop a profound reflection on their teaching preparedness, one of the aims of action research (Hendricks, 2017). More specifically, the implications of the aforementioned results are discussed below in relation to the research questions.

As for RQ1 (*What are the positive and negative aspects of designing ESoPC materials in ERLT settings according to pre-service bilingual primary teachers?*), the fact that the training experience has provided participants with a real, meaningful example of teaching and material design is the most highlighted idea. Respondents have claimed that learning and using the ESoPC approach has allowed them to feel like real teachers, which reveals the potential of material planning and designing for the preparedness of future teachers, an idea extensively discussed in the specialized scientific literature (Augusto-Navarro, 2015; Lou et al., 2012).

Peer collaboration and the development of teacher-specific competences (digital, linguistic, social, and cognitive) have also been referred to as beneficial aspects of designing ESoPC materials for ERLT situations. These have also been considered by scholars as essential skills of educators toward which teacher training programs must be directed (Hadar et al., 2020; Jan, 2017; Palacios-Hidalgo et al., 2020; Slapac & Navarro, 2011). Therefore, specific training in ESoPC is perceived by future teachers of English as necessary and useful in the current situation.

In relation to the negative aspects and the main challenges of designing ESoPC materials in ERLT settings, respondents have referred to their lack of expertise in designing this type of materials (in terms of selecting the appropriate contents and language) as the most significant problem. This concern is in line with previous studies on technology integration in education which expose the need to provide teachers with sufficient knowledge and means to fully use these resources in order to guarantee effective implementation (Domingo-Coscollola et al., 2020; Sipilä, 2014). Likewise, participants have also mentioned the potential technical issues associated with the use of the Internet and the design of online resources, a long-discussed negative aspect of using technology in the classroom (Caneva, 2020; Patel, 2017). Future ESoPC training experiences should consider these two aspects, and especially providing pre-service teachers with clear guidelines of how to appropriately select the contents and adapt the language when designing this sort of materials.

As for RQ2 (*What are the most important social concerns that pre-service bilingual primary teachers face when designing ESoPC materials in ERLT settings?*), helping others (including children, families and other teachers, since all educational stakeholders will suffer the consequences of the COVID-19 pandemic in the short term; UNESCO & IESALC, 2020), and considering students' learning needs in ERLT contexts are the most relevant and significant social aspects of the experience. This entails that respondents consider ESoPC a powerful educational option for enhancing language teaching and ensuring a quality and continuous learning process in times of crisis and difficulty. Moreover, the perceptions of the participants in the study show that a combination of action research and ESoPC has proved of merit for teacher training programs since both seek transformation and social interest as indispensable for improving educational practice (cf. Banegas & Consoli, 2020; Huertas-Abril, 2018).

These findings elicit the potential of ESoPC as an approach to English language teaching and for ERLT situation as pointed by the participants of the study. Therefore, universities and teacher educators should contemplate using it when training teachers of English. Furthermore, the revealed positive and negatives aspects, as well as the indicated social concerns to be faced when designing ESoPC materials ought to be considered by teacher educators interested in this approach.

FUTURE RESEARCH DIRECTIONS

The findings of this study are encouraging for future teachers and teacher educators for various reasons. On the one hand, they show how, according to pre-service teachers, the ESoPC approach constitutes a valid solution for ERLT situations in which face-to-face instruction has to be substituted by online teaching; nevertheless, the need for specific training in this approach and in how to appropriately introduce technology into the language classroom cannot be overlooked. On the other hand, they reveal the potential of action research for teachers, since it allows them to identify the strengths and limitations of their teaching practice, and for teacher educators, who can learn how to improve future teacher education experiences. In this light, training programs aimed at teachers of English as a foreign language should consider including ESoPC as part of their syllabuses, not only for it can constitute a teaching opportunity during a crisis or a health emergency, but also for its social and cultural focus. Likewise, further research should be developed on the potential of ESoPC.

The results presented in this chapter, however, should be interpreted considering three limitations. First, due to the nature of an exploratory study, only pre-service teachers from one university were considered as target population. Therefore, the findings may not be applicable to participants from other institutions, backgrounds or contexts. Future research should then consider recruiting participants from different institutions and sociocultural backgrounds to carry out comparisons with this piece of research. Second, the findings reported here were only based on self-reported data, so they may be affected by respondents' subjective opinions about the phenomena. For this reason, future studies should also consider obtaining data through additional sources (e.g., observations, tests, questionnaires, interviews, focus groups) in order to obtain more reliable and comparable data. Third, and considering the deep impact of the COVID-19 pandemic on education, it is possible that pre-service teachers' attitudes on designing ESoPC may change. Further studies should replicate this study after the COVID-19 pandemic to evaluate its effect.

CONCLUSION

This paper has attempted to reflect on the potential of ESoPC in a real ERLT context. This challenging situation has been the context in which pre-service teachers of English as a foreign language have designed real educational resources to help students continue with their learning process from their homes.

By doing so, they have been able to act as real teachers, experiencing the strengths and opportunities of ESoPC as well as its weaknesses and limitations. In this light, participants have engaged in action research, deepening their own understanding of their teaching and identifying problematic or puzzling aspects they will need to consider in their short-term professional future.

Although the basics of ESoPC are theoretically clear, no examples of implementation could be found previously in the scientific literature that allow proving its benefits for language learning. This chapter has shown an example of how using the approach in a teacher training program can improve their motivation and practice. Participants have revealed a generally positive attitude towards the design of socially- and culturally-responsive learning materials, considering the experience as an enriching opportunity to become teacher-researchers. This study has unveiled the need not only for specific training in material design but also for professional skills that allow teachers to adapt to the constant changes the world is facing and, ultimately, continue ensuring young generations' learning. Ultimately, it also seems necessary that countries ensure Internet access for learning to all citizens because, otherwise, teachers' and universities' initiatives may be lost efforts.

ACKNOWLEDGMENT

This paper was partially supported by the Spanish Ministry of Education (Resolución de 5 de diciembre de 2017, de la Secretaría de Estado de Educación, Formación Profesional y Universidades, por la que se convocan ayudas para la formación de profesorado universitario, de los Subprogramas de Formación y de Movilidad incluidos en el Programa Estatal de Promoción del Talento y su Empleabilidad, en el marco del Plan Estatal de Investigación Científica y Técnica y de Innovación 2013-2016).

REFERENCES

Arbeláez, M. C., & Onrubia, J. (2014). Análisis bibliométrico y de contenido. Dos metodologías complementarias para el análisis de la revista colombiana Educación y Cultura. *Revista de Investigaciones UCM, 14*(23), 14–31. https://bit.ly/31A2xbH

Asrifan, A., Zita, C. T., Vargheese, K. J., Syamsu, T., & Amir, M. (2020). The effects of CALL (Computer Assisted Language Learning) toward the students' English achievement and attitude. *Journal of Advanced English Studies, 3*(2), 94–106. https://bit.ly/3qjlmtg

Augusto-Navarro, E. H. (2015). The design of teaching materials as a tool in EFL teacher education: Experiences of a Brazilian teacher education program. *Ilha do Desterro, 68*(1), 121–137. doi:10.5007/2175-8026.2015v68n1p121

Banegas, D. L., & Consoli, S. (2020). Action research in language education. In J. McKinley & H. Rose (Eds.), *The Routledge handbook of research methods in applied linguistics* (pp. 176–187). Routledge. https://bit.ly/342YhB6

Beatty, K. (2010). *Teaching and researching Computer-Assisted Language Learning* (2nd ed.). Pearson.

Bogdan, R., & Taylor, S. J. (1975). *Introduction to qualitative research methods.* John Wiley & Sons.

Caneva, C. (2020). Do pre-service teachers feel ready to teach with digital technologies? A study in two teacher training institutions in Costa Rica. *Research. Social Development*, *10*(1), 1–14. doi:10.33448/rsd-v10i1.11436

Castells, M. (2010). *The rise of the network society* (2nd ed.). Wiley-Blackwell.

Chang, G.-C., & Yano, S. (2020). *How are countries addressing the Covid-19 challenges in education? A snapshot of policy measures.* https://bit.ly/2wgK6LO

Clark, J. T. (2020). Distance education. In E. Iadanza (Ed.), *Clinical engineering handbook* (2nd ed., pp. 410–415). Elsevier. doi:10.1016/B978-0-12-813467-2.00063-8

Denzin, N. K., & Lincoln, Y. S. (Eds.). (2017). *The SAGE handbook of qualitative research* (5th ed.). SAGE Publications.

Díaz-Larenas, C., Alarcón-Hernandez, P., & Ortiz-Navarrete, M. (2015). A case study on EFL teachers' beliefs about the teaching and learning of English in public education. *Porta Linguarum*, *23*, 171–186. https://bit.ly/35ywOZK

Dina, A., & Ciornei, S.-I. (2013). The advantages and disadvantages of Computer Assisted Language Learning and Teaching for foreign languages. *Procedia: Social and Behavioral Sciences*, *76*, 248–252. doi:10.1016/j.sbspro.2013.04.107

Domingo-Coscollola, M., Bosco, A., Segovia, S. C., & Valero, J. A. S. (2020). Fostering teacher's digital competence at university: The perception of students and teachers. *Revista de Investigación Educacional*, *38*(1), 167–182. doi:10.6018/rie.340551

Ellis, R. (2005). Principles of instructed language learning. *System*, *33*(2), 209–224. doi:10.1016/j.system.2004.12.006

Ellis, R., & Shintani, N. (2014). *Exploring language pedagogy through second language acquisition research*. Routledge.

European Commission. (1995). *White paper on education and training – Teaching and learning – Towards the learning society*. Commission of the European Communities.

Ezzy, D. (2002). *Qualitative analysis. Practice and innovation*. Routledge.

Ferreira-Barcelos, A. M., & Kalaja, P. (2012). Beliefs in second language acquisition: Teacher. In *The Encyclopedia of Applied Linguistics*. Wiley Online Library. doi:10.1002/9781405198431.wbeal0083

Ghanizadeh, A., Razavi, A., & Hosseini, A. (2018). TELL (Technology-Enhanced Language Learning) in Iranian high schools: A Panacea for emotional and motivational detriments. *International Journal of Applied Linguistics and English Literature*, *7*(4), 92–100. doi:10.7575/aiac.ijalel.v.7n.4p.92

Giannini, S. (2020,). *Three ways to plan for equity during the coronavirus school closures*. https://bit.ly/2XboNGv

Glaser, B., & Strauss, A. (1967). *The discovery of grounded theory. Strategies for qualitative research*. Aldine Press.

Hadar, L. L., Ergas, O., Alpert, B., & Ariav, T. (2020). Rethinking teacher education in a VUCA world: Student teachers' social-emotional competencies during the Covid-19 crisis. *European Journal of Teacher Education*, *43*(4), 573–586. doi:10.1080/02619768.2020.1807513

Hendricks, C. (2017). *Improving schools through action research. A reflective practice approach* (4th ed.). Pearson.

Hodges, C., Moore, S., Lockee, B., Trust, T., & Bond, A. (2020, March 7). The difference between emergency remote teaching and online learning. *EDUCAUSE Review*. https://bit.ly/2DwKOYM

Huertas-Abril, C. A. (2018). Inglés para fines sociales y de cooperación (IFSyC): Contextualización y justificación. In C. A. Huertas-Abril & M. E. Gómez-Parra (Eds.), *Inglés para fines sociales y de cooperación. Guía para la elaboración de materiales* (pp. 9–24). Graó.

Huertas-Abril, C. A. (2020a). Implementation of cooperative learning strategies to create 3D-videos in EFL teacher training. In L. N. Makewa (Ed.), *Theoretical and practical approaches to innovation in higher education* (pp. 17–41). IGI Global. doi:10.4018/978-1-7998-1662-1.ch002

Huertas-Abril, C. A. (2020b, December). *Telecollaboration in Emergency Remote Language Learning and Teaching* [Conference paper]. The Sixth International Conference on E-Learning (ECONF20), Sakhir, Bahrain.

Huertas-Abril, C. A., & Gómez-Parra, M. E. (2018). English for social purposes: A new approach to language learning. In M. I. Amor, M. Osuna, & E. Pérez (Eds.), *Fundamentos de enseñanza y aprendizaje para una educación universal, intercultural y bilingüe* (pp. 73–78). Octaedro.

International, Q. S. R. (2021). *NVivo. Qualitative data analysis software*. https://bit.ly/38EqKAN

Jan, H. (2017). Teacher of 21st century: Characteristics and development. *Research on Humanities and Social Sciences*, *7*(9), 50–54. https://bit.ly/3qhhZm5

Krippendorff, K. (2004). *Content analysis: An introduction to its methodology* (2nd ed.). SAGE Publications. https://bit.ly/2NR0V5i

Krystalli, P., Panagiotidis, P., & Arvanitis, P. (2020). Criteria for motivational Technology-Enhanced Language Learning activities. In M. R. Freiermuth & N. Zarrinabadi (Eds.), *Technology and the psychology of second language learners and users* (pp. 571–593). Springer. doi:10.1007/978-3-030-34212-8_22

Lan, Y.-J. (2020). Immersion, interaction, and experience-oriented learning: Bringing virtual reality into FL learning. *Language Learning & Technology*, *24*(1), 1–15. https://bit.ly/3jTNyPp

Lee, C., Yeung, A. S., & Ip, T. (2016). Use of computer technology for English language learning: Do learning styles, gender, and age matter? *Computer Assisted Language Learning*, *29*(5), 1033–1049. doi:10.1080/09588221.2016.1140655

López-Noguero, F. (2002). El análisis de contenido como método de investigación. *Review of Education*, *4*, 167–179.

Lou, S.-J., Chen, N.-C., Tsai, H.-Y., Tseng, K.-H., & Shih, R.-C. (2012). Using blended creative teaching: Improving a teacher education course on designing materials for young children. *Australasian Journal of Educational Technology, 28*(5), 776–792. https://bit.ly/2MZNUJw. doi:10.14742/ajet.816

Madani, S. (2017). Promoting multilingual communicative competence for the labor market. *European Scientific Journal, 13*(7), 201–214. doi:10.19044/esj.2017.v13n7p201

Milman, N. B. (2015). Distance education. In J. D. Wright (Ed.), International encyclopedia of the social & behavioral sciences (2nd ed., pp. 567–570). Elsevier. doi:10.1016/B978-0-08-097086-8.92001-4

Mishra, S. K. J. (2016). English language teaching: A shift from chalk to digitalization. *Critical Space, 4*(3), 45–50.

Negash, S., & Wilcox, M. V. (2008). E-Learning classifications: Differences and similarities. In S. Negash, M. E. Whitman, A. B. Woszczynski, K. Hoganson, & H. Mattord (Eds.), *Handbook of distance learning for real-time and asynchronous information technology education* (pp. 1–23). IGI Global., doi:10.4018/978-1-59904-964-9.ch001

Palacios-Hidalgo, F. J. (2020). TELL, CALL, and MALL: Approaches to bridge the language gap. In C. A. Huertas-Abril & M. E. Gómez-Parra (Eds.), *International approaches to bridging the language gap* (pp. 118–134). IGI Global., doi:10.4018/978-1-7998-1219-7.ch008

Palacios-Hidalgo, F. J., Gómez-Parra, M. E., & Huertas-Abril, C. A. (2020). Digital and media competences: Key competences for EFL teachers. *Teaching English with Technology, 20*(1), 43–59. https://bit.ly/2GHgDML

Patel, D. S. (2017). Significance of Technology Enhanced Language Learning (TELL) in language classes. *Journal of Technology for ELT, 4*(2). https://bit.ly/2E7G4qk

Patton, M. Q. (2003). *Qualitative evaluation checklist. Evaluation checklists project.* https://bit.ly/2F2sYOv

Pidgeon, N., & Henwood, K. (1997). Using grounded theory in psychological research. In N. Hayes (Ed.), *Doing Qualitative Analysis in Psychology* (pp. 245–273). Psychology Press.

Redecker, C., & Punie, Y. (2017). *Digital competence framework for educators (DigCompEdu)*. Publications Office of the European Union. doi:10.2760/178382

Reinhardt, J. (2019). Social media in second and foreign language teaching and learning: Blogs, wikis, and social networking. *Language Teaching, 52*(1), 1–39. doi:10.1017/S0261444818000356

Richards, M., & Guzman, I. R. (2016). Academic assessment of critical thinking in distance education information technology programs. In P. Ordóñez & R. D. Tennyson (Eds.), *Impact of economic crisis on education and the next-generation workforce* (pp. 101–119). IGI Global. doi:10.4018/978-1-4666-9455-2.ch005

Sert, O., & Li, L. (2017). A qualitative study on CALL knowledge and materials design: Insights from pre-service EFL teachers. *International Journal of Computer-Assisted Language Learning and Teaching, 7*(3), 73–87. doi:10.4018/IJCALLT.2017070105

Simonson, M., Zvacek, S. M., & Smaldino, S. (2019). *Teaching and learning at a distance: Foundations of distance education* (7th ed.). Information Age Publishing.

Sipilä, K. (2014). Educational use of information and communications technology: Teachers' perspective. *Technology, Pedagogy and Education, 23*(2), 225–241. doi:10.1080/1475939X.2013.813407

Slapac, A., & Coppersmith, S. A. (Eds.). (2019). *Beyond language learning instruction: Transformative supports for emergent bilinguals and educators*. IGI Global. doi:10.4018/978-1-7998-1962-2

Slapac, A., & Navarro, V. (2011). Shaping action researchers through a Master's capstone experience. *Teacher Education and Practice, 24*(4), 405–426. https://bit.ly/3uZgYCa

Tafazoli, D., & Golshan, N. (2014). Review of computer-assisted language learning: History, merits & barriers. *International Journal of Language and Linguistics, 2*(5–1), 32–38. doi:10.11648/j.ijll.s.2014020501.15

Tafazoli, D., Gómez-Parra, M. E., & Huertas-Abril, C. A. (2017). A cross-cultural study on the attitudes of English language students towards Computer-Assisted Language Learning. *Teaching English with Technology, 18*(2), 34–68. https://bit.ly/2q9YNtB

Tafazoli, D., Huertas-Abril, C. A., & Gómez-Parra, M. E. (2019). Technology-based review on Computer-Assisted Language Learning: A chronological perspective. *Pixel-Bit. Revista de Medios y Educación, 54*(54), 29–43. doi:10.12795/pixelbit.2019.i54.02

Ulbrich, F., Jahnke, I., & Mårtensson, P. (2011). Special issue on knowledge development and the net generation. *International Journal of Sociotechnology and Knowledge Development, 2*(4), i–ii.

UNESCO & IESALC. (2020). *COVID-19 and higher education: Today and tomorrow. Impact analysis, policy responses and recommendations*. https://bit.ly/34TOSvu

Valdemoros-San-Emeterio, M. Á., Ponce-De-León-Elizondo, A., & Sanz-Arazuri, E. (2011). Fundamentos en el manejo del NVIVO 9 como herramienta al servicio de estudios cualitativos. *Contextos Educativos: Revista de Educación, 14*, 11–29. https://bit.ly/3i503IA

ADDITIONAL READING

Bozkurt, A., & Sharma, R. C. (2020). Emergency remote teaching in a time of global crisis due to CoronaVirus pandemic. *Asian Journal of Distance Education, 15*(1), i–vi. doi:10.5281/zenodo.3778083

Gómez-Parra, M. E., & Huertas-Abril, C. A. (2018). *English for social purposes and cooperation (B1)*. Ministerio de Educación, Cultura y Deporte. https://bit.ly/39U320S

Mills, G. E. (2018). *Action research: A guide for the teacher researcher* (6th ed.). Pearson.

Mulyani, M., Fidyati, F., Suryani, S., Suri, M., & Halimatussakdiah, H. (2021). University students' perceptions through e-learning implementation during COVID-19 pandemic: Positive or negative features dominate? *Studies in English Language and Education, 8*(1), 197–211. doi:10.24815iele.v8i1.17628

Slapac, A., Song, K. H., & Chasteen, C. C. (2017). Introspections on in-service teachers' intercultural responsiveness skills for English language learners. In K. Jones & J. R. Mixon (Eds.), *Intercultural responsiveness in the second language learning classroom* (pp. 181–201). IGI Global., doi:10.4018/978-1-5225-2069-6.ch011

Trust, T., & Whalen, J. (2020). Should teachers be trained in emergency remote teaching? Lessons learned from the COVID-19 pandemic. *Journal of Technology and Teacher Education*, *28*(2), 189–199. https://bit.ly/2FslGUi

Whittle, C., Tiwari, S., Yan, S., & Williams, J. (2020). Emergency remote teaching environment: A conceptual framework for responsive online teaching in crises. *Information and Learning Sciences*, *121*(5/6), 311–319. doi:10.1108/ILS-04-2020-0099

KEY TERMS AND DEFINITIONS

Action Research: Process of inquiry carried out by the teaching and learning actors own their own practice with the aim of transforming and improving it.

Emergency Remote Language Teaching: Language teaching modality developed partially or totally online due to circumstances of crisis (such as natural disasters, wars, or health emergencies). It constitutes a temporary change in the way of teaching the language until the crisis or emergency has ended.

Emergency Remote Teaching: Teaching modality carried out partially or totally online due to circumstances of crisis (such as natural disasters, wars, or health emergencies). It constitutes a temporary change in the form of instruction until the crisis or emergency has ended.

English for Social Purposes and Cooperation: Approach to English language learning that explores social and cultural topics (e.g., gender equality, environmental problems, immigration and refugees). It aims at developing students' language proficiency, cultural awareness, and social responsibility.

ERLT: Emergency Remote Language Teaching.

ESoPC: English for Social Purposes and Cooperation.

Grounded Theory: Systematic methodology based on the application of inductive reasoning mainly used, but not exclusively, in qualitative research in the field of Social Sciences. This methodology involves the development of hypotheses and theories through data collection and data analysis.

ENDNOTES

[1] The materials designed by participants are available here: https://englishsocially.wixsite.com/covid.

[2] More information about this experience can be found at Huertas-Abril, C. A., & Palacios-Hidalgo, F. J. (2020). Uso del enfoque IFSyC para la elaboración de materiales didácticos online para Educación Primaria en tiempos de COVID-19. Paper presented at *Jornadas Internacionales de la pizarra a la ciber-educación*. University of Córdoba. Available at https://bit.ly/2NnFjAq.

Chapter 5
Assessment of Case-Based Instruction in a Graduate Educational Psychology Course:
Preparing P-12 Teachers for Classroom Management

Alpana Bhattacharya
https://orcid.org/0000-0002-5152-7748
Queens College and Graduate Center, CUNY, USA

ABSTRACT

This chapter showcases a teacher educator's assessment of case-based instruction in an advanced level educational psychology course. First, action research, self-study, and reflective practice are explained as constructs of practitioner inquiry. Then, case-based instructional models related to teacher candidates' classroom management proficiencies are reviewed. Next, the teacher educator's examination of own teacher preparation practice is described to highlight development, implementation, and improvement of the target educational psychology course geared towards advancement of teacher candidates' classroom management capacities. Thereafter, solutions and recommendations for promoting teacher candidates' P-12 grades classroom management expertise are discussed. Finally, future research directions are proposed for ascertaining effectiveness of case-based instruction as evidence-based pedagogical approach for strengthening teacher candidates' P-12 grades classroom management aptitudes.

INTRODUCTION

The Council for the Accreditation of Educator Preparation (CAEP) is currently the sole accrediting body for educator preparation programs in the United States. As such, CAEP standards are now implemented in several advanced-level programs to promote teacher candidates' teaching potential in P-12 schools (CAEP, 2020). Teacher preparation programs at the graduate level require that teacher candidates take

DOI: 10.4018/978-1-7998-6922-1.ch005

an educational psychology course for their professional certification. Often, courses such as classroom management, cultural differences, adolescent development, and instructional assessment are offered by educator preparation programs to develop teacher candidates' content and pedagogical knowledge in their field of professional specialization. This chapter shares my (i.e., a teacher educator's) self-study of an advanced-level educational psychology course, *Classroom Management*, completed by teacher candidates for their Master of Science in Education degree at a public college in the United States.

Since the CAEP (2020) standards for accreditation at the advanced-level programs are based on two principles: a) development of competent and caring P-12 teachers, and b) use of evidence for maintaining and enhancing the quality of teacher preparation programs, teacher educators, as education preparation providers, are expected to document evidence of teacher candidates' knowledge, skills, and dispositions appropriate for their professional specialty based on proficiency measures used in their courses. The goal is for teacher educators to then use the documented evidence to monitor, evaluate, and improve their courses and teacher preparation practices (Cochran-Smith & Villegas, 2016). Given that the accreditation process calls for self-assessment and evidence-based analysis of educator preparation programs, teacher educators are also expected to infuse research and development in their teacher preparation courses to expand their own knowledge base of effective teacher preparation practices.

This chapter showcases my self-assessment and analysis of evidence-based teaching practice and teacher preparation measures, as a teacher educator, from an advanced-level educational psychology course, *Classroom Management*, completed by P-12 teachers from 2016 through 2020. More specifically, my assessment and analysis related to conceptualization, development, implementation, and improvement of my teacher preparation practice are narrated to pinpoint impact of such practice on P-12 teachers' preparation to manage learning of diverse students in public school classrooms. Select case-based activities are illustrated to portray a trajectory of course development, implementation, and improvement of my teacher preparation practice in the classroom management course.

Due to increasing scrutiny and expectation of accountability from teacher preparation programs as producers of competent and caring P-12 teachers, professional development of teacher educators is crucial. Teacher educators' professional development related to teacher preparation therefore could be advanced through a framework connected to understanding of the challenges and expectations of the teacher education enterprise, and the place of scholarship in the academia (Loughran, 2014). Action research is a mode of investigation which enables practitioners to assess and reflect on effectiveness of existing practice in their own instructional setting with the goal of improving practice. Through a systematic cycle of planning, action, observation, and reflection, action research can lead to improvement in practice, thereby facilitating personal and professional development of practitioners (Koshy, 2005). Since action research serves as a venue for teacher educators to reflect on their own instructional practice, with the goal of advancing P-12 teachers' classrooms practice (Anwar, 2016; Casey, 2012; Kitchen & Stevens, 2008), this chapter illustrates action research for improving my teacher preparation practices.

BACKGROUND

Action research related to my teacher preparation, specifically case-based instruction for preparing P-12 teachers to effectively manage their classroom environment, is emphasized in this chapter. First, action research, self-study, and reflective practice concepts are discussed as key constructs of practice-based inquiry. Then, evidence-based models including *Web-Enhanced Case-Based Activity* (Kim & Hannafin,

2009), *Conceptual Framework of Teaching Case* (Kim et al., 2006), and *Hybrid Case-Learning* (Strangeways & Papatraianou, 2016) are examined as frameworks for case-based instruction. Next, action research pertaining to my case-based instruction for strengthening P-12 grade teachers' classroom management is illustrated to showcase development, implementation, and improvement of my teacher preparation practice. Thereafter, *Case-based Learning for Classroom Management Problem Solving* (Choi & Lee, 2009) and *Classroom Management Competencies* (Piwowar et al., 2013) models are reviewed as solutions and recommendations for promoting P-12 teachers' classroom management proficiencies. Finally, future research directions are proposed for examining effectiveness of teacher preparation practice for strengthening in-service teachers' classroom management aptitude.

Research Constructs: Action Research, Self-Study, Reflective Practice

Action Research

Action research serves as the structure for examining different instructional issues and for planning instruction to effectively address selected issues. For example, the research question "How can I provide a successful lesson for this particular group of students?" could enable systematic examination and analysis of instructional issues including "the nature of our students, the outcomes to be achieved, the content to be learned, the learning activities involved, and the means for assessing that learning" (Stringer et al., 2010, p. 10).

Willis and Edwards (2014) identify three major paradigms, positivism, interpretive theory, and critical theory, as theoretical foundations for action research. Of the three paradigms, interpretive paradigm is one of the more popular action research approaches at present. "Interpretive action research tends to emphasize reflection and practical research conducted by professionals such as teachers who are interested in solving a local problem of practice" (p. 34). Furthermore, teacher educators who draw on interpretive action research are able to develop their skills and expertise for solving problems in their own settings.

The interpretive paradigm of action research undertaken by Walker-Floyd (2014) included use of a *personal action research journal* as a tool for self-study. This action researcher created and used a *personal action research journal* to: "(a) record experiences and/or classroom challenges; (b) explore ideas and/or methods to address the challenges; (c) try the new practice; (d) monitor students; and (e) reflect upon the experience and new practice" (p. 95). My research investigation draws on the integrative paradigm of action research, specifically maintenance of a reflective journal, as a tool for self-study of my own teacher preparation practices in the classroom management course.

Self-Study

A key characteristic of self-study research is that the practitioner's research questions are embedded in dilemmas within the practitioner's practice, and the practitioner initiates research to solve the dilemma in their own practice. Since the practitioner is a participant in their own self-study, the research investigation always involves one's self, one's actions, and one's ideas. Similarly, data collection in self-study research involves one's own experiences and practices as a practitioner. For example, a teacher educator studying effectiveness of own instructional practice usually draws on personal experiences as data (i.e., lesson plans, meeting reports, discussion board comments, videotaped instructional activities, observations, assignments, and student outcomes) which are then analyzed and interpreted to address their research questions (Vanassche & Kelchtermans, 2015). My investigation of teacher preparation practice draws on analysis and interpretation of personal experiences embedded within the graduate course geared towards advancement of in-service teachers' knowledge, skills, and dispositions for classroom management. Accordingly, my observation of in-service teachers' case analysis, my reviews of in-service teachers' school-based strategy applications, and my evaluation of in-service teachers' exams were analyzed and interpreted to determine effectiveness of my teacher preparation practice.

Reflective Practice

Reflection is an important element of action research. Integration of planned and deliberate reflection within the action research process lends towards professional growth of the practitioner as well as their practice (Vaughan & Burnaford, 2016). Reflective practice therefore involves learning from experience; reflective practice, however, is not a continuous process and does not get initiated on demand. Although reflections can be planned and intentional as a part of the action research process, unexpected and unpredicted situations may emerge within the professional setting which could then call for reframing of the practitioners' action and lend towards learning from experience (Russell, 2018). Thus, experience in practice settings can lend towards development of reflective practice and reflective practice can contribute towards development of professional knowledge. Finally, development of professional knowledge and understanding of practice setting as well as ability to recognize and respond to such knowledge enable reflective practitioners to address needs, issues, and concerns in shaping practice (Loughran, 2002).

Reflection has been a salient attribute of my instructional practice. Assessment and analysis of in-service teachers' verbal and written communication emerging from case-based activities completed in the college classroom, application of classroom management strategies in the school setting, and problem-solving of simulated situations in take-at-home exams helped me identify effectiveness and fallacies of my teacher preparation practice, and subsequent modifications of my pedagogical approaches.

Teaching Case Frameworks: Components and Attributes

One goal of teacher preparation programs is to help P-12 teachers develop as professionals who can deal with real-world problems in complex and dynamic classroom situations, and who can make reasoned and reflective decisions. Case-based instruction therefore has been accepted by education researchers as an effective pedagogical approach for preparing P-12 teachers' ability to be reflective educators based on research evidence from varied field such as medicine, education, business, and law that attest to efficacy of case-based instruction (see Kim & Hannafin, 2009; Kim et al., 2006; Strangeways & Papatraianou, 2016). However, despite teacher preparation programs' recognition of the importance of promoting P-12 teachers' ability to problem solve as competent and caring professionals, teacher educators often find it challenging to redesign their teaching methods in ways that will enhance teachers' ability to problem solve due to limited research and resources available for incorporating instructional models in the college context to solve real-world issues (Choi & Lee, 2009).

One research supported case-based instructional approach is the *Web-Enhanced Case-Based Activity* (CBA) designed by Kim and Hannafin (2009). The structure and components of CBA include: *Scenario work, What's the story, Planning, Doing,* and *Telling your story.* Instructor coaching, peer feedback, and web resources are made available to learners throughout the CBA process. The first component, *Scenario work*, involves development of a project. The next component, *What's the story*, involves use of personal case knowledge or an expert's case to develop conceptual understanding for summarizing the case. *Planning* involves interpreting and analyzing the case and proposing preliminary solutions. The *Doing* component requires adapting and applying solutions to address the case. Finally, *Telling your story* emphasizes reflection and transference of the process for classroom application.

Another case-based instructional framework is Kim et al.'s (2006) *Conceptual Framework for Teaching Cases*. Their conceptual framework emphasizes five core attributes of cases that are of significance: *Relevant; Realistic; Engaging; Challenging,* and *Instructional*. First, teaching cases should be aligned with the goals and objectives of instruction, should be of interest for the learners, and should be embedded in settings that are aligned with the scenario to be deemed as "*relevant*". Next, cases that incorporate real-world settings and authentic materials tend to increase the likelihood of learners being able to generalize their case-based learning in real-life settings. Teaching cases that incorporate real-life experiences and resources tend to be "*realistic*". Furthermore, cases have to be engaging. Cases that provide learners with opportunities for multiple levels of analysis and interpretations, consider multiple perspectives, and allow learners to independently derive outcomes are deemed as "*engaging*". "*Challenging*" cases incorporate ambiguity, uncertainty, and multiple solutions. Presenting rare and unusual cases or presenting cases in non-sequential fashion or presenting a series of cases tailored for a given issue can make a case "*challenging*". Finally, teaching cases that are designed to extend leaners' prior knowledge, assess their knowledge and skills, integrate teaching aids, and offer feedback are "*instructional*". The five core attributes of a teaching case are integrated within four major categories of Kim and her colleagues' *Conceptual Framework of Teaching Case: Content* (i.e., case content), *Structure* (i.e., case layout), *Attribute* (i.e., case purpose), and *Process* (i.e., learning processes).

Finally, the *Hybrid Case-Learning (HCL) Model* designed by Strangeways and Papatraianou (2016) also makes a valuable contribute to case-based pedagogy. The *HCL* model is a multi-level pedagogical tool for analyzing and interpreting case stories. More specifically, in their model Strangeways and Papatraianou have built a venue for bridging practice and theory as a pedagogical tool for preparing preservice teachers for the classroom. The model consists of three components: *Platform and Place* (i.e., Face-to-Face and Website), *Structure* (i.e., case learning for classroom readiness), and *Resource Set* (i.e., case writing and case interpretation). The model offers teacher candidates with templates for writing and interpreting case-stories within the context of multiple perspectives and theoretical applications.

Teaching Case Frameworks: Analysis and Interpretation

Despite uniqueness of components and attributes embedded within the frameworks reviewed above (see Kim & Hannafin, 2009; Kim et al., 2006; Strangeways & Papatraianou, 2016), a common thread that could be spun across the three teaching case models is problem solving situations akin to real-life classroom context. A salient element of the three above identified teaching case frameworks is their emphasis on interpretation, reflection, and analysis of case stories from authentic academic context for preparing educators to acquire the knowledge, skills, and dispositions relevant for their professional fields. The acquisition and generalization of content knowledge and pedagogical skills for advancement of learning of all students in the diverse academic disciplines were to be supported and facilitated by course instructors and peers through collaborative problem solving as illustrated in *Web-enhanced Case-Based Activity* (Kim & Hannafin, 2009), *Conceptual Framework of Teaching Case* (Kim et al., 2006), and *Hybrid Case-Learning* (Strangeways & Papatrainaou, 2016) models. Thus, the "long history of teaching from cases challenge learners to analyze, problems presented in cases, make inferences based on limited information; and make decisions on uncertain, ambiguous, and conflicting issues that simulate a real-world, professional context" (Kim et al., 2006, p. 867). In closing, although theory and practice are expected to be inseparable and are to be emphasized in all teacher education programs and teacher candidates are to have opportunities to integrate theory and practice as a part of their professional preparation, there has been a disconnect between theory and practice in teacher education, which then often results in lack of teacher candidates' classroom readiness. Case-based instruction models therefore could address the theory and practice disconnect within the classrooms by scaffolding the complexity of professional practice, particularly the interpersonal and intrapersonal aspects, through reflective practice (Strangeways & Papatraianou, 2016).

MAIN FOCUS OF THE CHAPTER

Action Research Frameworks Guiding Self-Study of Teacher Preparation Practice

Although action research and self-study have different historical and epistemological traditions, these practitioner research have several commonalities. For instance, both research paradigms emphasize systematic examination and analysis of student learning and are interrelated with the practitioners' intentions, reactions, decisions, and interpretations. Planned and intentional collection and documentation of personal experiences in professional context enable the researcher to produce insightful analysis of educational outcomes (Cochran-Smith et al., 2009).

Willis and Edwards (2014) describe a four-moment model of action research which includes: reflect, plan, act, and observe. *Reflect* involves thinking of an issue or problem of interest and tentatively identifying goals for the project. *Plan* focuses on exploring ways to address the problem through gathering of information from literature, conferences, colleagues, and community. *Act* deals with implementation of plan with the resources, support, and collaboration. *Observe* requires collection of outcome data through qualitative and quantitative method and evaluation of change based on reflection.

Comparatively, Stringer and his colleagues' (2010) conception of action research includes three cyclical steps: *Look* (collect information – Data), *Think* (reflect on information – Analyze), and *Act* (use outcomes from reflection - Plan, Implement, Evaluate). For example, for the first step, *Look*, an action researcher could gather information for the research question by observing students. Next, *Think* would involve analyzing and reflecting on student activities. Finally, *Act* would focus on planning, implementing, and evaluating teaching and learning processes in the educational environment.

Figure 1 is a graphic illustration of course development, implementation, and improvement processes that informed my teaching practice in the classroom management course. The structure of my pedagogical process corresponds with Willis and Edwards (2014) and Stringer et al. (2010) action research models. More specifically, my *Course Development* phase is comparable to Willis and Edwards' *Reflect and Plan* moments and Stringer and his colleagues' *Look, Think,* and *Act* steps. Thereafter, my *Course Implementation* phase is equivalent to Willis and Edwards as well as Stringer et al. *Act* moment/step. Then, my *Course Evaluation* phase parallels Willis and Edwards' *Observe* moment and Stringer et al. *Act* step. Finally, my *Course Refinement* phase corresponds with Willis and Edwards's *Reflect* and *Plan* moments and Stringer et al.'s *Look* and *Think* steps.

Assessment of Case-Based Instruction in a Graduate Educational Psychology Course

As illustrated in Figure 1, my *Course Development* phase involved review of key course elements. This phase focused on course objectives, selection of weekly reading assignments, teaching approaches, weekly class activities, culminating course project, and formative as well as summative evaluation methods for judging effectiveness of instruction. The *Course Implementation* phase involved operationalization of teaching and learning processes aligned with the course objectives. For instance, one of my course objectives is that "teacher candidates will understand, apply, and value *behavior management models and strategies* as applicable to learning and instruction of P-12 grade students". To ensure that this objective was addressed in my course, I selected textbook chapters corresponding with specific topics as required reading in order for in-service teachers to actively participate in class discussion of behavior management models and practice application of strategies corresponding with selected topics (e.g., *Assertive Discipline* for analyzing and problem solving the case, *Forgetful Eighth Grader*). Similarly, specific course objectives guided implementation of course assignments and exams. The *Course Evaluation* phase focused on judging effectiveness of my teaching practice on in-service teachers' preparation for addressing academic and behavior issues in their P-12 grade classes. For instance, in-service teachers' individually written reflections related to case analysis of the *Forgetful Eighth Grader* aligned with the *Assertive Discipline* reading and their collaborative presentation of strategy-based solution for the case was examined to draw conclusions about the effectiveness of case-based learning on in-service teachers' preparation for management of P-12 classes. The *Course Refinement* phase of my self-study was based on evaluation of in-service teachers' performance during college-based activities, school-based assignments, and take-at-home exams. I modified my reading selections, course assignments, and evaluation measures based on analysis of in-service teachers' performance. For instance, when in-service teachers' written responses for the *Forgetful Eighth Grader* case reflected regurgitation of solutions offered in the chapter for *Assertive Discipline* rather than self-generated solutions based on the *Assertive Discipling Model*, the class activity was modified, and in-service teachers were engaged in collaborative case analysis. This was to ensure that in-service teachers self-generated solutions through dialogue, inquiry, reflection, and exchange of ideas with their peers.

Action Research in Teacher Educator's Classroom Management Course

Research Question

My research aimed at investigating effectiveness of case-based instruction on in-service teachers' efficacy for promoting P-12 grade students' learning through efficient management of classroom environment. The research question of interest was: Can case-based instruction promote in-service teachers' ability to effectively manage P-12 grade classroom environment and student learning?

Context

Although action research and self-study have common features including systematic examination and analysis of student learning which are interrelated with practitioners' intentions, reactions, decisions, and interpretations (Cochran-Smith et al., 2009), action research and self-study differ in terms of their contextual focus. While action research emphasizes collaboration, community, and activism (Rutten, 2021), self-study involves personal inquiry conducted within one's own teaching context based on alignment of one's own practice with adopted educational standards (Vanassche & Kelchtermans, 2015). This chapter therefore emphasizes examination of instructional practices implemented within the context of my own teacher preparation course.

Figure 1. Teacher preparation cycle related to teacher educator's action research

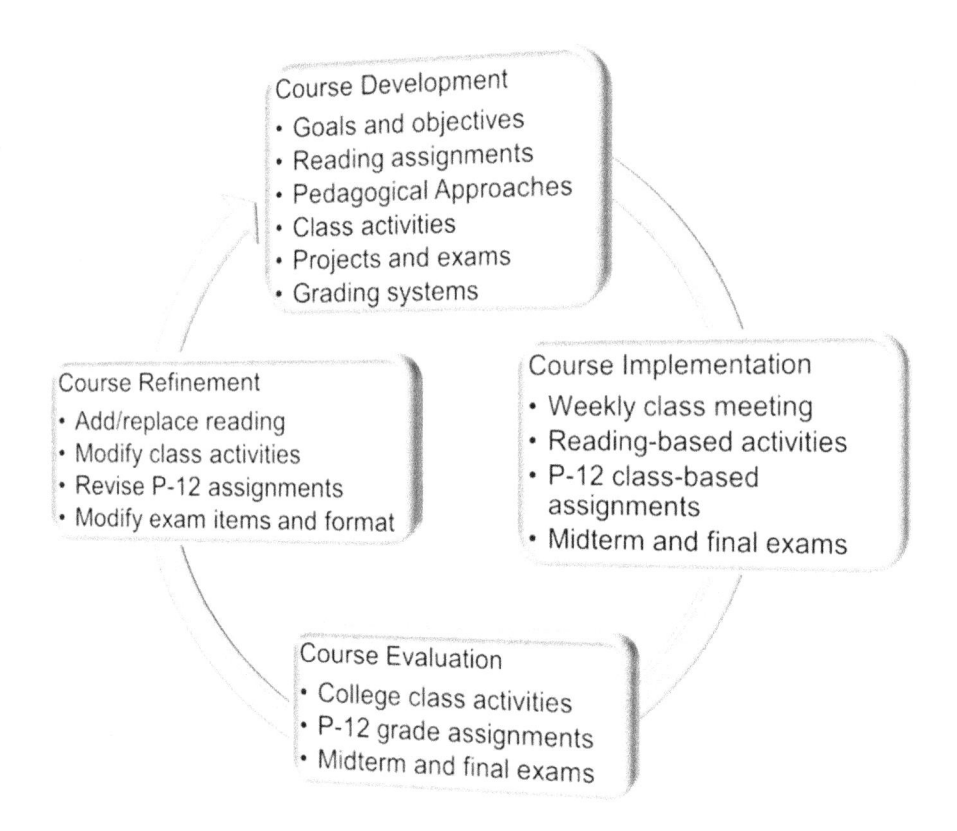

Course Development
- Goals and objectives
- Reading assignments
- Pedagogical Approaches
- Class activities
- Projects and exams
- Grading systems

Course Implementation
- Weekly class meeting
- Reading-based activities
- P-12 class-based assignments
- Midterm and final exams

Course Evaluation
- College class activities
- P-12 grade assignments
- Midterm and final exams

Course Refinement
- Add/replace reading
- Modify class activities
- Revise P-12 assignments
- Modify exam items and format

The educational psychology course, *Classroom Management*, wherein teacher preparation practice has been studied, is a 3-credits graduate course taught by me each spring semester, from 7:15 PM to 9:45 PM per week, over 15 weeks (i.e., February to May). My course prepares in-service teachers (i.e., P-12 grade classroom teachers) to support P-12 grade students' learning by attending to their cognitive, behavioral, and social-emotional needs. Furthermore, my course is open only to in-service teachers (i.e., P-12 teachers) who are in an advanced level teacher education program (i.e., Master of Science in Education), and hold an initial certificate to teach either in P-12 grades (i.e., art education, music education, or physical education) or 7-12 grades (i.e., English language, mathematics, science, social studies, or world languages). Examination of my teacher preparation practice between 2016-2020 (spring semesters only) in the classroom management course is described in this chapter.

Participants

This chapter focuses on assessment of my teacher preparation practice within my own educational psychology course. My investigation is based on Stringer et al. (2010) and Willis and Edwards (2014)

Assessment of Case-Based Instruction in a Graduate Educational Psychology Course

conceptual frameworks for action research. Although most models emphasize collaboration and cooperation in conducting action research, some forms of action research enable one person to be the sole researcher (Willis & Edwards, 2014). Accordingly, I am the sole researcher of my investigation, and also the only participant of my personal inquiry, despite it being contextualized within the educational psychology course, wherein usually 20-25 in-service teachers (P-12 grades) complete the course each spring semester. Enrollment of in-service teachers from 2016-2020 in my course is displayed in Table 1. Since my inquiry involved personal analysis and reflection of instructional approaches, assignments, and assessments that were planned, designed, and implemented by me, and are routine educational practice, my investigation does not involve human subjects and IRB review. Measures and outcomes derived from my inquiry are based on my own observations, anecdotal notes, and analysis of in-service teachers' written and verbal reports, which have all been anonymously discussed in this chapter.

Table 1. In-service teacher enrollment in my classroom management course during 2016-2020 semesters

	Spring 2016 N=20	Spring 2017 N=22	Spring 2018 N=12	Spring 2019 N=24	Spring 2020 N=25
Program	Art = 5 English = 2 Music = 2 Science = 3 Social Studies = 7	English = 4 Math = 6 PE = 2 Science = 3 Social Studies = 7	Art = 4 English = 1 Music = 1 Science = 3 Social Studies = 3	Art = 4 Languages = 7 Math = 6 Social Studies = 7	Art = 1 English = 6 Math = 2 Social Studies = 16

Measures

Table 2 illustrates select classroom management models, strategies, and measures included in my educational psychology course for advancing P-12 grade teachers' knowledge, skills, and dispositions for supporting their students' learning in an effectively managed classroom environment. Examples of classroom management items listed in Table 2 are grouped into two categories: models and strategies. As clarification, readings listed under the heading, *Management Models*, are theory-based frameworks that call for readers' ability to interpret and apply these models. Comparatively, items listed as *Management Strategies* include readings that specifically describe strategies for addressing behavioral and academic issues in the classrooms. The topics and readings shown in Table 2, as well as those that are essential for effectively preparing in-service teachers, are integrated within three central measures of my course: 1) case-based activities completed on college campus; 2) strategy-based activities completed in P-12 schools; and 3) case-based exams completed at home.

Table 2. Matrix of course content and pedagogical approach for teacher preparation

CLASSROOM MANAGEMENT COURSE			
MANAGEMENT MODELS		**MANAGEMENT STRATEGIES**	
ASSIGNED READING	**TEACHING APPROACH**	**ASSIGNED READING**	**TEACHING APPROACH**
Discipline with dignity: Curwin and Mendler Source: Hardin, C. J. (2008b). Discipline with dignity. In *Effective classroom management: Models and strategies for today's classrooms* (2nd ed., pp. 101–118). Pearson.	Case study: Schoolwide Discipline (Hardin, 2008b, pp. 102-103)	Congruent communication: Haim Ginott Source: Manning, M. L., & Bucher, K. T. (2007b). Exploring the theories of congruent communication: Haim Ginott. In *Classroom management: Models, applications, and cases* (2nd ed., pp. 77–93). Pearson.	Case study: Diffusing Anger (Manning & Bucher, 2007b, p. 86)
Assertive discipline: Canter and Canter Source: Hardin, C. J. (2008a). Assertive discipline. In *Effective classroom management: Models and strategies for today's classrooms* (2nd ed., pp. 43–61). Pearson.	Case study: Forgetful Eighth Grader (Hardin, 2008a, p. 59)	Instructional management: Jacob Kounin Source: Manning, M. L., & Bucher, K. T. (2007c). Exploring the theories of instructional management: Jacob Kounin. In *Classroom management: Models, applications, and cases* (2nd ed., pp. 94–109). Pearson.	Case study: Inconsistency in classroom (Manning & Bucher, 2007c, p. 105)
Noncoercive discipline: William Glasser Source: Charles, C. M. (2005b). William Glasser's noncoercive discipline. In *Building classroom discipline* (8th ed., pp. 73–92). Pearson.	Case study: Middle School History (Charles, 2005b, p. 91)	Positive classroom discipline: Fred Jones Source: Charles, C. M. (2005a). Fred Jones's positive classroom discipline. In *Building classroom discipline* (8th ed., pp. 55–72). Pearson.	Case study: Concept cases (Charles, 2005a, p. 70)

Outcomes

Based on my examination of three central course measures (i.e., in-class activities, P-12 grade assignments, and take-at-home exams), I drew conclusions regarding effectiveness of my own teacher preparation practice. More specifically, I reflected on the efficacy of my own teaching practice in terms of, 1) selection of reading resources, 2) conceptualization of activities and assignments, and 3) administration of formative and summative assessments. Casey (2002) utilized four different types of field notes as data sources to preserve authenticity of observations as a participant: reflective diaries, unit diaries, post-teaching reflective analysis, and post-cycle reflective analysis. My reflections were based on anecdotal notes written after each class meeting (weekly) and reflection notes written after each semester (15 weeks). These notes were based on observation of in-service teachers' engagement in college-based class activities and analysis of in-service teachers' completion of school-based activities as well as take-at-home exams. Being that this action research involved examination of my own teaching practice in the classroom management course between 2016-2020, development, implementation, and refinement of course reading, assignments, and assessments resulting from my inquiry helped me critically analyze and reflect on improvement of my own teaching practice for effectively preparing in-service teachers. Modifications to course components, following my investigation of outcomes, are described below.

Modification of Teacher Educator's Selected Course Reading

My course syllabus includes 14 topics and related reading. Table 3 showcases topics and literature selected for my course. Based on my anecdotal notes, class observations, and review of activities, assignments, and exams, the peaks and pitfalls of each assigned reading were identified to draw conclusions regarding effectiveness of selected literature as facilitator of in-service teachers' preparation for P-12 grade classroom management. Furthermore, recurring use of selected literature over multiple semesters enabled me to revise the reading list illustrated in Table 3; wherein, reading sources that were deemed to be beneficial were retained and additional sources were either included as supplementary sources to embellish exiting topics or as new sources to replace existing sources. For instance, new literature was added for culturally responsive classroom management; disabilities and discipline; bullying and school violence; and conflict resolution.

There were several reasons for including additional literature (see Table 3). One reason was to increase the rigor of my teacher preparation practice by emphasizing critical issues that currently challenge effectiveness of in-service teachers' classroom management. For instance, discussion of the sensitive topic, *Bullying and School Violence*, in my class, in recent years (i.e., 2019-2020), suggested that in-service teachers have limited knowledge of matters related to bullying and school violence in P-12 grades. According to many of the in-service teachers enrolled in my classroom management course, whatever knowledge of bullying and school violence they have, which was not much, was accrued from occasional professional development at work and from workshop (i.e., *School Violence Prevention and Intervention*) completed for their initial educator certification. Benefits of adding literature for bullying and school violence were gleaned through engagement of in-service teachers in collaboratively researching and designing interventions for addressing bullying and school violence reported by news media, thereby expanding their classroom management aptitude.

Another reason for reflecting on and updating reading sources was to present an in-depth and extensive coverage of key topics in my course. Exposing in-service teachers to diverse coverage of the same topic not only had the potential of enhancing their teaching practice, but also that of mine as a teacher educator. For example, I embellished on information pertaining to classroom management in the realm of diversity and disabilities by adding literature sources that offered comprehensive coverage of these two topics (see Table 3). Although teacher education programs require that preservice teachers complete one course for teaching students with disabilities and another for teaching English Language Learners, including advanced level literature for these topics contributed towards my efforts at preparing in-service teachers for supporting diverse learners through knowledge of diversity and disability issues. Such an expansion of in-service teachers' knowledge of diversity and disabilities also contributed towards my conceptualization of class activities and course exams, wherein knowledge of diversity and disabilities were measured.

Finally, scrutiny of literature sources selected for the classroom management course advanced my knowledge of current research and publications related to classroom management issues confronted by in-service teachers in P-12 classes. Inclusion of evidence-based literature also facilitated advancement of my teaching practice due to sharing of content knowledge and pedagogical strategies within the classroom management course by in-service teachers based on their everyday management of P-12 grade classes.

Table 3. Teacher educator analysis of literature sources selected between 2016-2020 for own course

Topic	Literature Source	Assigned Reading: Peaks	Assigned Reading: Pitfalls	Alternate Reading Selection	Semester(s) Source Assigned
Classroom Organization	Emmer & Evertson (2009a) Chapter 1: pp. 1–16	• Keys to room arrangements • Classroom layout	None	None	2016-2020
Classroom Rules and Procedures	Emmer & Evertson (2009b) Chapter 2: pp. 17–41	• Planning class rules • Planning classroom procedures • Case studies	None	None	2016-2020
Democratic Teaching: Dreikurs	Manning & Bucher (2007a) Chapter 4: pp. 62–76	• Key concepts of Dreikurs's theory • Addressing mistaken goals • Case studies	None	None	2016-2020
Noncoercive Discipline: Glasser	Charles (2005b) Chapter 5: pp. 73–92	• Meeting student needs • Quality teaching • Case studies	None	None	2016-2020
Assertive Discipline: Canter	Hardin (2008a) Chapter 3: pp. 43–61	• Basic teacher response styles • Steps in Assertive Discipline Plan • Sample class plan	None	None	2016-2020
Congruent Communication: Haim Ginott	Manning & Bucher (2007b) Chapter 5: pp. 77–93	• Communication applications • Management tips • Case studies	None	None	2016-2020
Discipline with Dignity: Curwin	Hardin (2008b) Chapter 6: pp. 101–118	• Three-Dimension Plan • Principles for consequences • Sample Contract	None	None	2016-2020
Positive Classroom Discipline: Jones	Charles (2005a) Chapter 4: pp. 55–72	• Skill clusters • Case studies	None	None	2016-2020
Instructional Management: Jacob Kounin	Manning & Bucher (2007c) Chapter 6: pp. 94–109	• Movement management techniques • Case studies	None	None	2016-2020
Conflict Resolution: Johnson	*Johnson & Johnson (2004) *Theory into Practice*, 43(1), 68-79	• Peacemaker Program Steps • Conflict Form	Johnson & Johnson (2004) Limited to discussion of Teaching Students Peacemaker Program (TSP)	**Johnson & Johnson (2011) Chapter 30: pp. 803 - 831 (Includes other models and theories)	*2016-2020 **2020
Culturally Responsive Classroom Management	*Cartledge, Singh, & Gibson (2008) *Preventing School Failure*, 52(3), 29-38	• Guidelines for establishing class environment for culturally and linguistically diverse (CLD) students	Cartledge et al. (2008) Discusses limited strategies for promoting learning of CLD students	**Gay (2011) Chapter 13: pp. 343–370 Discusses racial disproportionality in school discipline, cultural insensitivity, provocative interaction, and culturally responsive teaching	*2016-2019 **2020
Disabilities and Discipline	*Lock & Cooper Swanson (2005) *Intervention in School and Clinic*, 40(3), 182-187	• Guidelines for establishing class environment • Guidelines for setting rules nd procedure • Guidelines for organizing activities • Guidelines for providing choice	Lock & Cooper Swanson (2005) Offers general strategies for supporting students with learning and behavior disabilities	**Shepherd & Linn (2015) Chapter 2: pp. 33-60 Includes disability laws, legal mandates, and disciplinary procedures for behavior management	*2016-2019 **2020
Common Behavior Problems	*Foley (2006a) Chapter 5: pp. 43–66	• Problem solutions • Management techniques	Foley (2006a) General guidelines for managing common behavior problems	**Cangelosi (2014) Chapter 10: pp. 330–355 Supplements Foley (2006) with cases and strategies for dealing with nondisruptive off-task behaviors	*2016-2020 **2020
Chronic Disruptions	*Foley (2006b) Chapter 6: pp. 67–90	• Problem solutions • Management techniques	Foley (2006b) Discussion of bullying and violence is brief and guidance for addressing these issues is general/ sparse.	Bullying: **Tauber (2007a & b) Chapters 14 & 15: pp. 333–353 These readings supplement Foley (2006) discussion of bullying and violence.	*2016-2020 **2020

Figure 2. Teacher educator's PAGE structure for operationalizing collaborative case analysis

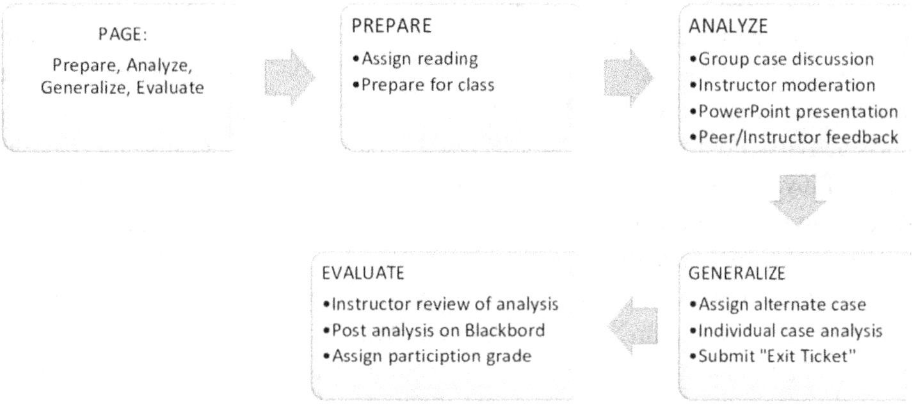

PAGE: Prepare, Analyze, Generalize, Evaluate

PREPARE
- Assign reading
- Prepare for class

ANALYZE
- Group case discussion
- Instructor moderation
- PowerPoint presentation
- Peer/Instructor feedback

GENERALIZE
- Assign alternate case
- Individual case analysis
- Submit "Exit Ticket"

EVALUATE
- Instructor review of analysis
- Post analysis on Blackbord
- Assign participation grade

Modification of Teacher Educator's Case-Based Class Activities

Class activities in my course require analysis of authentic classroom situations as case-based pedagogical approach for advancing in-service teachers' management of P-12 classes. Inspection of class activities resulted in my recognizing strengths and shortcomings of case-based teaching. Initially, in-service teachers were engaged in case-based learning through individual analyses, followed by whole class discussion and sharing of ideas. This teaching practice was limited in effectiveness as it inhibited effective evaluation of all in-service teachers' preparation for classroom management, as only some members shared their analyses with the class. As a result, the case analyses activity was extended, and in-service teachers were expected to submit written reflections for class participation grades.

Although requiring written responses for case analysis was improvement of class activity, written responses varied in quality as the format for written reflections was not established by me. Consequently, many in-service teachers were writing responses as quick writes rather than as analytic reflections. For example, one class activity, wherein in-service teachers had to analyze students' off-task behaviors in Teacher A's class, such as making irrelevant comments, talking during seatwork, refusing to do classwork, and complaining about homework, based on *Dreikurs's Democratic Teaching*, specifically his theory of mistaken goals (i.e., attention getting, power seeking, revenge, and feelings of inadequacy), some in-service teachers effectively analyzed student behaviors in relation to specific mistaken goal (e.g., interpreting making irrelevant comments as attention getting behavior; talking during seatwork as power seeking; refusing to do classwork as revenge; and complaining about homework as feelings of inadequacy), and suggested self-generated strategies for addressing students' mistaken goals (e.g., assigning classroom chores such as collecting homework to provide attention; providing choices for classwork such as oral report versus written report for sharing power; involving students in establishing grading system to curb revenge; and arranging peer-tutoring for homework to reduce feelings of inadequacy). Comparatively, others provided reflections that did not include analysis of mistaken goals and their suggested strategies were drawn from assigned reading rather than being self-generated or drawn from their own P-12 grade teaching experiences.

With the goal of further enhancing in-service teachers' case analysis aptitude for classroom management, collaborative analysis of cases was appended to individual case analysis. Figure 2 illustrates steps for collaborative case analysis resulting from my examination of in-service teachers' engagement in class activities. First, course readings are made available to in-service teachers via *Blackboard Learn* (Blackboard, 2021), a web-based Learning Management System, in order for them to come prepared for collaborative groupwork and class discussion. For example, the Hardin (2008a) chapter, *Assertive Discipline: Canter and Canter* (see Table 2), is posted on the *Blackboard Learn* for in-service teachers to prepare for class activity and discussion. Thus, "*Prepare*" is the first step of my case-based instruction.

The next step of my case-based instruction is *Analyze*. This step requires in-service teachers to work in collaborative groups to examine the assigned case (i.e., *Forgetful Eighth Grader*, Hardin, 2008a, p. 59) and recommend solutions to address the case. Group analyses of case and recommended solutions are aligned with the classroom management model assigned as reading (i.e., *Assertive Discipline: Canter and Canter, Hardin, 2008a),* and presented in class via PowerPoint slides. Groups' analysis of case is facilitated by me and culminates with peer and my questions and feedback for oral presentation.

The third step of my case-based instruction is *Generalize*. After in-service teachers have analyzed the case from their assigned reading (i.e., *Forgetful Eighth Grader*, Hardin, 2008a, p. 59), they are assigned a case written by me. In-service teachers write individual reflections and submit it as an "Exit Ticket" for class participation grade. The purpose is to determine in-service teachers' ability to apply content knowledge and pedagogical skills for analyzing and solving authentic cases.

The last step of my case-based activity is *Evaluation*. In-service teachers' collaborative oral presentation, wherein each member of the group is expected to share a component of their collaborative case analysis, and their individual written analyses (i.e., "Exit Ticket") of case are assessed as class participation. Collaborative case analysis PowerPoint slides are posted on *Blackboard Learn* (Blackboard, 2021) as course materials for in-service teachers. Table 4 illustrates the rubric created by me for evaluation of in-service teachers' weekly engagement in class activities. Performance (individual written reflections and collaborative oral presentations) related to case-based activities on average ranged from "Excellent" to "Good" for 2016-2020 semesters.

Table 4. Rubric for assessing in-service teachers' oral and written case analyses and reflections

ASSESSMENT RUBRIC					
EXCELLENT (A+ Grade)	**GOOD** (A to A- Grade)	**AVERAGE** (B+ to B- Grade)	**LIMITED** (C+ Grade)	**POOR** (C to C- Grade)	**MISSING** (F Grade)
1. Discussion of concepts is *excellent* 2. Description of examples is *excellent* 3. Analysis of scenarios is *excellent* 4. Design of plans is *excellent*	1. Discussion of concepts is *good* 2. Description of examples is *good* 3. Analysis of scenarios is *good* 4. Design of plans is *good*	1. Discussion of concepts is *average* 2. Description of examples is *average* 3. Analysis of scenarios is *average* 4. Design of plans is *average*	1. Discussion of concepts is *limited* 2. Description of examples is *limited* 3. Analysis of scenarios is *limited* 4. Design of plans is *limited*	1. Discussion of concepts is *poor* 2. Description of examples is *poor* 3. Analysis of scenarios is *poor* 4. Design of plans is *poor*	1. Discussion of concepts is *missing* 2. Description of examples is *missing* 3. Analysis of scenarios is *missing* 4. Design of plans is *missing*

Modification of Teacher Educator Generated P-12 Grades Application Activities

Application activities were written by me to facilitate in-service teachers' ability to transfer knowledge of theories, principles, and strategies from the classroom management course to P-12 grade school settings. Appendix 1 illustrates application activities which in-service teachers had to complete in their own class or in another teacher's class. Appendices 2, 3, 4, 5, and 6 illustrate templates that in-service teachers had to complete in relation to application activities completed in their own class or in another teacher's class.

Templates illustrated in Appendices 2 through 6 were designed by me in response to in-service teachers' questions during review of application activities between 2016-2020. Some in-service teacher questions were: "Can you share templates for recording teacher behaviors?" "What should be recorded as teacher behaviors?" "Can you review some recording forms?" Similarly, guiding questions were added for Activities 3 and 4 (see Appendix 1) based on my review of in-service teachers' written analysis, which were general rather than specific for verbal and non-verbal teacher behaviors and communication styles.

Comparatively, the questionnaire template was provided (see Appendix 3) to substantiate in-service teachers' inquiries such as, "What types of questions should we ask?" "How many questions should we ask?" "Can our questions cover topics from course reading?" Another reason for supplementing application activities with templates was to ensure that in-service teachers were appropriately applying classroom management theories, models, and strategies in P-12 grade settings. Review of in-service teachers' written reports and records confirmed advantages of providing templates and guiding questions. Their applications and analyses of classroom management strategies appeared more focused and comprehensive, rather than being generic and sparse as had been prior to my supplementing application activities with templates as a result of my inspection of these activities.

Modification of Teacher Educator's Course-Based Exams

Examination of my own teaching practice also influenced my assessment of in-service teachers' preparation in the classroom management course. As a result of my action research, development and implementation of my take-at-home exams also underwent changes. My review of in-service teachers' essay responses for take-at-home exam items reflected noticeable improvements from 2016-2020. I interpreted this change as a reflection of in-service teachers' understanding of central theories, principles, and strategies emphasized in my course. Furthermore, since the course exams are designed to tap in-service teachers' potential for bridging theory and practice, my revisions of the exams reflect transition from focus on assessing in-service teachers' knowledge of theories, principles, and strategies from course reading to focus on ability to demonstrate problem solving of authentic classroom situations.

Figure 3 illustrates exam items that evolved between 2016-2020. In addition to change in weightage assigned to course content, my exam format also underwent revisions, with the goal of streamlining the quality of in-service teachers' responses, and my objectively evaluating responses. In place of open-ended response format, the exam format was revised to include requirements such as page length, section heading, font size, and other features with the goal of lending structure and enhancing readability of in-service teacher responses. Furthermore, the time for completing take-at-home exams was extended from one week to two weeks. Finally, exam items were reviewed during class meetings and in-service teachers were provided opportunities to collaboratively discuss exam items in-class, with the caveat that each in-service teacher's exam response had to have explanations and examples that were distinct from those of their peers. Thus, the focus of my exams transitioned from evaluation of in-service teachers' content knowledge to evaluation of content knowledge and pedagogical practice related to P-12 classes.

Figure 3. Modification of teacher educator's take-at-home exams between 2016-2020 semesters

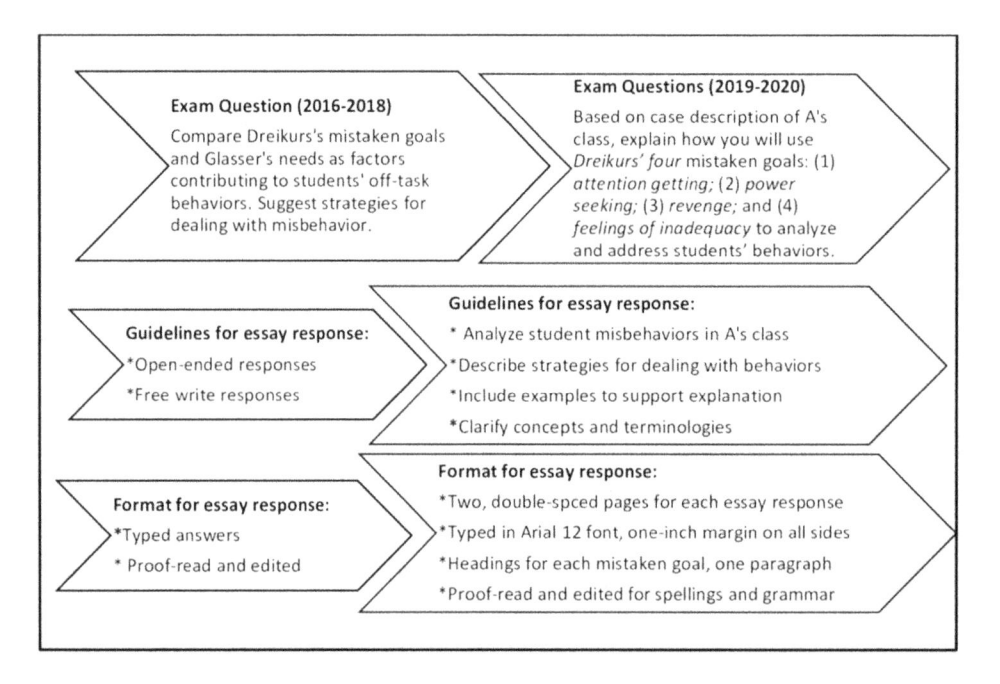

Exam Question (2016-2018)
Compare Dreikurs's mistaken goals and Glasser's needs as factors contributing to students' off-task behaviors. Suggest strategies for dealing with misbehavior.

Exam Questions (2019-2020)
Based on case description of A's class, explain how you will use *Dreikurs' four* mistaken goals: (1) *attention getting;* (2) *power seeking;* (3) *revenge;* and (4) *feelings of inadequacy* to analyze and address students' behaviors.

Guidelines for essay response:
*Open-ended responses
*Free write responses

Guidelines for essay response:
* Analyze student misbehaviors in A's class
*Describe strategies for dealing with behaviors
*Include examples to support explanation
*Clarify concepts and terminologies

Format for essay response:
*Typed answers
* Proof-read and edited

Format for essay response:
*Two, double-spced pages for each essay response
*Typed in Arial 12 font, one-inch margin on all sides
*Headings for each mistaken goal, one paragraph
*Proof-read and edited for spellings and grammar

In closing, my action research not only facilitated improvement of course measures, but also advanced in-service teachers' preparation for managing P-12 grade classes. Table 5 displays outcomes from administration of take-at-home exams between 2016-2020 that could be attributed to streamlining of exams based on my investigation. In-service teachers' performance and absence of their requesting explanation for the graded exams attest to effectiveness of my modified assessment measures.

Table 5. Teacher educator analysis of take-at-home exam between 2016-2020

	ACADEMIC SEMESTER					
TAKE-AT-HOME EXAMS	**SPRING 2016**	**SPRING 2017**	**SPRING 2018**	**SPRING 2019**	**SPRING 2020**	**2016 - 2020 TOTAL RANKING**
Outstanding Exams	N=2	N=2	N=2	N=6	N=6	N=18
Commendable Exams	N=8	N=10	N=4	N=14	N=15	N=51
Acceptable Exams	N=10	N=10	N=6	N=4	N=4	N=34
TOTAL EXAMS	N=20	N=22	N=12	N=24	N=25	N=103

Outstanding = Exam responses included 97%-100% comparison of theories/models (2016-2018); analysis of P-12 classroom situations (2019-2020); clarification of concepts; description of self-generated strategies; examples of strategy application for dealing with P-12 grade student behaviors.

Commendable = Exam responses included 90%-96% comparison of theories/models (2016-2018); analysis of P-12 classroom situations (2019-2020); clarification of concepts; description of self-generated strategies; examples of strategy application for dealing with P-12 grade student behaviors.

Acceptable = Exam responses included 89%-80% comparison of theories/models (2016-2018); analysis of P-12 classroom situations (2019-2020); clarification of concepts; description of self-generated strategies; examples of strategy application for dealing with P-12 grade student behaviors.

SOLUTIONS AND RECOMMENDATIONS

Based on my action research, I have arrived at the conclusion that case-based instruction can advance in-service teachers' ability to connect theory and practice through reflection and interpretation of real-life cases. Teacher educators therefore could integrate case-based learning to enhance in-service teachers' potential for addressing classroom management issues in their own classes.

Building Classroom Management Aptitude with Simulation and Video Analyses

Collaborative learning has been recognized as an effective pedagogical approach for promoting teacher candidates' potential as reflective educators (Kim et al, 2006). Although collaborative cased-based activities were incorporated in my course for strengthening in-service teachers' classroom management skills, most collaborative interactions emphasized analysis of simulations from printed sources. Alternate formats for case analyses and problem solving therefore could be incorporated in teacher preparation courses to advance teacher candidates' ability to deal with academic and behavior situations in P-12 classes.

One option is to promote in-service teachers' classroom management potential by engaging them in analysis of simulated situations via role play. Module 2, *Elaboration,* of the KODEK model (Piwowar et al., 2013) focuses on teacher candidates' application of role play as a problem-solving strategy in simulated settings by assuming four roles: a) the teacher, b) students who are on-task during class, c) students who are off-task and disrupting class, and d) an observer who evaluates the teacher's performance with an observation form. This approach allows teacher candidates to practice classroom management strategies in a sheltered environment and receive feedback from peers.

Another option is to use video analysis for advancing in-service teacher's classroom management aptitude. For example, Module 3, *Externalization,* of Piwowar et al. (2013) model involves analysis of two, 3-minute, segments from teacher candidates' videotaped lessons focused on implementation of their self-generated strategies in their own classrooms. The focus of such videotaped lesson segments by teacher candidates, identified as "video circles", is to analyze application of classroom management strategies and to co-construct alternate strategies to deal with classroom issues based on peer feedback. Based on their study findings, Piwowar and her colleagues contend that mediated analysis of videotaped lesson segments, related to applications of classroom management strategies, facilitated teacher candidates' knowledge of strategies for addressing classroom management situations in their own secondary school classes. Analyzing and addressing classroom management problems based on teacher candidates' videotaped lessons is of significance as it bridges the theory and practice gaps.

Case-Based Problem Solving from Multiple Perspectives

Case-based Learning for Classroom Management Problem Solving (CBL-CMPS) model (Choi & Lee, 2009) is an evidence-based framework which could be used for promoting teacher candidates' knowledge of solving ill-structured classroom problems (i.e., problems with multiple solutions). Choi and Lee's CBL-CMPS model comprises of five stages. *Stage 1: Reviewing Problems* involves teacher candidates being presented with audio stories of real-life classroom problems collected from teachers, which they have to solve on their own. *Stage 2: Analyzing Problems* focuses on different stakeholders such as principals, parents, and teachers sharing their opinion about the classroom problems. Teacher candidates listen to the multiple perspectives and are provided with the opportunity to revise their own analysis about the problem. *Stage 3: Creating Solutions* emphasizes sharing of multiple solutions by experienced teachers and the teacher candidates have the option of revising their own solution for the classroom problems. *Stage 4: Making Decisions* focuses on providing teacher candidates with literature related to classroom management in order for them to drawn on theories and principles to identify problems, generate solutions, and justify their decisions. Finally, *Stage 5: Reflecting on Results* involves teacher candidates receiving information about solutions implemented by teachers from whom the classroom cases were collected and comments from stakeholders regarding solutions for the problems provided by teachers. Teacher candidates then share their reflections about case-based learning process and comments regarding teachers' solutions for the reviewed problems. Emphasizing multiple perspectives and solutions from experienced teachers and other stakeholders is valuable as teacher candidates can benefit from diverse opinions and solutions and build up their repertoire of strategies for identifying, analyzing, and resolving ill-structed problems in their own P-12 grade classes.

FUTURE RESEARCH DIRECTIONS

Transfer of Problem-Solving from College Courses to P-12 Classes

Although teacher education researchers have examined effectiveness of engaging teacher candidates in interpreting and analyzing authentic P-12 classroom situations in relation to educational theories and models in teacher preparation courses on college campuses, transfer of problem solving to teaching and managing P-12 grade students by teacher candidates have not been extensively examined. Future research therefore could examine teacher candidates' application of problem solving in their own classrooms to see whether or not they draw upon content knowledge and pedagogical skills from teacher preparation course to deal with academic and behavioral problems of P-12 students in real-life settings. Future research examining transference of problem solving acquired by teacher candidates through case-based instruction in graduate teacher preparation courses to deal with academic and behavioral dilemmas in their own P-12 classrooms is essential because although such transference has been studied with preservice teachers during their fieldwork and student teaching experiences, it has not been extensively examined with in-service teachers in graduate courses, wherein fieldwork and practice teaching are not required.

Course Instructor Written Cases Versus Teacher Written Cases

Effectiveness of case-based instruction on teacher candidates' preparation to work with P-12 students has been investigated by several teacher educators in the United States (Harrington, 1995; Hemphill et al., 2015; Laframboise & Griffith, 1997). Investigation of teaching cases used as approaches for advancing teacher candidates' content knowledge and pedagogical skills have mainly focused on:1) cases selected by teacher educators from published sources such as books, chapters, journal articles, and newspapers (Kim et al., 2006) and 2) cases written by teacher educators themselves. A third form of teaching cases is those written by the teacher candidates. By engaging teacher candidates in the process of writing and interpreting cases, teacher educators support their metacognition to determine not only what they know about the cases, but also how they know about the cases. Furthermore, engaging teacher candidates in the case writing process enables them to add to the bank of cases that could be used to help them bridge the theory and practice space (Strangeways & Papatraianou, 2016). Future research could investigate effectiveness of teacher preparation by comparing performance on teacher educator generated versus teacher candidate generated cases.

CONCLUSION

Case-based instruction has been well-researched and supported as an effective pedagogical approach for advancing teacher candidates' P-12 grade teaching. Investigation of my case-based instruction implemented in an educational psychology course for advancing in-service teachers' classroom management capabilities has been emphasized in this chapter. Focus of my investigation has been limited to analyses of 1) college class activities, 2) P-12 grade application assignments, and 3) take-at-home exams. Interpretation of outcomes from my investigation suggests that individual and collaborative analysis of academic and behavior problems of P-12 grade students were effective approaches for promoting in-service teachers' classroom management competencies. Theories, principles, and strategies drawn from classroom management research were connected to in-service teachers' proficiencies for addressing academic and behavior problems in P-12 grade classes. Review of case-based instructional approaches drew attention to similarities and difference across models in relation to teacher preparation for classroom management. Results of my investigation have been supplemented with suggestions of pedagogical approaches for advancing in-service teachers' aptitudes for managing academic and behavior problems in P-12 grade classes. Future directions for research have been proposed for examining effectiveness of teacher preparation in advanced level education courses for classroom management.

REFERENCES

Anwar, N. (2016). Action research a tool to build capacity of teacher educators. *The Journal of Educational Research*, *19*(2), 105–116.

Blackboard. (2021). *Blackboard Learn*. Blackboard. https://www.blackboard.com/Learn

Cangelosi, J. S. (2014). Dealing with nondisruptive off-task behaviors. In *Classroom management strategies: Gaining and maintaining students' cooperation* (7th ed., pp. 330–355). John Wiley & Sons.

Cartledge, G., Singh, A., & Gibson, L. (2008). Practical behavior management techniques to close the accessibility gap for students who are culturally and linguistically diverse. *Preventing School Failure*, *52*(3), 29–38. doi:10.3200/PSFL.52.3.29-38

Casey, A. (2012). A self-study using action research: Changing site expectations and practice stereotypes. *Educational Action Research*, *20*(2), 219–232. doi:10.1080/09650792.2012.676287

Charles, C. M. (2005a). Fred Jones's positive classroom discipline. In *Building classroom discipline* (8th ed., pp. 55–72). Pearson.

Charles, C. M. (2005b). William Glasser's noncoercive discipline. In *Building classroom discipline* (8th ed., pp. 73–92). Pearson.

Choi, I., & Lee, K. (2009). Designing and implementing a case-based learning environment for enhancing ill-structured problem solving: Classroom management problems for prospective teachers. *Educational Technology Research and Development*, *57*(1), 99–129. doi:10.100711423-008-9089-2

Cochran-Smith, M., Barnatt, J., Friedman, A., & Pine, G. (2009). Inquiry on Inquiry: Practitioner Research and Student Learning. *Action in Teacher Education*, *31*(2), 17–32. doi:10.1080/01626620.2009.10463515

Cochran-Smith, M., & Villegas, A. M. (2016). Research on teacher preparation: Charting the landscape of a sprawling field. In D. Gitomer & C. Bell (Eds.), *Handbook of research on teaching* (5th ed., pp. 439–547). American Educational Research Association. doi:10.3102/978-0-935302-48-6_7

Council for the Accreditation of Educator Preparation (CAEP). (2020). *CAEP consolidated handbook*. CAEP. http://www.caepnet.org

Emmer, E. T., & Evertson, C. M. (2009a). Organizing your classroom and materials. In *Classroom management for middle and high school teachers* (8th ed., pp. 1–16). Pearson.

Emmer, E. T., & Evertson, C. M. (2009b). Choosing rules and procedures. In *Classroom management for middle and high school teachers* (8th ed., pp. 17–41). Pearson.

Foley, D. (2006a). Handling common problems. In *Ultimate classroom control handbook: A veteran teacher's on-the-spot techniques for solving adolescent student misbehavior* (pp. 43–66). JIST Publishing.

Foley, D. (2006b). Dealing with disruption. In *Ultimate classroom control handbook: A veteran teacher's on-the-spot techniques for solving adolescent student misbehavior* (pp. 67–90). JIST Publishing.

Gay, G. (2011). Connection between classroom management and culturally responsive teaching. In C. M. Evertson & C. S. Weinstein (Eds.), *Handbook of classroom management: Research, practice, and contemporary issues* (pp. 343–370). Routledge.

Hardin, C. J. (2008a). Assertive discipline. In *Effective classroom management: Models and strategies for today's classrooms* (2nd ed., pp. 43–61). Pearson.

Hardin, C. J. (2008b). Discipline with dignity. In *Effective classroom management: Models and strategies for today's classrooms* (2nd ed., pp. 101–118). Pearson.

Harrington, H. L. (1995). Fostering reasoned decisions: Case-based pedagogy and the professional development of teachers. *Teaching and Teacher Education*, *11*(3), 203–214. doi:10.1016/0742-051X(94)00027-4

Hemphill, M. A., Richards, K. A. R., Gaudreault, K. L., & Templin, T. J. (2015). Pre-service teacher perspectives of case-based learning in physical education teacher education. *European Physical Education Review*, *21*(4), 432–450. doi:10.1177/1356336X15579402

Johnson, D. W., & Johnson, R. T. (2004). Implementing the teaching students to be peacemakers program. *Theory into Practice*, *43*(1), 68–79. doi:10.120715430421tip4301_9

Johnson, D. W., & Johnson, R. T. (2011). Conflict resolution, peer mediation, and peacemaking. In C. M. Evertson & C. S. Weinstein (Eds.), *Handbook of classroom management: Research, practice, and contemporary issues* (pp. 803–831). Routledge.

Kim, H., & Hannafin, M. J. (2009). Web-enhanced case-based activity in teacher education: A case study. *Instructional Science*, *37*(2), 151–170. doi:10.100711251-007-9040-7

Kim, S., Phillips, W. R., Pinsky, L., Brock, D., Phillips, K., & Keary, J. (2006). A conceptual framework for developing teaching cases: A review and synthesis of the literature across disciplines. *Medical Education*, *40*(9), 867–876. doi:10.1111/j.1365-2929.2006.02544.x PMID:16925637

Kitchen, J., & Stevens, D. (2008). Two teacher-educators practice action research as they introduce action research to preservice teachers. *Action Research*, *6*(1), 7–28. doi:10.1177/1476750307083716

Koshy, V. (2005). Action research for improving practice: A practical guide. *Sage (Atlanta, Ga.)*.

Laframboise, K. L., & Griffith, P. L. (1997). Using literature cases to examine diversity issues with pre-service teachers. *Teaching and Teacher Education*, *13*(4), 369–382. doi:10.1016/S0742-051X(96)00034-0

Lock, R. H., & Cooper Swanson, T. (2005). Provide structure for children with learning and behavior problems. *Intervention in School and Clinic*, *40*(3), 182–187. doi:10.1177/10534512050400030801

Loughran, J. (2002). Effective reflective practice: In search of meaning in learning about teaching. *Journal of Teacher Education*, *53*(1), 33–43. doi:10.1177/0022487102053001004

Loughran, J. (2014). Professionally developing as a teacher educator. *Journal of Teacher Education*, *65*(4), 271–283. doi:10.1177/0022487114533386

Manning, M. L., & Bucher, K. T. (2007a). Exploring the theories of democratic teaching: Rudolph Dreikurs. In *Classroom management: Models, applications, and cases* (2nd ed., pp. 62–76). Pearson.

Manning, M. L., & Bucher, K. T. (2007b). Exploring the theories of congruent communication: Haim Ginott. In *Classroom management: Models, applications, and cases* (2nd ed., pp. 77–93). Pearson.

Manning, M. L., & Bucher, K. T. (2007c). Exploring the theories of instructional management: Jacob Kounin. In *Classroom management: Models, applications, and cases* (2nd ed., pp. 94–109). Pearson.

Piwowar, V., Thiel, F., & Ophardt, D. (2013). Training inservice teachers' competencies in classroom management. A quasi-experimental study with teachers of secondary schools. *Teaching and Teacher Education*, *30*(30), 1–12. doi:10.1016/j.tate.2012.09.007

Russell, T. (2018). A teacher educator's lessons learned from reflective practice. *European Journal of Teacher Education*, *41*(1), 4–14. doi:10.1080/02619768.2017.1395852

Rutten, L. (2021). Toward a theory of action for practitioner inquiry as professional development in pre-service teacher education. *Teaching and Teacher Education*, *97*, 103–194. doi:10.1016/j.tate.2020.103194

Shepherd, T. L., & Linn, D. (2015). Legal issues of behavior and classroom management. In *Behavior and classroom management in the multicultural classroom: Proactive, active, and reactive strategies* (pp. 33–60). Sage Publications. doi:10.4135/9781483366647.n2

Strangeways, A., & Papatraianou, L. H. (2016). Case-based learning for classroom ready teachers: Addressing the theory practice disjunction through narrative pedagogy. *The Australian Journal of Teacher Education*, *41*(9), 117–134. doi:10.14221/ajte.2016v41n9.7

Stringer, E. T., Christensen, L. M., & Baldwin, S. C. (2010). Action research in teaching and learning. In *Integrating teaching, learning, and action research: Enhancing instruction in the K–12 classroom* (pp. 1–14). Sage., doi:10.4135/9781452274775.n1

Tauber, R. T. (2007a). Bullying. In Classroom management: Sound theory and effective practice (4th ed., pp. 333–345 & 369–370). Praeger Publishers.

Tauber, R. T. (2007b). Violence in today's schools. In Classroom management: Sound theory and effective practice (4th ed., pp. 347–353 & 365–368). Praeger Publishers.

Vanassche, E., & Kelchtermans, G. (2015). The state of the art in self-study of teacher education practices: A systematic literature review. *Journal of Curriculum Studies*, *47*(4), 508–528. doi:10.1080/00220272.2014.995712

Vaughan, M., & Burnaford, G. (2016). Action research in graduate teacher education: A review of the literature 2000-2015. *Educational Action Research*, *24*(2), 280–299. doi:10.1080/09650792.2015.1062408

Walker-Floyd, L. K. (2014). Individual action research: The PARJ and self study. Academic Press.

Willis, C. E., & Casamassa, M. (2014). *Action research: Models, methods, and examples*. Information Age Publishing.

Willis, J., & Edwards, C. (2014). *Theoretical foundations for the practice of action research*. Academic Press.

Willis, C. E., & Casamassa, M. (2014). *Action research: Models, methods, and examples*. Information Age Publishing.

Willis, J., & Edwards, C. (2014). Varieties of action research. Academic Press.

Casamassa (2014). *Action research: Models, methods, and examples*. Information Age Publishing.

ADDITIONAL READING

Efron, S. E., & Ravid, R. (2019). *Action research in education: A practical guide* (2nd ed.). Guildford Press.

Jones, V., & Jones, L. (2015). *Comprehensive classroom management: Creating communities of support and solving problems* (11th ed.). Pearson.

Samaras, A. P. (2011). *Self-study teacher research: Improving your practice through collaborative inquiry* (1st ed.). Sage.

Schön, D. (1995). *The reflective practitioner: How professionals think in action.* Basic Books.

Slapac, A., & Navarro, V. (2011). Shaping action researchers through a master's capstone experience. *Teacher Education and Practice, 24*(4), 405–426.

Stringer, E. (2007). *Action research* (3rd ed.). Sage.

Willems, P. P., & Gonzalez-DeHass, A. R. (2017). *Case studies in educational psychology: Elementary school grades* (1st ed.). Rowman & Littlefield Publishers.

KEY TERMS AND DEFINITIONS

Action Research: Study of specific educational problems with the goal of solving them through inquiry and reflection.

Assessment Rubric: System for evaluating academic performance based on specified qualitative and quantitative criteria.

Case-Based Instruction: Real-life classroom episodes used as teaching tools for strengthening in-service teachers' content knowledge and pedagogical skills of their professional discipline.

Classroom Management: Creating an instructional environment to promote optimal learning by monitoring and attending to cognitive, behavioral, and social-emotional needs of P-12 students.

Course Measures: Educational tools used to determine outcomes of teacher preparation in a college course.

In-Service Teachers: College students who teach children in P-12 grade classes and are enrolled in a graduate level teacher preparation course.

Reflective Practice: Analyzing and tailoring one's own instruction to ensure effective learning outcomes.

Self-Study: Examining effectiveness of specific educational methods, measures, and materials within one's own teacher preparation course.

Teacher Candidates: P-12 grade teachers who are graduate students in accredited teacher education programs leading to professional teaching certificate.

Teacher Preparation: Teacher education courses that train college students to teach children in P-12 grade classes.

APPENDIX 1

Applications Activities: Part 1

Activity 1: Classroom Organization

First, observe a lesson at a grade level and subject you teach and record the amount of time the teacher spends on instructional and non-instructional matters during class. Use the *Teacher Monitoring Form* (see enclosed form for teacher monitoring) to record the teacher's instructional and non-instructional behaviors during the observed lesson. Then, write a report including, a) description of the observed lesson, b) narrative of your thoughts about the observed teacher use of class time for instructional and non-instructional elements, and c) discussion of actions that could be taken to reduce the amount of time spent on various non-instructional tasks during the observed lesson. Support your analysis of the observed lesson with information drawn from reading sources assigned for your classroom management course. Finally, **cite and attach the completed teacher monitoring form as illustration of your recordings of teacher's instructional and non-instructional actions during the observed lesson.**

Activity 2: Discipline System

First, interview a teacher at a grade level and subject you teach on the topic of classroom management and discipline as related to his or her teaching and students. Use the *Teacher Interview Questionnaire* (see enclosed questionnaire for teacher interview) to record "verbatim" the teacher's verbal responses during the interview. Then, write a report including: a) discussion of the interviewed teacher's perspective on classroom management and discipline, and how the teacher's perspective compares with those expressed in the reading sources assigned for your classroom management course, b) explanation of your own philosophy of classroom management and discipline as well as principles you follow or will follow as a teacher, and c) narrative of concerns that you have about classroom management and things you would like to learn about discipline. Finally, **cite and attach the completed questionnaire as illustration of responses you recorded ("verbatim") during the teacher interview.**

Application Activities: Part 2

Activity 3: Teacher Response Styles

First, in your own classroom or in another teacher's classroom, use the *Teacher Response Style Checklist* (see enclosed checklist for teacher response style) to record your own or the observed teacher's verbal and non-verbal behavior during one lesson or class period. Then, briefly describe the observed lesson, and provide a written analysis of behaviors recorded in the checklist, with particular emphasis on the following issues: Which response styles were used most of the time? Which teacher behaviors were appropriate? Which teacher behaviors were inappropriate? What suggestions do you have for improvement of teacher response styles? Support your analysis of teacher response styles with information drawn from reading sources assigned for your classroom management course. Finally, **cite and attach with your**

Assessment of Case-Based Instruction in a Graduate Educational Psychology Course

written report the completed response style checklist, including record of teacher statements and student behaviors.

Activity 4: Instructional Management

First, in your own classroom or in another teacher's classroom, use the *Instructional Management Checklist* (see enclosed checklist for instructional management) to record teacher behavior and movement management during one lesson or class period. Then, briefly describe the observed lesson, and provide a written analysis of the instructional management techniques recorded in the checklist, with emphasis on the following issues: Which behaviors were representative of appropriate instructional management techniques? Which behaviors were representative of inappropriate instructional management techniques? What are your reactions to observed instructional management techniques? What suggestions do you have for eliminating inappropriate management techniques? Support your analysis of teacher behavior and movement management with information drawn from Ginott's Congruent Communications Theory (Manning & Bucher, 2007, pp. 77–93). Finally, **cite and attach with your report the completed instructional management checklist, including record of teacher behaviors and contexts**.

Table 6.

Time Intervals	Grade/Subject _____ Time: _____ Date: _____	
	TEACHER BEHAVIORS	
	Instructional behaviors	**Non-instructional behaviors**
0-5 minutes		
Related Context		
5-10 minutes		
Related Context		
10-15 minutes		
Related Context		
15-20 minutes		
Related Context		
20-25 minutes		
Related Context		
25-30 minutes		
Related Context		
30-35 minutes		
Related Context		
35-40 minutes		
Related Context		
40-45 minutes		

Assessment of Case-Based Instruction in a Graduate Educational Psychology Course

APPENDIX 2

Teacher Monitoring Form (Activity 1)

APPENDIX 3

Teacher Interview Questionnaire (Activity 2)

Date/Time of interview: _____ Years of teaching: _____
Place of interview: _____ Subjects/Grades Taught: _____

1. How do you view discipline in the school where you work?

   _____
   _____
   _____
   _____

2. What do you think are the most important challenges for teachers regarding classroom management?

   _____
   _____
   _____
   _____

3. What advice do you have for someone entering the teaching field about classroom management?

   _____
   _____
   _____
   _____

4. What is your stance on consequence for disruptive classroom behaviors?

   _____
   _____
   _____
   _____

   <u>IMPORTANT REMINDER</u>: INCLUDE ADDITIONAL QUESTIONS RELATED TO SCHOOL DISCIPLINE POLICIES AND INTERVIEWEE CLASSROOM MANAGEMENT PRACTICES

APPENDIX 4

Teacher Response Styles Checklist (Activity 3)

Grade/Subject _____ Time: _____ Date: _____
VERBAL TEACHER BEHAVIORS PRESENCE OF BEHAVIOR_____
FREQUENTLY *SOMETIMES NEVER*

1. Statements were direct and specific _____ _____ _____

   Teacher statements and student behaviors:
   _____
   _____
   _____

2. Statements were firm but not hostile _____ _____ _____

   Teacher statements and student behaviors:
   _____
   _____
   _____

3. Statements showed respect or consideration of student _____ _____ _____

   Teacher statements and student behaviors:
   _____
   _____
   _____

4. Statements included sarcasm or were condescending _____ _____ _____

   Teacher statements and student behaviors:
   _____
   _____
   _____

5. Statements included preaching or lecturing _____ _____ _____

   Teacher statements and student behaviors:
   _____
   _____
   _____

APPENDIX 5

Teacher Response Styles Checklist (Activity 3)

NONVERBAL TEACHER BEHAVIORS
    ASSERTIVE NONASSERTIVE AGGRESSIVE

1. *Eye contact* Maintained eye contact Avoided eye contact Stared down

   _____ _____ _____

   Teacher behavior and related context: _____
   _____
   _____

2. *Voice volume* Appropriate loudness Too soft Too loud

   _____ _____ _____

   Teacher behavior and related context:
   _____
   _____
   _____

3. *Voice tone* Natural sounding Tremulous Shouting

   _____ _____ _____

   Teacher behavior and related context:
   _____
   _____
   _____

4. *Voice fluency* Even paced Pauses Fast paced

   _____ _____ _____

   Teacher behavior and related context:
   _____
   _____
   _____

5. *Facial Expression* Attentive, engaged Nervous, blinking Stoic, indifferent

   _____ _____ _____

   Teacher behavior and related context:

_____
_____
_____

6. *Body language* Alert, relaxed Trembling, fidgeting Pointing, gesturing

    _____ _____ _____

    Teacher behavior and related context:
    _____
    _____
    _____

APPENDIX 6

Instructional Management Checklist (Activity 4)

Grade/Subject _____ Time: _____ Date: _____
   PRESENCE OF BEHAVIOR_____
   Often Sometimes Never

A. Teacher Behavior

    1. Withitness _____ _____ _____

        Observed behaviors:
        _____
        _____
        _____

    2. Desists _____ _____ _____

        Observed behaviors:
        _____
        _____
        _____

    3. Overlapping _____ _____ _____

        Observed behaviors:
        _____
        _____
        _____

4. Satiation _____ _____ _____

   Observed behaviors:
   _____
   _____
   _____

B. Movement Management

   1. Jerkiness _____ _____ _____

   Observed behaviors:
   _____
   _____
   _____

2. Stimulus Bound _____ _____ _____

   Observed behaviors:
   _____
   _____
   _____

3. Thrust _____ _____ _____

   Observed behaviors: _____
   _____
   _____

Chapter 6
The Challenges and Benefits of Online Instruction:
Navigating the Rough Waters of Teaching College Classes During the COVID-19 Pandemic

Madalina F. Tanase
University of North Florida, USA

Shae Hammack
University of North Florida, USA

ABSTRACT

Because of the COVID-19 pandemic, educators everywhere transitioned to an online environment. This abrupt transition brought about some challenges: educators shifted their content and activities online, while their students attended classes and completed assignments online. This action research study analyzed the challenges experienced by an educator and her students during the summer and Fall 2020 semesters at a mid-size university. The researchers collected student surveys about their experiences with online learning. Results highlight the educator's struggle to make learning more interactive, as well as students' challenges with navigating the online platform and maintaining focus in class. Conversely, the online experience provided the following benefits: flexibility (logging in from different locations), comfort (joining class from home), and convenience (recorded class sessions). In alignment with the action research, the educator will continue to reflect on her practice in an attempt to make changes to the instruction and content of her classes.

DOI: 10.4018/978-1-7998-6922-1.ch006

INTRODUCTION

On March 11, 2020, the World Health Organization declared the coronavirus outbreak a pandemic (Rajab, Gazal, & Alkattan, 2020). This new virus, transmitted in just minutes through droplets or by touching surface metals or other materials which have been infected, can affect everyone, young or old, healthy or with pre-existing conditions (Bender, 2020; Meng, et al., 2020; Toquero, 2020). One after another, countries closed their borders, and governments issued stay at home orders (Rajab et al., 2020). As a result, businesses closed, many people lost their jobs and applied for unemployment, experiencing high levels of anxiety (Karademir, Yaman, & Saatçioğlu, 2020).

Educational systems worldwide have been adversely affected by the outbreak, as schools, universities, and colleges closed their doors (Huang, 2020; Rajab et al., 2020). As of April 06, 2020, United Nations Educational, Scientific and Cultural Organization (UNESCO) reported 1,576,021,818 affected learners out of 91.3% total enrolled learners in 188 countries in all levels of learning. These closures led to a transition to the online format, prompting educators all over the world "rapidly and suddenly to adapt to what can only be described as an unprecedented emergency educational response" (Assunção & Gago, 2020, p. 2). Due to the swiftness of this transition, in most cases, many educators felt they did not possess a fundamental knowledge of the components involved in the processes of online teaching (Karademir et al., 2020). Moreover, this process was also unfamiliar to many students and parents (Bakker & Wagner, 2020; Erduran, 2020; Wang, Horby, et al., 2020).

Rajab et al. (2020) discussed the two main reported predictions about the potential impact of the coronavirus pandemic on online education. One such prediction was that the pandemic would adversely impact online education, because of the challenge posed by transitioning to online education, the financial burdens that result from a collapsing economy and with this, the crude reality that some college students will not afford college after the pandemic. In addition, the teaching/learning from home may carry extra challenges, as some of the faculty and students now needed to manage their children, elders, or siblings in the house.

Rajab et al. (2020) also predicted that the pandemic would positively impact online education, which had experienced growth through the years. One of the positive reasons is "the reset button to the ailing traditional educational system" (Rajab et al., 2020, p. 2), a re-vamping of some sorts of the educational system, pushing educators to design assessments that are in sync to the online teaching and to ensure that students stay engaged. To ensure the success of this transition, higher education institutions supported educators with developing their online courses. As such, 80% of institutions surveyed in a study conducted in US confirmed that faculty members were offered support for their online courses (Rajab et al., 2020).

This study aims to discuss the first author's challenges with the transition to online teaching over the course of the summer and fall 2020 semesters. The authors reflect on the issues encountered while transitioning online in COVID times, and they propose solutions to remedy some of these challenges. In addition, this study presents challenges and benefits to online learning, as perceived by the students enrolled in the educator's fall 2020 classes. The authors would like to note that the purpose of the chapter is not to reflect on the myriad of effective online teaching strategies (abundant in the literature of online teaching), but to specifically discuss one educator's experience with online teaching during a highly stressful time period, as well as to offer some practical solutions to the encountered challenges.

LITERATURE REVIEW

Challenges with Online Teaching and Learning

The transition to the online environment was challenging for both students and educators. As universities began to operate fully online, students returned home, leaving their campus life and jobs behind (Karademir et al., 2020). This abrupt move meant a change in their lifestyles, adjustment to a limited freedom, and anxiety over the rapid spread of the disease (Brooks et al., 2020; Wang, Pan et al., 2020). Students who lived together with family members who have lost their jobs or faced a pay cut, experienced financial issues more profoundly (Karademir et al., 2020). In addition, the fear of catching the virus, the lack of outdoor activity, a limited personal space, and unfavorable conditions for learning, impacted students' physical, mental, and psychological health (Brooks et al., 2020; Wang, Horby, Hayden, et al., 2020; Wang, Zhang, Zhao, et al., 2020). The high levels of stress, anxiety, and depression had the potential to impact negatively the students' experiences with online learning, and to decrease their motivation (Brooks et al., 2020).

On the other hand, educators around the world—including the ones who had previously taught online classes and were more prepared for the transition—faced unprecedented challenges when transitioning their classes online in a matter of weeks. Examples of such challenges included inequalities in equipment and internet access, communication, student assessment, use of technology tools, online experience, pandemic-related anxiety, time management, and technophobia.

Student Challenges

A major challenge that affected both students and educators alike was the inequitable access to online teaching. Participation in the online activities required some type of technology (Barr & Miller, 2013). Researchers (Assunção & Gago, 2020; Wang, Horby, Hayden, et al., 2020; Zhang et al., 2020) pointed to the lack of technology in some cases, as students either did not have a laptop or tablet, or they shared the equipment with other family members. In other cases, students had no internet access, or they faced technical problems (Rajab et al., 2020; Zhang et al., 2020). In addition, some students had difficulties navigating the online platforms to locate course assignments. The age of the learners was yet another challenge, as older internet users experienced technophobia, feeling worried or not confident enough to deal with computer hardware and software in their classrooms. These inequities could further deepen the achievement gap, having irreparable effects on students' education (Bakker & Wagner, 2020; Zhang et al., 2020).

In addition, Huang (2020) discussed college students' struggle with the home learning environment. For example, some students could not find a quiet place at home, others felt lazier, and some could not concentrate because of various distractions, which all lead to inefficient learning at home. The inability to communicate face-to-face with classmates presented another challenge, as students believed that collaborating on assignments and communicating with their peers held them accountable and pushed them to meet and exceed expectations. Lastly, eye fatigue due to a prolonged screen exposure affected both students and educators (Huang, 2020).

Instructor Challenges

Educators faced challenges when adjusting their face-to-face content to the new situation (Choi & Park, 2006), as the online environment required a different approach to pedagogy (Islam et al., 2015). Huang (2020) stated, "Online education is not only about transferring traditional teaching to the internet; it requires us to change from the old teaching paradigm to a new teaching method that matches the functions of digitization" (p. 2811). Similarly, Leask (2004) discussed the inefficiency of "dumping large amounts of text onto a website" (p. 347). In this respect, Leask (2004) cautioned educators to not provide classes dense in information, but scarce in student-student and student-teacher interaction. Educators must also be able to interpret students' online written text, understand the context, and understand group dynamics with individual needs (Loveless, 2011; Turvey, 2008). This transition is even harder when the instructor is a novice in the online setting (Choi & Park, 2006; Kebritchy et al., 2017). Novice instructors believed online courses involved a heavy workload, technology issues, and a decreased student–teacher interaction (Choi & Park, 2006). An additional reported challenge for educators was understanding the different learning styles of their students in order to improve the learning outcomes (Donahue & Glodstein, 2013; Folley, 2010). These researchers believed that in order to respond to the individual needs of their students, educators should be aware of the diversity in their virtual classes. Similarly, Phipps and Merisotis (1999) argued that researcher on e-learning did not focus on individual needs, and they advocated for "more emphasis on individual differences such as gender, age, educational experience, motivation and learning style" (p.3). In addition, Islam et al. (2015) urged content providers to design courses and materials that acknowledge these differences in order to engage culturally diverse audiences.

On the other hand, Islam et al. (2015) and Cornelius and Macdonald (2008) addressed the difficulties educators faced when managing their time online (i.e. checking and responding to discussion boards). For example, educators in the UK became overwhelmed by the sheer volume of traffic in the discussion boards, which resulted in skimming over posted messages and becoming selective when traffic increased. Similarly, Clark (2001) discussed that when switching from face-to-face to online learning, verbal conversations were replaced by a permanent written discussion forum. According to Islam et al. (2015), online learning allows 24 hours a day for a class to run, placing extreme demands on educators, as students expect an immediate reply (Gustafson & Gibbs, 2010). When educators are overworked, student learning suffers. Reeder et al., (2004) argued that the cyber culture values speed, reach, and quick response. According to Burd and Buchaman (2004), an effective educator should visit the discussions' page at least once a day, while other researchers (Mayes et al., 2011; Nandi et al., 2012) contended that educators should maintain a vigorous presence on online discussion boards to facilitate discussion and to provide feedback, in order to keep the students engaged.

Adding to the above challenges, technical errors, bugs, and slowness can negatively impact the success of online learning (Islam et al., 2015). Moreover, educators struggled with the online 'presence' of their students. For example, Donitsa-Schmidt and Ramot (2020) discussed how some students did not have their camera on, while others, while on camera, appeared preoccupied with other things. This might be problematic, as learning generally requires a high level of engagement, collaborative and cooperative learning (Davidson & Major, 2014). Moreover, when students stay off camera, educators are unable to take their clues from the students' verbal and non-verbal interactions (Coppola et al., 2001). This may negatively impact the educator-student interaction (Kebritchy et al., 2017).

Some educators find the online environment cold and distant for students and have not yet made the connections between the content and how best to deliver their lessons online. For this reason, many are reluctant to teach online classes, as they struggle to connect with students (Kebritchy et al., 2017). In the same vein, Osika et al., (2009) found that while educators may use technology in their face-to-face classes, they might not feel that online courses hold the same value. In general, lack of training for faculty and administrators (Chang et al., 2014; Mbuva, 2014; Osika et al., 2009) was one of the reasons educators felt less comfortable to teach online. To facilitate the transition to online setting, educators need more support from the university to deliver effective online teaching, interact effectively with students, and keep their students motivated (Huang, 2020). When academics are not equipped technically to handle developments of materials and to deliver online modules, they are hampering progress, and they require extensive skills development (Ellis et al., 1998).

In summary, online education places high demands on both educators and students. Educators are expected to utilize effective instructional strategies for online teaching as well as to understand the group dynamics with individual needs and to facilitate educator-student and student-student communication (Loveless, 2011; Turvey, 2008). On the other hand, students are required to be proactive and independent, to become more self-disciplined and to manage their time effectively (Huang, 2020).

Benefits of Online Teaching and Learning

One of the obvious benefits of online education is that it breaks down geographical and social boundaries (Chen & Yang, 2006). As Islam et al., (2015) stated, "The rise of e-learning technology used by higher education institutions can be attributed to globalisation" (p. 102). In a globalized economy, and with the help of computing technology, it is becoming increasingly easy to teach audiences in different countries from the comfort of your home. Educators teach, attend professional development opportunities, present at conferences, and confer with colleagues from different states or countries from home.

When discussing the benefits of online instruction, Donitsa-Schmidt and Ramot (2020) focused on the creation of a community of learners in a college of education. Educators attended their colleagues' classes and invited other educators to observe their lessons. Lesson recordings and recordings of guest speakers' lectures became public. Many educators became part of professional learning communities, engaging in conversations about their courses and learning from one another: "Paradoxically, a period of social distancing and self-quarantine led to increased peer collaboration, shared learning and mutual aid" (p. 8).

Another benefit was the re-vamping of assessment techniques that were expected to be in sync with the online teaching (Donitsa-Schmidt & Ramot, 2020). Not being able to rely on the paper-and-pencil tests, educators designed assignments that enabled the students to create podcasts, write blogs, produce interactive digital posters, collate portfolios, etc. In addition, Huang (2020) believed that the greatest benefit for students were the lecture recordings via online teaching software. Unlike the traditional classes, where students attend the educator's lecture in real time, students have access to the online lectures after class ends. Moreover, these recordings capture the teacher's PowerPoint presentation as well as class discussions and student participation (Huang, 2020). In addition, these recordings benefit the students who missed class or were struggling with internet access. These students can follow the lecture at their own pace, without feeling disconnected from instruction.

In conclusion, online teaching and learning offer flexibility and convenience (Huang, 2020), enabling the students to stay in the loop and learn at their own pace. In a similar vein, Islam et al. (2015) argued that flexibility, expediency to learners, and opportunities for innovative teaching were among the most notable benefits of online teaching and learning. In addition, some researchers believed online learning to be superior to face-to-face instruction, allowing for higher student engagement (Hardaker & Singh, 2011; Macharia & Pelser, 2012), high quality interaction, and timely feedback (Chen & Yang, 2006). In essence, educators believed that they worked harder than ever before to ensure successful online experiences for their students (Donitsa-Schmidt & Ramot, 2020).

MAIN FOCUS OF THE CHAPTER

The Context of the Study

The first author, faculty in the College of Education at a mid-sized university in the southeastern United States, has been teaching face-to-face education classes for the past twelve years. Mid-March, with six weeks left of the semester, COVID-19 interrupted instruction and all classes were transitioned online. Having little experience with online teaching, and in an attempt to not overwhelm the students, the instructor finished the semester asynchronously, as some students relocated and had poor or no internet access. In the summer, the instructor taught one section of the Classroom Management course as distance learning (hereon DL). This was the first time in the last fifteen years the instructor taught a DL course, and she used Canvas to teach and to communicate with the students. Both the instructor and the students struggled with this format, mainly because of the lack of direct communication, which was enhanced by the students' busy schedules, and an overall poor attendance of the weekly office hours. These challenges with asynchronous teaching led the instructor to switch to remote instruction (hereon RI) in the fall, when the instructor taught an undergraduate section of the Classroom Management and Communications course, and a graduate section of the Principles of Instruction course synchronously.

The Classroom Management course assisted preservice teachers in obtaining knowledge about classroom management in a collaborative setting and applying this knowledge in practical situations that affect the success of the classroom. In addition, in this course, preservice teachers developed skills to design and implement an effective classroom management program (a culminating assignment titled The Classroom Management Plan). The emphasis of this culturally responsive classroom management course was on the development of knowledge about the cultural backgrounds of students and families, congruent and nonverbal communication practices, culturally appropriate management strategies, and the creation of caring, respectful classroom communities that ensure the physical and emotional safety of all. Specifically, this course addressed the challenges and opportunities in creating effective learning communities in the increasingly diverse classrooms in U.S. public schools.

The Principles of Instruction provided a foundation for pedagogical and professional knowledge based upon research, thoughtful discussion, reflection and inquiry. Just like the undergraduate section, this course emphasized culturally responsive classroom management (see above). Furthermore, this course prepared teachers and teacher candidates to impact the lives of children by developing and writing goals and objectives, planning and implementing lessons that addressed the needs of a diverse student population, developing and presenting instructional models with the use of technology, utilizing effective verbal communications, and conceptualizing motivational strategies.

Methodology

This study employed the methodological process of action research. Action research is defined as "a cyclical research process that may be used to improve instructional practice, assessment tools, and student outcomes" (Lari et al., 2019, p. 23). It is a collaborative process in which educators collect data about their students' educational experience, they then analyze the data and implement changes. Researchers (Hendricks, 2008; Wennergren & Ronnerman, 2006) identified the following steps of action research studies: formulating questions, collecting data, reflecting, writing, revising, acting, and evaluating. Action research has primarily been employed in academic settings to facilitate improvement by garnering the perspectives of every group involved in the pedagogical process.

In this study, we solicited the perspective of two groups of students with regards to their experience with the online class taught in the Fall 2020 semester. Creating an egalitarian relationship in which students are co-investigators of their educational outcomes is empowering (Stern, 2019). In addition, student perspectives may "offer relevant inside views and refer to issues which might remain inaccessible or invisible" (Stern, 2019, p. 436). By consulting these multiple perspectives, we facilitated "a more comprehensive overall picture of a complex situation" (Stern, 2019, p. 435). As Slapac and Navarro (2011) concluded, action research can be transformative and powerful, as it encourages educators "to explicitly solicit feedback from students, to share power by opening up to new ways of teaching and learning, and to collaborate with others" (p. 423). Perhaps this is why this methodological approach requires an openness on the part of educators; as they solicit feedback, educators need to accept critique and alter their methods if necessary (James & Augustin, 2018).

Action research puts the authors in the optimal position to hear and understand diverse issues being faced by their students, issues that typical research is less likely to uncover. These collaborative and empowering aspects of action research, between students and educators, lend a diverse perspective uniquely calculated to produce meaningful change. In this study, we considered and valued all student data, as the underlining goal were the positive changes made to the education outcomes to benefit both students and educator. The results generated by the student data resulted prompted the instructor to alter her practice (Guy et al., 2020).

The participants were six undergraduate students enrolled in the Classroom Management and Communications course, and ten graduate students enrolled in the Principles of Instruction and Classroom Management course offered remotely, in the Fall 2020 semester. The undergraduate participants were education majors and minors. The graduate participants were a mix of residents in their first year of teaching and international students, who had little teaching experience. Three teachers taught Exceptional Student Education, three Science, two English, and two Social Studies. To preserve participant anonymity, we used pseudonyms. When reporting the participant data, for clarification issues, we indicated whether the participant was undergraduate or graduate, by adding (UG) or (G) after their name. Age-wise, there were twelve females and four males of a mean age of twenty-nine. In terms of ethnicity, ten participants were Caucasians, one was Latinx, two were Asian, and three were Arabs. See Table 1 for the participant information.

Table 1. Participants

\multicolumn{5}{c	}{**Participants**}
Gender	Male: 4	Females: 12		
Ethnicity	Caucasians: 10	Arabs: 3	Latinx: 1	Asian: 2
Status	Graduate students: 10	Undergraduate students: 6		

The first author was also the class instructor. The second author, a Graduate Research Assistant (hereafter GRA), was involved in the data collection and the data analysis process. For data collection, the instructor devised two instruments: a survey and a demographic questionnaire. In the survey, the participants answered five open-ended questions discussing challenges and benefits of online learning, and suggested areas in which the instructor could improve the online teaching in the next semester. All the questions are included in Appendix 1. The authors used the demographic questionnaire to collect demographic data from participants (age, ethnicity, gender, major/minor). At the end of the Fall 2020 semester, the GRA administered and collected both instruments, in order to ensure the instructor did not have access to the data until the grades were posted. The following research questions guided the data collection in this qualitative study: 1) What are some challenges and benefits students have experienced in this class, as it pertains to online learning?; 2) What are some challenges and benefits the instructor has experienced with online teaching?; and 3) What changes can the instructor implement to improve the quality of online teaching in the next semester?

As discussed above, when using action research, educators should be open to critique and use this feedback to alter their methods if necessary. Consequently, the instructor identified her own challenges with online teaching, and discussed the accommodations she made when transitioning to online teaching. Data regarding the instructor's challenges with online teaching came from her personal notes while teaching in the Summer 2020 and Fall 2020 semesters. The instructor kept notes on the computer regarding her own challenges with teaching the DL summer class, as well as she reflected on the changes she implemented in the RI Fall classes in order to ensure a better experience in her future classes. These notes consisted of words and short sentences jotted down on the computer, and they came from her observations of the challenges encountered when teaching online classes. To analyze the data from personal notes, the instructor used content analysis to classify words that had similar meanings into categories (Cavanagh, 1997) with the aim "to attain a condensed and broad description of the phenomenon" (Elo & Kyngäs, 2008, p. 108).

Action research data are substantiated through triangulation (James & Augustin, 2018), a process undergone with multiple researchers, thereby upholding the quality of data analysis. For triangulation purposes, we first coded the data individually, then we discussed the similarities and inconsistencies in the categories, and finally reached a consensus about the data categories. To analyze the data from the student survey, we conducted a content analysis of the survey to identify the participants' challenges and positive experiences with online learning. While interpreting the data, we grouped the statements into categories, and further named these categories using content-characteristic words. To discover connections among the concepts, we analyzed the refined data sets from the participant surveys.

Three big themes emerged from the instructor's personal notes and the student survey: a) the participants' perceived challenges and benefits of online learning, b) the instructor's challenges with teaching online, and c) proposed changes to improve the quality of instruction for the next semester. We further

The Challenges and Benefits of Online Instruction

assigned the data from the three themes discussed above into four categories: 1) the participants' perceived challenges with online learning, 2) the participants' perceived benefits of online learning, 3) the participants' suggestions for improving online teaching in the next semester, and 4) the instructor's challenges in teaching online in the Fall 2020 semester and the changes made the next semester. Each category contained sub-categories. These categories and sub-categories are included in Table 2.

Table 2. Participant and instructor challenges with and benefits of online instruction

	Instructor		Participants	
Challenges with online instruction and changes made to new classes	*Challenges with DL* (Summer 2020) • Feeling disconnected from students • Misunderstandings with deadlines and assignment requirements *Changes made to teaching RI (Fall 2020)* • Switching to synchronous teaching • Posting deadlines under each assignment on Canvas • Breaking up big lectures in smaller chunks; stopping for Qs and As • Frequent break-out sessions (1-3/week) • Weekly office hours • Staying after class to talk to students	*Challenges with RI* (Fall 2020) • Technology issues • Weak presence on camera • Unprofessional behavior on camera • Time management (a lot of time spent after class with students) *Changes made to teaching RI (Spring 2021)* • Requiring a camera presence • Explaining etiquette for presence on camera	*Instructional challenges* (n = 8G + 2 UG) • Unclear deadlines and assignment requirements • Navigating Canvas • Staying focused • Less interaction with peers and instructor	*Personal challenges* (n = 4G + 3 UG) • Home distractions • Technology issues • Being on camera • Time management
Benefits of online instruction	*Benefits of teaching RI* • Stronger relationships with students • Few misunderstandings of assignments and deadlines		*Instructional benefits* (n = 5G + 3UG) • Improved communication with peers and instructor • Recorded lectures • Higher use of technology • Easiness to navigate Canvas	*Personal benefits* (n = 8G + 4UG) • Saving money and time • No driving • Flexibility with joining class • Comfort of home
Suggestions for improving online instruction			*Suggestions* (n = 7G + 4UG) • Incorporating more interactive activities • Making Canvas more user friendly	*No changes needed* (n = 1G + 1UG)

Participants' Perceived Challenges of Online Learning

Challenges with Online Learning

Participants struggled online for a variety of reasons. Some of these reasons were instructional, while others were of a personal nature.

Instructional Issues

While the instructor ensured all assignment requirements and deadlines were accurate by posting deadlines on Canvas under each individual assignment and including the due dates in the syllabus, one graduate participant found the deadlines unclear, while another graduate participant stated, "There were a few areas of confusion regarding requirements of assignments." On the other hand, despite the instructor's high level of organization, one graduate and one undergraduate participant indicated they had problems locating information on Canvas. For example, Jacob (UG) stated: "Another difficulty was finding information on canvas. Some classes are better organized than others, but occasionally I would find mention of an assignment, but could not find the document outlining expectations for the assignment." Although Jacob talks about classes in general, in a conversation with the instructor, he indicated he was not able to find information on an assignment. When checking, the instructor realized she did not upload that particular assignment.

Other participants faced challenges with online learning in general. Some found it more difficult to focus in an online class. For example, Miriam (G) wrote: "Online classes don't provide me with the mood of studying. It is hard for me to focus," while Wendy (G) explained that she found the online class more distracting, and she was not "focusing on the whole class." The loss of focus was due, in part, to the length of the class. The class met once a week at 4:30 pm, for two hours and forty-five minutes. As Mitchell (UG) explained, "At over two hours, it's difficult to maintain focus and control distractions during class, even with a break," and Mary (G) reflected: "Looking at a screen for so long is hard on the eyes and to stay focused." Andrea and Caroline, two other graduate students, shared similar concerns with the length of the class. Andrea found it "difficult at times to sit on a Zoom call for three hours after teaching all day," while Caroline explained that her biggest challenge with staring at a computer screen for multiple hours was due to her brain injury: "it's hard for me to stay engaged and stare at the computer screen for so long without getting tired and having a terrible headache."

In addition to the length of the class, some participants found the online session less interactive than face-to-face classes, despite the fact that the instructor utilized breakout sessions in every class, engaging the students in small group discussions. Samantha (G) commented on the fact that the class had little social interaction, while Claire (G) discussed the fact that there was "No true social interaction." Mary and Caroline, both graduate participants, felt that the format of the online classes in general lacked "the feeling of connectivity, organic conversation, and rich interaction between humans" (Mary), and it took away "the joy of human engagement and being around people physically" (Caroline). On the other hand, Samantha (G) and Wendy (G) mentioned that the online format made it harder to foster interaction with the instructor: "Online classes take more time for the professor and the student to understanding each other. The communication is harder than the face-to-face class," explained Wendy.

Overall, more graduate than undergraduate participants struggled with instructional issues. For example, eight graduate participants struggled in the following areas: unclear deadlines and assignment requirements (n=2); navigating Canvas (n=1), staying focused for a long time (n=5), and less interaction with peers and instructor (n=5), whereas two undergraduate participants only reported challenges with navigating Canvas (n=1) and staying focused (n=1).

Personal Challenges

One of the most common problems with online learning were home distractions. For example, Samantha (G) stated: "Being at home can be distracting, people coming in and out of the house, easier to pick up your phone to text," while Andrew (G) was "easily distracted by things in my house or household tasks that need to be done. That's why I prefer sitting in class or not doing schoolwork at home."

Other participants identified technology-related issues: "Technology does and will break down, and it isn't easy to learn when the internet keeps breaking in and out," reflected Andrew (G). Chloe (UG) also discussed the obstacles she experienced "due to having an older laptop. My Zoom would freeze, but not every class, and occasionally my computer would have an issue with the internet. But these challenges were minor and didn't cause me to miss any class."

Time management was another challenge, as Jacob (UG) explained: "The biggest hurdle for me was time management. Staying on top of what is due, especially for bigger projects was challenging for me." On the other hand, Wendy (G) felt uncomfortable being on camera: "seeing myself in the camera makes me uncomfortable, but if I turn my camera off, that may show that I'm not in class, which is embarrassing because the professor could think I am not in attendance," and Bridget (UG) found it "challenging to share my thoughts in a whole-class setting because I prefer sharing with a partner first."

Overall, seven participants discussed personal challenges. While the graduate participants struggled with home distractions (n=2), technology issues (n=1), and being on camera (n=1), undergraduate participants struggled with technology issues (n=1), being on camera (n=1), and time management (n=1).

Participants' Perceived Benefits of Online Learning

Participants discussed both the personal and professional benefits of online learning.

Instructional Benefits

When discussing the professional benefits of online instruction, five participants found the class interactive, and believed that the group work improved communication between students. Hope (G) stated, "I liked the Zoom class. I feel like being together is interacting and helpful," and Mitchell (UG) shared that "Dr. T.'s frequent use of breakout rooms effectively simulated in-class small group discussion, enabling students to learn from each other." Similarly, Madison (G) reflected on the difference between DL and RI, finding the latter more beneficial: "it improved communication between the teacher and students as well as among students, comparing to online only learning. We were able to do group discussions and presentations to a whole class via Zoom." Madison was the only participant who addressed how this format improved not only student-student, but also instructor-student communication. Moreover, Chloe (UG) stated that she liked the small breakout sessions, as she was able "to get to know a little bit about the other students who were in my class instead of just seeing their faces." Lastly, Victor (UG) believed that the instructor fostered a community resembling the traditional class: "Some teachers this semester, such as yourself, did that really well, creating the environment without the physicality of it, but others not so much, unfortunately."

Other participants reflected on the benefit of having recorded lessons they could watch, in case they missed class. For example, Mary (G) stated: "Having a recorded lesson means that you can go back and review, or if you miss a class you can go see it as well," and Samantha (G) commented: "Recorded lessons make it easy to go back and review a lecture." In addition, Caroline (G) thought that the "recording feature helps, as it allows one to watch the video if they had to miss class, for whatever reasons."

Chloe (UG) and Victor (UG) enjoyed the high use of technology of the class. Victor shared: "I also enjoyed the higher use of technology; I feel like half of my teachers did their best to learn a lot about using Zoom and Canvas and more, and for that, I am very grateful." On the other hand, while confessing that she preferred the traditional setting, Chloe stated that she "did gain confidence communicating with classmates through the computer."

Finally, two participants found Canvas easy to access. Madison (G) reflected: "I loved how the instructor organized all the contents such as assignments and lesson materials for better viewing and content clicking," and Victor (UG) believed that "it was very easy for me to check on assignments and view the requirements and just be more attentive. Seeing a clear organized schedule and the supplement of easily accessible resources as well were a huge help."

In total, five graduate and three undergraduate participants reflected on the instructional benefits of online learning, such as: improved communication between students through group work (n=2G and n=3UG), having the lectures recorded (n=3G); a higher use of technology (n=2UG); the easiness to access Canvas (n=1G and n=1UG), and improved communication with the instructor (n=1G).

Personal Benefits

The most common benefit, as discussed by most of the participants, was saving time and money by not driving to campus. For example, two graduate participants and three undergraduate participants talked about saving money by not paying for gas, parking, or food while out on campus, while another graduate participant saved money by not sending her baby to daycare. On the other hand, seven participants (four G and 3 UG) found online classes to save them time by cutting down travel. Some, like Wendy (G) and Andrew (G), had long drives to school. "It would have taken me four hours back and forth, because I don't live in this town," said Wendy, and Andrew reflected, "I didn't have to drive over an hour to and from campus and to be fatigued in class after work and a long drive". In addition, Victor (UG) appreciated only spending three hours in class, versus the whole day on campus: "It definitely saved me on gas money and time, just having to pop on the computer a couple hours each day rather than practically spending the day on campus. I thoroughly enjoyed this newfound efficiency of my schedule." Other participants talked about how travel time was better spent on working on assignments. For example, Samantha (G) explained that less time and resources spent on commuting meant "extra time to get things done at home," and Jacob (UG) commented that "The time spent driving and walking to class has been entirely eliminated, offering more time for study and preparation of assignments." Finally, Brooke (UG) was completely candid: "The only real benefits to me is saving gas, mileage, and travel time to the school. I hate to be a Debby downer, but I don't see much benefit."

Another benefit to online learning was its flexibility, as participants logged in from different locations. Caroline (G) said: "One of the few benefits of online learning is that you can access the class anywhere. So, if I had an inconvenient situation or an emergency came up, I would still be able to log on and be in class." Jacob (UG) also discussed how he enjoyed "the flexibility of doing homework in local coffee shops." This flexibility enabled participants to attend class even when feeling sick, like Brooke (UG) commented: "You can attend class even if you are ill and you won't get anyone else sick!" In addition, Wendy (G) liked this format, as she felt "freer to eat and drink during the online class."

Five participants (three G and two UG) also discussed the practicality of the online learning, as they enjoyed being in the comfort of their home. Jacob (UG) commented: "I enjoy building a comfortable learning environment in my own home," and Claire (G) shared that she enjoyed the comfort of her home, "In my own space, I set up everything on my kitchen table. I like to spread out all my papers and books." Andrea (G) commented on the positive of working from home, which allowed her brain "to destress from the workday and I didn't feel like I was constantly on the go, going from work to class, and getting home late at night from UNF."

Overall, eight graduate and four undergraduate participants reported personal benefits of online learning, such as: saving time and money (n=3G and n=3UG), not having to drive and using that time on assignments (n=5G and n=4UG); flexibility with attending class from anywhere (n=2G and n=2UG); and the comfort of learning from your own home (n=3G and n=2UG).

Suggestions for Improving Online Learning

When discussing improvements for the following semester, five graduate and two undergraduate participants recommended the class be more interactive, and the instructor use more discussion boards, breakout rooms, and interactive programs. For example, Hope (G) suggested the instructor change "some assignments to a discussion board so that students can benefit from their friends' experiences in dealing with school situations," while Claire (G) recommended more breakout rooms, as a "small environment is easier to participate in." Similarly, Mary (G) suggested the use of "online polls and questioning to make sure students are engaged," while Bridget (UG) suggested incorporating videos and interactive activities, if the class continued to be taught for three hours. Andrew's (G) recommendation was the instructor use programs "like pear deck, near pod, drag and drops assignments, to make the course more engaging. I use these programs and creative assignments in my class to engage the students." And while some participants had trouble being engaged for three hours, Mitchell (UG) suggested the class met twice a week.

A few other participants recommended the instructor make Canvas more user friendly and maintain all documents updated. Samantha (G) suggested: "Having very clear calendars and making Canvas more user friendly, helps to stay on track while virtual," while Jacob (UG) reflected:

Organize the online format of everything. Making sure important documents are easy to find and clearly labeled. The professor did a good job with this, but I believe there is always room for improvement. A master document of assignment expectations may be nice for students to refer to rather than referring to an individual document for each task.

In addition, Madison (G) stated:

It would be great if the instructor kept all the related document and announcements updated as the semester moves on. For example, the changes occurred as we made adjustments to our weekly schedule should be reflected on the syllabus, so students can accurately refer them for due dates or activities. For online learning, accurate, explicit and up to date sharing of information is the key for students to follow the track.

Lastly, two participants were satisfied with the layout of the course, and they did not suggest any changes. Miriam (G) stated: "I think Dr. T. did a great job in this course, so I don't think anything needs to change," and Chloe (UG) suggested the instructor continue to teach synchronously and include breakouts sessions.

In conclusion, seven graduate and four undergraduate participants provided suggestions on how the instructor can improve the class, such as: incorporating more interactive activities (n=5G and n=2UG), making Canvas more user friendly (n=2G and n=1UG). Two participants (n=1G and n=1UG) believed the instructor did not need to change anything.

Instructor Perceived Challenges and Benefits of Online Teaching

All the instructor data come from the instructor's notes from teaching online in the summer and fall 2020 semesters. After the Spring Break, the instructor transitioned to online teaching, feeling somewhat unprepared for not having taught online classes in the past fifteen years. The instructor finished the last six weeks of the semester online, without facing too many challenges.

Challenges with Distance Learning

The DL undergraduate course the instructor taught in the summer proved problematic for a variety of reasons. Firstly, as the course was asynchronous, the instructor did not meet the students, the only interaction being through emails and discussion boards. Because of this general lack of communication, the instructor struggled to develop meaningful relationships with students, as she would in face-to-face classes. Despite the fact that the instructor had weekly office hours, few students attended those. Overall, the instructor finished the course feeling that she did not get to know her students well.

Another significant challenge were several misunderstandings related to assignments requirements and deadlines. Every Monday morning, the instructor uploaded assignments and lectures on Canvas. All assignments were due on Sunday afternoons. In order to facilitate understanding and to establish online presence, the instructor created videos for each major assignment, walking the students through the requirements of the assignments. In addition, every Monday morning, the instructor created a 5-minute video announcement, reminding the students about the assignments and readings due that week. This short announcement was followed by a written announcement, containing the same information. Lastly, the syllabus contained all this information. While the instructor felt that her course expectations were transparent and clear, misunderstandings happened frequently. These misunderstandings were due in part, to the fact that students did not familiarize themselves with the syllabus (requirements and/or deadlines). In addition, since the instructor did not meet with the students, she could only communicate important information through announcements. However, this proved ineffective in some cases, as students did not watch the introductory videos or read the weekly announcements. Yet another factor that led to misunderstandings was the fact that not all Canvas assignments had deadlines (due dates, available from/to), although all these deadlines were listed in the syllabus and mentioned in the weekly announcements.

Lastly, the first author experienced with a general feeling of disconnect with students (enhanced by the lack of communication), and a weak knowledge of the students, as a result of not meeting the students weekly. This disconnect also transpired in the student-student interactions, as the instructor felt somewhat unsuccessful in developing a community of learners, given that the students only communicated with each other once a week through the discussion boards. In addition, the instructor implemented only a few group work assignments. More such projects would have allowed students to bond more.

Transitioning to Remote Instruction: Changes and Benefits

Given these considerable challenges, the instructor made some changes in teaching the same class in the following semester. Perhaps the most important change was switching to RI, which enabled her to meet

The Challenges and Benefits of Online Instruction

students every week at a predetermined day/time. The instructor emphasized course attendance, discussing the penalties for missing classes. Class attendance and participation in discussions have always been a part of the course requirements, but they were difficult to implement in the DL course. Attendance and participation provided for rich discussions, enabling students to ask questions, and ensuring they develop misunderstandings. In addition, all class sessions were recorded, allowing the students to catch up in their own time.

Equally significant, all Canvas assignments had listed deadlines (due dates, open from/to) to prevent misunderstandings. Consequently, few students were late with assignments. In the live sessions, the instructor broke down the lectures into 20-minute chunks, stopping for questions and comments to gauge student understanding. This was a change from the summer course, when some of the recorded lectures reached forty minutes.

To boost student-student interaction, the instructor engaged students weekly in break-out sessions, allowing them to get to know each other in a small group format (4-5 students/group). This also enabled shy students to contribute to the discussion, as some are more reluctant to open up in front of 30+ students. In these break-out groups, students responded to prompts, questions, or scenarios assigned by the instructor, and then shared their group's answers with the whole class. These breakout sessions lasted 5-15 minutes; the instructor visited each group for 1-2 minutes to answer questions and establish presence. In addition to these breakout sessions, the instructor assigned a few group projects outside of class, being mindful of the students' busy schedules. Lastly, to boost instructor-student interaction, the instructor held weekly office hours. While not all students attended office hours, some stopped by, enabling the instructor to get to know them on an individual level. In addition, quite a few students stayed after class to ask questions and chat with the instructor.

Overall, the instructor was pleased with the RI experience in the fall semester, as she felt that she bonded better with her students, and that she developed a community of learners. Overall, there were very few misunderstandings about assignments and deadlines, as the instructor explained the assignments and reminded the students about the deadlines in each class, and answered any questions at the end of every class. In addition, there was a noticeable difference in the quality of assignments in the fall semester, when compared to the summer semester.

In spite of all the changes and the many positive experiences, there were still a few challenges with online teaching in the fall semester. Because all class sessions were live, at given times throughout the semester both the instructor and the students experienced the inevitable internet issues. When the students experienced internet/connection issues, the instructor did not penalize them for missing parts of the class. Most students let the instructor know as soon as they connected again that they experienced internet issues.

In addition to internet issues, the instructor did not enforce a camera presence in the syllabus, so throughout the semester, some students were constantly off camera. While most of them were present, contributing to class discussions and group projects, others took advantage of being off camera and occasionally disappeared, missing the breakout sessions. One undergraduate participant logged in and out after an hour of class. When this behavior became a pattern, the instructor reached out to the student, and the student apologized and attended all classes through the end of the semester.

Lastly, the instructor noticed a decreased level of professionalism for some students who had their cameras on. Pets and children got in the way at times; children would come ask their parents for things, and pets would jump on the beds, desks, or tables, distracting the students. In addition, some students got comfortable, snuggling in bed with their blankets. Although the instructor reminded the students to remain professional in dress, talk, and class behavior, these reminders were sometimes disregarded. In general, the positive aspects overpowered the challenges in the fall semester. Given the improved experience with the RI in the fall semester, the instructor felt confident that the spring semester would be even more successful.

SOLUTIONS AND RECOMMENDATIONS TO IMPROVE ONLINE TEACHING AND LEARNING

The instructor experienced some foreseeable challenges with the online teaching. Most of these challenges were not unique, such as students having internet connection issues, which obstructed course attendance (Assunção & Gago, 2020; Rajab et al., 2020; Zhang et al., 2020). In addition, at times online teaching felt like a sub-par-learning experience, as some students were distracted, others made themselves comfortable, perhaps forgetting they were in class, and yet others were not present on camera (Donitsa-Schmidt & Ramot, 2020; Huang, 2020). While the instructor could not prevent technical difficulties from happening, one solution and future teaching recommendation in order to improve student online (professional) presence is to implement the following course expectations in the spring semester: students should be on camera at all times, students should find a place where they will not be disturbed by pets and/or children, they should sit down at a desk/table, and they should mute themselves until they want to share their thoughts with the class.

Another challenge generally experienced in teaching online is adjusting face-to-face content to meet the online environment, which requires a different pedagogical approach (Choi & Park, 2006; Islam et al., 2015). Teaching online does not mean transferring face-to-face content to the internet (Huang, 2020), and providing classes dense in information, but scarce in interaction (Leask, 2004). In this respect, the instructor felt the summer class was quite dense in information and scarce in interaction, a challenge posed, in fact, by the format of the DL course. To foster more interaction in the fall class, the instructor provided more opportunities for students to interact with each other and the instructor, and chunked lectures into 20-minute sessions. In addition, some assignments posed challenges when transferred to the online environment, as they were not online friendly (such as doing teaching presentations). Consequently, some of these assignments suffered gentle modifications to meet the online requirements (Donitsa-Schmidt & Ramot, 2020). For example, the instructor allowed the students to record some assignments and present them to class.

The instructor also struggled with time management. Researchers (Clark 2001; Cornelius & Macdonald, 2008) have long addressed the difficulties educators faced when managing their time online, as students generally expect immediate replies (Gustafson & Gibbs, 2010). While the instructor managed her time better in the discussion boards (responding to a few students a week), the after-class conversations became lengthy, extending at times for an hour. The instructor ultimately saw this challenge as a benefit, which improved instructor-student interaction.

Perhaps the most significant challenge was a weak interaction with the students in the DL class, which was not conducive to developing strong relationships and to getting to understand the individual student needs. This challenge was also reported by Turvey (2008) and Loveless (2011), who discussed the need for the instructors to understand the group dynamics with individual needs. To remedy this challenge, in the fall semester the instructor established a strong online presence (teaching a weekly class, having office hours, and staying after class with students).

The Challenges and Benefits of Online Instruction

In addition, to foster a stronger student-student interaction, the instructor implemented weekly breakout sessions and assigned students to work on projects outside of class, which fostered student accountability and pushed students to meet expectations (Huang, 2020). Some participants enjoyed the interactive approach of the class, which helped improve student-student and student-instructor communication (Hardaker & Singh, 2011; Macharia & Pelser, 2012), and fostered a community of learners, similar to that of traditional classes (Hardaker & Singh, 2011; Macharia & Pelser, 2012). However, one participant felt there was no true social interaction, in spite of instructor's repeated use of the breakout sessions.

One last reported challenge was the misunderstandings with assignments/deadlines in the summer class, due to the fact that some assignments did not have listed deadlines in Canvas. To remedy this for the fall semester, the instructor listed all the deadlines on Canvas and the syllabus, reminding students at the end of each class what readings and assignments were coming due. As a result, very few students missed deadlines, and the quality of the assignments improved. To ensure that students would not be confused by the course organization on Canvas, in the fall semester, the instructor walked the students through Canvas, showing them where to find course related materials. As a stark contradiction, while some participants were still confused with Canvas layout and documents, others found the platform easy to navigate.

FUTURE RESEARCH DIRECTIONS

Given the challenges addressed above, the instructor's lack of preparation with teaching online classes was obvious. The instructor had not taught an online course in fifteen years, which reflected in the frequent misunderstandings, leaving the instructor feeling inadequately prepared to teach the DL class. On the other hand, right before the pandemic, the instructor underwent some minor training for teaching online (eight class sessions). The findings reflect, however, that this training did little to prepare the instructor for the online transition. This lack of preparation, coupled with the hasty transition to the online environment, and the stress of the pandemic, made for a rather unsuccessful first experience with teaching online classes. Undergoing more training with online teaching might have created a better first experience with online teaching for the instructor.

From this perspective, future studies could investigate what training different institutions of higher education offer their faculty to help them successfully teach online. The researchers can, for examples, look at the different classes offered by institutions of higher education, analyzing content of the training, contact hours, as well as faculty satisfaction with the training and level of preparedness. In addition, researchers could analyze different training opportunities conducted at different institutions since the pandemic began, to account for how faculty and staff were supported throughout these challenging times, as well as account for faculty satisfaction with these trainings and their level of preparedness to teach online.

CONCLUSION

Conducting action research (Guy et al., 2019; Lari et al., 2019) enables educators to reflect on what worked and what did not work, and improve their learning experience for future students. This action research study enabled the instructor to analyze her practice by reflecting on the challenges she encountered when teaching the DL class in the summer. Some of these challenges were due, in part to the nature of the DL course, such as: frequent miscommunications regarding assignments and deadlines, a general disconnect from students, and a weak student-student interaction. This analysis informed the changes she made in the Fall, in order to eliminate or decrease some of these challenges. The biggest change spurred by this reflection on practice was the transition to the RI format in the Fall, which enabled the instructor to bond with her students more, and to increase the amount of student-student interaction both in class, and for out of class projects.

Perhaps the most important part of this study was inviting student perspectives. Through her students' lenses, the instructor identified her students' personal challenges with online learning, as well as the challenges that directly related to the Fall RI class. In this study, student perspectives offered "relevant inside views" (Stern, 2019, p. 436). When coupled with the instructor's perspective, the student perspectives offered a comprehensive understanding of challenges in the online environment (Stern, 2019).

When conducting action research, educators alter their practice after analyzing student data (Guy et al., 2020). The student data gathered informed the instructor that in spite of the changes implemented in the Fall RI class, students continued to face some challenges: such limited student-student and student-instructor interaction, confusion with deadlines and assignment requirements. This indicated a need for the instructor to continue to *reflect on her practice, in an attempt to make changes to the instruction and content of her classes* for the Spring 2021 semester. In conclusion, the use of action research in educational settings allows educators and students to collaboratively improve their interactions and learning outcomes. By consulting stakeholders at every level of the educational experience, diverse and unknown perspectives are revealed, education is democratized, and beneficial modifications are made.

ACKNOWLEDGMENT

This research received no specific grant from any funding agency in the public, commercial, or not-for-profit sectors.

REFERENCES

Assunção Flores, M., & Gago, M. (2020). Teacher education in times of COVID-19 pandemic in Portugal: National, institutional and pedagogical responses. *Journal of Education for Teaching*, *46*(4), 1–10. doi:10.1080/02607476.2020.1799709

Bakker, A., & Wagner, D. (2020). Pandemic: Lessons for today and tomorrow? *Educational Studies in Mathematics*, *104*(1), 1–4. doi:10.100710649-020-09946-3

Barr, B., & Miller, S. (2013). *Higher education: The online teaching and learning experience*. files.eric.ed.gov/fulltext/ED543912.pdf

Bender, L. (2020). *Key messages and actions for COVID-19 prevention and control in schools*. Unicef Romania. https://www.unicef.org/romania/documents/key-messages-and-actions-covid-19-prevention-and-control-schools

Brooks, S. K., Webster, R. K., Smith, L. E., Woodland, L., Wessely, S., Greenberg, N., & Rubin, G. J. (2020). The psychological impact of quarantine and how to reduce it: Rapid review of the evidence. *Lancet*, *395*(10227), 912–920. doi:10.1016/S0140-6736(20)30460-8 PMID:32112714

Burd, B. A., & Buchanan, L. E. (2004). Teaching the teachers: Teaching and learning online. *RSR. Reference Services Review*, *32*(4), 404–412. doi:10.1108/00907320410569761

Cavanagh, S. (1997). Content analysis: Concepts, methods and applications. *Nurse Researcher*, *4*(3), 5–16. doi:10.7748/nr.4.3.5.s2 PMID:27285770

Chang, C., Shen, H.-Y., & Liu, E. Z.-F. (2014). University faculty's perspectives on the roles of E-instructors and their online instruction practice. *The International Review of Research in Open and Distributed Learning*, *15*(3), 72–92. doi:10.19173/irrodl.v15i3.1654

Chen, C. C., & Yang, S. C. (2006). The efficacy of online cooperative learning systems, the perspective of task-technology fit. *Campus-Wide Information Systems*, *23*(3), 112–127. doi:10.1108/10650740610674139

Choi, H. J., & Park, J. (2006). Difficulties that a novice online instructor faced: A case study. *Quarterly Review of Distance Education*, *7*, 317–322. https://www.learntechlib.org/p/106761/

Clark, J. (2001). Stimulating collaboration and discussion in online learning environments. *The Internet and Higher Education*, *4*(2), 119–124. doi:10.1016/S1096-7516(01)00054-9

Coppola, N. W., Hiltz, S. R., & Rotter, N. (2001). Becoming a virtual professor: Pedagogical roles and ALN. *Proceedings of the 34th Annual Hawaii International Conference on System Sciences*. 10.1109/HICSS.2001.926183

Cornelius, S., & Macdonald, J. (2008). Online informal professional development for distance tutors: Experiences from The Open University in Scotland. *Open Learning*, *23*(1), 43–55. doi:10.1080/02680510701815319

Davidson, N., & Major, C. H. (2014). Boundary crossings: Cooperative learning, and problem-based learning. *Journal on Excellence in College Teaching*, *25*(3–4), 7–55.

Donahue, N., & Glodstein, S. (2013). Mentoring the needs of nontraditional students. *Teaching and Learning in Nursing*, *8*(1), 2–3. doi:10.1016/j.teln.2012.07.003

Donitsa-Schmidt, S., & Ramot, R. (2020). Opportunities and challenges: Teacher education in Israel in the Covid-19 pandemic. *Journal of Education for Teaching*, *46*(4), 1–10. doi:10.1080/02607476.2020.1799708

Ellis, A., O'Reilly, M., & Debreceny, R. (1998). *Staff development responses to the demand for online teaching and learning*. Southern Cross University. http://epubs.scu.edu.au/tlc_pubs/39/

Elo, S., & Kyngäs, H. (2008). The qualitative content analysis process. *Journal of Advanced Nursing*, *62*(1), 107–115. doi:10.1111/j.1365-2648.2007.04569.x PMID:18352969

Erduran, S. (2020). Science education in the era of a pandemic: How can history, philosophy and sociology of science contribute to education for understanding and solving the Covid-19 crisis? *Science and Education*, *29*(2), 233–235. doi:10.100711191-020-00122-w PMID:32292244

Folley, D. (2010). The lecture is dead long live the e-lecture. *Electronic Journal of e-Learning, 8*(2), 93-100.

Gustafson, P., & Gibbs, D. (2000). Guiding or hiding? The role of the facilitator in online teaching and learning. *Teaching Education, 11*(2), 195–210. doi:10.1080/713698967

Guy, B., Feldman, T., Cain, C., Leesman, L., & Hood, C. (2020). Defining and navigating 'action' in a participatory action research project. *Educational Action Research, 28*(1), 142–153. doi:10.1080/09650792.2019.1675524

Hardaker, G., & Singh, G. (2011). The adoption and diffusion of e-learning in UK universities: A comparative case study using Giddens's theory of structuration. *Campus-Wide Information Systems, 28*(4), 221–233. doi:10.1108/10650741111162707

Hendricks, C. (2008). *Improving schools through action research: A comprehensive guide for educators* (2nd ed.). Pearson.

Huang, J. (2020). Successes and challenges: Online teaching and learning of chemistry in higher education in China in the time of COVID-19. *Journal of Chemical Education, 97*(9), 2810–2814. doi:10.1021/acs.jchemed.0c00671

Islam, N., Beer, M., & Slack, F. (2015). E-learning challenges faced by academics in higher education. *Journal of Education and Training Studies, 3*(5), 102–112. doi:10.11114/jets.v3i5.947

James, F., & Augustin, D. S. (2018). Improving teachers' pedagogical and instructional practice through action research: Potential and problems. *Educational Action Research, 26*(2), 333–348. doi:10.1080/09650792.2017.1332655

Karademir, A., Yaman, F., & Saatçioğlu, O. (2020). Challenges of higher education institutions against COVID-19: The case of Turkey. *Journal of Pedagogical Research*, 1-22. doi:10.33902/JPR.2020063574

Kebritchy, M., Lipschuetz, A., & Santiague, L. (2017). Issues and challenges for teaching successful online courses in higher education: A literature review. *Journal of Educational Technology Systems, 46*(1), 4–29. doi:10.1177/0047239516661713

Lari, P., Rose, A., Ernst, J. V., Clark, A. C., Kelly, D. P., & DeLuca, V. W. (2019). Action research. *Technology & Engineering Teacher, 79*(2), 23–27.

Leask, B. (2004). Internationalisation outcomes for all students using information and communication technologies (ICTs). *Journal of Studies in International Education, 8*(4), 336–351. doi:10.1177/1028315303261778

Loveless, A. (2011). Technology, pedagogy and education: Reflections on the accomplishment of what teachers know, do and believe in a digital age. *Technology, Pedagogy and Education, 20*(3), 301–316. doi:10.1080/1475939X.2011.610931

Macharia, J. K., & Pelser, T. G. (2012). Key factors that influence the diffusion and infusion of information and communication technologies in Kenyan higher education. *Studies in Higher Education, 39*(4), 1–15. doi:10.1080/03075079.2012.729033

Mayes, R., Luebeck, J., Yu Ku, H., Akarasriworn, C., & Korkmaz, O. (2011). Themes and strategies for transformative online instruction. *Quarterly Review of Distance Education*, *12*(3), 51–166.

Mbuva, J. M. (2014). Online education: Progress and prospects. *Journal of Business and Educational Leadership*, *5*(1), 91–101.

Meng, L., Hua, F., & Bian, Z. (2020). Coronavirus Disease 2019 (COVID-19): Emerging and future challenges for dental and oral medicine. *Journal of Dental Research*, *99*(5), 481–487. doi:10.1177/0022034520914246 PMID:32162995

Nandi, D., Hamilton, M., Chang, S., & Balbo, S. (2012). Evaluating quality in online asynchronous interactions between students and discussion facilitators. *Australasian Journal of Educational Technology*, *28*(4), 684–702. doi:10.14742/ajet.835

Osika, E. R., Johnson, R. Y., & Buteau, R. (2009). Factors influencing faculty use of technology in online instructions: A case study. *Online Journal of Distance Learning Administration*, *12*, •••. https://www.westga.edu/_distance/ojdla/spring121/osika121.html

Phipps, R., & Merisotis, J. (1999). What's the difference: A review of contemporary research on the effectiveness of distance learning in higher education. *Journal of Distance Education*, *14*(1), 102–114.

Rajab, M. H., Gazal, A. M., & Alkattan, K. (2020). Challenges to online medical education during the COVID-19 pandemic. *Cureus*, *12*(7), 1–11. doi:10.7759/cureus.8966 PMID:32766008

Reeder, K., Macfadyen, L. P., Chase, M., & Roche, J. (2004). Negotiating culture in cyberspace: Participation patterns and problematics. *Language Learning & Technology*, *8*(2), 88–105.

Slapac, A., & Navarro, V. (2011). Shaping action researchers through a Master's capstone experience. *Teacher Education and Practice*, *24*(4), 405–426.

Stern, T. (2019). Participatory action research and the challenges of knowledge democracy. *Educational Action Research*, *27*(3), 435–451. doi:10.1080/09650792.2019.1618722

Toquero, C. M. (2020). Challenges and opportunities for higher education amid the COVID-19 pandemic: The Philippine context. *Pedagogical Research*, *5*(4), em0063. Advance online publication. doi:10.29333/pr/7947

Turvey, K. (2008). Student teachers go online; the need for a focus on human agency and pedagogy in learning about 'e-learning' in initial teacher education (ITE). *Education and Information Technologies*, *13*(10), 317–327. doi:10.100710639-008-9072-x

UNESCO. (2020). *How to plan distance learning solutions during temporary schools closures*. https://en.unesco.org/news/covid-19-10-recommendations-plan-distance-learning-solutions

Wang, C., Horby, P. W., Hayden, F. G., & Ga, G. F. (2020). A novel coronavirus outbreak of global health concern. *Lancet*, *395*(10223), 470–473. doi:10.1016/S0140-6736(20)30185-9 PMID:31986257

Wang, C., Pan, R., Wan, X., Tan, Y., Xu, L., Ho, C. S., & Ho, R. C. (2020). Immediate psychological responses and associated factors during the initial stage of the 2019 coronavirus disease (COVID-19) epidemic among the general population in China. *International Journal of Environmental Research and Public Health*, *17*(5), 1729. Advance online publication. doi:10.3390/ijerph17051729 PMID:32155789

Wang, G., Zhang, Y., Zhao, J., Zhang, J., & Jiang, F. (2020). Mitigate the effects of home confinement on children during the COVID-19 outbreak. *Lancet*, *395*(10228), 945–947. doi:10.1016/S0140-6736(20)30547-X PMID:32145186

Wennergren, A., & Ronnerman, K. (2006). The relation between tools used in action research and the zone of proximal development. *Educational Action Research*, *14*(4), 547–568. doi:10.1080/09650790600975791

Zhang, W., Wang, Y., Yang, L., & Wang, C. (2020). Suspending classes without stopping learning: China's education emergency management policy in the COVID-19 outbreak. *Journal of Risk and Financial Management*, *13*(3), 55–61. doi:10.3390/jrfm13030055

ADDITIONAL READING

Allen, L., Kiser, B., & Owens, M. (2013). Developing and refining the online course: Moving from ordinary to exemplary. In R. McBride & M. Searson (Eds.), Proceedings of society for information technology & teacher education international conference 2013. (pp. 2528–2533). Chesapeake, VA: Association for the Advancement of Computing in Education (AACE).

Almala, A. H. (2005). A constructivist conceptual framework for a quality e-learning environment. *Distance Learning*, *2*, 9–12.

Baran, E., Correia, A., & Thompson, A. (2011). Transforming online teaching practice: Critical analysis of the literature on the roles and competencies of online teachers. *Distance Education*, *32*(3), 421–439. doi:10.1080/01587919.2011.610293

Broszik, D., & Zapalska, A. (2006). Learning styles and online education. *Campus-Wide Information Systems*, *23*(5), 325–335. doi:10.1108/10650740610714080

Cavanaugh, J. (2005). Teaching online – A time comparison. *Online Journal of Distance Learning Administration*, *8*, 1–9.

Conrad, D. (2004). University instructor's reflections on their first online teaching experience. *JALN*, *8*(2), 31–44.

Hathaway, K. L. (2013). An application of the seven principles of good practice to online courses. *Research in Higher Education*, *22*, 1–13.

Jacobs, P. (2014). Engaging students in online courses. *Research in Higher Education*, *26*, •••. https://files.eric.ed.gov/fulltext/EJ1055325.pdf

Miller, M. D. (2014). *Minds online: Teaching effectively with technology*. Harvard University Press. doi:10.4159/harvard.9780674735996

Tanis, C. J. (2020). The seven principles of online learning: Feedback from faculty and alumni on its importance for teaching and learning. *Research in Learning Technology, 28*(0). Advance online publication. doi:10.25304/rlt.v28.2319

KEY TERMS AND DEFINITIONS

Action Research: Research conducted by educators in their own classes, collecting data about their students' educational experience, analyzing these data, and implementing changes in their practice and assessments as informed by their findings.

Breakout Sessions: Small group discussions used by educators to engage students in the online and face-to-face courses.

Canvas: A web-based platform used by students and educators to access and manage course materials for online and face-to-face classes.

Distance Learning: An asynchronous method of instruction where educators conduct teaching by sharing course materials on different educational platforms, without meeting formally.

Face-to-Face Instruction: A synchronous method of instruction where educators conduct teaching in a traditional class setting, meeting formally with students once or twice a week, on a predetermined course day/time.

Remote Instruction: A synchronous method of instruction where educators conduct teaching on different educational platforms, meeting formally with students once or twice a week, on a predetermined course day/time.

Zoom: An online platform used by people to communicate online to collaborate, hold meetings, hold classes, share documents.

Chapter 7
Online Teaching:
Taking Advantage of Complexity to See What We Did Not Notice Before

Anne Carr
Universidad del Azuay, Ecuador

Patricia Ortega-Chasi
https://orcid.org/0000-0003-4251-7588
Universidad del Azuay, Ecuador

Monica Martinez-Sojos
Universidad del Azuay, Ecuador

ABSTRACT

The purpose of this participatory action research study was to investigate if teaching in virtual spaces could offer the opportunity to exercise reflexivity and transform pedagogy by including new roles, modes of interaction, and authentic practice to increase connectivity with students. The study was conducted with a small convenience group of university teachers in a private university in the south of Ecuador. Data was triangulated through individual and group interviews, a specifically designed blog, and participation in three learning-teaching modules. Certain dialogic characteristics in the data demonstrate epistemological and pedagogical transformations. Short-term results show that the complexity of teaching in virtual spaces indicates more research is necessary on the role of professional development that focuses on both pedagogy, effective communication, and technical abilities with discipline content.

INTRODUCTION

The title of this paper involves the concept and practice of reflexivity, that is, the examination of university teachers' own beliefs, judgments and practices involving the questioning of their own taken for granted assumptions. Can the shift to online teaching be a potential opportunity for teachers to develop new ideas about teaching and learning to restructure traditional roles and relationships in the virtual classroom?

DOI: 10.4018/978-1-7998-6922-1.ch007

Faculty ranked redesign and rethinking of teacher roles as the most important aspect of professional development for online teaching as well as relatively difficult concept shifts regarding outcomes expected from learning and the directionality of teaching or content control (Samuelowicz, 2001). In a review of the adult education and faculty development literature and research to discover what is known about changes or transformation in teaching assumptions and beliefs when faculty prepare to teach online or when they are engaged in online teaching, McQuiggan (2009) identified framing faculty development within adult education and faculty development models as most important.

Borup and Evmenova (2019) identify two sets of barriers for professional development to achieve effective online teaching: the first is concerned with issues that are external to the teacher, such as the professional development available; and the second are internal such as teacher beliefs and attitudes. Teachers' perceptions of their roles may also impact their willingness to engage in professional development, "persons who saw their role as guides to learning were more likely to complete all of the faculty development modules than faculty who saw their role as providers of content" (Meyer, 2013, p.11). Baran and Correia (2014) highlighted that the lack of technology skills can impact teachers' ability to engage with aspects of online teaching such as student engagement. They suggest that technology support is required, particularly when they are transitioning from face-to face to online. Teachers with experience in using technology due to past practice had no difficulty in creating digital artefacts (Adnan, 2018). This was also reflected in the use of the VLE (Virtual Learning Environments) during a training program where those unfamiliar with Moodle took some time to grasp it (Adnan et al., 2017). Borup and Evmenova (2019) found that those teachers who were not ready with the technological skills had a deep learning curve and may not have benefited from the exposure to new tools as much as teachers who had prior experience. In addition, evaluating the impact of professional development Brinkley-Etzkorn (2018) noted that there are many ways to approach the evaluation of the impact of professional development but that they fall into two broad categories: 1. Beliefs, confidence, and attitudes; and 2. Teaching behaviors, abilities, and effectiveness. Using teacher perceptions of changes in knowledge and attitudes when evaluating the impact of a professional development program, Borup and Evmenova (2019) acknowledge the need to take observable measures of those changes.

Teacher professional development focuses on adult education which puts all the theory, research and literature in the field of adult education and its various principles, practices, strategies, and applications in the hands of developers. However, regarding technological infrastructure, some critique that online platforms that are often presented as "empty spaces for others to interact on" when as textually mediated literacies they are actually political and increasingly can "gain control and governance over the rules of the game" (Selwyn, 2015, p.47). For education, the collection of digital data through online education platforms has "raised concerns over power, control and performativity....reinforcing and intensifying the culture of managerialism within education" (p.72) with the potential risk of reducing teachers, students and their interactions to measurable data sets that increasingly shape educational processes, for example, standardization and competitiveness.

We were curious if an action research professional development model could intentionally provide activities to integrate what and how teachers were learning about online teaching to inform their teaching practice and how these activities might transform their assumptions and beliefs about teaching both online and face to face. The answers to these questions could inform university administrators and specialists in developing programs within an adult learning framework that support change opportunities to go beyond standardized plans.

The research questions that guided this research study included:

1. What aspects of professional development activities do teachers perceive to be most effective in helping them reflect on and question their assumptions and beliefs about teaching?
2. Have teachers experienced changes in their assumptions and beliefs in their practice as a result of online teaching?
3. What characteristics of teacher discussion and reflection are demonstrated when epistemological and pedagogical perspectives appear to transform?
4. Does transformative learning explain any changes?

BACKGROUND

The 2030 Agenda for sustainable development includes among its 17 goals, set out in 2015 to achieve a better and more sustainable future for all, quality education. This goal aims to ensure inclusive and equitable quality education and promote lifelong learning opportunities that touch on the social, humanistic, and moral purposes of education, explicitly linking education to other Sustainable Development Goals and capturing the new global development agenda's transformative aspirations (UNESCO, 2015).

Institutions of higher education have significant potential to prepare learners as global citizens with stamina, critical literacy, humility and self-reflexivity to face the complexities, tensions, and uncertainties that are inherent to any effort to address the challenges of contemporary, overlapping global issues rooted in "past and present colonial and imperialist processes" (Andreotti, 2011, p.307) that up to the present health pandemic, have been unprecedented in their scope, scale, and intensity. These factors place the spotlight on faculty and research about how global citizenship education can be responsive, rigorous, and relevant in the context of today's matrix of social, political, economic, health, and ecological challenges.

During 2020, COVID-19 complications have exacerbated the driving force for change in higher education teaching and changing the way we gather and share information, gain knowledge, do business, collaborate with communities, design and deliver instruction. Within the concept of sustainability are the effects that the university has both inside and outside of its organization or academic boundaries, on its stakeholders, the natural environment, the economy, and society in general, as well as activities that take place in education, research, outreach, campus operations, and campus experiences. Various factors including "mission, student population, faculty profile, geographic location, funding sources, level of resources and orientation to local, national and international interests" (Knight 2004, p.25) influence why and how a university contextualizes its role in sustainable development goals. The activities both inside and outside of the university can strengthen the ties between the university community and its environment, guiding them in unity towards the improvement of the quality of life, harmony with nature, the rescue of indigenous and ancestral customs, and the promotion of interculturality.

In this chapter, we discuss two research projects that illustrate the university's role both inside and outside of the university. The authors of the first research project collaboratively constructed an 'insider' (Herr & Anderson, 2004) participatory action research study involving four teachers, all of whom had graduate degrees (three masters' degrees and one doctorate) to investigate if online teaching could be a potential opportunity for them (and us as their peers) to reflect and develop new ideas about teaching and learning on and offline. This hermeneutic 'insider' collaboration with our peers was to increase our local knowledge base to improve and critique practices with a view to individual and organizational transformation of professional development (Heron, 1996).

The second project involved students who were in classes taught by the action research study teachers. The students' assignment was to teach basic English online to artisans for touristic purposes and to members of the local authority who sought strategies for the internationalization process required by UNESCO for their communities to collectively be named a "Creative City." Within this project, the students learning about online teaching and extending into participatory social advocacy did not occur in isolation, but in a continuous process within the same community members learning from each other as apprentices and from their expert teachers (Lave & Wenger, 1991).

FRAMEWORK AND LITERATURE REVIEW

Five key learning theories and frameworks, Technological Pedagogical Content Knowledge (TPACK), Communities of Practice Theory, Connectivism Theory, Situated Learning, and Threshold Concepts, provide the foundation to examine higher education teachers' questioning of their assumptions and ideas about teaching and learning to restructure traditional roles and relationships in the virtual classroom.

Technological Pedagogical Content Knowledge (TPACK)

Mishra and Koheler (2006) identified the specific knowledge required to effectively teach with technology, providing a conceptual model. The seven types of knowledge they have identified include Content Knowledge (CK), Pedagogical Knowledge (PK), Technology Knowledge (TK), Pedagogical Content Knowledge (PCK), Technological Content Knowledge, Technological Pedagogical Knowledge (TPK), and Technological Pedagogical Content Knowledge. Mishra and Koehler (2006) posit that learning environments are more effective when the teacher understands the interactions among these identified knowledges. Hence, the core of a meaningful learning experience is the balance of these types of knowledge.

The Technological, Pedagogical, and Content Knowledge (TPACK) framework enables teachers to consider how their knowledge of content, pedagogy and technology interact to enable them to develop effective teaching strategies. It provides a lens through which to examine effective online teaching (Mishra & Koehler, 2006). Additionally, it has been used as a framework to design professional development opportunities for teachers (Northcote et al., 2015). Brinkley-Etzkorn (2018) carried out a similar study of a professional development program for online teachers in a large U.S. university. Data was gathered from three sources: 1) student evaluations pre and post teacher professional development; 2) teacher course material and 3) a teacher completed survey one year after the professional development assessing their self-rated level of TPACK skills. While the student ratings had not changed significantly, the teachers' course materials demonstrated evidence of incorporation of the professional development training. Teachers rated their skill development higher in pedagogy than technology. The authors consider that this points to a lack of understanding of how technology and pedagogy are interrelated or that the TPACK framework is not reflective of the actual way educators learn to teach online (Brinkley-Etzkorn, 2018).

Community of Practice

Lave and Wenger (1991) were first to discuss the idea of a community of practice in educational terms. The benefits of these communities of practice are many, from providing mutual support to colleagues about frustrations they encounter in the online environment to sharing best practice (Baran & Correia,

2014). Wenger's (1998) Communities of Practice theory provides insight to understand adults' learning in terms of participation in practices and identity.

Figure 1. Technological, pedagogical content knowledge (Mishra & Koehler, 2011)
Source: http://tpack.org/

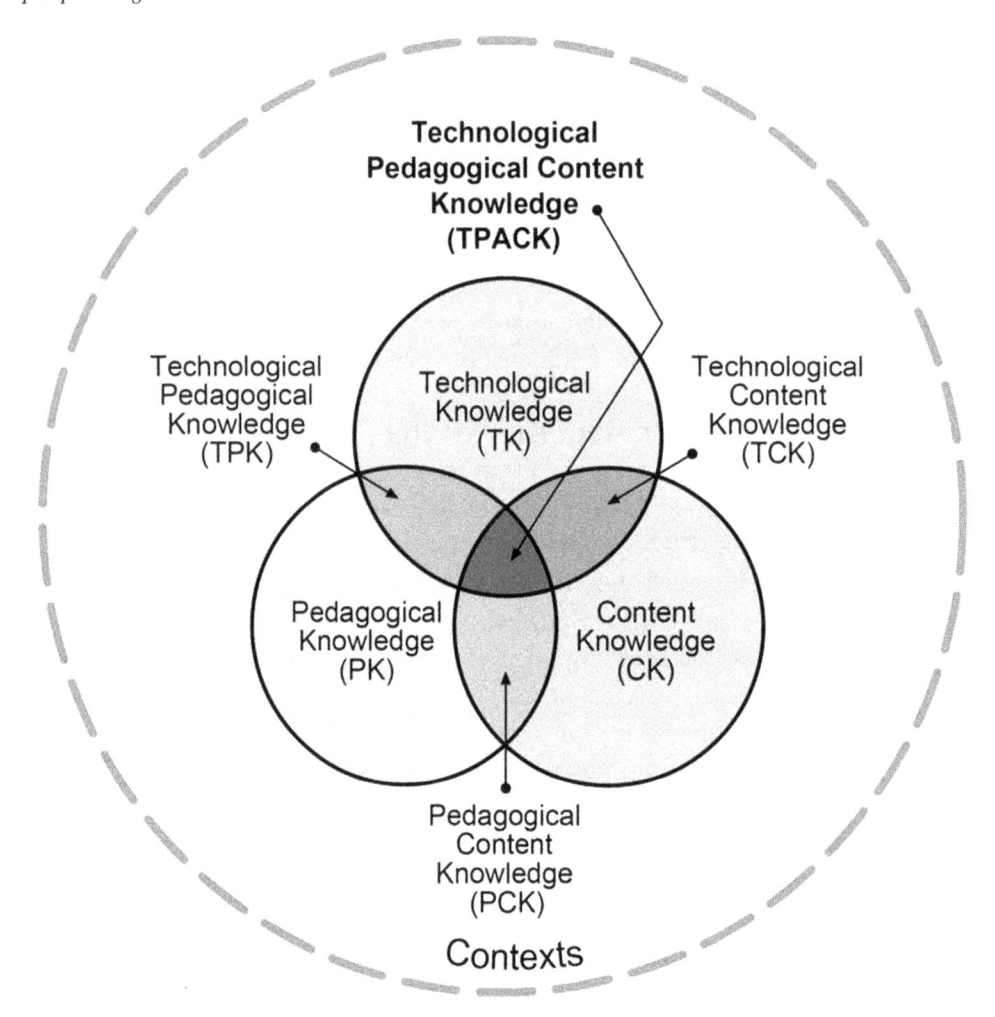

Connectivism

De Metz and Bezuidenhout (2018) identify the need for professional development that enables teachers to facilitate online learning communities amongst their students and make connections between the different complex information they encounter during their learning. It relates to Siemens' (2005) Connectivism theory, which advances a learning theory consistent with the needs of the 21st century and e-learning. It is based on the notion of learning as a network phenomenon shaped by technology and socialization into the "learning community," which is ultimately considered a "node" of a more extensive network that includes organizations, libraries, databases, and websites.

Situated Learning

Situated learning was first proposed by Jean Lave and Etienne Wenger (1991) as a model of learning in a community of practice, that is, learning that takes place in the same context in which it is applied. For example, Lane (2013) acknowledged that professional development for online teachers should be provided in the same modality as their teaching environment. Further, Bell and Morris (2009), discuss the importance of reflection in action and provided opportunities to reflect on authentic practices captured in video clips. The use of social networking sites to support learning activities was found to be a very useful authentic practice in an online teacher professional development program in Canada (Oastashewski et al., 2011). Feedback from participants in the e-tutor professional development program requesting more opportunities to perform authentic tasks was noted. "Hands-on, real-world experience was reiterated, and the lack of immediate practice opportunities was frequently raised" (Adnan, 2018, p.103). Aligned with the idea of situated learning is the belief that professional development for online teachers should model best practice, for example, participation in discussions which have both a pedagogical and technical focus (Borup & Evmenova, 2019).

Threshold Concepts

Threshold concepts are those understandings that are difficult to grasp and may alter previously held conceptions, but once grasped they will open doors to new and further levels of knowledge (Kilgour et al., 2018). For example, a comprehensive theory of adult learning that facilitates a process of examination, questioning, validation, and review of perspectives is that of transformative learning. Originated by Jack Mezirow (2003), transformative learning is a theory that utilizes disorienting dilemmas to challenge participants' beliefs defined as broad sets of predispositions resulting from psycho-cultural assumptions which determine the horizons of expectations.

For Mezirow (2011), reflection involves a critique of assumptions to determine whether the belief, often acquired through cultural assimilation in childhood, remains functional for us as adults. Reflection for Mezirow (2011) is similar to problem-solving. He describes how we reflect on the content of the problem, the process of problem-solving, or the premise of the problem. Through this reflection we are able to understand ourselves more and then understand our learning better. Mezirow (2011) also proposed that there are four ways of learning which are refining or elaborating meaning schemes, learning new meaning schemes, transforming meaning schemes, and transforming meaning perspectives. Kitchenham (2006), for example, demonstrates how teachers transform their perspectives during self-reflective learning to resolve conflicting teaching situations experienced while using educational technologies. Perspective transformations occur when people become critically aware of how and why their psychocultural assumptions are constrained and determine what to do to revise those assumptions to make meaning from given situations, and then take some form of action to incorporate their revised frames of reference. Taking a closer look at actual examples of teacher discussion and reflection can demonstrate what the characteristics are when epistemological and pedagogical perspectives appear to transform (Lee & Brett, 2015).

Many different roles have been considered for the online teacher. There have also been many different approaches to defining them. For example, Gómez-Rey, Barbera, and Fernández-Navarro (2018) used a 69-item Likert scale survey, administered to students, to complete a bottom-up approach to compiling the online teacher role descriptions. A new role, the life skills promoter was identified by the students which requires transversal skills such as teaching values and empathy. Badia et al. (2017), examined the roles of online teachers with respect to different approaches to teaching in a survey of part-time online teachers. They identified a new role, that of learning support. When acting in the learning support or the social role online teachers often use a collaborative learning approach. A number of studies also examined the roles from the point of view of being central and/or peripheral (Carril et al., 2013; González-Sanmamed, et al., 2014; De Metz & Bezuidenhout, 2018). For example, Carril et al. (2013) considered the pedagogical role as central and all seven others as peripheral. According to De Metz and Bezuidenhout (2018), the content facilitator, metacognition facilitator, technologist, process facilitator, assessor, advisor and resource provider are all central roles, and manager/administrator, designer, co-learner, and researcher are peripheral.

MAIN FOCUS OF THE CHAPTER

The primary purpose of this participatory action research study was to investigate the potential of an online development program to find out if it can support teachers' changing reflections about their beliefs and practices of teaching and learning at an Ecuadorian University. The data collection methods selected for this study included online group interviews, a reflection blog, and a participatory observation. Specifically, our research is oriented to a cycle of actions as an opportunity for teachers to see if changes occur within themselves. The modules or cycles of activities form an action research spiral (plan, act, observe, reflect) in which each cycle increases the evidence and our knowledge of the original questions leading to their solutions.

Methodology

Location Action Research Project

The research was conducted in a medium-sized private, non-profit full-time university in the south of Ecuador, with an enrollment of 5,500 undergraduate students, 381 full-time faculty, offering 29 bachelor's degrees including Medicine, Business, Law, Design, Education, Tourism and Engineering.

The instruction mode is primarily face-to-face; however, due to the COVID-19 pandemic, all the courses needed to be moved to the online format. The Learning Management System used in this university is the Moodle platform known as the Virtual Campus.

Participants in the Action Research Project

A convenience sample was invited to participate and provide information-rich cases from which we might learn a great deal of central importance to the research purpose. The criteria for participant selection included current employment, limited teaching online experience, and at least two years of experience teaching at the university level to have accumulated some assumptions and beliefs about teaching in higher education that would be later called into question. The selected participants signed an informed consent form. A scheduled group meeting with all participants was held for the first data collection.

Although initially six participants engaged in the project, only four remained throughout the whole process. Three had a master's degree, one in Political Science, one in Applied Linguistics, one in International Business, and one a Ph.D. in Statistics. Participants were from Ecuador and Italy. The length of teaching practice varied from two years to 20 years. The following table presents the participants' demographic information.

Table 1. Action research project participants' demographic information

Alias	Age	Gender	Degree	Department	Years of Experience
G	30	Female	Masters	International Studies	2
D	33	Male	Masters	International Studies	8
J	33	Male	PhD	Engineering	5
A	50	Female	Masters	International Studies	20

Location of the Community Project

To date (2020), 180 cities around the world have obtained the UNESCO Creative City nomination and joined the Network, a space which promotes international collaboration while constituting a space for reflection on the role of creativity in sustainable development. Within a framework strategic of twinning processes of action for bilateral cooperation to stimulate the artisanal sector and to promote the exchange of experiences and knowledge with another UNESCO Creative City in areas of mutual interest as well as internationalization processes and para-diplomacy, it was necessary for both artisans and their families to learn English primarily for touristic purposes, and the local municipality employees to be informed about the formal processes of internationalization to promote sustainable economic growth (Sustainable Development Goal # 8).

Participants in the Community Project

The 25 students who participated in the Chordeleg Community Project belong to the School of International Studies. They are in third and fifth level of their career. Four of them participated in the focus group sessions for this research.

Table 2. Community project participants' demographic information

Alias	Gender	Major	Level	Role in the Chordeleg community project
Student D	Female	International Studies	Fifth	Facilitator/tutor for municipality workers in the internationalization area
Student M	Female	International Studies	Fifth	Facilitator/tutor for municipality workers in the internationalization area
Student C	Female	International Studies	Fifth	Facilitator/tutor for children or adults in elementary English
Student J	Female	International Studies	Third	Facilitator/tutor for children or adults in elementary English

Data Collection: Action Research-Teachers

Data was collected from October 2020 to January 2021 through three online group interviews, a writing reflection blog, and three participatory observation sessions. Within the action research design, participants received readings, additional resources and three planned two-hour video-recorded group sessions. Participants had access to a specifically designed blog to discuss, ask questions, and reflect on the process. The three video-recorded group interviews took place during September and November with final video-recorded group interview during the first week of January 2021. These three sources of data allowed for data triangulation. Data from blog reflections, video-taped interviews and discussion yielded certain themes some of which related to our research questions and others that were new, for example, roles and dialogue.

Participatory Action Research Plan

The plan was developed to be responsive to the initial interviews with participants and in recognition of the essential attributes for an adult education-based teacher professional development program. Our strategic planning for the modules was developed using the four principles of action that incorporate an adult learning framework and reflect the adult learning principles developed by Mezirow (2003).

First, responsiveness to the individuality of the faculty member is essential. Second, sessions that are offered only once are not as effective as those provided continuously or developed gradually. Third, building a community based on peer sharing provides a necessary support structure. Finally, teachers must experience the teaching and learning conditions they plan to create for their own students through constructive activities, providing an authentic context for their learning.

These principles, together with the assumptions about the adult learner proposed by Malcolm Knowles (2011), and the strategies for incorporating an adult learning perspective in teacher professional development raised by Lawler and King (2001), form a set of essential attributes for an adult education-based teacher development program.

Figure 2 shows the three participatory action research cycles designed for this project, including the activities carried out during the four phases for each cycle (planning, executing, observing, and reflecting).

- Module 1: During the first video-recorded group interview, participants shared how their needs and concerns regarding teaching online were influenced by their professional narratives. For example, how they had become a teacher, what events and experiences had made them the kind of teacher they are today, students they had encountered, teaching practices they had employed. To demonstrate reflexivity, they were asked to share an example. Based on these themed reflections, the second module was planned, and the cycle repeated with observations collected from the reflection blog as well as prompted group and individual interviews.
- Module 2: group interview prompts concerned any new insights that connected to the initial questions, especially the ones related to changes in teaching practices with the new shared resources, as well as the impact of students' feedback. These questions were intended to support the participants sharing about how they reflected on their thinking and practice with the new tools and strategies from Module 1.
- Module 3: consisted of student perspectives, summative and formative assessment and online management strategies. It was constructed from themed data collected from group interviews and

reflective blogging from Module 2. In the final group interview, teachers were asked to reflect on any new strategies that had affected the way they think and teach, as well as to what extent their discipline had and/or continued to direct or inform their thinking about practice.

Figure 2. Three participatory action research cycles

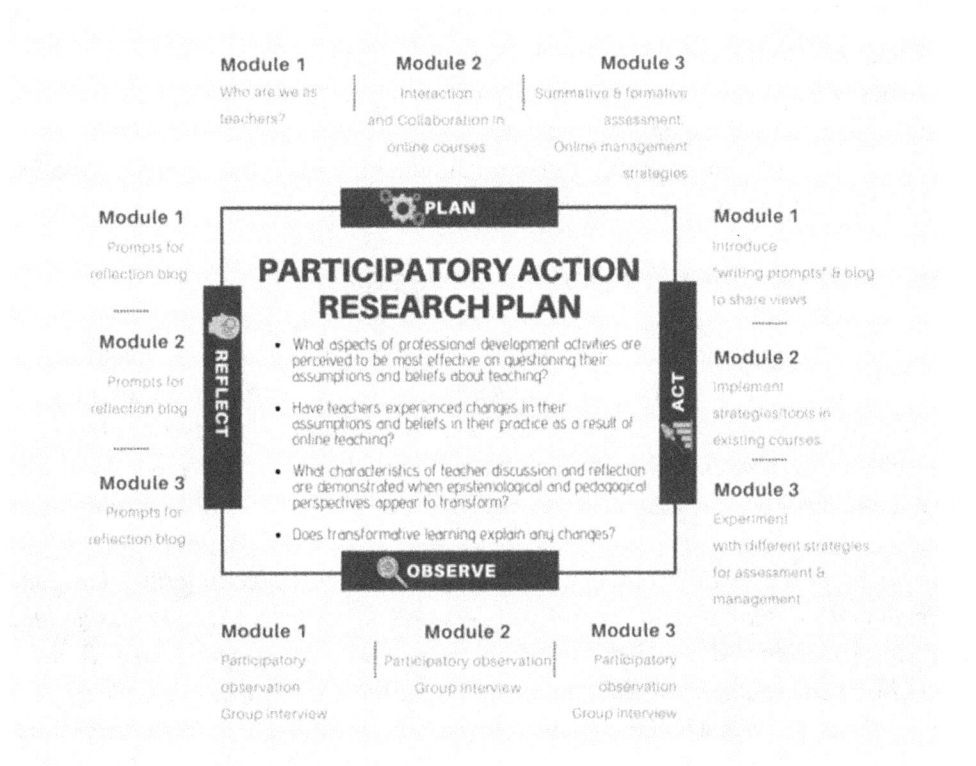

Data Analysis

Analysis of the emerging themes derived from the initial group interview began immediately and guided further explicit data gathering and decision making. An ongoing tension was that decisions for action needed to be made sometimes before we reached a thorough understanding of the data since participants were involved in the ongoing process of classes. For example, from the emerging themes identified in the first cycle of the participatory action research process, we designed a module addressing participants' beliefs about teaching in general and about teaching online in particular. During the group interview, participants were asked about their needs for learning about teaching methodologies, online tools, and strategies for teaching in online settings. Data was also collected from the blog reflections, and participant-observation during the interview session. The transcription of the group interview was verbatim.

RESULTS

The next section consists of the three Action Research Modules developed during the collection of data in the course of the first three months of a twelve-month design.

Module 1

The first module was designed for meeting the participating teachers as they responded to how they became a teacher, what events and experiences make them the kind of teacher they are and how they feel about and approach teaching online.

The data analysis of this initial group interview and the blog reflections provided the foundation to construct Modules 2 and Module 3. From this data, the following collective issues emerged:

Views About the Role of the Teacher and Students

Teacher G was an undergraduate student at the University of Azuay and received a Master's Degree in International Business at the University of South Carolina. She has two years of teaching experience.

From her narration, we noted her beliefs and assumptions are in process as described by Feiman-Nemser (2001), probably due to short experience as it seems she is still figuring out her identity as a teacher with interests that are related to content knowledge, students' characteristics, and classroom management.

...I'm still in the process of understanding what kind of teacher I am, but in terms of my teaching techniques, my goal is always for students to really understand the topics we see in class and that knowing how and in what situation this knowledge will help them in their professional lives. To achieve this, in my classes I always use examples and situations from real life, I also make the students get involved in the process by being the ones who investigate, analyze and draw their own conclusions, opinions and solutions to problems. (Teacher G)

For Teacher D, who has undergraduate and graduate degrees in Political Science from the University of Padua, Italy (8 years teaching experience), his identity has been influenced by his former teachers, posing dialogism as his primary teaching method:

(My teachers) were people who based everything on the creation of a dialogue, an exchange of opinions, a critical vision and above all in the consideration of being able to consider the ideas of the classics not as immutable and absolute truths, but as a starting point for the mental formation of the individual. So, when I started my work at the University in my early days, I decided to simply be "who I am", not imposing myself on the students, although maintaining the proper academic distance, but conversing with it, opening up to their reflections and ideas and always valuing them. (Teacher D)

Regarding this topic, Teacher J, who has undergraduate degree in Industrial Engineering in Ecuador, Master of Science specializing in Quality and Productivity Systems in Mexico, and a Ph.D. in Engineering Sciences from Instituto Tecnológico de Monterrey (5 years teaching), shared:

Online Teaching

I realized that several of my teachers did not teach me as I would have liked, some were very rude, others very relaxed, others were not properly prepared, but I also had teachers who were incredible and I wanted to be like them. In my childhood, I had several learning disabilities due to language difficulties, so I had a significant number of teachers and tutors. I remember what their teachings were like and the different types of exercises they taught me to learn better. That is why when I grew up I decided that science and teaching was the way I wanted to go.

I studied in a public school where we had a large number of classmates in the courses. My course was 52 people in one subject (Physics). My teacher had several problems teaching due to his attitude, he proposed us the idea that if those with the highest grades supported their classmates with private lessons, he would "pay" us with grades. And that's how I started in a formal way, I had to prepare the classes, I studied in the morning so I gave classes in the afternoons. I had 5 classmates who studied with me every day until we graduated. Being in contact with them I learned about their lives, their problems, their ideas for the future, and little by little I changed and I liked to support them. It was an experience that at first challenged me, but now that I look back, I know that it was the trigger for each idea to try to learn to become a better teacher. (Teacher J)

Loss of Relationships

Teacher A has undergraduate and graduate degrees in Applied Linguistics in Ecuador, and 20 years teaching experience. For her, virtual classes do not afford the connection of a two-way relationship between teacher and students.

It is this relationship that I feel has been lost with virtual classes. There is no longer a two-way relationship, because although I try to get the students to participate in the class as much as possible, I do not feel that there is the same connection. What's more, I'm not even sure I'd recognize them if I saw them go by on the street. Academically, perhaps not as much has been lost as what is lost in the interpersonal relationship. (Teacher A)

In spite of the differences in terms of years of teaching experience, Teacher A and Teacher G share a similar view regarding the loss of relationships in online settings.

…Virtual classes constitute a new challenge, the lack of personal contact with students has been a demotivating fact not only for students but also for teachers. With the aim of making them feel that everyone is important and that we are aware of everyone and their progress in class, I have chosen to divide the course into four groups and connect with them at different times. That allows everyone to participate and ask the questions that they do not dare to ask when they are with all the classmates. (Teacher G)

A similar view is shared for Teacher J, for him connecting with students is the biggest loss in virtual classes, he explained:

Personally, I do not like teaching online. It is possible to do it but the guidance of a tutor and teacher in person is not a substitute for the coldness of a video or a document with questions. The connection with students is one of the great advantages of being a teacher, but that is lost online. (Teacher J)

On the other end of the spectrum, for Teacher D, the virtual classes did not provoke a change in his way of teaching. However, he also acknowledges the lack of direct and frequent interaction with students.

...the academy is a space with two directions: students learn from the teacher as the teacher from the students. Virtuality has not changed much - I would say almost nothing - my way of teaching, and I consider that I have been able to take advantage of this complexity. However, what is most lacking is the most direct and frequent interaction with students, which in virtuality is transformed only into interaction with a few, and often not visual. (Teacher D)

Complexity of Technology and Virtuality for the Few and Related Assessment Issues

The participants pointed out some shortcomings of the technology of virtuality, such as the difficulty of assessing students' understanding due to the inability to perceive their cues through the screen, and the diminished opportunities to interact with students, since "… virtuality is transformed only into interaction with a few, and often not visual." (Teacher D)

There are times when in face-to-face classes I explain a topic and looking at the faces I know that it is easy, difficult, or not and I knew how to explain. This ability is not possible to use in online classes, despite having the cameras on, I cannot be watching 40 students from a laptop and at the same time directing the class, it is very complex. (Teacher J)

Module 2

In this section, as explained previously, based on the observed collective emerging themes in Module 1, we designed Module 2 to introduce new tools and strategies in an attempt to extend and/or provoke interruption of the teachers' assumptions (Mezirow, 2003).

New strategies and tools that were introduced to the participants are explained with comments on their use. In addition, in Module 2 we added anecdotes from the students participating in the Chordeleg community project.

Flipgrid + Rubrics

FlipGrid allows the creation of video discussion experiences in a free, straightforward, and accessible way. Students can share their ideas and reflection on a topic on their schedule, enabling teachers to hear from students who may not usually share. Students can also use Flipgrid for documenting their hands-on learning anytime, anywhere through the iOS and Android app. Teachers can respond to student questions at any time with a video when convenient.

The participants' experience implementing this tool in their classes were varied. For Teacher G, who had described the importance of active involvement of students in their own learning, it was surprising to see the effort students put into creating the videos and how the students' interaction spiked. She attributed this outcome to the combination of FlipGrid and rubrics. The rubric helped students to perform a better analysis and Flipgrid helped them in planning the activities related to the analysis, she shared:

Both, Flipgrid and having a rubric were very useful, the first to speed up the planning of activities and the second to motivate students to carry out a good analysis and reflection as well as listening to the analysis of other groups and commenting on them. The students made videos explaining their analysis of an article and later everyone left a comment on the videos of the other groups. I was surprised to see the effort they put into conducting the analyses, perhaps because they knew that this time they were going to be seen and heard by their colleagues. The videos also made it much easier for students to really take an interest in hearing what other groups had to say since they do not have the possibility of meeting in person. (Teacher G)

Teacher D was apprehensive of introducing a new tool not known by his students. However, in a Vygotskian scaffolding (1978), he took the main Flipgrid idea and crafted it with tools he already used in his classes. In Module 1, Teacher D had also mentioned his concerns about virtuality for the few who were present synchronously and assessment challenges.

I particularly liked Fipgrid, although reflecting on the tool I found it somewhat dubious to use yet another application compared to the ones that students already know and handle in my classes. I had a negative experience with an application that in theory I had liked a lot and I had asked students to download it, but it turned out to be very complex and impractical in the "test run" so I had to abandon it. For this reason, I decided to take the FlipGrid idea and apply it in a context already known to students: in two courses I asked them to record a video of their group exhibitions, upload them to Google Drive and share the link through the Virtual Campus in a dedicated forum, then I asked each group to "co-evaluate" the work of their classmates through comments and a grade assigned by each group. (Teacher D)

Students participating in the Chordeleg community project who were mentored by the teachers that were part of the action research project found Flipgrid a useful tool. Their use of what Teacher J described as the "complexity of technology" could be interpreted as novices teaching experts in the broader community of learners. For example, Chordeleg students used Flipgrid to prepare short videos in English of a product they wanted to sell to a small group of students in the U.S. who were learning Spanish. The students in the U.S. watched the videos and then participated in a zoom discussion with the Chordeleg students about the effectiveness of their videos. (Student C)

Google Docs + Zoom Breakout Rooms

The breakout rooms are ideal for small group work or sharing-type activities with one partner. In combination with Google Drive, breakout activities can be set up in advance and collect and share student work with the entire class after everyone reconvenes when the small group session finishes.

For Teacher D this tool is not new:

I have used Breakout rooms constantly, as it ensures the participation of all students when the groups are small. Padlet is also a good tool for collaboration, since the platform is updated every time the student writes something and everyone in the class can see it. I have use Padlet and Breakout rooms together so the students can post what they are doing and the teacher can see and comment on their progress. (Teacher D)

Teacher G also shared the same view as Teacher D regarding the usefulness of this tool to promote students' active participation. She explained:

With the aim of making students main actors in learning, I have used tools such as the Breakout Rooms in Zoom, where each student collaborates with their knowledge and research on the assigned tasks, for example case analysis, problem solving, article analysis, documentaries or interviews. This tool has helped me a lot to motivate students to get involved in the topics and work in groups. other groups and commenting on them. Working with multiple Zoom groups has helped me a lot, in addition to allowing me to enter and exit between rooms. (Teacher G)

For Teacher J, the breakout rooms are a way to provide the more personalized instruction that students are eager for. He also has explored Google Meets as an alternative to Zoom, finding an easier way to manage groups. However, as Teacher D, he also has combined the use of Zoom breakout rooms with Padlet, as a way to share in real time the results of the work in small groups. He described his experience in these words:

Several students indicate that they would like the class more personalized, so they usually suggest working with other people and for that reason, I do not assign the groups randomly. I have found that Google Meets has several functions and plugs that allow the management of groups.

Padlet is also a good tool for collaboration, since the platform is updated every time the student writes something and everyone in the class can see it. (Teacher J)

Students in the Chordeleg community project also used these tools during their instruction activities in the English classes they taught. For instance, Student D found document sharing through Google docs useful mainly with groups of learners that had mixed abilities and learning styles. Because of the variety of document modality, and because the material is available to access on demand, Student M explained that: "Google Docs are especially helpful for pacing activities for different groups when you have mixed abilities and styles of learning. Padlet is very useful too because everyone can make the content they want whatever their age, level or ability."

The previous descriptions of the use of breakout rooms have addressed student-student collaboration. Teacher D pointed out that breakout rooms also contribute to nurturing student-student and student-teacher dialogue (Bahktin, 1981) to foster students' involvement in their learning process. He explains how it can be achieved:

In the current semester, I have had the possibility to deepen the use of some online tools to make the classes even more dynamic. I believe, and I underline it, that the cooperation of the students, not only in a student-student sense but also in a student-teacher sense, is key to making students feel involved. To this end, I have repeatedly used Zoom's breakout rooms which I find to be an excellent tool so that students can cooperate with each other in small groups and then point out their views in the general class. I have been working a lot with the possibility of applying what I call "parliamentarism applied to the classroom": students meet in small groups through breakout rooms (parliamentary committees), groups in which they bring personal instances as well as opinions of third parties (e.g. relatives) trying to find a theoretical basis. Then, they take these opinions and common considerations of the group to the classroom (the parliament) where an exchange of opinions is carried out between students and with the participation of the teacher who, and it is very important, does not try to impose their point of view but rather as "one more opinion", valuing the contributions of the students and refuting them only when necessary. (Teacher D)

Bahktin's dialogism can inform us how to facilitate teacher-to-teacher, and as Teacher D illustrates, student-to-student and student-to-teacher discussions. The nature of dialogue required for transformative learning is distinguished from both discussions aimed at consensus and debate seeking better ideas (Rule, 2011). Although Bakhtinian dialogue too involves interactions with others, it is distinct from "interaction" in social constructivist learning theories (e.g., Hannafin, 2009; Vygotsky, 1978; Woo & Reeves, 2007), which often focus on constructing a homogeneous piece of knowledge (Matusov, 2011). Rather, Bakhtin (1981) would argue that knowledge is neither absolute nor can be predefined as an instructional goal. Thus, the dialogue of ideological becoming is ultimately an individualized process so that individuals participating in dialogue do not necessarily construct a shared knowledge as a result. Most importantly, a central focus of transformative learning is not to construct shared knowledge but to develop alternative perspectives for understanding one's practices and awareness of the socio-political settings in which these practices are involved (Brett, 2015).

Module 3

In Module 3, based on prompted blog reflections, we continued to pursue themes identified in Modules 1 and 2 to include assessment and classroom management that may contradict teachers' assumptions about the roles of teachers and students in online teaching and learning.

Three collective themes had previously been identified in Module 1 and built on in Module 2. Paying closer attention to the emerging theme of teacher roles identified in Module 1 and extended in Module 2, we began to expand two perspectives that reflect teachers' roles in Module 3. However, whilst there are references to teacher roles in the literature review, for example, Carril (2013) on central or peripheral roles, we had not included a specific research question on teacher roles.

We designed Module 3 from two perspectives that reflect teachers' roles: thinking of students as collaborative partners, and specific teacher assessment strategies both formative and summative. What strategies can foster interdependence, create awareness of thoughts and challenges and at the same time encourage help seeking in formative ways? How can trust be built while using assessment through Flipgrid and breakout rooms as it requires thoughtful organization on the teacher's part for both individual and group tasks keeping in mind De Metz & Bezuidenhout's (2018) premise that the content facilitator, metacognition facilitator, technologist, process facilitator, assessor, advisor and resource provider are all central roles and manager/administrator, designer, co-learner, and researcher are peripheral?

First, we considered the teacher's peripheral role as manager/administrator and central roles as assessor and process facilitator in formative assessment that serves to continuously provide feedback to students on progress in their learning, for example, surveys (several times to measure where students are), one-minute summaries (very short writing activities at the end of each class), voting (Mentimeter, Zoom Polls), conceptual mapping, peer review and self-reflection, for example, Kulthau's Information Search Process (metacognition facilitator) which help students identify the cognitive steps involved as well as the potential emotions they may experience.

Rubrics

Rubrics define criteria for evaluation using clear headings and provide examples aligned with those headings so that students know what is being required of them. In addition to rubrics designed and administered by the teacher, they can be designed by teacher for use by students in pairs or collaborative groups and designed by students for teacher use. This process in and of itself is formative in concept. Two participants shared their views about rubrics, for teacher A, "rubrics are useful to convey clear guides of evaluations to students and help her provide feedback to students based on its criteria." (Teacher A) For teacher G:

Rubrics were very useful to motivate students to carry out a good analysis and reflection as well as listening to the analysis of other groups and commenting on them. The students made videos explaining their analysis of an article and later everyone left a comment on the videos of the other groups. (Teacher G)

Groupwork

From the blog-based reflection question in Module 2 about how the new strategies were affecting thinking and doing in the process of teaching and learning, the introduced topic that was most provocative representing a 'dilemma' (Mezirow, 2003) to the participants was group work and assessment.

The participants agreed that group work was a very effective learning strategy but also presented many complications, a solution, for example, that teacher appointed "leaders" apparently intuitively chosen to peer-assess and ensure participatory interdependence took away attention from what strategies are necessary for effective group work. None of the participants had ever considered group work as a developing process. For example, a teacher could run an initial survey to find out individual experience, such as students who consider themselves "lone wolves," that is, they always do all the work, rather than teaching investigation, critiquing, and ongoing feedback to group members as a kind of formative assessment. None of the participants had considered placing all the "lone wolves" together in a group! Semester-long groups were not popular, even though longer-term relationships can build interdependence and accountability among group members. However, the pairing was described as an initial builder for negotiation, even forcing task completion. Pairs can then be added to each other to expand the group size and build increased negotiating strategies over time. Regarding the teacher's role, one participant captured the others' attention by declaring that he never entered groups in the process but rather evaluated the assigned outcome, a summative assessment strategy. However, if invited by the group, he would accept.

Teaching Online Reflections and Interim Analysis

In our last meeting with the teachers, before writing this chapter, we wanted to explore our research questions:

- Did the teachers experience changes in beliefs and assumptions?
- What aspects of activities/strategies provoke questions that run counter or contradict current assumptions?

Online Teaching

The chart shown in Figure 3 prompted the opportunity to take a closer look at actual examples of teacher discussion and reflection in which we could demonstrate what the characteristics were when epistemological and pedagogical perspectives appeared to transform (Lee & Brett, 2015).

Figure 3. Three participatory action research cycles

1. E-learning Leadership, Work-life motivation, Work-life balance
2. Getting to know your classroom management strategies
3. Peer collaboration Work group strategies
4. Online games & apps Guest speackers
5. Evaluation: Formative & Summative
6. A time of unknowns?

Are there particular strategies that may run counter to your assumptions about online and/or face-to-face teaching?

Socio-cultural understanding of learning as active participation in shared practices of social communities has been suggested as one of the most promising approaches to teacher professional development (Lave & Wenger, 1991; Wenger, 1998). A teacher community of practice, and particularly one which has created a shared trust among its members, enables teachers to learn new knowledge and perspectives through interacting with other teachers and transforming their teaching practices with community supports (Hawkins, 1996; Lock, 2006; MacDonald, 2006; Wang & Lu, 2012; Wei et al., 2009). By taking a closer look at actual examples of teacher discussion and reflection we could demonstrate what the characteristics were when epistemological and pedagogical perspectives appeared to transform (Lee & Brett, 2015). This process includes dialogic interactions among participants such as representing the self to others, sharing different perspectives, assessing various values, and reconstructing new beliefs (Mezirow,

2003). For example, Teacher D's description of his role during groupwork is somewhat different from that of Teacher J. In fact, groupwork whether how groups are designated or what skills need to be made explicit besides the content aspect underscores how the central pedagogical role is co-constructed with peripheral roles from different perspectives (De Metz, 2018).

During this semester, I have come to the conclusion that "less is better" for both the student and the teacher. A myriad of different instruments makes the student and teacher "overwhelmed" by various things to watch for (I report this from a conversation I had with the students). For this reason, as a tool I can suggest the use of Mentimeter that allows you to create a large number of presentations, polls, word clouds, graphics, quizzes, among other things. For example, I have used it a lot to encourage student participation through open questions that require a written response the size of a "tweet" and from that short answer I ask them to deepen it by voice. On the other hand, I have been deepening my knowledge of Zoom, realizing that it has greatly expanded its possibilities by presenting tools such as polls, for example, which before I used only through Mentimeter but now I use more agilely through Zoom. So, I think I investigate in greater depth all the options offered by Zoom which are extremely useful. It's a challenge not seeing students so how to know if they are following, for example, using questions or surveys can help. (Teacher D)

And on guest speakers and group work, Teacher D affirms his belief that zoom facilitates the active learning of individuals as well as collaborators within groupwork. Provoked by the ideas of a guest speaker, he instructed the students to use the wide appeal of social media for metacognitive purposes and suggests that these participation strategies assist him in relating to and evaluating students.

In this respect guest speakers are voices to be heard from outside, different points of view. For example, I invited one of my professors in Padua to give a zoom class to my students here on human rights. Guest speakers have the power to inspire group work discussion. After the class, I asked the students to go on Twitter to move forward the idea of citizenship to reach more people. This certainly changed how the students looked at social media for more serious issues. Then I divided them into small groups to discuss and reach a definition in the group. Group work is easier with zoom ... I believe from the beginning that the best strategy is and continues to be the assessment of the student as an individual capable of thinking and contributing, and not just as a "sponge" capable of receiving and absorbing. At the moment in which the student feels that he is being valued, it is where he understands that he can contribute actively to the class, and not only passively participate in it.

In this framework I believe that several of the participation strategies as well as group work contributed during the sessions were for me a help, perhaps not to implement certain tools directly in the classroom space (in some cases, yes) but also to improve the way of relating to and evaluating students. (Teacher D)

Teacher A on peer collaboration and group work seems to be on the edge of a positive dilemma about group participation and application of entertaining online strategies with face-to-face teaching and evaluation.

I think the strategies aimed at working in groups are very interesting. Group work is very peculiar, since it always happens that some student takes advantage of the work of others, or instead, that some student does not let others have an opinion. So, it is important to apply some strategy that teaches the students to participate actively in the group, to accept the opinions of others and to present their own opinion. In real life, they'll have to work with other people and they won't always be to everyone's liking, so it's a good workout. (Teacher A).

During the discussion on group work, the belief of demand-organization-discipline of Teacher J may have been challenged to include new group strategies that extend adaptations for different learning styles that he noted previously.

I really liked the strategy of working according to leaders when we make teams. I would think that it could be very useful in semesters where the level of maturity of the students is more developed, but in the first levels, it is quite complex, some are afraid, and as it was said in the discussion "they have never been taught to work as a team".

DISCUSSION

This chapter content represents the first three months of a twelve-month project to investigate what aspects of professional development activities and strategies teachers perceive to be most effective in helping them reflect on and question their assumptions and beliefs about teaching practices. Did, in fact, they experience any changes resulting from online teaching and, if so, does transformative learning explain these changes?

We can read from the anecdotal material elicited through the prompted reflections on the blog and the narrative from interviews and discussions, that each teacher has begun engagement in the transformative process of describing how their reflection on the content of the problem (who may have initially influenced their beliefs and practices), the process of problem-solving (evolving roles, relationships and groups) or the premise of the problem (what kind of protagonist to be in these "unknown times"). In these processes, they are scaffolding self-understanding, that according to Mezirow (2011), leads to a better understanding of their learning that can guide potential change in beliefs and practices. For example, teacher J's statement that some teachers he did not like were either rude, very relaxed or not properly prepared but his "amazing" teachers that motivated him were those who supported the development of his learning difficulties with "different types of exercises." Or Teacher D, regarding the evolving role of the teacher, captured his peers' attention by declaring that he never entered groups in the process but rather evaluated the assigned outcome, a summative assessment strategy. However, if invited by the group, he would accept. Within this community of teachers as peer learners he described the role of the teacher as protagonist with parliamentarism applied to the classroom where an exchange of opinions is carried out between students and with the participation of the teacher who, and it is very important, does not try to impose their point of view but rather as "one more opinion", valuing the contributions of the students and refuting them only when necessary.

The importance of Chordeleg community student teaching reflections in practice echoes some of the beliefs and practices of their mentors as they document their evolving roles and relationships with the community groups they were teaching. The following anecdote illustrates that learning does not occur in isolation, but is a continuous process, whereby learners from within the same communities learn from each other, as apprentices learn from other apprentices and experts on their way to becoming global citizens.

The initial zoom class with municipal employees was challenging. We were in the process of teaching to others what we were learning. Although we were mentored by our teachers it was difficult to engage those who seemed less interested. Also, we were students and they were local government employees. We tried to present how change can change perception and interacting more cooperatively with us and each other can lead to international recognition and increased sales. At the beginning, they seemed a bit scared and with no immediate results from learning about internationalization some gave up early. Is this cultural? Low self-esteem? So, we made the class schedule more flexible and changed how we presented. There was more affirmation and motivation when we visually linked the process to other artisans' cooperatives in, for example, Colombia where they could see people like themselves producing beautiful products and learn about the related internationalization processes. (Student D Chordeleg community project)

SOLUTIONS AND RECOMMENDATIONS FOR FUTURE RESEARCH

Our action research project has some similar results to a large international study with transformative learning theory as the theoretical framework (McLoughlin, 2017). The international study was designed to investigate and explore the perceptions of experienced teachers about the skills and knowledge essential for online teaching and the capacities they considered most important for effective learning. Results from both the large international study and our action research study demonstrate that the complexity of teaching in virtual spaces indicates more research is necessary to transform pedagogy to include new roles, modes of interaction and the discovery of and authentic practice with strategies that increase connectivity and interaction with students. Professional development needs to focus on both pedagogy, that is, the beliefs, confidence and attitudes of teachers as well as effective communicative and technical abilities with discipline content. Individually tailored based on authentic evidence, structured but allowing for flexible participation, and focused on situated delivery, professional development for online teaching can support community building and integration into an institution.

CONCLUSION

Our small participatory action research in a developing country, where all students do not necessarily have access to digital resources, helped us realize what we had not seen before in the complexity of online teaching. In the short-term, the four participating teachers from diverse disciplines found the process of three modules, dialoguing and blogging helpful in reflecting about what they had not seen before in their previous practice. From a long-term perspective, will they continue with their self-reflexivity alone? Has a community of learners begun?

ACKNOWLEDGMENT

This research received no specific grant from any funding agency in the public, commercial, or not-for-profit sectors.

REFERENCES

Adnan, M. (2018). Professional development in the transition to online teaching: The voice of entrant online instructors. *ReCALL*, *30*(1), 88–111. doi:10.1017/S0958344017000106

Adnan, M., Kalelioglu, F., & Gulbahar, Y. (2017). Assessment of a multinational online faculty development program on online teaching: Reflections of candidate e-tutors. *Turkish Online Journal of Distance Education*, *18*(1), 22–22. doi:10.17718/tojde.285708

Andreotti, V. (2011). Towards decoloniality and diversity in global citizenship education in globalisation. *Social Education*, *9*(3-4), 3–4. doi:10.1080/14767724.2011.605323

Badia, A., Garcia, C., & Meneses, J. (2017). Approaches to teaching online: Exploring factors influencing teachers in a fully online university: Factors influencing approaches to teaching online. *British Journal of Educational Technology*, *48*(6), 1193–1207. doi:10.1111/bjet.12475

Bakhtin, M. M. (1981). *The dialogic imagination* (C. Emerson & M. Holquist, Trans.). University of Texas Press., doi:10.2307/1770763

Baran, E., & Correia, A.-P. (2014). A professional development framework for online teaching. *TechTrends*, *58*(5), 95–101. doi:10.100711528-014-0791-0

Bell, A., & Morris, G. (2009). Engaging professional learning in online environments. *Australasian Journal of Educational Technology*, *25*(5), 700–713. doi:10.14742/ajet.1116

Borup, J., & Evmenova, A. (2019). The effectiveness of professional development in overcoming obstacles to effective online instruction in a College of Education. *Online Learning*, *23*(2), 1–20. doi:10.24059/olj.v23i2.1468

Brinkley-Etzkorn, K. E. (2018). Learning to teach online: Measuring the influence of faculty development training on teaching effectiveness through a TPACK lens. *The Internet and Higher Education*, *38*, 28–35. doi:10.1016/j.iheduc.2018.04.004

Carril, P. C. M., Gonzalez Sanmamed, M., & Hernandez Selles, N. (2013). Pedagogical roles and competencies of university teachers practicing in the E-learning environment. *International Review of Research in Open and Distributed Learning*, *14*(3), 462–487. doi:10.19173/irrodl.v14i3.1477

De Metz, N., & Bezuidenhout, A. (2018). An importance–competence analysis of the roles and competencies of e-tutors at an open distance learning institution. *Australasian Journal of Educational Technology*, *34*(5), 27–42. doi:10.14742/ajet.3364

Feiman-Nemser, S. (2001). From preparation to practice: Designing a continuum to strengthen and sustain teaching. *Teachers College Record*, *103*(6), 1013–1055. doi:10.1111/0161-4681.00141

Gómez-Rey, P., Barbera, E., & Fernández-Navarro, F. (2018). Students' perceptions about online teaching effectiveness: A bottom-up approach for identifying online instructors' roles. *Australasian Journal of Educational Technology*, *34*(1), 116–130. doi:10.14742/ajet.3437

González-Sanmamed, M., Muñoz-Carril, P.-C., & Sangra, A. (2014). Level of proficiency and professional development needs in peripheral online teaching roles. *The International Review of Research in Open and Distributed Learning, 15*(6), 162–187. doi:10.19173/irrodl.v15i6.1771

Hannafin, M. J. (2009). Interaction strategies and emerging instructional technologies: Psychological perspectives. *Canadian Journal of Educational Communication, 18*(3), 167–179. doi:10.21432/T2GK6G

Heron, J. (1996). Quality as primacy of the practical. *Qualitative Inquiry, 2*(1), 41–56. doi:10.1177/107780049600200107

Herr, K., & Anderson, G. (2004). *The action research dissertation: A guide for students and faculty.* SAGE. doi:10.4135/9781452226644

Kilgour, P., Reynaud, D., Northcote, M., McLoughlin, C., & Gosselin, K. P. (2019). Threshold concepts about online pedagogy for novice online teachers in higher education. *Higher Education Research & Development, 38*(7), 1417–1431. doi:10.1080/07294360.2018.1450360

Kilgour, P., Reynaud, D., Northcote, M., McLoughlin, C., & Gosselin, K. P. (2019). Threshold concepts about online pedagogy for novice online teachers in higher education. *Higher Education Research & Development, 38*(7), 1417–1431. doi:10.1080/07294360.2018.1450360

Kitchenham, A. (2006). Teachers and technology: A transformative journey. *Journal of Transformative Education, 4*(3), 202–225. doi:10.1177/1541344606290947

Knight, J. (2004). Internationalization remodeled: Definition, approaches, and rationales. *Journal of Studies in International Education, 8*(1), 5–31. doi:10.1177/1028315303260832

Knowles, M. S., Holton, E. F., & Swanson, R. A. (2011). *The adult learner: The definitive classic in adult education and human resource development* (7th ed.). Elsevier Inc.

Lave, J., & Wenger, E. (1991). *Situated learning: Legitimate peripheral participation.* Cambridge University Press. doi:10.1017/CBO9780511815355

Lawler, P. A., King, K. P., & Wilhite, S. C. (2004). Living and learning with technology: faculty as reflective practitioners in the online classroom. *Leadership, Counseling, Adult, Career and Higher Education Faculty Publications, 239*, 328-332. https://scholarcommons.usf.edu/ehe_facpub/239

Lee, K., & Brett, C. (2015). Dialogic understanding of teachers' online transformative learning: A qualitative case study of teacher discussions in a graduate-level online course. *Teaching and Teacher Education, 46*, 72–83. doi:10.1016/j.tate.2014.11.001

Lock, J. V. (2006). A new image: Online communities to facilitate teacher professional development. *Journal of Technology and Teacher Education, 14*(4), 663–678. https://www.learntechlib.org/primary/p/21030/

MacDonald, J. (2006). *Blended learning and online tutoring.* Gower. doi:10.1111/j.1467-8535.2007.00749_10.x

Matusov, E. (2011). Irreconcilable differences in Vygotsky's and Bakhtin's approaches to the social and the individual: An educational perspective. *Culture and Psychology, 17*(1), 99–119. doi:10.1177/1354067X10388840

McLoughlin, C., & Northcote, M. (2017). What skills do I need to teach online? Researching experienced teacher views of essential knowledge and skills in online pedagogy as a foundation for developing professional development. In *Search and Research: Teacher Education for Contemporary Contexts, Proceedings of the 18th Biennial International Conference on Teachers and Teaching, 3-7 July, 18th Biennial International Study Association on Teachers and Teaching (ISATT) Conference 2017* (pp. 1119-1129). Ediciones Universidad de Salamanca.

McQuiggan, C. A. (2012). Faculty development for online teaching as a catalyst for change. *Journal of Asynchronous Learning Networks*, *16*(2), 27–61. doi:10.24059/olj.v16i2.258

Meyer, K. A. (2013). An analysis of the research on faculty development for online teaching and identification of new directions. *Online Learning*, *17*(4), 93–122. doi:10.24059/olj.v17i4.320

Mezirow, J. (2003). Transformative learning as discourse. *Journal of Transformative Education*, *1*(1), 58–63. doi:10.1177/1541344603252172

Mezirow, J. (2011). Transformative dimensions of adult learning. *International Journal of Adult Vocational Education and Technology*, *2*(4), 58–66. doi:10.4018/javet.2011100105

Mishra, P., & Koehler, M. J. (2006). Technological pedagogical content knowledge: A framework for teacher knowledge. *Teachers College Record*, *108*(6), 1017–1054. doi:10.1111/j.1467-9620.2006.00684.x

Northcote, M. T., Reynaud, D., Beamish, P., Martin, T., & Gosselin, K. P. (2011). Bumpy moments and joyful breakthroughs: The place of threshold concepts in academic staff development programs about online learning and teaching. *ACCESS: Critical Perspectives on Communication, Cultural &. Policy Studies*, *30*(2), 75–89.

Ostashewski, N., Moisey, S., & Reid, D. (2011). Applying constructionist principles to online teacher professional development. *International Review of Research in Open and Distance Learning*, *12*(6), 143–156. doi:10.19173/irrodl.v12i6.976

Samuelowicz, K., & Bain, J. D. (2001). Revisiting academics' beliefs about teaching and learning. *Higher Education*, *41*(3), 299–325. doi:10.1023/A:1004130031247

Selwyn, N. (2013). Discourses of digital "disruption" in education: a critical analysis. In *Fifth International Roundtable on Discourse Analysis*, City University Hong Kong.

Siemens, G. (2005). Connectivism: A learning theory for the digital age. *International Journal of Instructional Technology and Distance Learning*, *2*(1). http://www.itdl.org/Journal/Jan_05/article01.htm

UNESCO. (2015). *Rethinking education: Towards a global common good*. UNESCO. https://unesdoc.unesco.org/images/0023/002325/232555e.pdf

UNESCO. (n.d.). *UNESCO*. Obtenido de https://en.unesco.org/creative-cities/home

Vygotsky, L. S. (1978). *Mind in society: The development of higher mental processes*. Harvard University Press.

Wang, Q., & Lu, Z. (2012). A case study of using an online community of practice for teachers' professional development at a secondary school in China. *Learning, Media and Technology, 37*(4), 429–446. doi:10.1080/17439884.2012.685077

Wei, R. C., Darling-Hammond, L., Andree, A., Richardson, N., & Orphanos, S. (2009). *Professional learning in the learning profession: A status report on teacher development in the United States and abroad.* National Staff Development Council. https://edpolicy.stanford.edu/

Wenger, E. (1998). *Communities of practice.* Cambridge University Press. doi:10.1017/CBO9780511803932

Woo, Y., & Reeves, T. C. (2007). Meaningful interaction in web-based learning: A social constructivist interpretation. *The Internet and Higher Education, 10*(1), 15–25. doi:10.1016/j.iheduc.2006.10.005

ADDITIONAL READING

Bao, W. (2020). COVID-19 and online teaching in higher education: A case study of Peking University. *Human Behavior and Emerging Technologies, 2*(2), 113–115. doi:10.1002/hbe2.191 PMID:32510042

Collay, M. (2017). Transformative learning and teaching: How experienced faculty learned to teach in the on-line environment. *Journal of Transformative Learning, 4*(2), 21–42. https://jotl.uco.edu/index.php/jotl/article/view/187/130

Elçi, A., Beith, L. L., & Elçi, A. (Eds.). (2019). *Handbook of research on faculty development for digital teaching and learning.* IGI Global. doi:10.4018/978-1-5225-8476-6

Hora, M. T. (2014). Exploring faculty beliefs about student learning and their role in instructional decision-making. *The Review of Higher Education, 38*(1), 37–70. doi:10.1353/rhe.2014.0047

Johnson, N., Veletsianos, G., & Seaman, J. (2020). U.S. faculty and administrators' experiences and approaches in the early weeks of the COVID-19 pandemic. *Online Learning, 24*(2), 6–21. doi:10.24059/olj.v24i2.2285

Kim, S., & Slapac, A. (2015). Culturally responsive, transformative pedagogy in the transnational era: Critical perspectives. *Educational Studies, 51*(1), 17–27. doi:10.1080/00131946.2014.983639

McQuiggan, C. A. (2007). The role of faculty development in online teaching's potential to question teaching beliefs and assumptions. *Online Journal of Distance Learning Administration, 10*(3), 1–13. https://www-westga-edu.gate.lib.buffalo.edu/~distance/ojdla/fall103/mcquiggan103.htm

Mezirow, J. (1997). Transformative learning: Theory to practice. *New Directions for Adult and Continuing Education, 74*(74), 5–12. doi:10.1002/ace.7401

Quezada, R. L., Talbot, C., & Quezada-Parker, K. B. (2020). From bricks and mortar to remote teaching: A teacher education program's response to COVID-19. *Journal of Education for Teaching, 46*(4), 472–483. doi:10.1080/02607476.2020.1801330

Rahim, A. F. A. (2020). Guidelines for online assessment in emergency remote teaching during the COVID-19 pandemic. *Education in Medicine Journal, 12*(2), 59–68. doi:10.21315/eimj2020.12.2.6

KEY TERMS AND DEFINITIONS

Adult Learning: A specific philosophy about learning and teaching based on the assumption that adults can and want to learn, that they are able and willing to take responsibility for the learning, and that the learning itself should respond to their need.

Critical Literacy: Critically analyze and evaluate the meaning of texts as they relate to topics on equity, power and social justice.

Epistemic Technologies: Information providing and gathering increasingly involve technologies like search engines which actively shape their epistemic surroundings but there is no account of the associated epistemic responsibilities.

Global Citizenship Education: Aims to empower learners of all ages to assume active roles, both locally and globally, in building more peaceful, tolerant, inclusive and secure societies. GCED is based on the three domains of learning - cognitive, socio-emotional and behavioral.

Hermeneutic: A method or theory of interpretation.

Managerialism in Education: Digital technologies subtle reinforcement of wider trends that local enactments of such governance can be shaped by schools' relatively unsophisticated data processing technologies and techniques.

Rubric: An assessment tool that clearly indicates achievement criteria across all the components of any kind of student work, from written to oral to visual. It can be used for marking assignments, class participation, or overall grades. There are two types of rubrics: holistic and analytical.

Self-Reflexivity: Examination of one's own beliefs, judgments and practices during the research process and how these may have influenced the research. If positionality refers to what we know and believe then reflexivity is about what we do with this knowledge.

Transformative Learning: Learners who are getting new information are also evaluating.

Chapter 8
Applying Online Instructor Presence Amidst Changing Times

Michelle L. Rosser-Majors
University of Arizona Global Campus, USA

Sandra Rebeor
University of Arizona Global Campus, USA

Christine McMahon
University of Arizona Global Campus, USA

Stephanie L. Anderson
University of Arizona Global Campus, USA

ABSTRACT

Online learning can be challenging for both the students and instructors. Students can feel isolated or intimidated by the asynchronous environment, and instructors may find it difficult to connect with students as well as encourage active learning and critical thinking. Instructor presence (IP), as presented by the community of inquiry model (CoI), suggests that there are three areas of presence that must be applied cohesively to create an environment that is satisfying to students and the instructor: teaching, social, and cognitive. In this chapter, the authors report their findings of applied IP on student pass rates, drop rates, and satisfaction after exposing online instructors to IP training that provided immediate application examples. The findings suggested that when IP is applied effectively, student outcomes are significantly improved and are sustainable. This chapter will also share specific strategies, based on this model, that were utilized in the authors' research protocol.

DOI: 10.4018/978-1-7998-6922-1.ch008

INTRODUCTION

Online learning has struggled to support retention and student success since its inception (Allen & Seaman, 2015; Hamann et al., 2020; Jaggars, 2012; Xu & Jaggars, 2014). Engaging students in an online modality can be challenging even for seasoned instructors. Diverse students with a multitude of needs increase the necessity for proactive engagement by instructors to maintain successful outcomes. Identifying sustainable strategies to apply in the online context is essential to improvement (in both K-12 and higher education) and to provide the quality of educational experience more pursuant to traditional institutional outcomes. And although research on applying Instructor Presence (IP), based on the Community of Inquiry (CoI) model, has had promising results, the initial model was developed over two decades ago (Garrison et al., 1999). This means that how these crucial areas (teaching, social and cognitive presence) can be applied, should be evaluated and updated, based on increasingly more technological sophistication.

It is with this knowledge that our team of fulltime instructors strategized and developed an IP training series as an intervention to improve retention and success rates. The series purposefully included up-to-date application examples to more effectively equip instructors, as well as self-assessment activities, with the goal of improving outcomes in their classrooms. Once the instructors were IP trained, our analysis focused on the effects to drop rates, success rates, and satisfaction to determine if the IP strategies successfully resulted in an immediate improvement. To our knowledge, this training series was the first of its kind, explicitly demonstrating immediate-based strategies that instructors could apply to their classrooms, resulting also in a certification program disseminated to the entire institution, and, as a response to the pandemic-associated educational crisis, to the global educational community though social-networking communications.

Specific to this chapter, strategies included in the training series will be highlighted to support the readers who may be part of the global educational community who have been forced to move their courses online, as the current state of social distancing and heightened feelings of insecurity have mandated (Hodges et al., 2020). For these educators, the transition from traditional to online educational settings has created barriers that must be addressed with timely development and support. In addition, the long-term challenges encountered by experienced online institutions are similar to those being faced by educators and learners (both K-12 and in higher education) who have been forced to learn online due to the pandemic: perceptions of increased instructor workloads, feelings of isolation, anxiety due to lack of resources (Angdhiri, 2020), lowering math achievement (Kuhfeld et al., 2020), disadvantages of online learning associated with low-income students (García & Weiss, 2020), increased dropout risks (De La Rosa, 2020), and feelings of unpreparedness for learning online, reducing likelihood of success (Zhao, 2020). It has been suggested that "[at] least 24 million children are projected to drop out of school due to Covid-19" (Feuer, 2020, para 1). This situation incites online professionals to support their traditional counterparts by sharing research and best practices to overcome these challenges (Bond et al., 2018; Sandkuhl & Lehmann, 2017), especially as the long-term consequences of moving traditional learning to online are still unknown (Kuhfeld et al., 2020). Also, support for those moving online is limited, offering an opportunity for seasoned online educators to play a pivotal role in helping to support the challenges faced by these instructors and institutions (Bond et al., 2018; Sandkuhl & Lehmann, 2017).

It is with this mindset that we share our action research findings and highlight some of the immediately applicable strategies that were included in the research protocol that can support seasoned online instructors as well as those new to online learning. Our suggested research-based strategies included in this chapter, although associated with a university level learning environment, are universally applicable and can be integrated into the K-12 environment. Suggestions for applying the variables, based on age, development, and culture, are included.

BACKGROUND

The Community of Inquiry

The IP training modules that will be discussed in this chapter were the primary intervention in our research and were created based on the CoI (Figure 1) for the purpose of identifying strategies that encouraged improvement of retention, student success, and satisfaction (Garrison et al., 2000). CoI is based on constructivist principles and "encourages the construction of a social context in which collaboration creates a sense of community, and that teachers and students are active participants in the learning process" (Tam, 2000, p.51). CoI includes three areas of instructor presence (IP) that must be applied to better support learners: teaching, social, and cognitive. This model was chosen because previous research has suggested that these applications positively affect the following areas:

- Improved retention and success (Boston et al., 2009; Rebeor et al., 2019a, 2019b; Rosser-Majors et al., 2020)
- Increased satisfaction (Carr, 2000; Sliwinski & Rosser-Majors, 2018; Rosser-Majors et al., 2020)
- Improved persistence and perceptions of instructor psychological support (Roberts & Styron, 2010).
- Enhanced human connection and belonging/relatedness (Gunawardena & Zittle, 1997; Hart, 2012; Lieberman, 2013; Reeve & Lee, 2019; Vansteenkiste et al., 2020).

In addition, the CoI model specifically inspires an environment that fosters intellectual curiosity, creativity, and critical and skeptical thinking, encouraging students to explore and participate in ways that efficaciously support their success through the process of inquiry. CoI also suggests that instructors must have a learning context that invokes trust, and once obtained, will better support the needed comfort level for learners to feel safe to ask questions. CoI proposes that an online course must be "an active, constructive process whereby learners set goals for their learning and then attempt to monitor, regulate, and control their cognition, motivation, and behavior, guided and constrained by their goals and the contextual features in the environment" (Pintrich, 2000, p. 453). Hence, most important to the CoI model when adapting to online contexts, is the application of all three areas of presence in conjunction (UVA Center for Teaching Excellence, 2020), using innovative tools to achieve optimal success.

The CoI variables, teaching, social, and cognitive presence, are conveyed as an integrated application via the intentional use of available tools that can contribute to improvements in performance and retention based on students' perceptions. Perceptions are based on experiences (Jaggars et al., 2013) and mediate the relationship between the use of interactive technology tools and student engagement in the course, contributing to student satisfaction (Park & Kim, 2020). In addition, student satisfaction conspicuously affects performance and retention (Gray & DiLoreto, 2016). Therefore, as we developed our intervention we maintained that while a vast array of tools exist, instructors must fully consider each element of presence when selecting and implementing technology, avoiding the practice of using a new tool or method simply for the sake of it, or relying on an old one out of sheer habit (Rebeor, et al., 2019;

Rosser-Majors et al., 2020). In preparing our intervention we discovered that current IP findings were not specific in nature, implicitly suggesting potential strategies, decreasing the likelihood of success by some to effectively apply to the classroom. Our team spent significant time identifying specific strategies and developing examples of how these would look in a classroom to more effectively develop the instructors' teaching applications. We contend that the explicit inclusion of IP examples of teaching, social, and cognitive presence, as applied online, were instrumental to our findings.

Figure 1. Community of inquiry (CoI) model (Garrison et al., 2001)
Adapted from Garrison et al., 2001

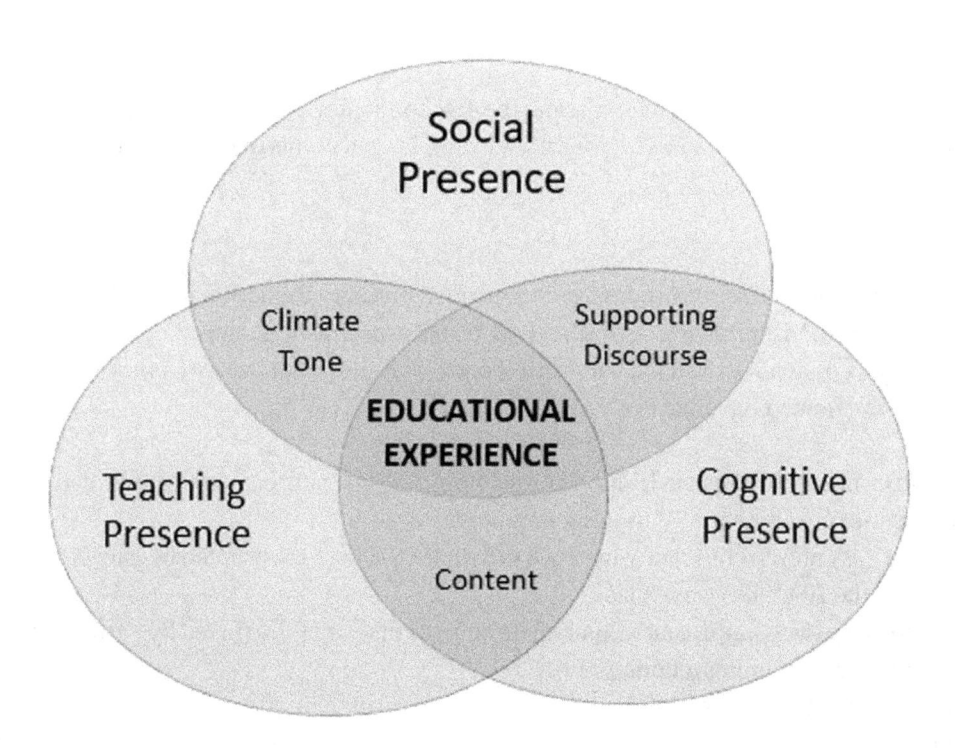

Developing Effective Instructional Techniques

Although much research was available about the positive outcomes of applying IP, very little research has noted the importance of how professional development is disseminated to effectively address outcome concerns using IP strategies. However, research does suggest that online instructors must have support in developing their craft. Lehman and Conceição (2014) state, "[a]s online courses continue to grow in number, it is essential to provide quality course design, exemplary instructional strategies, and strong support to increase online retention" (p. 11). Fortuitously, extensive research in the online educational sector has suggested that without this poignant development in online teaching applications, the prospect of executing increased presence strategies efficaciously can be daunting and often result in negative outcomes, including, but not limited to, class failures and dropouts (Xu & Jaggars, 2014). Also, virtual instructors often may not have the knowledge of the behaviors needed within the online context to increase their success (Revere & Kovach, 2011). For instructors to have success in this context, one's knowledge must be crucially scrutinized and continually developed (Rose, 2012; Rebeor et al., 2019; Rosser-Majors et al., 2020). Edwards et al. (2011) state, "[t]o develop quality online teachers, we need to understand what makes online educators not only effective but also exemplary and to consider changes face-to-face teachers need to make in order to succeed in the online milieu" (p. 102). With this information, our research centered around a self-paced series of modules supporting knowledge about IP and the CoI model that were concise, example driven, and metacognitively ambitious.

APPLYING THE COMMUNITY OF INQUIRY MODEL

In this section we will describe our methods and the 18-month process of creating and disseminating the strategy-based intervention, as well as highlight key examples and points that were used in the intervention.

Methods

The methods for our research followed the recommended protocol for action research (Sagar, 2020) and utilized a mixed methods approach, specifically, a quasi-experimental, causal comparative design and a thematic analysis of qualitative data. To fulfill the goals of the action research protocol, the following research questions framed the analysis:

1. Is a significant improvement in IP applications within the learning environment evident pre-exposure versus post-exposure to the IP training modules?
2. Do course pass rates significantly improve in courses that were instructed by participants who were exposed to the IP training modules?
3. Do course drop rates significantly improve in courses that were instructed by participants who were exposed to the IP training modules?
4. Will instructors be open to exploring IP strategies within their courses?
5. Will instructors find benefit in applying the IP strategies in their courses?
6. Will student surveys reflect positive experiences in courses where instructors are applying effective IP?

This mixed methods approach was utilized based on the suggestion that for some action research, "mixing methods has particular value when the issue under investigation is embedded in a complex educational or social context" (Bielska, 2011, p. 86). For our study, this level of complexity existed as numerous extraneous variables needed to be controlled. In addition, analyzing the effects of instructors' behaviors was necessary to evaluate how they potentially affect the learners' behaviors in the online classroom. Further, "[e]xperimental studies in action research, therefore, serve the purpose of enabling teachers to make, evaluate, or justify their choices concerning classroom instruction by testing hypotheses related to the contextualised use of pedagogical procedures" (Bielska, 2011, p. 88).

Our research team consisted of seven full-time online institutional faculty members. Once the modality for delivering the intervention, a seven module self-paced training series based on the CoI model, was determined, the research protocol was established, and IRB approval was obtained. The study followed OHRP guidelines (https://www.hhs.gov/ohrp/) for protection of human subjects.

Once approved, we recruited participants from the college to complete the intervention. It was also important to identify participants who were willing to allow us to rate their levels of applied IP strategies prior to receiving the intervention and afterwards, as well as complete two self-assessments. All participants were given the same intervention opportunity. Initially, 81 instructors agreed to participate.

Our next step was to develop the intervention. We focused on how the IP training series for instructors should be organized to be most effective. We chose to present the information in a way that emphasized the goal of increased cognitive presence by both the instructor and the student that could be obtained by utilizing the supporting areas of social and teaching presence:

1. Module 1: Introduction to Instructor Presence and CoI
2. Module 2: Cognitive Presence- Part 1
3. Module 3: Cognitive Presence- Part 2
4. Module 4: Social Presence – Part 1
5. Module 5: Social Presence – Part 2
6. Module 6: Teaching Presence
7. Module 7: That's a Wrap – Applying all 3 Areas of Presence (Included a post-assessment.)

Next, we worked in pairs with a media specialist to create immediately-applicable strategy examples to be included in each module. Each module was designed to walk instructors through the essential applications of cognitive, social, and teaching presence. During the development of our first two modules, a pre-assessment was sent to the participants evaluating their knowledge and predispositions about IP. These results guided our design so that any concerns or inaccurate understanding of IP were addressed within the modules.

The seven modules were then disseminated to the research participants (81), all of whom were online instructors for the fully online institution. The modules were completed over a period of 18 months, and each module was released upon availability during the development period. Forty-seven participants completed the module series and were included in our analysis.

To analyze improvement and effects, we designed a rubric, which was calibrated to establish inter-rater reliability (intraclass correlation coefficient [ICC = .9]) and utilized it to measure the level of each area of IP demonstrated by the participating instructors in their courses, both prior to being exposed to the IP strategy-based development series and following the exposure. Five members of our team were assigned to utilize the rubric to evaluate IP applications. To prevent unconscious bias and substantiate rigor, three members were assigned to review each course. Two courses per participant (i.e., instructor), two before and two after the training series intervention, were evaluated using the rubric. The number of courses reviewed for IP applications, based on completion of the modules, were 94 courses prior to receiving the intervention and 94 courses post treatment. Total reviews completed were 282 pre-exposure and 282 post-exposure. Once an instructor's courses had been evaluated by our team, the identifiers were coded and removed. Next, using the rater scores, numerical ratings were averaged for each area of presence applied, and one holistic score that averaged all three areas of presence, for each participant.

Lastly, data associated with course drops, student pass rates pre- and post-training, satisfaction, and perceptions of the courses from the student perspective (end-of-course surveys) were collected by our primary investigator. The collection of data included pre- and post-intervention three months, as well as one-year post training. Using SPSS, the data were analyzed using paired samples two-tailed *t* tests and ANOVA. The multivariate test, Wilks' Lambda, was utilized to increase the rigor of the analysis and account for instructor characteristics that could potentially affect improved pass rates and drops: degree level (masters or doctoral degree), program alignment level (undergraduate versus graduate), instructors' department alignment (health versus behavioral sciences, performance scores (instructional quality review scores + faculty activity scores + end of source student survey scores), experience (low: 2-6 years; high: 7+ years), and longevity with the institution. Student and instructor comments were also analyzed using interpretive qualitative methods to triangulate the findings.

Intervention Development

As noted, key to this research was the intervention offered to all of our participants: seven online self-paced development modules that were created using Articulate Storyline 2 software (https://articulate.com). In addition, Animaker (https://www.animaker.com) was used to create the animated videos that were included to support the application of example scenarios. Each module took approximately one hour for each instructor to complete.

The following sections highlight the specific strategies and summarizations that were included in each module. The disseminated information was based on the CoI model (Garrison et al., 2000, 2001, 2007, 2010), and included innovative examples, created by our team, for applying each area. Our training series followed the guidelines suggested by previous research that emphasized that higher levels of IP applicability are related, both directly and indirectly, to student satisfaction (Garrison, 2007; Akyol & Garrison, 2008, 2013; Martirosyan et al., 2014), reduced feelings of isolation (Collins et al., 2019), and improved attrition and retention (Wanstreet & Stein, 2011; Xu & Jaggars, 2014). Inclusive of all modules, interactive self-practice activities were utilized to substantiate a clear understanding of IP and CoI, and how these could be applied in the online classroom.

Module 1: Introduction to Instructor Presence and CoI

The first module introduced the participants to the CoI model and explained how each area of presence built upon one another, and were dependent upon each other, much like the building of a house (Figure 2). We included significant research findings, such as shared in this chapter previously, to create a solid understanding of the theoretical findings that supported the IP protocol, as well as the final outcomes and applications that were desired by our team. Specifically, we also shared how we, as instructors, are crucial to promoting an online environment where student behaviors are cultivated and may improve their engagement, substantiating and improving overall learning outcomes, retention, and satisfaction.

Applying Online Instructor Presence Amidst Changing Times

Figure 2. IP construct dependence

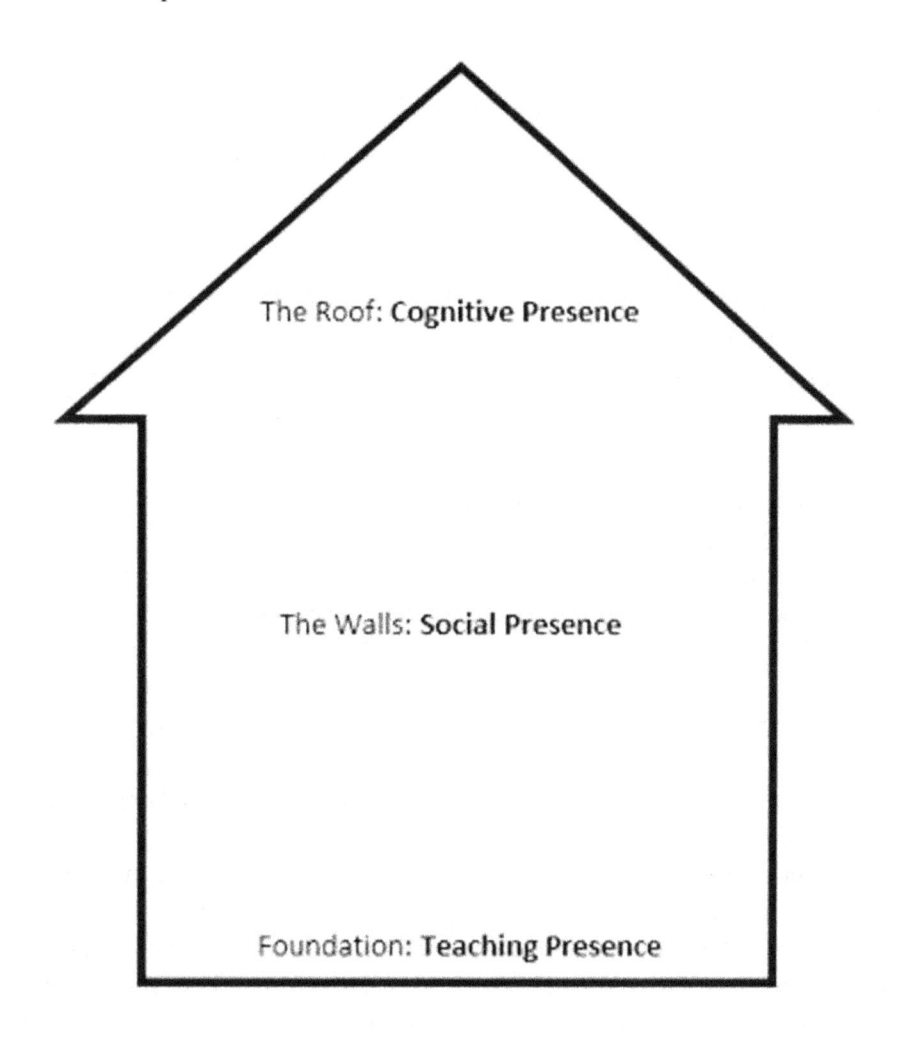

The Roof: **Cognitive Presence**

The Walls: **Social Presence**

Foundation: **Teaching Presence**

Figure 3. Cognitive presence: A reciprocal process

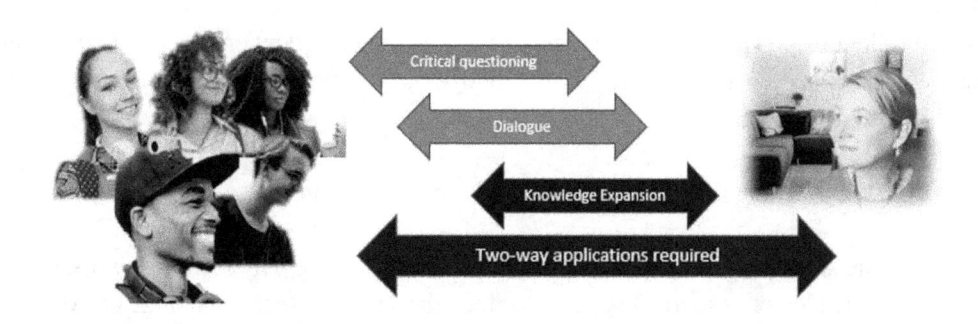

Critical questioning

Dialogue

Knowledge Expansion

Two-way applications required

Modules 2 and 3: Cognitive Presence

Modules Two and Three covered cognitive presence: the process of constructing meaning through discourse and reflection (Akyol & Garrison, 2008, 2013; Garrison et al., 2001; Garrison & Arbaugh, 2007; Garrison et. al., 2010). These modules focused on how cognitive presence requires reciprocal inquiry from both the instructor and the student (Figure 3), and is a challenge to fulfill if trust (discussed in Modules Four and Five) has not been established in the learning community. We posed that cognitive presence should be applied, using very specific strategies for increasing critical inquiry and skeptical thought, engagement, and dialogue throughout the learning environment, suggesting that when students and instructors both create meaningful contributions, increased understanding is cultivated, and a cognitively stimulating environment (where inquiry drives the engagement for knowledge) is encouraged.

Discussion Forums

In our modules about cognitive presence applied to discussions, we focused on how online discussion forums can quickly get boring as they may appear to not be mentally stimulating or repetitive in that a response to one or more questions is required, resulting in the same or similar responses by students. To address, we modeled strategies that instructors and course designers could apply to keep discussions vibrant and diverse. The below-mentioned strategies are but an example of the inclusions:

1. Provide students with choices (i.e. case studies, scenarios) to create autonomy, foster creativity, and share interests.
2. Provide multiple platforms for learning (i.e. audio, video, relevant research/examples, interactive texts, etc.).
3. Provide reflection-based assignments, as they naturally create diverse responses and allow students to connect the learned content to their experiences.
4. Require peer replies to foster peer-to-peer learning and networking. We suggest requiring a minimum word count and number of resources utilized to reduce the likelihood of short, shallow responses.
5. Clearly state expectations to avoid uncertainty or confusion among students. Examples can be useful as well.
6. Respond with intellectual and critical thought by sharing expertise, knowledge, research, and resources to further clarify content or concepts and increase content mastery.
7. Promote inquiry by asking a variety of critical thinking questions to encourage deeper topic exploration.
8. Integrate student responses in replies to encourage additional student engagement and community.
9. Proactively reach out to students who are not engaged or missing and/or misunderstanding certain elements of their assignment.

We also suggested avoiding the following "pitfalls" applicable to many groups of learners:

1. Avoid using the statement "great job" without further explaining why students' work was "great."
2. Do not share articles or resources if they do not relate to the weekly content or course content (unless the relationship to the content is explicitly explained) as this may create confusion among students. Be sure to connect the resources/reply to the student's initial work.

Applying Online Instructor Presence Amidst Changing Times

3. Avoid using "canned" responses. Instead, tailor responses to individual students.
4. When a student misunderstands a concept/theory/definition, etcetera, do not ask questions that may further create confusion or that add unnecessary information without clarifying the misunderstood element. Let students know that your "door" is open if anything is unclear, and encourage students to ask questions when they arise.
5. Do not just "check the boxes" by making a brief appearance, without providing substantive feedback, knowledge, and content. Efforts and time invested in the cognitive presence component will very likely be noted and appreciated by learners.

The aforementioned examples present only a sampling of options and advice that we shared to encourage the fostering of cognitive presence within discussion forums. Instructors' expertise and creativity were encouraged to create and facilitate uniquely engaging online discussions. We recommended that all instructors teaching online, be cognizant of how applied strategies, utilized by educators, may "look" diverse, based on age, development, and content, to name only a few.

Grading Feedback

In addition, we connected our cognitive presence strategies to grading feedback, recommending that cognitive presence is crucial when providing feedback for discussions and other assignments. Various strategies were included for the instructors to effectively apply when grading students' work to demonstrate cognitive presence. Here are some strategies for success that were shared in these two modules:

1. Is it enough? Merely stating "Good job on this assignment", followed by a grade and rubric, rarely demonstrates interest, expertise, or cognitive involvement on behalf of the instructor. Students may question the instructor's value, sincerity, and expertise.
2. Is it too much? As an instructor, it is critical to provide sufficient feedback without being too long-winded as students may not read all of the feedback if it is excessive in length.
3. Point out strengths while offering opportunities for improvement.
4. Ask questions to increase critical thinking and reflection (i.e. Based on..., as specified in Chapter 3 of our course text, how would you apply this in the real world?).
5. Ensure feedback is balanced in terms of quality and quantity. Quantitative elements are always an important consideration, but the quality of the knowledge shared should be fully addressed.
6. Provide direct links and attachments to resources to further encourage critical thinking, effective knowledge acquisition, and reflection (i.e. additional articles, credible sources, and institutional resources that support content understanding and academic writing practices).
7. Clarify concepts that are misunderstood by reframing them in terms that may be easier to grasp (i.e. by providing examples).
8. Conduct similarity checks to uphold your institution's academic integrity by identifying plagiarism, collusion, and other incidents early on during the student's program of study.
9. Refer to the assignment prompt and grading rubric within the paper and/or summative feedback so that students understand the connection between their work and the rating on the rubric, based on the requirements.

Figure 4. Example postings—high versus low cognitive engagement

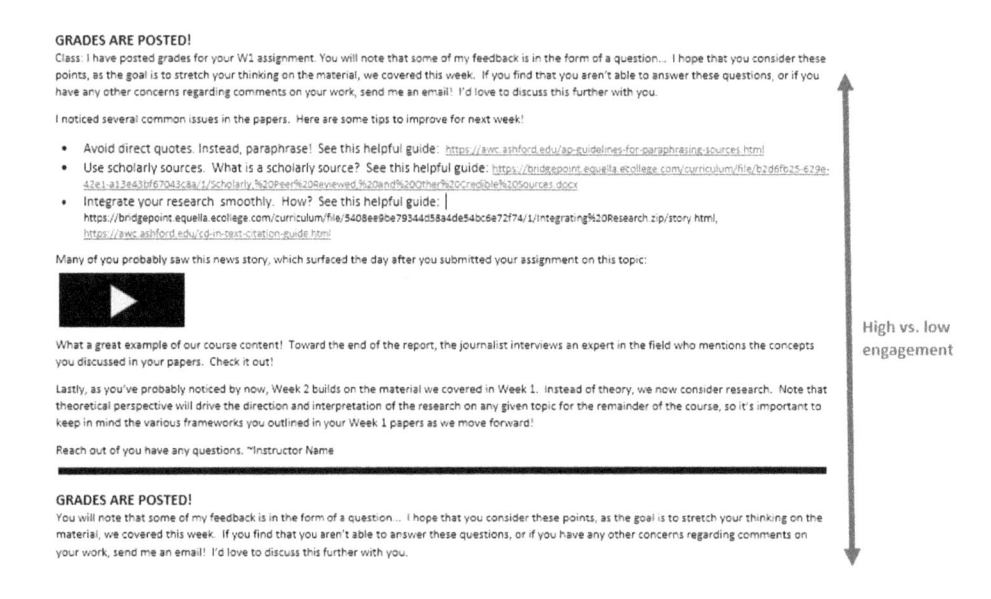

By applying these cognitive presence strategies via grading feedback on discussions and other assignments, research suggested that students would more effectively engage with the content in the online course.

Announcements and Email Communications

Announcements and email communications were also a facet of these two modules, suggesting an opportunity to foster cognitive presence through explicit inquiry-driven inclusions. We encouraged thinking beyond one-liner announcements and instead, giving students important, relevant, and informative content that allows them to truly engage. We encouraged the instructors to post announcements that motivate their students to actively seek knowledge and engage with the topics at hand, which can then be shared via discussions with peers and other assignments. We suggested the following strategies:

1. Include tips, recorded and written, to help students complete upcoming assignments successfully without simply repeating the instructions.
2. Offer encouragement, clarifications, and supporting resources.
3. Offer holistic feedback on graded assignments that includes praise as well as opportunities for improvement.
4. Refer students to resources to improve their understanding of the content and academic writing skills.
5. Provide additional in-house and global resources (i.e. links to articles, websites, recent news, and videos) as applicable to the content material.
6. Make access to additional resources easy by embedding videos or providing direct links to resources.
7. Ask questions! Encourage students to think critically about the content by asking questions in the announcements. Use phrases that encourage a response (i.e. I look forward to your thoughts.)

8. Connect the course content to the "real world", making the new information more relevant and more easily scaffolded (Mahan, 2020; Pitkänen et al., 2020).
9. Communicate the "big picture" by connecting to the previous weeks' content.
10. Offer your explicit help! Remind students that you are there to support their success.

Figure 5. Social presence components

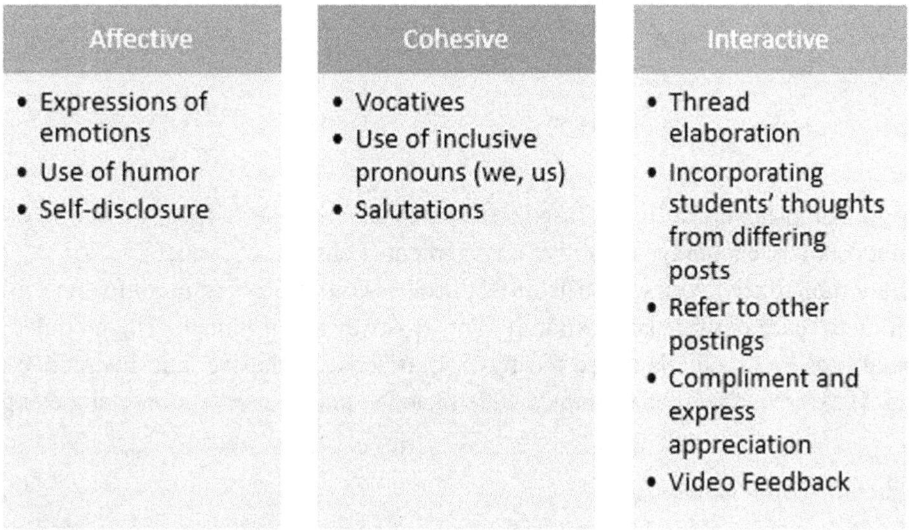

Affective	Cohesive	Interactive
• Expressions of emotions • Use of humor • Self-disclosure	• Vocatives • Use of inclusive pronouns (we, us) • Salutations	• Thread elaboration • Incorporating students' thoughts from differing posts • Refer to other postings • Compliment and express appreciation • Video Feedback

We shared also how announcements and email communications can provide instructors with opportunities to share their knowledge and expertise, as students often appreciate the personal perspectives and may be more encouraged to seek critical knowledge, substantiating that creating high level versus low level cognitive engagement opportunities must be purposeful and notably helpful to the students. Figure 4 was one example shared in the modules.

Modules 4 and 5: Social Presence

Modules Four and Five were based on social presence: the ability of instructors to show their real self in the online classroom, which is suggested to help develop a trusting relationship with the student and provides the instructor with an opportunity to add their own personality into the classroom. In addition, it supports the building of a community of learners by improving relationships through expression of individual identities that create the whole (Garrison et al., 2001). These two modules highlighted how social presence can also pique student interest and enthusiasm about what will be learned, reduce feelings of isolation (Collins et al., 2019), improve attrition and retention (Wanstreet & Stein, 2011; Xu & Jaggars, 2014), and improve efficacy for learning in the environment. We also suggested that there are diverse strategies for applying social presence and that instructors should be creative, innovative, and open. Thinking outside the box was highly recommended and should include purposeful support, sharing of experiences, and real-life examples to build the foundation of trust.

Figure 6. Affective and cohesive method examples.

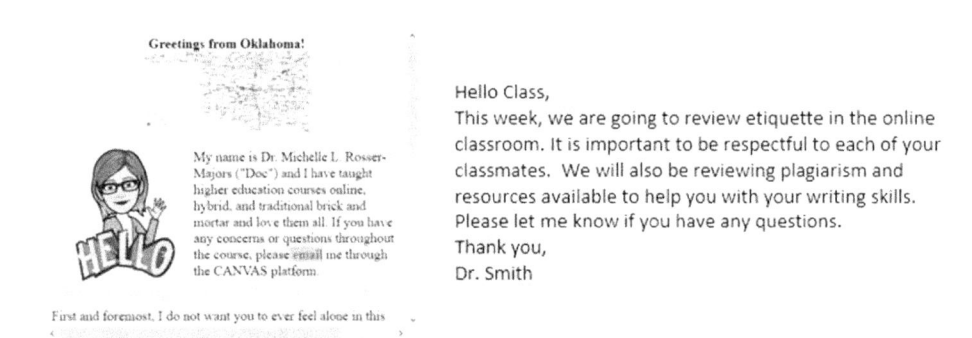

Our strategy examples were designed based on research that suggests that a sense of trust built by social presence is important to encourage cognitive engagement (Lehman & Conceição, 2013). CoI suggests that students are more likely to view instructor feedback as constructive or if confusion arises, students are more willing to reach out for clarification if they "trust" the environment. The modules highlighted the three social presence methods suggested by CoI: affective, cohesive, and interactive (Whiteside, 2015) (Figure 5). Affective method examples were included in our intervention include expressions of

Figure 7. Personalized Message.

emotion, humor, and self-disclosure in the online learning environment. For example, we suggested that instructors could post an introductory video that provides information about family, hobbies, and interests. Examples such as these further elaborated on how students, who know more about their instructor, may develop an increased level of trust and be more likely to reach out to the instructor when they have a question or problem in the course. Another example we used of an "affective" method was the use of humor, such as posting a cartoon or funny video through an announcement. Cohesive methods included using vocatives, inclusive pronouns, and salutations. We demonstrated through examples how instructors could personalize communications with their students, showing them that they are valued and recognized as an individual, reinforcing respect and fostering a trusting relationship in the online environment (Figure 6).

Finally, the interactive approach, suggested as bringing humanization to the online classroom, was addressed. Effective ways that we suggested to provide interactive social presence methods included: 1) providing audio and video grading feedback and 2) discussion forum participation that contains audio, video, or other resources to enhance the weekly learning concepts. However, we acknowledged, based on the pre-assessment, how this can be challenging to some (i.e. videoing oneself), and identified many options for presenting information creatively in a more personal manner, addressing a person's needs for increased privacy. For example, we suggested using an online avatar to welcome the class to the online classroom. (See examples at https://www.voki.com.) We also included creating a Bitmoji or a self-created personalized message (Figure 7) to promote belonging and trust. A list of possible software for creating audio, videos, and using vokis can also be found in the Additional Resources section of this chapter.

Along with audio and visual components in the discussion threads, we elaborated on how instructors can integrate other students' comments into their responses and promote peer collaboration. Example: "Great posting, John. You and Moesha both highlighted important areas of this concept. Consider reviewing your peer's posting to help elaborate on your initial thoughts..." We substantiated how this method also encourages students to collaborate with the instructor, sharing their own views on the concepts. Additionally, as suggested by CoI, we outlined how connections could be created between student to student and student to instructor using strategies; thus, strengthening the relationship among the course community and improving the trust factor within the environment. We also suggested that these social connections increase students' perceptions of the course.

Discussions

In the social presence modules, we also advocated that discussions could be utilized to help students feel comfortable in the more public area of an online course. With the goal of increasing cognitive exchange, this area can often be neglected by students, as they may not understand the purpose and value (Aloni & Harrington, 2018). Using social presence strategies successfully, we identified how these applications demonstrated attention, effort, care, and commitment to one's students, increasing a student's willingness to participate. The following are example strategies we included to help instructors in supporting their students' feelings of connection, safety, and efficacy to ask questions and share information.

1. Purposefully create a warm and inviting tone when you reply to students.
2. Reread (out loud) what you wrote, putting yourself in the position of the student.
3. Add gifs and images that encourage students.
4. When students reply, acknowledge their efforts by responding, either "closing" the dialogue or further discussing the response and content (more about this later, in connection to cognitive presence).
5. Integrate personal examples to build trust with students increasing trust, transparency, and a sense of belonging (Gunawardena & Zittle, 1997; Hart, 2012; Lieberman, 2013; Reeve & Lee, 2019; Vansteenkiste et al., 2020).
6. Use *vocative case* and *valediction* (i.e. "Thanks for your posting, Tremaine... I look forward to your thoughts and hope your week has gone well. ~Instructor Name").

Announcements

In the area of social presence, we also suggested using the announcement area in the online course. We outlined how and why it is best to start this early in a course to encourage shared communication engagement, and substantiate the instructor's support, especially as increased cognitive presence strategies are added. In cases where an announcement area may not be available, we suggested emailing students with similar uplifting and supportive messages as a potential option. Examples:

1. Provide words of encouragement, such as inspirational quotes, uplifting videos, or your own messages to keep students encouraged and motivated. Humorous content, such as jokes, are generally enjoyed by students.
2. Share institutional events with students, such as webinars, career fairs, conferences, and club activities.
3. Create "catchy" announcement titles to get students curious about reading the content, such as "What's happening in Week 3? – Check this out!"; "Have you heard the news yet? – A New Resource was created for YOU!"; "Week 5 Tips to End this Course with a Home Run!"

To connect the three-facet CoI model we emphasized that once social presence was established, trust of the environment should increase (Flock, 2020), supporting both teaching and cognitive presence.

Module 6: Teaching Presence

Module 6 addressed teaching presence, the process by which those involved in the course construction (i.e. an instructor and/or content team) promote a quality online environment and facilitate an effective CoI, including audience age-based design and organization, facilitation of discourse, and direct instruction (Figure 8) (Garrison et al., 2000, 2001, 2007, 2010).

Figure 8. Components of teaching presence

The module also elaborated on the instructional practices of sharing clear expectations and specific feedback. We presented teaching presence as the foundation that must be solid to fully develop its partners: social and cognitive presence. The module suggested the following areas as important to success: course design, facilitation, and direct instruction (Garrison et al., 2000, 2001, 2010).

Course Design

The module first elaborated on how the course design creates the basis for effective teaching presence and is a priority to successful IP integration (Castellanos-Reyes, 2020). We demonstrated how clear and concise assignment directions, appropriate activity prompts, and logical content presentation are key. In addition, we highlighted the following based on the CoI model:

1. Directions for assignments and discussions must take into consideration students' development throughout their course and the academic program.
2. Terminology and wording for a lower-level course should be simplified as compared to an upper-level course.
3. Evaluation of student performance throughout a course gives designers and instructors a better understanding as to whether an element of a prompt is too wordy or unclear.
4. At times, aspects of an assignment may need to be clarified after the course-live date as discrepancies relating to content directions and/or content to rubric alignment may exist.
5. Instructors and course designers should view a course from the perspective of the learner, also addressing the developmental and previous experiences and knowledge of all students (Birgbauer, 2016).

Assessment rubrics were also addressed in this model as key to improving a student's understanding of expectations and should be utilized and align with the assignment/activity prompt, defining what the various ratings are, denoting what "distinguished" (or another descriptor) looks like (Garrison et al., 2000, 2001, 2010). Rubric examples were highlighted in the modules as valuable in guiding students in the completion of the content, but also as a self-assessment tool, based on the course expectations. We noted that rubrics should accompany discussion prompts and other assignments to further clarify expectations. The instructors were guided through a process of evaluating the effectiveness of using the rubrics. The following strategies were suggested in the module to integrate teaching presence into online activities:

1. Link content to external and real-life experiences, such as current events or personal/professional student experiences.
2. Create a connection to the field of study via case scenarios, recent events, or research, allowing students to demonstrate their knowledge as if they were working in the field.
    a. For younger learners, games and interesting facts about the subject matter may be utilized.
3. Connect content to the textbook and other useful resources to further engage students and make the weekly information more relevant and memorable.
4. Create educational experiences by designing discussion prompts to improve interactions between students and the instructor.
5. Design assignments prompting reflection to allow students to evaluate content based on their past experiences and/or future goals.

Facilitation

For discussions and assignments, Module Six also indicated how clear expectations, both written and verbal, should be used to avoid confusion and frustration. Directly stating the late policy and rationale for actions when grading and enforcing policies, such as academic integrity, were also addressed. Instructors were encouraged to provide additional examples and links to resources whenever possible to clarify expectations. Suggestions included embedded links to a paper review service, such as Grammarly (https://www.grammarly.com), or tutoring services. Announcements were also noted as an excellent way to post policies and expectations prior to the course and as needed throughout the course. When announcements are not available in the learning management system (LMS), our suggested strategies included the use of email communications.

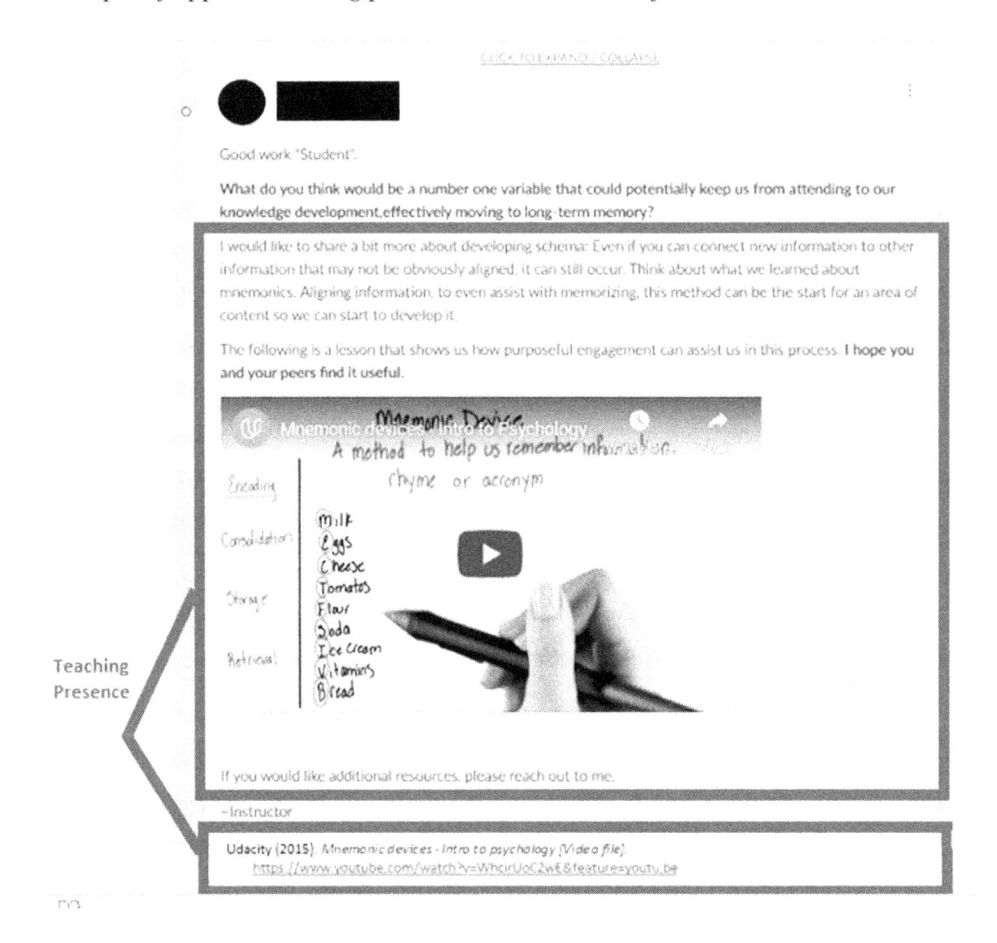

Figure 9. Example of applied teaching presence in a discussion forum

Direct Instruction

Direct instruction, based on CoI, entails any direct communication between the instructor and students, such as instructive feedback. The instructors were encouraged to think about how to increase their success when communicating with students. Various strategies were noted, such as the modeling of expectations and the importance of specificity. For instance, we suggested that instructors should model citation and reference formatting guidelines, a respectful tone, inclusive communication, use of resources (i.e. by embedding videos, outside links, and utilizing scholarly articles to support responses to students), and clear, yet detailed contributions that are thought-provoking, when facilitating a course. Effective direct instruction was also suggested as applied to announcements, discussion forum responses, when grading assignments, and even communicating with students via email, in-classroom messaging, phone, or virtual conferencing platforms (Figure 9).

We also addressed how teaching presence suggests that timely and clear feedback is of the upmost importance, as students must know how to apply development to ongoing assignments. Self-assessment of teaching practices, to allow for improvement of presence techniques in the courses we teach, was also suggested with particular focus on the value students have placed on receiving an education; and hence, best practices should be applied consistently.

Lastly, this module guided instructors through the area of giving feedback, which we suggested should respect and embrace students' individual cognitive styles and learning preferences, since students have unique needs in terms of problem solving, thinking, perceiving, and remembering, as well as how this unique style or preferred method is applied to a specific learning situation (Allport, 1937; Riding & Cheema, 1991). In alignment to diverse needs, the module also noted the multitude of theories that exist pertaining to learning styles and preferences, such as Gardner's Multiple Intelligences (Gardner, 2000). This theory suggests different areas of strength and weakness for individuals and promotes the use of various modes of learning in application to designing, facilitating, and communicating with students with respect to factors, such as cultural backgrounds, age, and experiences. The module also highlighted the importance of being sensitive to such factors. We suggested the inclusion of audio, video, text-based, and visual content within feedback, to support student preferences and learning styles to encourage success in the classroom.

Module 7: That's a Wrap

The final module reviewed the information from past modules and reinforced the unification of strategies, being cognizant of the importance for how each area of presence builds upon one another. Key points were made addressing why all three must be applied in one's courses. Examples of key points included:

1. An environment devoid of social presence is unlikely to engage students and build trust in the learning environment, hence, teaching and cognitive presence may go unappreciated.
2. If teaching presence is lacking, students can be confused and frustrated as the information is not clear and even missing. No amount of trust (social presence) can reduce a confused learner, struggling to understand the content.
3. If successful teaching and social presence are not established, students may feel less able to engage with the instructor, and their peers, critically (cognitive presence).
4. Without cognitive presence, the student may successfully access materials and feel trust for the environment, but may only engage in rote, or at best, shallow learning.
5. Students in online courses equally value qualities aligned with IP (Sheridan & Kelly, 2010). Hence, creating cohesive IP strategies are essential to fully capitalize on the benefits of applying IP, improving performance and retention (Park & Kim, 2020).

Lastly, based on the self-assessment results taken prior to the intervention launch, predispositions of the instructors, which will be further addressed in the section titled "Challenges", were strategically addressed making note of the potential improvement of outcomes, level of engagement by students, and increased satisfaction of the instructors, making the level of effort applied worthwhile.

FINDINGS

Our research findings suggested that instructors' behaviors affect student behaviors that promote improved outcomes. Specifically, instructors who are successfully applying IP have a significant impact on the success that students experience in online courses. Moreover, the three areas of presence (teaching, social, and cognitive), working in unity, encourage meaningful engagement from students. Student drop and pass rates significantly improved in courses where the instructor had been exposed to IP training: pass rates ($p = .05$); drop rates ($p < .001$). In addition, all of the instructors who had completed the training intervention (47) had applied the strategies in their courses. The improvement of applying each area was significant for these participants: social presence ($p = .000$); cognitive presence, ($p=.000$); and teaching presence ($p =.008$). Most extraneous variables were found not to be significant with regard to drops and pass rate improvement. There was a marginally significant interaction effect of performance on both, pass and drop rates ($p =.05$), suggesting a greater improvement pre-to-post by high performing instructors. Based on our qualitative analysis, instructors also found benefit in applying the strategies and self-reported feeling motivated and excited about the IP practices.

Statement Example 1: "Thank you for offering such an incredible training. I think that we can all get a little bit stuck doing things just one way, and this has certainly opened my eyes to some amazing new strategies to apply in my classroom. I am so excited to get started!"

Statement Example 2: "I found it a good learning experience to give me the scholarly background for why these interrelated concepts are important for student learning and retention. I find myself already using some of these techniques in my current class."

Statement Example 3: "…Just a short note on my experience with video responses and the impact on instructor surveys and retention. My survey percentages for the 1/22 course were the best I have ever had. … according to student responses it was directly connected to video responses for all DQ's and announcements. I believe that retention was better too because of personal touch…Glad I did the training modules to find out this option existed."

Lastly, our team analyzed student end-of course surveys associated with the instructors (pre- and post-intervention) who had completed the training. It was noted that there was an increase in student comments suggesting that the instructor engagement was appreciated and helpful, pre-intervention versus post-intervention. The following are but a sample of the comments made by students:

- "The instructor has been very active and provides feedback in her own unique way, which is very engaging and interactive. Her feedback is very informative and helpful. This is the best instructor I have had so far…"
- "…the instructor has been pivotal in my success... She is a wonderful instructor that further explains material, asks thought-provoking questions, and really helps guide the classroom. She is always willing to help, and will reach out to you if she feels you need some extra help. Her encouragement truly made a difference in my education!"
- "This course was challenging but the instructor's feedback and course structure made it clear what was required in order to succeed. I really appreciate the instructor's feedback because he pushed the class to think critically!"

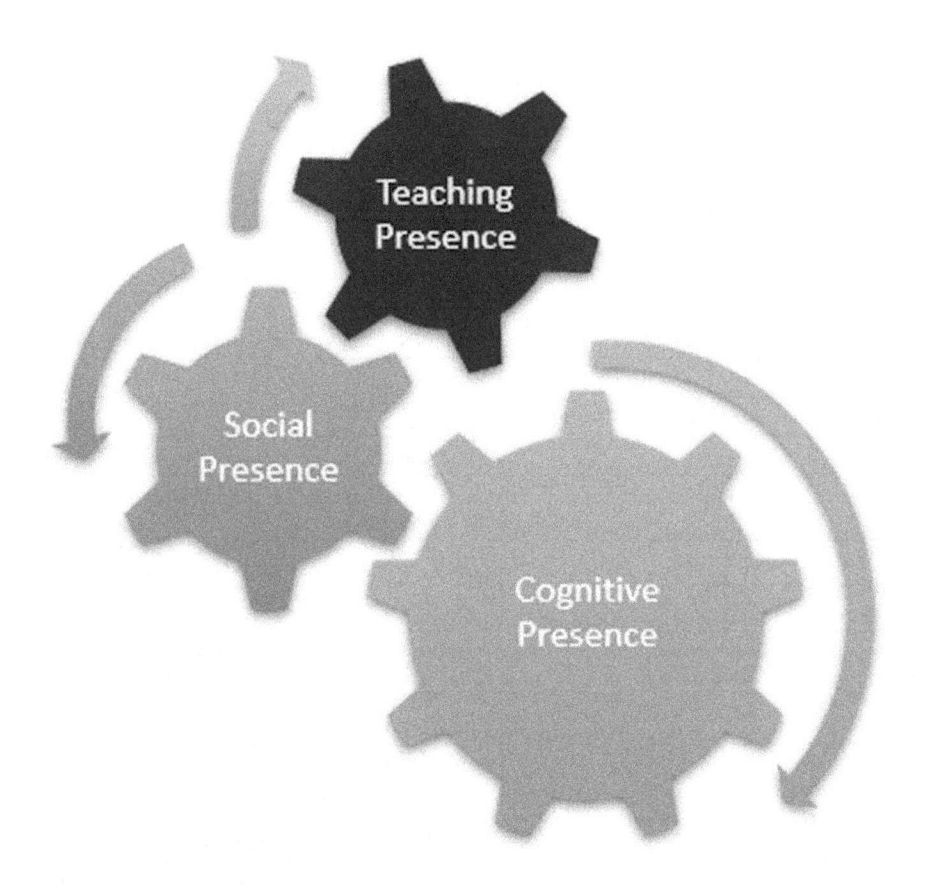

Figure 10. All areas of CoI must work in a unified manner for maximum success

Further analysis demonstrated that effective IP was still being applied by the trained instructors one-year post-exposure, suggesting sustainability of the intervention.

Challenges

Our research, as well as previous research, has proposed that the application of teaching, social, and cognitive presence is a key component of a successful online course and should be cohesively applied; therefore, this was the focus of our module development intervention series. However, developing training that supports diverse teaching philosophies, personalities, predispositions, purpose, or other factors was a key challenge in designing the intervention. Two key obstacles, based on the qualitative analysis of pre- and post-assessments by all participants, were identified: 1) unconscious bias towards one area of presence over another, and 2) predispositions associated with applying IP.

Table 1. Free online software resources

General Educational Resources (Resources, Tools, Activities, etc.)		Specific Content Areas
123 Homeschool for ME: https://www.123homeschool4me.com/home-school-free-printables/	**Physical Health**	Go Noodle: movement and mindfulness videos https://www.gonoodle.com/# Physical Activity for Youth: https://food.unl.edu/physical-activity-youth
Amazing Educational Resources: https://www.amazingeducationalresources.com/	**Music**	Chrome Music Lab: activities https://musiclab.chromeexperiments.com/ Music Theory: exercises and tools https://www.musictheory.net/
Discovery K12: http://discoveryk12.com/dk12/	**Art**	Sketchpad: online tools to create digital art https://sketch.io/sketchpad/ Sumopaint: drawing tool and image editor https://sumo.app/paint
Exploratorium: websites, activities, apps, videos, and more https://www.exploratorium.edu/explore	**Literacy**	Storyline Online: videos of illustrated books read aloud https://www.storylineonline.net/ Typing.com: keyboarding, coding, and digital literacy https://www.typing.com/
Funbrain: games, videos and more https://www.funbrain.com/	**History & Geography**	National Geographic Kids: games, videos, and more https://kids.nationalgeographic.com/ The Hidden Worlds of the National Parks: videos https://artsandculture.withgoogle.com/en-us/national-parks-service/parks American Panorama: atlas of United States history https://dsl.richmond.edu/panorama/ Big History Project: general history course https://www.oerproject.com/Big-History World History Project: world history course https://www.oerproject.com/World-History
Learning Games for Kids: educational games on a variety of topics https://www.learninggamesforkids.com/		
PBS Kids: games, videos, and more https://pbskids.org/		
Purple Mash: https://2simple.com/blog/using-purple-mash-when-school-closed/	**Math**	Prodigy: math games https://www.prodigygame.com/main-en/ Cool Math: learning games and information https://www.coolmath.com/ Cool Math for Kids: learning games https://www.coolmath4kids.com/
PBS Learning Media: videos, interactives, and more https://ca.pbslearningmedia.org/ Teaching Online: Best Practices, Technology & Tools https://www.nagc.org/teaching-online-best-practices-technology-tools	**Science**	Highlights Kids: games, activities, information, and more https://www.highlightskids.com/ The Old Farmer's Almanac for Kids: stories, activities, information https://www.almanac.com/kids San Diego Kids Zoo: activities, videos, games, and more https://kids.sandiegozoo.org/ San Diego Zoo: live cam https://zoo.sandiegozoo.org/live-cams Mystery Science: activities and videos https://mysteryscience.com/distance-learning Nick Jr.: games and videos http://www.nickjr.com/ Toy Theater: art creation tools and educational activities https://toytheater.com/category/art/ Access Mars: explore the surface of Mars: https://accessmars.withgoogle.com/
	Stress Management	Stress Management for Children: https://www.mottchildren.org/health-library/aba5971 Stress Management Resources for Teens: https://www.healthychildren.org/English/healthy-living/emotional-wellness/Building-Resilience/Pages/For-Teens-Creating-Your-Personal-Stress-Management-Plan.aspx

Unconscious Bias

Based on the self-assessments, it was evident that some instructors found one strategy, or area of IP, more natural or easier to apply. This unconscious bias was most prevalent in two identified themes: 1) preferred past practices and 2) one's past teaching experiences. However, as has been suggested, the IP strategies are to be applied in unity (Figure 10) to obtain optimal results; hence, discovering ways to effectively communicate this importance was a challenge. We addressed this by using the final module to substantiate how the three areas of presence should be applied as one, using examples and applied practice activities.

Predispositions

As we prepared the training series for this project, a pre-assessment suggested that the predisposition of instructors associated with their knowledge about applying the IP strategies were also a challenge. One such area was about the use of software, especially in the areas of difficulty of use and cost, which has also been noted by other researchers as an instructor concern (Eiland & Todd, 2019). Thus, it was important for us to identify online tools that could support each area of presence that reduced these concerns. The following resources (Table 1) have been adapted for this chapter, to bring awareness of free resources that not only support those in higher education, but also for the readers who may be associated with K-12 online learning modalities. We encourage the readers to search online to identify additional resources that further support specific content and the target learner age group.

Another area of instructor predisposition that we identified was that of time. Instructors suggested that too much time might be needed to successfully apply the unified strategies of IP, increasing feelings of being overwhelmed and of decreased satisfaction. However, after applying techniques, we found that a significant number of instructors indicated that they are more satisfied with their teaching experience and the students' level of engagement (Rebeor et al., 2019a, 2019b; Sliwinski & Rosser-Majors, 2018). It was suggested by some instructors that by more effectively applying IP, time spent answering questions, clearing up miscommunications, and re-explaining instructions were replaced with inspiring learning participation and a development for a love for learning.

SOLUTIONS AND RECOMMENDATIONS

Our research was dependent upon the treatment intervention which was a self-paced training series that identified applicable strategies associated with IP, and provided opportunities for self-assessment and practice. Based on our findings and our experience developing the modules, we recommend that online and hybrid instructors, seeking to improve outcomes in their courses, be exposed to similar training and applications, such as described previously in this chapter. It is also recommended that administrators consider similar training that can support instructor enthusiasm and enhance student outcomes. We propose that the foundational components of IP are an important aspect of consideration associated with improving outcomes for online learners.

FUTURE RESEARCH DIRECTIONS

As the global community continues to be impacted by threats that may force learners to engage online more frequently, it will be important to continue to develop tools and software that can create online learning opportunities to support learning success for all. We suggest that further research be conducted to evaluate students' beliefs of what each type of presence would, or should, look like in an online classroom, further supporting the success of outcomes associated with IP. This approach will also identify diverse strategies based on student needs that can be implemented.

In addition, we propose that the personality characteristics of instructors may be an important variable to consider when addressing effective training and mentoring opportunities. As highlighted in research, an instructor's personality traits can have both positive and negative effects on the learner and learning success (Maazouzi, 2019; Noreen et al., 2019). Giamatti (1988) emphasizes that "[t]eaching is an instinctual art, mindful of potential, craving of realizations, a pausing, seamless process" (p. 194). Palmer (2007) points out that "[g]ood teachers join self, subject, and students in the fabric of life.... they can weave a complex web of connections between themselves, their subjects, and their students so that students can learn to contrive a world for themselves" (p. 11). By identifying whether specific personality characteristics of educators indicate an ability to apply differing areas of IP (teaching versus social versus cognitive presence) with greater success, or less success, training can be developed that explicitly provides accommodating strategies for diverse instructors. Lastly, monitoring sustainability of IP practices can support the evaluation of continuing professional development needed by instructors that will positively impact online learning outcomes.

CONCLUSION

The goals for this chapter were two-fold:

1. Share examples of the strategic applications of IP that were included in our intervention, supporting the readers' immediate ability to apply in their own classrooms.
2. Disseminate the findings of our action research that supports previous research connected to applying IP in the online platform to improve retention variables and student success rates in the online learning environment.

As has been suggested, the online environment can feel uninviting, intimidating, and overwhelming to both the learner (Farrell & Brunton, 2020) and the instructor (Schaffhauser, 2020). To provide effective instruction in the online setting, teaching, social, and cognitive presence are critical (Gardner et al., 2010, Rebeor et al., 2019a; Rosser-Majors et al., 2020). Without these elements, student and program success rates can suffer (Rebeor et al., 2019a, 2019b). Student enrollment in online classes continues to grow with 934,000 more students taking online courses in 2016 compared to 2012 (Seaman et al., 2018), yet institutions across the globe continue to struggle with drop rates, failure rates, student satisfaction, and demotivated instructors. IP strategies have shown great promise in improving these areas, yet, most online instructors never receive any formal training in effective online instructional practices. In addition, most institutions do not require set engagement requirements of their instructors, such as frequency or quality of discussion posts, response timelines, or grading due dates (Magda, 2019). Instructors must be given the tools to effectively engage their students, supporting their success in the online learning platform, as well as be held accountable for consistent teaching standards.

To have success teaching online, IP implicitly suggests that instructors must utilize their motivation for teaching. These include inspiration, positivity, dedication, love for teaching, passion for their subject matter, compassion for their students, and expertise. Given the challenges and uncertainty of the current times and future, effective IP is more important than ever to help students feel safe and allow them to look forward to connecting virtually. Instructors must be purposeful in creating content with the learner in mind and then manage their learning environment with the upmost diligence. While instructors may not be in control of events outside of the classroom, they are in full control of what they do inside the online environment. It is this factor, controlling controllable factors using IP strategies, that can increase success in the online learning environment.

ACKNOWLEDGMENT

Thank you to our fellow researchers Dr. Yolanda Harper (University of Arizona Global Campus), Dr. Laura Sliwinski (Colorado Technical University), and Dr. Andrea Wilson (Walden University), as well as our media expert/designer who supported the development of our intervention, Rebecca Hayes (University of Arizona Global Campus). In addition, the authors appreciate all of the instructors across the country who have taken the opportunity to participate in the UAGC Instructor Presence Online Certification Development series.

This research received no specific grant from any funding agency in the public, commercial, or not-for-profit sectors.

REFERENCES

Akyol, Z., & Garrison, D. R. (2008). The development of a community of inquiry over time in an online course: Understanding the progression and integration of social, cognitive and teaching presence. *Journal of Asynchronous Learning Networks*, *12*(3), 3–23. doi:10.24059/olj.v12i3.66

Akyol, Z., & Garrison, D. R. (2013). *Educational communities of inquiry: Theoretical framework, research and practice*. IGI Global. doi:10.4018/978-1-4666-2110-7

Allen, I. E., & Seaman, J. (2015). Grade level: Tracking online education in the United States. *Babson Survey Research Group*. https://eric.ed.gov/?id=ED572778

Allport, G. W. (1937). *Personality: A psychological interpretation*. Holt.

Aloni, M., & Harrington, C. (2018). Research based practices for improving the effectiveness of asynchronous online discussion boards. *Scholarship of Teaching and Learning in Psychology*, *4*(4), 271–289. doi:10.1037tl0000121

Angdhiri, R. P. (2020). Challenges of home learning during a pandemic through the eyes of a student. *The Jakarta Post*. https://www.thejakartapost.com/life/2020/04/11/challenges-of-home-learning-during-a-pandemic-through-the-eyes-of-a-student.html

Bandura, A. (1986). *Social foundations of thought and action: A social cognitive theory*. Prentice-Hall, Inc.

Bembenutty, H., & Karabenick, S. A. (2004). Inherent association between academic delay of gratification, future time perspective, and self-regulated learning. *Educational Psychology Review*, *16*(1), 35–57. doi:10.1023/B:EDPR.0000012344.34008.5c

Bielska, J. (2011). The experimental method in action research. In W: D. Gabryś-Barker (Ed.), *Action research in teacher development: an overview of research methodology* (pp. 85-119). Wydawnictwo Uniwersytetu Śląskiego. https://core.ac.uk/download/pdf/197740124.pdf

Birgbauer, E. (2016). Student assisted course design. *Journal of Undergraduate Neuroscience Education*, *15*(1), E3–E5.

Bond, M., Marín, V. I., Dolch, C., Bedenlier, S., & Zawacki-Richter, O. (2018). Digital transformation in German higher education: Student and teacher perceptions and usage of digital media. *International Journal of Educational Technology in Higher Education*, *15*(1), 48. doi:10.118641239-018-0130-1

Boston, W., Diaz, S. R., Gibson, A. M., Ice, P., Richardson, K., & Swan, K. (2009). An exploration of the relationship between indicators of the community of inquiry framework and retention in online programs. *Journal of Asynchronous Learning Networks*, *14*(1), 3–19. https://www.researchgate.net/publication/330985126

Carr, S. (2000). As distance education comes of age, the challenge is keeping the students. *The Chronicle of Higher Education*, *46*(23), A39–A41.

Castellanos-Reyes, D. (2020). 20 Years of the Community of Inquiry Framework. *TechTrends*, *1–4*(4), 557–560. Advance online publication. doi:10.100711528-020-00491-7

Collins, K., Grroff, S., Mathena, C., & Kupczynski, L. (2019). Asynchronous video and the development of instructor social presence and student engagement. *Turkish Journal of Distance Education*, *20*(1), 53–70. doi:10.17718/tojde.522378

Day, S. L., & Connor, C. M. (2017). Examining the relations between self-regulation and achievement in third grade students. *Assessment for Effective Intervention*, *42*(2), 97–109. doi:10.1177/1534508416670367 PMID:28439211

De La Rosa, S. (2020). Ed experts fear rise in dropouts as remote learning continues. *K12 Dive*. https://www.k12dive.com/news/ed-experts-fear-rise-in-dropouts-as-remote-learning-continues/585558/

Edwards, M., Perry, B., & Janzen, K. (2011). The making of an exemplary online educator. *Distance Education*, *32*(1), 101–118. doi:10.1080/01587919.2011.565499

Eiland, L. S., & Todd, J. D. (2019). Considerations when incorporating technology into classroom and experiential teaching. *The Journal of Pediatric Pharmacology and Therapeutics: JPPT: the Official Journal of PPAG*, *24*(4), 270–275. doi:10.5863/1551-6776-24.4.270 PMID:31337989

Farrell, O., & Brunton, J. (2020). A balancing act: A window into online student engagement experiences. *International Journal of Educational Technology in High Education*, *17*(1), 25. doi:10.118641239-020-00199-x

Feuer, W. (2020). *At least 24 million students could drop out of school due to the Coronavirus pandemic, U.N. says.* https://www.cnbc.com/2020/09/15/at-least-24-million-students-could-drop-out-of-school-due-to-the-coronavirus-un-says.html

Flock, H. (2020). Designing a community of inquiry in online courses. *The International Review of Research in Open and Distributed Learning, 21*(1), 134–152. doi:10.19173/irrodl.v20i5.3985

García, E., & Weiss, E. (2020). Covid-19 and student performance, equity, and U.S. education policy: Lessons from pre-pandemic research to inform relief, recovery, and rebuilding. *Economic Policy Institute.* https://www.epi.org/publication/the-consequences-of-the-covid-19-pandemic-for-education-performance-and-equity-in-the-united-states-what-can-we-learn-from-pre-pandemic-research-to-inform-relief-recovery-and-rebuilding/

Gardner, H. E. (2000). Intelligence reframed: Multiple intelligences for the 21st century. Hachette UK.

Garrison, D. R., Anderson, T., & Archer, W. (2000). Critical inquiry in a text-based environment: Computer conferencing in higher education model. *The Internet and Higher Education, 2*(2-3), 87–105. doi:10.1016/S1096-7516(00)00016-6

Garrison, D. R., Anderson, T., & Archer, W. (2001). Critical thinking, cognitive presence, and computer conferencing in distance education. *American Journal of Distance Education, 15*(1), 7–23. doi:10.1080/08923640109527071

Garrison, D. R., Anderson, T., & Archer, W. (2010). The first decade of the community of inquiry framework: A retrospective. *The Internet and Higher Education, 13*(1–2), 5–9. doi:10.1016/j.iheduc.2009.10.003

Garrison, D. R., & Arbaugh, J. B. (2007). Researching the community of inquiry framework: Review, issues, and future directions. *The Internet and Higher Education, 10*(3), 157–172. doi:10.1016/j.iheduc.2007.04.001

Giamatti, A. B. (1988). *A free and ordered space: The real world of the university.* W.W. Norton.

Gray, J. A., & DiLoreto, M. (2016). The effects of student engagement, student satisfaction, and perceived learning in online learning environments. *International Journal of Educational Leadership Preparation, 11*(1).

Gunawardena, C. N., & Zittle, F. J. (1997). Social presence as a predictor of satisfaction within a computer-mediated conferencing environment. *American Journal of Distance Education, 11*(3), 8–26. doi:10.1080/08923649709526970

Hamann, K., Glazier, R. A., Wilson, B. M., & Pollock, P. H. (2020). Online teaching, student success, and retention in political science courses. *European Political Science.* Advance online publication. doi:10.105741304-020-00282-x

Hart, C. (2012). Factors associated with student persistence in an online program of study: A review of the literature. *Journal of Interactive Online Learning, 11*(1), 19–42.

Hodges, C., Moore, S., Lockee, B., Trust, T., & Bond, A. (2020). The difference between emergency remote teaching and online learning. *EDUCAUSE Review, 27.* https://er.educause.edu/articles/2020/3/the-difference-between-emergency-remote-teaching-and-online-learning

Jaggars, S. S. (2012, April). *Beyond flexibility: Why students choose online and face-to-face courses in community college.* In American Educational Research Association Annual Meeting, Vancouver, Canada. https://ccrc.tc.columbia.edu/media/k2/attachments/online-outcomes-beyond-flexibility.pdf

Jaggars, S. S., Edgecombe, N., & Stacey, G. W. (2013). *Creating an Effective Online Instructor Presence.* Community College Research Center, Columbia University. https://files.eric.ed.gov/fulltext/ED542146.pdf

Kuhfeld, M., Soland, J., Tarasawa, B., Johnson, A., Ruzek, E., & Lewis, K. (2020). How is Covid-19 affecting student learning? Initial findings from fall 2020. *Brown Center Chalkboard.* https://www.brookings.edu/blog/brown-center-chalkboard/2020/12/03/how-is-covid-19-affecting-student-learning/

Lehman, R. M., & Conceição, S. C. O. (2013). *Motivating and retaining online students: Research-based strategies that work.* John Wiley & Sons.

Lieberman, M. D. (2013). *Social: Why our brains are wired to connect.* Oxford University Press.

Maazouzi, K. (2019). Impact of teacher's personality and behavior on students' achievement. *Global Journal of Human Social Science, 19*(9), 2249–2460.

Magda, A. J. (2019). Online learning at public universities: Recruiting, orienting, and supporting online faculty. *The Learning House.* https://www.learninghouse.com/knowledge-center/research-reports/online-learning-at-public-universities/

Mahan, K. (2020). The comprehending teacher: Scaffolding in content and language integrated learning (CLIL). *Language Learning Journal,* 1–15. Advance online publication. doi:10.1080/09571736.2019.1705879

Martin, F., & Bolliger, D. U. (2018). Engagement matters: Student perceptions on the importance of engagement strategies in the online learning environment. *Online Learning, 22*(1), 205–222. doi:10.24059/olj.v22i1.1092

Martirosyan, N. M., Saxon, D. P., & Wanjohi, R. (2014). Student satisfaction and academic performance in Armenian higher education. *American International Journal of Contemporary Research, 4*(2), 1–5.

Noreen, S., Ali, A., & Munaw, U. (2019). The impact of teachers' personality on students' academic achievement in Pakistan. *Global Regional Review, 4*(3), 92–102. doi:10.31703/grr.2019(IV-III).11

Palmer, P. J. (2007). *The courage to teach: Exploring the inner landscape of a teacher's life.* Jossey-Bass.

Park, C., & Kim, D. G. (2020). Perception of instructor presence and its effects on learning experience in online classes. *Journal of Information Technology Education, 19,* 475–488. doi:10.28945/4611

Pintrich, P. R. (2000). The role of goal orientation in self-regulated learning. In *Handbook of self-regulation* (pp. 451–502). Academic Press., doi:10.1016/B978-012109890-2/50043-3

Pitkänen, K., Iwata, M., & Laru, J. (2020). Exploring technology-oriented Fab Lab facilitators' role as educators in K-12 education: Focus on scaffolding novice students' learning in digital fabrication activities. *International Journal of Child-Computer Interaction, 26,* 100207. Advance online publication. doi:10.1016/j.ijcci.2020.100207

Rebeor, S., Rosser-Majors, M., McMahon, C., Anderson, S., Harper, Y., & Sliwinski, L. (2020). *Applying instructor presence*. https://www.instructorpresence.com/

Rebeor, S., Rosser-Majors, M. L., McMahon, C. L., & Anderson, S. L. (2019a). Social, cognitive, & teaching presence: Impact on faculty and AU's diverse student body. *TCC Worldwide Online Conference*.

Rebeor, S. M., Rosser-Majors, M. L., McMahon, C. L., Anderson, S. L., Harper, Y., & Sliwinski, L. J. (2019b). Effective instruction in virtual higher education: Ensuring cognitive, social and teaching presence. *International Conference on Education and New Developments*, Porto, Portugal. 10.36315/2019v1end118

Reeve, J., & Lee, W. (2019). A neuroscientific perspective on basic psychological needs. *Journal of Personality*, *87*(1), 102–114. doi:10.1111/jopy.12390 PMID:29626342

Revere, L., & Kovach, J. (2011). Online technologies for engaged learning: A meaningful synthesis for educators. *Quarterly Review of Distance Education*, *12*, 113–124.

Riding, R., & Cheema, I. (1991). Cognitive styles–an overview and integration. *Educational Psychology*, *11*(3–4), 193–215. doi:10.1080/01443419910110301

Roberts, J., & Styron, R. (2010). Student satisfaction and persistence: Factors vital to student retention. *Research in Higher Education*, *6*, 1–18.

Rose, R. (2012). What it takes to teach online: While some instructors think online teaching will be a breeze, the truth is that the best teachers work very hard to connect with students. here are seven tips from an online insider. *T.H.E. Journal*, *39*(5), 28–30.

Rosser-Majors, M., Rebeor, S., McMahon, C., & Anderson, S. (2020). *Instructor presence training: Sustainable practices supporting student retention and success*. Teaching and Learning Conference, University of Arizona Global Campus (virtual). https://www.youtube.com/watch?v=4zrFNOtp198

Sagar, R. (2000). *Guiding school improvement with action research*. Association for Supervision and Curriculum Development. http://www.ascd.org/publications/books/100047.aspx

Sandkuhl, K., & Lehmann, H. (2017). Digital transformation in higher education – the role of enterprise architectures and portals. *Digital Enterprise Computing*. https://eprints.win.informatik.uni-rostock.de/516/1/Sandkuhl,%20Lehmann%202017.0%20-%20Digital%20Transformation%20in%20Higher%20Education.pdf

Schaffhauser, D. (2020). Educators feeling stressed, anxious, overwhelmed and capable. *THE Journal*. https://thejournal.com/articles/2020/06/02/survey-teachers-feeling-stressed-anxious-overwhelmed-and-capable.aspx

Seaman, J. E., Allen, I. E., & Seaman, J. (2018). *Grade increase: Tracking distance education in the United States*. Babson Survey Research Group. https://onlinelearningsurvey.com/reports/gradeincrease.pdf

Sheridan, K., & Kelly, M. A. (2010). The indicators of instructor presence that are important to students in online courses. *Journal of Online Learning and Teaching*, *6*(4), 767–779.

Sliwinski, L., & Rosser-Majors, M. L. (2018). Faculty development and student learning: A deep dive into instructor presence. OLC Accelerate: Online Learning Consortium, Orlando, FL.

Tam, M. (2000). Constructivism, instructional design, and technology: Implications for transforming distance learning. *Journal of Educational Technology & Society*, *3*(2), 50–60.

UVA Center for Teaching Excellence. (2020). *Applying the community of inquiry framework.* https://cte.virginia.edu/resources/applying-community-inquiry-framework

Vansteenkiste, M., Ryan, R. M., & Soenens, B. (2020). Basic psychological need theory: Advancements, critical themes, and future directions. *Motivation and Emotion*, *44*(1), 1–31. doi:10.100711031-019-09818-1

Wanstreet, C. E., & Stein, D. S. (2011). Presence over time in synchronous communities of inquiry. *American Journal of Distance Education*, *25*(3), 1–16. doi:10.1080/08923647.2011.590062

Whiteside, A. L. (2015). Introducing the social presence model to explore online and blended learning experiences. *Online Learning*, *19*(2), n2. doi:10.24059/olj.v19i2.453

Xu, D., & Jaggars, S. S. (2014). Performance gaps between online and face-to-face courses: Differences across types of students and academic subject areas. *The Journal of Higher Education*, *85*(5), 633–659. doi:10.1353/jhe.2014.0028

KEY TERMS AND DEFINITIONS

Avatar: Customized character used online to relay a message, in place of one's self being disclosed.

Cognitive Presence: The two-way engagement in an online course that exhibits application of critical and skeptical thinking, questioning, and higher-order knowledge development.

Community of Inquiry (CoI) Model: The model, suggested by Garrison et al. (2000) that exemplifies three types of instructor presence to increase success in an online course.

Gardner's Multiple Intelligences: Harvard psychologist Howard Gardner's (1983) theory suggests strengths in differing areas of knowledge development capabilities: verbal–linguistic, logical-mathematical, spatial, musical, bodily–kinesthetic, interpersonal, intrapersonal, and naturalistic.

Grammarly: A digital writing service online tool designed to improve writing. The platform works across multiple platforms and devices. https://www.grammarly.com/

Instructor Presence (IP): The process of creating an online community in learning environments through applications of teaching, social, and cognitive presence techniques.

Rubric: An assessment measurement that communicates expectations for learning activities.

Social Presence: The application of strategies that create a warm inviting tone and feelings of belongingness within a classroom.

Teaching Presence: The design, facilitation, and teaching strategies applied to an online learning environment that when applied effectively, create clarity of learner expectations.

Valediction: The ending of a communications. Example: "Let me know if you have questions and have a great week! ~Instructor Name."

Vocative Case: Addressing someone in a communication by name. Example: "Great start on your post, Jenni…"

Chapter 9
Critical Participatory Action Research in a Rural Community Committed to Peacebuilding in Times of Crisis

Lina Trigos-Carrillo
Universidad de La Sabana, Colombia

Laura Fonseca
Universidad de La Sabana, Colombia

ABSTRACT

Conducting critical community research during the COVID-19 pandemic has brought unexpected challenges to academic communities. In this chapter, the authors analyze the obstacles faced in a Critical Participatory Action Research (CPAR) education project with a rural community of former guerrilla members in the Amazon piedmont in Colombia. After this analysis, the authors present four CPAR principles to support critical community work during difficult times. The authors argue that communicative action, horizontal community participation in all the stages of the research process, time commitment, and the leverage of other competing needs should be guaranteed and maintained during times of crisis. CPAR offers opportunities to advocate better conditions for the most affected communities in moments of increasing inequality.

INTRODUCTION

In the context of the 2016 Peace Agreement signed between the Colombian government and the FARC-EP guerrilla group, 24 Territorial Spaces for Training and Reincorporation (ETCR in Spanish) provided a space for the former guerrilla members reintegration to civil society (nearly 6.000 people). In the Caquetá region, ETCR Héctor Ramírez (ETCR-HR) became a successful rural community of former guerrilla members and their families who based their economy on sustainable projects. In December 2019, the

DOI: 10.4018/978-1-7998-6922-1.ch009

community transitioned from ETCR to the new-born town Centro Poblado Héctor Ramírez (CP-HR). Due to a growing children and young population who attended half-day school in distant towns, there was a need of an education project that incorporated the community values, empowered children and youth in the community, and could further promote social cohesion in the Colombian post-conflict setting.

The partnership between researchers from a private university near the capital city of Colombia and the CP-HR community started in July 2018 with an agreement to cooperate in projects of mutual interest. The community, organized by former FARC-EP guerrilla members and their families, expressed their desire to collaborate with the university in the co-construction of an education project for this rural community committed to peacebuilding in Colombia. In April 2019, a group of researchers and university students visited CP-HR, located 614 kms away from campus in the Caquetá Department, near the Amazon piedmont. Grounded in the tenets of Critical Participatory Action Research (CPAR), the university team started an alliance with the community to co-construct an education project aimed to provide relevant education that sustains the community cultural values. During 2019, the university team travelled four times with students and research assistants to CP-HR. The community also conformed an education committee in charge of working collaboratively in the research process. However, in March 2020, the pandemic crisis unraveled in Colombia with a strict lockdown for six months.

The COVID-19 pandemic has posited several challenges for the community and for the research process. In this chapter, we analyze the challenges of the CPAR methodology while working with a rural community in process of reincorporation in times of crisis. Throughout the text, the reader will find some of the challenges of working with a geographically distant community in a complex sociopolitical landscape during the pandemic, as well as the CPAR principles (communicative action, horizontal relationships, time commitment, and the leverage of other competing needs) that have supported the critical community work during these times. These four principles will be elucidated further throughout the paper.

The analysis revolves around the action research spiral before and after the pandemic. We reflected on the different stages of the spiral process within the research project: 1) Planning a change, 2) acting and observing the process and consequences of the change, 3) reflecting on these processes and consequences, 4) replanning, and 5) acting and observing (Kemmis, McTaggart, & Nixon, 2014). We analyzed three loops of the spiral process: 1) the initial phase of trust building with the community members, and the beginning of the systematization of the community values and principles that served as the basis for the education project; 2) the consolidation of the research team and securing funding for the project; and 3) the consolidation of the community education committee through virtual meetings since March 2020, due to the pandemic and the national regulations that prevented the planned visits to CP-HR. Then, we present four principles that have supported our community work during these difficult times: (1) Communicative action is more than a theoretical concept; (2) horizontal relationships should prevail; (3) time is of the essence; and (4) other competing needs should be leveraged. We hope other groups of researchers and community leaders find some light in our experience, and institutions become more aware of the challenges communities and researchers face when conducting critical research in times of crisis.

BACKGROUND

Context of the Community in the Process of Reincorporation

Colombia has endured an internal armed conflict for almost 60 years. This conflict has involved both legal (National Army) and illegal armed actors (left-wing guerrillas and dissidences, right-wing paramilitary, and drug traffickers) particularly in rural areas. Over the past three decades, different Disarmament, Demobilization and Reintegration (DDR) processes have been implemented with paramilitary and guerrilla groups (CNMH, 2018). The most recent one was the peace agreement signed in 2016 between the Colombian government and the Revolutionary Armed Forces of Colombia - People's Army (FARC-EP in Spanish), the oldest guerrilla in the continent. Based on the previous DDR experiences, this agreement is a comprehensive document that includes specific actions to tackle the roots of the conflict: land distribution and effective social reincorporation for FARC-EP members and their families.

In the case of reincorporation, former guerrilla members initially lived in one of the 24 ETCR, small villages in rural areas built specifically to provide a safe space for reincorporation in different areas of the country, specifically where the FARC-EP had been historically present. Currently, only 30 percent of former FARC-EP members live in these territories (Kroc Institute, 2020). Some of them decided to create their own spaces for reincorporation (currently known as New Areas of Reincorporation), and some others are doing their process individually. Either way, most of the reincorporation process occurs in rural areas, where there is still lack of State presence, and the implementation of pivotal elements of the peace agreement, such as the rural reform, are not prioritized by the current government (Kroc Institute, 2020). This scenario creates uncertainty among former guerrilla members, which, in some cases, results in recidivism (Kaplan & Nussio, 2018) and the creation of armed dissidences. Therefore, it is crucial to support people in process of reincorporation, particularly those who are building peaceful communities with the development of income-generating and family sustainable projects.

The legal figure of ETCR ended in December 2019. In some cases, the ETCR had to be reallocated due to security reasons (assassination of social leaders and former guerrilla members); in others, the former guerrilla members managed to buy the land and further consolidated their life project. This is the case of the ETCR Héctor Ramírez (ETCR-HR), located in La Montañita, a municipality in the Caquetá Department, Colombia (Figure 1). Currently, the ETCR-HR is constituted as a small village named Centro Poblado Héctor Ramírez (CP-HR), and it is one of the few former ETCR communities who bought the land they inhabited using community resources.

Not only former guerrilla members live in CP-HR. They are building their houses and their families there. Therefore, the children population is rapidly growing, with babies being born after the peace agreement signature, and older children being reunited with their parents. Additionally, other family members such as grandparents, siblings and nephews are now part of the village. Despite all the efforts to build this village in peace, there are still multiple barriers and obstacles to access basic services, such as education and health care. This is in line with one of the key drivers of the armed conflict in Colombia: a historical inequality, with the rural settings disconnected from the urban ones (Molano, 2015). The State has developed different initiatives to reduce the urban-rural gap in terms of access to and quality of education services, by focusing on participatory actions in planning and designing rural curriculums. However, most of the cases fail to offer training to local leaders, which in turn prevents people's participation once the projects have ended (Parra, Mateus & Mora, 2018). As a result of the lack of flexible curriculums and nearby secondary education schools, most children living in rural areas only reach primary education (Ministerio Nacional de Educación, 2018).

Figure 1. Map of Colombia. The red dot indicates the location of the CP-HR in Caquetá, Colombia.
Source: Google maps

The role of education in a post-accord setting is outlined in the peace agreement (Alto Comisionado para la Paz, 2016). In the document, the Special Plan of Rural Education is one of the solutions agreed

Critical Participatory Action Research in a Rural Community Committed to Peacebuilding in Times of Crisis

by the Colombian government and the FARC-EP. This plan highlights the importance of community participation and the recognition of sociocultural values for children's education, as well as the improvement of infrastructure and resources in these areas (Ministerio de Educación Nacional, 2018). However, the plan has not been a priority for the current government and is not being implemented. To contribute to the solution of this structural problem, the aim of our research project is to co-construct the design and implementation of own and relevant education to sustain the cultural identities and practices of a community in a rural area where former guerrilla members are in the process of reincorporation (Paris, 2012).

The research project involves recognizing the urgent need to provide youth with sustaining and alternative models of development, based on the local needs of the population in accordance with their community ideologies and values. The construction of an education model between members of the CP-HR community and a university research team can be an example of a reconciliation process in a post-conflict setting by recognizing the core values of a community that has previously sought social change using violence as one of their action mechanisms, and now it is consolidating their political ideals through democratic and participative means, as well as through decolonial epistemologies and practices. A Critical Participatory Action Research (CPAR) project implies building a public sphere with different actors from the community such as former guerrilla members, community education committee members, children and youth, as well as from the university, such as faculty, junior researchers and undergraduate and graduate students (see Table 1). In this research project, we focus on deconstructing hegemonic ways of understanding education and the incorporation of local understandings of education and development into the education project.

Table 1. CPAR research team

CPAR Research Team	
Community-based team	**University research team**
Former guerrilla members who are in the process of reincorporation (who participate in the design and implementation of the project)	Leading researchers (university faculty, who are in charge of the direction, implementation and evaluation of the project)
Community Education Committee (formed by community members, particularly women, who oversee the sustainability of the project)	Junior researchers (who contribute with fieldwork)
Volunteers (people, usually college students, from outside the community who conduct social work in CP-HR)	CSL course students (who travel to the community as part of the course and support research activities)
Children and youth (who are the beneficiaries and actively participate in the project and in its educational initiatives)	Undergraduate and graduate students (part of research seedbeds, who support research activities)

CPAR

Critical Participatory Action Research (CPAR) is a research approach that fits within community work towards social justice. Beyond a methodological approach, CPAR is an epistemological stance towards research and community work, one that places the community in the center and looks to comprehend social reality to transform it (Colmenares, 2012). According to Kemmis, McTaggart, and Nixon (2014), "the purpose of critical participatory action research is to change social practices, including research practice itself, to make them more rational and reasonable, more productive and sustainable, and more just and inclusive" (pp. 2-3). Since CPAR is oriented towards making social change with the different members of the communities, it implies taking decisions collectively and following the model of a self-reflective spiral of cycles of planning, acting and observing, reflecting and then re-planning in an improved iteration (Kemmis et al., 2014).

Therefore, CPAR implies a deep comprehension of the community and their practices, a trustful relationship, and the intention to sustain the community culture while fostering social change that aligns with the community's values. To achieve this, the process requires us to adopt a critical stance and to generate communicative action, that is "to reach (a) intersubjective agreement about the ways we understand the situation (the language we use), (b) mutual understanding of one another's points of view (and situations), and (c) unforced consensus about what to do" (Kemmis, McTaggart, & Nixon, 2014, p. 68). Then, we act to achieve social change and document the process to make changes when needed. In this process, the social actors become active researchers, people who make decisions, take actions, and reflect about the process (Colmenares, 2012). Community members' participation entails a dialogue where different knowledges are put into conversation to create new knowledge (Ahumada, Antón, & Peccinetti, 2012). It recognizes the community values and knowledge as well as the academic knowledge as part of the research epistemology (de Oliveira Figueiredo, 2015).

Even though the CPAR process is outlined in the literature, another story is to implement it in a particular community due to their history, their geographical and sociopolitical context, and the social tensions within. The challenges start to emerge as soon as the social realities and dynamics in the community intersect with the research process. Further, the difficulties intensify in times of crisis, for example, during the COVID-19 pandemic, when the community's interests and priorities shift towards more pressing needs. However, the research process should continue if we genuinely seek to achieve social change.

The CPAR Process in Caquetá

The consolidation of the alliance between the CP-HR and the Universidad de La Sabana (ULS) team started in December 2018 through the design and implementation of a Critical Service-Learning (CSL) course called "Community Psychology Applied to Post-Conflict Settings". This course was co-constructed with one of the social leaders of the CP-HR (a former guerrilla member) and two professors from the Psychology School at ULS (Fonseca & Trigos-Carrillo, in press). The general objective of the course was to create a dialogical communication between two historically distant social groups: former guerrilla members and urban youth from Bogota, the capital city (Fonseca & Reinoso, 2020). The implementation of the CSL course created a safe space for encountering the "unknown other", to challenge common stereotypes around former guerrilla members, as well as providing a service-learning experience in community psychology (Trigos-Carrillo, Fonseca & Reinoso, 2020). Moreover, spending two weeks living with the CP-HR community and sharing their daily routines, enabled collaborative relationships where it was possible to identify the education of children as an important community need.

After the CSL course, the community members expressed their desire to start a partnership with the university to design and implement an education project in the community. The aim of the CPAR research project is to co-construct relevant and own education initiatives to improve access to education in a rural area and TO sustain the community cultural values during the peacebuilding process. During 2019, the research team visited the CP-HR four times. During those visits, the university team met with community leaders of the CP-HR and a group of four volunteers, who oversaw the education activities for children at the Popular Library Alfonso Cano located in the community (BPAC in Spanish). The community leader and the volunteers were our liaison with the rest of the community, as they were recognized for their work with children and had a direct line with other community's social leaders. During the first year, we consolidated ideas around the education project with the community.

The first visits were the basis for the creation of a CPAR research project to design and implement an education project that recognizes the values, practices and beliefs of the community. The BPAC volunteers had initially designed after-school activities for the children in the community, and we facilitated spaces for discussion about the potential of those activities to contribute to the education project. The regular visits, along with continuous communication about the project, were key to consolidate a collaboration between the ULS and the community teams. Undergraduate university students supported the community team activities with children, and our role as professors was to provide tools to systematize the experience as well as to plan and execute the activities in line with the community values. Nevertheless, ensuring the systematization of the activities from the volunteers was difficult sometimes, as they had other responsibilities in the community and lacked the time to effectively write and reflect on every educational activity.

Despite this, we managed to articulate the community efforts towards applying for funding, which could provide economic recognition for the time community members spent working on the project, as well as basic supplies for designing and implementing the education project. It is worth noting, however, that the formulation of a CPAR project involves previous stages of concertation, trust-building and effective communication, which took, in our case, almost two years before we received funding from international agencies.

When the COVID-19 arrived in Colombia, in mid-March 2020, we were already dealing with one important change in the community: the group of volunteers had had some disagreements with the community that involved their alignment with the political ideals of the community, and the four members of the team decided to leave the process and moved away from the town. Additionally, just when the research team was planning a trip to work with the community in the consolidation of an education committee who could replace the volunteers' role in the project, the Colombian government ordered a national lockdown and domestic travel was restricted. All university work was moved online and the research team as well as the community faced an unexpected reality.

In this context, our relationship with the community was virtual while a member of the team was able to travel to Caquetá in October 2020. Two community leaders organized an education committee with members of the community, and we established weekly online meetings. At the end of July, we were notified of an important grant we had been waiting for, and in September we received another grant that would complement the project. We were enthusiastic about these new opportunities, but we also needed to organize and coordinate with the community to achieve the project goals while responding to the needs imposed by the pandemic.

ANALYSIS OF THE REFLECTIVE SPIRAL CYCLE

In this section, we present the analysis of three loops of the CPAR reflective spiral cycle. We identified four meaningful moments in the research project: (1) Trust-building process, (2) consolidating a research team, (3) securing and managing funding, and (4) implementing the project in times of a pandemic.

Trust-Building Process

Building trust with the community is a continuous process that requires encountering the other, their representations, and understanding their communication styles and their projects (Aveling & Jovchelovitch, 2014). The development of a CPAR process starts even before formulating the research question. A community of former guerrilla members is a hard-to-reach group, as there is still stigma around the peace agreement and the Colombian society is politically divided. Left- and right-oriented groups and institutions remain suspicious of one another and this is translated to private universities, which in some cases, hold a more conservative view on the society's problems.

In this context, a research project, a collaboration between a research group from a private university and a group of former guerrilla members involved an immersion in the community without a pre-determined research agenda. Previous research has pointed out the importance of this approach with groups that have been historically marginalized, because the relationship with researchers can be problematic (Mohebbi, Linders & Chiffos, 2018). Moreover, it is necessary to critically reflect about the "inherent privilege, often due to race, class and the history of academic elitism" (Hebert-Beirne et al., 2017, p. 416) and to look for methodological strategies to promote a power shift. Community psychology provides an interesting framework to understand the potential of building horizontal relationships, reflecting on our own positionality, but also engaging from a genuine interest of getting to know the unknown other (Reinoso & Fonseca, 2020).

In our case, the first collaboration was the construction of the syllabus for the optional CSL course, which was the first opportunity to understand the representations that the social leaders held about the students, the ideas around encountering with people from a private university and how it could fit in their long-term community building project. One of the community's social leader was very keen on creating a syllabus that would allow students to get to know the former combatants in everyday interactions, as he wanted them to challenge previous stereotypes, which, according to him, were brought by mass media through the years. Moreover, there was a great interest in producing a book with narratives from the students after the encounter. As a result, the CSL course was flexible enough to create safe spaces for the encounter and to invite students and former guerrilla members to meet and to know one another (Reinoso & Fonseca, 2020). The development of the course was the second level of trust-building. Once in the field, the social leader, as the initial gatekeeper of the community, discussed our visit with the former guerrilla members and arranged our arrival. Once there, we had to communicate with one of the BPAC volunteers who was in charge of our visit. She was not a former guerrilla member, but she had gained enough trust with the community to manage our activities and our agenda for the following weeks. She first asked about our agenda for the visit, which was an initial marker of representations about universities as having their own agenda, which reproduces power imbalance. The development of the CSL course was fluid as our approach was to participate in daily activities, and to engage in dialogue through sharing the day-to-day tasks rather than a rigid approach with specific places to have conversations (Trigos-Carrillo et al., 2020). At the end of the course, students wrote narratives of the encounter, which were read by the community and an editorial board conformed by the BPAC volunteers (Fonseca & Reinoso, 2020). This process ensured another important aspect of the trust-building process: transparency.

After this first experience, subsequent visits were planned with the BPAC volunteers and the social leader, who prioritized the development of an education project for the community as something we could support them with. Nevertheless, each visit posed different challenges. In the first visit, they were eager to organize the different activities they were implementing with the children and we supported that idea with specific workshops. However, they were still cautious about inviting other members of the community to participate in the meetings: that first gate was still closed. In the second visit, with a second cohort of the CSL course, a new gate opened: they invited us to participate in the children's activities. That moment was important as we could observe the different pedagogical strategies used with the children, as well as potential elements to support the construction of the education project. We also discussed the possibility of participating in the application to an international grant and translated the draft from English to Spanish to ensure transparency in the application process. We also conducted an exercise of participatory budget to include all the costs they deemed necessary for the project. After we left, our first recommendation was to systematize the activities and start writing their own views on the education project. We tried to start virtual communications between June and September (our third visit in 2019) to support the systematization process. Nevertheless, this first writing exercise was not conducted by the BPAC volunteers, who felt overwhelmed with multiple tasks within the community. Additionally, and after subsequent discussions with the social leader, the team was reluctant to write because they were afraid that we, as researchers, would take credit for their job. This distrust was specifically shared by the BPAC volunteers, and not by the community. One of the reasons for this was probably a distrust towards academia and "academic extractivism." This tension has endured in the whole trust-building process and it requires active reflections from both the community and the researchers every time there is a disagreement.

But perhaps the most challenging situation was the shift from the BPAC volunteers to the consolidation of the education committee. After internal tensions between the four volunteers and the community, they decided to leave the project in February 2020. This rupture involved not only distrust with external agents but also starting again with other people who joined the education committee, this time guided by two social leaders of the community. In order to deal with the previous tensions, we created virtual meetings with the education committee and the university team to discuss the agenda, and collaboratively decided next steps for the education project. One specific strategy was to create a study group, open to students, researchers and the education committee, to reflect about theoretical and methodological issues. These meetings, along with the weekly general meeting with both teams, provided an initial platform to enter a dialogic partnership.

Consolidating the Research Team

Planning and implementing a research project require a team committed to the principles, goals and values of the project. This team should be formed with people from the university and community people. At the university, at the beginning of the project, two faculty members with a similar vision of social research and agenda, although different research topics and experience, joined together to think about the possibility of working with the community. On the other side, a community leader, who served as a gatekeeper, showed interest in working with the people from the university. However, we needed to consolidate a stronger team in order to accomplish the initial goals and secure community participation.

At the university, students from a research seedbed on social and community psychology joined the team, as well as another faculty member with expertise in gender studies. We also had two undergraduate research assistants who supported data collection and management (see Table 1). The main challenge in consolidating the research team at the university was to find the people who would align epistemologically and methodologically to CPAR, and with experience working with communities. For the students, we designed a formation plan that included activities in the research seedbed, a study group, a research internship, fieldtrips, and research assistantships.

In the community, the education committee has been a key ally of the university team because they have permanent contact with the community through the public library and other educational initiatives. The community team became community co-researchers. Community co-researchers are people from the community who do not necessarily have received formal training to conduct research although they are central to the research process (Vaughn et al., 2017). We, thus, designed a training plan on popular education that included a module on CPAR for community members. The importance of including people from the community as co-researchers is that they have privileged knowledge about the community and the leadership to sustain research initiatives for longer periods of time. Further, including community co-researchers is a decolonizing act where equal participation is fostered through four principles (Stanton, 2014): respect, relevance, reciprocity, and responsibility. This process implies a shift in power and participation throughout all the research process. Our desire was to build the human capacities for the community to implement and maintain the project with the support of professionals and scholars willing to work collaboratively. In this case, most former guerrilla members lived in the jungle before the reincorporation process and their participation in a research project represented an opportunity to voice their views about education. Nonetheless, time is a major constrain for community co-researchers since they have multiple responsibilities, including work in sustainable productive projects, their families and other projects. Finally, another challenge to consolidate the research team in the community was associated to internal tensions between members of the community. For example, the initial BPAC volunteers withdraw from the research process and a new education committee shared different views about the activities carried out by the volunteers. Adaption to social change required strong trust bonds and flexibility in the research design.

Securing and Managing Funding

There is a large inequality between Latin American and developed countries research funding. "Although Latin American institutions have high expectations for their investigators and require them to publish in high impact journals (Thomaz & Mormul, 2014), the financial support for research is inadequate to meet these high standards" (Ciocca & Delgado, 2017, p. 848). First, Latin American governments offer limited research funding in comparison with developed countries (in Colombia, only 0,25% of the GDP was assigned to Research and Development in 2018); second, most private companies are not interested in financing research; and third, there are not clear rules about the distribution of research funding (Ciocca & Delgado, 2017). Besides, additional barriers are placed for those conducting social research. Therefore, most CPAR projects start without funding to support research activities, materials and personnel.

Due to the importance and scope of the project, since the beginning we acknowledged the importance of securing funding to guarantee the sustainability of the education project. For that reason, early in the process, the research team started the application to international research grants. All the planning and application process was conducted collectively with the community. However, two of the faculty members who were participating in the project were also in the process of securing tenure at their university, and their participation in the project entailed difficult decisions about time allocation and commitment, sometimes at the great risk of putting in jeopardy their scholarly careers if funding was not obtained.

After two rounds of applications, our project received a large grant from a U.S. foundation that funds educational research. Having external funding has resulted in a significant support for the project in times of a pandemic, just when university and national resources for research are even more limited. Managing external international funding has also presented some learning opportunities: the university has had to adjust their traditional research funding procedures to accommodate to a community-based approach to funding, and the community has had to assume the responsibility of managing funding through a community cooperative.

In sum, securing and managing research funding in developing countries poses several challenges during the CPAR process that should not be overlooked, because sometimes funding could make the difference between a successful and an unsustainable project.

Implementing the Project in Times of a Pandemic

Qualitative research, and particularly CPAR, involves fieldwork and in-person interactions. These interactions are key for trust-building, collaborative data collection and capacity building, which are central tenets of this methodological approach (Salerno Valdez & Gubrium, 2020). Yet, the recent global health emergency as a result of COVID-19 has had an impact on the way researchers conceive fieldwork (Howlett, 2020), particularly given the strict measures of lockdown and travel restrictions to prevent risks of further spreading the virus. In this context, the advantages of doing in-person research, linked with being physically present within the communities (Howlett, 2020) has been challenged and, in our case, it transformed our own approach to the CPAR project.

In Colombia, the pandemic regulations started in March 2020, when national and local governments decided to implement total lockdown in the country. National and international transportation was restricted, which had a great impact on the poorest communities as they relied on informal jobs and in-person interactions. In the case of CP-HR, they decided to self-isolate given the lack of essential health care access within the community and the low number of ICU beds in the nearby hospital. As a result, our original plan to travel in April and June 2020 was cancelled, and we had to design a new approach to continue our fieldwork. This posed uncertainty over the development of the project, mainly because of the restrictions for group encounters within the community but also because of the traditional view of fieldwork as staying *with* the communities, not the process behind it, such as meetings and overall planning from the office (Howlett, 2020). This dichotomy of fieldwork and office work was soon challenged, and we designed weekly meetings with the community social leaders and two more people who worked at the BPAC. As presented above, the initial BPAC volunteers left the project and the new challenge, on top of the pandemic, was to re-build a community team focused on education. Therefore, the weekly virtual meetings were a strategy which served to invite other community members to gather once a week to discuss the future of the project, and eventually, to consolidate an initial Education Committee for the community. However, we still considered that the virtual encounters were not enough as the multiple responsibilities of the community team prevented them to fully commit to the meetings.

Opportunities and Challenges of Virtual Encounters in a CPAR Project

The implementation of weekly virtual meetings was an opportunity to engage in continuous dialogue with the community, instead of waiting until our visit to have face-to-face work and analysis of the activities developed in the previous months. The selected platform was Zoom, as the project leaders had access to a pro version, which enabled more security, unlimited time for the meeting and the possibility of audio/

video recording. Additionally, this platform does not require downloading the app for participants, which is more user friendly (Lobe, Morgan & Hoffman, 2020).

Meetings were initially a mechanism to explain the project to the new members of the Education Committee, and to introduce other university team members who had not previously travelled to the community. This was a positive outcome from the online experience, as students, researchers, community participants and social leaders were able to visit together in one place, at the same time, regardless of the possibility to travel 600 Km to see each other. This process enabled collaborative action, co-constructing the minutes after each meeting, assigning specific responsibilities to be developed during the week, as well as a space to sort day-to day difficulties. Another strategy was to create an online study group, not only for the students but also open to the Education Committee. This space served as a place for academic encounter, based on different materials, such as academic papers, videos and films, to discuss the theoretical underpinnings of the project (CPAR, critical education projects, epistemologies of the south, among others). Initially, members of the Education Committee were silent during the conversations, but over the course of the group meetings, they started to actively participate by giving their opinions and ideas. We also created a WhatsApp group with the university team and the education committee, which was useful for constant communication and opened the communication to members of both teams. This was an interesting shift in power, as the professors were not solely in charge of the communications with the community.

Despite the positive outcomes of the virtual strategy implemented, there were also difficulties in the process. Online encounters in a hard-to-reach community can be difficult given their historical marginalization, which is seen in the lack of access to stable internet services, the multiple roles they have to fulfill, and their expertise using virtual platforms (Howlett, 2020; Salerno Valdez & Gubrium, 2020). As the community is located in the Amazon piedmont, intense rain affects electricity, which makes the internet connection unstable. Moreover, moving from an in-person intensive quarterly visit to a weekly basis diminished the attention from the community leaders to the meetings, as they started to delegate some functions to the younger education committee members. This was particularly difficult, as some of the decisions had to be taken with the community leaders, and sometimes communication was not quite effective.

Extended Period of Fieldwork

During the strict lockdown measures in the country, from March to September, we continued our weekly online meetings and the study group. Once the national government restored domestic transportation, we adjusted our methodological approach both to ensure minimum risk of spreading the virus but also to reflect on the importance of providing a more rigorous support to the community and the research process. As a result, one of the lead researchers traveled to the CP-HR for two months following all the biosecurity protocols (pre-visit COVID-19 test, use of face mask and hand sanitizer). This was an opportunity to share everyday experiences of implementing the project with the community, as well as to prevent risks of bringing the virus to the community if we had quarterly visits as originally planned. This first experience was successful because we had an experienced researcher on site, while having all the research team joining in virtual meetings with the community and jointly designing the next steps. Based on this new approach, we decided to maintain a blended CPAR methodology: two junior researchers and one senior researcher would spend longer periods of time (three months) in the community for the first year. This approach enabled to consolidate the community's Education Committee with a permanent support from the university research team.

SOLUTIONS AND RECOMMENDATIONS

Principles and Practices to Implement CPAR in Times of Crisis

The following principles and practices have been useful during the times of crisis, particularly during the COVID-19 pandemic, to maintain the CPAR project afloat and overcome the challenges we presented above.

Communicative Action is More than a Theoretical Concept

Communicative action is "what happens when people interrupt what they are doing to ask, 'What is happening here?'" (Kemmis, McTaggart, & Nixon, 2014, p. 34). Communicative action requires a communicative space and public spheres. A public space is created when people from the research team and from the community gather to sincerely, respectfully, and openly reflect, analyze and discuss together their practices and the consequences of such practices to make decisions (Kemmis & McTaggart, 2005). Additionally, public spheres are necessary to achieve legitimacy; that is, "public spheres are constituted as actual networks of communication among actual participants" (Kemmis, McTaggart, & Nixon, 2014, p. 37). The participation in public spheres is voluntary, horizontal and safe. People gather around a theme and a view of the future to achieve community change. However, opening a communicative space where people gather to talk about the project and the desired transformations in practice is very challenging in times of a pandemic. After meeting for periods of between 4 and 15 days, four times a year with the community, in March 2020 the research team could not travel to the territory as planned.

At the beginning of the COVID-19 pandemic, we knew that maintaining communicative action was essential to keep the project afloat; therefore, we decided to have virtual encounters. Some of the challenges of virtual meetings with the community were: people did not have a stable internet connection, they could not gather in the library where internet access was easier to obtain, they had other pressing needs, and time was a constrain. The solution was to maintain constant communication with one of the community leaders and to agree upon one day to meet every week. The chat apps also supported our mission to stay connected. In the meantime, we planned that a research team member would travel to the community for a longer period than usual. In October 2020, one of the professors visited the territory for three months.

Having one research team member in the community during the crisis resulted very useful because she was in charge of maintaining communicative action in the community, as she functioned as a liaison between the university and the community teams. For this reason, we also decided to hire two junior researchers who could travel most of the year to support fieldwork. When working with rural communities in distant geographical areas, fieldwork personnel could be key to read and understand the social realities of the community, to strengthen communication, to support the daily struggles in times of crisis, and to maintain the focus towards shared goals.

In sum, communicative action is at the core of the relationship between the research team and the community. Beyond an abstract concept, communicative action should be created and maintained during the research implementation. In this process, the researchers must listen to people, legitimize their concerns and knowledge, generate open participation, shift power dynamics, and build trust.

Horizontal Relationships Should Prevail

In academia, power relationships are hierarchical and most of the times vertical. Faculty members are accustomed to hold some power and prestige among the academic community. Often, they are authorities in one area of study and their knowledge is highly valued. CPAR puts into question these notions about academic knowledge and power when working with communities. Decolonizing research implies a shift in power relationships and notions of knowledge and expertise (Stanton, 2014). It requires a different positionality, one where community people become co-researchers and scholars become community supporters. Then, knowledge is redistributed and revalued; disciplinary knowledge may be as necessary as ancestral or local knowledge to solve specific community problems.

In the case of CP-HR, designing and implementing an education project that not only recognizes but also sustains the community values and culture, or their community cultural wealth (Trigos-Carrillo, 2019), requires deep knowledge about educational values and practices in the FARC-EP guerrilla group and pedagogical knowledge to adapt some of these values and practices into the peacebuilding process. In this exercise, we fostered a dialogue of knowledges and epistemologies to co-construct an education project that sustains the community's cultural wealth while incorporating flexible pedagogical approaches. We noticed that although the community has strong educational values and hoped-for visions of the future that look to decolonize traditional education, their pedagogical practices still maintain traditional power structures and educational practices. Therefore, we had to question some of those practices and imagine others that align better to creating a critical community education project.

Finally, horizontal participation entails cultural humility (Trigos-Carrillo et al., 2020), open and candid communication, the recognition of everyone's knowledges and experiences, transversality in the decision-making process, unabridged community participation in all the stages of the research process, and dialogic negotiation. Cultural humility is enacted throughout the different encounter mechanisms we create to engage in meaningful dialogue with the community. Weekly meetings, the study group and extended periods of fieldwork are methodological and epistemological strategies to create a safe space for encountering knowledge diversity and to foster collaborative work to advance the education project.

Time is of the Essence

As we have previously outlined, a CPAR approach starts before formulating a project. To have a clear research question requires spending time with the community, which, in most cases, is not possible. Indeed, most of the approaches that follow a participatory design are planned by the researchers before going to the field (Salerno Valdez & Gubrium, 2020). In our case, the trust-building process is a first loop in the reflective spiral, which is often an under-explored moment in the research process. Bearing in mind that there is a tension in academia between fieldwork, publication, service and teaching, the time faculty members can spend with the communities gets severely reduced. Nevertheless, by combining teaching and research in CP-HR, this tension became blurred. The development of the CSL course was the first step towards securing a collaborative partnership with the community, but also creating a training space for students interested in community psychology who could then join the research team. In this regard, a research project also requires time to consolidate a research team that is flexible enough to adapt to methodological shifts. This time must be included throughout the development of the CPAR cycle, as future researchers are central to this process, and the possibility to participate and be part of the project is a central tenet for CPAR (Fals Borda, 1998).

Moreover, understanding the importance of fieldwork in CPAR is key, which raises questions about academia and the obstacles linked to long-term visits of researchers to the community. In our case, the consolidation of a flexible research team enabled us to deal with internal travel restrictions. The researcher visiting the community is currently pursuing a PhD degree, which is an asset as she has more flexibility for fieldwork and living with the community. Additionally, the junior researchers are professionals who were former students in the CSL course, which provides them with contextual knowledge and facilitates the encounter when they started fieldwork. Trust-building and implementation require long time in the community and a consistent time commitment that does not easily align with other academic demands at the university. As Stanton (2014) states, "respectful entry into the cross-cultural research context further increases time commitment demands: It can take years to develop trusting relationships" (p. 577). At some point, scholars must negotiate with the university leadership their goals and responsibilities to make a CPAR project attainable under the current pressures for publishing and administrative demands.

Another facet of time is the community members' time commitment with the research project. This is particularly challenging in rural areas, where people work the land to provide a sustainable living for the community. At CP-HR, many women are having children for the first time after the armed conflict, people work in different productive projects, people are building a new community, which requires planning and community consensus, and people are reconnecting with their extended families. Time is a scarce resource among them. However, this should not be an excuse to guaranteeing full participation in the research and decision-making process. As a result, it is important for the research team to reach agreements about the community team's time commitments, to be flexible, and to make an effective use of time. If people are personally invested in the project, they will carve out time from their busy schedules and find satisfaction in the process.

Other Competing Needs Should be Leveraged

Funding is central to the research process. This is particularly true in communities with limited economic resources. In times of a pandemic, inequalities become larger. Many people have lost their jobs, others have had food insecurity, and others have faced health problems. Then, basic needs become pressing needs for the rural communities. At CP-HR, children had to study online without personal computers or other electronic devices and unstable internet access. In this context, providing funding to support community participation, capacity building, educational resources and infrastructure, and research personnel, is essential to leverage other competing needs. In this sense, the research process should acknowledge social change and the research team must provide community support and comprehension in the face of these new demands.

Moreover, in the peacebuilding context, external agencies are key actors that offer different types of community support. As a result, there are numerous programs targeting different social groups within the community. While these supportive actions are meant to benefit the communities, sometimes there is an overload of programs which starts to create difficulties for people's participation. In the CP-HR case, they are the target of multiple programs which offer economic and material benefits, which creates conflicting decisions to participate in certain projects where the economic benefit does not match what others are offering. This is a particularly problematic issue for a CPAR approach as the sustainability of the project cannot lie on economic compensation. For the research project, balancing economic compensation and community participation and investment is one of the key elements to be explored and discussed during the research process.

FUTURE RESEARCH DIRECTIONS

As a result of the global health emergency in 2020, there is a transformation of the methodological and epistemological approaches to research (Howlett, 2021). Recent research experiences highlight the potential of virtual interactions and the possibilities they offer for research (Lobe et al., 2020; Salerno Valdez & Gubrium, 2020), challenging past notions of in-person fieldwork as the gold standard of research (Howlett, 2021). In this chapter, we argue that CPAR projects can indeed benefit from virtual interactions, but in-person fieldwork cannot be fully replaced. Instead, we propose a blended methodological approach, with frequent online communications between the community project team and the research team, but also extended periods of fieldwork of research personnel who can offer continuous support to the community's efforts. To our knowledge, this blended strategy is yet to be explored in CPAR projects, and we believe that it is worth exploring the opportunities and challenges of its implementation.

CONCLUSION

The aim of this chapter was to critically analyze the opportunities and challenges of the implementation of a CPAR project in the middle of a global health emergency as a result of the COVID-19 pandemic. We identified key elements throughout the reflective spiral cycle of the project such as: trust-building, consolidation of a research team, securing and managing funding, and the impact of the pandemic on the development of the CPAR project. Overall, these dimensions highlighted the importance of four principles that have guided our community work during times of crisis. First, maintaining communicative action is at the core of our methodological decisions because it fosters community participation. Second, closely related to communicative action is the construction of horizontal relationships based on trust and respect. Third, time is literally of the essence. The consolidation of the alliance throughout the years between the community and the research team has been an important factor to overcome the challenges posed by the pandemic. Finally, recognizing the pressing needs of the community and the research team, as well as designing new spaces to meet, provides opportunities to engage in effective dialogue and to achieve social transformation. In addition, adjusting to a blended approach to CPAR, combining online and in-person interactions, is an interesting new strategy which can further contribute to a supportive and collaborative research process.

We hope this chapter will shed light on CPAR strategies in complex sociopolitical contexts and in times of crisis. We also hope this chapter will provide contextual information about the opportunities and challenges of community research for higher education institutions. We argue that the university leadership should take steps towards supporting (senior and junior) scholars who are interested in building community relationships and conducting long-term social research and innovation. CPAR offers principles to achieve social change and empower communities to lead their own educational processes and decolonize research practices.

ACKNOWLEDGMENT

This research was supported by the Spencer Foundation [grant number 202100090].

We also acknowledge the support of the community in the Centro Poblado Héctor Ramírez, Caquetá, Colombia, especially the leadership of Federico Montes and Esperanza Fajardo.

REFERENCES

Ahumada, M., Antón, B. M., & Peccinetti, M. V. (2012). El desarrollo de la investigación acción participativa en psicología. *Enfoques*, *24*(2), 23–52.

Alto comisionado para la Paz. (2016). *Acuerdo final para la terminación del conflicto y la construcción deuna paz estable y duradera*. http://www.altocomisionadoparalapaz.gov.co/Paginas/inicio.aspx

Aveling, E. L., & Jovchelovitch, S. (2014). Partnerships as knowledge encounters: A psychosocial theory of partnerships for health and community development. *Journal of Health Psychology*, *19*(1), 34–45. doi:10.1177/1359105313509733 PMID:24195915

Centro Nacional de Memoria Histórica. (2018). *Sujetos victimizados y daños causados. Balance de la contribución del CNMH al esclarecimiento histórico*. Centro Nacional de Memoria Histórica.

Ciocca, D. R., & Delgado, G. (2017). The reality of scientific research in Latin America; an insider's perspective. *Cell Stress & Chaperones*, *22*(6), 847–852. doi:10.100712192-017-0815-8 PMID:28584930

Colmenares, E. A. M. (2012). Investigación-acción participativa: Una metodología integradora del conocimiento y la acción. *Voces y Silencios. Revista Latinoamericana de Educación*, *3*(1), 102–115.

de Oliveira Figueiredo, G. (2015). Investigación Acción Participativa: Una alternativa para la epistemología social en Latinoamérica. *Revista de Investigacion*, *39*(86), 271–290.

Fonseca, L., & Reinoso, N. (2020). *Punto de encuentro: Reflexiones sobre la construcción de paz en el Centro Poblado Héctor Ramírez*. Universidad de La Sabana. doi:10.5294/978-958-12-0561-5

Fonseca, L. & Trigos-Carrillo, L. (in press). Critical Service-Learning amidst conflict: Tensions and opportunities for peacebuilding in divided societies. In *Pursuit of liberation: Critical service-learning as capacity building for historicized, humanizing, and embodied action*. Academic Press.

Hebert-Beirne, J., Felner, J. K., Kennelly, J., Eldeirawi, K., Mayer, A., Alexander, S., Castañeda, Y. D., Castañeda, D., Persky, V. W., Chávez, N., & Birman, D. (2018). Partner development praxis: The use of transformative communication spaces in a community-academic participatory action research effort in a Mexican ethnic enclave in Chicago. *Action Research*, *16*(4), 414–436. doi:10.1177/1476750317695413

Howlett, M. (2021). Looking at the 'field' through a Zoom lens: Methodological reflections on conducting online research during a global pandemic. *Qualitative Research*, 1–16. doi:10.1177/1468794120985691

Kaplan, O., & Nussio, E. (2018). Explaining recidivism of ex-combatants in Colombia. *The Journal of Conflict Resolution*, *62*(1), 64–93. doi:10.1177/0022002716644326

Kemmis, S., & McTaggart, R. (2005). Participatory action research: Communicative action and the public sphere. In N. Denzin & Y. Lincoln (Eds.), Handbook of qualitative research (3rd ed., pp. 559-604). Sage.

Kroc Institute for International Peace Studies. (2020). *Tres años después de la firma del Acuerdo Final en Colombia: Hacia la transformación territorial. Diciembre 2018 a Noviembre 2019*. http://peaceaccords.nd.edu/wp-content/uploads/2020/06/200630-Informe-4-resumen-final.pdf

Lobe, B., Morgan, D., & Hoffman, K. A. (2020). Qualitative data collection in an era of social distancing. *International Journal of Qualitative Methods, 19*, 1–8. doi:10.1177/1609406920937875

Ministerio de Educación Nacional. (2018). *Plan Especial de Educación Rural hacia el desarrollo rural y la construcción de paz*. MinEducación.

Mohebbi, M., Linders, A., & Chifos, C. (2018). Community immersion, trust-building, and recruitment among hard-to-reach populations: A case study of Muslim women in Detroit Metro area. *Qualitative Sociology Review, 14*(3), 24–44. doi:10.18778/1733-8077.14.3.02

Molano, A. (2015). *50 años de conflicto armado*. El Espectador.

Paris, D. (2012). Culturally sustaining pedagogy: A needed change in stance, terminology, and practice. *Educational Researcher, 41*(3), 93–97. doi:10.3102/0013189X12441244

Parra, A., Mateus, J., & Mora, Z. (2018). Educación rural en Colombia: El país olvidado, antecedentes y perspectivas en el marco del posconflicto. *Nodos y Nudos, 6*(45), 52–65.

Reinoso, N., & Fonseca, L. (2020). Introducción al Encuentro: enseñar psicología comunitaria para la construcción de paz en Colombia. In L. Fonseca & N. Reinoso (Eds.), Punto de encuentro: Reflexiones sobre la construcción de paz en el Centro Poblado Héctor Ramírez (pp. 17-29). Bogotá: Universidad de La Sabana.

Salerno Valdez, E., & Gubrium, A. (2020). Shifting to virtual CBPR protocols in the time of Corona Virus/COVID-19. *International Journal of Qualitative Methods, 19*, 1–9.

Stanton, C. R. (2014). Crossing methodological borders: Decolonizing community-based participatory research. *Qualitative Inquiry, 20*(5), 573–583. doi:10.1177/1077800413505541

Trigos-Carrillo, L. (2019). Community cultural wealth and literacy capital in Latin American communities. *English Teaching, 19*(1), 3–19. doi:10.1108/ETPC-05-2019-0071

Trigos-Carrillo, L., Fonseca, L., & Reinoso, N. (2020). Social impact of a transformative service-learning experience in a post-conflict setting. *Frontiers in Psychology, 11*(47), 1–12. doi:10.3389/fpsyg.2020.00047 PMID:32038445

Vaughn, L. M., Jacquez, F., Zhen-Duan, J., Graham, C., Marschner, D., Peralta, J., García, H., Recino, M., Maya, M., Maya, E., Cabrera, M., & Ley, I. (2017). Latinos Unidos por la Salud: The process of developing an immigrant community research team. *Collaborations: A Journal of Community-Based Research and Practice, 1*(1). http://scholarlyrepository.miami.edu/ collaborations/vol1/iss1/2

ADDITIONAL READING

Chaves, M., McIntyre, T., Verschoor, G., & Wals, A. E. (2018). Radical ruralities in practice: Negotiating buen vivir in a Colombian network of sustainability. *Journal of Rural Studies*, *59*, 153–162. doi:10.1016/j.jrurstud.2017.02.007

Fals Borda, O. & World Congress of Participatory Convergence in Knowledge, Space, Time. (1998). *People's Participation: Challenge's Ahead*. New York: Apex. Intermediate Technology Publications.

Loewenson, R., Laurell, A. C., Hogstedt, C., D'Ambruoso, L., & Shroff, Z. (2014). *Participatory action research in health systems: A methods reader*. Equinet.

Morrison, J., Akter, K., Jennings, H. M., Nahar, T., Kuddus, A., Shaha, S. K., Ahmed, N., King, C., Haghparast-Bidgoli, H., Costello, A., Khan, A., Azad, K., & Fottrell, E. (2019). Participatory learning and action to address type 2 diabetes in rural Bangladesh: A qualitative process evaluation. *BMC Endocrine Disorders*, *19*(1), 118. doi:10.118612902-019-0447-3 PMID:31684932

Rahman, M. A., & Fals-Borda, O. (1991). *Action and Knowledge: Breaking the Monopoly with Participatory Action-research*. Intermediate Technology Publications.

Rettberg, A., & McFee, E. (2019). *Excombatientes y acuerdo de paz con las FARC-EP en Colombia: balance de la etapa temprana*. Bogotá: Ediciones Uniandes-Universidad de los. *Andes (Salta)*.

Versmesse, I., Derluyn, I., Masschelein, J., & De Haene, L. (2017). After conflict comes education? Reflections on the representation of emergencies in 'Education in emergencies.'. *Comparative Education*, *53*(4), 538–557. doi:10.1080/03050068.2017.1327570

KEY TERMS AND DEFINITIONS

COVID-19: Coronavirus disease or COVID-19 is an infectious disease caused by a newly discovered coronavirus in 2019. Most people infected with the COVID-19 virus will experience mild to moderate respiratory illness and recover without requiring special treatment. Older people, and those with underlying medical problems like cardiovascular disease, diabetes, chronic respiratory disease, and cancer are more likely to develop serious illness.

CPAR: Critical Participatory Action Research is rooted in the belief that those most impacted by research should take the lead in framing the questions, design, methods, analysis and determining what products and actions might be most useful in securing social change.

Crisis: A time of great disagreement, confusion, or suffering.

ETCR: In English, Territorial Spaces for Training and Reincorporation are spaces created by the government to facilitate the reincorporation process of former FARC-EP guerrilla members in the context of the 2016 Peace Accord in Colombia.

Guerrilla Member: It is a member of a small independent group taking part in irregular fighting, typically against larger regular forces. In Colombia, the FARC-EP guerrilla group was created in 1964.

Peacebuilding: From a critical lens, peacebuilding is not reduced to the absence of war. Peacebuilding is related to achieving social justice and transformation in Colombia.

Reincorporation Process: This process is geared at people who laid down their arms within the framework of the Final Peace Agreement and transitioned to legality.

Rurality: In Colombia, rurality implies social and political dimensions. Rural people or *campesinos* are affected by lack of land ownership, violence, limited access to basic public services, health and education, and other social inequalities.

Chapter 10
Between Two Crises:
Identity Reconstruction Through Critical Action Research Self-Study

Kathryn G. O'Brien
University of Missouri-St. Louis, USA

ABSTRACT

The purpose of this chapter was to critically examine the reconstruction of professional identity between two crises: The Great Recession of 2008 and the COVID-19 pandemic of 2020. Using a critical participatory action research self-study design, the author deconstructs the transition from for-profit behavioral health care business leadership to adjunct professor. Data sources include U.S. government job classification profiles, syllabi from courses taught, and the university's corresponding student surveys to answer the primary research question: How can teaching action research contribute to the reshaping of professional identity? Data analysis revealed that iterative cycles of reflection and action in teaching action research supported the development of identity as an academic across time. The knowledge, skills, and abilities required for a career in business supported, and also interfered with, career transition. Lastly, the author understood that the problem of practice stemmed from lack of recognition of her own privilege.

INTRODUCTION

This chapter details a critical action research self-study, the purpose of which was to examine and understand the transition of the author's professional identity between The Great Recession of 2008 through the end of 2020 during the COVID-19 pandemic. Much has been written about career transitions, but little research is available from the insider perspective of a transition from business operations to teacher educator. During those 12 years I evolved from corporate director in international behavioral health care business operations to Adjunct Associate Professor of education in a state university but found that I could only superficially recognize myself in the contexts of academia. This troubled me to the extent that I experienced it as a problem of practice.

DOI: 10.4018/978-1-7998-6922-1.ch010

From the completion of my master's degree in counselor education in 1984, I moved through a succession of early-career work settings and earned my clinical license. I provided psychotherapy to individuals, couples, and families in an agency setting and then made a transition to the oversight of contracted counselors. I advanced upward and in 1998 I was a director of Employee Assistance Program (EAP) services for more than 6 million employee households in a large behavioral health care organization. The company was purchased, and the new owners began to eliminate layers of management, putting my director-level position at risk. I was laid off and as it turned out, due to a non-compete agreement between that U.S. organization and a job I *really wanted* with an international EAP company, layoff was the *only* way I could have gone from where I was to the next job.

I viewed my new job as the holy grail of professional opportunities in corporate international behavioral healthcare management. The goal of company leadership was to build a solid International Organization for Standardization (ISO) (ISO, 2000) certified organization, signifying its highest quality standardized services and practices, and then when the time was right the owner would sell, and we would all profit handsomely. Throughout the next ten years I focused on that objective, as I worked and traveled to Canada, the U.K., South Africa, Mexico, and China with the same small team of colleagues, who became like family members. I also benefited from a virtual office that made it possible for me to meet day or night with colleagues in disparate time zones. I authored operations manuals, I participated in sales presentations, and when I went to industry conferences, I was recognized by colleagues and competitors. I grew at ease in diverse cultural contexts. I designed and implemented the clinical operations, created performance metrics, contributed as content expert to proprietary software for clinical management, implemented reorganization initiatives, and stayed over one or two extra nights wherever I went on company business, since the overnight hotel and food were my only out-of-pocket costs. My professional identity solidified, and I acquired expertise.

Then, almost to the exact date, ten years after my start with the organization, the clock stopped. I answered my phone on a Friday morning and heard the voice of the Chief Executive Officer, who briefly explained that my position was being eliminated, effective immediately. In an instant, although I did not recognize it as such, my identity was stripped away. Gone were my familiar language set, my daily practices, my work family, the relationships with professional colleagues around the world, and my retirement plan. At every level to the depths of my being, this change was unwanted.

I negotiated for six months of severance pay and began searching diligently for a job. Overqualified, and older than average, I struggled as the six months passed, and then a year. Finally, after two and a half personally and financially devastating years of unemployment I was hired for an entry-level position in social work. I also returned to academia to pursue a graduate certificate in gender studies, which led me into a PhD program in education in teaching and learning, and a second graduate certificate in social justice in education. I transitioned to full-time student, supporting myself with graduate assistantships and student loans. My doctorate was conferred four months after I was eligible for Medicare. Now as an adjunct professor, I teach master's students in education in the social justice and action research classrooms. I also work as a psychotherapist in private practice.

T. S. Eliot (1968) wrote, "For last year's words belong to last year's language, and next year's words await another voice" (p. 54). This is where I found myself stuck, and why I took up this inquiry. Discourses can be troubling. The loss of familiar language sets and daily practices were grievous occurrences that led to loneliness, anxiety, hopelessness, and depression. What makes it possible for someone to lose the familiar and to begin again after investing a lifetime of hope and energy in a career? Through my engagement in academia, the feeling of not belonging persisted. I taught graduate students in education, yet I had not worked in a K-12 classroom. Was I, or could I be credible? I perceived myself as not quite belonging with colleagues who possessed deep experience and lifelong engagement with teaching. This had little to do with their responses to me, as they uniformly demonstrated welcome. For me, it was an expressive issue. A conundrum of language as social practice. I couldn't explain to them who I was, because we had no shared professional spaces of discursive pasts. I continued to grieve the loss of my previous professional identity and didn't know how to fix that. This was my problem of practice.

I am confident that I am not alone in having made such a transition as an older woman, and so I believe this research may benefit others like me who have traversed such spaces, as well as students of action research and critical discourse studies, other academics, career transition professionals, and psychotherapists working with clients who are making similar life changes.

LITERATURE REVIEW

At the outset of this review, I noticed a gap in the literature related to older women in business transitioning to careers in academia. My professional identity comprised years of practice through which I developed the daily habits and shared language of the workplace, the structures of meetings, phone calls, written and oral communications, taking and giving direction, instructions, mentorship, and the creation and construction of the minutiae of daily business operations. To explore my identity construction and career transition in the literature, I relied first on theory and research related to discourse and identity for focus on professional identity construction. Next, I explored literature about career derailment and its effects on executives. Finally, to focus my research methods, I analyzed resources related to self-study and critical action research.

Discourse and Identity

Discourse is related to distinctive elements of social practice including the linguistic elements (texts, talk), and non-linguistic components such as ideologies, behaviors, and ways of expression (Fairclough, 2003). Texts take place within contexts, or social events where individuals engage in "interactive processes of meaning making" (Fairclough, 2003, p. 10). This connection is explicated by Bakhtin (1986), who described texts as "any coherent complex of signs" (p. 103) and who theorized that such complexes formed contextually understood speech genres, which encompass more than merely the spoken utterances. Examples include such things as discourses of the crowd at a baseball game and discourses of a congregation at worship. Vygotsky (1978) viewed context as essential to making meaning based on the operations of signs, may include language, behavior, artifacts, and all other elements that contribute to meaning within context. Norris (2004) asserted that context is defined by language plus all other elements that contribute to meaning making, which happens within the contexts of discourses.

Kress (2010) views discourse as dealing with, "the production and organization of *meaning* about the world from an institutional position" (p. 110). He argues that discourses are a society's resource for meaning making in various contexts including at the national, regional, local, and even the family levels. What "we" know may not be the same in every context. He explains,

Discourse refers to 'institutions' and the knowledge they produce about the world which constitutes their domain. Knowledge about the world which is the institution's domain of relevance and responsibility is

continuously produced. Examples of such institutions are education, medicine, science, law, 'the church', and more often and somewhat less tangibly, institutions such as 'the family'. Knowledge is produced in and shaped by the perspectives of a particular institution. 'Discourse' names both the complex as well as the understandings derived in encounters with such knowledge. In these encounters 'we' produce what we then hold as our knowledge about our world. Discourse shapes and names the routes through which we (have come to) know the socially shaped world as one kind of knowledge. (Kress, 2010, p. 110, italics in original)

Kress (2010) further describes Discourse as a continuous and evolving set of social practices. Fairclough (2011) posits that social practices "articulate discourse…along with other non-discoursal elements" (p. 25) and that any social practice comprises these elements: "Action and interaction, social relations, persons (with beliefs, attitudes, histories, etc.), the material world, and discourse" (Fairclough, 2011, p. 25). Furthermore, the term, discourse, refers to connections in language: "saying (informing), doing (action), and being (identity)" (Gee, 2011a, p. 2). Rogers (2007) describes these connections as *ways of interacting, ways of representing, and ways of being*. I argue that the identity of an individual is context dependent, including what the individual brings to the setting (e.g., what Fairlough, 2011, above refers to as persons), and the constitutive (myriad other) elements of that context. Such contexts are political, because language is political. Gee (2011b) asserts,

When we speak or write, we always risk being seen as a "winner" or "loser" in a given game or practice. Furthermore, we can speak or write so as to accept others as "winners" or "losers" in the game or practice in which we are engaged. In speaking and writing, then, we can both gain or lose and give or deny social goods. (p 7)

Discourse *does* things (Austin, 1975). First, social relations and social subjects are constituted in and by discourse, which is viewed as socially constructive. Second, each instance of discourse is considered to have three components: text, interaction, and social action that occur within a specific context at a particular time. Identity contributes to and is simultaneously shaped by discourse, and discourses are contextually limited. Bronfenbrenner (1979) wrote,

The ecology of human development involves the scientific study of the progressive, mutual accommodation between an active, growing human being and the changing properties of the immediate settings, in which the developing person lives, as this process is affected by relations between these settings, and by the larger contexts in which the settings are embedded. (p. 21)

An individual in context is "a growing, dynamic entity that progressively moves into and restructures the milieu in which it resides" (Bronfenbrenner, 1979, p. 21). The environment, however, exerts influence in return, the phenomenon Bronfenbrenner called reciprocity. This becomes evident, for example, in ongoing striving for equity among people of varying intersections such as skin color, national origins, ethnicity, religious beliefs, sexual orientation, gender identity, sex, and so forth. Annamama (2015) asserts that, while intersectionality is important, caution must be used to avoid de-centering race as a primary concern for rebalancing contexts in support of equity. This caution is inextricable from the purpose of this research, which seeks to produce solutions and insights that can be accessible and allowable for everyone.

Borba and Osterman (2007) consider identity as having to do with context-based, gendered bodily meanings such as mannerisms, dress, tone of voice, expressions through language, and verbal transmission. The communication of one's identity in any given context raises the matter of intelligibility. Identities may be understood, or not understood, based upon specific contextual discourses, and such understanding depends upon ongoing interchanges with others. Social interactions are necessary for any concept of human identity whatsoever (Lemke, 2000), and identities carry meanings. Lemke (2000) contends, "Meanings are not made by organisms but by persons, and they are not made within organisms but within an ecosocial system that minimally includes other persons and the things they make meaning about" (p. 283).

Gergen (1994) proposes that identity is relational, rather than something an individual possesses apart from a specific context connecting it to, "the performance of languages available in the public sphere" (p. 247). Instead of looking at categories like self-concepts, schemas, self-esteem, Gergen (1994) considers "the self as a narration rendered intelligible within ongoing relationships" (p. 247). Davies and Harré (1990) assert that identity is a persistently open question, and that the answer shifts based upon positions possible based on one's own, and others' discursive practices and the narratives used to make sense of life as it is lived. As articulated by Shotwell and Sangrey (2009) "To understand the full complexity of identity requires a more nuanced account of how people's self-formation is multiply constituted" (p. 66).

Based on critical language theories, and constructivist and sociocultural perspectives discussed in this section, discourse(s) and identity are inextricable: identity cannot be understood apart from context. Since unplanned and unexpected career derailment prompted the need for identity work, literature related to that topic was also essential.

Career Derailment

The Great Recession of 2008 marked, "The highest yearly job-loss total since 1945" (Goldman, 2009, p. 1). By the end of that year the number of jobs lost reached 2.6 million (Goldman, 2009) and underemployment was "at a record high" (Goldman, 2009, p. 1). The Great Recession stretched from December 2007 to June 2009 (Ahn & Song, 2017). Ahn and Song (2017) wrote, "The Great Recession was the most severe downturn in a generation, and one distinguishing feature of this event from previous recessions was the degree of job loss among older workers" (p. 250). These authors cited difficulties faced by older adults (ages 50-61) including material hardship related to food insufficiency, housing insecurity, lack of funds to pay basic utility bills, delaying medical or dental care, loss of health insurance coverage, and a lower likelihood of their becoming re-employed. McCormack, Abou-Hamdan, and Joseph (2017) add that, "The cost of derailment to the individual is also high, including a catastrophic loss of identity often impacting on family life, income, and psychological wellbeing" (p. 24).

McCormack, Abou-Hamdan, and Joseph (2017) focused on career derailment of corporate executives from 38 to 50 years of age, "a critical time in which self-reflection and an evaluation of former dreams and current achievements often occurs" (p. 25). These authors assert that the wellbeing of professionals and executive-level employees is closely aligned with job loss, including that which is related to organizational restructuring. Despair and major depression are common among executives experiencing such unplanned disruption (McCormack, et al., 2017). Shameful loss of reputation, psychological vulnerability and distress, feeling unwanted at the workplace, lack of validation, powerlessness and isolation, feeling that others did not understand their situation, and irreparable damage to relationships were among the experiences reported to McCormack, Abou-Hamdan, and Joseph (2017). Although career derailment can have severe and sometimes chronic negative psychological effects, it is also possible for an individual to engage in growth through making "sense of this highly challenging period, which has shattered previous goals, beliefs, and expectations" (McCormack, et al., 2017, p. 26). Participants in McCormack, Abou-Hamdan, and Josephs' (2017) research mentioned mobilization of internal agency, addressing irrational fears, orientation toward an opportunity for increased self-knowledge, positive and genuine professional and social support, increased empathy, and helping others going through similar struggles as mechanism that contributed to healing and a focus on the future after career derailment.

Kaiser, Hennecke, and Luhmann (2020) explored: 1) the interaction effects between life satisfaction and domain satisfaction, and 2) perceived control. They describe affective well-being as referring to "People's emotional experiences as reflected by how often they experience negative and positive affect" (Kaiser, Hennecke, & Luhmann, 2020, p. 5). Kaiser, Hennecke, and Luhmann (2020) asserted, "People low in life satisfaction reported a greater desire to change their life circumstances, underpinning the assumption that people self-initiate changes due to dissatisfaction" (p. 2). Kaiser, Hennecke, and Luhmann (2020) mention that "For some people…major life changes just happen…with little control over whether and when they occur" (p. 1). Alessandri, Truxilly, Tisak, Fagnani, and Borgnoni (2020) describe what they term *event-driven* forms of change as "changes attributable to the influence of major and minor work and life events" (p. 664). But when someone transitions to a new career, they are once again a beginner.

Pinnegar (1995) addresses the issue of being a beginner. "It appears to me that being a beginner brings with it certain feelings and emotions. Two of these are a pervading sense of vulnerability and an uncertainty about what things mean and how to make sense of them" (Pinnegar, 1995, p. 80). Furthermore, he asserts, "These feelings and emotions may limit the beginners' ability to use the expertise they have… there is a chasm of lived experience between entering a new setting and being able to understand and work with that context in powerful ways" (Pinnegar, 1995, p. 80). To further complicate an unexpected midlife career transition, it is necessary to take into account that younger adults typically possess more cognitive resources compared to middle-aged and older adults (Teshale & Lackman, 2016). This does not necessarily mean that middle-aged and older adults have cognitive deficits. For example, as Teshale and Lackman (2016) indicate, middle-aged adults may need to balance multiple demands including elder care, children leaving the home, care of the home and family relationships, and work.

Career derailment in mid-to-late adulthood involves significant challenges. Starting over, being once again a beginner, carries consequences for identity including view of self, and how one is viewed by others. For the purposes of this inquiry, to document the trajectory from beginner to competency, an examination of the research method is necessary.

Critical Action Research and Self-Study

Kemmis, McTaggert, and Nixon (2014) describe action research as "a 'disciplined' way of making change" (p. 18), which works as, "A spiral of self-reflective cycles of: *planning* a change, *acting* and *observing* the process and consequences of the change, *reflecting* on these processes and consequences, and then *re-planning, acting* and *observing, reflecting,* and so on" (Kemmis, McTaggert, & Nixon, 2014, p. 18). They emphasize the participatory nature of action research, meaning that participant(s) are 'insiders' to the research being conducted (Kemmis et al., 2014). Participatory action research can "transform the conduct and consequences of…practice to meet the needs of changing times and circumstances by confronting and overcoming…*untoward consequences* of…practice" (Kemmis et al., 2014, p. 5). These same authors describe those consequences as being irrational, unsustainable, or unjust (Kemmis et al., 2014)).

This constitutes the critical component of critical participatory action research. Kemmis, McTaggert, and Nixon (2014) write, "Critical participatory action research aims to help people to understand and to transform 'the way we do things around here'" (p. 67), making a strong connection between this form of research and Discourse, as described above. They furthermore assert that through critical participatory action research participants may transform,

(1) their understandings of their practices; (2) the conduct of their practices, and (3) the conditions under which they practice, in order that these things will be more rational (and comprehensible coherent and reasonable), more productive and sustainable, and more just and inclusive. (Kemmis et al. 2014, p. 67)

Research that is just and inclusive links practice and theory (Levin & Greenwood, 2013), and positions the researcher to abide by "disciplined material practices that produce radical, democratizing transformations in the civic sphere (Denzin & Lincoln, 2013, p. 43). Such transformations are inextricable from the shaping of identities and connect with Tan's (2021) three discursive identities of teacher educators.

(a) a practitioner identity, based on a discourse that positioned the practitioner within school and placed practitioners above academics in terms of ability to prepare teachers for classroom teaching; (b) a teaching identity with a discourse about teaching as the core purpose of secondment, sidelining an identity as a learner; and (c) an individualistic identity based on an individualistic framing of teaching work. (Tan, 2021, p. 104).

Comprehension of identity necessarily includes a reflexive position. Patton (2002) writes that the engagement with reflexivity is "[T]o undertake an ongoing examination of *what I know* and *how I know it*" (p. 64). As Lather (1986) writes, "[T]here is no neutral research" (p. 257) and "[R]esearch that is explicitly committed to critiquing the status quo and building a more just society — that is, research as praxis — adds an important voice" (p. 258). Lather (1986) refers to the "reciprocal shaping of theory and practice" (footnote, p. 258), which I argue is essential to critical (anti-oppressive) perspectives and practices. Reflexivity shapes the data, "but in conversation with it, so that the researcher's own methods and appreciations are also shaped" (Schön, 1987, p. 73) by it.

Lather (1986) argues that, "Our best tactic at present is to construct research designs that demand a vigorous self-reflexivity" (p. 268). In regard to the telling of one's own story Rubin and Rubin (2012) explained, "Stories are as important in research as they are in everyday life" (p. 97). The action research cycle provided the structure for this self-study.

"Making one's self the unit of study in teacher education is transformative in that it increases introspection and reflection" (Kindle & Schmidt, 2019, p. 86). Necessarily, tension is involved. Bullough and Pinnegar (2001) locate this tension between "self and the arena of practice" (p. 15). Self-study is dialogical. Friere (2011) contends that a word is not merely a tool for talk, but a symbol comprising multiple elements and meanings. "Within the word we find two dimensions, reflection and action, in such radical interaction that if one is sacrificed—even in part—the other immediately suffers" (p. 87). Leaning into the research process, Kristeva's (1986) perspective becomes helpful. "Dialogism… does not strive towards transcendence but rather toward harmony, all the while implying an idea of rupture (of opposition and analogy) as a modality of transformation" (p. 58). Thus, it becomes apparent that introspection and reflection produce tension between self and practice as the self-study must be dialogical. Remaining in the weeds rather than floating above the horizon of self-study allows the tension to produce resolution, leading to change. Finally, a critical perspective permits liberatory outcomes as the researcher considers situating the self in juxtaposition with others. Lather (1991) agrees: "[T]he creation of emancipatory theory is a dialogic enterprise" (p. 59).

Zeichner (2007) affirms the significance of self-study research: "Self-study research can potentially make an important contribution to the knowledge base in teacher education…about the important role of practitioner-generated knowledge in building a knowledge base in education" (p. 37). Furthermore,

It is the balance between the way in which private experience can provide insight and solution for public issues and troubles and the way in which public theory can provide insight and solution for private trial that forms the nexus of self-study. (Bullough & Pinnegar, 2001, p. 15)

To combine self-study and action research positions my lived action within the cycle of action research (Stewart, et al., 2020, p. 437).

Understanding the context-specific operation of discourses, the devastating effects of career derailment, and the benefits of self-study dovetailed with my action research practice that was in operation from 2015 and onward, and led me to ask these questions: *How can teaching action research contribute to the reshaping of professional identity? How can knowledge, skills, and abilities from three professional identities coalesce in career transition? What can be learned about identity and career transition through critical action research?*

MAIN FOCUS OF THE CHAPTER

Methods: Setting and Participants

This inquiry used qualitative action research self-study methods to address my research questions. I was the sole participant in the research. I identify as a white cisgender lesbian and acknowledge that my experiences are situated within layers of white privilege, such as having two parents who completed master's degrees, a lifetime of 100% access to medical care, stable employment (until 2008), transportation to get everywhere I needed to go, food security, four adult children whose lives are stable and happy, five well-nurtured grandchildren, and much, much more. I recognize that the experience I sought to tease apart in this research, while catastrophic for me, pales in comparison to daily challenges of those who lack access to what should be commonly accessible social goods.

Methods: Data Sources and Data Analysis

To answer my research questions, I selected three sources of data. First, I looked at U.S. Government Occupational Summary Reports (OSRs) for my three professions, syllabi from six sections of the university's Introduction to Action Research course that I taught from 2015 to 2020, and quantitative data from the corresponding six university student course surveys.

Between Two Crises

OSRs

To provide an objective overview of my professional origins (Mental Health Counselor, MHC), my previous career (Operations Manager, OM) and my current work (Education Teachers, Postsecondary, ETP), I selected as my first data source, "the O*NET database, containing hundreds of standardized and occupation-specific descriptors on almost 1,000 occupations covering the entire U.S. economy" (National Center for O*NET Development, a; see also job-specific descriptors in National Center for O*NET Development b, c, and d). From the online details page associated with each of the above-mentioned occupations I captured the knowledge, skills, and abilities from each professional category. I first identified all common traits and observed that shared traits occurred only in the top 50% of the descriptors. All traits below the 50% sharing level were increasingly specific to the role. Therefore, I eliminated all descriptors at 50% and lower. I then created three tables in order to examine common features across all three professions: one table for knowledge, one for skills, and one for abilities (see Tables 1-3). Definitions for all included traits are available in Appendix 1.

Table 1. Traits across professions: Knowledge

Knowledge	MHC	ETP	GOM
Psychology	X	X	-
Therapy and Counseling	X	-	-
Customer and Personal Service	X	X	X
Sociology and Anthropology	X	X	-
English Language	X	X	X
Education and Training	X	X	-
Clerical	X	-	-
Philosophy and Theology	X	X	-
Law and Government	X	-	-
Administration and Management	X	X	X
Communications and Media	-	X	-
Mathematics	-	X	X
Personnel and Human Resources	-	X	X
Computers and Electronics	-	X	-
Clerical	-	-	X
Economics and Accounting	-	-	X
Sales and Marketing	-	-	X
Production and Processing	-	-	X
Public Safety and Security	-	-	X
	\multicolumn{3}{c}{3 traits in common}

Table 1 shows the aggregate list of aspects of knowledge from all three professional categories: Mental Health Counselor (MHC), Education Teachers, Postsecondary (ETP), and General and Operations

Managers (GOM). Knowledge traits for each profession are marked with an X beneath each profession, bringing to the forefront traits that are common across all three. Table 1 shows that the professions share three common knowledge areas: customer and personal service, English language (presumably because this is a U.S. government endeavor), and Administration and management. In the findings I will explore in depth the commonalities across knowledge, skills, and abilities of the three professional descriptions, and make application to my research questions. Tables 2 and 3 illustrate professional skills and abilities in the same way Table 1 reveals common traits for professional knowledge.

Table 2. Traits across professions: Skills

Skills	MHC	ETP	GOM
Active Listening	X	X	X
Social Perceptiveness	X	X	X
Speaking	X	X	X
Service Orientation	X	X	X
Writing	X	X	X
Critical Thinking	X	X	X
Monitoring	X	X	X
Judgment and Decision Making	X	X	X
Reading Comprehension	X	X	X
Persuasion	X	-	X
Active Learning	X	X	X
Learning Strategies	X	X	X
Coordination	X	X	X
Complex Problem Solving	X	X	X
Negotiation	X	-	X
Systems Evaluation	X	X	X
Science	X	-	-
Instructing	X	X	X
Systems Analysis	X	X	X
Operations Analysis	X	-	-
Time Management	X	X	X
Management of Personnel Resources	X	-	X
Management of Material Resources	-	-	X
Management of Financial Resources	-	-	X
		17 traits in common	

Table 2 shows the aggregate list of aspects of skills from all three professional categories. This table reveals that the professions share 17 common skills: active listening, social perceptiveness, speaking, service orientation, writing, critical thinking, monitoring, judgement and decision making, reading comprehension, active learning, learning strategies, coordination, complex problem solving, systems evaluation, instructing, systems analysis, and time management.

Table 3. Traits across professions: Abilities

Abilities	MHC	ETP	GOM
Oral Comprehension	X	X	X
Oral Expression	X	X	X
Problem Sensitivity	X	X	X
Written Comprehension	X	X	X
Written Expression	X	X	X
Inductive Reasoning	X	X	X
Deductive Reasoning	X	X	X
Speech Recognition	X	X	-
Speech Clarity	X	X	X
Fluency of Ideas	X	-	X
Information Ordering	X	X	X
Category Flexibility	X	X	X
Selective Attention	X	-	X
Originality	X	X	X
Near Vision	X	X	-
	\multicolumn{3}{c}{11 traits in common}

Table 3 shows the aggregate list of aspects of abilities from all three professional categories. This table reveals that the professions share 11 common abilities: oral comprehension, oral expression, problem sensitivity, written comprehension, written expression, inductive reasoning, deductive reasoning, speech clarity, information ordering, category flexibility, and originality.

Syllabi

For the second data source, I relied upon syllabi from seven sections of the Introduction to Action Research course that I taught in different semesters across five years, beginning in the Fall Semester of 2015 and ending with the Fall Semester of 2020. Although I also now teach the Action Research Capstone course that follows the Action Research I course, I did not enter that classroom until several years later. For the purposes of this research, I limited the data to the introductory course, because that class was my earliest experience in university teaching, and also the moment in time when I felt most vulnerable, before my teaching skill began to take shape. Additionally, my teaching of that course continues in the present, allowing for representation of my development across time.

I conducted content analysis of my syllabi, searching in detail for changes in my teaching strategies, including assignments, point values, and texts. I also critically examined how in writing I positioned myself in relationship with students. I reviewed the syllabi in detail, making notes of changes across the semesters, and then I created a table to make my observations more accessible. Figure 1 illustrates an example of my raw note taking.

Figure 1. Example of raw notes from syllabus review

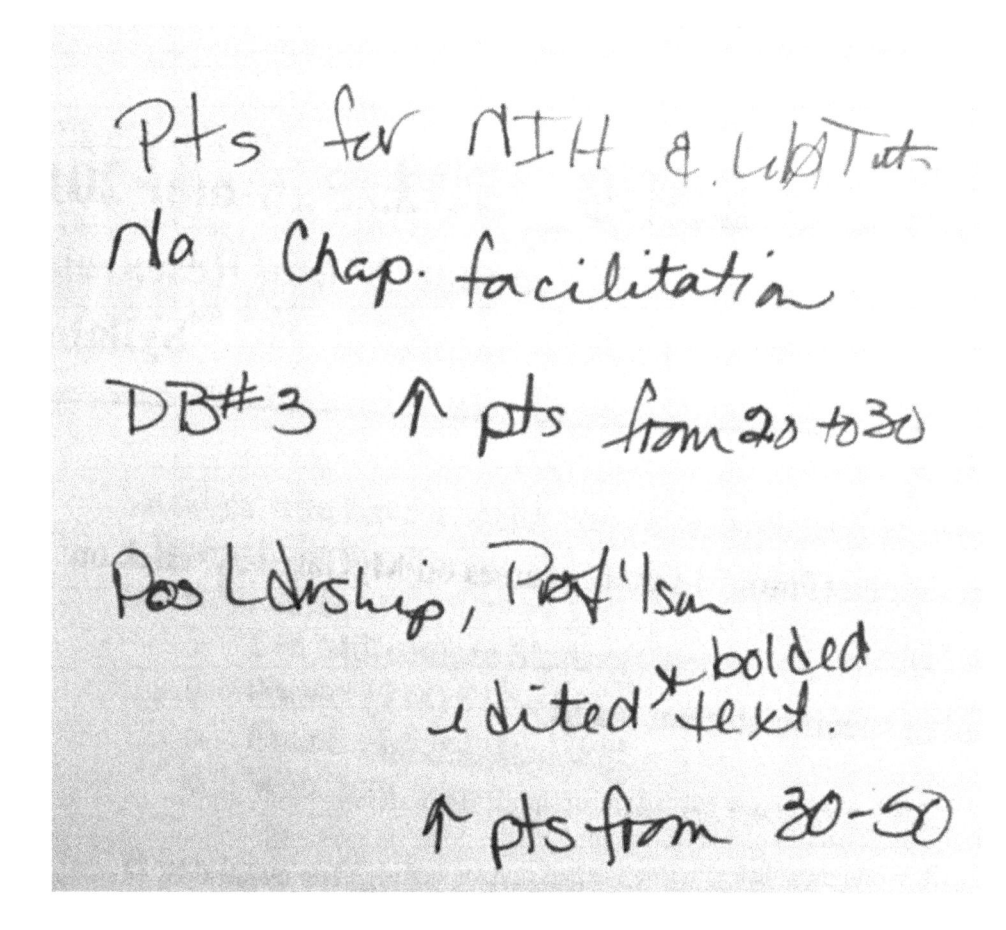

This raw note represented my decisions to assign points to students' completion of the training in working with human subjects (NIH), and for the completion of library tutorials to support research for their literature reviews. I noted, also, an increase of points for a specific Discussion Board assignment that was significant for the course, and also an increase of points for positive leadership and professionalism, that I noted in the syllabus with bolded text.

I created a spreadsheet to analyze the evolution of my syllabi across time. A section of the spreadsheet is included in Table 4.

Between Two Crises

Table 4. Evolution of syllabi data sample

Syllabus Review Notes	• I felt awkward, old, and underprepared	• I took some initiative. I was trying to get students to go more deeply into their literature reviews. I made a poster presentation through which I experienced a way of synthesizing a project that was different from immersion in the details, and in the writing. I felt that I could force (as with a spring bulb) students' ways of thinking about their work similarly. that's why I added the slide presentation - 5 slides exactly, with brief information - 5 minute presentation, with digital feedback from the class members to one another.
Ext Additions/Changes	• My first time teaching the course • This is the basic syllabus provided to me, except for the insertion of my contact information • I was learning along with the students	• I added my picture • I made explicit instructions to students to print the syllabus and bring it to the first class • I added to each week of the class schedule a section called "Ongoing Work" • I added to the class schedule assignment descriptions for some key projects • I added one new assignment, a brief presentation to the class of each student's literature, with feedback delivered electronically from class members
# Assign-ments	9	9
Format	In person	In person
Length	16 Weeks	16 Weeks
Semester	FS2015	SP2016

This example of my analysis of syllabi shows the changes I made across time, and also my decision-making process in regard to those changes. This was helpful in learning about my growth as a teacher educator as I will explain in the findings.

Course Surveys

The final data source was student surveys from the Introduction to Action Research course, which are conducted by the university. I analyzed surveys corresponding to all sections taught, except the survey from Summer Semester 2018, which was missing from the university archive. I used the remaining six surveys, each of which corresponds to a syllabus from my files, and also are related with the university's roster of courses I taught. The survey uses a Likert Scale response protocol to questions about the student, the course, and the instructor. I excluded the narrative comments (which ranged from scathing to laudatory), due to the changing wording of narrative prompts across the semesters. Additionally, I focused my analysis only on numeric items specifically related to the instructor, rather that other aspects of the course.

Table 5. Survey scores 2015-2016. % Change

% Change	FS2015 to SP2016	6%	8%	3%	-4%		-11%	-6%	17%	-5%	-4%			8%
SP2016	Course Mean (out of 5) (3 respondents/7 enrolled)	4.33	4.67	3.33	3.33		3.33	3.33	3.33	3.00	3.33			3.67
FS2015	Course Mean (out of 5) (13 respondents/15 enrolled)	4.08	4.31	3.23	3.46		3.69	3.54	2.77	3.15	3.46			3.38
Question		Knowledge of subject matter	Interest and enthusiasm in the subject	Ability to create enthusiasm and a desire to learn	Ability to stimulate critical thinking, opinions	Ability to encourage student opinions	Openness to views of students	Fairness in dealings with students	Clarity of explanations	Value of class discussion	Use and variety of resources, presentations	Sensitivity to student concerns	Availability for help with problems	General rating of instructor

Between Two Crises

Table 6.

	Course Mean (out of 5) (12 respondents/15 enrolled)	4.50	4.50	4.25	4.42	4.58					4.33	4.17	4.33
% Change SS2016 to SP2019		5%	3%	5%	7%	New					New	New	3%
SP2019 Course Mean (out of 5) (14 respondents/24 enrolled)		4.71	4.64	4.36	4.50	4.57					4.38	4.57	4.36
Question		Knowledge of subject matter	Interest and enthusiasm in the subject	Ability to create enthusiasm and a desire to learn	Ability to stimulate critical thinking, opinions	Ability to encourage student opinions	Openness to views of students	Fairness in dealings with students	Clarity of explanations	Value of class discussion	Use and variety of resources, presentations	Sensitivity to student concerns	Availability for help with problems	General rating of instructor

233

Statistical data described general trends in my teacher educator work across six of the seven semesters comprising five years. An aggregate total of 90 students were enrolled in my sections. Of those, 64 students participated in the survey, comprising 71% of the total enrollment. Because of the relatively small sample size, I did not take into account differences in the way the courses were structured such as the length of the course (ranging from four to sixteen weeks), or the format of the course (online or in person). I looked strictly at the aggregated feedback scores on the end-of-course surveys. During the time span from 2015 to 2020, the university amended the survey format twice. I limited my analysis to those items directly related to the instructor, in order to gain a close view of how students assessed my work as their instructor. These are illustrated in Tables 5 and 6 which follow.

Since I edited the syllabi, I sought to balance that subjective aspect with external data. To maximize reliability and validity I selected OSR descriptors and student surveys as objective resources. I triangulated the data, using both textual (OSR and syllabi) and numeric (survey) data sources.

Findings

My problem of practice led me to seek answers to specific research questions related to the interplay between teaching action research from 2015-2020, and the reshaping of my professional identity. In the sections that follow, I explain the findings in two subsections: syllabus changes and student feedback, and personal and professional fit. Limitations of the research are described.

Syllabus Changes and Student Feedback

Close examination of the course syllabi across the semesters exposed three categories of revisions I made across the semesters. Those revisions comprised textual changes, assignment changes, and point value changes students could earn for attendance and participation. "Textual changes" refers to edits and revisions within the body of the text of the syllabus, all elements of the syllabus that do not describe assignments or other aspects of the course that are scored based on student performance. Textual changes were of two primary types: 1) Human equity and diversity, and 2) Increased clarity for students about course policies and/or expectations. Assignment changes occurred when I added new tasks that I felt would enhance student learning, or when the course transitioned from the in-person to the online environment. I made point value changes when I felt students weren't following through on ungraded activities, such as keeping a reflective journal of their action research processes. I assigned points to the activities and added them to the course grade book. Student feedback gave me some indication of the effectiveness of those changes.

The first semester I taught the course, Fall Semester 2015, the only changes I made to the syllabus were the replacement of the Course Steward's name and contact information with my own and edits to the due dates for assignments. In later semesters, however, that was not the case. The student survey indicated that my highest score (4.31) was related to *interest and enthusiasm in the subject*, while the lowest score (2.77) was related to *clarity of explanations*, which isn't too surprising since I was just getting accustomed to the subject and to my classroom role. The *general rating of instructor* was 3.38 out of 5.

I focus heavily on planning and scheduling at the outset of the class and textual changes supported this practice. After my first teaching semester, I inserted instructions at the top of the course calendar for Class #1. This excerpt is from the Spring 2016 section: "**Print** syllabus and **bring to class**. We will review the coming semester in detail, and so it would be a very good idea to organize your thoughts around the syllabus content *before* coming to class…" (O'Brien, Unpublished a, p. 8). In class the students and I walked through the syllabus, and I gave suggestions for managing the workflow, so that they could stay on task. I felt they would benefit from the tactile experience of holding the document in their hands, hearing me talk about it, asking questions, making notations, and adding dates to their calendars to keep up with a rigorous schedule of assignments. That same semester I added my photo to the first page, and three sections of text including a welcome to class, my bio, and my teaching philosophy. The philosophy served to establish the high importance I attach to student attendance and participation, self-motivation, and the on-time completion of work. I emphasized my commitment to prompt feedback, and the classroom as a safe and respectful space for all students. In the Class Schedule I added a section associated with each class period called "Ongoing Work" which pointed students forward with tasks they should focus on in the immediate future. I hoped this addition would keep them "thinking forward" throughout the course. This last item, however, fell short and I felt I needed to further emphasize the significance of due dates in future sections of the class. I also felt that students could benefit from having to do a high-level overview of their literature reviews. Therefore, I added a workshop that required each student to do a 5-slide overview of their literature review in class one week before the due date. All students brought laptops, and all students sent electronic feedback to each presenter using a Google form. Thus, every presenter received feedback from me and from every other student colleague in the class. Through this assignment I tried to force (in the sense of forcing a spring bulb indoors in winter) students' thinking at a higher and broader (meta) level, rather than allowing their minds to dwell within the weeds of detail. The Spring 2016 student survey showed that my high score was 4.67, again for *interest and enthusiasm in the subject,* and the lowest score (3.00) corresponded to *value of class discussions*. The *general rating of instructor* was 3.67 out of 5, indicating an 8% gain.

As I developed the Summer 2016 syllabus, I felt I needed to solve a problem related to students lagging on two critical tasks due early in the semester: 1) the completion of research with human subjects training (required by a specific due date to continue in the course), and 2) library research tutorials that teach them how to locate peer reviewed literature in the databases. The problem affected me, because I found the previous two semesters that I was having to nudge students to do their work, when I wanted *them* to manage their work. Therefore, I attached point values to these activities. I also increased points for attendance and participation from 30 to 50 points, because students disrupted class by arriving late, and looked at websites on their computers during class. I wanted to move in the direction of making it more desirable to participate than to underachieve in that regard. Additionally, these habits annoyed me, and I felt that letting the students bear the brunt of coming in late or of not engaging would remove me from the loop of graduate student behavior management. The survey feedback indicated that my highest score (4.48) was a tie between *knowledge of subject matter* and *interest and enthusiasm in the subject*. My lowest score (4.04) was for *clarity of explanations*, and the *general rating of instructor* was 4.22, a gain of 12% over the spring semester scores.

In the interest of the aggressive assignment schedule (and therefore, my aggressive grading schedule) I inserted text relating grades to on-time submissions: "All assignments must be submitted at or before the assigned due date. Contact the instructor before the due date if there is a problem" (O'Brien, Unpublished b, p. 5). I took initiative with assignments in small ways, reflecting on the previous semester and revising my approaches, as I worked to get students to go more deeply into their literature reviews. I again assigned the 5-slide workshop with feedback, because it appeared that students dug into the literature somewhat earlier to make the presentations, and this time I allowed them to earn minimal points for this activity. Upon reflection at the end of the course, I felt they would benefit from a more deliberate pace with the literature. I resolved to devise something different for the next time I taught the course.

The next term during which I taught the action research class was in the summer of 2018. By this time, I had completed my doctorate and felt confident in the classroom. Since this was a four-week course for which I included strict on-time submission instructions in the syllabus. To encourage students to be more deeply and consistently engaged with the literature, I introduced four literature review matrix assignments (5 peer-reviewed articles per matrix), that would be due in rapid succession, two matrices per week across two weeks. My goal was to pace students through the work, rather than allowing them to crash into a literature review deadline that would undoubtedly result in lack of depth in their reviews and less than excellent writing. Although I knew requiring the matrices would increase pressure on students, I also thought it help them achieve great pride in their finished work. Every aspect of this short class had to run like clockwork. Students applied themselves diligently and their literature reviews demonstrated thoughtful synthesis. There is no survey available for this course in the university archives.

Spring 2019 was my next opportunity in the Introduction to Action Research I classroom. Parallel to teaching this course I also taught social justice in education classes, and I felt that my syllabus for this course would benefit from language related to equity. Therefore, I added text related to equity under the Learning Environment heading, and again in my teaching philosophy statement, based on examples from a colleague (sj Miller, personal communication, December 23, 2018). Since this was an online section, I added a Zoom Research Roundtable where students could review progress in small groups, offering insight and feedback to one another, with my input as needed. Due to the course length, I relaxed the matrix submission schedule, with one matrix due each week across four weeks. Because action research is a reflective process, and also because I doubted that most of the students were doing much in the way of written reflection, I added brief weekly research reflections to the schedule. I also added a required assignment for students to submit literature review final drafts to TurnItIn for their own learning. I did not review the feedback at all, but the students earned ten points for doing it. My goal was to get them to take responsibility for ethics in the literature review process, to benefit from TurnItIn feedback, and to prevent myself from having to guess at the integrity of their writing. The TurnItIn data was available in each student's assignment if I needed to access it. Survey feedback for that semester indicated that my highest score (4.71) was for *knowledge of subject matter*, and the lowest score (4.36) was for *ability to create enthusiasm and a desire to learn*. The *general rating of instructor* was 4.36, a gain of 3% over the summer 2016 rating.

I taught the course twice more, in the fall of 2019 and in the fall of 2020, making only one change to the class, which was the addition of a Plan of Action Roundtable conducted in small groups on Zoom. High scores on the survey were *ability to encourage student opinions* (4.58, fall 2019) and *knowledge of subject matter* (4.73, fall 2020). Low scores on both were associated with *availability for help with problems* (4.17, fall 2019 and 3.73, fall 2020). *General rating of instructor* scores was 4.33 and 4.09 respectively, marking a 3% decline for fall 2019 and a 6% decline for fall 2020.

Personal and Professional Fit

Specific knowledges, skills, and abilities that I practiced in business also served me well in academia. I understand that my expertise in *administration and management* helped me with structuring courses, providing rationale to students, and engaging them in dialogue and meetings. *Customer and personal service, social perceptiveness, service orientation, writing, complex problem solving, time management, written expression, and category flexibility* all supported my transition from corporate director to adjunct professor, and now are evident in my teaching and in colleague relationships. A high level of expertise in one career domain supported my transition into another domain, because I relied on strengths I previously developed in presenting myself as professional and capable. My move into academia included my own education in classroom pedagogy and social justice. I saw these as transitional tools, which bridged the divides between *learning strategies* for workplace training, and those for active learning in the university, and human resource policies for equity in the workplace and *social perceptiveness*. I devised specific strategies for challenging myself, while also protecting myself. *Customer and personal service* was critical, as I was schooled in business to resolve issues immediately. I also understood that I could not solve all issues for students, whose job it was to *learn*, and so I needed to provide the underpinnings, the structure and constraints in a way directed them toward learning.

In behavioral health care one cannot "walk in late" when a life might hang in the balance. In the classroom, for good or for ill, attendance and participation might as well be the matador's red cape if I am the bull. Try as I might, I could not enter a psychological space where the concepts of time and of engagement could be optional as key professional skills of graduate students in education. I view these as key elements of citizenship, although I also am able to allow for exceptions under extraordinary circumstances. *Social perceptiveness* and *complex problem solving* were helpful with this, but the heart of my struggle – my Whiteness – deserved critique. I was fortunate to have a Black colleague, who helped me understand that students of color would not always initiate discussion with me about personal limitations (for example, lack of access to Internet services or the need to care for a younger sibling, which interfered with on-time arrival for in-person classes). I grew to understand the difference between "being late" and "not being able to get to class on time," and that I must take into account students' individual circumstances rather than focusing exclusively on their foregrounded behaviors. This shift made it possible for me to invite a student who was failing the course to discuss her class performance. I learned that she didn't understand the final, most critical assignment, and that she was afraid to ask for help. Five days before the end of the semester I offered her a delayed grade when I understood her problem. The student worked until she had the assignment done and submitted it on time. I felt ashamed that I had not reached out to her earlier in the semester.

Apart from circumstances like these, when a student fails to show up for class, doesn't complete work on time (or arrange for off-time submissions ahead of the due date/time), and doesn't offer peers the respect of timely participation in online posts and discussions, that student will not earn enough points to make the top grade in a class I teach. The attribute from the OSRs that applies most directly here is *customer and personal service*. My practices from business dominated here, as I focused so strongly on consistency and precision in working with people. I reacted with inner shock as I observed students overlooking what I considered key elements of respect for the group processes, and I set about to raise consciousness. At the same time, I recognized that they were learning while I had 25 years of experience. As the instructor, I show up on time, I give prompt feedback, I make myself available on very short notice (often within a few hours) for Zoom meetings, and more. Apart from teaching I have the rest of my life. Early on as a new counselor, I learned to maintain separateness to refuel. This principle holds true as well in teaching, and I believe it is important to show students how to do it.

As I reflected on the findings I saw clear signs of my growth as an academic, and the impact of the action research classroom on my professional development. Fall Semester 2015 teaching action research was also my first opportunity to teach in a school classroom. I trained employees, and I trained counselors in workshop and in-service programs, but never had I taught in a school classroom. Furthermore, it was a graduate classroom full of teachers. According to my notes I felt "awkward, old, and underprepared." This did not mean that other faculty, including the course steward who in fact *did* prepare me, did a poor job. It meant that I was a beginner who was accustomed to being an expert. Girded with the syllabus provided to me, I set to work with the students, learning about action research as they learned. Self-reflexivity, and working with theory and practice (Lather, 1984) situated within academia supported my identity work.

SOLUTIONS AND RECOMMENDATIONS

How can teaching action research contribute to the reshaping of professional identity? The creation of syllabi to support the spiral of action research was in itself action research-based, as I considered what worked, and what didn't work in the previous semester(s). Work with students who are learning to practice the action research cycle and reflecting *about* my teaching while simultaneously *doing* the teaching, created a dialogical and iterative spiral (Kemmis et al., 2014). As the students and I co-created discourses in our communities of practice, so my identity was transformed as a community actor.

How can knowledge, skills, and abilities from three professional identities coalesce across career transition? Knowledge, skills, and abilities from my corporate work set the structures in place for those of teaching. Strengths I developed through the years in business provided support for my identity work as I tried out new practices and strategies for teaching, student motivation, and engagement. However, there was also a liability. In business I found I must always appear in control, be strong and somewhat demanding, due to being a woman in a male-dominated realm. I quickly discovered that in the classroom that approach felt harsh and unnecessary and I turned to strategies such as the adjustment of point values to influence student learning. I gained insight into students' access to optimal circumstances for learning, such as on-time arrival and Internet availability, and through reflective practice changed the way I positioned myself as instructor, from a manager/director-instructor to an educator-instructor.

What can be learned about identity and career transition through critical action research? As I reflected on my journey from one career to another, I pondered my problem of practice, the issue of feeling disconnected due to separate discourses. I recognized the business persona that I brought with me into academia, and as I considered openness and equity, I realized that I was less than transparent. The effect of this was that I could keep myself *above* the issues as I maintained anger about my previous job loss. At last, I understood that my problem of practice related to privilege, to the power I experienced in past employment and ways I expressed myself in my new workplace. *I created the boundaries that held me apart from my colleague. I* held on to entitlement. As I reflected about this insight, I started to question my expectations of students. Was I too authoritarian? Too much like a manager/superior, and not enough of co-learner? My problem was myself. Most importantly, I grew better able to recognize and check my privilege, as nothing at all has been withheld from me due to my skin color, sexual orientation, religious affiliation, or ability.

Limitations

Limitations of this research included inconsistencies in the university student surveys, which changed somewhat over time, although the core questions remained the same. Narrative feedback from the surveys could have added depth, but due to the inconsistency in narrative prompts across the five years, they were not included as data for this research. Changes of term length for the Action Research I course probably made a difference in the student experience, but I did not take that into consideration. Term lengths were four, six, eight, and sixteen weeks. In addition, the earlier sections that I taught were in-person, while the later sections were exclusively online. This, too, might have made a difference in the students' experiences. As insider research, action researcher is inherently subjective. However, as mentioned earlier, I made every effort to minimize subjectivity by using data sources (two of three) that were external to my direct influence. Finally, there was a missing evaluation, which might have been important to my analysis, but equally likely, might not have made any difference at all.

Future Research Directions

Based on this action research self-study, I suggest that more inquiry in the areas of older women and career change could provide insight and also perhaps a resounding rebuff to ageism in the workplace. Starting over later in life is no small matter. Additional research with people who have transitioned between same-level careers (those with similar educational levels required) could be interesting to illustrate fluidity and an emphasis on capability and skill migration. Self-study and personal narratives focused on individuals' lived experiences can productively be placed in dialogue with large quantitative studies to tell on-the-ground stories that add depth to big numbers.

CONCLUSION

I offer suggestions to other teachers who are not yet familiar with action research. First, begin with *you*. You *are* the narrative. Engage with action research in order to identify your own problems of practice, and then set out to solve them. In this way, you will remain self-aware and also student aware. You will be able to see what happens when you try out strategies, and then revise those strategies and try again. Second, review your syllabi and celebrate your accomplishments. Third, embrace anonymous student feedback. Fourth, take time for yourself and through doing so, show your students how to do it, too. Last, conquer your fear of looking inward and in doing so, create equitable existence with others.

From my experience in the graduate classroom, I suggest that our practices are the best when we take time to deconstruct minutia of our work with students so that we can learn what motivates and inspires them, what makes it less painful to achieve than to underachieve, and how to participate as active members of a learning community of practice.

Sandwiched between the Great Depression of 2008 and the COVID-19 Pandemic of 2020 my identity transformed. Conducting this critical action research self-study led me to a deeper understanding of, reconciliation with, and contentment in my current profession. Through the analysis of OSRs, syllabi from across the semesters I taught the Introduction to Action Research course, and student surveys from those courses, I learned that iterative cycles of reflection and action in teaching action research supported the development of my identity as an academic across time. I deconstructed ways in which the knowledge, skills, and abilities required for my career in business supported, and also interfered with, my transition into academia. Finally, I came to understand that my problem of practice was related to my own privilege, an insight that holds great promise for my ways of working with others as a team member, or as a professor.

ACKNOWLEDGMENT

This research received no specific grant from any funding agency in the public, commercial, or not-for-profit sector. I wish to acknowledge Dr. Alina Slapac for extending to me the privilege of teaching in the graduate action research classroom across the semesters.

REFERENCES

Ahn, S., & Song, N. K. (2017). Unemployment, recurrent unemployment, and material hardships among older workers since the Great Recession. *Social Work Research*, *41*(4), 249–260. doi:10.1093wrvx020

Alessandri, G., Truxillo, D., Tisak, J., Fagnani, C., & Borgnoni, L. (2019). Within-individual age-related trends, cycles, and event-driven changes in job performance: A career-span perspective. *Journal of Business and Psychology*, *35*(5), 643–662. doi:10.100710869-019-09645-8

Annamama, S. A. (2015). Whiteness as property: Innocence and ability in teacher education. *The Urban Review*, *47*(2), 293–316. doi:10.100711256-014-0293-6

Austin, J. L. (1975). *How to do things with words*. Harvard University Press. doi:10.1093/acprof:oso/9780198245537.001.0001

Bakhtin, M. M. (2010). *Speech genres & other late essays*. University of Texas Press.

Borba, R., & Ostermann, A. C. (2007). Do bodies matter? Travestis' embodiment of (trans)gender identity through the manipulation of the Brazilian Portuguese grammatical gender system. *Gender and Language*, *1*(1), 131–147. doi:10.1558/genl.2007.1.1.131

Bronfenbrenner, U. (1979). *The ecology of human development: Experiments by nature and design*. Harvard University Press.

Bullough, R. V. Jr, & Pinnegar, S. (2001). Guidelines for quality in autobiographical forms of self-study research. *Educational Researcher*, *30*(3), 13–21. doi:10.3102/0013189X030003013

Davies, B., & Harré, R. (2014). Positioning: The discursive production of selves. In M. Wetherell, S. Taylor, & S. J. Yates (Eds.), *Discourse theory and practice: A reader* (pp. 261–271). Sage Publications.

Denzin, N. K., & Lincoln, Y. S. (2013). *The landscape of qualitative research*. Sage Publications.

Eliot, T. S. (1968). *Four quartets*. Mariner Books.

Fairclough, N. (2011). Discourse and social change. *Polity*.

Friere, P. (2011). *Pedagogy of the oppressed*. Continuum International Publishing Group.

Gee, J. P. (2011a). *An introduction to discourse analysis: Theory and method*. Routledge.

Gee, J. P. (2011b). *How to do discourse analysis: A toolkit*. Routledge.

Gergen, K. J. (1994). Self-narration in social life. In M. Wetherell, S. Taylor, & S.J. Yates (Eds.), *Discourse theory and practice: A reader* (pp. 247-260). Sage Publications.

Goldman, D. (2009, January 9). *Worst year for jobs since '45*. CNNMoney.com. https://money.cnn.com/2009/01/09/news/economy/jobs_december/

ISO. (2020). *Standards*. Retrieved January 16, 2021, from https://www.iso.org/standards.html

Kaiser, T., Hennecke, M., & Luhmann, M. (2020). The interplay of domain-and life satisfaction in predicting life events. *PLoS One*, *15*(9), e0238992. doi:10.1371/journal.pone.0238992 PMID:32941489

Kemmis, S., McTaggart, R., & Nixon, R. (2014). *The action research planner: Doing critical participatory action research*. Springer. doi:10.1007/978-981-4560-67-2

Kindle, K. J., & Schmidt, C. M. (2019). Developing preservice teachers: A self-study of instructor scaffolding. *Reading Improvement*, *56*(2), 70–88.

Kress, G. (2010). *Multimodality: A social semiotic approach to contemporary communication*. Routledge.

Kristeva, J. (1986). Revolution in poetic language. In T. Moi (Ed.), The Kristeva Reader (pp. 89-136). Blackwell Publishing.

Lather, P. (1986). Research as praxis. *Harvard Educational Review*, *56*(3), 257–277. doi:10.17763/haer.56.3.bj2h231877069482

Lather, P. (1991). *Getting smart: Feminist research and pedagogy with / in the postmodern*. Routledge. doi:10.4324/9780203451311

Lemke, J. (2000). Across the scales of time: Artifacts, activities, and meanings in ecosocial systems. *Mind, Culture, and Activity*, *7*(4), 273–290. doi:10.1207/S15327884MCA0704_03

Levin, M., & Greenwood, D. (2013). Revitalizing universities by reinventing the social sciences: Bildung and action research. In N. K. Denzin & Y. S. Lincoln (Eds.), *Landscape of qualitative research* (pp. 55–88). Sage Publications.

McCormack, L., Abou-Hamdan, S., & Joseph, S. (2017). Career derailment: Burnout and bullying at the executive level. *International Coaching Psychology Review*, *12*(1), 24–36.

National Center for O*NET Development. (n.d.a). *About O*NET*. O*NET Resource Center. https://www.onetcenter.org/overview.html

National Center for O*NET Development. (n.d.b). 11-1021.00 - General and Operations Managers. *O*NET OnLine*. https://www.onetonline.org/link/details/11-1021.00

National Center for O*NET Development. (n.d.c). 21-1014.00 - Mental Health Counselors. *O*NET OnLine*. https://www.onetonline.org/link/details/21-1014.00

National Center for O*NET Development. (n.d.d). 25-1081.00 - Education Teachers, Postsecondary. *O*NET OnLine*. https://www.onetonline.org/link/details/25-1081.00

Norris, S. (2004). *Analyzing multimodal interaction: A methodological framework*. Routledge. doi:10.4324/9780203379493

O'Brien, K. G. (2016a). *Teacher Action Research 1 Course Syllabus, Spring 2016*. Unpublished.

O'Brien, K. G. (2016b). *Teacher Action Research 1 Course Syllabus, Summer 2016*. Unpublished.

Patton, M. Q. (2002). *Qualitative research and evaluation methods* (3rd ed.). SAGE.

Pinnegar, S. (1995). (Re-)Experiencing beginning. *Teacher Education Quarterly*, *22*(3), 65–81. https://www.jstor.org/stable/23475835

Rogers, R. (2007). *A critical discourse analysis of family literacy practices: Power in and out of print.* Routledge.

Rubin, H. J., & Rubin, I. S. (2012). *Qualitative interviewing: The art of hearing data.* Sage Publications.

Schön, D. A. (1987). *Educating the reflective practitioner: Toward a new design for teaching and learning in the professions.* Jossey-Bass.

Scollon. (2008). *Analyzing Public Discourse*. Routledge.

Shotwell, A., & Sangrey, T. (2009). Resisting definition: Gendering through interaction and relational selfhood. *Hypatia*, *24*(3), 56–76. doi:10.1111/j.1527-2001.2009.01045.x

Stewart, H., Gapp, R., & Houghton, L. (2020). Large online first year learning and teaching: The lived experience of developing a student-centered continual learning practice. *Systemic Practice and Action Research*, *33*(4), 435–451. doi:10.100711213-019-09492-x

Tan, M. Y. (2021). Discourses and discursive identities of teachers working as university-based teacher educators in Singapore. *Journal of Teacher Education*, *72*(1), 100–112. doi:10.1177/0022487119896777

Teshale, S. M., & Lackman, M. E. (2016). Managing daily happiness: The relationship between selection, optimization, and compensation strategies and well-being in adulthood. *Psychology and Aging*, *31*(7), 687–692. doi:10.1037/pag0000132 PMID:27831710

Vygotsky, L. S. (1938/1978). *Mind in society: The development of higher psychological processes.* Harvard University Press.

Zeichner, K. (2007). Accumulating knowledge across self-studies in teacher education. *Journal of Teacher Education*, *58*(1), 36–46. doi:10.1177/0022487106296219

ADDITIONAL READING

Bartlett, T. (2014). *Analysing power in language: A practical guide.* Routledge. doi:10.4324/9781315851938

Bourdieu, P. (2003). *Language & symbolic power.* Harvard University Press.

Gee, J. P. (1998). Identity as an analytic lens for research. *Review of Research in Education*, *25*(2000-2001), 99–125. http://www.jstor.org/stable/1167322

Hendricks, C. (2017). *Improving schools through action research: A reflective practice approach.* Pearson Education.

Kalliola, S., & Mahlakaarto, S. (2020). Methods of promoting professional agency at work. *Challenges*, *11*(30), 1–15. doi:10.3390/challe11020030

Lave, J., & Wenger, E. (2011). *Situated learning: Legitimate peripheral participation*. Cambridge University Press.

Miller. (2019). *About Gender Identity Justice in schools and communities (School: Questions)*. Teachers College Press.

Nordahl, H. & Wells, A. (2018). In or out of work: A preliminary investigation of mental health, trait anxiety, and metacognitive beliefs as predictors of work status. *Clinical Psychologist, 23*(2019), 79-84. doi:10.1111/cp.12153

Rogers, R. (2007). *A critical discourse analysis of family literacy practices: Power in and out of print*. Routledge.

Stetson, G. F., Kryzhanovskaya, I. V., Lomen-Hoeth, C., & Haure, K. E. (2020). Professional identity formation in disorienting times. *Medical Education, 54*(8), 765–766. doi:10.1111/medu.14202 PMID:32344447

KEY TERMS AND DEFINITIONS

Cisgender: Refers to gender identity that is aligned with an individual's assigned sex at birth.
Discourse: Context-based connections in language, which include informing, doing, and identity.
General and Operations Manager: One who plans, directs, or coordinates the day-to-day activities of an organization.
Identity: Context-based, gendered bodily meanings such as mannerisms, dress, tone of voice, expressions through language, and verbal transmission.
Mental Health Counselor: One who counsels and advises individuals and groups to promote optimum mental and emotional health, with an emphasis on prevention.
Postsecondary Teacher: One who teaches courses related to education, such as counseling, curriculum, guidance, instruction, teacher education, and teaching English as a second language.
Privilege: Access to human rights and social goods such as housing, jobs, health care, education and the like, because of belonging to a certain racial group, sex, or class.
Self-Study: Insider research focused on the self.
Social Goods: Anything that is considered worth having, including access to healthcare, jobs, education, visibility of personal identity, food, housing, and so forth.
Systemic Racism: Access to social goods based on nothing more than an individual's appearance of having white Western European origins.

APPENDIX 1

OSR Definitions		
Category	Criteria	Definition
Knowledge	Customer and Personal Service	Knowledge of principles and processes for providing customer and personal services. This includes customer needs assessment, meeting quality standards for services, and evaluation of customer satisfaction.
	English Language	Knowledge of the structure and content of the English language including the meaning and spelling of words, rules of composition, and grammar.
	Administration and Management	Knowledge of business and management principles involved in strategic planning, resource allocation, human resources modeling, leadership technique, production methods, and coordination of people and resources.
Skills	Active Listening	Giving full attention to what other people are saying, taking time to understand the points being made, asking questions as appropriate, and not interrupting at inappropriate times.
	Social Perceptiveness	Being aware of others' reactions and understanding why they react as they do.
	Speaking	Talking to others to convey information effectively.
	Service Orientation	Actively looking for ways to help people.
	Writing	Communicating effectively in writing as appropriate for the needs of the audience.
	Critical Thinking	Using logic and reasoning to identify the strengths and weaknesses of alternative solutions, conclusions or approaches to problems.
	Monitoring	Monitoring/Assessing performance of yourself, other individuals, or organizations to make improvements or take corrective action.
	Judgment and Decision Making	Considering the relative costs and benefits of potential actions to choose the most appropriate one.
	Reading Comprehension	Understanding written sentences and paragraphs in work related documents.
	Active Learning	Understanding the implications of new information for both current and future problem-solving and decision-making.
	Learning Strategies	Selecting and using training/instructional methods and procedures appropriate for the situation when learning or teaching new things.
	Coordination	Adjusting actions in relation to others' actions.
	Complex Problem Solving	Identifying complex problems and reviewing related information to develop and evaluate options and implement solutions.
	Systems Evaluation	Identifying measures or indicators of system performance and the actions needed to improve or correct performance, relative to the goals of the system.
	Instructing	Teaching others how to do something.
	Systems Analysis	Determining how a system should work and how changes in conditions, operations, and the environment will affect outcomes.
	Time Management	Managing one's own time and the time of others.
Abilities	Oral Comprehension	The ability to listen to and understand information and ideas presented through spoken words and sentences.
	Oral Expression	The ability to communicate information and ideas in speaking so others will understand.
	Problem Sensitivity	The ability to tell when something is wrong or is likely to go wrong. It does not involve solving the problem, only recognizing there is a problem.
	Written Comprehension	The ability to read and understand information and ideas presented in writing.
	Written Expression	The ability to communicate information and ideas in writing so others will understand.
	Inductive Reasoning	The ability to combine pieces of information to form general rules or conclusions (includes finding a relationship among seemingly unrelated events).
	Deductive Reasoning	The ability to apply general rules to specific problems to produce answers that make sense.
	Speech Clarity	The ability to speak clearly so others can understand you.
	Information Ordering	The ability to arrange things or actions in a certain order or pattern according to a specific rule or set of rules (e.g., patterns of numbers, letters, words, pictures, mathematical operations).
	Category Flexibility	The ability to generate or use different sets of rules for combining or grouping things in different ways.
	Originality	The ability to come up with unusual or clever ideas about a given topic or situation, or to develop creative ways to solve a problem.

Chapter 11
Investigating Inquiry-Based, Technology-Rich Global Education Through Action Research

Nada Zaki Wafa
North Carolina State University, USA

Meghan McGlinn Manfra
North Carolina State University, USA

ABSTRACT

As teachers increasingly face new challenges related to the COVID-19 pandemic and instructional adjustments related to digital and online learning, action research may provide a more effective approach for bringing about change. In this chapter, the authors provide an example of an innovative project in which a university-based researcher worked alongside an elementary school teacher to implement and assess a technology rich, global education program. The case followed the global education teacher from the initial stages of the curriculum implementation through teaching a complete unit. Using a collaborative inquiry model, the authors merged action research with qualitative case study methodology to develop a rich description of instruction. The aim was to understand teacher and student outcomes, while also exploring the benefit of engaging practitioners as co-researchers. The authors offer this project as a representative example of the myriad ways educators can leverage action research to develop innovative approaches to teaching and learning global education.

INTRODUCTION

During the 2020-2021 school year, educators faced unprecedented challenges due to the COVID-19 pandemic. As schools closed, teachers were called upon to radically alter their instructional practices by adopting digital and on-line approaches. Many found it difficult to provide students with engaging and

DOI: 10.4018/978-1-7998-6922-1.ch011

effective learning environments in the new digital format due to a variety of factors, including a lack of high-quality digital resources, little time to plan, and logistical difficulties.

At the same time, the enormous challenges posed by the pandemic led to new innovations in teaching and learning. Educators were eager to develop new strategies for integrating digital technologies for learning and sought out the professional knowledge of teachers. The pandemic also demonstrated the importance of understanding our increasingly interdependent world.

In this chapter, we describe a collaborative action research project conducted in an elementary classroom prior to the pandemic. Since the study focused on developing effective strategies for the integration of inquiry and digital tools to teach global education, findings from this study provide educators today with insights about adapting global education for virtual classrooms. Much like Shulman's (1999) "visions of the possible" (p. 13) this case contributes to the "scholarship of teaching" and provides a "source for specific [teaching] ideas and as a heuristic to stimulate new thinking" (1986, p. 12).

We describe our study here to also spur conversation about the extent to which action research may be an effective framework for bringing about change in teaching while engaging the "insider knowledge" of teachers. As Dervin et al. (2020) remark, it is necessary to equip teachers to dig into reconstructing alternative ways of thinking about "interculturality [and global education], in times of crisis and beyond" (p. 94). In our study, the classroom teacher participated actively in the design and implementation of a re-designed global education curriculum. The university-based researcher was involved face-to-face with the global education teacher during the initial process of re-designing the curriculum to the observation and implementation of the curriculum.

As a result, the need to help foster more global knowledge, understanding, and building bridges between individuals and the world has been increasing through the years. In schools, global education classes are a way for educators to empower students to think globally and bring about change in society and the world. There is much that can be explored within global education, however when planning a global education curriculum, teachers should select topics in an informed way that will honor children's interest and needs.

Overall, the school in which this curriculum was developed follows a four key design element model that provides students with authentic learning, a nurturing environment, collaboration, and technology skills. The school's mission is to provide authentic learning to improve the lives of students through a collaborative, nurturing environment, and its aim is to build a foundation for students' success in school, career, and life. One of the unique aspects of this school is that it offers global education as a course for kindergarten through sixth grade students.

The university-based researcher in this study was actively involved in the school as a parent, volunteer, room-parent, substitute, and a co-developer of the curriculum with the global education teacher. observed the global education students thinking creatively, critically, purposefully, as well as problem-solving real word situations to take further action. The global education class offered at the school is student-centered and revolves around discussions, hands-on projects, inquiry-based learning, and technology integration. Students expand their knowledge and understanding of the world around them, which helps them become more globally competent, informed, and active global citizens.

The primary goal and core process of this action research is to learn how does global education classes and teachers prepare students for the diversified world we live in and the ways in which this global education teacher is able to foster global knowledge and understanding among a group of first grade students. Both the methodology of our study as well as the content of the curriculum provide practical strategies for improving elementary global education.

BACKGROUND

Global Education in the Elementary Classroom

Recent calls to foster global education include a focus on preparing educators to empower students to think globally and bring about change in society and the world (Crawford & Kirby, 2008). In this project, we collaborated with an elementary grade teacher to develop a technology-infused, inquiry-based global education curriculum. By merging global education with technology and inquiry, we were able to leverage new strategies for engaging students.

The aim of the global education curriculum in this study was to encourage students to understand various perspectives, and create a more prosperous, productive, sustainable, and meaningful world through action (Burnouf, 2004). It is critical for us, as action researchers, to see how teachers are able to influence students' thinking through global topics to expand perspectives, and work through their interests in connecting with inquiry and technology.

The researcher and global education teacher sought to nurture students to think creatively, critically, purposefully, as well as engage in problem-solving relevant to real-world situations. We used digital tools to implement pedagogical strategies relevant to inquiry-based learning including, whole group discussions, hands-on projects, visualization, and storytelling. Findings suggest that through these learning experiences, students expanded their knowledge and understanding of the world around them.

A key aspect of this curriculum is creating an active learning environment that focuses on the universal values of equality, tolerance, cooperation, and inclusion. The global education class does not have a textbook; rather, it is student-led through discussions, projects, dialogue, and student-driven interest in topics. Many students have not been exposed to the technology use and inquiry-based learning in global education, therefore, this action research proved to be invaluable to researchers and teachers who are looking for ways to integrate inquiry-based learning and technology simultaneously in their global education class.

MAIN FOCUS OF THE CHAPTER

The Promise and Practice of Global Education

In our increasingly interdependent work, educating our students to become global learners and global citizens is now a responsibility of educators everywhere (Schukar, 1993). Future generations depend on thinking, working, and moving across diverse environments with a range of people. In order to be successful, students need to develop new skills such as intercultural communication and conflict resolution. They must develop cross-cultural understanding and seek out multiple perspectives. Global education unites "us all when we begin to ask questions about our roles and responsibilities as educators, learners or students in pursuit of global citizenship" (Dei, 2014, p. 10).

Global educators make educational and instructional decisions that influence students' understanding of others, as well as global issues. These decisions become more important when a community, a state, a country, or the world is feeling the effects of a global change, such as a pandemic, economic instability, sociocultural, environmental, or technological changes (Merryfield, 2002). When teaching global education, teachers may cover a range of topics, building in new knowledge each year. This requires teachers to have deep content knowledge. According to Burnouf (2004), "teachers must educate themselves first in local, global and national knowledge systems of the world and continue learning about global issues together with their students" (p.10). In order to develop content knowledge, teachers can take advantage of the rich digital resources available that provide background knowledge as well as tools for facilitating inquiry-based global education. The global aspect of inquiry-based learning is important for three reasons. First, engaging students in global issues allows them to endure challenges and problem solve global issues of our present time (OECD, 2018). Second, teachers and students are encouraged to focus on the pressing challenges that are aligned with the United Nations Sustainable Development Goals. Through this focus, the outcome could result in having the next generation continue on the path to acquire knowledge, as well as "expertise and passion for global problem solving" (Spires et al., 2019, p. 52). Nonetheless, teaching through C3 inquiries using global learning context is one of the paths to the development of global education.

Integrating Technology in Global Education

Teachers can leverage rich digital resources to develop background knowledge and to facilitate active student engagement in the global education classroom. Bell-Rose and Desai (2005) encourage "the creative use of technology and new media to promote international knowledge and understanding and expand global citizenship opportunities for young people" (p. 36). Modeling the use of technology in the classroom prepares students for the digital age (Gaudelli, 2006).

Digital technologies offer many ways to connect students to the world outside of the classroom. Infusing technology into global education can help "foster students' understanding of interrelationships of people worldwide, thereby preparing them to participate meaningfully as global citizens" (Crawford & Kirby, 2008, p. 56). Teachers should consider effective strategies to incorporate technologies into their teaching through various sources, including multimedia, to positively impact students' ability to engage in inquiry and make connections to their world. For example, using technology, students can participate in service learning projects, social action projects, digital pen pal projects, and virtual field trips. These types of activities can provide a virtual network for students and teachers to cultivate global knowledge. Access to technology, plus the right tools that match the content, provide teachers and students with the opportunity to build a deeper understanding and appreciation of the world. However, it is important to note that, "giving students access to multiple sources or multimedia learning environments will not guarantee any meaningful learning. This type of knowledge needs to be acquired through participation in highly structured guided activities with clear problem-solving and inquiry goals" (Wiley & Ash, 2005, p. 385). In other words, the integration of technology must be paired with rich, inquiry-based pedagogy.

Integrating C3 Inquiry into Global Education

The College, Career and Civil Life (C3) Framework is an instructional framework developed to reform social studies teaching by providing a model or template for teachers to engage students in inquiry. The C3 Framework is based on an "inquiry arc" that includes compelling and supporting questions (NCSS, 2013, pp. 82-91). The first dimension of the inquiry arc in the C3 Framework focuses on planning inquiries by posing compelling and supporting questions to students. "Compelling questions focus on enduring issues and concerns" (NCSS, p. 23). These questions go beyond mundane information; they are "both intriguing and intellectually honest" (p. 17). In addition to the compelling questions, teachers are to design "supporting questions" that scaffold students towards answering the compelling questions. The second dimension of the C3 Framework involves taking the various disciplinary concepts and tools of the social studies and applying them in such a way that a student can better understand the content and engage in analysis. The third dimension of the C3 Framework requires students to "analyze information and come to conclusions in an inquiry" (p. 53). Students examine, evaluate, and find evidence to support the arguments they will make to answer the inquiry questions from Dimension 1. The final dimension of the C3 Framework describes the culmination of the Inquiry Arc. Here, students are required to communicate their conclusions based on their analysis. The goal is to give students authentic opportunities to take informed action - taking what they have learned and using it to do something in the world based on their conclusions.

In summary, the Inquiry Design Model (IDM) of the C3 Framework (NCSS, 2013) aims at "organizing the curriculum around the foundations of inquiry: questions, tasks, and sources" (Swan, et al., 2018, p. 137). Using IDM, teachers are able to facilitate students' knowledge development, expand their opportunities to develop literacy skills, and find meaningful ways to express themselves through argumentation. Students are naturally curious and "curiosity drives interest and interest drives knowledge, understanding, and engagement" (Grant, 2013, p. 322). Inquiry education provides students with "opportunities to answer those questions more through disciplinary (civic, economic, geographical, and historical) and multidisciplinary venues" (Grant, 2013, p. 322).

The Global C3 Hub (http://c3teachers.org/global-hub/) provides a wealth of inquiries aligned with the United Nations Sustainable Development Goals (see Appendix 1). These inquiries purposely link the United Nations goals with state standards for curriculum. The Global C3 hub is designed to be a collaborative workspace for educators around the world who are interested in developing globally-relevant, internationally-focused C3 Framework instructional materials. Materials available through the hub provide examples of inquiry-based learning using technology. Each inquiry focuses on global knowledge through compelling questions that are challenging and address a range of topics that enable students to think critically, creatively, and proactively.

Collaborative Practitioner-Based Action Research

Our study was premised on the notion that pursuing inquiry enables higher-level thinking for students, particularly when teachers provide appropriate digital resources. The authors pursued a collaborative action research study (Herr & Anderson, 2014; Manfra, 2019, 2020) with a first-grade teacher. Using a nested approach to conducting research, the university-based researchers conducted a wrap-around qualitative research study to understand the teacher and student experiences. The classroom-based teacher collaborated actively in the design and implementation of the teaching activities. The researchers relied on her insider knowledge to develop and implement the re-designed curriculum, as well as to help analyze and interpret data from this study.

Action research refers to systematic and intentional inquiry designed to bring about change. Similar to other approaches to educational research, action research emerges from a problem related to practice and pursues a cycle of inquiry, including data collection and analysis. According to McNiff (2016), "action research is about improving learning in order to influence improvement in a particular social context" (p. 20). In this study, the aim was to improve global education in a 1st grade classroom by integrating inquiry-based teaching strategies and technology. This was accomplished by pairing an "outsider" - a university-based researcher - working collaboratively with an "insider" (see Herr & Anderson, 2005) for various positionalities in action research. By pursuing action research methods, the authors were able to bring about change through action (Manfra, 2019) and developed a "dynamic practice-based theory" (McNiff, 2016, p. 19) to inform other practices.

Methodology

This was an action research project that examined the ways in which a teacher was able to help students develop as global citizens who will serve their community, nation, and world. This year-long study consisted of a collaboration between the university-based research and the global education teacher and a 1st grade classroom with 30 students. This study was designed from the initial stages of the curriculum development to the implementation and teaching of the complete unit. Three interviews were conducted with the teacher as well as classroom observations of her teaching practice. A semi-structured interview was conducted at the beginning of the unit that focused on the implementation of the curriculum. A second and third interview covered the details of the implementation of the unit, as well as, expectations and focused reflections. The first interview occurred before the unit was taught. The second interview occurred mid-way through the lessons. The third interview occurred at the end of the unit.

The purpose of the first interview was to gather a baseline of information regarding the research questions in regards to implementing the unit study planned in the curriculum. It also allowed the researcher to better understand any assumptions, beliefs, or experiences that might serve as a reference point to compare this inquiry-based, technology infused unit with prior units. In addition, the researcher was able to receive responses about what was planned compared to what will be observed when the inquiry is taught and technology is used.

The purpose of the second interview was to gather formative data after the implementation of two lesson plans, in particular to the research questions about the implementation of the lesson plans in the unit through teaching inquiry and infusing technology.

The purpose of the third interview was to gather summative data after the implementation of the unit in reference to the research questions in regards to how the unit was implemented through inquiry and technology. This allowed the researcher the opportunity to reflect on the process of implementing a unit and better understand the global education teacher's pedagogy through inquiry-based learning and technology integration.

Curriculum materials were analyzed using open-ended, inductive coding techniques. Copies of all the notes and transcriptions were coded as primary data. After organizing all of the transcripts by data type and completing preliminary coding, the data were reorganized according to categories. As categories began to emerge, the smaller pieces of data were matched to the categories, and as new data came in, the categories were altered accordingly. After organizing and analyzing the data, more formal codes were generated. As the findings became more concrete, themes in the data were color-coded making it easier to incorporate new data as it was collected. The findings were triangulated between interview transcriptions, field notes, and curriculum data. This approach allowed a thorough examination of the data to ensure the conclusions were valid and trustworthy.

Data for this research was derived from interviews, observations, and the curriculum. For the three interviews, a digital recorder was used. The interviews were transcribed, and the information organized according to the research questions and sub-questions. The data were analyzed using a grounded theory approach, which provided a way to develop explanations supported by evidence

Study Context

This collaborative action research project was undertaken in a unique school setting with a mission to create an active learning environment for students, focused on the universal values of equality, tolerance, cooperation, and inclusion. School-wide learning themes included global literacy, environmental science, financial literacy, global demographics and geography, cultures, and endangered species. The global education curriculum was taught as part of a "specials class" for the first graders. The framework for the global education classes at the school were developed based on unique topics for each grade level (see Table 1).

Table 1. Global education curriculum

Grade	Topics (Tagline)
Kindergarten	Fun: Learning Through Literacy (Fiction & Non-fiction)
1st grade	Traveling Around the World- Learning All the Way
2nd grade	Endangered species: Research & Study
3rd grade	Learning, Caring, Protecting: Activists in the Making
4th grade	International Geography: Demographic & Culture
5th grade	Financial Literacy: Budgets, Stocks, and Business
6th grade	World Change: See it, Feel it, Be it

The primary goal of this global education class research study was to see how students are being prepared for the diversified world we live in and the multicultural society they are surrounded with each day. The need to educate our students on how to become global citizens is in high demand. When this study was conducted, students were well versed in classroom procedures for participating in student-led discussions and projects focused on the theme of *Traveling Around the World*.

Demographics of Students and Classroom Background

The participant in this study, Ms. Z was a K-6th grade teacher at a charter school in the Southeastern United States. Ms. Z was in her 2nd year teaching at the charter school and had no previous teaching experience. She earned her degree in History. The duration of the class was 45 minutes of instruction. The school was located in an upper middle- class community. The global education class was taught as a "specials" class, which is an elective class that is taught once or twice a week to a group of about 30 students at one section in grade level. Each lesson was taught for one a week, resulting in four to five classes per unit study.

Teaching global education was new to Ms. Z. She was hired in the summer of 2017 after submitting a proposal to her administrators in the school about a potential elective class. She envisioned a course that cultivated students' understanding of the universal values of inclusion, cooperation, equality, and tolerance, as well as environmental science, cultural studies, financial literacy, endangered species, and global demographics and geography. During Ms. Z's interview conducted on January 9, 2019, she recognized that the course would be a work in progress and that "in practice, I keep learning, and

I'm having things added in all the time." She relied on her personal teaching style and implied that she doesn't follow a specific curriculum, as Ms. Z stated in the interview, "it's my own curriculum" (personal communication, January 9, 2019). Ms. Z emphasized that in planning the overall curriculum she "tried to choose one country per continent, a country that the students would be interested in" (personal communication, January 9, 2019).

Ms. Z was familiar with the structure of the Inquiry Design Model (IDM) after she was introduced to some of the online IDM materials and connected her with another teacher who uses IDM. Teaching through inquiry required that students remain engaged in their learning, thus allowing the teacher to provide a student-centered lesson. Inquiry provides the opportunity for students to share their thoughts in a safe space, connect content with personal experiences, and explore new ideas and deepen their knowledge. The inquiry-based learning method helped Ms. Z understand her students better and focus students' learning on outcomes. When Ms. Z was asked about her thoughts regarding the inquiry-based structure of the unit, she said, "I haven't done anything like that so I'll have to see how it goes...that will be a new thing to try" (personal communication, January 9, 2019). When she referred to the Inquiry Design Model and the inquiries that I shared with her, she said, "I haven't done that inquiry method like the ones we've seen online. I need to try one, but with so many classes, it's hard" (personal communication, January 9, 2019). When asked if she would be using inquiry in the future, her response was, "my problem is finding time to like really plan it and do it" (personal communication, January 9, 2019).

In general, the 1st grade curriculum was about *Traveling Around the World*. Students were introduced to world geography and cultural studies through a "monthly adventure" taken to a country in the world. The students had a world map in their classroom, and throughout the school year, the countries visited were marked with a pushpin and a string, illustrating the miles and distance traveled from one country to the other. The eight countries studied throughout the year were: Chad, Pakistan, Italy, Brazil, Canada, Australia, Russia, and China. This research study focused on one unit in the curriculum, Brazil.

Students also learned about the country's flag and other symbols. As an opening, the teacher reviewed content about the previous country. This set up the exploration of each new country. Students maintained a global education folder that consisted of their work and provided evidence about what they learned about the country. Within the notebook, each country section had a title page that included the country flag, with lines underneath the image for the students to write and reflect about the country they were learning about.

During the unit examined in this research, the teacher highlighted important information about the country and facilitated student learning about various facts and information from numerous sources. Each unit was framed by a compelling question, and each lesson had a supporting question. Students were able to answer the supporting questions by completing formative assessments, such as discussions and other tasks. Units also included summative assessments, such as writing a few sentences to indicate what the students had learned.

At the time of the study, the classroom teacher considered herself to be a novice teacher, still learning about global education. Nonetheless, she was eager to develop a specials course for her students that would introduce them to contemporary global issues as well as cultivate students' understanding of the universal values equality, tolerance, cooperation, and inclusion, as well as learning about the world around them.

The curriculum included non-fiction and fiction books which students used to learn about the chosen country. Students' work with these books helped them to develop a deeper connection and understanding of the country and helped to support their literacy development and creativity.

During the unit examined in this research, the teacher highlighted important information about the country and facilitated student learning about various facts and information from numerous sources. Each unit was framed by a compelling question, and each lesson had a supporting question. Students were able to answer the supporting questions by completing formative assessments, such as discussions and other tasks. Units also included summative assessments, such as writing a few sentences to indicate what the students had learned.

The curriculum included multimedia materials that supported visual learning and innovative technologies incorporated in the lessons. An active learning environment was supported by technology and enriched by creating a strong connection among the various countries studied. Technology enhancements included one activity where the teacher provided a live online camera shot of a city in the focus country, as well as other educational videos that enriched students' learning. The teacher also incorporated robotics (Ozobot) that enabled a focus on the geography of the country. The use of technology was designed to help students to become more actively engaged and helped them build curiosity to learn more about the world.

Redesign of the Curriculum

The first author, a university-based teacher educator and researcher, and the global education teacher participant met weekly to plan and design instruction using the C3 framework and related to the theme of *Traveling Around the World*. Together they compiled resources, non-fiction and fiction children literature, and brainstormed lesson plans together. They also discussed resources related to the C3 Framework, including journal articles and the C3teachers.org website. The inquiry curriculum materials planned and implemented in this research were focused on the needs of students, and framed by efforts to "determine what students need to know, what they actually know, and what activities might be needed to bolster their knowledge" (Lee, 2008, p.63). Ultimately, the Brazil unit, under focus here, included five inquiry lessons centered on one compelling question and five supporting questions.

Compelling Question

Developing an effective compelling question can be difficult. Teachers often experience a tension between creating a question that focuses on content standards while also making the content relevant to students. The compelling question can "come in all sizes and shapes. Some address wide swaths of content, while others take a more focused approach; some feature deep analysis, while others are more playful" (Swan, Lee, & Grant, p. 34). Ultimately, the determined compelling question for the Brazil unit was - "How do we impact Brazil?" - and the question encouraged students to reflect on what they learned throughout the unit and to think about ways to make a difference.

Supporting Questions

The compelling question was paired with five supporting questions:

- Compelling Question: How do we impact Brazil?

  ◦ Supporting Question #1: What is Brazil?

- Supporting Question #2: Why are rainforests important?
- Supporting Question #3: How can technology impact the rainforest?
- Supporting Question #4: Is the relationship between humans and the rainforest good or bad?
- Supporting Question #5: How can we help Brazil?

The role of the compelling question was to encourage students to think about the ways they can impact Brazil and distinguish the commonalities and differences between the U.S. and Brazil based on the information presented throughout the lessons. The negotiated process of developing the question began as a thought process to encourage students to think about the ways we impact Brazil and distinguish the commonalities and differences between the U.S. and Brazil based on the information presented throughout the lessons. The supporting questions addressed various aspects of the compelling question. When completing the formative tasks, students gathered basic information about Brazil and identified and expressed their ideas about the rainforest, deforestation, and how changes in the rainforest affect animals. They categorized the layers of the rainforest and expressed how our relationships with animals affected their lives. The students then formulated and organized their ideas about how to best conserve the rainforest.

The compelling question challenged Ms. Z as she presented it to the students. She was focused on the order of tasks in each lesson, but could not connect with the question. "I don't love that [compelling] question. I don't see it myself, but I'll ask it," since students "might surprise me" when asked a compelling question. Ms. Z asked the compelling question in the last lesson: "How do we impact Brazil?" Students responded,

"We can leave [trees] the way they are."

"We can plant more trees, when they fully grow, animals can live there."

At the end of the unit, when asked for her thoughts on teaching the unit for this inquiry, she said,

I think it went well. I think maybe the [compelling] question might not have been the right question, How do we impact Brazil? I think that went way above of them, I could have thought of maybe a different question. I don't know that they really made a connection with that so much, a little bit. Maybe a few kids did.(personal communication, February 8, 2019)

In practice, the supporting questions created the focus for each of the five lessons for the unit and aligned with the compelling question. Throughout the unit, the teacher highlighted important information about the country and facilitated student learning about various facts and information from numerous sources. Each lesson included non-fiction and/or fiction books which students used to learn about the chosen country as "featured sources." This appeared to help students develop a deeper understanding and connection to the country under study. This also helped students develop literacy skills, comprehension, and creativity.

The supporting questions in the unit were designed to scaffold students' thinking. When students were provided with the opportunity to expand their thoughts, they engaged in thoughtful discussions and were willing to participate because their voices were being heard. Despite having no prior experience teaching global education through inquiry, Ms. Z expressed excitement about students' positive experiences with inquiry-based learning. She also needed some time to adjust to this new teaching method and emphasized "I think I'll add questions for sure like that, I'm thinking when I'm starting my unit" (personal communication, February 8, 2019).

The curriculum also included multimedia materials that supported visual learning. For example, students could access Chromebooks to conduct individual research. The teacher also would screen digital footage from a city in the focus country, as well as other educational videos that enriched students' learning.

Integrating Robotic Technology

The teacher participant and researcher also incorporated robotics using Ozobot in the unit of study in order to build curiosity as well as demonstrate for students the interaction of rainforest animals with their environment. The Ozobot robots were used in a simulation to represent animals in the Amazon rainforest (OzoCapuchin Monkey, OzoSloth, OzoBeetle, OzoJaguar) that students used to navigate through a map of the four-layers of the rainforest. As the animals navigated through the map, color-codes were generated. The robotic simulation also had accompanying print resources, including 16 maps that were colored and labeled as the layers of the rainforest.

Although the teacher was initially "nervous about the technology part" and "didn't feel like that fit in," in the end she reported "it went well and they did fine with it...they got the overall message" (personal communication, February 8, 2019). In contrast to other activities in the unit, she viewed students' use of robots as enabling them to gain a better understanding of where the animals live. They "got the idea of moving between layers" (personal communication, February 8, 2019).

Summative Performance Task

The summative performance task posed to students focused on engaging in civic action. The students were divided into small groups to discuss ways people use and/or misuse the rainforest. Each group was provided a question from the following:

- How can we stop cutting down trees in the rainforest?
- How are animals affected by deforestation?
- Why is the Amazon rainforest being destroyed?
- What can we do, as 1st grade students, to help the rainforest?

Students were then prompted to consider action strategies that extend to family, friends, and community members. For example, they could send a request to the city mayor or contribute to an organization that plants trees in Brazil (e.g. WWF in Brazil, Rainforest Alliance, Rainforest Action Network, StandForTrees, and/or OneTreePlanted). To conclude the unit, students each returned to the compelling question and wrote and drew responses. They presented their summative projects to the whole class. Examples of student responses included wanting to make "posters that say don't cut down trees;" "We can leave [trees] the way they are." "We can plant more trees, when they fully grow, animals can live there."

SOLUTIONS AND RECOMMENDATIONS

Major findings from this study point to the benefits of action research as a professional development approach. These three findings emerged from the analysis of the data: although the teacher did not implement all of the elements of the curriculum, she considered using inquiry in the future; she did not use inquiry from the unit in some lessons, and thought they were too rigid; and she believed students responded well to inquiry. In addition, she was reluctant to using technology, nonetheless, she found that students were imaginative and responded very well to technology- integration in the classroom. She appreciated the learning process between the integration of technology and inquiry in global education and stated that she would definitely be using inquiry in the future.

The focus on inquiry and digital tools provide classroom-tested strategies that may be adopted for a virtual classroom, including resources from the C3 Teachers Global hub (http://c3teachers.org/global-hub/). At the same time students seem to have benefited in particular from the authentic approaches to global education that occurred in the classroom. Rather than learn disparate facts, students were able to engage in depth of study about topics relevant beyond the classroom.

Collaborative Action Research

By pursuing a collaborative action research approach, the university-based researcher was able to engage the classroom teacher as an active participant in the design of the project. The teacher played a significant role throughout the entire curriculum development process, especially during the planning and implementation stages, and provided important insights about what worked "best" in the school context. Through on-going collaboration, the researchers pursued an iterative approach to modifying and improving the C3 inquiry design. It is important to note that this was the teacher's first time using an inquiry-based teaching method and innovative technology in her first grade classroom. She valued what she had learned throughout the process, and although she was initially reluctant, when asked if she will use inquiry in the future, she replied, "yes, I would, definitely" (personal communication, January 9, 2019).

Reflecting back on her experience, the teacher participant expressed an appreciation for the experience of designing and implementing the inquiry-based, technology infused unit and reported that she learned and benefitted from the collaboration. She valued the support and collaboration with the researcher in designing the unit, and claimed to learn new teaching strategies. She also expressed a new-found comfort in talking about the content and methods of the unit. The teacher and the researcher created a personal connection with the curriculum. Clandinin (1985) notes that teachers who construct their own way of thinking through a "personal practical knowledge" method "develop and use a special kind of knowledge (p. 362). This knowledge is neither theoretical, in the sense of theories of learning, teaching, and curriculum, nor merely practical, in the sense of knowing children" (Clandinin, 1985, p. 361).

Through the process of conducting collaborative action research, the researchers also uncovered important issues related to practice. These included limited fidelity to the C3 Framework and difficulty developing compelling and supporting questions appropriate for early elementary school. Despite these limitations, the teacher believed students exceeded expectations and that they responded well to the inquiry. While at the beginning, students "were not all ready" to answer the compelling question, it was "something good for me to do moving forward" (personal communication, January 29, 2019). Overall, Ms. Z thought that it was good to have a compelling question that "we don't have a concrete answer to…

just open-ended" (personal communication, January 29, 2019). She felt like such a question would allow students to develop their global understanding of the country chosen for the unit.

Furthermore, when asked about teaching another inquiry lesson, Ms. Z said, "I think I will think of questions to add into my lessons moving forward with 1st grade" (personal communication, February 8, 2019). She noticed that students did respond well to inquiry, especially for one student who "never raised his hand for anything. I had him for two years, and he was really eager to participate, which is happy to see. I've never seen him raise his hands" (personal communication, February 8, 2019).

Technology Rich Global Education

Our findings suggest that educators can effectively integrate inquiry in global education through the use of multimedia and technological tools and that the C3 Framework provides an effective instructional approach (see appendix 2). An important part of our project was carefully considering which tools foster learning and match the learning goals of the teacher. For example, teachers may have students engage in an open-ended web search or use multimedia to support their knowledge development as a means to help them connect to others around the world. If the goal is to encourage perspective taking or expand their understanding of diversity, such approaches to using technology would make sense.

Through digital learning, students can participate in service learning projects and social action projects virtually or at a distance. They can communicate with a classroom in another country and participate in virtual field trips. These activities provide a virtual network for students and their teachers to cultivate global knowledge. Access to technology and digital learning, plus the right tools that match the content, provide teachers and students with the opportunity to build a deeper understanding and appreciation of the world.

In reality, digital learning and technology seem to be touching every aspect of our lives. Schools are currently fully dependent on digital teaching. As teachers teach global education through technology, students stand to be better prepared to become stronger global learners. By incorporating inquiry-based instruction, as well as various types of technologies into concepts and frameworks necessary to teach the content, teachers are able to further expand students' global knowledge and awareness in a meaningful way, thereby preparing them to think, act, and become global citizens.

Cohesive Global Education

Global education extends beyond teaching bits of knowledge about the culture, geography, demographics, folklore, food, and more. Rather, the aim of global education is to instill cross-cultural and intercultural understanding through empathy, tolerance, humanity, and awareness of diverse peoples. The authors recommend focusing on topics through the lens of cooperation, respect for human rights, cross-cultural communication, cultural diversity, and tolerance. Global education allows teachers and students to learn through different worldviews to live effectively in a multicultural, interconnected, and diversified world (Mansilla, 2017).

A core tenet of the United Nations Sustainable Development Goals is providing a quality education for all. This includes empowering all students to become global citizens by developing new ways of teaching and learning. In order to achieve the goal of infusing global education in schools, we will need teachers who are qualified to teach students through various forms of resources and can individualize instruction and learning. Furthermore, focusing on the community and parent relationships is a significant contribution to creating powerful learning experiences for students. In addition, teachers need to be fully supported by strong, effective, and productive leaderships that support growth, improvements, and profound learning systems.

FUTURE RESEARCH DIRECTIONS

Future research would engage more teachers in action research to refine their integration of technology-rich, inquiry-based education into the global education curriculum. This will likely include exploring strategies in response to the changing context of education, especially related to the Covid-19 pandemic. For example, this might include creating micro-school settings with social distancing measures or connecting students from all around the world in World-School pods. Through action research, educators will develop strategies for helping students develop the global competence, awareness, and understanding they need to become global citizens. Working alongside educators who are willing to incorporate global C3 inquiries into their teaching would help expand student's understanding of the world and allow perspective-taking into students' learning experience.

In this particular example, the researchers pursued a collaborative action research method in which the university-based researcher partnered with a classroom teacher to develop and design a global education curriculum. As with any approach, there are affordances and limitations. For example, by collaborating with a university-based instructor, the teacher received outside support and resources. Yet, at the same time, she opened up her classroom to outside scrutiny - an experience that may seem risky or uncomfortable to teachers. Nonetheless, the researchers and global education teacher continued to learn about the benefit of inquiry and technology, as well as the impact it can have on students. In addition, we were able to support our action research through the data gathered from the global education teacher because she was passionate about this field of study and because she valued the opportunity to share her knowledge about the world with her students. This global education class provided an enriching environment for children to learn about and express understanding of the world around them. Further action research studies could continue to incorporate additional inquiry-based learning and technology integration into the more mainstream classrooms and develop learning through global education.

CONCLUSION

The collaboration between the researcher and the global education teacher provided a representative example of the power of merging research into practice. By using a nested approach to conducting educational research, we were able to positively impact classroom practice while also developing a better understanding of the teacher's insider knowledge. There are other permutations of action research that might prove fruitful for teachers as they continue to explore strategies for improving the effectiveness of the teaching and learning in their classrooms. Teachers may choose to conduct action research projects independently or in collaborative groups. Each variation will warrant new insights and understandings.

As we continue to make sense of the impact of the Covid-19 pandemic on education, we may benefit from seeking collaborative relationships between university-based researchers and practitioners. Rather than assume research should impact practice, we recommend pursuing approaches to educational research that engage university-based researchers and practitioners improving practice. This will enable us to understand effective approaches to integrating digital tools to teach global education through the crucible of classroom practice and bring about change through action.

ACKNOWLEDGMENT

Thanks to Dr. John K. Lee, Dr. Meghan M. Manfra, and Dr. Candy Beal for their inspiration, mentorship, encouragement, support, and guidance through this research. Their valuable insights and continuous contribution to advance research in global education has been immeasurable. I am forever grateful for their support and guidance.

The global education teacher deserves a special mention, as she has given me the opportunity to learn from and with her through my research. She is a passionate educator in global education. She has welcomed me into her classroom, and provided me with invaluable insights on how the course works. It was an honor to observe her teaching and class, and I appreciate her being vulnerable enough to allow me to document how and what she had learned through the process. Thank you to the school, Head of the School, and Principal for accepting my research idea and allowing me to move forward with this project.

Sincere thank you to my dear family and friends who have stood by my side through this research. It has been a blessing to have such a supportive family and friends who stand by my side with their unconditional, constant support.

REFERENCES

Bell-Rose, S., & Desai, V. (2005). *Educating leaders for a global society*. Retrieved from: http://www.internationaled.org/publications/GSF_EducatingLeaders.pdf

Burnouf, L. (2004). Global awareness and perspectives in global education. *Canadian Social Studies*, *38*(3), 1–12.

Crawford, E. O., & Kirby, M. M. (2008). Fostering students' global awareness: Technology applications in social studies teaching and learning. *Journal of Curriculum and Instruction*, *2*(1), 56–73.

Dei, G. (2014). Global education from an 'indigenist' anti-colonial perspective. *Journal of Contemporary Issues in Education*, *9*(2), 4–23.

Dervin, F., Chen, N., Yuan, M., & Jacobson, A. (2020). COVID-19 and interculturality: First lessons for teacher educators. *Education and Society*, *38*(1), 89–106. doi:10.7459/es/38.1.06

Gaudelli, W. (2006). Convergence of technology and diversity: Experiences of two beginning teachers in a web-based distance learning for global/multicultural education. *Teacher Education Quarterly*, *33*(1), 97–116.

Grant, S. G. (2013). From inquiry arc to instructional practice: The potential of the C3 Framework. *Social Education*, *77*(6), 322–326, 351.

Herr, K., & Anderson, G. (2014). *The action research dissertation: A guide for students* (2nd ed.). Sage.

Lee, J. (2008). *Visualizing elementary social studies methods*. John Wiley & Sons, Inc.

Manfra, M. M. (2019). Action research and systematic change in teaching practice. *Review of Research in Education*, *43*(1), 163–196. doi:10.3102/0091732X18821132

Manfra, M. M. (2020). Action research for classrooms, schools, and communities. *Sage (Atlanta, Ga.)*.

McNiff, J. (2016). *You and your action research project* (4th ed.). Routledge. doi:10.4324/9781315693620

Merryfield, M. M. (2002). The difference a global educator can make. *Association for Supervision and Curriculum Development*, *60*(2), 18–21.

National Council for the Social Studies. (2013). *The College, Career, and Civic Life (C3) framework for the social studies state standards: Guidance for enhancing the rigor of K-12 civics, economics, geography, and history*. NCSS.

Schleicher, A. (2018). *The future of education and skills*. OECD.

Schukar, R. (1993). Controversy in global education: Lessons for teacher educators. *Theory into Practice*, *32*(1), 52–57. doi:10.1080/00405849309543573

Shulman, L. S. (1986, February). Those who understand: Knowledge growth in teaching. *Educational Research*, *15*(2), 4–14. doi:10.3102/0013189X015002004

Shulman, L. S. (1999). Course anatomy: The dissection and analysis of knowledge through teaching. In P. Hutchings (Ed.), *The Course Portfolio: How Faculty Can Examine Their Teaching to Advance Practice and Improve Student Learning* (pp. 5–12). American Association for Higher Education.

Spires, Himes, M. P., Paul, C. M., & Kerkhoff, S. N. (2019). Going global with project-based inquiry: Cosmopolitan literacies in practice. *Journal of Adolescent & Adult Literacy*, *63*(1), 51–64. doi:10.1002/jaal.947

Swan, K., Lee, J., & Grant, S. G. (2018). Questions, tasks, sources: Focusing on the essence of inquiry. *National Council for Social Studies*, *82*(3), 133–137.

Wiley, J., & Ash, I. K. (2005). Multimedia learning in history. In R. E. Mayer (Ed.), *The Cambridge handbook of multimedia learning* (pp. 375–392). Cambridge University Press. doi:10.1017/CBO9780511816819.025

ADDITIONAL READING

Axford, B. (2020). *Where globalities are made*. https://www.21global.ucsb.edu/global-e/february-2020/where-globalities-are-made

Featherstone, M. (2020). Problematizing the Global: An Introduction to Global Culture Revisited. *Theory, Culture & Society*, *37*(7-8), 157–167. doi:10.1177/0263276420957715

Juergensmeyer, M. (2011). *What is global studies?* https://www.21global.ucsb.edu/global-e/may-2011/what-global-studies

Kaplowtiz, R. D., Griffin, S. R., & Seyka, S. (2019). *Race dialogues: A facilitator's guide to tackling the elephant in the classroom*. Teachers College Press.

Kornelsen, L., Balzer, G., & Magro, K. M. (2020). *Teaching global citizenship: A Canadian perspective*. Canadian Scholars.

Richards, P. (2014). Decolonizing globalization studies. *Global Society*, *8*(2), 139–154.

KEY TERMS AND DEFINITIONS

Action Research: The form of applying research approaches to real issues faced by practitioners and researchers as it has an emphasis on inquiry and dialogue to develop practical and meaningful teacher experiences (Manfra, 2019).

C3 Framework: Based on the National Council for Social Studies, it is a powerful guide to help frame instruction in the social studies education for instruction through various context of civics, economics, history, geography, and more from Kindergarten through high school years.

Compelling Question: As inquiry-based learning occurs, the compelling question is developed carefully as a provocative and engaging question that frames a specific unit.

Digital Learning: A type of teaching and learning practice that constructs of establishing innovative, instructional, and engaging learning that is accompanied by technological tools and advances through the application of student learning.

Formative Assessment: A form of assessment that summarizes what students learned over a specific period of time. In particular to the C3 Framework, each supporting question has a formative assessment that allows students to share their learning within each task.

Global Education: The incorporation of learning about the world as it engages students in learning about various cultures, histories, geographies, and current issues of the world through inquiry and action that would lead students to become change agents to become citizens of the world.

Inquiry-Based: The concept of asking students thought-provoking, engaging questions that trigger their curiosity of the world, ultimately, leading to taking informed action.

Summative Assessment: A form of assessment that is usually after the compelling question based on the C3 Framework, in particular to what students had learned from a specific unit.

Supporting Questions: Through inquiry-based learning, the supporting questions address various aspects of the compelling question. In the C3 Framework, the supporting questions are around 4 to 5 questions that follow guided formative tasks. The supporting questions align with the compelling questions and allow students to connect the unit to their personal experiences.

APPENDIX 1

United Nations Sustainable Development Goals[1]

Goal 1. No Poverty (in all its forms)
Goal 2. Zero Hunger (achieving food security, sustainable agriculture, and better nutritional guides)
Goal 3. Good Health and Well-being (promoting healthy lives and well-beings for all)
Goal 4. Quality Education (equitable high quality education and learning opportunities for all)
Goal 5. Gender Equality (bringing about gender equality and empowering young girls and women all around the world)
Goal 6. Clean Water and Sanitation (sanitation and sustainability in water consumption in the world)
Goal 7. Affordable and Clean Energy (ensuring sustainable, modern, affordable energy for all).
Goal 8. Decent Work and Economic Growth (inclusivity, sustainable economic development, as well as productive employment growth and work opportunities for all).
Goal 9. Industry, Innovation, and Infrastructure (sustainable industrialization that help foster innovation and continuing to build adaptable, strong infrastructures)
Goal 10. Reduce Inequality (reducing inequality among people around the world)
Goal 11. Sustainable Cities and Communities (creating safe, sustainable, inclusive communities)
Goal 12. Responsible Consumption and Production (sustainable consumption and production)
Goal 13. Climate Action (combat climate change and its major impacts on the world)
Goal 14. Life Below Water (conserve, protect, and sustain the oceans, seas, and water resources in the world)
Goal 15. Life on Land (conserve, protect, and sustain the ecosystem, forests, desertification; end land degradation and loss of biodiversity)
Goal 16. Peace and Justice Strong Institutions (establish inclusive, peaceful, and tolerant societies that integrate justice for all and build inclusive institutions around the word for all).
Goal 17. Partnerships to Achieve the Goal (strengthen relationships between global partnerships with an aim for sustainable development around the world)

APPENDIX 2

Digital Learning Platforms that Support Global Education

Table 2.

Resource	Brief Description
Belouga: https://belouga.org/	Teachers can sign up at no cost. This platform provides a personalized global education journey that is followed through by action to have students put their learning to work.
Big History Project: https://www.oerproject.com	Year-long social studies course that enables teachers and students to connect to the past, present, and future.
Bunk History: https://www.bunkhistory.org/	An archive of digital media and an exploration of the connection between the past and present.
The Compassion Project: https://thecompassionproject.com/	A national initiative to incorporate compassion education with the intent to practice and improve perspective taking skills to make a difference in the world.
Culture Kits: https://navigators.unc.edu/kit-checkout/	1 kit per teacher as everyone is transitioning to remote learning. Kits are shipped (for free) to your home to help support your teaching and students learning.
Empatico: https://empatico.org/	This digital platform empowers teachers and students to connect with other classrooms across the world at no cost.
EverFi https://everfi.com/partners/k-12-educators/social-emotional-learning/	Digital social and emotional learning resources that equip teachers and students with leadership skills, as well as empathy, conflict resolution, and global awareness.
Facing History and Ourselves: https://www.facinghistory.org/	Primary sources that include multimedia materials and resources that can be incorporated in lesson plans and teaching strategies.
Global C3 Inquiries: https://c3teachers.org/global-hub/	A digital workspace available for all educators to develop, use, and implement global C3 inquiries in their classroom to promote global education and instructional practice materials that are aligned with the UN Sustainable Development Goals.
iCivics: https://www.icivics.org/	A free learning kit is available for enrichment for parents, teachers, and students. This digital platform contains games, and lesson plans that incorporate civics education and motivate students to become active citizens.
National Geographic Learning: https://ngl.cengage.com/assets/html/covid19/	National Geographic Learning through Cengage is providing free resources and lessons for online learning.

Chapter 12
An Action Research Study on Globally Competent Teaching in Online Spaces

Shea N. Kerkhoff
University of Missouri-St. Louis, USA

Fatemeh Mardi
University of Missouri-St. Louis, USA

Han Rong
University of Missouri-St. Louis, USA

ABSTRACT

Research shows that teachers understand why global competence is important but do not necessarily know how to implement global teaching. One way to address this problem of practice is integrating global competence with teacher education. Education abroad is an effective method to internationalize teaching, but travel is suspended due to the global pandemic. At the same time, the pandemic also highlights how global cooperation and global competence are vital in mitigating the effects of the virus. The purpose of this action research study was to investigate the impact of infusing global learning in an online education methods course. Data sources included products of learning and reflections from 24 master's students. Findings include five themes (multilingual communication, current event awareness, content-aligned integration, utilizing students' identities, and practicing local-global inquiry) that describe the prerequisites, barriers, challenges, and successes as teachers develop global competence and implement globally competent teaching in their K-12 classrooms.

Globalization 3.0 makes it possible for so many more people to plug in and play,

DOI: 10.4018/978-1-7998-6922-1.ch012

and you are going to see every color of the human rainbow take part.

-Thomas Friedman in The World is Flat

INTRODUCTION

Our world is increasingly digital and global. Technology makes connections across the globe faster and easier than ever before. Digital and global competence is thus important for success in the modern world. Digital competence refers to the ability to *leverage technology* to participate, communicate, and work, while global competence, similarly, refers to the ability to participate, communicate, and work *worldwide* (Kerkhoff, 2017; Kerkhoff, 2020).

A 2018 Sodexo Global Workplace Trends report points to cross-cultural competence, virtual collaboration, and new media literacy as key skills for the 2020 workforce. Similarly, according to an American Association of Colleges and Universities' (2018) sanctioned report on the importance of college learning outcomes in the business world, 65% of business executives and 73% of hiring managers believe that the ability to "analyze/solve problems w/people from different backgrounds/cultures" is of high importance and 60% and 73% respectively believe "stay current on changing technology/applications to workplace" is of high importance (p. 13). Business leaders perceived gaps in terms of graduate preparedness with both of these outcomes, and both held or increased in importance since the 2014 report. To help prepare students for 21st-century careers and community life, teachers themselves need to know how to collaborate with people from different cultures and stay current on technology applications.

Various communication and telecollaboration tools enable interaction and professional collaboration (Lips et al., 2017; Starkey, 2020), and allow teachers the opportunity to create engaging lessons with global and diverse perspectives (Broere & Kerkhoff, 2020; Goodwin, 2020; Kaempf, 2018). Educators need to be able to use technology tools and resources to maximize and support 21st- century learning (ISTE, 2017).

In addition to digital competence, global competence is important. This combination of digital and global competence is mentioned by Yemini et al. (2019) as their review of the literature on global education identified a gap in research at the intersection of the digital and the global. The researchers state a need for "scholarship to take a greater interest in ICTs [Information and Communication Technologies], as well as in the infusion of GCE [Global Citizenship Education] into pre-existing approaches" (p. 87). Reimers (2009) defines global competence as:

The knowledge and skills people need to understand today's flat world and to integrate across disciplines so that they can comprehend global events and create possibilities to address them. Global competencies are also the attitudinal and ethical dispositions that make it possible to interact peacefully, respectfully, and productively with fellow human beings from diverse geographies. (para 4)

The authors appreciate how Reimers' (2009) definition broadens the discussion beyond career-readiness to include ethical and peaceful living. The extant research shows that teachers understand why global competence is important for their students' future careers and community lives, but that they do not necessarily know how to implement global teaching in their classrooms (Kerkhoff, et al., 2019; Kerkhoff & Cloud, 2020; Rapoport, 2010). One way to address this problem of practice is through integrating globally competent teaching with formal teacher education in universities. According to the Longview Foundation (2008), colleges of education are among the least internationalized on campus. Education abroad is touted as an effective method to reflect on practice (Alfaro & Quezada, 2010; Kissock & Richardson, 2010); develop personally and professionally (Pence & Macgillivray, 2008; Zhao et al., 2009); and enhance knowledge of and appreciation for cultural diversity (Doppen, 2010; Kinginer, 2009). However, traveling abroad is a large investment of time and money. In addition, there is not a body of evidence yet that teaching abroad is associated with increases in one's global competence (Byker, 2016) nor one's future students' global competence. Although there have been qualitative and longitudinal studies that are beginning to show a relationship, in fact, Kerkhoff and colleagues' (2019) survey research found that travel was not correlated to global competence nor teaching for global competence. After teaching abroad, participants reported introducing authentic cultural experiences for their students (Biraimah & Jotia, 2012; Cook, 2009), including students' cultures in the curriculum (Slapac & Kim, 2020; Slapac, 2021; Zhao et al., 2009), and "decentering" the US from the curriculum (Patterson, 2013, p. 107).

Globally competent teaching from home is especially important during the current pandemic when global travel is prohibited, and yet global cooperation and global competence is vital in mitigating the effects of the virus. The purpose of this action research study was to investigate the impact of a masters-level online education methods course infused with global learning. The study aimed to determine what participants perceived as the prerequisites, barriers and successes when developing and enacting globally competent teaching.

REVIEW OF RELEVANT LITERATURE

Teacher education programs are responsible for preparing pre-service and in-service teachers to teach their students to interact and function in a globalized, digitized world (Longview Foundation, 2008; Asia Society & OECD, 2018; Yemini et al., 2019). In the United States, where this study is situated, education organizations (i.e., United States Department of Education Office of Educational Technology, International Society of Technology in Education, Society for Information Technology and Teacher Education, Council for the Accreditation of Educator Preparation, National Technology Leadership Coalition, and American Association of Colleges of Teacher Education) developed the Teacher Educator Technology Competencies (Foulger et al., 2017). The eighth competence listed for teacher educators is to use technology to connect globally with various regions and cultures. Research has shown that technology can be a successful medium to foster global competence among teachers and their students (Carr, 2016).

Online Global Learning with Teachers

Online collaboration has played an important role in fostering global competence among teacher candidates. Zong (2009) found that by participating in a multinational online collaboration project, preservice teachers gained an understanding of global education and a deeper level of global awareness through the project. Russian (Dugartsyrenova & Sardegna, 2019) and South Korean (Kim et al., 2018) teacher candidates collaborated with teacher candidates in the United States (U.S.) resulting in an increase in intercultural awareness and transformative learning in both studies. Kopish et al., (2019) researched the integration of cross-cultural experiences in their local community in their teacher education courses designed to develop the global competencies of teacher candidates. They found that establishing human connections was core to participants' development of global competence.

Carr (2016) researched an online platform, eTutor, through which pre-service teachers and grades kindergarten through 12 students across four countries interacted. The objective was to enhance the PSTs' intercultural and educational technology capabilities. The eTutor project successfully shows how an online platform can provide opportunities for teacher candidates to engage in authentic cross-cultural experiences and foster the competencies needed to teach in a digital and global world.

Online Global Learning with Students

Kerkhoff's (2017) mixed methods study found three K-12 instructional practices that used technology to develop students' global readiness: students utilize technology for virtual interviews (with experts, community members, etc.); students utilize synchronous technology (e.g., Skype, Google Hangouts) for international collaborations; and students utilize asynchronous technology (e.g., email, blogs) for international collaborations.

Spires and colleagues (2019) explained that the global aspect of the curriculum helped students learn to consider different perspectives. Students utilized technology to research a global issue from international sources and to interview an expert to learn more about the issue.

Sánchez and Ensor's (2020) qualitative study of U.S. elementary media center classes examines communicating online with children in a refugee facility in Europe. Through their viewing of each other's experiences, students in the U.S. engaged in deep and active listening to the experience of diverse others and "restor(y)ing social futures" by committing to action to help one another (p. 272). Even through space and distance, the digital stories and videos prompted U.S. students to respond with empathy to make a positive impact.

Kaempf (2018) researched the Global Read Aloud (Ripp, 2021) virtual learning environment and found it impacted the third-grade students' interest in learning more about other countries. Participants in her study had collaborated over shared reading with classes in Egypt, India, and Canada. Carpenter and Justice (2017a; 2017b) researched potential technology-enhanced global collaboration using the Global Read Aloud project. Educators (primarily from North America) utilized social media to interact with other classes using synchronous and asynchronous technologies. This study revealed some teachers need preparation and support to participate in activities related to the Global Read Aloud (GRA), which is a complicated process requiring Technological Pedagogical Content Knowledge (TPACK) (Mishra & Koehler, 2006) as well as "cross-cultural interaction, networking, collaboration, global citizenship and digital citizenship" (Carpenter & Justice, 2017a, p. 298). Carpenter et al. (2018) conclude that technology provides a potential space for building students' global readiness. Teachers are required to learn how ICT relates to content and pedagogy (Mishra & Koehler, 2006; Koehler & Mishra, 2009). Technology skills can help teachers to weave in global citizenship education throughout all subject areas (Tichnor-Wagner et al., 2016). Therefore, teacher educators are challenged with designing authentic learning experiences for teacher candidates that foster their global and digital competencies.

CONCEPTUAL FRAMEWORK

Our conceptual framework joins TPACK (Mishra & Koehler, 2006; Koehler & Mishra, 2009), globally competent learning (Tichnor-Wagner, et al., 2016; Tichnor-Wagner et al., 2019), and teaching for global readiness (Kerkhoff, 2017; 2018).

TPACK

TPACK by Mishra and Koehler (2006) builds on Shulman (1986)'s pedagogical content knowledge which describes effective teachers as having: a) content knowledge, i.e., deep knowledge about the subject they teach, b) pedagogical knowledge, i.e., a thorough understanding of how students learn, and c) pedagogical content knowledge, i.e., an expert knowledge-base for pedagogy specific to their content area. In response to the digital turn in education, Mishra and Koehler used a five-year design experiment methodology to add technological skills and knowledge to Shulman's theory. In the same vein as Shulman, assert that in addition to knowledge about technology, teachers need to learn how technology relates to their particular content area and can enhance their pedagogy (Mishra & Koehler, 2006; Koehler & Mishra, 2009). Experts in education technology research, Albion and Redmond (2008) agree, stating that effective teachers "infuse ICTs using authentic and pedagogically appropriate approaches" (p. 1). See Figure 1 for an illustration of TPACK.

The TPACK model is foundational in education and has been cited over 10,000 times. However, the TPACK model also has been critiqued for being highly theoretical, not being student-centered, and being hard to enact practically (Mirra, 2019). In addition, while the TPACK model acknowledges that learning does not happen in a vacuum but is situated within a context, the model tends to equate context with limitations and does not expound on how context can be related to teaching as an asset. This leads to the next concept where context is explicitly linked to teaching and learning.

Global Competence and Readiness

Globally competent learning and global readiness are related concepts that were developed around the same time by different researchers. Globally competent learning is based on qualitative analysis of interviews with expert global teachers (Parkhouse et al., 2015; Tichnor-Wagner et al., 2016, 2019) and defines global competence as "the knowledge, skills and dispositions needed to thrive in a diverse, interconnected world" (Tichnor-Wagner & et al., 2019, p. 2). Global competence includes cultural knowledge, intercultural skills, and a positive attitude towards multiple perspectives and global interconnectedness. Globally competent teachers "recognize their own perspective, culture, language, and context before extending outward to recognize the perspectives, cultures, languages, and contexts of others. This embraces a 'glocal' mindset that recognizes the intersecting cultural, regional, national, and global identities and affiliations" (Tichnor-Wagner et al., 2019, p. 13). Teachers use a glocal mindset to integrate global learning with the standard course of study. In this way, globally competent teaching is situated in the local context, connected to global systems, and integrated with the curriculum (Slapac, 2021).

Likewise, the first two dimensions of teaching for global readiness are situated relevant learning and integrated global learning, as demonstrated in the first row of Figure 2. Critical and intercultural are the last two dimensions. Teaching for global readiness was operationally defined and empirically validated through quantitative analysis (Kerkhoff, 2017; Kerkhoff, et al., 2019; Kerkhoff & Cloud, 2020). Global readiness refers to the digital literacy and global citizenship needed in 21st-century private and public life to participate, communicate, and work anywhere with anyone in the world.

Figure 1. Technological Pedagogical Content Knowledge used with permission from Mishra & Koehler (2006)
Source: (Mishra & Koehler, 2006)

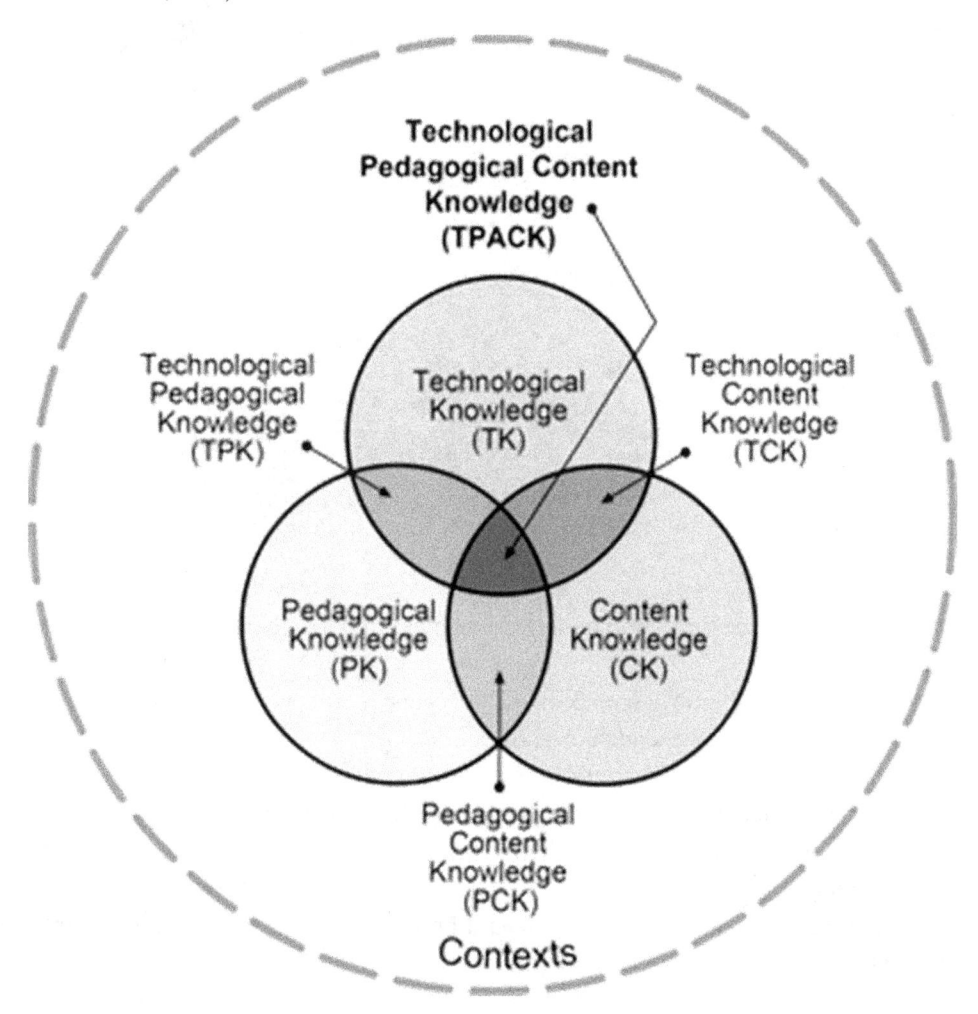

METHODS

We utilized action research as our inquiry method (Cochran-Smith & Lytle, 2015). Action research involves a teacher investigating a problem of practice, in our case infusing global competence with teacher learning. The teacher-researcher acts as a participant-observer in the study, systematically and iteratively examining their own practice designing the study and the learning; observing and collecting data; analyzing data and reflecting; and generating findings to improve their own practice with hope of transferability to other teachers as well (Kemmis et al.,2014). As such, action research creates a cycle between research and practice, "where research impacts practice and practice influences research" (Putman & Rock, 2018, p. 12). The research questions for this study include:

Figure 2. Four dimensions of teaching for global readiness
Source: (Kerkhoff & Cloud, 2020)

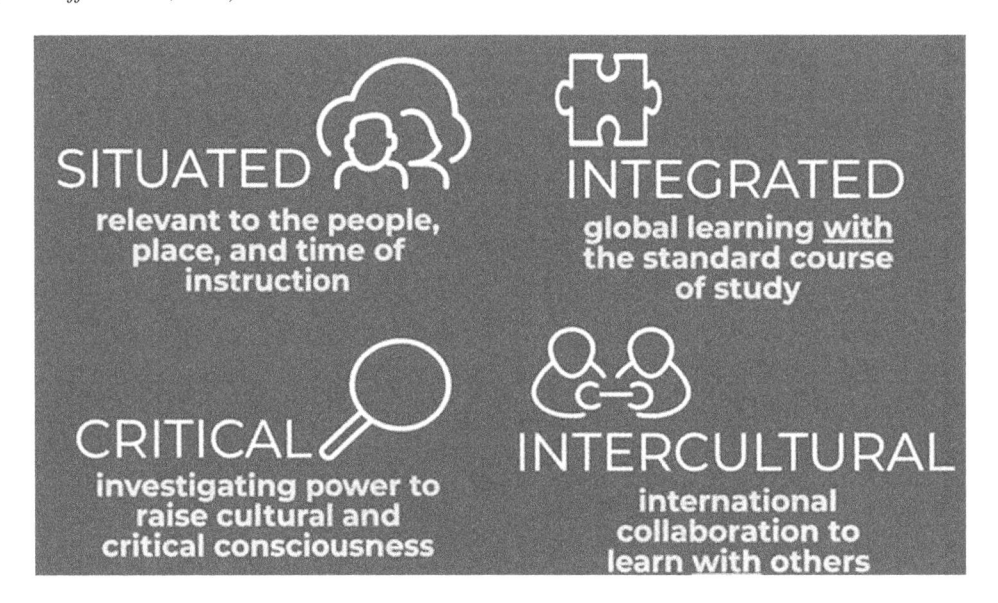

- What prerequisites, successes, and barriers do teachers report when developing a global competent teaching practice?
  ○ What dispositions, knowledge, skills do teachers report as being foundational to globally competent teaching? (prerequisites and successes)
  ○ What do they perceive as barriers to developing global competence? (barriers)
- What experiences do teachers report when enacting global learning?
  ○ What challenges do teachers face when enacting globally competent teaching? (prerequisites and barriers)
  ○ What methods do teachers perceive would be beneficial when teaching students for global competence? (desired or successful practices)

Context and Participants

The context of this study is an education methods course in an online curriculum and instruction master's degree program at a large urban land-grant university. Participants included 24 teachers with 1-20 years of experience, teaching in grades 1-12, in content areas including English, mathematics, science, social studies, music, and art. Participants identified as 84% White, 8% African-American, 4% Asian-American, and 4% Hispanic or Latinx. Participant demographics can be found in Table 1. The course, called "Learning through Inquiry", included modules on collaborative learning, culturally relevant teaching, inquiry-based learning, and global teaching. In Figure 3, we outline the global teaching module objectives and content.

An Action Research Study on Globally Competent Teaching in Online Spaces

Table 1. Table of participant demographics

Identity	Variable	Percentage	Number
Gender	Male	38	9
	Female	62	15
Race and Ethnicity	Asian and Pacific Islander	4	1
	Black and African American	8	2
	Hispanic and Latinx	4	1
	White	84	20
Age	18-24	42	10
	25-34	38	9
	35-44	17	4
	45-54	4	1

Figure 3. Global teaching module objectives and learning activities

Global Teaching Module

Learning Objectives

The learning objectives for this module were adapted from the Global-Ready Teacher Competency Indicators (VIF International, 2014).

- Pedagogy - The teacher demonstrates and models expertise in inquiry- and design-based learning theories and practices that build learners' knowledge, creativity, innovation, critical thinking, perspective-taking and problem-solving skills through consistent implementation of global projects.
- Content - The teacher demonstrates knowledge of global content, curriculum and instructional practices that cultivate new knowledge through ongoing interdisciplinary global investigations.
- Technology - The teacher is confident in experimenting with and consistently integrating next-generation technology throughout teaching and learning processes that build learners' global content knowledge, communication and media literacy skills.

Agenda

1. Watch the Asia Society video Global Competence
2. Read Veronica Boix Mansilla's article Global Thinking
3. Discuss the video and reading using the Global Thinking 3Ys Routine
4. Watch minilecture video captured on Voicethread
5. Complete a collaborative Case Study on global teaching
6. Participate in FlipGrid Discussion on productive collaboration
7. Take the Teaching for Global Readiness self-reflection instrument again. Compare to your answers at the beginning of the semester. Reflect on how you grew. Set goals on what you would like to continue to work on

Data Collection

We collected multiple sources of data to provide convergence of evidence in relation to our findings (Miles et al., 2014). We collected products of learning from the online course that related to global teaching. Primary data sources included assessments that were intentionally added to the course to integrate globally competent teaching throughout the courses as well as assessments of the Global Teaching Module. Secondary data sources were used to contextualize and triangulate analysis of primary sources. See Figure 4 for descriptions of each source.

Figure 4. Data sources of online interactions

> Primary data sources:
> - Concentric Circles of Identity Discussion board posts where students listened to the TED Talk "Don't ask where I'm from, ask where I'm a local" by Taiye Selasi (https://www.youtube.com/watch?v=LYCKzpXEW6E) and described their identity as connected to multiple places, starting with local and moving out to national and global.
> - Globally Competent Teaching Continuum (Tichnor-Wagner, et al., 2019) pre-assessment and self-reflection on their responses, setting goals for the semester.
> - Global competence discussion board post and replies following the 3 Whys global thinking routine: Why does global competence matter to you, Why does global competence matter to the people around you (e.g., your students), and Why does global competence matter to the world?
> - Teaching for Global Readiness collaborative case studies where participants worked in collaborative groups to evaluate a teaching vignette from World of Words or PBI Global.
> - Globally Competent Teaching Continuum post-assessments and self-reflections on growth over the course of the semester.
>
> Secondary data sources:
> - Definitions of teaching at the beginning of the semester and self-reflections on definition of teaching at the end of the semester captured via images and audio on Voicethread.
> - Asynchronous FlipGrid discussions on productive collaboration with pre-service teachers from another university.
> - Project-Based Inquiry Global (see Author, 2020) culminating assessments where teachers designed and completed personal inquiry projects around a question they were intellectually curious about and integrated global perspectives as they gathered and synthesized resources.
> - Anonymous course evaluations after the course was completed.

Data Analysis

We used Google Drive to collaborate on data analysis. We copied and pasted all data into Google Docs organized in a collaborative Google Drive folder. With Google Drive, we could show our views on the same material while dividing the work and cooperating. We could also see each other's views, evaluate each other, and help and inspire each other. As for the coding methodology part, we applied both descriptive and values coding (Saldaña, 2016).

In the first round of coding, we divided this part of the work into three parts. Focusing on the research questions, we launched the first round of coding for the four main data sources: Pre-Globally Competent Teaching Continuum Reflections, Post-Globally Competent Teaching Continuum Reflections, Discussion Board, and Final Projects. For the first round of data analysis, we highlighted sentences in the text that showed insights into the research questions (Yin, 2018). In this coding process, we chose different colors to relate the data to the different research questions, for example prerequisites were yellow, successful practices were green, and barriers were red. The use of different colors during coding made it easier to recognize for all the collaborators. Below, we use Table 2 to illustrate the first encoding process.

Table 2. Data extract with codes applied

Data Extract	Coded for
Overall, I do continue to strongly promote equity for both my students and their families in both education and community interactions.	Equity and equality
Develop local, national, or international partnerships that provide real world contexts for global learning opportunities and Develop and use appropriate methods of inquiry to assess students' global competence development.	Inquiry
I feel like my biggest weaknesses are Integrate learning experiences for students that promote content-aligned explorations of the world and Facilitate intercultural and international conversations that promote active listening, critical thinking, and perspective recognition. I teach math so I do feel like these are harder for me to incorporate in my classroom than they would be in a social studies or language arts classroom.	Challenge in math and science

After the first coding, we summed up 48 initial codes. We created a codebook, giving each initial code an operational definition and example from the data. We use Table 3 to illustrate this process. At last, we combined similar initial codes through pattern matching to develop five themes, as seen in Table 4: (a) communicating in multiple languages a prerequisite for globally competent teaching, (b) awareness of global issues and current events: prerequisites for globally competent teaching, (c) challenges in integrating content-aligned explorations and discussions, (d) success practice of diversity of students identities a resource for global learning, and (e) successful practice of local-global inquiry.

FINDINGS

The first two themes answer the research question 1. *What prerequisites, successes, and barriers do teachers report when developing a global competent teaching practice?* The first theme is *Communicating in Multiple Languages: A Prerequisite for Globally Competent Teaching*, and the second theme is *Current Events: A Success for Some and Barrier for Others*. Following explanation of these two themes, we then explain three themes that answer research question 2: *What experiences do teachers report when enacting global learning?*

Communicating in Multiple Languages and Awareness of Current Events: Prerequisites for Globally Competent Teaching

Of the 24 participants in this study, ten chose to reflect on the ability to communicate in multiple languages in the pre-survey. Two identified their ability as a strength, while the rest expressed interest in improving this aspect of global competence. The specific languages mentioned were Spanish, French, German, Bosnian, Mandarin, and Arabic. As the participants reflected on their language abilities, they mentioned how the importance of using multiple languages is intertwined with students' backgrounds and the need for effectively communicating with students and families.

Table 3. Codebook sample from collaborative analysis

Research Questions	Initial Codes	Operational Definition	Examples/Research Notes
Prerequisite	Value multilingualism	Value multilingualism. Indicate that they know another language and/or understand that language is foundational to culture and global teaching.	"I really would like to take some time out to learn more Arabic phrases, I know that I will not be fluent, but I need to be able to communicate with my student's parents a little easier."
Successful Practice	Equity and equality	Value education that itself is equitable, and education that promotes equity and justice worldwide	"I do continue to strongly promote equity for both my students and their families in both education and community interactions."
Successful Practice	Families as resources	Value that their students' families are cultural resources	"I establish strong relationships with the parents in which I truly believe they would participate and assist their children in global competence inquiries as well as projects to determine how the issues could be addressed."
Barrier	Challenge in math and science	Value global learning and have global competence themselves but not knowing how to teach for global competence in the discipline, ex. math, physics	"I don't know how to do it even though I want to."
Barrier	Assessing global learning	Not realizing that global competence should be assessed or not knowing how to assess global learning.	"As the year continues, I plan to work on assessing my students' global competence so that I have a better understanding of where they are and how they grow as I implement more global inquiry in my classroom. Prior to taking the survey and this course, I had never considered the importance of measuring this, but rather thought that implementing cultural awareness into my classroom was enough. However, I now realize that global readiness is far more than ensuring my students are ware of other cultures and that measuring their growth is the key to learning."

Language and Cultural Diversity: Chicken or the Egg?

One teacher reflected on the need to learn a specific language to better communicate with his/her/their student's family: "I really would like to take some time out to learn more Arabic phrases. I know that I will not be fluent, but I need to be able to communicate with my student's parents a little easier." The student's background prompted the need for global competence growth in this teacher. Another teacher reflected at the beginning of the semester on a very different case. Without multicultural student backgrounds, the need for communicating in multiple languages is not as important to everyone.

One area that I, as well as my school, needs to improve is the use of multiple languages. I teach in a very rural school district with little to no diversity. Currently, we offer Spanish, but very few students take it. They do not understand the impact it can have on their understanding of the world.

This teacher goes on to connect the lack of diversity to students' low interest in multiple languages. These two reflections show how student diversity affects how multiple languages are valued.

An Action Research Study on Globally Competent Teaching in Online Spaces

Table 4. Data analysis progression from codes to themes

Initial Code	Operational Definition	Theme
Value multilingualism	Ts value multilingualism. Ts indicate that they know another language and/or understand that language is foundational to culture and global teaching	Communicating in Multiple Languages a Prerequisite for Globally Competent Teaching
Need intercultural communication strategies	Want to learn intercultural communication strategies, believe communication interculturally is important for communicating with families	
Barrier is communication	Not knowing enough about other languages and cultures	
Families' languages	Value that their students' families are cultural resources, value communicating with parents but aware that language barriers may interfere, want to do more	
Activate students' language awareness	Aware that cultures have different language practices, but need to know strategies in how to implement, apply, activate the knowledge to inspire students to be globally competent	
Not aware of current events	Barrier to including global connections and real world problems is teacher lack of awareness about international current events	Awareness of Global Issues and Current Events: Prerequisites for Globally Competent Teaching
Using current events	Ss read about current international events that relate to the curriculum they are studying	
Values real world problem-solving	T appreciates that global learning involves real world problem-solving of global issues	
Personally globally competent but not teaching it	Knowledge of interconnectedness of world and global issues. Difference between being globally competent personally and teaching global competence	
Assess global learning	Not realizing that global competence should be assessed or not knowing how to assess global learning.	Challenges in Integrating Content-aligned Explorations and Discussions
Not in curriculum	Global learning is currently not in the curriculum, and curriculum jam packed then not enough time and need creativity to implement global learning district lack of resources and district approval	
Too many priorities	Still seeing global learning as add-on, juggling too many things, time is already tight because so much is already required, trying to integrate so many things at same time, standards not having global learning in them	
Challenge in math and science	Value global learning and have global competence themselves but not knowing how to teach for global competence in the discipline, ex. math, physics	
No international partners	Teachers do not have international partners or know ways to establish international partnerships	
Student as resource	Ss diverse identities and experiences are seen as a resource for teachers to utilize to teach all students about different cultures and countries	Success Practice of Diversity of Students Identities a Resource for Global Learning
Incorporate global/multiple perspectives	include other voices, either through researching diverse perspectives, listening to guest speakers from the community, or each other	
Diversity of identities	T is aware of and appreciates the cultural and global diversity present through the transnational identities of their students	
Equity and equality	T values education that itself is equitable, and education that promotes equity and justice worldwide	
Value students collaborating with diverse others	T wants students to collaborate and think it's important that they learn to collaborate in culturally diverse teams	
Empathy	Believe that global learning should be from and about empathy and that global learning can help students develop empathy across cultural differences	
Inquiry	Open-ended learning, ss conducting research, constructivism framing. Want students to come to their own conclusions about controversial or political issues, based on understanding of the facts. Understand other's perspective and piece it together with one's own viewpoints	Successful Practice of Local-Global Inquiry
Students challenge their own perspectives	Wants students to challenge their own perspectives. Values that global learning helps students' breakdown stereotypes about people from other countries	
Zooming out first	Looking globally first, then coming in to personal	
Local-global connection	Connecting study of global issues to the local context and issues too	
PBL	Ss engage in Project-based learning and the engineering design process, collaborative learning on projects	
Action	Ss take critically framed and informed action for social justice through service learning or projects either locally or globally	

Supporting Linguistically Diverse Families, Enforcing Equity

Valuing efficient communication with families of different backgrounds was also seen in the reflections as a strength. A teacher reflected on their strength: "I am fluent in two languages, English and Bosnian. Working at a diverse school has helped me use both languages to help the students and their parents feel more successful at school." This reflection shows the impact of being able to communicate effectively with families in diverse schools.

Another teacher reflected on the need to improve their ability to communicate more with parents in multiple languages. "While I am fairly capable in terms of Spanish, I am incapable in other languages which makes me think I am not providing the families with enough insight on their child's academic performance or needs." Even though language acquisition was not part of the graduate course, this teacher focused on refreshing their Spanish proficiency throughout the semester. They reflect on their progress in the post-survey reflection about parents communicating more often and more openly than before. The teacher intended to learn more languages to "become somewhat capable in Chinese and Arabic as it would be helpful for some of the parents. Overall, I do continue to strongly promote equity for both my students and their families in both education and community interactions." Through this educator's lens of equity, one can prioritize effective global teaching by improving communication with families.

Students as Resources to Increase Cultural and Linguistic Awareness

The other in-service teacher who reflected on the ability to communicate in multiple languages in response to both surveys (at the beginning and end of the semester) reflected on their language acquisition progress, "The only portion I haven't changed very much in was with language. I, unfortunately, am limited in my learning, as two elementary students are trying to teach me Spanish." Regardless of the amount of progress, the method they chose is positioned students as resources and experts of their language. Another teacher intended to increase cultural awareness of their class through a new student. "This year, I have an exchange student from Japan. I am hopeful that Mai cannot only teach me about her culture, but also her peers." These two reflections show the potential of utilizing the rich linguistic and cultural backgrounds of students to increase global competencies of the teacher and other students.

Beyond Language: Intercultural Communication and Facilitation

Of the survey items, some in-service teachers identified intercultural communication as a foundational prerequisite related to globally competent teaching. Many of them chose communicating in multiple languages and intercultural communication together (as a weakness or strength). One teacher, fluent in English and Bosnian, reflected on their understanding of intercultural communication, "I can relate as I know that learning a new language has social, emotional and cognitive aspects." Through this reflection, they identify how they have first-hand experience that learning a language is intertwined with other domains.

Another teacher reflected on the need to improve their intercultural communication to be a better educator, "I am aware that different cultures communicate differently, but I would like to work on some strategies so that I can be more effective in my communications with those students." This goes beyond linguistic barriers and refers to the cultural factors that can make communicating (and teaching) more effective. They continued by explaining the need to form a cultural bridge between teacher and students;

An Action Research Study on Globally Competent Teaching in Online Spaces

"Very few students are like me, and I love it, but if I could bridge that gap a little more and be a little more culturally responsive, that would be excellent." These reflections show how the teachers value their students' diversity and the importance of communicating effectively with them.

Awareness of Global Issues and Current Events: Prerequisites for Globally Competent Teaching

Awareness of global issues and current events was a success for some and barrier for others, but all participants demonstrated that being globally aware was a value. When talking about strengths and areas to improve on the end of course survey, a total of thirteen participants mentioned understanding of current events. Among them, seven participants thought that the understanding of the current event is what they are good at. The other five participants believed that understanding of current events is what they need to strengthen.

Seven participants who thought they were good at understanding of current events gave examples to prove their points. For example, on the reflection of the survey results one said, "One of my strengths is my understanding of current events, both at a local and global level. I enjoy learning new things and I think that this translates into an openness toward other people as well." A different participant stated, "One of my strengths is that I am aware of global issues and how they affect culture."

On the other hand, five participants who thought they needed to strengthen their understanding of current events gave their reasons in the reflection. In one teacher's opinion, "Understanding global conditions and current events is something that I am interested in, but just like learning a new language, I do not give as much time as I need to truly access multiple resources that portray current events." Among the participants who stated global awareness as a weakness, one made an insightful comment, "The interesting part is that I already am proficient in actively seeking out multiple sources of news for global events and try to understand the impact, but I don't push my students to do this also." This teacher thought about this problem not only from the perspective of himself/herself but also teaching global competence to the students.

Challenges in Integrating Content-Aligned Explorations and Discussions

The next theme answers the research question: *What do teachers feel they need in order to enact globally competent teaching?* Participants described desires to integrate content-aligned global explorations and discussions but found doing so challenging, particularly in math and science and certain school cultures where the focus was solely on content standards.

The first challenge was a set daily curriculum. On a discussion board, a teacher stated, "There is not much time for me to be creative and incorporate global issues." Another teacher agreed, "I teach math, and often struggle to find opportunities to open conversation to my students about relevant issues while remaining on my content timeline." Focusing on and prioritizing content is a challenge in implementing global learning even to teachers who understand the importance of cross-cultural or international interaction. One teacher stated: "Involving my students in global issues and making it a part of the curriculum would engage them, but from a mathematical perspective that alignments with the standards is what I'm finding challenging." On the end of the semester survey, this educator felt they were still in the processing stage. Going from understanding the need to integrate global learning to learning how to apply these concepts practically is more challenging in subjects where there are not standards explicitly making connections.

The second reason was how the subject was not inherently integrated with global learning. A teacher stated on the post-survey reflection, "Math is more of a reach to have a discussion about such things, when usually we are just working with numbers and talking about numbers." Similarly, another math teacher stated, "These are harder for me to incorporate in my classroom than they would be in a social studies or language arts classroom. I do not have intercultural conversations in my classroom."

Not knowing how to incorporate global learning was also mentioned by a math teacher who showed passion and a sincere desire to incorporate diversity, "As a math teacher I do not know where to do this as we do not really have discussions about these issues naturally through the curriculum." A different teacher reflected, "I would like to see or know more about how to integrate these [global] opportunities into an upper-level math classroom where it is not always as inherent in how to do so."

In chemistry, a teacher optimistically reflected on the possibility of adding a global lens. "I would like to be able to bring more of these worldviews to my students. It is something that I discuss in passing with students, but it is not an integrated part of my curriculum." This educator realized they need to actively seek out ways to incorporate global learning into the curriculum. A distinction between subjects within science was made by another teacher; "It's relatively easy to get my environmental science students to have a conversation about global perspectives, but it's not as easy for physics." Like math educators, they continue, "I always tend to focus on the content only and am not sure how to use that content in a global context." Discussions that are content-relevant and provide global perspectives were challenging for the participants in this study. As such, Table 5 provides examples of global topics for math and science.

Table 5. Global topics for math and science

Discipline	Global Topic
Mathematics	Global digital divide; currency conversion; Fahrenheit to Celsius conversion
Biology	HIV/AIDS; global pandemics; cloning; clean water
Environmental Science	Green schools project; deforestation in Tennessee, Brazil, and Kenya
Physics	Clean energy; clean water

Two Successful Practices for Globally Competent Teaching Across Disciplines

The last two themes answer the research question: *What methods do teachers perceive would be beneficial when teaching students for global competence?*

Diversity of Students' Identities Resource for Global Learning

At the beginning of the semester, several teachers reflected on their strengths in creating a classroom environment that values diversity and global engagement and their commitment to promoting equity worldwide. They both had students that come from all over the world. One shared how they frequently had discussions with their diverse students "about respecting each other's languages, cultures, and thoughts. Everyone's ideas are valued equally in my classroom and I remind students that every one of us has the power to promote a more equitable world." The other teacher described their class context of diverse English abilities working together to promote equity: "It is my passion to ensure that every student believes and know that he or she can and will learn unashamedly in my classroom." Another participant stated: "I choose to focus on the students' cultural background and allow them to share important pieces of it with their peers." A fourth participant shared a similar value of students sharing their cultures with one another: "Appreciate the connection made to the diverse cultures in your room, even amongst students who may share a lot of identities. It's crucial we remember this and help students explore this."

One elementary teacher was in the process of implementing a global project called Holidays Around the World. They chose Laos and two other first grade teachers chose different countries to learn about with their first-grade students. "We can all collaborate and learn about three different countries. We will learn about the different traditions/customs, politics, holidays, foods, etc. This will help students learn about different cultures." One teacher shared that their students learned so much from a similar project, "This really helps everyone connect and find a common bond." They replied to the post with three suggestions: creating a Cultural Potluck, share presentations with other grades, and have family members read a story from their home country. Another teacher stated, "Overall, I do continue to strongly promote equity for both my students and their families in both education and community interactions." Connecting with students' and families' cultures provides rich resources for classrooms with diversity. As one participant articulated on the post-survey reflection, "I establish strong relationships with the parents in which I truly believe they would participate and assist their children in global competence inquiries as well as projects to determine how the issues could be addressed." Addressing global issues through inquiry leads to the next theme.

Local-Global Inquiry

At the end of the semester, two teachers reflected on global learning inquiries they had started and how they utilized technology to support students' learning. "I had an Apple design rep video chat with my students to discuss how she uses various skills she learned in order to fulfill various design ideas and advertise products on a global scale." The teacher reports that many of the students were engaged in the lesson and it "helped them think about how communication on a global scale could help them become more marketable now that the world is so interconnected due to social media." A science teacher planned a unit that also focused on the interconnectedness of students' personal lives with global systems.

She designed for students to utilize technology to collaborate with a class in another country to solve an environmental sustainability issue at their schools. On the Project-Based Inquiry Global unit plan, a science teacher stated that in addition to learning the course content, she valued that an inquiry project on sustainable schools would enable students to collaborate with diverse others, perhaps even internationally,

Teaching students to collaborate with one another in the classroom, especially in diverse groups, provides an opportunity for them to practice these skills as well as be exposed to differing points of view. ... Through this project, my goal is for my students to understand that while environmental sustainability is a challenge that directly affects them, it also occurs on a global scale and the most effective approach to creating a more sustainable world that directly affects the society at large is through global collaboration.

An English as a second or other language teacher enacted a unit on immigration utilizing technology to allow students to collect facts on the issue. "The goal for this unit is to not only teach the students' basic information about immigration but to provide them with the information required to really think about and understand this issue and develop an educated, research backed opinion." This teacher decided to zoom out to a global scale first before zooming in on immigration in the U.S. so that students could focus on fact gathering and analysis rather than on their preconceived notions. When describing the Project-Based Inquiry Global assignment, he stated:

Many teachers (myself included) have had problems bringing up immigration in the classroom because we tend to focus on immigration in the United States. If we shift our focus to immigration worldwide, we can avoid the political debate and help our students learn about the various aspects of immigration. In the past, we have attempted to bring up different issues regarding Hispanic immigration in our classes but things quickly turned into a political debate. Rather than going down this road, we decided to begin our immigration unit from a more international approach rather than just focusing on Latin America.

Throughout the unit, the teacher utilized technological resources to support students' meeting of the unit objectives. The teacher included an interactive map of immigration stories, satellite map of the U.S./Mexico border, and the simulation project titled "Roadmap to Immigration." On the post reflection, a teacher states: "I want them to see how things that happen on a local level can make an impact on a global level. Example: How the war in Syria impacted the world, How immigrating to a new country doesn't just make an impact on their own life but impacts the world as a whole." Teachers felt that the open-ended nature of inquiry provided space for students to discover the local connections and root causes of global issues in a way that would lead to positive changes in attitude towards those issues. And moving forward, teachers hoped that students would take action on global issues, as represented by this participant who stated that they wanted to teach "students what it means to be a global citizen of an inequitable world. These types of curricular opportunities will create globally ready members of society that are prepared to act against these multifaceted issues." Taking action leads to the next section that describes solutions to the problem of practice investigated in this study and recommendations as to next steps in the context of teacher education.

SOLUTIONS AND RECOMMENDATIONS

Research on integrating global learning and teacher education curricula is a growing area. In addition, online teaching and integrating technology in teacher education holds potential for transcending geographic and metaphorical borders. Transcending borders necessitates moving beyond the local when considering the real-world context of the curriculum and our students' identities. Each of these ideas will be discussed in detail below.

Explicitly Naming the Global in Education Contexts

The TPACK model (Mishra & Koehler, 2006) is explicit in naming context as an essential consideration in education. MacKinnon (2017) highlights the importance of context in the TPACK model and believes context (CTX) drives the other knowledges (technological, content, and pedagogical). He bases his claim on three global cases in non-traditional settings and explains how the context determines any technological, content, or pedagogical decision making on behalf of the teacher. "Using a plant metaphor, one

An Action Research Study on Globally Competent Teaching in Online Spaces

could posit the notion that T, P and CK actually grow out of and are simultaneously constrained by the possibilities that the context affords" (p. 12). However, the global is not explicitly named. To remedy this, we renamed the TPACK circle of contexts as local contexts and add a larger circle named global contexts, as seen in Figure 5. Our TPACK model that considers local and global contexts is aligned with this view. Unlike Urban et al. (2018) who suggest replacing technological knowledge with global knowledge, this [our] model recognizes the need for integrating technology to meet learning goals, while infusing global citizenship education within each of the knowledge domains.

The new outer circle serves as a reminder for educators to consider the global implications and contexts as they design collaborative experiences and refine learning for their specific contexts. This global circle also signals the mindful integration of the global context within all knowledges (pedagogical, content, and technological). Examples of the global aspect of each knowledge domain are shown in Figure 5.

This echoes the report published by the Longview Foundation (2008), stating a globally competent teacher should have a "commitment to assisting students to become responsible citizens both of the world and of their own communities" (p. 7). Teachers need knowledge of global contexts as a prerequisite to make global connections to the curriculum. To build teachers' knowledge of the global, they can utilize students, families, and local communities as resources. Diversity of student identities means that within the local, there is already a global context.

Figure 5. The global and digital integration model of intersecting knowledge domains for effectively teaching in the 21st century based on Mishra and Koehler (2006)

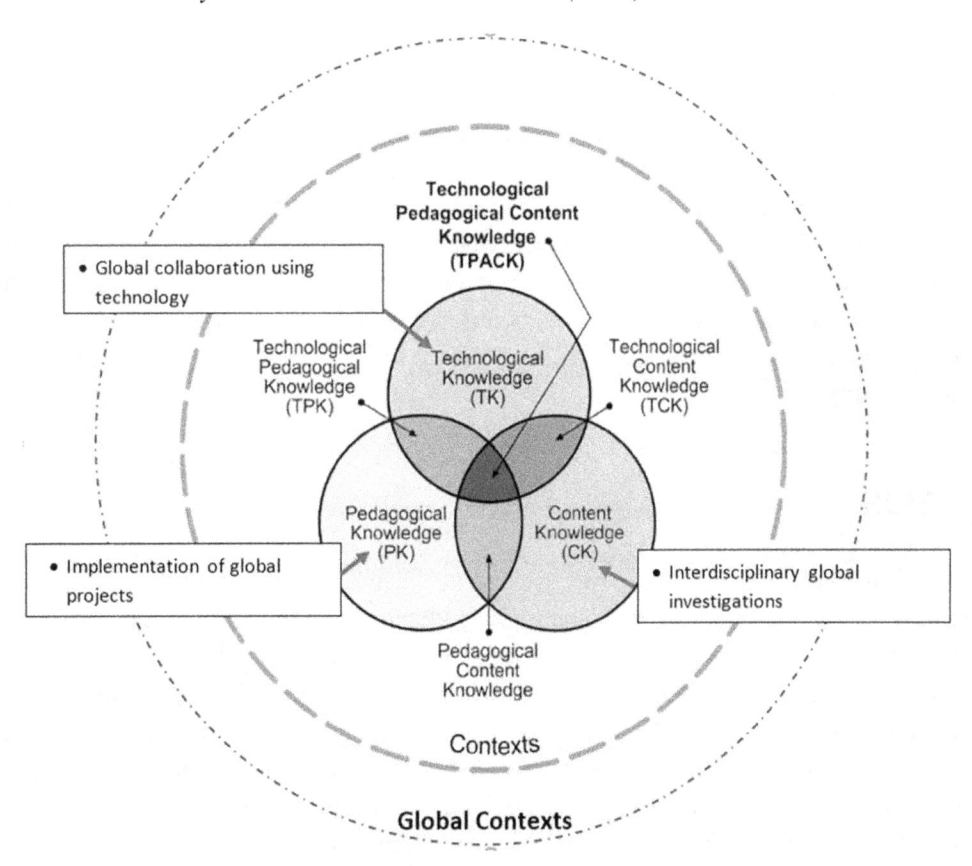

Students, Families, and Communities as Global Resources in the Local Context

Our data showed that teachers from culturally diverse schools recognized their students and families as resources for global literacy learning, but were curious about how to invite students and their families to share their knowledge in ways that promoted the curriculum. Ghiso and colleagues (2016) assert teachers can partner with parents and community organizations to enrich the curriculum with "the robust multilingual counterpublics of their students' home and neighbourhood communities into the curriculum" (p. 24). However, some teachers perceived the communities that they worked in as monocultural or as too transient to establish meaningful partnerships. A teacher stated that a challenge to building partnerships in the community is "because of the difficulty of developing partnerships in the classroom that my school faces due to administration transitions, lack of community support, and a community divided between two separate schools." Another challenge to building partnerships during the Covid-19 pandemic is that communication with families and communities has become digital, which means the digital divide can impact teachers' ability to communicate successfully.

LIMITATIONS AND FUTURE RESEARCH

Fundamental to action research, the first author was both the course instructor and researcher. It is possible that students' intrinsic interest in global education may have elicited their interest in participation or that students may have produced what they believed would earn them a high grade, meaning that findings could include a possible positive-leaning skew. However, to mitigate concerns, all protocols were IRB-approved and informed consent received for all participants. The identity of those students who consented to the research was not revealed to the instructor until after final grades were posted. In addition, the data only included self-report of practices and beliefs. Future research could include observations of classroom practice to examine the successful practices as they are implemented in K-12 online and physical settings to determine whether what teachers' beliefs around global learning align to the practices that they implement in their classrooms and to determine whether the practices that teachers report are the same practices that researchers observe. In addition, future research could describe how teachers can encourage all students in a class to share knowledge as a means of fostering values of diversity and equality.

CONCLUSION

The purpose of this action research study was to examine the influence of integrating global competence with an online education methods course. The findings demonstrate the prerequisites, barriers and successes of K-12 teachers when developing and enacting globally competent teaching. Conducting action research during this course helped to identify barriers participants perceived. Now that this is known, future iterations of the course can focus on providing more math and science resources and more support around multilingual and intercultural communication. Our study contributes the successful practices of embracing students' diverse cultures as resources and inquiry on local-global issues as providing space for globally competence learning. Future research in online teacher education can explore multilingualism as a prerequisite and/or barrier for globally competent teaching and for relationship building with globally diverse families. Future research can also explore topics to integrate global competence in mathematics and science classrooms that align to state standards in those courses. As our world continues to become increasingly digitized and globalized, teachers will also need to be globally competent themselves and to be able to support students in becoming globally competent too.

ACKNOWLEDGMENT

This research was supported by the Longview Foundation.

REFERENCES

Albion, P., & Redmond, P. (2008, September). Teaching by example? Integrating ICT in teacher education. In *Proceedings of the 2008 Australian Computers in Education Conference.* Australian Council for Computers in Education.

Alfaro, C., & Quezada, R. L. (2010). International teacher professional development: Teacher reflections of authentic teaching and learning experiences. *Teaching Education*, *21*(1), 47–59. doi:10.1080/10476210903466943

American Association of Colleges and Universities. (2018). *Fulfilling the American dream: Liberal education and the future of work.* https://www.aacu.org/research/2018-future-of-work

Asia Society & OECD. (2018). *Teaching for global competence in a rapidly changing world.* https://asiasociety.org/education/teaching-global-competence-rapidly-changing-world

Biraimah, K. L., & Jotia, A. L. (2012). The longitudinal effects of study abroad programs on teachers' content knowledge & perspectives: Fulbright-Hays in Botswana and SE Asia. *Journal of Studies in International Education*, *17*(4), 433–454. doi:10.1177/1028315312464378

Broere, M., & Kerkhoff, S. N. (2020). Discussing the word and the world: Discussion prompts for critical global literacies. *Voices from the Middle*, *27*(3), 50–53. https://library.ncte.org/journals/vm/issues/v27-3

Byker, E. J. (2016). Developing global citizenship consciousness: Case studies of critical cosmopolitan theory. *Journal of Research in Curriculum and Instruction*, *20*(3), 264–275. doi:10.24231/rici.2016.20.3.264

Carpenter, J., Weiss, S., & Justice, J. (2018). Opportunities and Challenges of Using Technology to Teach for Global Readiness in the Global Read Aloud. In *Society for Information Technology & Teacher Education International Conference* (pp. 822-831). Association for the Advancement of Computing in Education.

Carpenter, J. P., & Justice, J. E. (2017a). Can technology support teaching for global readiness? The case of the Global Read Aloud. *LEARNing Landscapes*, *11*(1), 65–85. doi:10.36510/learnland.v11i1.923

Carpenter, J. P., & Justice, J. E. (2017b). Evaluating the roles of technology in the Global Read Aloud project. *Computers in the Schools*, *34*(4), 284–303. doi:10.1080/07380569.2017.1387464

Carr, N. (2016). Pre-service teachers teaching about and across cultures using digital environments: The case of eTutor. *Educational Media International, 53*(2), 103–117. doi:10.1080/09523987.2016.1211336

Cochran-Smith, M., & Lytle, S. L. (2015). *Inquiry as stance: Practitioner research for the next generation.* Teachers College Press.

Cook, R. (2009). *The effects of a short-term teacher abroad program on teachers' perceptions of themselves and their responsibilities as global educators* (Doctoral dissertation). Retrieved from https://digitalcommons.usu.edu/etd/375

Doppen, F. H. (2010). Overseas student teaching and national identity: Why go somewhere you feel completely comfortable? *Journal of International Social Studies, 1*(1), 3–19.

Dugartsyrenova, V. A., & Sardegna, V. G. (2019). Raising intercultural awareness through voice-based telecollaboration: Perceptions, uses, and recommendations. *Innovation in Language Learning and Teaching, 13*(3), 205–220. doi:10.1080/17501229.2018.1533017

Foulger, T. S., Graziano, K. J., Schmidt-Crawford, D., & Slykhuis, D. A. (2017). Teacher educator technology competencies. *Journal of Technology and Teacher Education, 25*(4), 413–448.

Ghiso, M. P., Campano, G., Player, G., & Rusoja, A. (2016). Dialogic teaching and multilingual Counterpublics. *International Perspectives on Dialogic Theory and Practice, 16*(Dial. Ped.), 1–26. doi:10.17239/L1ESLL-2016.16.02.05

Goodwin, A. L. (2020). Globalization, global mindsets and teacher education. *Action in Teacher Education, 42*(1), 6–18. doi:10.1080/01626620.2019.1700848

ISTE. (2017). *International Society for Technology in Education standards for educators.* Retrieved from: https://www.iste.org/standards/for-educators

Kaempf, R. C. (2018). *A Phenomenological Study of the Influence of a Virtual Learning Project on an Elementary Class in the USA* (Doctoral dissertation). Texas Wesleyan University.

Kemmis, S., McTaggart, R., & Nixon, R. (2014). *The action research planner: Doing critical participatory action research.* Springer. doi:10.1007/978-981-4560-67-2

Kerkhoff, S. N. (2017). Designing global futures: A mixed methods study to develop and validate the teaching for global readiness scale. *Teaching and Teacher Education, 65*, 91–106. doi:10.1016/j.tate.2017.03.011

Kerkhoff, S. N. (2018). Teaching for global readiness: A model for locally situated and globally connected literacy instruction. In E. Ortlieb & E. H. Cheek (Eds.), *Addressing diversity in literacy instruction* (pp. 193–205). Emerald. doi:10.1108/S2048-045820170000008009

Kerkhoff, S. N. (2020). Collaborative video case studies and online instruments for self-reflection in global teacher education. *Journal of Technology and Teacher Education, 28*(2), 341–351. http://learntechlib.org/primary/p/216212/

Kerkhoff, S. N., & Cloud, M. (2020). Global teacher education: A mixed methods self-study. *International Journal of Educational Research, 103*. Advance online publication. doi:10.1016/j.ijer.2020.101629 PMID:32834467

Kerkhoff, S. N., Dimitrieska, V., Woerner, J., & Alsup, J. (2019). Global teaching in Indiana: A quantitative case study of K-12 public school teachers. *Journal of Comparative Studies and International Education, 1*(1), 5–31. https//www.jcsie.com/ojs/dir/index.php/JCSIE/article/view/14

Kim, J., Wong, C. Y., & Lee, Y. (2018). Transformative learning through an online global class project in teacher education. *Teacher Educator, 53*(2), 190–207. doi:10.1080/08878730.2017.1422577

Kinginger, C. (2009). *Language learning and study abroad: A critical reading of research*. Springer. doi:10.1057/9780230240766

Kissock, C., & Richardson, P. (2010). Calling for action within the teaching profession: It is time to internationalize teacher education. *Teaching Education, 21*(1), 89–101. doi:10.1080/10476210903467008

Koehler, M., & Mishra, P. (2009). What is technological pedagogical content knowledge (TPACK)? *Contemporary Issues in Technology & Teacher Education, 9*(1), 60–70.

Kopish, M. A., Shahri, B., & Amira, M. (2019). Developing globally competent teacher candidates through cross-cultural experiential learning. *Journal of International Social Studies, 9*(2), 3–34.

Lips, M., Eppel, E., McRae, H., Starkey, L., Sylvester, A., Parore, P., & Barlow, L. (2017). *Understanding children's use and experience with digital technologies*. Final research report. https://www.victoria.ac.nz/__data/assets/pdf_file/0003/960177/

Longview Foundation. (2008). *Teacher preparation for the global age: The imperative for change*. Retrieved on 2 July 2019 from: https://longviewfdn.org/programs/internationalizing-teacher-prep

MacKinnon, G. (2017). Highlighting the importance of context in the TPACK model: Three cases of non-traditional settings. *Issues and Trends in Educational Technology, 5*(1), 4–16. doi:10.2458/azu_itet_v5i1_mackinnon

Mansilla, V. B. (2017). *Global thinking*. http://www.pz.harvard.edu/sites/default/files/Global%20Thinking%20for%20ISV%202017%2006%2023_CreativeCommonsLicense.pdf

Miles, H., Huberman, A. M., & Saldaña. (2014). *Qualitative data analysis: A methods sourcebook* (3rd ed.). Sage.

Mirra, N. (2019). From connected learning to connected teaching: Reimagining digital literacy pedagogy in English teacher education. *English Education, 51*(3), 261–291.

Mishra, P., & Koehler, M. J. (2006). Technological pedagogical content knowledge: A framework for teacher knowledge. *Teachers College Record, 108*(6), 1017–1054. doi:10.1111/j.1467-9620.2006.00684.x

Parkhouse, H., Glazier, J., Tichnor-Wagner, A., & Montana Cain, J. (2015). From local to global: Making the leap in teacher education. *International Journal of Global Education, 4*(2), 10–29. http://www.ijtase.net/ojs/index.php/ijge/article/view/409/492

Parkhouse, H., Tichnor-Wagner, A., Glazier, J., & Cain, J. M. (2016). "You don't have to travel the world:" Accumulating experiences on the path toward globally competent teaching. *Teaching Education*, *27*(3), 267–285. doi:10.1080/10476210.2015.1118032

Patterson, T. (2013). *Stories of self and other: Four in-service social studies teachers reflect on their international professional development* (Doctoral dissertation). Retrieved from https://digitalcommons.sacredheart.edu/ced_fac/112

Pence, H. M., & Macgillivray, I. K. (2008). The impact of an international field experience on preservice teachers. *Teaching and Teacher Education*, *24*(1), 14–25. doi:10.1016/j.tate.2007.01.003

Putman, S. M., & Rock, T. (2018). Action research: Using strategic inquiry to improve teaching and learning. *Sage (Atlanta, Ga.)*.

Rapoport, A. (2010). We cannot teach what we do not know: Indiana teachers talk about global citizenship education. *Education, Citizenship and Social Justice*, *5*(3), 179–190. doi:10.1177/1746197910382256

Reimers, F. (2009). Leading for global competence. *Educational Leadership*, *67*(1). http://www.ascd.org/publications/educational-leadership/sept09/vol67/num01/Leading-for-Global-competence.aspx

Ripp, P. (2021). *The Global Read Aloud*. https://theglobalreadaloud.com/

Saldaña, J. (2016). *The coding manual for qualitative researchers* (3rd ed.). Sage.

Sánchez, L., & Ensor, T. (2020). "We want to live": Teaching globally through cosmopolitan belonging. *Research in the Teaching of English*, *54*(3), 254–280.

Shulman, L. S. (1986). Those who understand: Knowledge growth in teaching. *Educational Researcher*, *15*(2), 4–14. doi:10.3102/0013189X015002004

Slapac, A. (2021). Advancing students' global competency through English language learning in Romania: An exploratory qualitative case study of four English language teachers. *Journal of Research in Childhood Education*, *35*(2), 1–17. doi:10.1080/02568543.2021.1880993

Slapac, A., & Kim, S. (2020). Negotiating teaching cultures and developing cultural competency towards classroom communities in early childhood (K-2) language immersion schools. In International Perspectives on Modern Developments in Early Childhood Education (pp. 77-93). IGI Global.

Sodexo. (2018). *Global workplace trends*. https://www.sodexo.com/workreimagined/2018-global-workplace-trends

Spires, H. A., Himes, M., Paul, C. M., & Kerkhoff, S. N. (2019). Going global with project-based inquiry: Cosmopolitan literacies in practice. *Journal of Adolescent & Adult Literacy*, *63*(1), 51–64. doi:10.1002/jaal.947

Starkey, L. (2020). A review of research exploring teacher preparation for the digital age. *Cambridge Journal of Education*, *50*(1), 37–56. doi:10.1080/0305764X.2019.1625867

Tichnor-Wagner, A., Parkhouse, H., Glazier, J., & Cain, J. M. (2016). Expanding approaches to teaching for diversity and social justice in K-12 education: Fostering global citizenship across the content areas. *Education Policy Analysis Archives*, *24*(59), 1–31. doi:10.14507/epaa.24.2138

Tichnor-Wagner, A., Parkhouse, H., Glazier, J., & Cain, J. M. (2019). *Becoming a globally competent teacher*. ASCD.

Urban, E. R., Navarro, M., & Borron, A. (2018). TPACK to GPACK? The examination of the technological pedagogical content knowledge framework as a model for global integration into college of agriculture classrooms. *Teaching and Teacher Education, 73*, 81–89. doi:10.1016/j.tate.2018.03.013

VIF. (2014). *Global-ready teaching indicators by grade level*. Partnership for 21st Century Learning.

Yemini, M., Tibbitts, F., & Goren, H. (2019). Trends and caveats: Review of literature on global citizenship education in teacher training. *Teaching and Teacher Education, 77*(1), 77–89. doi:10.1016/j.tate.2018.09.014

Yin, R. K. (2018). *Case study research: Design and methods* (6th ed.). Sage.

Zhao, Y., Meyers, L., & Meyers, B. (2009). Cross-cultural immersion in China: Preparing pre-service elementary teachers to work with diverse student populations in the United States. *Asia-Pacific Journal of Teacher Education, 37*(3), 295–317. doi:10.1080/13598660903058925

Zong, G. (2009). Developing preservice teachers' global understanding through computer-mediated communication technology. *Teaching and Teacher Education, 25*(5), 617–625. doi:10.1016/j.tate.2008.09.016

ADDITIONAL READING

Chappel, J. (2019). *Engendering cosmopolitanism through the local: Engaging students in international literature through connections to personal experience and culture*. Peter Lang. doi:10.3726/b14960

Myers, J. P. (Ed.). (2020). *Research on teaching global issues: Pedagogy for global citizenship Education*. Information Age Publishing.

Reimers, F. M. (2020). *Educating students to improve the world*. Springer. doi:10.1007/978-981-15-3887-2

Spring, J. (2008). Research on globalization and education. *Review of Educational Research, 78*(2), 330–363. doi:10.3102/0034654308317846

Tiven, M. B., Fuchs, E. R., Bazari, A., & MacQuarrie, A. (2018). *Evaluating global digital education: Student outcomes framework*. Bloomberg Philanthropies and the Organisation for Economic Cooperation and Development.

KEY TERMS AND DEFINITIONS

Action Research: A disciplined investigation process conducted by and for those taking the action. Assisting the "actors" in improving and refining their actions is the main reason for conducting an action research.

Digital Literacy: The capacity to locate, read, create, and communicate texts in online and digital environments.

Global Competence: The knowledge, skills, and attitudinal and ethical dispositions needed to understand, interact, and problem-solve globally.

Global Learning: Through strategic institutional partnerships and innovative academic, experiential, and co-curricular programming expressed in diverse and challenging global contexts, students learn to think critically, observe skillfully, reflect thoughtfully, and participate meaningfully.

Global Readiness: Possessing the digital and global literacies necessary for career, community, and civic life in our digitized, globalized world.

Globally Competent Learning Continuum: A rubric of 12 dimensions of global competence as related to teaching and learning.

Globally Competent Teaching: Being globally competent oneself and fostering students' development of global competence.

Teaching for Global Readiness Scale: A 21 item self-reflection survey on teaching practices that can promote students' global readiness.

TPACK: The technological, pedagogical, and content knowledge needed to be an effective teacher.

Chapter 13
Teaching Action Research to International Educators:
Transitioning Professional Development Online

Ruhi Khan
Arizona State University, USA

Alejandra Enriquez Gates
Arizona State University, USA

Rebecca Grijalva
Arizona State University, USA

Ann Nielsen
Arizona State University, USA

ABSTRACT

This chapter examines how a team of university experts within the field of education adjusted the focus of a professional development (PD) model to teach action research to 60 international educators. Three key educational elements were used to create the PD model: 1) transformational learning theory, 2) language acquisition and learning methodologies, and 3) a personalized system of instruction (PSI). When the unexpected worldwide pandemic caused a shift to remote learning, the team was tasked with adjusting the original face-to-face model. Evidence from meeting agendas, action plan tracking spreadsheets, and personal communication were analyzed as the program moved to an online learning environment. Based on this data, the team recognized that the theoretical principles and conceptual framework did not change but were refocused and emphasized a more human-centered approach. Future research should explore continued long-term professional development after action research has been implemented to support reflective practice and inquiry.

DOI: 10.4018/978-1-7998-6922-1.ch013

INTRODUCTION

Action research has frequently been used as a means to make change in education. This type of research provides educators with the opportunity to learn, reflect and find solutions to educational challenges. In 2019, the Arizona State University (ASU) Building Leadership for Change (BLC) team designed a professional development (PD) model to train 60 international educators from the Kingdom of Saudi Arabia (KSA) in leadership development and pedagogy using action research as a strategy to promote change.

The importance of having a professional development model is to help support educators to critique, improve and implement a new idea or strategy and customize their learning to their own context (Burns, 2011). Action research for educators is a process of inquiry that focuses on teaching and learning to explore a topic, involves data collection and analysis followed by implementing change (Mertler, 2014). The emphasis of using a model for professional development in this chapter provides insight into how to train educators in establishing the foundation for using action research while enhancing professional practice.

In July 2019, a group of educators traveled to the United States to participate in a yearlong program that consisted of 1500 hours of academic engagement. The main goal of the program was for the international educators to transfer the knowledge and skills gained from training and K-12 school experiences in the United States into an action research plan. Created around educational challenges in Saudi Arabia, the action research plan served as a capstone project to advocate for change. The BLC team responsible for creating and delivering the PD model consisted of experts within the fields of K-12 education and English language instruction who collectively have extensive experience in educational coaching and mentoring at national and international levels. The PD model was designed using the Whole Teacher approach (Chen & McCray, 2012), which emphasizes qualities essential to educator practice. Additional considerations for the needs of the educators and delivery methods were strengthened by a conceptual framework grounded in (a) transformational learning theory, (b) language acquisition and learning methodologies, and (c) a personalized system of instruction (PSI). These components and elements were believed to offer the international educators with the greatest opportunities to grow professionally.

In March 2020, the impact of the COVID-19 pandemic accelerated transitions to online learning for adults and children. In the case of higher education institutions, the pandemic prompted the "forced adoption of technology driven instruction" (Lederman, 2020, para. 1). Knowing that online education has been at the forefront of instructional design in supporting the overall needs of 21st century learners all around the world, the BLC team explored: *What adjustments need to be made to transition a face-to-face professional development training into an online setting?* Shifts in program implementation involved drawing upon the successes of the face-to-face professional development model prior to the pandemic and reinforcing the strategies for adult learners within more individualized online settings. This heightened reflection of strategic change and adaptation of the existing model reaffirmed the strength of the conceptual framework, the needs of the educators, and the delivery methods as the driving forces behind the online PD model. When planning in the future, educators should consider the fundamental principles behind meaningful professional development, and how those principles are not abandoned but refocused to meet the needs in an online learning environment.

This chapter will outline how the university team at ASU adjusted the focus of the face-to-face PD model to teach action research into an online environment to support and address the needs of the international educators. Detailed information about the components and elements of the PD model, including its design and implementation, will be summarized and discussed. Practical recommendations will illustrate how refocusing the elements of the face-to-face PD model for an online environment resulted in educators exceeding program expectations. Furthermore, the chapter focuses on using professional development as a conduit to support the educators in developing action research plans. Evidence from meeting agendas, action plan tracking spreadsheets, and personal communication were analyzed to substantiate claims made about the success of the PD model, as the program moved to an online learning environment during the pandemic.

BACKGROUND

Professional Development Model

Professional development is a means to strengthen educator proficiency in teaching and learning (Desimone, 2009; Wei et al., 2010). Research suggests that effective PD advances knowledge, introduces new concepts, nurtures educator efficacy, and fosters continued growth (Desimone, 2009). High quality PD moves away from the traditional method of addressing what professionals should be taught toward advocating for professional practices (Chen & McCray, 2012) that produce change in education. Following the review of research into effective PD and determining the needs of the educators, the BLC team identified theories, methodologies, and approaches as the framework to design the model. The remainder of this section will outline how the face-to-face PD model was created.

The Whole Teacher Approach

The Whole Teacher approach (Chen & McCray, 2012) was used to develop the PD model. The premise of this approach acknowledges four qualities of PD as the underlying standards that strengthen educator professional practice. These qualities reinforce that PD should be multidimensional, integrated, developmental and contextualized (Chen & McCray, 2012). The multidimensional quality provides educators with the opportunity to access learning in several ways. As outlined by Chen and McCray (2012), "Addressing multiple learning pathways allows PD to build on teachers' motivations and respond to their needs rather than requiring that all teachers follow the same course of learning" (p. 20). In addition, the integrated quality of the Whole Teacher approach moves beyond traditional PD by supporting instructional knowledge of content, while simultaneously building confidence and motivating the implementation of new learning leading to advanced professional practice (Chen & McCray, 2012). Furthermore, the developmental quality of this approach emphasizes the recognition of individual differences, which are accommodated by coaching to meet the developmental needs of each teacher and their distinctive pathway to grow and learn. Lastly, contextualized PD is important so that educators can recognize applications to their specific teaching and learning environments.

The BLC team explored how the qualities of the Whole Teacher approach could be used to create the PD model that addressed the specific needs of the international educators while meeting the objectives of planning and designing their action research plans. Using the Whole Teacher approach outlined above as a blueprint, the PD model designed to teach action research emphasized three components: the conceptual framework, the needs of the educators, and the delivery, as essential to guiding the international educators. Figure 1 provides a graphic representation of the BLC team's model of professional development for action research. These components were critical for the international educators to learn, reflect and find solutions to educational challenges while simultaneously addressing language acquisition, individual learning, and planning needs.

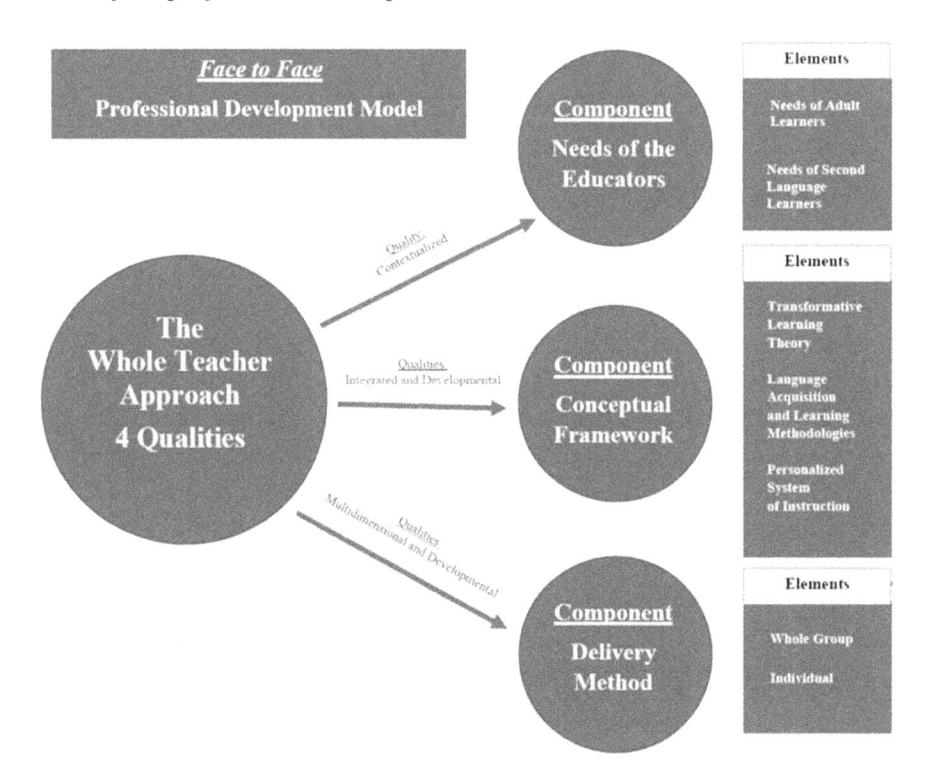

Figure 1. Face-to-face professional development model in action research

The conceptual framework was founded on the elements of: (a) transformative learning theory (b) language acquisition and learning methodologies, and (c) personalized system of instruction (PSI). By designing the conceptual framework using these three elements, the integrated and developmental qualities of the Whole Teacher approach would be addressed. The visiting educators would be able to learn content while developing their English language skills to transform their professional practice using action research. The developmental quality was emphasized through intentional implementation of the elements by the team as they would be supporting the educators in developing and experiencing the transformation of their practice at their own rate.

When considering the delivery method as a component of the PD model, the BLC team combined the multidimensional and developmental qualities of the Whole Teacher approach. Multiple access points to the content would be provided through whole group instruction and individualized support, including coaching sessions. Recognizing individual differences solidified the importance of the developmental quality of this approach and would guide the international educators as they set their action research goals.

The BLC team was purposeful in designing the PD model so that the qualities of the Whole Teacher approach were interconnected within some of the components. The elements of the conceptual framework were carefully selected to ensure that each international educator would engage in high quality

PD that would produce change in education. The needs of the educators, the elements of the conceptual framework, and the delivery method will be discussed in more detail to demonstrate how the PD model successfully guided the international educators in creating their action research plans.

The Elements of the Conceptual Framework Component

Transformative Learning Theory

Embedding transformative learning theory would provide a rationale for how PD can evoke change in perspectives or frame of reference (King, 2009), also defined as points of view, behavior and action. This theory would challenge the educators to think critically about their philosophy and worldview with respect to their professional practice (Taylor & Cranton, 2012). Examining previous assumptions and developing new understandings would equip the educators with diverse perspectives. If acted upon, these new understandings would lead to transformative learning. In the context of the PD model (Figure 1), this would involve developing an action research plan based on acquiring new knowledge and making changes to professional practice. According to Timperly (2011), transformation does not occur if new professional learning is believed to be an existing part of the educators' perspectives and frame of reference. This emphasizes that change is not only occurring while acquiring knowledge but necessitates action based on the new knowledge learned.

Transformative learning theory explains the process through which an adult learner changes the way they think, feel and act based on the transformation of the learner's frame of reference. It is purposeful to guide critical reflection so that learners make meaning of an experience as part of the learning process (Mezirow 1997). The theory provides adult learners with the critical steps and reasoning needed to shift their understanding or assumptions to manage new information (King, 2005; Mezirow & Rose, 1978). Glisczinski (2007) revised Mezirow's original 10 stages into four quadrants: disorienting dilemma, critical reflection, rational dialogue, and action. These quadrants are considered "the foundation components of transformative learning" (Glisczinski, 2007, p. 320). Figure 2 provides an overview of the transformative learning process of an adult learner.

Adult learners need to understand and make sense of experiences, build on previous knowledge, reflect critically on assumptions, and engage in rational reasoning to validate meaning of new learning (Glisczinski, 2007). Glisczinski's (2007) model identifies the first quadrant as a disorienting dilemma. This quadrant is considered the catalyst for a transformative learning process; it is an "ah-ha" moment, a disconnect between the frame of reference and the disorienting encounter. The experience might be a positive or negative one that would challenge their worldview. The international educators would participate in a number of experiences planned by the BLC team that might not be in harmony with their culture and established educational schemes. This disconnect could be experienced during guided school visits and full day-school immersion experiences. Each "dilemma" could help the educators define problems of practice and identify questions that would inform their action research plans.

Transformative learning theory inspires educators to critically reflect and improve their teaching (Taylor & Cranton, 2012). The second quadrant in transformative learning involves critical reflection and is considered a key element in the transformative learning process. During this phase, learners question themselves, their roles, their actions, and their feelings. Cranton and King (2003) discuss how critical reflection occurs in PD when educators are aware of their frame of reference and confront their personal beliefs about teaching and learning. Through this process, educators become receptive to new strategies and approaches.

Figure 2. Quadrants of transformative learning (Adapted from © 2007, Glisczinski. Used with permission).

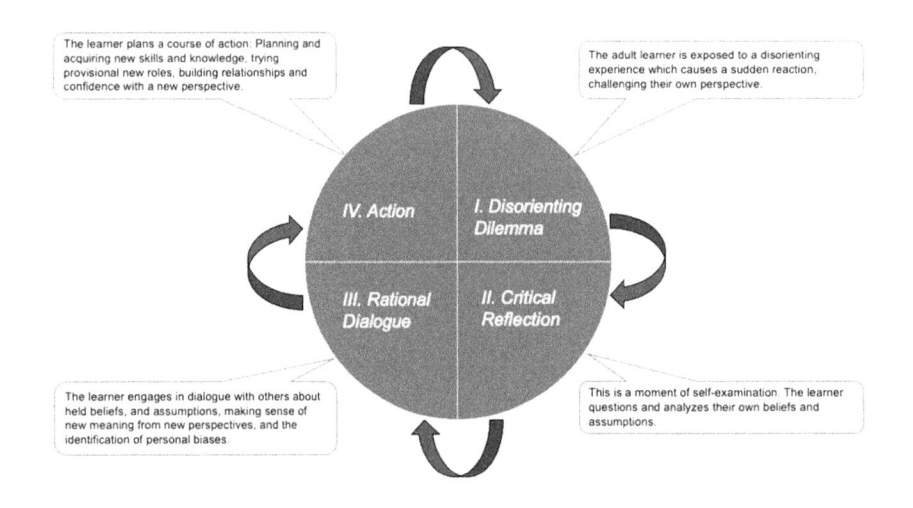

The process of transformation in the third quadrant is known as rational dialogue. During the rational dialogue phase, learners externalize their thoughts by engaging in discussion of discontent through critical reflection and the discovery of new information which supports the development of a new perspective. It is during the rational dialogue phase that learners visualize their own selves in different roles and with different worldviews. Visits to school immersion sites, discussions with district mentors, school administrators, and the BLC team would provide opportunities for the visiting educators to build meaning and understanding of new learning. Through discussion and dialogue about these experiences, the international educators would have opportunities to develop a deeper understanding and consider additional points of view. Hirsh (2012) affirmed the need for PD to incorporate rational dialogue as the next steps for instituting change into action.

Action is the last quadrant of Mezirow's (1990) theory and focuses on change, planning next steps, and acquiring new knowledge for the implementation of the plan. During this time, the learner discovers, and experiments with new roles while building confidence. The learner considers how to integrate the new perspective and schemes into one's own life under new conditions. For the international educators, this would mean transitioning from engaging in rational dialogue with their mentors to creating a plan of action. This would provide educators with the motivation to move from their previous mindsets and implement change (Mezirow, 1990).

Transformative learning theory acknowledges that an individual critiques their original frame of reference when new learning takes place (Gravett, 2004). The PD model embedded transformative learning theory as a means to examine educators' assumptions and expectations to build an awareness of how their context affects teaching and learning. Engaging in critical reflection and discussion could help the international educators increase awareness of their beliefs and consider alternative approaches to professional practices. This awareness would be part of the 'disorienting dilemma' that led to a realization that a previous approach to teaching or learning required change.

Language Acquisition and Learning Methodologies Component

Language is used to teach culture and convey the message of economic, social, and cultural norms. Language acquisition and language learning methodologies are deeply linked to culture, as culture is embedded in context (Nieto, 2009). With this in mind, the BLC team designed the PD model using English language vocabulary and acquisition practices to prepare international educators to learn about the U.S. education system, school policies, and practices. It would also be through these language experiences that the educators would learn about cultural values, attitudes, and behavior expectations (Slapac, Kim & Coppersmith, 2019; Negrea, 2013).

The language acquisition process requires meaningful interaction in the selected language, where the learner is focused on the message that is being conveyed and the understanding, instead of the form (grammar), the rules, or error correction of the message. English language instructors would plan and provide highly interactive learning environments for second language adult learners (Kim & Slapac, 2015). Classes would be designed for discovering learning through thematic experiences to simulate social settings for a natural language acquisition experience (Krashen, 1981).

The design of the program based on the grant from the Ministry of Education in KSA required English language learners to be fully immersed in a sheltered English environment. According to Freeman and Freeman (1988), Sheltered English Immersion is an instructional approach to make academic content comprehensible for English language learners and frequently used when all students in the classroom are non-native English speakers. Instructors used multiple strategies to promote language: repetitions and pauses during speech, comprehension checks in between interactive lectures, the integration of visuals, props and body language, thinking maps, and cooperative learning strategies. For example, when presenting information about action research, the English instructors would ensure that they repeated concepts and used formative and summative assessments. Additionally, when generating ideas about action research topics with the international educators, the English instructors could incorporate the circle map to brainstorm ideas. The circle map, also known as the "defining in context map" is commonly used as a strategy to support English language learners. It helps define a word based on prior knowledge or in context, the learner can write any information that comes to mind: keywords, phrases, or illustrations (Sigueza, 2020).

The use of the primary language for instruction is also a component of this approach (Freeman & Freeman, 1988). Although the instructors did not speak the primary language of Arabic, they would encourage the educators to use translation apps or check for understanding with colleagues. Instructors use metacognitive strategies, cognitive, and social/affective strategies to promote language acquisition (Collier, 1995). Similarly, the BLC team planned model think alouds to demonstrate how to complete each section of the action research plan. The educators were then able to internalize the process of completing these sections.

Exposure to language and culture plays a noticeable role when learning a new language (Nieto, 2009). During school immersion, the international educators improved their language learning skills while preparing to deliver an action research plan for future implementation. Experiencing the dynamics of the U.S. school culture would also strengthen their action research plans. Throughout this type of experience possible changes in an individual's identity could lead to perspective transformation (Kim &

Slapac, 2015; King, 2009). Using this information, the BLC team and English instructors continuously revised the opportunities for educator exposure to educational and social experiences to support their language acquisition and cultural understanding (Slapac, Kim & Coppersmith, 2019).

Personalized System of Instruction Component

In conjunction with transformative learning theory and the language acquisition and language learning methodologies, the BLC team took into consideration how to individualize educator achievement in developing the action research component of this international program. Keller (1968) highlighted the importance of mastering sequenced course material with specific objectives, using proctors, self-pacing, immediate feedback, credit for success and lectures for motivation. Personalized system of instruction (PSI) has been shown to be more successful than using a conventional lecture approach to enhance student learning experiences (Kulik et al., 1990). According to Svenningsen and Pear (2011), PSI demonstrated a significant impact on student achievement when performance was measured on essay exams. In this study, learners received less lecture-based instructional time and found their learning to be more enjoyable than traditional teaching methods (Svenningsen and Pear, 2011). Comments from the international educators were used to demonstrate evidence of this trend:

"My message to all of Arizona State University's teachers and instructors, you are the reason for my success" (Personal Communication, June 25, 2020).

"I learned a lot from you and benefited a lot from the topics you chose for us and the method of discussion that you used" (Personal Communication, June 29, 2020).

"Thank you for everything. I'll always remember you with deepest respect and affection for your efforts in making each workshop enjoyable and educational" (Personal Communication, July 10, 2020).

As part of PSI, mastery learning is divided into smaller segments followed by an assessment component (Dempsey, 2007). For example, when learners were unable to reach mastery, they reviewed the material and retook the assessment until they were able to achieve the level of mastery outlined by the instructor. In this model, there was no penalty for the number of attempts. The intention of not providing consequences for unsuccessful attempts emphasized a focus on mastery learning. Furthermore, mentors provided individualized feedback and tutoring to support program objectives. Another essential component of PSI is self-pacing so that learners spend less time on material they understand and additional time on areas that seem more challenging. As the educators engaged with the course material, the instructor served as a facilitator to clarify material and motivate learners.

Technology has fundamentally changed the nature of PSI and has increased the flexibility of teaching and learning based on its essential principles (Dempsey, 2007). With the use of technology, asynchronous and synchronous chats, discussion board postings and virtual meetings, the role of the mentor and instructor have transformed (Ross & McBean, 1995). The BLC team took into consideration the opportunity for faculty mentors to communicate with the international educators using Zoom when face-to-face interaction was not feasible. Content was also delivered using Google docs, slides etc. so that they could be archived and referenced later. Instruction with the use of technology fosters written communications, which can lead to greater opportunities for reflection and problem solving (Garrison & Kanuka, 2004). Pear and Kinsner (1988) discuss how using technology in a PSI model provides immediate feedback and supports virtual participation. With the use of live Google docs, faculty mentors could provide feedback to help support developing and writing the action research plan. More recently, Pedreira and Pear (2015) explored the effectiveness of a computer-aided personalized system of instruction (CAPSI) on motivation and overall performance. The findings indicated that CAPSI demonstrated higher motivation levels than those who did not learn using this type of instruction. It was concluded that because motivation is a predictor of performance that CAPSI has the potential to increase achievement (Pedreira & Pear, 2015). For this reason, technology resources were included in the PD model prior to transitioning the program online to ensure that the international educators would be engaged in more personalized learning that helped meet their individual needs.

Planning and Designing the Professional Development Model

University Team

The BLC team consisted of university faculty and staff with global expertise who served as mentors for the international educators. This team assisted in providing a contextualized understanding of the U.S. education system and coached the visiting educators in the design and creation of their action research plans. In addition, the BLC team initially immersed the international educators in a face-to-face professional development model based on a conceptual framework to deepen the educators' understanding of how to implement and manage change through action research by examining their own educational practices.

In order to support the international educators, the PD model highlighted theories and practices that met the needs of adult learners and second language learners. Members of the BLC team at ASU collaborated and used their expertise to strategically build the capacity of the individual educators. Originally, participants would be placed into whole group settings so that they received the same message about the expectation of the action research plan. After delivering this initial instruction to heterogeneous groups, the BLC team would meet to identify the needs of the educators to tailor individual instruction. This personalized approach involves taking into consideration how adult learners have distinct experiences that enhance their learning of new knowledge, which can reinforce and build relationships. Based on the transformative theory, adult learners need to understand and make sense of experiences, build on previous knowledge, reflect critically, and engage in rational dialogue to make meaning of new learning (Glisczinski, 2007).

Profile of International Educators

The international educators who were selected to participate in the grant were provided scholarships to attend the program at ASU and were also provided with additional living wage stipends to pay for teach family's cost of living. The program was based on a grant from the Ministry of Education in KSA and consisted of academic engagement delivered through five phases with a final sixth phase implemented upon completion of the program in Saudi Arabia. Upon arrival in the U.S., the international educators received an orientation to educational institutions, English language training, cultural awareness sessions, and technical knowledge and skills development workshops. In addition, guided K-12 school visits and full day-school immersion experiences with specific school placements were provided with the support of district mentors. Each phase of the program was a requirement of the grant. The main goal of this partnership was for the international educators to transfer the skills and knowledge gained from field experiences in the United States into action research plans that would be implemented upon return to their home country.

Since this was ASU's second cohort, the BLC team had previous experience working with educators from Saudi Arabia that traveled with their families. This informed many of the decisions made in regards to the program. For example, scheduling breaks to honor prayer times, modified schedules for the month of Ramadan, and considerations for aligning the program calendar with local school districts to accommodate those who had children attending local schools. The BLC team also enlisted guidance from faculty who have worked with educators from the Middle East & North Africa (MENA) region.

Table 1 displays the demographic data of the international educators who participated in the partnership program. The 60 visiting educators included content teachers, special education teachers, counselors and school administrators in K-12 Saudi Arabian schools. The educators had a minimum of a bachelor's degree and five years of educational experience. Table 1 illustrates that a relatively equal number of males and females were represented in the group. The table also displays comparisons between the numbers of educators who were administrators versus those who were teachers and shows the highest level of education reached by each of the individuals prior to coming to the U.S. The international educators' ages ranged from 24 to 40 years with the youngest female at 25 years old and the youngest male at 24 years old. It should be noted that 46% of the educators were between the ages of 36-40, 42% were in the age group 31-35, while only 12% were between the ages of 23-30. There was not a minimum age requirement to join the program but five years of teaching was required. Over 72% of the group identified as teachers, 23% identified as administrators, and 5% of the group identified as "other" which included supervisors and school counselors. A total of 5% of the male administrators and 7% of the female administrators identified themselves as working in the secondary level. In Saudi Arabia, teachers and administrators do not work in schools of the opposite gender, with the exception of mixed gender classrooms in grades K-3 headed by female teachers and administrators. Based on the data, 89% of educators earned a bachelor's degree prior to arriving in the U.S., and 11% had a graduate degree. Position and level of education refer to corresponding roles as teacher, principal or other (supervisors and counselors) and whether the educators are employed in elementary, middle or secondary schools.

When planning and designing the PD model for action research, the BLC team took into consideration the demographic characteristics of the Saudi educators to best determine their needs. For example, based on segregated schooling after third grade, some educators explored gender specific topics for their action research plans. Taking into account years of experience, additional support was provided for early and mid-career educators. In addition, categorizations of roles (i.e. teacher, administrator, or other) were also considered, so action research topics could be aligned and relevant to their professional practice. By using the data based on the educators' respective professional settings in Saudi Arabia, PD was contextualized to meet their specific learning needs.

Teaching Action Research to International Educators

Table 1. Demographic characteristics of international educators

Group Characteristics	International Educators	
	N	%
Gender Totals	60	100
Female	28	47
Male	32	53
Ages		
Female Ages 23-30	1	2
Male Ages 23-30	6	10
Female Ages 31-35	10	17
Male Ages 31-35	15	25
Female Ages 36-40	17	28
Male Ages 36-40	11	18
Position and Level of Work		
Male Admin. Total	4	6
Elementary	0	0
Middle	1	1
Secondary	3	5
Female Admin. Total	10	17
Elementary	4	7
Middle	2	3
Secondary	4	7
Male Teachers Total	25	42
Elementary	9	15
Middle	6	10
Secondary	10	17
Male Other Total	3	5
Middle/Secondary	3	5
Female Teachers Total	18	30
Elementary	6	10
Middle	2	3
Secondary	10	17
Highest Educational Attainment		
Bachelor's Degree/Male Admin.	4	6
Bachelor's Degree/Female Admin.	9	15
Master's Degree/Male Admin.	0	0
Master's Degree/Female Admin.	1	2
Bachelor's Degree/Male Teachers	25	42
Bachelor's Degree/Female Teachers	14	23
Master's Degree/Male Teachers	0	0
Master's Degree/Female Teachers	4	7
Bachelor's Degree/Other	2	3
Master's Degree/Other	1	2

Note. $N = 60$

ISSUES, CONTROVERSIES, PROBLEMS

Key Transitions from Face-to-Face to Online Learning Environment

In March 2020, with the threat of the Covid-19 virus spreading, ASU pivoted from face-to-face instruction to a fully online setting. This immediate transition was a result of recommendations from health officials to limit in-person interactions and adhere to guidelines preventing the transmission of the virus. Additionally, the face-to-face K-12 school immersion experiences were suspended for the majority of the educators with the exception of a few who continued to interact with their district mentors online. The international educators were able to transition, at their own pace based on their previous knowledge and cultural experiences. As the educators adapted to new ways of living during the pandemic and immersed themselves in unfamiliar professional and personal lives, they challenged preconceived assumptions and perspectives in educational paradigms, gender roles, and mindsets. In order to explore the question: *What adjustments need to be made to transition a face-to-face professional development training into an online setting*? Data collected for this study was drawn from a variety of informal resources that faculty used to support teaching activities (Jirojwong & Wallin, 2002). This type of informal data such as personal communication was readily available and provided the information to meet research needs (Katz, 1992). Personal communications, meeting agendas, action plan tracking spreadsheets, TOEFL test scores were among the various resources that were analyzed. Axial coding allowed the BLC team to make connections between the various data sources to strategically examine the shift in the focus of professional development as it related to the participant's experiences (Corbin & Strauss, 2008).

Critical to transitioning to an online setting, the BLC team evaluated different options for how the PD model could evolve yet continue with the same rigor as pre-pandemic settings. The team explored challenges, and a proactive approach was taken to address potential obstacles that may be encountered. As summarized by the Organization for Economic Co-operation and Development (OECD, 2020), it is important to ensure that adults benefit from online learning experiences despite challenges. In a report titled, *The potential of online learning for adults: Early lessons from the COVID-19 crisis*, the OECD (2020) outlines the following challenges:

- developing basic digital skills
- motivating online learners
- training teachers to deliver online courses.

In an effort to address these challenges, the visiting educators were provided with Zoom and Google training in order to be equipped with tools necessary to navigate the online environment. This training helped to motivate learners in an area with which they may have been inexperienced. Also, providing flexibility of deadlines and schedules, and moving to asynchronous learning increased motivation and aligned with PSI's focus toward mastery learning (Dempsey, 2007). Assumptions about access to learning devices and digital pedagogy as a solution to online learning do not take into consideration the anxiety that transpires after the challenges of a pandemic (Adam, 2020). Because of the context learners are in, it is important to focus on emotional support and be aware of their situations by providing regular check-ins to help alleviate anxiety and provide social-emotional support to create a sense of stability and community. The flexibility of the online learning experience helped to address challenges such as sharing technology devices with children who were also home during school closures. Furthermore, wellness checks and social-emotional support were provided which contributed to increased motivation and participation. This included story time sessions using Zoom to engage with the international educators' children, physical activity workouts, chat sessions, and an additional layer of check-ins with the faculty mentor. With respect to technology training to deliver online courses, English instructors were invited to Google training sessions and were given access to Zoom training. This helped the instructors ensure they had the tools for a smooth transition to meet the needs of the educators in the online space.

The convenience of online PD provided access anytime and from anywhere (King & Dunham, 2009). The BLC team explored how the "forced adoption of technology driven instruction" (Lederman, 2020, para. 1) as a result of the COVID-19 could meet the demands of the PD model in action research. Lawler and King (2000) reinforced the importance for adult learners when participating in online PD to be provided with opportunities to build on prior experiences, apply new learning, and encourage active participation. The validation of adult experiences and importance of learning for applications embedded within online learning was essential (Lawler & King, 2000). Based on a study conducted with 324 educators in focus groups, King and Dunham (2009) recommended that online PD should have clear expectations, support technology skills, and recognize varying levels of motivation. This research affirmed that the face-to-face model would easily transition to an online model as clear expectations and the recognition of motivation were already in place within the conceptual framework.

SOLUTIONS AND RECOMMENDATIONS

Adjusting the Focus of the Professional Development Model

Although the initial discussion began with a focus on digital learning tools and platforms, the BLC team realized that the transition to online learning continued to lead them back to their original conceptual framework, the needs of the educators, and the delivery method that was designed for face-to-face interactions. The team aligned strategic and intentional online adjustments to the PD model originally designed for face-to-face adaptation. In maintaining the Whole Teacher approach, the BLC team adjusted the professional development model to focus on PSI, the needs of adult learners and individualized instruction and support. Figure 3 provides a revised overview of the professional development model when it transitioned to online. With continued collaboration and revisiting of the PD model, it was ensured that the international educators could complete the action research requirements of the program in an online environment.

Supporting participants beyond sharing technological tools was essential to address challenges faced when moving to online instruction during the pandemic (Bozkurt & Sharma, 2020). By focusing on learning context and the needs of the participants, it was recommended that the BLC team didn't rely on "purely technology-centered solutions" (Bozkurt & Sharma, 2020, p. ii). It was noted that in challenging times characterized by trauma and stress that collaboration and support should be emphasized. Noddings (2002) discusses that all humans need basic care. By creating an environment of empathy and elevating emotional support, the BLC team focused on the learner and learner engagement (Bozkurt & Sharma, 2020).

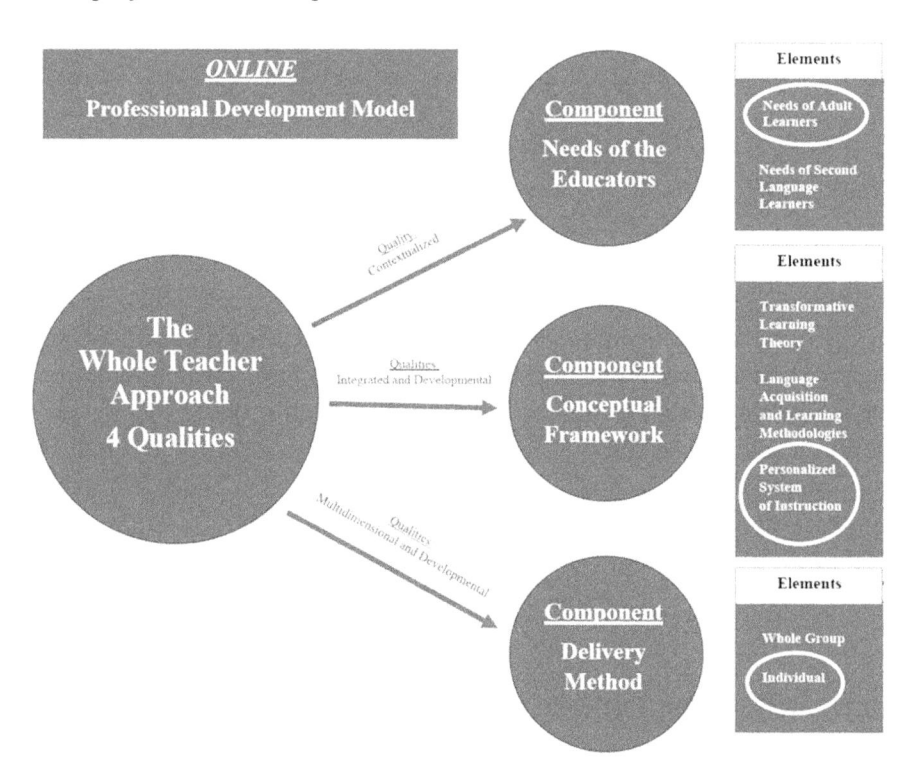

Figure 3. Online professional development model in action research

Figure 4. Interventions during the on-line instruction

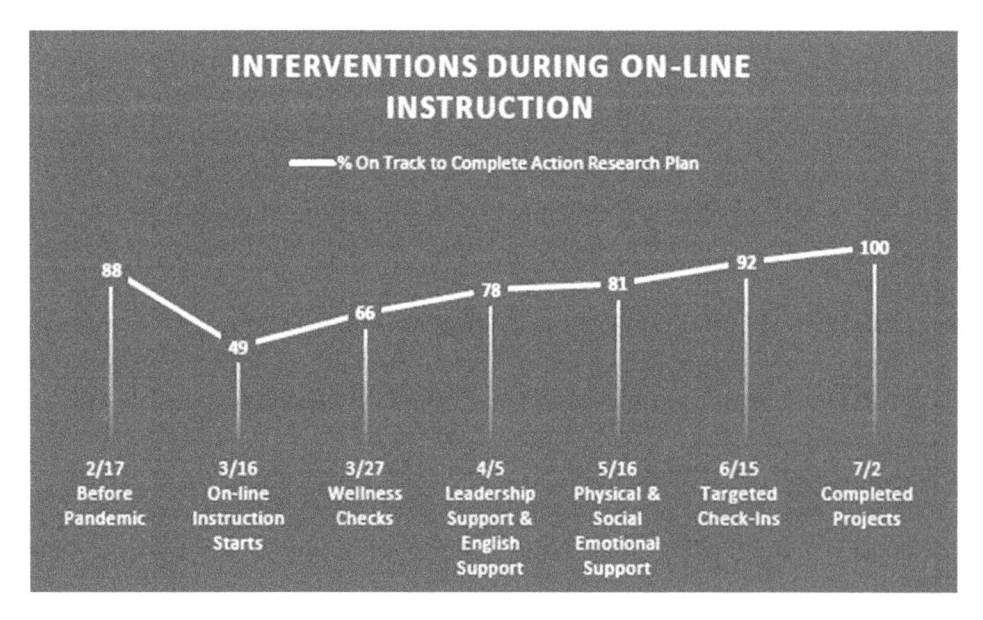

Teaching Action Research to International Educators

The chart below outlines the trajectory of the participants on track to complete the action research plan before the pandemic and their progression during the pandemic when online instruction began. Before online instruction officially started, many of the participants were faced with concerns about their children's school closing down, being exposed to COVID-19, the possibilities of returning to Saudi Arabia and completing the program, the trauma of being away from home when faced with the pandemic and stress about their family back home to name a few. Their attention to complete their action research plans had been diverted to focus on how they would navigate their lives through the pandemic. The BLC team worked together to provide interventions to help the participants complete their action research plans. Figure 4 summarizes the progression of interventions. The BLC team implemented and the data gathered from meeting agendas and the completion spreadsheet.

Additional information about the international educators' struggles was captured in email communication from English instructors, the educators themselves, and faculty mentors. The personal communication highlighted in Table 2 outlines issues with technology, stress, requests for extensions, concerns about returning home, physical health, and having children at home:

Table 2. Personal communications

English Instructor	It was a challenge with Zoom. We both had a lot of issues with Zoom, ... because of the bandwidth and having so many people on it (Personal Communication, March 25, 2020).
International Educators	Actually I don't know how I can write to you but I feel stress and tired. Because of many reasons. I never feel it in my life. So, I can't think and do any things. could you please extend the due date for the assignment ... (Personal Communication, April 10, 2020).
	I would like to start by presenting my deep apology for the late submission of tasks. ... if you look at my record before the spring break, you will see my commitment to the Khebrat program. However, my technology less experience pushed me back. I spent long time trying to understand the technology (Personal Communication, May 7, 2020).
	I hope to know the ... response regarding returning home and completing the study remotely. A grant for travel has arrived. Tickets to return on May 28, and I do not want to lose my research and work at the university due to travel (Personal Communication, May 15, 2020).
	I am afraid of any infection because the problems that I suffer from ... with the possibility of transmission (Personal Communication, May 20, 2020).
Faculty Mentors:	I received an email from ... requesting additional time to finish his assignments. I also Zoomed with ... yesterday and she had not started any of the assignments. She was super busy with the kids. (Personal Communication, April 1, 2020).

Baran and Alzoubi (2020) discuss the importance of a human-centered approach when transitioning to remote educator training during the COVID-19 pandemic. It is human-centered solutions that help address problems and issues that may arise during this transition. This approach promotes empathy (Luka, 2014) optimism, opportunities to grow from adversity and endure failure (Henriksen, et al., 2018; Razzouk & Shute, 2012). The BLC team mirrored this process to support the Saudi educators. Furthermore, it was emphasized that creating an online community was essential to learner success. The online learning community included individual check-ins and supports based on challenges faced by the learners (Baran & Alzoubi, 2020). Prioritizing students' needs, understanding context, determining their social and emotional well-being and access to resources are key components of a human-centered approach (Bozkurt & Sharma, 2020).

The importance of whole group, small group and individual interactions in conjunction with collaboration was fundamental to the success of the educators. The BLC team continued using these interactions while working online with the international educators to develop action research questions and design their action research plans. The individual meetings, which formally took place during a structured time in the original program schedule, became more flexible in the online environment. This allowed the educators to structure their interactions with their faculty mentors based on what they had accomplished in their action research plan. These one-to-one meetings with the educator provided targeted support in the areas of autonomous thinking and negotiating new meanings and perspectives as part of the transformative learning process (Mezirow, 1997). During the yearlong residency program, the individual educators experienced the transformative learning quadrants (Glisczinski, 2007) at their own pace and time. This aligned with the quality of developmental PD in the Whole Teacher approach to experience transformation at varying rates.

Once the English language training phase was completed in December 2019, the BLC team used English language assessment data to inform decisions made about the PD model for the visiting educators. The international educators were given a pre-test in August and a post-test in December in the areas of listening, structured written expression, and reading. The TOEFL ITP was used to measure (TOEFL ITP Test Taker Handbook, 2016):

- Listening Comprehension: the ability to understand spoken English as it is used in colleges and universities.
- Structure and Written Expression: recognition of selected structural and grammatical points in standard written English.
- Reading Comprehension: the ability to read and understand academic reading material written in English.

With the support of the English language instructors at ASU, the BLC team was able to use the data from the TOEFL ITP to ensure that the language development needs were being addressed as PD for action research was delivered. This also helped to develop the PSI in the conceptual framework in an online environment.

Highlighting Three Elements

During the face-to-face experience, the university English language instructors integrated action research elements into language classes and the educators were grouped by language ability levels: reading/writing and listening/speaking. There was an emphasis on academic writing with integrated language development as well as a focus on communicative competence and grammar structures. Once COVID-19 mandated a transition to online education, the strategies for English language development shifted to individualized support focused on the production of language for the specific purpose of the action research design and writing process.

The decision to focus on the message educators were trying to convey vs. form, grammar and error correction was made during the process. Sheltered English language immersion continued to be embedded throughout this more individualized approach. Members of the BLC team collaborated to support the educators to meet their individual needs with a personalized approach that took into consideration adult learners' distinct experiences. Therefore, the BLC team focused on the specific learning needs of the educator and did not generalize English language learning instruction. Individual meetings offered the opportunity for the international educators to ask questions or request clarification for any grammar corrections and assistance in editing. The developmental quality of individual support helped ensure the Whole Teacher approach was implemented. In some cases, the educators would reflect on their mistakes as part of the language acquisition process (Krashen, 1981).

When designing and delivering the initial professional development for action research, the BLC team organized learning experiences that mimicked concepts presented in Keller's (1968) personalized system of instruction (PSI). This system of instruction was evident through presenting the action research in chunks so that the international educators could master the material at their own pace. As Pear and Kisner (1988) discuss, the PSI philosophy promotes active engagement and is highly flexible in terms of how material is presented. Professional developmental material was broken down into smaller sections sequentially with expectations outlined. Delivering instruction in this manner ensured that it was developmental in quality, to adhere to the Whole Teacher approach. Even though the intent was to use the fundamental principles of PSI, it was important to note that issues of procrastination and pacing were avoided by setting soft deadlines for the action research plan with a hard deadline to ensure work was completed. Pacing contingencies were put into place with a timeline that helped the visiting educators meet the action research plan requirements (Ross & McBean, 1995). Ross and McBean (1995) examined the efficacy of multiple deadlines against single deadlines for unit mastery, as deadlines are often needed in a time-limited course. Adding the soft deadlines option was inconsistent with the constraints of Keller's (1968) approach to self-pacing but was used to ensure that individual action research plan deliverables were met. A sample of the timeline is outlined in Table 3.

Table 3. Sample timeline to meet action research plan deadlines

Action Research Deliverables	Due Date
Final Topic Refinement	February 17
Literature Review	March 6
Discussion Conclusion	March 27
Plan of Action Outline	May 29
Formatting and Bibliography	June 1
Abstract	June 4
Introduction	June 8
Final Review	June 12
Final Approval	June 15

Soft deadlines and asynchronous instruction were cemented during the online transition to professional development. Providing this flexibility of the online learning experience, the visiting educators assumed greater responsibility for their academic work and were not required to sit through hours of synchronous sessions. They accessed and scheduled learning when available, taking into consideration their family's needs. This was particularly important in many cases since children were sharing technology with their parents, because of their school closures due to the pandemic.

Table 4. Shifts made as a result of online transition

Shifts	Focus	Action Taken
Technology considerations	Developing basic digital skills	• Provided Zoom and Google training
	Motivating online learners	• Implemented technology trainings • Conducted wellness check-in and social-emotional support
	Flexibility of deadlines	• Moved to asynchronous learning so educators could access it at their own time
	Training teachers to deliver online courses	• Extended technology training to English instructors
Programmatic adjustments	Strategic and intentional adjustments	• Combined PSI with transformative learning theory and second language development
	Sharing leadership and team collaboration	• Aligned action research expectations from face-to-face an online environment • Assigned additional supports (faculty mentor, English instructor, leadership team member) to all educators to finalize action research plan
	Structuring individual meetings	• Provided flexible time to work on necessary action research plan as needed • Targeted support in the areas of autonomous thinking and negotiating new meanings and perspectives as part of the transformative learning process
English language team collaboration	Addressing challenges	• Individualized support in how to write the action research paper including paraphrasing, citations and how to complete a literature review • Focusing on the message educators were trying to convey vs form, grammar and error correction

The online asynchronous learning materials were available in a variety of digital formats including videos, presentations, and interactive digital documents. The PowerPoint presentations included audio and could be watched several times to reinforce the information presented. The added audio helped support the English language development, so the international educators could meet the requirements for each section of the action research plan.

After each section was completed, it was sent to a faculty mentor for approval. In order to proceed to the next section, mastery was required. Once approval was received, new asynchronous learning material was sent to the international educator for the next section. Immediate feedback with an opportunity to edit and revise was provided by the mentors to guide the educators as they completed the various parts of the action research plan. Transitioning to an online environment reinforced individualized instruction. For the purposes of mastery learning and self-pacing, the international educators were provided with an outline to complete the various sections of the action research plan. Furthermore, the 1:5 ratio of support evolved into a 3:5 ratio, in which five educators were provided with three layers of direct support from their mentor, an English instructor and a leadership team member. This evolved as the leadership team and English instructors provided additional support (see Figure 3). This structure magnified the role of the faculty mentor in PSI so that adequate feedback and support could be provided. By adjusting the focus of the PD model, the international educators were able to continue developing their action research plans online.

Table 4 summarizes the shifts made as a result of the online transition. The emphasis of the PD model was transformed to a focus on PSI, adult learning needs and individual support as outlined in Table 5.

The online PD focused on integrating transformational learning theory and language acquisition into PSI. This was a result of transformation experiences and language learning that took place at a magnified level during personal interactions.

Overcoming Unexpected Challenges

Near the end of the yearlong program, the international educators were faced with difficult choices that would impact finishing the program. These included opportunities or requests to return to Saudi Arabia. Beginning in May of 2020, some of the educators began departing Arizona for health and safety concerns that stemmed from the pandemic and travel restrictions. Time differences and quarantine measures taken as a result of international travel concerned the BLC team because program expectations outlined that all submissions for the action research plans needed to occur by the final deadline. Table 5 demonstrates how despite these challenges, all of the international educators were able to receive final approval and successfully completed their action research plans before the end of the program on July 14, 2020.

Table 5. Action research plan submissions

Submitted Before Final Deadline	Submitted by Final Deadline	Submitted and Approved Before Program End Date
86%	92%	100%

The impact of completing the action research plan was noted in the international educators' comments. For example, "I have developed a growth mindset that allowed me to see possibilities and want to make changes. I truly believe that I am not the same person as I was before the experience started," and "I am excited to return to Saudi Arabia and improve my school and help teachers to develop into change agents to achieve our goals." These quotes highlight the intention of the Whole Teacher approach to the PD model, putting a spotlight on the transformation of learning into action. The feedback also reinforced the BLC team's goal to provide several opportunities for the international educators to embody the roles and responsibilities of being an educational leader, lead learner, researcher and change agent.

FUTURE RESEARCH DIRECTIONS

Action research empowers educators to improve their professional practice by planning for change through inquiry, asking questions and analyzing data focused on continuous improvement in a cyclical manner (Mertler, 2014). This chapter provided readers with recommendations and insights for implementing PD for action research that was originally created for face-to-face learning and then adjusted the focus for an online environment. The COVID-19 pandemic thrust the program into a challenging time that brought about social distancing while maintaining expectations for educators to advance their teaching and the quality of learning students experienced.

By nature, the partnership between ASU and the Ministry of Education in Saudi Arabia was established to focus on creating individual action research plans that would be implemented upon the educators' return home. The program did not extend beyond the educators' experience in the United States, resulting in an inability to evaluate the effectiveness of the action research implementation. The Ministry of Education in KSA outlined that implementation of the action research plan would occur back in their home country. Moving beyond PD as a short term to "a long-term process that includes regular opportunities and experiences planned systematically to promote growth and development in the profession" (Villegas-Reimers, 2003, p.12) is an important aspect of professional practice. Recognizing PD as a long-term process reinforces that educators do not learn intermittently but continuously reflect on prior knowledge and experiences (Cochran-Smith & Lytle, 2001; Dudzinski et al., 2000; Ganser, 2000). Future research should consider evaluating continued PD after the action research has been implemented to explore how ongoing support could help educators engage in a reflective cyclical practice that supports inquiry.

The concept of the educator as a reflective practitioner who obtains new knowledge and builds on prior knowledge over the course of their professional practice is a shift from traditional PD, setting a new precedent in teaching and learning (Cochran-Smith & Lytle, 2001). This promotes PD that moves beyond skill training and establishes a culture of continuous improvement. Follow-up and support are important variables in teacher success (Guskey, 1995) that open up the possibilities for reflection, application, and additional professional growth (King & Dunham, 2009). Villegas-Reimers (2003) recommends that PD is a long-term process that starts during initial educator preparation programs and continues until retirement so that educators can be supported in an ongoing manner to grow in the profession. Lifelong learning and practice support "a vision of learning that evaluates the past, looks at new possibilities and carefully develops approaches to teaching and learning" (King & Dunham, 2009, p. 136). As a result, PD moves beyond a short-term solution.

Obtaining data that informs the implementation of action research will solidify the connection between theory and practice and recognize the impact that research-based practices can have on teaching and learning. Multi-year programs that involve multiple phases of PD show formidable evidence that educator practice and student achievement can be improved and show significant growth (Borko & Putnam, 1995). It is for this reason, the authors of this chapter advocate for additional research in long-term PD that moves beyond the initial implementation of action research.

CONCLUSION

Action research is a process of inquiry that involves learning and reflection to address challenges in multiple educational settings around the world. With this in mind, the BLC team at ASU designed a PD model using the Whole Teacher approach (Chen & McCray, 2012) that engaged international educators for action research as an opportunity to monitor and evaluate change. This approach helped ensure the professional development embraced the qualities of the Whole Teacher approach that was multidimensional, integrated, developmental, and contextualized to strengthen educator professional practice. Using this approach as a guide, the PD model emphasized a conceptual framework that narrowed its focus toward the needs of the educators and the delivery model as essential components in the international educators' success.

By designing the conceptual framework to focus on transformative learning theory, language acquisition and learning methodologies and a personalized system of instruction, the visiting educators were able to understand action research content while developing their English language skills, transforming their professional practice and progressing at their own rate. Strategies appropriate for adult and second language learners ensured individual needs were being met in both whole group and individualized instruction. The BLC team used the conceptual framework to extend the international educators' understanding of action research as a means to implement and manage change by examining their own educational practices.

The unexpected interruption from delivering face-to-face professional development into an online format was the result of the COVID-19 pandemic. This phenomenon required the BLC team to strategically shift from working in a traditional face-to-face format to an online setting. In order to address this shift, the BLC team committed to ensuring the educators had adequate digital skills, computer equipment and internet access. During this time, considerations were also made for the international educators' children, who needed to complete their schooling online due to school closures.

Despite the transition to an online environment, the underlying components and elements of the online PD model remained the same as the original face-face model. The BLC team maintained the Whole Teacher approach and adjusted the professional development model to focus on the needs of adult learners through individualized instruction. By revisiting and adjusting the focus, the BLC team was still able to uphold the rigor and expectations of the face-to-face PD model through individualized and strategic programmatic adjustments. In emphasizing the human-centered approach in the PD model, the international educators were able to complete a comprehensive action research plan, ready to implement on or before the program deadline. Comments such as "I would like to say to the Educational Administration thank you very much ... we have learned a lot from you, whether in attendance or online education ... you were really great and professional (Personal Communication, July 9, 2020) and "I took a long time thinking about what I should write. All thanks words are not enough. We learned a lot from you, much more than you can imagine. I have gratitude for all people who supported us (Personal Communication, July 10, 2020) affirmed the impact on the international educators.

Educational support systems were key to ensuring that the international educators made sense of new concepts and designed their action research plans to promote change in education once they returned to their home country. For this reason, it was important to maintain the PD model that encompassed the conceptual framework, the needs of the visiting educators, and delivery methods. The adjustments of the components and elements of the PD model were based on the shifting needs of the educators. The authors suggest, however, that the original components and elements in the face-to-face PD model continue to be the driving force behind developing an action research plan.

The authors of this chapter leave you the parting words of one of the international educators at the final certificate ceremony:

"I thank you all for everything you did to me in the program and I had the honor to communicate with you and sit with all of you and very grateful for all you presented to me in this fruitful program that greatly developed me from what I was previously and I thank you for your good treatment and your wonderful style in helping me in all stages of the program (Personal Communication, July 11, 2020).

ACKNOWLEDGMENT

The Ministry of Education in Saudi Arabia and the Saudi Arabian Cultural Mission in Washington D.C. supported this research. We would also like to thank our local school district partners, English instructors from Global Launch and the Building Leadership for Change (BLC) team for their continued efforts in supporting the visiting educators from Saudi Arabia in developing their action research plans. A special thank you to Arizona State University and the Mary Lou Fulton Teachers College for supporting our international partnerships.

REFERENCES

Adam, T. (2020, April 22). The privilege of #pivotonline: A South African perspective. *Open Development & Education.* https://opendeved.net/2020/04/22/the-privilege-of-pivotonline/

Baran, E., & Alzoubi, D. (2020). Human-centered design as a frame for transition to remote teaching during the COVID-19 Pandemic. *Journal of Technology and Teacher Education, 28*(2), 365–372. https://eric.ed.gov/?id=EJ1257151

Borko, H., & Putnam, R. T. (1995). Expanding a teachers' knowledge base: A cognitive psychological perspective on professional development. In T. R. Guskey & M. Huberman (Eds.), *Professional development in education: New paradigms and practices* (pp. 35–66). Teachers College Press.

Bozkurt, A., & Sharma, R. C. (2020). Emergency remote teaching in a time of global crisis due to the Coronavirus pandemic. *Asian Journal of Distance Education, 15*(1), i–vi. doi:10.5281/zenodo.3778083

Chen, J., & McCray, J. (2012). A conceptual framework for teacher professional development: The whole teacher approach. *NHSA Dialog, 15*(1), 8–23. doi:10.1080/15240754.2011.636491

Cochran-Smith, M., & Lytle, S. L. (2001). Beyond certainty: taking an inquiry stance on practice. In A. Lieberman & L. Miller (Eds.), *Teachers caught in the action: Professional development that matters* (pp. 45–58). Teachers College Press.

Collier, V. P. (1995). *Promoting academic success for ESL students: Understanding second language acquisition for school.* New Jersey Teachers of English to Speakers of Other Languages.

Corbin, J., & Strauss, A. (2008). Basics of qualitative research (3rd ed.). Sage Publications.

Cranton, P., & King, K. P. (2003). Transformative learning as a professional development goal. *New Directions for Adult and Continuing Education, 98*(1), 31–37. doi:10.1002/ace.97

Dempsey, H. (2007). Keller's personalized system of instruction: Was it a fleeting fancy or is there a revival on the horizon? *The Behavior Analyst Today, 8*(3), 317–324. doi:10.1037/h0100623

Desimone, L. M. (2009). Improving impact studies of teachers' professional development: Toward better conceptualizations and measures. *Educational Researcher, 38*(3), 181–199. doi:10.3102/0013189X08331140

Dudzinski, M., Roszmann-Millican, M., & Shank, K. (2000). Continuing professional development for special educators: Reforms and implications for university programs. *Teacher Education and Special Education, 23*(2), 109–124. doi:10.1177/088840640002300205

Fernandez, M, Sturts, J., Duffy, L. N., Larson, L. R., Gray, J., & Powell, G.M (2019) Surviving and thriving in graduate school. *A Journal of Leisure Studies and Recreation Education, 34*(1), 3-15. doi:10.1080/1937156X.2019.1589791

Freeman, D., & Freeman, Y. (1988, September 30). *Sheltered English Instruction.* ERIC Digest. https://eric.ed.gov/?id=ED301070

Ganser, T. (2000). An ambitious vision of professional development for teachers. *NASSP Bulletin, 84*(618), 6–12. doi:10.1177/019263650008461802

Garrison, R., & Kanuka, H. (2004). Blended learning: Uncovering its transformative potential in higher education. *The Internet and Higher Education, 7*(2), 95–105. doi:10.1016/j.iheduc.2004.02.001

Glisczinski, D. J. (2007). Transformative higher education: A meaningful degree of understanding. *Journal of Transformative Education, 5*(4), 317–328. doi:10.1177/1541344607312838

Gravett, S. (2004). Action research and transformative learning in teaching development. *Educational Action Research, 12*(2), 259–272. doi:10.1080/09650790400200248

Guskey, T. R. (1995). Professional development in education: In search of the optimal mix. In T. R. Guskey & M. Huberman (Eds.), Professional development in education: New paradigms and practices (pp. 1–35). Teachers College Press.

Harbecke, D. (2012, October 8). *Following Mezirow: A roadmap through transformative learning.* RU Training @ Roosevelt University in Chicago. https://rutraining.org/2012/10/08/following-mezirow-a-roadmap-through-transformative-learning/?blogsub=pending

Henriksen, D., Gretter, S., & Richardson, C. (2018). Design thinking and the practicing teacher: Addressing problems of practice in teacher education. *Teaching Education, 1*(21), 209–229. doi:10.1080/10476210.2018.1531841

Hirsh, S. (2012). The Common-Core contradiction. *Education Week, 31*(19), 22–24.

Jirojwong, S., & Wallin, M. (2002). Use of formal and informal methods to gain information among faculty at an Australian regional university. *Journal of Academic Librarianship, 28*(1-2), 68–73. doi:10.1016/S0099-1333(01)00284-1

Johnson, B. (1993). *Teacher as researcher.* ERIC Clearinghouse on Teacher Education.

Katz, W. A. (1992). *The "invisible college," Introduction to reference work.* McGraw-Hill.

Keller, F. S. (1968). Good-bye teacher. *Journal of Applied Behavior Analysis, 1*(1), 79–89. doi:10.1901/jaba.1968.1-79 PMID:16795164

Kim, S., & Slapac, A. (2015). Culturally responsive, transformative pedagogy in the transnational era: Critical perspectives. *Educational Studies, 51*(1), 17–27. doi:10.1080/00131946.2014.983639

King, K. P. (2005). *Bringing transformative learning to life.* Krieger.

King, K. P. (Ed.). (2009). *The handbook of the evolving research of transformative learning: Based on the Learning Activities survey.* IAP.

King, K. P., & Dunham, M. D. (2009). Anytime? Anywhere? What needs face us in teaching professional educators online? In K. P. King (Ed.), *The handbook of the evolving research of transformative learning: Based on the Learning Activities survey* (pp. 133–135). IAP.

Krashen, S. D. (1981). *Second language acquisition and second language learning*. Pergamon Press.

Kulik, C.-L., Kulik, J. A., & Bangert-Drowns, R. L. (1990). Effectiveness of mastery learning programs: A meta-analysis. *Review of Educational Research, 60*(2), 265–299. doi:10.3102/00346543060002265

Lederman, D. (2000, March). The shift to remote learning: The human element. *Inside Higher Ed*. https://www.insidehighered.com/digital-learning/article/2020/03/25/how-shift-remote-learning-might-affect-students-instructors-and

Luka, I. (2014). Design thinking in pedagogy. *The Journal of Education, Culture, and Society, 1*(2), 63–74. doi:10.15503/jecs20142.63.74

Mertler, C. A. (2014). *Action research: Improving schools and empowering educators* (4th ed.). Sage Publications.

Mezirow, J. (1990). *Fostering critical reflection in adulthood: A guide to transformative and emancipatory learning* (1st ed.). Jossey-Bass Publishers.

Mezirow, J. (1997). Transformative learning: Theory to practice. *New Directions for Adult and Continuing Education, 1*(74), 5–12. doi:10.1002/ace.7401

Mezirow, J., & Rose, A. (1978). *An evaluation guide for college women's re-entry programs*. Distributed by ERIC Clearinghouse.

Negrea, V. (2013). Education policy, applied language learning, and economic development. *The European Integration - Realities and Perspectives, 8*(1), 313–317.

Nieto, S. (2009). *Identity and belonging: Culture and Learning. In Language, culture, and teaching: Critical perspectives* (2nd ed.). Routledge. doi:10.4324/9780203872284

Noddings, N. (2002). *Starting at home: Caring and social policy*. University of California Press.

OECD. (2020). The potential of online learning for adults: Early lessons from the COVID-19 crisis. In *OECD tackling coronavirus (COVID-19): Contributing to a global effort*. OECD Publishing. https://read.oecd-ilibrary.org/view/?ref=135_135358-ool6fsocqtitle=The-potential-of-Online-Learning-for-adults-Early-lessons-from-the-COVID-19-crisis

Pear, J., & Kinsner, W. (1988). Computer aided personalized system of instruction: An effective and economical method for short- and long-distance education. *Machine-Mediated Learning, 2*(3), 213-37. https://www.researchgate.net/profile/Joseph-Pear/publication/234597931_Computer-Aided_Personalized_System_of_Instruction_An_Effective_and_Economical_Method_for_Short-_and_Long-Distance_Education/links/58864a3992851c21ff4d5991/Computer-Aided-Personalized-System-of-Instruction-An-Effective-and-Economical-Method-for-Short-and-Long-Distance-Education.pdf

Pedreira, K., & Pear, J. (2015). Motivation and attitude in a computer-aided personalized system of instruction course on discrete-trials teaching. *Journal on Developmental Disabilities, 28*(1), 45–51.

Razzouk, R., & Shute, V. (2012). What is design thinking and why is it important? *Review of Educational Research, 82*(3), 330–348. doi:10.3102/0034654312457429

Ross, L. L., & McBean, D. (1995). A comparison of pacing contingencies in classes using a personalized system of instruction. *Journal of Applied Behavior Analysis*, *28*(1), 87–88. doi:10.1901/jaba.1995.28-87 PMID:16795855

Sigueza, T. (2020, March 4). *Using graphic organizers with ells*. Retrieved from https://www.colorincolorado.org/article/using-graphic-organizers-ells

Slapac, A., Kim, S., & Coppersmith, S. A. (2019). Preparing and enriching linguistically and culturally responsive educators through professional development. In A. Slapac & S. Coppersmith (Eds.), *Beyond language learning instruction: Transformative supports for emergent bilinguals and educators* (pp. 282–304). IGI Global Disseminator of Knowledge.

Svenningsen, L., & Pear, J. J. (2011). Effects of computer-aided personalized system of instruction in developing knowledge and critical thinking in blended learning courses. *The Behavior Analyst Today*, *12*(1), 34–40. doi:10.1037/h0100709

Taylor, E. W., & Cranton, P. A. A. (2012). *The handbook of transformative learning: Theory, research, and practice* (1st ed.). Jossey-Bass.

Timperley, H. (2011). *Realizing the power of professional learning*. McGraw-Hill.

TOEFL ITP Test Taker Handbook. (2016). Education Testing Service.

Villegas-Reimers, E. (2003). *Teacher professional development; an international review of literature*. UNESCO: International Institute for Educational Planning. http://www.unesco.org/iiep

Wei, R. C., Darling-Hammond, L., & Adamson, F. (2010). Professional development in the United States: Trends and challenges (Technical report). Stanford Center for Opportunity Policy in Education.

ADDITIONAL READING

Freeman, D., & Freeman, Y. (2020). *Teaching diverse learners: Sheltered English instruction*. The Education Alliance. https://www.brown.edu/academics/education-alliance/teaching-diverse-learners/strategies-0/sheltered-english-instruction-0

Harbecke, D. (2012, October 8). *Following Mezirow: A roadmap through transformative learning*. https://rutraining.org/2012/10/08/following-mezirow-a-roadmap-through-transformative-learning/?blogsub=pending

Lieb, S. (1991). *Principles of adult learning*. Vision-South Mountain Community College. https://petsalliance.org/sites/petsalliance.org/files/Lieb%201991%20Adult%20Learning%20Principles.pdf

Mezirow, J. (1981). A critical theory of adult learning and education. *Adult Education Quarterly*, *32*(3), 3–24. doi:10.1177/074171368103200101

Mezirow, J. (1991). *Transformative dimensions of adult learning*. Jossey-Bass.

National Training Coordinating Council (NTCC) and AARP/Legal Counsel for the Elderly. (1993). *What's so special about teaching adults?* (Vol. 8). Fast Track Training Series.

Trivett, C. M., Dunst, C. J., Hamby, D. W., & O'Herin, C. E. (2009). Characteristics and consequences of adult learning methods and strategies. *Winterberry Research Syntheses*, *3*(1), 1–32.

KEY TERMS AND DEFINITIONS

Building Leadership for Change (BLC) Team: University faculty and staff who are experts within the K-12 education field or English language instruction and who also have an average of 18 years in coaching and mentoring experience at a national and international level.

Conceptual Framework: The framework used in designing the professional development model grounded in elements from the transformative learning theory, language acquisition, and personalized system of instruction.

Delivery Method: The way in which educational material is transferred from instructor to others through face-to-face, web-enhanced courses or through online learning.

Education Experts: Individuals with special skill or knowledge in the field of study that deals mainly with the methods of teaching and learning in schools.

Needs of Educators: What facilitators know or need to know about the educators participating in the program and what they individually need in order to be successful.

Programmatic Adjustments: Corrections, modifications or changes that need to be made relating to the program.

Section 2

Chapter 14
Reflecting on Self-Reflection:
Overcoming the Challenges of Online Teaching in a Romanian School Through Action Research

Andreea Roxana Bell
Colegiul Național "Andrei Șaguna", Romania

Elena Corina Bularca
Colegiul Național "Andrei Șaguna", Romania

Diana Elena Banu
Colegiul Național "Andrei Șaguna", Romania

Elena Diana Lazăr
Colegiul Național "Andrei Șaguna", Romania

Constanța Bordea
Colegiul Național "Andrei Șaguna", Romania

Lorena Mirela Spuderca
Colegiul Național "Andrei Șaguna", Romania

ABSTRACT

This chapter discusses the challenges of online teaching faced by six English teachers in a state school in Romania in the context of the COVID-19 pandemic. As first-time action researchers, these teachers self-reflected on their challenges to make sense of their experiences as they transitioned from face-to-face to online teaching in a collaborative research self-study. Reflective practice is the conceptual framework within which the complexities and tensions of online teaching will be explored, as well as the process by which the authors have responded to the social and technological changes caused by the pandemic. Excerpts from the authors' voices highlight their personal views and experiences as online teachers. It is hoped that not only will this self-study reflection-in-action research provide some useful lessons regarding online teaching, but it will also showcase the benefits of collaboration and reflective practice and the action it led to.

INTRODUCTION

Teaching is a fascinating but unpredictable experience. Sometimes too unpredictable... In March 2020 I instantly realized that I had been invited to ride a bike without a chain. My educational objectives were

DOI: 10.4018/978-1-7998-6922-1.ch014

clear, but I felt I had not been appropriately trained to face the challenges of online teaching. (LMS, teacher, author of self-reflection)

Many teachers in Romania and around the world probably experienced the same realization as the Covid-19 pandemic unfolded, bringing about major changes not only in the way we interact on a daily basis, but also in the way we teach. In this new context created by the pandemic, education in Romania shifted focus towards online and hybrid teaching, with significant implications for teaching and learning. During the initial stages of the breakout, March-June 2020, all schools in Romania closed and some form of online teaching was adopted in most schools, across a range of subjects. A lot of teachers were not prepared for such a challenge, especially as they received little to no support from their schools. In September 2020, when the new school year started, a new teaching format was introduced in many schools – the hybrid format – which raised additional barriers for teachers to overcome.

This action research self-study aims to highlight the challenges of online teaching that the English teachers at Colegiul Național "Andrei Șaguna" (CNAS), a state school from Romania, have experienced since the pandemic, and the changes they have adopted to be better prepared for both hybrid and online teaching. The main research question is what lessons can be learned from the authors' own lived experiences of online teaching. The authors chose action research because it is the methodological approach that seems most suited to the authors' educational context, allowing for reflection and enabling the authors to identify weaknesses in their own online teaching practice and to develop solutions collaboratively to address them.

BACKGROUND

Online Teaching

Online teaching has been embraced by many schools and universities with the rapid spread of the use of the Internet and there are many for whom this format is a choice. However, in the context of the COVID-19 pandemic, "online teaching is no more an option, it is a necessity" (Dhawan, 2020, p. 7) and teachers have had to use technology for teaching, regardless of the level of their e-learning competence (Babić et al., 2020). Online teaching and learning can occur in synchronous or asynchronous environments using different devices connected to the Internet (Singh & Thurman, 2019). In synchronous online classes students are all online and learning at the same time, while in asynchronous online classes students log on to a platform and work on it in their own time and at their own pace (Tallent-Runnels et al., 2006). According to the same authors, hybrid or blended learning combines online components with traditional, face-to-face components.

The rapidly changing nature of technology has had a striking impact on students' modes of expression (Swenson & Taylor, 2012) and has altered the way they learn. Rather than listening passively to lectures, students want to be doing and creating (Boettcher & Conrad, 2016), so teachers must make creative use of these technological developments and avoid the tendency of replicating traditional educational practices in online classrooms (Kreber & Kanuka, 2006). In rethinking their current teaching practices, teachers must gradually 'relinquish the role of "sage on the stage" and assume one as "guide on the side," leading students through information gathering, practice, and knowledge construction'. (Baylen & Zhu, 2009, p. 242). In an online environment, teachers are expected to create more learner-centered classrooms (Salmon, 2004) and to engage students in actively constructing knowledge and co-creating the educational experience (Baylen & Zhu, 2009; Swenson & Taylor, 2012). However, online teachers often feel uncertain, uneasy, and unprepared for the challenges of teaching online (Major, 2010).

Challenges of Online Teaching

Some authors argue that challenges associated with online teaching can be classified into four areas: online course design; technology tools and course management systems; faculty development; and technical and administration support (Berge, et al., 2002). For Dhawan (2020) "distance, scale, and personalized teaching and learning are the three biggest challenges for online teaching" (p. 8). Clearly, moving teaching online involves working through a whole new set of challenges that are as much pedagogic as they are technological (Williamson, et al., 2020). Other aspects of online teaching that can be challenging are, what platforms to use, what tools and apps are most suitable, and how to design course content and assessments. Above all, the use of technology can be problematic, and such issues range from installation and login problems to audio and video problems, downloading errors (Dhawan, 2020), or simply Internet failures and power outages. The latter can be a barrier for teachers, discouraging them from implementing new technologies in online classrooms (Yadav, et al., 2018).

Other obstacles that must be overcome are "reduced teaching time due to more management tasks, lack of effective assessment tools, [...] and the challenge of material development" (Hakim, 2020, p. 38), increased frustration and confusion, and loss of direct communication and human touch (Dhawan, 2020). All this, along with online lessons that are too theoretical or too passive, can lead to student disengagement. Students feel that "lack of community, technical problems, and difficulties in understanding instructional goals are the major barriers for online learning" (Song et al., 2004, p. 66). According to Yandell (2020), one cannot ignore the social dimension of teaching and learning, real classrooms being "extraordinarily complex, unpredictable and exciting places" whereas "[t]he interactions that happen online [...] are much less intricate, nuanced and multidimensional" (p. 263). Dhawan (2020) and Yandell (2020) argue that the overall quality of online teaching is the real challenge. In one teacher's words, "What I have learned is: I cannot teach well via the Internet' (Evans et al., 2020, p. 244).

Best Practices for Online Teaching

Despite all the challenges, "using technology facilitates teaching and helps teachers maintain a positive attitude towards their profession" (Hakim, 2020, p. 38), nowadays, when online teaching has become a necessity. Dhawan (2020) attributes accessibility, affordability, and flexibility to online teaching, and sees it as "a panacea in the time of crisis" (p. 6). Among the strengths and opportunities of online teaching identified by Dhawan (2020) are student-centeredness, a diversity of online tools, collaborative and interactive learning, immediate feedback, scope for digital development, enhancement of students' problem-solving skills, critical thinking and adaptability, and development of innovative pedagogical approaches.

Baylen and Zhu (2009) state that one must not make teaching fit into an online platform, "but [...] take advantage of a system's functions to support teaching activities that facilitate student learning" (p. 242). Google products and tools such as Gmail, Forms, Calendar, Drive, Hangouts, Slides or Jamboard can be successful alternatives to face-to-face classes (Basilaia et al., 2020) and emerging online activities have created new opportunities for skillful teachers (Raghavendra, 2020). Baran et al. (2011) argue that "it is through the integration of technology into the pedagogical inquiry that teachers can go through a transformative process of examining the pedagogical potential of online technologies" (p. 433). However, adequate teacher training in the use of technology [...] is essential (Hakim, 2020). For Boettcher and Conrad (2016) some of the best practices for teaching online include being present online, creating a supportive online community, developing clear expectations, using a variety of group formats, using synchronous and asynchronous activities, asking for informal feedback early in the term, preparing discussion posts, assessing as you go, and planning a good closing activity for the course.

Other solutions to overcome the challenges of online teaching are pre-recording and testing the content, having a plan B, setting time limits to keep students alert and attentive, humanizing the learning process, providing personal attention to students (Dhawan, 2020). In addition, there should be an emphasis on collaborative learning, case learning, and project-based learning (Kim & Bonk, 2006). Finally, "teachers should be encouraged to promote community building around online teaching" (Baran et al., 2011, p. 436) and to create room for open dialogue in a dynamic interactive environment - the core of a successful online classroom (Swenson & Taylor, 2012).

This action research project seeks to explore to what extent such best practices have been adopted by the six authors during the switch to online teaching and whether they were successful in overcoming some of the challenges associated with online teaching. It will also identify a future course of action for self-change in the six teachers' professional practice.

Reflective Practice

Reflective practice involves "repeated cycles of examining practice, adjusting practice and reflecting upon it, before trying it again" (Grushka et al., 2005, p. 239). In a study conducted ten years ago on the literature around the roles and competencies of online teachers, one aspect that was found to need further research was promoting critical reflection (Baran et al., 2011). Critical and subjective reflection is what enables teachers to ask themselves questions and make important decisions about their own practice and its impact on their students (Eilers, 2006), and is a key factor for improving a teacher's practice (Baran et al., 2011).

Mortari (2015) argues that "learning the practice of reflection is fundamental because it allows people to engage into a thoughtful relationship with the world-life and thus gain an awake stance about one's lived experience" (p. 2). This applies to any type of research practice, therefore also to teachers as reflective practitioners, since teaching is a complex process and "lived experience" (Van Manen, 1991). As adult learners, teachers constantly transform their approach to online teaching through an ongoing process of critical reflection and action (Baran et al., 2011). Schön distinguishes between "reflection-in-action" and "reflection-on-action", where the first concept refers to professionals' ability to solve problems as they occur, and the second means "reflecting on experience after the event, drawing out lessons, implications and understandings that will inform future action." (Costley et al., 2010, p. 123). What is worth retaining is that the self-reflective research process is transformative and focuses on the individual's need for self-change (Mezirow, 1990).

Based on the literature review and the authors' personal reflections some questions arise. What makes online teaching successful? How can teachers best engage their students in the subject matter? How can the quality of education be maintained? What lessons can be learned from the authors' own lived experiences of online teaching? This self-reflective action research will provide some answers to these questions as well as show how the authors were motivated to take transformative action.

MAIN FOCUS OF THE CHAPTER

Context and Participants

The present self-study action research project was conducted by the six English teachers at Colegiul Național "Andrei Șaguna" (CNAS), a highly selective state school in Brașov, Romania, and one of the top ten schools nationally from the point of view of high school entrance and Baccalaureate examination scores. It is a public school with 170 years of tradition in education, the first Romanian boys' school in Brașov, whose name is connected to the names of many of its teachers and alumni who made history, including 49 members of the Romanian Academy.

CNAS has around 800 students annually, of whom around 120 are in middle school (5th-8th grades) and around 680 are in high school (9th-12th grades). Admission to the 5th grade and 9th grade is based on a highly-selective entrance exam in Romanian and Mathematics. There are six specializations at high school level (two Mathematics and Intensive Computer Science, one Science, one Bilingual French - Science, one Intensive English - Science, and one Bilingual English - Social Science). For the bilingual and intensive English classes, students must pass an additional national English language exam or hold an internationally recognized English language certificate. Class size is typically 30 students in both middle school and high school, across all specializations. The school year is divided into two semesters (mid-September to end of January, and February to mid-June).

The six authors are teachers in the English Department, all female within the age range of 40-48. We teach subjects such as general English for young learners and teenagers, English for exams, the geography / history / culture and civilization of the English-speaking world, as well as literature, public-speaking and debate skills. We have individual teaching experience ranging from 15 to 28 years in various settings, from primary to middle school and high school (2), middle and high school (6), university (2) and private schools (1). We were all exposed to online teaching tools through training courses, still, we had no online teaching experience prior to March 2020. Moreover, we were all confronted with other pressures outside our professional lives (young children, elderly parents, distanced families because of the pandemic), which made online teaching even more challenging.

The project arose from the need of the authors to share the common challenges posed by online and hybrid teaching during the pandemic, as well as, most importantly, the solutions and changes they implemented to transition to online teaching and to make a difference in their individual practice. Aware that action research is "a disposition toward improvement and self-directed problem solving" (Slapac & Navarro, 2011, p. 417), the authors decided to take the "ultimate 'mirror test'" (Eilers 2006, p. 14) and to attempt self-reflection as a research tool and a means of self-change.

The study focuses on the three different periods of online teaching between March and December 2020: synchronous and/or asynchronous online teaching (March-June, October-December), hybrid teaching (September-October), and synchronous and asynchronous online teaching (October-December). Three so-called scenarios were considered between September and December 2020: "green" (whereby all the students were at school, being taught face-to-face), "red" (where all the students were at home studying online) and "yellow" or "hybrid" (where the teacher simultaneously taught half of the students in class, and the other half online, the students changing formats on alternate weeks).

The hybrid teaching format was adopted by CNAS on 14th September 2020, at the start of the new school year, based on the epidemiological context (the number of cases in one given area per 1,000 inhabitants), and was implemented in most of the classes. Depending on the number of English classes

Reflecting on Self-Reflection

per week at high school level, which determines the profile of a class, English was taught in all three formats, face-to-face, hybrid and online. It was the "yellow", or hybrid, teaching format that presented most of the challenges for the whole of the English department.

Table 1. The profile of the six teachers at CNAS as research authors and participants

Teachers' pseudonyms	Years of experience	Courses taught Mar.-Jun. 2020	Teaching format	Courses taught Sep.-Dec. 2020	Teaching format
ARB	18	EAL (English as an Additional Language) in a South-East Asian country	online synchronously	General English for middle and high school; a class on *Stories* for 5th graders	hybrid online synchronously
CB	21	General English for middle and high school; a class on *Stories* for 6th graders	online synchronously	General English for middle and high school; a class on *Ready for exams* for 6th graders	hybrid online synchronously
DEB	17	General English for middle and high school; a class on *Ready for exams* for 6th graders	online synchronously	General English for middle and high school	hybrid online synchronously
ECB	13	General English for high school; *Debate Skills* for 11th graders	online synchronously asynchronously	General English for middle and high school; British and American Culture and Civilization for 11th graders	hybrid online synchronously
EDL	16	General English for high school	online synchronously	General English for high school	hybrid online synchronously
LMS	28	General English for high school; British and American Culture and Civilization for 12th graders; Geography of the UK and USA for 9th graders	asynchronously	General English for high school; British and American Culture and Civilization for 12th graders; Geography of the UK and USA for 9th graders	hybrid online synchronously

Methodological Procedures

This action research lies within a constructivist paradigm, which views reality and knowledge as socially constructed by those involved in the research process, and where understanding of reality and knowledge arises from lived experience (Costley et al., 2010). "Learning to do action research [...] successfully can be a complex process." (Ponte, 2002, p. 420) so we are aware of our own ontological and epistemological position, as first-time researchers sharing and exploring our own lived experiences and constructing knowledge from a multiplicity of perspectives. Our authentic voices have been accurately recorded and presented in this study. We are also aware of the limitations of our research, in that an analysis of our own reflections may convey deeply personal and subjective views of our experiences, which will not necessarily be relevant to other teaching contexts.

The main body of data of the present study comes from the six authors' personal reflections (which draw on personal experience of online and hybrid teaching), informal conversations held during the school breaks, face-to-face and online discussions at department meetings and email correspondence. During the hybrid teaching period, we used to meet daily at school and discuss our problems, attempt to overcome barriers, and support one another. Once teaching moved online, we started meeting once or twice a week for two or three hours, depending on our needs and time constraints. The isolation generated by the online teaching format prompted the authors to meet online and to continue to provide support to one another.

The reflections were written in Google docs and stored in a shared drive, so that all six teachers could access them. We individually color-coded the challenges and adaptations before collaboratively extracting the common themes across all the data sources. We then compared the data thus labelled into categories and analyzed them from the perspective of the literature review. The research tasks were assigned in such a way among the group members that everybody had an equal share of data to analyze and discuss. During the writing process, acronyms were used instead of the authors' names to make the coding and analysis easier. We held regular online meetings to discuss the collaboration in terms of the research methodology, the coding process, and the analysis.

Findings

Challenges Related to Hybrid and Online Teaching

The present action research study revealed a set of challenges that the six teachers experienced related to the online and hybrid teaching formats, and the solutions they identified. The challenges are in the thematic areas of legislation and school policy, technology integration, professional development and pedagogy. In the light of the literature review, these resemble the areas in which teachers elsewhere have experienced challenges because of the pandemic.

Legislation and School Policy

One of the main challenges which heavily impacted online education during the March-June 2020 period was the lack of clear guidelines provided by the authorities. Once schools closed, the teaching system in Romania was overthrown into uncertainty, anxiety and the unknown. As most teachers felt, there was no immediate reaction or clear direction, locally or nationally, as to how school was going to continue or what approach the Ministry would adopt. Added to all the other challenging issues, it was felt as a strong demotivator, generating confusion and opportunities for online misconduct:

[...] as a result, some teachers, myself included, continued their activity conscientiously, whereas others waited for clear instructions which did not come, so they did not do their classes. To further deepen the injustice, the ministry decided that we could not consider the students absent during the online classes and if we assessed them during that time, we had to ask for their or their parents' permission to write those grades in the register, which made our work even more difficult. (CB)

The legal context concerning online behavior was absent or vague; the duration of a class or the overall number of classes were not specified, students and teachers did not have to have their cameras on [...]. (DEB)

The students, no matter how diligent and hard-working, are children [...], so they tended to "skip" classes physically or mentally due to the lack of immediate consequences and because they probably thought that not covering that part of the curriculum would not have a great impact on their future education. (CB)

However, there were also students who, *[d]espite all this, [...] were receptive, willing to learn and share, and active. (DEB)*. The impact of the pandemic on the students was perceived differently by the teachers, probably due to the difference in the age or personality of the students. Since CNAS is a state school, the lack of adequate legislation meant a lack of clear guidelines for the educational activities and, in turn, a lot of freedom for the teachers. The recommendation was to continue teaching remotely, but a lot of flexibility was allowed. This was felt as positive by some of the staff, but for others stricter control would have rendered the activity more organized and, as a result, more efficient.

When the lockdown started, we did not exactly know how school was going to go [...]; we [...] had a period of accommodation when we attended a series of seminars and training sessions to prepare for remote teaching. And since there was no clear set of instructions as to how we should all proceed, each teacher had the flexibility to choose one platform or another to continue their teaching. (ECB)

At school level we established a new timetable depending on how each teacher decided to meet their classes [...]: exclusively in synchronous learning; assigning tasks to students in asynchronous learning; or having classes in both synchronous and asynchronous learning. (ECB)

During the same time a different experience was undergone by a teacher who was employed by a private school in a South-East Asian country which had no official ministry guidelines but started planning early on and bridged the digital divide.

Every department conceived an action plan for online teaching and the timetable was adapted, as well as a class content, resources and assessment. Therefore, when the school closed and we started our online classes, Google Classroom was used by everyone, via Meet and Hangouts. For the few students who did not have a stable Internet connection and could not join the online classes, the school prepared a weekly pack of materials that was collected by parents and returned to school the next day for the teachers to mark and provide feedback. (ARB)

This period, however disorganized, proved invaluable for the start of the 2020-2021 school year, in September, when the government finally provided teachers with the legislation necessary to coordinate school activities and three scenarios were possible according to the epidemiological context: face-to-face, hybrid and online. On the other hand, having had clear guidelines and having switched from private to state education, one teacher felt the need for the same type of instructions in her present activity.

[...] there was no clear set of guidelines nor a strategy at institutional level regarding the use of G Suite or other platforms. Everyone was given the freedom to choose how to organize their own teaching,

what platforms to use and how to adapt their own classes from face-to-face to hybrid teaching. [...] so even the apparently simple task of generating a link or a code was really frustrating in the absence of a clear direction as to who generates the links – the students or the teachers, from Classroom or not – and whether the link is the same for all the classes students have daily, or specific to the English class. (ARB)

With or without clear rules, for education to continue, either the school or the Ministry had to provide the means necessary to sustain teaching and learning, because quality face-to-face classes were impossible. This was also the case in other countries, where "authorities seem to have no option other than technology integration in order to be able to maintain the flow of the teaching and learning process" (Hakim 2020, p. 34). Fortunately, at CNAS most of the students have access to a stable Internet connection and a device that gives them access to online education. Only 11 students out of around 800 met the eligibility criteria to receive tablets from the government on loan, starting with November 2020.

Technology Integration

In March 2020, at the beginning of the pandemic, most of the teachers were not professionally trained to use the online teaching tools exclusively. Even those who had access to high-tech equipment had never used it intensively and extensively, with many students. One of the teachers' major concerns was how to communicate with more than 200 students via different online tools they were not particularly familiarized with. Thus, the teachers had to experiment, utilize technology, and rethink their educational strategies. Additionally, teachers had to find viable solutions to many problems, including technical ones.

We had to prepare and deliver our classes from home, with all the practical and technical difficulties this involves, and often without proper technical support. On top of that, a significant challenge for me has been the lack of the pedagogical knowledge needed for teaching online (using different platforms, apps, and tools). (EDL)

The lack of experience [...] together with the lack of proper technical equipment and conditions posed many problems that affected mainly the groups of students that were online. (DEB)

Another issue was that some students did not have access to reliable Internet connection or a microphone at home, so could not participate in class when invited to speak. (ARB)

Although our school offered the teachers fully available technical support and assistance, the hybrid format proved to be the most detrimental to an efficient teaching-learning process, both students and teachers having to deal with a variety of technological drawbacks.

[...] It was this system that was the most disturbing for everyone mostly because the students online at home were in some cases overlooked by teachers, and in others, they either did not have proper technology to connect or the school did not provide high-tech equipment for them [...]. (ECB)

The students who are at home frequently experience technical problems: they cannot hear the teacher and their classmates well or they cannot see what is written on the board. (LMS)

The teachers faced technical difficulties even during synchronous online teaching and learning, which is more homogenous than the hybrid format, such as not being able to share the sound via Google Meet [...] The solution [...] was to use an external speaker but this was obviously quite costly. (ECB) Another significant drawback of the online system is that the students can take a break during the class, claiming some technical problems. (LMS)

The youngest group of students represented a teacher's ongoing challenge because of their age peculiarities and lack of technical experience. Compared to the high school students, who are frequently demotivated, some of the younger students are very energetic. Thus, the teacher had to keep the optimum balance between the hyperactive students and the shy ones, who are reluctant to participate in the educational activities, simultaneously considering the quality of technology.

[...] the lack of adequate technology and equipment in some classrooms [...] made it difficult to communicate with the students learning online from home. This was the case in the fifth grade, the youngest students at our school, who are not used to learning independently and who need a lot of support and explanations, clear writing on the board etc. The lack of a good quality camera meant that lessons were of a low standard for those learning online. (ARB)

The authors have reached the same conclusion as others, namely that "any meaningful work in a classroom has to be done with and alongside others, and online learning is a real detriment to that." (Evans et al., 2020, p. 246). Therefore, the hybrid teaching and learning format posed the greatest challenge to all the teachers involved in the research process as it was impossible to offer equal learning opportunities to the students at home as compared to those in class.

Professional Development

Professional development is an ongoing process throughout a teacher's career, but it was in March 2020, more than ever, that the need for training was felt by everyone. Teachers in Romania were recommended and offered free online training courses to be able to cope with the new situation; the training provided information about different platforms such as Google Meet, Zoom or Microsoft Teams.

[The national, European-funded training course] was implemented for all disciplines, on a national level, [...] and three of the authors benefited from it. About 40% of the course was on Google Meet, so it basically introduced the participants to the use of the platform later to be recommended on a national level [...]. (DEB)

[...] we learned how to create Google classrooms. Using all this information, on 17th March I created my Google classrooms and, communicating with the students via WhatsApp, I asked them to enlist. Using Google calendar, I planned my first classes and via Google Meet, I saw my students online for the first time. I think that being familiarized with those platforms was a great help, because my experience was a lot better than what most of my colleagues experienced. (CB)

At school level, however, due to a visionary math teacher, some work had already been done to create the school Moodle platform, www.saguna.eduas.ro and *[...] several teachers in my school met and exchanged information and experiences related to using these two resources we had at our disposal: EduAS (the Moodle platform) and G Suite for education.* (CB). With all these resources at hand, teachers still felt the need for further professional development, for equipping themselves with the necessary information to adjust to the new situation, thus adding the online component to their pre-existing pedagogical expertise:

The educational target was certainly known, but I experienced the feeling of being inadequately equipped to reach it. We [...] were encouraged to attend courses to be familiarized with a multitude of educational online tools and everybody supposed that we had already had fully developed technical expertise. (LMS)

It was the transfer of pedagogical skills from a real environment to a virtual one that posed the real challenges, as further discussed. Traditional pedagogy did not envision the possibility of online mass teaching, which is why teachers themselves had to resort to their already acquired experience, common sense, and available online training, in order to find the necessary tools and resources to adapt their teaching techniques, methods and approaches to a new reality.

Pedagogy

March 2020 - Mid-September 2020

At the beginning of the pandemic the teachers involved in this study overcame a multitude of problems in what concerns their teaching, in terms of methods, techniques and approaches. They realised that these can no longer be used as they had been in the traditional, face-to-face class. Questions that were no longer in focus, such as "Does this method work?", "Will the students learn better through this method?", "Will they engage in the activity?" became all of a sudden extremely relevant again and required action and reaction from the teachers. They basically reshaped their methods of teaching, adopted new tools and techniques, broadened their perspective on teaching in order to meet the needs of the students and the demands of online teaching:

The challenges were not insurmountable obstacles, but they epitomized the process of ongoing adapting and reshaping the teaching, learning, and assessing strategies. Since March 2020 I have experienced different teaching techniques: asynchronous, using Google Classroom platform to send assignments and feedback to my students; blended lessons, and synchronous classes in Google Classroom. (LMS)

Such challenges involved managing time in order to cover the remaining syllabus by the end of the school year or to adapt the teaching methods, approaches and activities to the new dynamic of the online learning environment:

I had not predicted that our teaching would move almost completely online so I had very little time [...] to adjust my "ways" to the virtual medium. (CB)

The activities [...] involved: using the interactive software to teach and practice textbook content, delivering information using Google slides and PowerPoint presentations, watching videos, predicting and analyzing content through pre-watching and post-watching tasks (on Netflix, YouTube – mainly TED talks), Google docs for paragraph and functional writing. (DEB)

In this new, virtual context, intuitive approaches to teaching that imply spontaneous decisions or changes made by the teacher in the classroom, based on the students' reaction and level of participation, could no longer be used. Instead, teachers had to be clearer and more precise in their explanations:

When teaching face-to-face, I sometimes rely on intuition and spontaneity, but in an online environment this approach may be confusing rather than helpful. Therefore, I realized that I needed to be more organized than ever before and that I had to explain everything very clearly and carefully, as further interactions were hardly possible. (EDL)

Asynchronous teaching implied a new perspective in what concerns offering feedback to students' work, which was via this medium more detailed and more precise, though time-consuming:

[T]he asynchronous system is more flexible and allows the students, [...] to revise or clarify the concepts necessary to fulfill the tasks. This is the most time-consuming process for the teacher, but it is useful for the students who receive individual feedback that can be read whenever necessary. (LMS)

Alternatively, synchronous teaching challenged teachers to be even more creative and flexible in the use of their methods and approaches, which, overall, were more diverse and appealing to students in the online environment. A challenge would often be using techniques and activities that would involve all the receptive and productive skills and, most importantly, encourage interaction between students – often difficult to do for teachers inexperienced in online teaching, prior to the pandemic:

The teacher can coordinate the whole class of 30 students in a more efficient way, can alternate the educational strategies and expose all the students to the same amount of information or encourage most of them to express their opinions. Thus, the students can practice more and learn through a wider variety of stimuli if the teacher is creative enough to adapt diverse teaching techniques to the new educational context. (LMS)

[H]aving found out about a site where students could choose books to listen to, I encouraged the students to listen to whichever book they liked, to summarize and review it. I also encouraged discussions among students about the books they had listened to, thus ensuring that all the skills were covered. (CB)

For one teacher, who was teaching English as an Additional Language at a private school in a South-East Asian country, the beginning of the pandemic meant a complete change in terms of teaching role, content and format, which made the experience even more challenging:

My role as an EAL teacher, teaching English to a small group of students [...] changed – I became a support-teacher: I no longer taught my students grammar, vocabulary and spelling in pairs or small groups, but instead I supported them individually in writing their essays and analyzing their poems in the English literature classes, completing their research projects in science or art. Since I was expected to work with my students individually, I did not use Google Classroom, but I made use of Google Docs,

Google Hangouts and Google Slides, offering students feedback in real time, collaborating creatively, and helping them to improve their English. (ARB)

September 2020 - December 2020

The beginning of the 2020-2021 school year brought about new challenges for the teachers: they had to teach some of the classes face-to-face and some in the hybrid format, i.e. teach simultaneously half of the students in a class at school, face-to-face, and the other half online. The latter was perceived as challenging, even demanding, by most teachers included in this research, as they had to be present in two learning environments at once: in the classroom and online. Thus, they were challenged to adopt new strategies, compared with the beginning of the pandemic, in order to primarily offer equal opportunities to all students. The methods and techniques used implied active participation of all students in the activities, instant feedback to both those in class and at home, more technology used in the classroom environment (which required therefore good or improved computer skills from the teachers):

[T]he difficult aspect was that [...] I had to make sure both the students in class and those at home could hear, understand me, and participate. [...] I made a strategy to involve all the students in equal measure. [S]o I used PowerPoint presentations, or I opened Word documents which could be seen by all students. Working that way proved to be a lot more demanding for me than working exclusively online and my fellow teachers felt the same way. (CB)

The blended system is unanimously associated by students and teachers with the mission (almost) impossible, being considered extremely counterproductive. Even the most experienced teachers cannot provide the information equitably and help the students practice and check their progress instantly. It is difficult for the teacher to offer a fair chance to students to express their opinions, especially if a student who is in the classroom and the other one who is at home wants to answer a question simultaneously. (LMS)

In order to encourage collaboration and participation, one of the techniques used was flipped classroom – an occasion for students to develop research skills (data collection, data analysis, synthesis), online presentation and computer skills. (DEB)

Assessment

In terms of assessment, transitioning from paper-based tests to online ones presented its own challenges. One of them was during the hybrid format at the beginning of the school year 2020-2021, when [t]*he initial evaluation was [...] problematic to organize with only half of the students always present in class.* (ARB) What the same teacher found most difficult was to administer her first online test as a Google form quiz to the fifth graders after only one month of hybrid teaching:

Even though by then I had learned how to create and administer a test of this type as part of my online training course, and despite being helped by one of my colleagues in choosing the right settings, it was a failure. While everyone solved the paper-based version of the test in good time in class, only three students managed to complete the whole test online, the rest got stuck either because of the technical difficulties involved (had never taken a quiz of that type before) or the lack of time or were confused by the fact that the questions were shuffled. (ARB)

Though it was generally perceived by the teachers as a useful tool: *I could not check my students' work in synchronous lessons,* [but] *I started using Google forms, which helped me enormously* (ECB), designing online tests often proved to be *time-consuming and disappointing* (LMS) because of cheating, communicating results and answers via WhatsApp or other messenger apps:

Even when writing skills were assessed, there was no way to ensure that it was done in a way to prevent cheating, since I did not think it fair to force students to keep their cameras on. (ARB)

Students can easily communicate using other online tools such as WhatsApp to fulfill the tasks posted on educational platforms. Thus, the results of certain types of assessment like multiple choice items are inaccurate and they do not reflect the students' [...] level of knowledge and understanding. (LMS)

Overcoming all these methodological issues required a concerted effort from teachers and students alike, and the determination to continue to provide quality education for all in times of crisis was what motivated everyone to adapt, ask for and provide support when needed.

Psychological Impact on Teachers and Students

The pandemic generated a period of time characterized by a bewildering psychological complexity, the teachers and students constantly facing the significant challenge of adapting their own strategies to online teaching and learning. The novelty of the process puzzled all the participants who had to face it, from students, teachers, and parents to authorities:

The students' (and for that matter, the teachers' as well) mental state was affected. Not knowing what we were up against, being more or less locked in our homes affected everybody to a certain extent. A degree of stability in one's life most surely prevents people from losing their balance. (CB)

The problem that remained was the difficulty, mainly technical, in creating the proper atmosphere in the class for collaboration and sharing of ideas. (DEB)

The teachers had to deal with the cumulative impact of the lack of face-to-face communication and the unpredictable reactions of the students. As documented in research (Pöysä & Lowyck, 2009), the online environment provides intimacy for introverted students so, as one teacher states:

[...] students who rarely participated in class, even when prompted to do so, seemed to be less inhibited during the online classes. At the same time, students who had been active during face-to-face classes felt less challenged and did not engage as much [...]. (EDL)

Students can easily become unmotivated in the online classroom, so building community is a vital part of keeping them engaged. Students can no longer use the time before and after class to check in with their teachers and this lack of interaction makes it difficult for teachers to sense whether students feel motivated and involved during classes. Teaching in the hybrid format between September and October 2020 proved helpful as it allowed teachers to reconnect with their students and get to know the new ones. The new online environment also triggered some changes in what rules and expectations are concerned.

Agreeing on ground rules ensured that students engaged in proper Internet etiquette and helped them feel more connected to their class. While most of these rules were similar to those we set in the face-to-face learning environment, some adjustments were made to better suit the online learning environment:

In the classroom, these rules may include "put away our phones" or "don't talk to your desk mate". With online teaching, norms become: "mute your microphone" or "turn your cameras on" (EDL)

This online teaching and learning, especially the hybrid format, reflected the value of the acquisition of social skills for teenagers' healthy mental and emotional development. For adolescents, whose character is being shaped and who are peculiarly vulnerable at this age, communicating their emotions is of paramount importance, definitely more important than communicating information, so a tool, not even a high-tech one, cannot facilitate this laborious process:

The psychological impact of the hybrid format on the students should also be taken into account, because some of their close friends are in the other group, not in the classroom, and they cannot communicate efficiently. The special educational environment generated by the pandemic forced the students to experience the concept of the zone of proximal development and the sociocultural theory formulated in the 20th century by Lev Vygotsky, proving the tremendous impact of the social interaction on the development of cognition. The conclusion is the same, no matter the context: people, especially the young ones, are sometimes inextricably connected and this process helps them to enhance their knowledge and interpersonal skills. At the beginning of online teaching and learning the students and I experienced an emotional roller-coaster because they could not see my face covered with a protective facial mask, and I could see only the faces of the students who were at home. (LMS)

As the weeks and months passed, the greatest problem was that most of the students, especially the teenagers, seemed to be oblivious to the long-term deleterious consequences of their lack of involvement in their own educational process. Some teachers noticed this considerable change of attitude and tried to encourage the students to participate in a variety of activities:

[...] students became more disengaged and passive. They responded when asked but interaction was cumbersome, and it was tiring and time-consuming for me to keep calling out their names to get them to participate. (ARB)

Unfortunately, activating students during e-learning classes is not easy. Although online platforms have a range of options to engage the audience, these only work if students participate. For example, whenever I played a video in the classroom, it was easy to tell how students reacted and related to it. But while online, I cannot even be sure that the students are actually watching the video. (EDL)

One of the most serious challenges is the unpredictability of the long-term emotional impact on the students, as a result of the pandemic. No one can accurately estimate this impact on individuals:

Although some of the older students from 11th grade and the high school leavers, from the 12th grade, considered not attending face-to-face school a dream that came true, they soon felt the dramatic effect of the social and, consequently, emotional seclusion. I have noticed a significant change in my students' attitude, the vast majority of them becoming more mature, adopting a different life perspective and dramatically losing their sense of humor. (LMS)

Being affected by the pandemic in many various ways, the students need uniquely tailored measures and teaching strategies that can help them to be effectively reintegrated in their educational environment.

Solutions Related to Hybrid and Online Teaching

Technology Integration

In unexpected distance learning environments few things can be done without substantial logistics support that cannot be completely replaced by teachers' enthusiasm, creativity, or expertise. In the authors' school, teachers, students, parents, managers, technical staff and even alumni worked together to provide and improve adequate technical facilities, demonstrating power sharing among community members:

Overall, I managed to overcome these issues by asking my computer science colleagues to help me whenever I needed to or simply involving tech savvy students in such matters. (ECB)

This issue [lack of a good quality camera] was resolved with the contribution of the parents, who invested in new technology and reinstalled the whiteboard so that online teaching and learning were enhanced. (ARB)

Some of these steps were taken, fortunately, early on in January, before the pandemic: Colegiul National "Andrei Şaguna" applied for a domain @saguna.ro and, thus, provided all teachers and students with accounts which made it possible for the users to fully benefit from the advantages of G Suite for Education. (DEB)

The authors identified feasible and creative solutions to the problems of hybrid teaching – the most problematic and challenging of all – such as *to teach the students [...] in the classroom while those at home read a text, do some exercises or research for the next task and vice versa. (LMS)*. Thus, they demonstrated great flexibility and adaptability to the new educational context and, even when they could not verify the students' claims about technology issues, they had to find workable solutions by *[...] assigning to the [online] students some tasks to fulfill and inviting them to upload the answers (LMS)* or *[...] asking them to type their answers in the chat box or resolve a speaking task on the phone with a partner before presenting it in class.* (ARB)

Any viable solution had to be implemented, although it was considered less conventional, especially if the teacher did not have access to high-tech systems. The teachers had to be more efficient than during face-to-face interaction and support their students during such unusual circumstances:

Even if the vast majority of the teachers consider that it is absolutely vital for them and their students to have their computer cameras on, I have experienced the opposite and I can conclude that the students and I were not exposed to a myriad of distractions, thus students being able to be better focused on fulfilling their tasks. I encourage them to attend the classes giving them supplementary marks for their class activity and asking them questions randomly. The utmost important fact for me is to have the students involved in their own learning process [...]. (LMS)

The online teaching and learning system consolidated the teachers' professional relationship with their students, who proved eager to support the teachers in order to optimize the technical facilities and share power while exchanging roles.

My students and I have enjoyed interchanging our traditional roles. During the blended and online classes, they have always helped me to improve, select and adapt the technology in order to provide more interesting teaching and assessing strategies. In difficult circumstances they cooperated and then taught me how to use a system more efficiently. It was a major chance for them to cooperate and change roles with their teacher, so they were delighted to experience the power of taking a certain decision regarding their access to education. Some of them worked after the regular classes to improve the technology provided by the school and facilitate their classmates' access to modern equipment. (LMS)

The need to know how to make the best of the new online learning environment also increased communication among colleagues. Having their support and guidance helped a lot in understanding how to make better use of different teaching platforms and help the students as well.

I cooperated intensely with my colleagues, including those of different subjects, for example the computer science or mathematics teachers, in order to identify the online systems that could facilitate the students' access to attractive means of acquiring specialized information. (LMS)

Great achievements are sometimes the result of teamwork, cooperation, and flexibility; having always had close relations within the English department, another solution the teachers found, at the beginning of the 2020-2021 school year, was to collaborate even more intensely in such trying times, and to share ideas acquired at the training sessions they attended, as the majority suggest:

What helped a lot in the process, was the informal discussions within the English department, since my colleagues had already had the experience of using Google Classroom. Early on, at the beginning of the school year, we had decided to establish weekly online meetings to discuss our challenges and find solutions to overcome them. (ARB)

Although I was pretty confident and my first online classes were successful, I (...) kept exchanging ideas and tools with my colleagues from the English department. Since all the teachers had to cope with the same problems, we, the teachers of English, tried to discuss the problems we were undergoing and came up with several ways of helping each other [...] That way we found out about Google Attendance, which, when we resumed all our classes online, reduced the time needed to call the roll. (CB)

During the pandemic, the weekly online meetings of the staff of the English department of the school facilitated sharing the knowledge and skills gained. (DEB)

Although the unpredictable time of this pandemic generated a substantial amount of uncertainty, anxiety or confusion juxtaposed with the novelty and intensive use of online teaching, we adapted our traditional teaching methods and implemented new ones compatible with online teaching. We also recalibrated the importance of the cutting-edge technology and human factors involved in education.

Professional Development

Despite having the necessary tools at hand in March 2020 (whole-school G Suite for Education, EduAS Moodle platform and the national training course completed by three of the teachers), we were not able to use them properly (or at all, in some cases), so we had to resort to different types of training sessions found online or MOOC courses on the FutureLearn platform:

[We], as most teachers, turned to the media [...] for information and suggestions on how to deal with the crisis. Luckily, the pages [...] focusing on teaching [...] promoted online workshops and courses, most of them offered for free, in order to support teachers in using various methods and techniques, and most importantly, online tools [...]. Publishing houses, [...] teachers' associations and organizations focused on online platforms (Google Classroom, Zoom, Microsoft Teams), their pluses and minuses, using whiteboards, sharing video and audio materials, creating various online materials using special sites (Canva, Genially, Mentimeter, liveworksheets etc.). (DEB)

Although I could not use all the facilities provided by Google Classroom because I experienced technical problems from March to June 2020, I attended specialized courses and watched tutorials that helped me to be able to create some activities that motivated my students to learn. Jamboard, Mentimeter or the software for the students' books and other supplementary sources, facilitated my students' access to relevant information in a format adapted to their needs and interests. (LMS)

Whereas many of the professional development courses were free at the beginning of the pandemic, this was not the case in September 2020, at the start of the new school year, as one of the authors states:

I invested in an online course about the use of Google suite for Education, so it was a question of putting everything that I was learning into practice as quickly and efficiently as possible. (ARB)

At the beginning of the pandemic, another teacher decided to purchase a certificate in order to maximize the benefits of an otherwise free online course, specialize as an online teacher and continue the work she was previously doing in class:

[...] so I attended the online course "Teaching English Online" offered by the FutureLearn platform. There were loads of information and every bit and piece helped me: I found out about 'the flipped classroom', Padlet, and a variety of other resources that I could use with my students. (ECB)

With a clear purpose all the teachers had in mind, that it being able to use all the features of the platforms with ease and confidence in order to maintain the quality standards, training continued even during the summer as one of the teachers mentions:

The summer holiday offered the opportunity to attend more online courses, workshops and conferences, which dealt with the use of [...] Google Meet, Zoom, Microsoft Teams, [...] Jamboard, Whiteboard etc. for synchronous learning and the use or creation of resources (liveworksheets, Google slides and docs, Google quizzes, Kahoot, Mentimeter, Bookcreator, Livresq, Wordwall) for both synchronous and asynchronous learning. [...] The variety and multitude of tools were generally perceived as a stage of confusion and an imperative need to stop, reflect, test and select, then, perfect. (DEB)

Absorbing the available information was for the teachers only the first step into the process of adapting to a new reality. A second step was to implement and adjust the newly acquired set of skills to each particular class and school context.

Pedagogy

Among the solutions related to challenges raised by hybrid teaching during September-October 2020, the most important one focused on using teaching methods that would ensure equity for students at home and would offer equal opportunities for all the students to be involved in class activities:

Through the use of interactive software in all the contexts [hybrid and online], I adapted the textbook content and started creating and using tools and materials that could be shared online. (DEB)

In this context, the teachers felt that the switch from hybrid learning to online learning at the end of October 2020 *[...] came as a relief as it somehow ensured equal opportunities for all students.* (DEB) In terms of teaching methods and approaches, the switch marked a stage in which the teachers perceived themselves more confident in using appropriate tools for the online environment, as they had already been trialled and improved since the pandemic started, so they *focused on testing new materials and apps, together with more emphasis on methods of evaluation (online debates, project presentation, Google quizzes).* (DEB)

Google Classroom offers me the chance of communicating rapidly with all my students and of using an efficient mixture of synchronous and asynchronous teaching strategies. (LMS)

Also, the use of open educational resources for online learning helped to develop various skills in students and encouraged introspection, self-discovery, communication, and the improvement of social skills: *For example, my 11th grade students' project about revolutionary discoveries generated intense debates and my 10th grade students' presentations help them to know further details about their classmates' and their common interests.* (LMS). Similarly, overcoming assessment problems was not an easy task, nor was it devoid of creativity. For the initial assessment of all her new students within the hybrid teaching format, one teacher only gave students a writing test, *which was easier to administer, mark and return with feedback to both those in class (paper-based) and at home (Google doc in Classroom).* To improve the continuous assessment experience for her youngest students, she decided to *expose the fifth graders to several quizzes before administering another online test.* (ARB). To deter cheating, several solutions have been suggested by various teachers such as *evaluating them on their ability to research a topic of their interest, create a presentation and deliver it to the class in an engaging manner* (ARB) or *writing essays, [...] debating on a given topic* (LMS) or *project-based assessment, as it is relatively easy to co-ordinate and assess online.* (EDL). One teacher effectively used quizzes:

To ensure fairness and lack of cheating, I used the school platform or Google classroom for tests, which both gave me the opportunity to shuffle the order of the questions, to assign a time limit and to have instant results when the students had submitted their tests. (CB)

Instead of the final assessment at the end of one unit or chapter, one teacher decided to run short tests assessing different skills, every two weeks, thus ensuring the attention of the students all through the classes. (CB)

For asynchronous online teaching and learning, one teacher found the following solution:

I started entering almost everything from my students' books into these forms and I assigned a form per lesson. […] my students got used to them and now I conduct all my tests online. They are an immense benefit […] since tests can be corrected almost automatically when there are multiple choice questions or matching questions. Reading, listening and use of English tests can be very well conducted using such forms; they are an easy way to keep students informed of their progress. (ECB)

The benefits of such a form of evaluation can be easily underscored – testing receptive skills, grammar and vocabulary is fast and easy, even though not always reliable, and items from different Google forms can be used for subsequent tests. As for testing writing skills, Google docs allow for detailed feedback by providing the in-built suggestions feature. The authors also attempted to make assessment enjoyable to students because it should not be done solely for grading but for students' growth and development. And, as some of the authors of this research state, using projects and presentations, writing essays and organizing debates as alternative methods of assessment fosters teamwork, communication and a sense of community among students.

Psychological Impact on Teachers and Students

One of the positive outcomes of online teaching in terms of the psychological impact on teachers and students was the adaptation to the new environment and the new means of communication:

The focus at the very beginning of the pandemic was not on input, acquisition, and assessment, but mainly on online collaboration, on returning to a form of routine, while, at the same time, developing a sense of continuity and responsibility both in the teaching and learning process. (DEB)

Creating a classroom community meant that standard classroom rules and norms needed to be adapted for online learning. Thus, agreeing upon new terms proved essential to developing a solid working rapport with students.

A major change was that of reshaping the rapport with my students, especially with the new ones whose faces I was able to see only during the hybrid educational process. (LMS)

Teachers in general were severely criticized for their lack of technical expertise – rightly so since they were not specifically trained to use the technology in their classes. However, despite such great pressure and high expectations, we managed to reshape our educational strategies, adapting them to the new teaching and learning context, and experimenting with new ones:

In some of the writing classes we used a Google doc and students wrote a collective story in class, which enabled me to give them feedback and make corrections in real time. With the fifth-grade students and the ninth-grade students in the literature class I also used Jamboard to encourage collaboration and creative thinking, as well as video materials to stimulate discussions. (ARB)

Reshaping their face-to-face teaching and identifying efficient motivational strategies adapted to the students' age and educational needs had a positive impact on students' motivation in the new online environment. Communication represented a major challenge for everyone but the authors felt that they succeeded in filling a yawning gap between a teaching-learning system based on real interaction and the one facilitated by technology:

I focused on how to keep students motivated and my solution was [...]varying the approach for every lesson so as not to bore the students, but also to keep them "on their toes". I made it clear that I cared whether they were present or not, by both stating how important it was for them to keep attending and learning English and by keeping track of their attendance. I also involved the ones who were shy or not so eager to answer and I rewarded their contributions, establishing a system of continuous assessment. The same principle was the basis of their portfolio, which became a virtual one. [...] Other strong motivators are prizes so I encouraged students to participate in all the contests I considered worthwhile [...], thus ensuring that they had the chance to use their English not only for homework or classwork [...] (CB)

One solution that I found in order to increase student participation was including a short quiz at the end of the activity or class, which the students have to complete immediately and for which some participation marks are awarded. (EDL)

A viable solution [...] can be encouraging the students to offer feedback to their classmates randomly and ask questions about the presentations or projects. I always try to select the themes according to my students' interests. (LMS)

For the six authors, as well as for a significant majority of educators, online teaching has been a milestone in their professional lives that revealed their creative potential, empathy, adaptability, and an ability to reshape their well-established teaching and assessment methods as well as identifying new ways of motivating students by offering them suitable psychological support.

Reflecting on Self-reflection

Using self-reflections as part of the research process proved to be one of the greatest benefits, on both a personal and a professional level for all six teachers. Not only did it allow for an in-depth exploration of our own subjective views and experiences of online teaching, but it also brought out our individual and collective voices:

Reflecting on Self-Reflection

Having reflected upon my own activity and finding mainly similarities with not only the teachers in my school, but also with teachers all over the world has made me realize that, since the problems are general, one can find solutions not only by oneself but by sharing and creating communities of like-minded teachers. (CB)

Looking back on the beginning and continuation of the pandemic, i.e. what the experience of online and hybrid teaching meant for me, was an interesting undertaking, which made me realize the multiple aspects involved in online teaching, besides the particular outlook each author has on the situation. [...] What ultimately summarizes how I feel now is that drawbacks can be overcome when willingness and collaboration is involved. (ECB)

Having the chance to reflect on my own teaching experience has helped me assess more deeply the changes I have made to adjust to online teaching. I believe that the ability of teachers to keep adapting and innovating is essential in order to successfully embrace the new online learning environment. (EDL)

Reflecting on one's action is inherent to the process of teaching in general; it is what we teachers do at the end of the day, before embarking on a new journey the next day. 'Have I done what I intended to?', 'Will my students remember and use anything taught in the future?', 'Have they felt involved and listened to?' are some of the questions that teachers try to answer. Writing about this self-reflection, on the other hand, meant an internalization of the above and a better understanding of my role as a teacher, especially during extraordinary contexts, such as the pandemic. (DEB)

Reflecting has meant, for me, looking back at myself as objectively as I could to find the blockages and the benefits that I encountered on my way to becoming an online teacher. It was in many ways liberating to be able to write about the whole experience, as it unfolded during the pandemic. Reflecting on self-reflection means the realization that my lived experience has value and resembles that of my colleagues and of other teachers around the world. (ARB)

The whole experience of self-reflection, of introspection, helped me to assess and reshape my teaching strategies, to identify the weaknesses of the system, to learn new things, to rediscover my creative potential and ability to adapt myself to a new educational context. At the same time, I understood in a better, but also more painful way, the value and the power of the professional relationship between teachers and students who should be intrinsically connected and support each other in this arduous but rewarding process called EDUCATION. (LMS)

As revealed by the literature review, this research has been a reflection-in-action process, which meant that the authors reflected on the problems and solved them as they occurred. As a result of this research process, the authors have set the basis for future transformative individual and collective action, such as continuing to reflect on their teaching and adapt their strategies, collaborating within the English department and with other colleagues, continuing to build community with their students and listen to their voices and lived experiences of online learning.

FUTURE RESEARCH DIRECTIONS

What this self-reflective study revealed was the voices, views and lived experiences of the six authors, teachers at CNAS, a state school in Romania, during the COVID-19 pandemic, and the solutions they found in order to overcome the barriers encountered. Further research could capture and explore the students' voices and lived experiences of online learning. This is an area that could yield surprising results, with significant impact on current online teaching practices.

CONCLUSION

This self-reflective action research project explored six English teachers' experiences while transitioning from face-to-face to online teaching at a state school in Romania, during the COVID-19 pandemic. The study identified the challenges we encountered in the areas of legislation and school policy, technology integration, professional development, pedagogy, community and the psychological impact of the pandemic, and the adaptations we made to improve our online teaching practice ("reflection-in-action"). Like other teachers elsewhere, the authors understood that technology integration was a necessity during the pandemic. We did our best to prepare ourselves for online teaching, despite the multitude of challenges ranging from technical issues to pedagogical or psychological barriers. We struggled during the hybrid teaching period the most and, after many professional development sessions and intense collaboration within the English department, with the IT and other departments, we acquired the know-how and developed the skills necessary to overcome most barriers of online teaching. As professional educators, the authors regularly collaborate and exchange ideas and examples of good practice, and during this unprecedented global crisis we managed to provide support for each other to improve our practice as well as to advance student learning. This reflection-in-action study reveals that a positive attitude towards combining solid pedagogy and new technology and tools could ensure a quality education in times of crisis. Self-reflection proved to be a useful tool for us as first-time researchers, enabling us to explore our lived experiences as online teachers, as well as to grow professionally and improve our practice as we went along. We will continue to use reflections in our teaching practice to trigger transformative self-change.

ACKNOWLEDGMENT

The authors would like to thank Dr. Alina Slapac from the University of Missouri – St. Louis for the opportunity to have their views and lived experiences captured as part of this anthology of action research, and for all her support, resources and feedback provided along the way.

REFERENCES

Babić, S., Križan Sučić, S., & Sinković, G. (2020). Understanding the factors that influence secondary school teachers' intention to use e-learning technologies for Teaching After the COVID-19 Pandemic. In *MIPRO International Convention 2020*. Croatian Society for Information, Communication and Electronic Technology.

Baran, E., Correia, A. P., & Thompson, A. (2011). Transforming online teaching practice: Critical analysis of the literature on the roles and competencies of online teachers. *Distance Education*, *32*(3), 421–439. doi:10.1080/01587919.2011.610293

Basilaia, G., Dgebuadze, M., Kantaria, M., & Chokhonelidze, G. (2020). Replacing the classic learning form at universities as an immediate response to the COVID-19 virus infection in Georgia. *International Journal for Research in Applied Science and Engineering Technology*, *8*(3), 101–108. doi:10.22214/ijraset.2020.3021

Baylen, D. M., & Zhu, E. (2009). Challenges and issues of teaching online. In P. L. Rogers, G. Berg, J. Boettcher, C. Howard, L. Justice, & K. Schenk (Eds.), *Encyclopedia of distance learning* (2nd ed., pp. 241–246). Information Science Reference. doi:10.4018/978-1-60566-198-8.ch034

Berge, Z. L., Muilenburg, L. Y., & Van Haneghan, J. (2002). Barriers to distance education and training: Survey results. *Quarterly Review of Distance Education*, *3*(4), 408–418. http://citeseerx.ist.psu.edu/viewdoc/download?doi=10.1.1.462.6499&rep=rep1&type=pdf

Boettcher, J. V., & Conrad, R. M. (2016). *The online teaching survival guide: simple and practical pedagogical tips* (2nd ed.). John Wiley & Sons, Inc. https://ebookcentral.proquest.com/lib/open/detail.action?docID=4659728

Costley. (2010). *Doing work based research. Approaches to enquiry for insider-researchers*. Sage Publications. doi:10.4135/9781446287880

Dhawan, S. (2020). Online learning: A panacea in the time of COVID-19 crisis. *Journal of Educational Technology Systems*, *49*(1), 5–22. doi:10.1177/0047239520934018

Eilers, L. H. (2006). Action research: The ultimate 'mirror test'. *The Delta Kappa Gamma Bulletin*, *72*(3), 14-29. http://web.b.ebscohost.com.ezproxy.umsl.edu/ehost/pdfviewer/pdfviewer?vid=1&sid=a9d60907-a62e-4c75-9d3e-c56de96bd50a%40sessionmgr101

Evans, C., O'Connor, C. J., Graves, T., Kemp, F., Kennedy, A., Allen, P., Bonnar, G., Reza, A., & Aya, U. (2020). Teaching under lockdown: The experiences of London English teachers. *Changing English*, *27*(3), 244–254. doi:10.1080/1358684X.2020.1779030

Grushka, K., McLeod, J., & Reynolds, R. (2005). Reflecting upon reflection: Theory and practice in one Australian university teacher education program. *Reflective Practice*, *6*(2), 239–246. doi:10.1080/14623940500106187

Hakim, B. (2020). Technology integrated online classrooms and the challenges faced by the EFL teachers in Saudi Arabia during the COVID-19 pandemic. *International Journal of Applied Linguistics and English Literature*, *9*(5), 33–39. doi:10.7575/aiac.ijalel.v.9n.5p.33

Kim, K.-J., & Bonk, C. J. (2006). The future of online teaching and learning in higher education: The survey says. *EDUCAUSE Quarterly, 29*(4), 22–30. http://faculty.weber.edu/eamsel/Research%20Groups/On-line%20Learning/Bonk%20(2006).pdf

Kreber, C., & Kanuka, H. (2006). The scholarship of teaching and learning and the online classroom. *Canadian Journal of University Continuing Education, 32*(2), 109–131. doi:10.21225/D5P30B

Major, C. (2010). Do virtual professors dream of electric students? College faculty experiences with online distance education. *Teachers College Record, 112*(8), 2154–2208. http://www.tcrecord.org

Mortari, L. (2015). Reflectivity in research practice: An overview of different perspectives. *International Journal of Qualitative Methods, 14*(5), 1–9. doi:10.1177/1609406915618045

Ponte, P. (2002). How teachers become action researchers and how teacher educators become their facilitators. *Educational Action Research, 10*(3), 399–421. doi:10.1080/09650790200200193

Pöysä, J., & Lowyck, J. (2009). Communities in technology-enhanced environments for learning. In P. L. Rogers, G. Berg, J. Boettcher, C. Howard, L. Justice, & K. Schenk (Eds.), *Encyclopedia of distance learning* (2nd ed., pp. 345–351). Information Science Reference. doi:10.4018/978-1-60566-198-8.ch051

Raghavendra, C. (2020). The impact of COVID-19 lockdown on English language teaching & learning in India. *Language in India, 20*(8), 283–286.

Singh, V., & Thurman, A. (2019). How many ways can we define online learning? A systematic literature review of definitions of online learning (1988-2018). *American Journal of Distance Education, 33*(4), 289–306. doi:10.1080/08923647.2019.1663082

Slapac, A., & Navarro, V. (2011). Shaping action researchers through a Master's capstone experience. *Teacher Education and Practice, 24*(4), 405–426.

Song, L., Singleton, E. S., Hill, J. R., & Koh, M. H. (2004). Improving online learning: Student perceptions of useful and challenging characteristics. *The Internet and Higher Education, 7*(1), 59–70. doi:10.1016/j.iheduc.2003.11.003

Swenson, P., & Taylor, N. A. (2012). Online Teaching in the Digital Age. *Sage (Atlanta, Ga.)*. Advance online publication. libezproxy.open.ac.uk/. doi:10.4135/9781452244174

Tallent-Runnels, M. K., Thomas, J. A., Lan, W. Y., Cooper, S., Ahern, T. C., Shaw, S. M., & Liu, X. (2006). Teaching courses online: A review of the research. *Review of Educational Research, 76*(1), 93–135. doi:10.3102/00346543076001093

Van Manen, M. (1991). Reflectivity and the pedagogical moment: The normativity of pedagogical thinking and acting. *Journal of Curriculum Studies, 23*(6), 507–536. doi:10.1080/0022027910230602

Williamson, B., Eynon, R., & Potter, J. (2020). Pandemic politics, pedagogies and practices: Digital technologies and distance education during the Coronavirus Emergency. *Learning, Media and Technology, 45*(2), 107–114. doi:10.1080/17439884.2020.1761641

Yadav, N., Gupta, K., & Khetrapal, V. (2018). Next education: Technology transforming education. *South Asian Journal of Business and Management Cases., 7*(1), 68–77. doi:10.1177/2277977918754443

Reflecting on Self-Reflection

Yandell, J. (2020). Learning under lockdown: English teaching in the time of Covid-19. *Changing English*, *27*(3), 262–269. doi:10.1080/1358684X.2020.1779029

ADDITIONAL READING

Andriivna, B. O., Vasylivna, K. O., Pavlivna, K. O., & Mykhaylivna, S. V. (2020). Using distance EdTech for remote foreign language teaching during the COVID-19 lockdown in Ukraine. *Arab World English Journal: Special Issue on English in Ukrainian Context*. 4–15. doi:10.24093/awej/elt3.1

Cardullo, V., Wang, C., Burton, M., & Dong, J. (2021). K-12 teachers' remote teaching self-efficacy during the pandemic. *Journal of Research in Innovative Teaching and Learning*, *14*(1), 32–45. doi:10.1108/JRIT-10-2020-0055

King, K. P. (2002). Educational technology professional development as transformative learning opportunities. *Computers & Education*, *39*(3), 283–297. doi:10.1016/S0360-1315(02)00073-8

König, J., Jäger-Biela, D. J., & Glutsch, N. (2020). Adapting to online teaching during COVID-19 school closure: Teacher education and teacher competence effects among early career teachers in Germany. *European Journal of Teacher Education*, *43*(4), 608–622. doi:10.1080/02619768.2020.1809650

Mpungose, C. B. (2020). Emergent transition from face-to-face to online learning in a South African University in the context of the Coronavirus pandemic. *Humanities & Social Sciences Communications*, *7*(113), 1–9. doi:10.105741599-020-00603-x

Ortlipp, M. (2008). Keeping and using reflective journals in the qualitative research process. *Qualitative Report*, *13*(4), 695–705. https://nsuworks.nova.edu/tqr/vol13/iss4/8/

Robertson, S. (2020). Going hard and early: Tertiary teaching under lockdown in New Zealand. *International Studies in Educational Administration*, *48*(2), 107–113. http://web.b.ebscohost.com.ezproxy.umsl.edu/ehost/pdfviewer/pdfviewer?vid=2&sid=6e3b61b8-02ab-45c2-8272-abed063781fe%40pdc-v-sessmgr03

Warschauer, M. (2002). Reconceptualizing the Digital Divide. *First Monday*, *7*(7), 1–16. doi:10.5210/fm.v7i7.967

KEY TERMS AND DEFINITIONS

Asynchronous Online Classes: Classes where students log on to a platform and work on it in their own time and at their own pace.

Collaboration: Working well together to identify solutions to common problems.

Community: Building rapport between students, teachers, and parents.

Face-to-Face Teaching: Teaching that is conducted in a physical classroom.

Flipped Classroom: Students collaborate and solve problems in class, while the bulk of the work that can be done independently is done at home, asynchronously.

Hybrid Teaching: Teaching that is conducted with half of the students in the physical classroom while the other half is online, at home, changing on alternate weeks.

Online Teaching: Teaching that is conducted online, in synchronous or asynchronous classes, using various devices connected to the Internet.

Reflective Practice: The transformative process of critically reflecting on one's lived experiences as the result of the need for self-change.

Synchronous Online Classes: Classes where students are all online and learning at the same time.

Chapter 15
Transitioning the Elementary Mathematics Classroom to Virtual Learning:
Exploring the Perspectives and Experiences of Teachers

Christie Lynn Martin
University of South Carolina, USA

Kristin E. Harbour
University of South Carolina, USA

Drew Polly
https://orcid.org/0000-0003-2370-4409
University of North Carolina at Charlotte, USA

ABSTRACT

In this chapter, the authors explore the experiences of K-12 teachers as they navigated an abrupt transition from a traditional face-to-face mathematics classroom to virtual learning. The authors used a survey to ask teachers to explain what effective mathematics instruction meant for their classroom. Their responses most closely aligned with four of the National Council of Teachers of Mathematics (NCTM) effective practices. The survey continued to prompt teachers to share their concerns for the transition, the most effective virtual tools they implemented, support they received, how their virtual classrooms would influence their return to face, and where they needed more support. The authors offer recommendations for supporting teachers as the virtual classroom currently remains in place for many and for transitioning back to the traditional face-to-face classroom. Technology use and digital competence continues to expand in K-12 education.

DOI: 10.4018/978-1-7998-6922-1.ch015

INTRODUCTION

Schools all over the world faced difficult decisions for in-person learning as "107 countries implemented national school closures by March 18, 2020" (Viner et.al, 2020, p.1). These unexpected school closures led to instructional delivery continuing in multiple ways. Since these first closures, many schools have operated in virtual form, hybrid classes, and faced sudden shutdowns due to a spike in the COVID-19 cases. In addition to concerns about the modes of instructional delivery, long term school closures are also raising concerns about exacerbating issues of equality, equity, and access (Van Lancker & Parolin, 2020).

Teachers and administrations are currently charged to meet all these needs, while simultaneously working to continue supporting students' learning. This time has been challenging; however, there is an opportunity in this space that may create long-lasting change in schools and teacher preparation (Darling-Hammond & Hyler, 2020). Teachers are in the midst of taking their years of in-person classroom expertise developed through education, teaching, and professional development and transitioning to an online, virtual classroom. They are examining pedagogical practices for each content area while being cognizant of the additional stress families are facing. In essence, teachers and administrators are actively engaging in action research, finding solutions and pathways to meet the needs of their students. Sagor (2000) defines action research as "a disciplined process of inquiry conducted *by* and *for* those taking the action. The primary reason for engaging in action research is to assist the "actor" in improving and/or refining his or her actions" (p.3). This pilot study, conducted by mathematics teacher educators, was designed using the framework of action research as this study is collecting data from practicing teachers. We wanted to understand how to best support teachers in providing effective and equitable mathematics instruction in the new virtual classroom. The data will be used to inform our work with teacher candidates (future teachers) in course work and with practicing teachers during professional development that we facilitate. We acknowledge that this study may differ from traditional action research since we are not evaluating our own teaching or use of interventions, but the goals of this study align to those of action research since this data is being used to inform our practice as designers of professional development experiences and teacher education courses.

BACKGROUND

The next section offers a synthesis of effective practices identified by the National Council for Teachers of Mathematics ([NCTM], 2014) pertaining to teaching mathematics conceptually, using high-quality mathematics tasks during instruction, facilitating productive mathematical discourse, and teaching with multiple representations of mathematical concepts.

Effective Mathematics Teaching Practices Overview

As we consider the teaching practices that participants noted using prior to the COVID-19 pandemic, we must first consider what research indicates as effective practices for the teaching and learning of mathematics. In the following section, we outline four effective teaching practices. While NCTM (2014) indicates eight effective teaching practices, we keep our review to the following four as they encompass many of the practices our teacher participants indicated engaging with prior to the shift to virtual instruction.

Conceptual Understanding and Procedural Fluency

For students to know and do mathematics, both procedural and conceptual knowledge are necessary. Procedural knowledge can be defined as the "action sequences for solving problems" (Rittle-Johnson & Alibali, 1999, p. 175); whereas conceptual knowledge can be defined as a

"connected web of knowledge, a network in which the linking relationships are as prominent as the discrete pieces of information" (Hiebert & Lefevre, 1986, p. 3). In other words, procedural knowledge is more focused on how a problem is solved, whereas conceptual knowledge refers to the connections or relationships among ideas, strategies, and information. Both procedural and conceptual knowledge are necessary for the development of conceptual understanding and procedural fluency (NCTM, 2014; Van de Walle et al., 2019), and these two types of knowledge do not develop independent of one another (Rittle-Johnson & Alibali, 1999). Effective mathematics instruction integrates and balances the development of both conceptual knowledge and procedural knowledge (National Mathematics Advisory Panel, 2008; National Research Council [NRC], 2001), and emphasizes the development of procedural fluency through a foundation of conceptual understanding (NCTM, 2014).

Conceptual understanding is the "comprehension of mathematical concepts, operations, and relations" (NRC, 2001, p. 5). Conceptual understanding involves the ability to understand the relationships, connections, and representations of mathematical concepts and interpret this information in a meaningful way. Students who have a conceptual understanding of a mathematical concept engage in problem-solving and reasoning, and can communicate, represent, and justify their thinking (e.g., CCSM, 2010). Procedural fluency is the "skill in carrying out procedures flexibly, accurately, efficiently, and appropriately" (NRC, 2001, p. 5).

A critical point in understanding procedural fluency is that procedural fluency is far more than simply being able to follow a procedure to find an answer. A student who has a strong procedural fluency can determine the most appropriate and efficient way to solve a problem, rather than solely relying on one set way to solve a problem using only one procedure. This student is also able to move flexibly in their problem-solving approach, as they select different strategies based on the given problem. Conceptual understanding and procedural fluency work in tandem, with one supporting the development of the other, and with both being crucial for students to become mathematical proficient (NRC, 2001; Van de Walle et al., 2019). Despite the integration of conceptual understanding and procedural fluency, scholars advocate that the teachers initially focus on conceptual understanding and develop procedural fluency through activities focused on conceptual understanding. Over time and through this emphasis on conceptual development, students build their procedural fluency (NCTM, 2014).

Developing Understanding through Mathematical Tasks

One way to support teaching for conceptual understanding is through the use of mathematical tasks (Boston & Smith, 2009; NCTM, 2014; Polly, 2016a; Stein et al., 1996). Research on mathematical tasks has led to a seminal classification of mathematical tasks based on their cognitive demand (NCTM, 2014; Smith & Stein, 1998).

A task-centric approach to mathematics teaching provides opportunities for students to engage in solving word problems, explore mathematical concepts embedded in real-life contexts, and make sense of mathematics while exploring various tasks and problems (Polly et al., 2010; Smith & Stein, 1998). The 2014 NCTM *Principles to Action* document calls for students to engage in productive struggle by exploring mathematical tasks during lessons. Rather than being told directly how to solve tasks, scholars have found that conceptual understanding as well as problem solving skills can be developed through this approach (NCTM, 2014; Polly et al., 2014; Wang et al., 2013). Research indicates that teachers often pose tasks, but during class, teachers frequently decrease the cognitive demand of them by providing rote procedures to follow, launching the task by modeling the exact way to solve tasks, and decreasing the amount of time that students engage in a task (Polly, 2016b; Stein et al, 1996). There is a lack of research about how K-12 teachers enact mathematical tasks while teaching in a virtual environment.

Mathematical Discourse

While task-based instruction provides the setting in which effective teaching and learning of mathematics can occur, engaging students in rich, productive, mathematical discourse around these high-quality tasks is critical in developing mathematical thinkers and doers (e.g., Smith & Stein, 2018; Van de Walle et al., 2019). Effective mathematics teaching engages students in mathematical discourse wherein students are able to enhance and formalize their learning through purposeful dialogue involving everyone in the classroom community (NCTM, 2014; Smith & Stein, 2018). Mathematical discourse can occur in various ways, including verbal and written communication; although, verbal communication is often the most common way in which mathematical discourse is facilitated. Effective facilitation of mathematical discourse provides the vehicle for students to engage in reasoning, justifying, and explaining their problem-solving approaches, providing for more opportunities for students to develop a conceptual understanding of mathematical concepts (Carpenter et al., 2003; Michaels et al., 2008; Smith & Stein, 2018; NCTM, 2014). Additionally, mathematics classrooms that promote mathematical discourse can create a more inclusive environment where all students' ideas are represented, shared, valued, and encouraged (e.g., NCTM, 2014; Walshaw & Anthony, 2008).

A common way in which our participants facilitated mathematical discourse prior to the COVID-19 pandemic is through number talks: "Classroom number talks, five- to fifteen-minute conversations around purposefully crafted computation problems, are a productive tool that can be incorporated into classroom instruction to combine the essential processes and habits of mind of doing math" (Parrish, 2010, p.199). Parrish notes several classroom environment structures needed to promote effective number talks: (a) a supportive classroom environment that promotes risk-taking, and (b) a classroom environment where students can question, be critical of their own thinking and their classmates, and be open to new strategies. When the environment is designed for number talks to take place the next component needed for effective number talks is the actual communication. During the enactment of number talks, discourse helps students to address clarity and consider the ideas of others. The teacher moves from a stance of modeling, confirming correct answers, and explaining to questioning and listening to promote students' reasoning. The crafted computation problems are designed for students to use mental math to solve by tapping into the mathematical relationships we use to make sense of computation problems. Moreover, Sun et al. (2018) suggest that number talks are an important tool for learning that extends through high school. The longevity of this type of discourse practice is promising for vertical alignment.

Multiple Representations

To support students' conceptual understanding and procedural fluency, effective mathematics instruction provides students with ample opportunities to engage with multiple representations of mathematical concepts and to explore the connections among the various representations (NCTM, 2000, 2014). "Representations embody critical features of mathematical constructs and actions, such as drawing diagrams and using words to show and explain the meaning" of various mathematical concepts (NCTM, 2014, p. 24). Representations allow for us to communicate and share our mathematical ideas and understandings to others (National Research Council, 2001; NCTM, 2000). Mathematical representations are generally described as falling into the following classifications: (a) contextual, (b) visual, (c) verbal, (d) physical, and (e) symbolic (Lesh et al., 1987). Through the use of multiple representations, students are able to become more flexible problem-solvers and thinkers, reason about mathematical concepts in a variety of ways, and appreciate the varied problem-solving approaches used by themselves and their peers (e.g., Fuson et al., 2005; NRC, 2001).

Visual and physical representations of mathematical ideas are particularly important for young learners (NRC, 2001). A common way to include both visual and physical representations is through the use of manipulatives. "Manipulative materials are objects designed to represent explicitly and concretely mathematical ideas that are abstract" (Moyer, 2001, p. 176). These concrete models allow for physical manipulation by students to provide a hands-on learning experience (Moyer, 2001). Concrete models, both in physical and virtual form, have been found to help students understand mathematical relationships as they are able to visually explore and manipulate the models to *see* these relationships (Roschelle et al., 2010).

Based on the recommendations from scholars in mathematics education and the context of the COVID-19 pandemic, this study aimed to examine mathematics teachers' uses of specific technologies to support their virtual mathematics teaching in order to inform our future work as designers of professional development and mathematics education courses. Since a majority of the participants were teachers who have either graduated from our teacher education programs or participated in professional development that we had facilitated, we situate this action research as a collection of data on teachers' current practices that we use to inform our future work.

This paper is grounded in the broad research questions: How do teachers reflect upon their mathematics teaching during the pandemic? This question was used to inform our future work as designers and instructors of mathematics professional development efforts and mathematics teacher education courses for future teachers.

METHODS

This is an action research study that uses qualitative content analysis of survey data. To examine our broad research question, the authors designed, refined, and then collected data from mathematics teachers about their experiences in the pandemic. We situated this study in the framework of action research (e.g., Mills, 2014; Putman & Rock, 2017) since this exploratory, pilot study is used to inform our work as teacher educators and professional development facilitators who support mathematics teaching and learning. Mills (2014) defines action research as a systematic inquiry conducted by teacher researchers or other stakeholders in teaching and learning to gather information with goals such as gaining insight and developing reflective practice (p.10).

This study was designed as a pilot to help us refine our questions and decide on subsequent methods for conducting a larger study in the future (Crossman, 2019). We moved forward with several considerations in mind. First, at the time of development we were approximately seven months into the pandemic with limited access to schools. We wanted to gain insight into how this experience unfolded for mathematics teachers, and how this might continue to impact their teaching. Second, we recognized the stress and time constraints teachers face and continue to face in the midst of the pandemic. We noticed from other projects and feedback from colleagues that teachers were reluctant to participate in research at this time. This was considered when designing the survey, as explained in Data Collection below. The survey was completed by 40 teachers ranging from kindergarten to high school.

Data Collection

Through our survey, teachers (a) identified their initial concerns, (b) indicated where and who provided support for these transitions to their instruction, (c) described what tools and practices they find more effective than others, and (d) considered what pedagogical shifts in their mathematics instructional practices will be long lasting. The eleven questions that were sent out through google are included in the Appendix. The researchers recognize that in-person learning as invaluable, and that shifting to online instruction in such a short time was not an easy feat. However, there is much to learn and take away from this effort.

Specifically, this study focuses on the transition that teachers made in their mathematics instructional practices and how this process, experiences, tools, and reflection will impact their pedagogy moving forward. A researcher-created survey was sent to elementary mathematics teachers across grade levels and stated via e-mail to teachers who were part of both universities' school partnership network. The survey included three questions to identify demographic information, including (1) the state teachers were located, (2) grade level taught, and (3) years of teaching experience. We purposely limited the demographic information to ensure that the survey was not overly taxing, our objective was to begin to examine the experiences teachers shared in the transition to virtual learning.

Data Analysis

The survey included three demographic questions and eight open-ended questions focused on what the participating teachers found to be effective mathematics instructional practices in-person (i.e., prior to the COVID-19 pandemic), their concerns about moving to a virtual classroom, the technology tools they found helpful and why, and how they believe their future in-person mathematics instruction will be impacted by this transition. Teachers' responses were read through several times, and while reading the researchers began memo-ing with notes in the margins (Mills, 2014). An example of memo-ing from our analysis is in Figure 1 below. Color-coded highlighting was used to begin the open coding process (Miles et al., 2019). The codes were condensed into broader themes. For example, the first question identified practices that teachers found most effective for teaching mathematics. Within the responses, similar phrases were highlighted such as "the use of hands on manipulatives," "hands on learning strategies," "hands on manipulatives for kids, blocks, cubes, fraction pieces" and "lots of manipulatives, concrete-representation-abstract" were collapsed into the theme of mathematical representations. This analysis and coding continued for the first question and became the basis of our literature review. We continue this analysis process for the remaining seven open ended questions and will discuss the findings.

Figure 1. Memo-ing notes

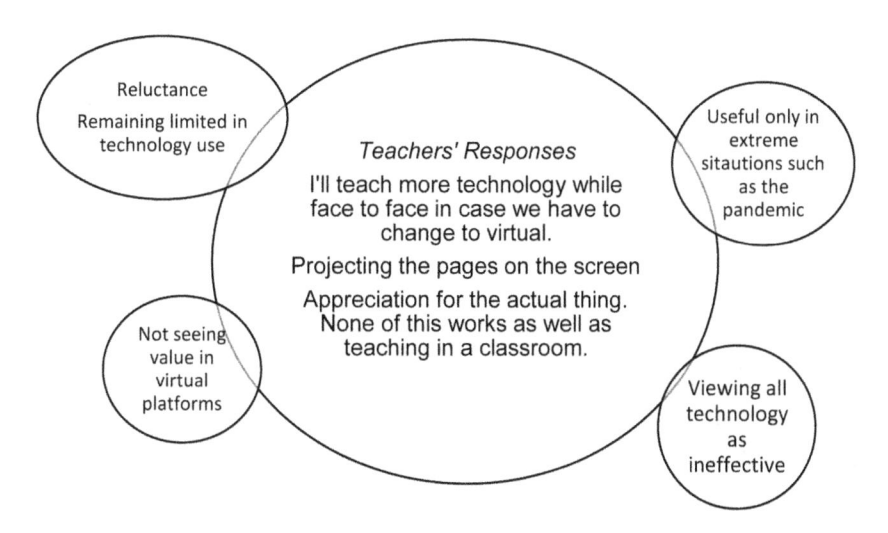

[Figure: Diagram showing "Teachers' Responses" in center with surrounding bubbles. Center contains: I'll teach more technology while face to face in case we have to change to virtual. Projecting the pages on the screen. Appreciation for the actual thing. None of this works as well as teaching in a classroom. Surrounding bubbles: Reluctance Remaining limited in technology use; Useful only in extreme situations such as the pandemic; Not seeing value in virtual platforms; Viewing all technology as ineffective.]

FINDINGS

Transitioning to Virtual Learning

Following the initial survey question in which teachers indicated effective mathematical practices, teachers were asked to identify their initial concerns when transitioning from traditional face-to-face instruction to virtual learning. The concerns raised were the lack of manipulatives, being able to work collaboratively, providing authentic feedback and addressing misconceptions immediately, and providing student choice. These concerns aligned with key elements of the effective instructional practices they were using in face-to-face instruction, including multiple representations (i.e., manipulatives) and collaboration (i.e., discourse). Teachers developed an environment in their traditional, face-to-face classrooms with mathematics teaching practices they found effective; as they made their transition to virtual settings, teachers looked to technology to address their concerns and recreate an environment where effective mathematics teaching still occurs.

Question six focused on determining how teachers implemented the use of virtual tools to create high-quality mathematics learning opportunities. Several common tools emerged in participant responses. The common virtual tools/platforms were cross-checked with the survey question that asked which tools and practices would continue to influence their instruction going forward. There were 39 responses to this survey question that were analyzed to identify tools that were mentioned several times. One response might contain a number of virtual tools. Table 1 provides the tools mentioned in responses and the frequency they were mentioned.

Table 1. Frequency of virtual tools and/or platforms used in virtual instruction

Virtual Tool/Platform	Frequency of Mentions
Virtual manipulatives	13
Google platform (forms, slides, & meet)	12
Zoom	6
Jamboard	6
Interactive whiteboards	5
Document cameras	5
Nearpod	4
Kahoot!	3
Peardeck	3
Edmodo	2
Flipgrid	2
Bitmoji	2

Virtual Manipulatives

The continued ability to incorporate the use of manipulatives into virtual instruction was noted as an area of concern for teachers. As virtual learning became a reality, virtual manipulatives were then selected as a helpful tool that would continue to be used when in-person instruction returned. While manipulatives, in general, are often considered a physical representation, the use of virtual manipulatives continues to represent the use of multiple representations in instruction but may shift more to a visual type of representation as opposed to a physical one (Lesh et al., 1987). Additionally, the use of manipulatives, either physical or visual representations, aligns with a focus on instruction to support the development of conceptual understanding (e.g., NCTM, 2000, 2014) wherein students are provided the opportunity to explore relationships and connections among mathematical ideas and concepts. The use of manipulatives provides experiential learning, which is noted as especially important for young learners (NRC, 2001). It is widely accepted that manipulatives assist learners in their development from the concrete to the abstract representations of mathematical ideas and concepts; this sentiment holds true for both physical and virtual manipulatives. For instance, Burns and Hamm (2011) conducted a study to compare the use of concrete and virtual manipulatives for a fraction unit in third- and fourth grade. They note that virtual manipulatives have potential for teaching mathematics, but there is a lack of empirical studies. They found both groups made improvements between pre - and post-tests, and there were no statistically significant differences. Moreover, Olkun (2003) examined the difference between concrete and virtual manipulatives in geometry for fourth- and fifth grade and found the fifth-grade students improved more with the virtual manipulatives. The research suggests that virtual manipulatives can offer the positive impact that concrete (i.e., physical) manipulatives have in supporting students' conceptual understanding and may potentially provide greater impact on a particular grade levels and content. Although virtual manipulatives were frequently indicated as a tool being used during virtual learning, there was only one response that included virtual manipulatives as a tool teachers would continue to use upon returning to face-to face-instruction.

Interactive Platforms

Teachers' responses to how they implemented virtual tools to create high-quality mathematics learning opportunities highlighted various platforms that provide synchronous interactions, including: (a) Google Meet, (b) Zoom, (c) Jamboard, (d) Interactive Whiteboards, (e) Nearpod, and (f) Peardeck. These virtual platforms served as instructional tools noted to be effective in teachers' virtual instruction. Some responses indicated platforms are also being used in combination. For instance, a teacher noted: "I am able to use Jamboards with my iPad presented on the Google Meet to demonstrate how to solve problems when students need intervention and extension." (T13, 2020) As we consider the four effective teaching practices that teachers indicated using in their face-to-face instruction (i.e., conceptual learning, high-quality tasks, mathematical discourse, and use of multiple representations), we can infer that the use of these synchronous platforms were used as a way to continue teaching mathematics effectively in a virtual learning environment. For instance, synchronous platforms can provide the space for the use of tasks and encouragement of mathematical discourse to occur. As indicated in the teachers' response of integrating various platforms, we see the focus on solving problems. The coupling of platforms may have provided a way in which teachers could present a high-quality mathematical task to students, as well as promote in-the-moment discourse around said task, both of which are associated with the development of conceptual understanding surrounding mathematical concepts and ideas (e.g., NCTM 200, 2014; Carpenter et al., 2003; Michaels et al., 2008; Smith et al., 1996).

Data indicated that Google platforms and Zoom were most frequently used during virtual instruction. Google Meet and Zoom are familiar video conferencing tools that allow the participants to share their screen, use chat features, and breakout rooms to talk with one another. Jamboard, also a product of Google released in 2017, is an app and interactive whiteboard that allows everyone on the board to edit and add to the board. It connects to Google files and Google search engines to pull in images and pictures. The Jamboard files are automatically saved to the cloud. There is currently minimal research on the use of Jamboard in elementary mathematics; however, Jamboard was noted in teacher responses as effective for virtual instruction and as one of the tools that will continue to influence face-to-face instruction.

Another interactive platform that appeared in the results was Nearpod (www.nearpod.com). Nearpod provides flexibility, allowing one to upload slides and videos from other platforms. It also has premade lessons that are searchable by state, content area, and standard. Once a lesson is created, Nearpod has nine different types of formative assessment options that are inserted at chosen points during the lesson. These formative assessments allow teachers to assess students' understanding at various points in the lesson, thus providing ample opportunities for feedback to students (a concern expressed by teachers in the transition to virtual learning). Nearpod also offers virtual reality and simulations to engage students. Nearpod access is free and includes all of the discussed components; however, there are two levels that require payment and an option for a school or district to purchase access. It was not specified in the responses which version of Nearpod the teachers were using or if the platform was being used school wide. Nearpod was launched in 2012; although the number of users have increased, there is little empirical research on the impact on elementary learners. Delacruz (2014) conducted a qualitative study of using Nearpod for guiding reading instruction. The study included nine fourth students, four of which were noted as English Language Learners. The findings indicated that students preferred using Nearpod for guided reading and noted they could interact with the pages, answer questions, and draw what they thought words meant. Although this is a small study in language arts, it suggests the interactive platform is engaging for students. Nearpod was also selected by the American Association of School Librarians

(AASL) as one of the best apps for 2019. Like Nearpod, Pear Deck offers comparable features and pricing scale, and was selected as a best website in 2015 by AASL; however, limited studies on its use in the elementary classroom exist.

Flipgrid, a free tool by Microsoft that offers a space for video discussion, was another interactive platform teachers noted using during their virtual instruction. The Flipgrid platform ensures each student can individually respond to specific prompts from their teachers. Video posts can be shared with classmates, and classmates can respond to others' videos. This feature can be turned on and off as needed. Research studies continue to be limited on these platforms. Even so, there are some examples of how Flipgrid is being used and suggestions for its use in the literature. For instance, Flipgrid was used with fifth- and sixth-grade students to share book talks with one another (Batchelor & Cassidy, 2019). In this study, students provided feedback to one another about their talk. In another example Johnson and colleagues (2019) shared their work with kindergarten students implementing a Project-Based Learning (PBL) Inquiry using Flipgrid within the project. The central focus of this research was PBL; however, it was noted that Flipgrid was easy to use, allowed for easy editing and revising, alleviated anxiety for presentations, and offered a platform to give feedback. Additionally, Miller et al. (2020) shared suggestions for using Flipgrid in the elementary classroom across content areas. Their piece presents ideas moving through the four Depth of Knowledge (DOK) levels: (1) recall, (2) basic application, (3) strategic thinking, and (4) extended thinking (Webb, 1997). Miller and colleagues' suggestions included students recording themselves doing tasks such as, counting money to show basic recall, as well as recording themselves engaging in complicated tasks such as multi-digit multiplication and division to share with classmates. The mathematical tasks elevated to collecting data, sharing data, and conducting analyses of the data. Collectively, these articles provide insight into how Flipgrid supports student learning and may be a potential tool for engaging in high-quality mathematics tasks and mathematical discourse. In addition to the promising, but limited research, Flipgrid was also selected in 2017 as a best app and website from AASL.

Kahoot! is a widely used interactive quiz game, designed in Norway, with 70 million users globally (Videnovik et al., 2018). Teachers can design their own quizzes or choose ready to play games within the system. A teacher can create a Kahoot to administer at any time during a unit, at the beginning to access prior knowledge, as a formative assessment during the unit, or as a review or summative assessment. Students' procedural knowledge, a type of knowledge related to both conceptual understanding and procedural fluency (Rittle-Johnson & Alibali, 1999) may be developed by tools such as Kahoot! Another tool shared in the participating elementary mathematics teacher responses was Edmodo. Trust (2017) described Edmodo as a management tool that creates a safe space for class interactions. She highlighted the subject community feature in her research of mathematics teaching and learning. Trust's (2017) study sought to understand Edmodo's online space of a virtual community Professional Development Network (PDN). Results showed teachers felt empowered by being in this community and were able to access the community at times that were best for them. The survey and interview data in Trust's study indicated teachers' teaching and learning practices were shifted by participating in this community. While our participating teachers' survey data showed Edmodo as a tool they found effective, the responses were limited in detail and it remains unknown whether they were participating in the communities available through this platform.

In addition to using specific platforms to engage students, teachers noted the use of Bitmoji. A Bitmoji is a personal avatar emoji with a large selection of stickers to convey mood, emotion, and quotes. The Bitmoji virtual classroom has grown into a large network of teachers using Google Slides coupled with Bitmojis to create interactive slides. Facebook pages dedicated to Bitmoji classroom resources such as the private group Bitmoji Craze for Educators have over half a million followers and https://www.weareteachers.com/virtual-bitmoji-classroom/ is filled with Bitmoji classrooms across grade levels. The growth and popularity of this platform and its impact on student engagement is yet to be studied.

Transitions: Growth and Challenges

The transition from in-person mathematics teaching to virtual mathematics teaching was a large shift for both teachers and students; however, when meeting a challenge, there is bound to be growth. The next survey question sought to understand how this experience impacted the participants as mathematics teachers. Several responses indicated teachers grew in several ways. Responses showed teachers reflected on their own communication skills and how to engage, observe, support, and encourage their students. Jacobs et al. (2010) defined professional noticing as observing students, using those observations to interpret students' thinking, and using that interpretation to respond. The quotes indicate teachers were grappling with how to build the expertise necessary to effectively engage in professional noticing virtually: "I recognize how essential it is for me to watch students as they are working in order to correct misconceptions." (T1, 2020)

It has made me appreciate being with students as they work. So much of what I do as a math teacher isn't explicitly planned, but a reaction to what the students in front of me are doing. Only seeing their work once they are "done" allows for lots of mistakes to go unchecked for too long.(T29,2020)

In the responses noted above, the teachers recognized that watching students is essential for the purpose of correcting misconceptions. In addition to addressing misconceptions, research on professional noticing examines how teachers interpret evidence of students' thinking and understanding to respond and support that understanding. Prior research with 131 participants ranging from prospective teachers to emerging teacher leaders showed that the emerging teacher leader group had the most participants that provided robust evidence of professional noticing expertise (Jacobs et al., 2010). The teacher leader groups' evidence focused on interpreting children's understanding, whereas the remaining categories of teachers provided responses that did not capture students' understanding. Instead, these responses were related more to general observations. This study highlights the complexity of making sense of students' strategies and being able to identify their understanding based on what was noticed. Teachers build their noticing expertise to enhance discourse and choose appropriate tasks. The responses from our survey reveals the challenges teachers faced building those skills and adapting to the virtual environment. The next responses highlight teachers' experiences and growth in communication. "This experience has challenged me to become a better math teacher. I have had to find more ways to explain skills to my students and really break down the "why" behind the processes we use". (T3, 2020) or

"I am more mindful of encouraging/supporting mathematical communication and encouraging students to openly explore math and develop their own strategies. "(T21, 2020). Another teacher explained:

It has allowed me to be very intentional with my teaching and very visual. I have also prerecorded lessons which is a great way for me to multiply myself in the classroom for kids to refer back to the lesson again and again if needed. (T18, 2020)

The responses included "become a better math teacher", "more mindful", and "be very intentional." The move to a virtual platform prompted teachers to reflect on their instruction with conceptual understanding, exploration of mathematics, visual representation, and encouragement for their students at the center. These responses connect back to the earlier discussion of multiple representations and discourse being important pedagogical practices in the mathematics classroom. As teachers were challenged by a virtual platform they continued to reflect on their practice and grow.

"This experience has definitely made me stretch my creativity and get out of my comfort zone. It has also motivated me to learn different technology platforms." (T34, 2020)

"It has caused me to be more innovative. I still don't have it all figured out, but I will not give up. "(T8, 2020)

"It has helped me to EXPLAIN/ MODEL better and to think how I will explain it a lot more." (T7, 2020)

The responses above contain words like "stretch", "creativity", "motivation", "innovation", and "not giving up". Teachers shared a desire to persist and persevere and use technology to engage their students.

"Made me want to have a flipped classroom where students can receive self- paced lessons but use classroom time to discuss and work together." (T13, 2020)

Struggled at first with limited formative assessment in Google forms or in photographs of worksheets uploaded to a document. But now I see added engagement and movement forward due to shared thinking and added evidence of student understanding in Jamboard or Kami. (T12, 2020)

The responses indicate that the transition increased intentionality, use of multiple platforms, critically examined explanations, and creativity. These areas of growth will now be transitioned back into a face-to-face model and may provide ways of being more responsive to other situations that interrupt the lives of our students.

While the majority of teachers' responses indicated positive takeaways from virtual learning, there were responses that highlighted the challenges teachers faced and showcased clear tensions remain as teachers reflect on using technology in their mathematics instruction. The responses below were to the questions which tools do you find effective for virtual learning and how will these tools influence your face-to-face instruction.

"Being virtual is so much less efficient than being in person." (T31, 2020)

"Students do less paper and pencil thinking, bad!" (T15, 2020)

"Appreciation for the actual thing. None of this works as well as teaching in a classroom."(T19, 2020)

"Possibly using google slides more, but nothing virtual I have found will replace students manipulating something with their hands."(T10, 2020)

"None-unless we have to resume virtual education; I was already using the practices that I tried to apply virtually." (T2,2020)

These responses indicate several teachers felt virtual learning was a poor substitute for in person learning. This sentiment may have been shared by more teachers that were surveyed; however, a majority of their responses showed they did find aspects of this experience to be positive and able to be transitioned back to their face-to-face classrooms. The response above stating "None of this works" seemed closed off to the idea that there are virtual tools and platforms that enhance learning for students. Pensky (2005) describes today's students as digital natives, they have been immersed in technology from a young age and are fluent in the digital language. Pensky suggests "As educators, we must take our cues from our students' 21st century innovations and behaviors, abandoning, in many cases, our own pre digital instincts and comfort zones" (p.2). Resnick (2002) also notes that schools should make changes to support students that are proficient users of technology. It is not to minimize the value in paper and pencil or hand-on manipulatives, but to consider how various technology tools and platforms can be used to address the needs of learners considered digital natives.

Dietrich and Balli (2014) conducted a qualitative study of classroom learning and technology with fifth grade students. The study explored how technology engages students considered digital natives in authentic learning. The researchers also sought to examine what lesson qualities are important for authentic engagement and if they are the same as previously noted in the research. Their findings indicated that engagement increased when new technology was introduced; however, if it was used as a prop for direct instruction that engagement quickly waned. The data indicated that sustained authentic engagement was generated when technology use was controlled by the students. The researchers identify control, choice, and real-world tasks as essential lesson qualities for technology to increase engagement and learning. Additionally, the importance of teacher training was highlighted. Student comments indicated they recognized when teachers continued a delivery style lecture with a document camera without revising their delivery to student centered strategies. Training, support, and learning opportunities are important for teachers to transition to effective and engaging virtual learning. Our survey asked participants to discuss where they received support or training; the results were mixed.

Current and Desired Supports

Transitions are usually more successful when there is a support system in place. This was another question on the survey: Where did teachers find support for this work and where would they like to receive more? The survey indicated, as often is the case, that teachers had varied levels of support.

A number of responses (below) showed teachers were finding support from one another and seeking out videos, social media, forums and online teaching groups. One participant noted, "There are a multitude of how to videos both on [our district] platform and on YouTube that provided support." (T1, 2020) Other participants commented on the benefit of social media, with specific references to Facebook and Twitter to get ideas and resources. Lastly, some participants commented that their Professional Learning Communities and colleagues on their grade level figured it out together using approaches like trying new things and seeing if it worked.

These responses coincide with increases of videos and Facebook groups designed to support the rapid transition to virtual learning. The next group of responses indicates support coming from within schools and districts. This support included technology-specific specialists as well as district-based and school-based mathematics specialists and coaches who provided resources and ongoing support as teachers learned how to teach mathematics virtually.

One participant noted that the benefit of having a mathematics expert who also was adept at teaching with technology. She wrote, "My math coach has been really helpful! She has helped create meaningful activities, support us in planning, answer tech questions related to Canvas." (T17, 2020) District personnel, math coaches, math specialists, technology specialists, and professional development were included as support provided outside fellow teachers and social media. This includes developing lessons, activities, providing resources, and technology support.

While teacher-participants commented about the inclusion of multiple examples of support, six of the 40 respondents indicated that there was a lack of support. One teacher wrote, "Our Instructional Coach can literally never be found, and colleagues are too busy dealing with their own problems, that I have not sought out help. Therefore, I really have not received any support to speak of." (T28, 2020)

Desired Support

The next survey question, number 11, asked teachers to reflect on this transition and consider what kind of support they wanted to have more of. The responses showed teachers wanted support in a number of areas. One of the areas where teachers noted was technology support. One teacher-participant wrote on the survey, "[I] need more step-by-step technology support. Technology is a huge learning curve for me and others in my age group. No resources [were] available for when I have questions about how to upload, download, or send items."

Others asked for someone to do the resource cultivation and creation. One teacher commented how they would like "someone to research different technology tools and actually teach us how to use them." Ten teachers noted that there was a need for more technology expertise related to teaching with technology and resources to use. Most teacher-participants asked for professional development on these topics.

One teacher commented, "If we are going to be teaching this way for a while there is an immediate need for some professional development on how to do it well." These responses indicate teachers have reflected on their experiences and consider professional development and workshops may help them enhance their teaching.

In addition, several responses suggest greater collaboration with colleagues is also a desired area of support. One teacher-participant wrote, "I would like more collaboration with colleagues in my district because we are working with the same population of kids and we should be building stronger collective efficacy." Another commented about her desire to "connect with other teachers to see what they are doing, what games they are playing." While a few found resources and examples via social media and their Personalized Learning Network most teachers desired more opportunities to learn and collaborate with others.

Teachers cited in the survey that they found support for this transition with their colleagues. The term Professional Learning Communities (PLC) is nuanced being represented differently across schools, but central to these communities is the idea that teachers come together and reflect on their practice. These communities exist within pre-service teaching programs as well. Research indicates that these communities support teachers in developing their instructional practices (Wahlstrom & Louis, 2008). School closings and schedule changes may have limited teachers' ability to plan for PLC meetings. There were also a few responses that were centered on resources.

One teacher said that it would be ideal for her district to make "a library of virtual tools and paced lessons that combine virtual tools and hands-on using household manipulatives, pacing and sequencing of skills for 100% virtual compared to standard in-person learning."

Another teacher wrote about her need for "support in making materials / assignments that can be ready to go for lessons." Teachers' responses focused on resources that are already created, access to paid versions of technology platforms, and assistance to create the resources to engage their students. The request for support in creating materials may be met with collaboration or professional development.

SOLUTIONS AND RECOMMENDATIONS

There are several areas to consider as we reflect on the experience of abruptly transitioning to online instruction and move forward to enhance the learning environment for our students.

Teachers' Successful Uses of Technology

Despite the sudden shift to teaching mathematics virtually, our data indicate that many teachers have not only taken on these challenges but have found successes in doing so. Data also indicate tensions and clear challenges associated with these efforts. *So what can we take from this and how do we move forward?* As we write this chapter in late 2020 and early 2021, the COVID-19 pandemic continues, leaving us to consider how to best support teachers in their efforts to provide effective and equitable mathematics virtual learning experiences now, as well as how to support the continued use of effective virtual pedagogical practices as school communities transition back to in-person instructional delivery.

Teachers are resilient and with access to technology being at an all-time high (Educause, 2017), the participants in this study reported using a wide variety of technologies and approaches to enhance their teaching and support their students' learning. While it is intuitive, the technologies used to support live synchronous virtual teaching (e.g., Zoom and Google Meets) were frequently used. Future research needs to be more nuanced with alternative ways to collect data, such as analyzing live or retroactive evidence of how teachers are teaching mathematics. Furthermore, there is a need to examine teachers' and students' perceptions and reactions to this experience, as well as evidence from students during virtual lessons. Further, research suggests that there is a lot of potential by increasing technology access, especially one-to-one learning environments where each child has a device (Harper & Milman, 2016). There is a need to further document the successes and barriers encountered by teachers during the pandemic and the shift to teaching mathematics virtually.

Opportunities to Support Teachers with Resources

One of our major findings was teachers' desire for immediate support. One way in which we can provide timely support is through creating shareable resources. Data indicate teachers need "ready-to-go" or "just in time" resources to support their virtual mathematics instruction. The creation of shareable resources is recommended to occur at various levels, including school, district, and national levels. In other words, curating resources to allow for easy and equitable access, as well as providing resources for specific school and district level needs, is important. Importantly, resources should be organized in a way that allows teachers to search easily, finding topics of interest, as well as platforms of interest.

While these types of shareable resources do exist on some levels, making sure that shareable resources are easily accessible and evidence-based is critical. Resources created by individuals that are qualified to provide recommendations, who know effective mathematics instructional practices, and who know effective virtual learning practices are needed.

In addition to shareable resources, teachers also need the time and space to share, explore, and use new resources (Dufour & Fullan, 2012; Polly, 2011, 2012). The transition to online learning has only heightened the time intensive job of teaching. To better support our students' learning opportunities, we also need to consider systems, structures, and processes to support the sharing of ideas, resources, strategies, and technology-based platforms. Further, it is critical to allow teachers the time and space to learn these strategies. It can be overwhelming when too many resources are provided at once. Therefore, it is important for leaders to empower those who are more comfortable with this technology and working collaboratively to determine a few platforms/resources coupled with the time to implement them until teachers are comfortable is important. Then, teachers can continue examining resources and implement new ones along the way. Our data also indicated that several teachers have received little to no support during the shift to virtual learning. Suddenly having to learn not only how to navigate online platforms but teach using them presents many challenges. Technology support is an important consideration for schools and districts.

The Role of Professional Development and Teacher Education

As we transition back to in-person learning with the hopes of continuing to leverage effective pedagogy related to technology, continued support is needed. One way in which this support can be provided to teachers is through well-designed professional development opportunities. Professional development (PD) is a way to provide continual support and structured learning opportunities for teachers (Koellner et al., 2011). Through PD, changes in teachers' attitudes, beliefs, and practices can be achieved in the hopes of affecting student learning (Guskey, 2002). Research-supported tenets of effective professional development include: (a) focus on specific content, (b) sustained duration, (c) active learning, (d) collaboration, (e) coherence, (f) modeling, (g) feedback and follow up, and (h) coaching and support (Darling-Hammond et al., 2017; Desimone, 2009; Garet et al., 2001; Guskey, 2003; Hill, 2009; Ingvarson et al., 2005; Polly & Hannafin, 2010). High-quality PD that makes connections between the key components of a PD system, which include the facilitator (e.g., coach), teacher, and the context, heightens the impact on teacher learning (Borko, 2004). Coupling effective mathematics teaching practices (e.g., high-quality tasks, discourse, multiple representations, etc.; NCTM, 2014) and newly learned technology platforms provide an avenue for future PD opportunities. For instance, we saw a disconnect among research on virtual manipulatives, teachers' use of virtual manipulatives in their transition to online instruction, and tools that will continue to be used upon returning to face-to-face instruction. Specifically, research supports the use of virtual manipulatives (e.g., Burns & Hamm, 2011; Olkun, 2003) and virtual manipulatives were a tool teachers relied on during their online teaching. However, teachers did not indicate the use of virtual manipulatives would continue in their face-to-face instruction. Professional development could be used to explore this disconnect, and support teachers in leveraging their experience with virtual manipulatives and integrating this within their face-to-face practice.

As mentioned, teachers want and need support and collaboration as they navigate these abrupt changes to their teaching practices. If we are to continue to leverage newly learned practices as we transition back to face-to-face classroom, we must provide additional learning opportunities to support the continued development, implementation, and alignment to effective mathematics practices as well. Additionally, responses from the surveyed teachers indicated that teachers were finding support within communities of teachers within their schools and through social media. Research supports professional learning communities as effective, collaborative learning environments for helping teachers develop new skills and instructional practices (Smylie & Wenzel, 2003). Therefore, professional learning communities may be a way of fostering collaboration and supporting teachers' effective mathematics and technology practices, as well as providing the potential for teacher leaders to emerge within schools.

CONCLUSION

The data in this initial study provide information about how teachers responded to the pandemic by using a variety of technologies and teaching strategies to support their students' mathematics learning. While the data is self-reported in a survey, the data indicates the resilience and adaptability of the teacher-participants as well as the hardships in having access to high-quality instructional materials and professional development experiences to enhance their online virtual mathematics teaching.

Using the action research framework, this initial pilot study provided us with information to inform our practice in the future. In our mathematics teacher education courses, there is a need to ensure that teacher candidates not only learn about mathematical representations, high-quality tasks, and the value of mathematical discussions, but that they also participate in experiences to find free resources, such as Open Educational Resources or other materials that can support their development of knowledge and skills related to these topics. Further, there is a need to ensure that practicing teachers are aware of opportunities to deepen their learning through informal experiences such as Personal Learning Networks using influential mathematical educators or teachers who share resources and information via social media, YouTube, blogs, or other venues. For example, in one of the states in which data was collected, one influential teacher-leader began posting YouTube videos of mathematics lessons that have been viewed and liked thousands of times. Teachers and teacher-leaders are looking to these alternative venues for resources, support, and informal professional learning experiences.

Likewise, as researchers who designed this study to gather data from teachers to inform our practice in teacher education, we plan on sharing this data with our students. We recognize the need for pre-service teachers and teachers to have opportunities to learn how to and practice using online virtual manipulatives and different platforms. The responses showed teachers were interested in having a place for shared resources. In our practice, we will implement recording videos where candidates record mathematics lessons that include tasks to create a bank of resources. While the pandemic may be going away, it would be naive to not take what teachers and teacher educators have learned in the past 12 months to improve mathematics teacher education and professional development experiences for current teachers.

ACKNOWLEDGMENT

This research received no specific grant from any funding agency in the public, commercial, or not-for-profit sectors.

REFERENCES

Batchelor, K. E., & Cassidy, R. (2019). The lost art of the book talk: What students want. *The Reading Teacher, 73*(2), 230–234. doi:10.1002/trtr.1817

Borko, H. (2004). Professional development and teacher learning: Mapping the terrain. *Educational Researcher, 33*(8), 3–15. doi:10.3102/0013189X033008003

Boston, M. D., & Smith, M. S. (2009). Transforming secondary mathematics teaching: Increasing the cognitive demands of instructional tasks used in mathematics classrooms. *Journal for Research in Mathematics Education, 40*(2), 119–156. doi:10.2307/40539329

Burns, B. A., & Hamm, E. M. (2011). A comparison of concrete and virtual manipulative use in third- and fourth-grade mathematics. *School Science and Mathematics, 111*(6), 256–261. doi:10.1111/j.1949-8594.2011.00086.x

Carpenter, T. P., Franke, M. L., & Levi, L. (2003). *Thinking mathematically: Integrating arithmetic and algebra in elementary school.* Heinemann.

Crossman, A. (2020). *Pilot study in research.* https://www.thoughtco.com/pilot-study-3026449

Darling-Hammond, L., & Hyler, M. E. (2020). Preparing educators for the time of COVID… and beyond. *European Journal of Teacher Education, 43*(4), 457–465. doi:10.1080/02619768.2020.1816961

Darling-Hammond, L., Hyler, M. E., & Gardner, M. (2017). *Effective teacher professional development.* Learning Policy Institute.

Delacruz, S. (2014). Using Nearpod in elementary guided reading groups. *TechTrends, 58*(5), 62–69. doi:10.100711528-014-0787-9

Desimone, L. M. (2009). Improving impact studies of teachers' professional development: Toward better conceptualizations and measures. *Educational Researcher, 38*(3), 181–199. doi:10.3102/0013189X08331140

Dietrich, T., & Balli, S. J. (2014). Digital natives: Fifth-grade students' authentic and ritualistic engagement with technology. *International Journal of Instruction, 7*(2), 21–34.

Dufour, R., & Fullan, M. (2012). *Cultures built to last: Systemic PLCs at Work.* Solution Tree.

Educause. (2017). *2017 Horizon Report: K-12 Edition.* Retrieved from: https://library.educause.edu/~/media/files/library/2017/11/2017hrk12EN.pdf

Fuson, K., Kalchman, M., & Bransford, J. (2005). Mathematical understanding: An introduction. In M. S. Donovan & J. D. Bransford (Eds.), *How students learn: History, mathematics, and science in the classroom* (pp. 217–256). National Academies Press.

Garet, M. S., Porter, A. C., Desimone, L., Birman, B. F., & Yoon, K. S. (2001). What makes professional development effective? Results from a national sample of teachers. *American Educational Research Journal, 38*(4), 915–945. doi:10.3102/00028312038004915

Guskey, T. R. (2002). Professional development and teacher change. *Teachers and Teaching: Theory and Practice, 8*(3/4), 381-390. doi:10.1080/135406002100000512

Guskey, T. R. (2003). What makes professional development effective? *Phi Delta Kappan, 84*(10), 748–750. doi:10.1177/003172170308401007

Hiebert, J., & Lefevre, P. (1986). Conceptual and procedural knowledge in mathematics: An introductory analysis. In J. Hiebert (Ed.), *Conceptual and Procedural Knowledge: The Case of Mathematics* (pp. 1–27). Erlbaum.

Hill, H. C. (2009). Fixing teacher professional development. *Phi Delta Kappan, 90*(7), 470–477. doi:10.1177/003172170909000705

Ingvarson, L., Meiers, M., & Beavis, A. (2005). Factors affecting the impact of professional development programs on teachers' knowledge, practice, student outcomes & efficacy. *Education Policy Analysis Archives, 13*(10), 1–28. doi:10.14507/epaa.v13n10.2005

Jacobs, V. R., Lamb, L. L. C., & Philipp, R. (2010). Professional noticing of children's mathematical thinking. *Journal for Research in Mathematics Education, 41*(2), 169–202. doi:10.5951/jresematheduc.41.2.0169

Johnson, L., McHugh, S., Eagle, J. L., & Spires, H. A. (2019). Project-based inquiry (PBI) global in kindergarten classroom: Inquiring about the world. *Early Childhood Education Journal, 47*(5), 607–613. doi:10.100710643-019-00946-4

Koellner, K., Jacobs, J., & Borko, H. (2011). Mathematics professional development: Critical features for developing leadership skills and building teachers' capacity. *Mathematics Teacher Education and Development, 13*(1), 115–136.

Michaels, S., O'Connor, C., & Resnick, L. B. (2008). Deliberative discourse idealized and realized: Accountable talk in the classroom and in civic life. *Studies in Philosophy and Education, 27*(4), 283–297. doi:10.100711217-007-9071-1

Miles, M. B., Huberman, A. M., & Saldaña, J. (2019). *Qualitative data analysis: A methods sourcebook. Sage (Atlanta, Ga.)*.

Miller, S. C., McIntyre, C. J., & Lindt, S. F. (2020). Engaging technology in elementary school: Flipgrid's potential. *Childhood Education, 96*(3), 62–69. doi:10.1080/00094056.2020.1766677

Mills, G. E. (2014). *Action research: A guide for the teacher researcher* (6th ed.). Pearson.

Moyer, P. S. (2001). Are we having fun yet? How teachers use manipulatives to teach mathematics. *Educational Studies in Mathematics, 47*(2), 175–197. doi:10.1023/A:1014596316942

National Council of Teachers of Mathematics. (2000). *Principles and standards for school mathematics*. National Council of Teachers of Mathematics.

National Council of Teachers of Mathematics. (2014). *Principles to actions: Ensuring mathematics success for all*. National Council of Teachers of Mathematics.

National Mathematics Advisory Panel. (2008). *Foundations for success: The final report of the national mathematics advisory panel*. U.S. Department of Education.

National Research Council. (2001). *Adding it up: Helping children learn mathematics*. The National Academies Press., doi:10.17226/9822

Polly, D. (2011). Teachers' learning while constructing technology-based instructional resources. *British Journal of Educational Technology*, *42*(6), 950–961. doi:10.1111/j.1467-8535.2010.01161.x

Polly, D. (2012). Supporting mathematics instruction with an expert coaching model. *Mathematics Teacher Education and Development*, *14*(1), 78–93.

Polly, D. (2016a). Exploring the relationship between the use of technology with enacted tasks and questions in elementary school mathematics. *The International Journal for Technology in Mathematics Education*, *23*(3), 111–118. doi:10.1564/tme_v23.3.03

Polly, D. (2016b). Examining elementary school teachers' enactment of mathematical tasks and questions. *Research in the Schools*, *23*(2), 61–71.

Polly, D., & Hannafin, M. J. (2010). Reexamining technology's role in learner-centered professional development. *Educational Technology Research and Development*, *58*(5), 557–571. doi:10.100711423-009-9146-5

Polly, D., McGee, J. R., & Martin, C. S. (2010). Employing technology-rich mathematical tasks to develop teachers' technological, pedagogical, and content knowledge (TPACK). *Journal of Computers in Mathematics and Science Teaching*, *29*(4), 455–472.

Polly, D., Neale, H., & Pugalee, D. K. (2014). How does ongoing task-focused mathematics professional development influence elementary school teacher's knowledge, beliefs and enacted pedagogies? *Early Childhood Education Journal*, *42*(1), 1–10. doi:10.100710643-013-0585-6

Putman, S. M., & Rock, T. C. (2017). Action research: Using strategic inquiry to improve teaching and learning. *Sage (Atlanta, Ga.)*.

Resnick, M. (2002). Rethinking learning in the digital age. In G. Kirkman (Ed.), *The Global Information Technology Report: Readiness for the Networked World* (pp. 32–37). Oxford University Press.

Rittle-Johnson, B., & Alibali, M. W. (1999). Conceptual and procedural knowledge of mathematics: Does one lead to the other? *Journal of Educational Psychology*, *91*(1), 175–189. doi:10.1037/0022-0663.91.1.175

Sagor, R. (2000). *Guiding school improvement with action research*. ASCD.

Smith, M. S., & Stein, M. K. (1998). Selecting and creating mathematical tasks: From research to practice. *Mathematics Teaching in the Middle School*, *3*(5), 344–350. doi:10.5951/MTMS.3.5.0344

Smith, M. S., & Stein, M. K. (1998). Reflections on practice: Selecting and creating mathematical tasks: From research to practice. *Mathematics Teaching in the Middle School*, *3*(5), 344-350. doi:10.5951/MTMS.3.5.0344

Smith, M. S., & Stein, M. K. (2018). *5 practices for orchestrating productive mathematics discussions* (2nd ed.). National Council of Teachers of Mathematics.

Smylie, M. A., & Wenzel, S. A. (2003). *The Chicago Annenberg Challenge: Successes, failures, and lessons for the future* (Final Technical Report of the Chicago Annenberg Research Project). Consortium on Chicago School Research.

Stein, M. K., Grover, B. W., & Henningsen, M. (1996). Building student capacity for mathematical thinking and reasoning: An analysis of mathematical tasks used in reform classrooms. *American Educational Research Journal, 33*(2), 455-488. doi:10.2307/1163292

Trust, T. (2017). Motivation, empowerment, and innovation: Teachers' beliefs about how participating in the Edmodo math subject community shapes teaching and learning. *Journal of Research on Technology in Education, 49*(1–2), 16–30. doi:10.1080/15391523.2017.1291317

Van de Walle, J. A., Karp, K. S., & Bay-Williams, J. M. (2019). *Elementary and middle school mathematics: Teaching developmentally* (10th ed.). Pearson.

Van Lancker, W., & Parolin, Z. (2020). COVID-19, school closures, and child poverty: A social crisis in the making. *The Lancet Public Health, 5*(5), e243–e244.

Videnovik, M., Kiønig, L. V., Vold, T., & Trajkovik, V. (2018). Kahooting and learning: A study from Macedonia and Norway. In *Proceedings of the European Conference on Games Based Learning*. Academic Conferences International Limited.

Viner, R. M., Russell, S. J., Croker, H., Packer, J., Ward, J., Stansfield, C., Mytton, O., Bonnell, C., & Booy, R. (2020). School closure and management practices during coronavirus outbreaks including COVID-19: A rapid systematic review. *The Lancet Child & Adolescent Health, 4*(5), 397–404.

Wahlstrom, K. L., & Louis, K. S. (2008). How teachers experience principal leadership: The roles of professional community, trust, efficacy, and shared responsibility. *Educational Administration Quarterly, 44*(4), 458–495. doi:10.1177/0013161X08321502

Walshaw, M., & Anthony, G. (2008). The teacher's role in classroom discourse: A review of recent research into mathematics classrooms. *Review of Educational Research, 78*(3), 516–551. doi:10.3102/0034654308320292

Wang, C., Polly, D., LeHew, A. J., Pugalee, D. K., & Lambert, R. (2013). Supporting teachers' enactment of an elementary school student-centered mathematics pedagogies: The evaluation of a curriculum-focused professional development program. *New Waves- Educational. Research for Development, 16*(1), 76–91. PMID:23154410

ADDITIONAL READING

Amidon, J., Chazan, D., Grosser-Clarkson, D., & Fleming, E. (2017). Commentary: Meet me in Azul's room: Designing a virtual field placement for learning to teach mathematics. *Mathematics Teacher Educator, 6*(1), 52–66. doi:10.5951/mathteaceduc.6.1.0052

Dobie, T. E., & Anderson, E. R. (2021). Noticing and wondering to guide professional conversations. *Mathematics Teacher: Learning and Teaching PK-12, 114*(2), 94-102. doi:10.5951/MTLT.2020.0210

Langsdorf, A. (2021). Pandemic innovations worth keeping. *Mathematics Teacher: Learning and Teaching PK-12, 114*(2), 90-91. doi:10.5951/MTLT.2020.0339

Mangram, C., & Sun, K. L. (2021). Supporting preservice secondary mathematics teachers' professional judgment around digital technology use. *Mathematics Teacher Educator, 9*(2), 145–159. doi:10.5951/MTE.2020.0046

Moyer, P. S., Bolyard, J. J., & Spikell, M. A. (2002). What are virtual manipulatives? *Teaching Children Mathematics, 8*(6), 372–377. doi:10.5951/TCM.8.6.0372

Otten, S., Zhao, W., de Araujo, Z., & Sherman, M. (2020). Evaluating videos for flipped instruction. *Mathematics Teacher: Learning and Teaching PK-12, 113*(6), 480-486. doi:10.5951/MTLT.2019.0088

Ross, M. A. (2011). Creating digital partnerships with parents. *Teaching Children Mathematics, 18*(4), 260–262. doi:10.5951/teacchilmath.18.4.0260

KEY TERMS AND DEFINITIONS

Conceptual Fluency: Comprehension of mathematical operations and being able to flexibly use procedures competently.

Mathematical Discourse: Students articulating their ideas to build understanding of mathematics.

Mathematical Representations: Visible or physical productions of mathematical expressions, such as models, manipulatives, number lines, etc.

National Council of Teachers of Mathematics (NCTM): Founded in 1920, it is the largest mathematics education organization.

Procedural Fluency: Being able to use procedures accurately and efficiently.

Professional Learning Communities: A way to organize teachers to collaborate and engage in professional learning.

Virtual Manipulatives: Enhanced versions of objects for students to manipulate using technology.

APPENDIX

Transitioning the Elementary Mathematics Classroom to Virtual Learning Survey

1. In what state are you currently teaching?
2. What grade level do you teach?
3. How many years have you been teaching?
4. Prior to the COVID-19 pandemic, what instructional practices did you find most effective for the teaching and learning of mathematics?
5. During the transition from traditional face-to-face mathematics instruction to virtual mathematics instruction, what were your initial concerns?
6. What technology/virtual tools did you use to create high-quality (e.g., pedagogically sound) virtual learning environment for your mathematics teaching? Explain why.
7. What instructional practices have been most effective in your virtual mathematics instruction?
8. What tools or instructional practices have you engaged in virtually that will influence your face-to-face mathematics instruction as you move forward?
9. How has this experience impacted you as a mathematics teacher?
10. Where have you received the most support in learning how to teach mathematics virtually? What made that so supportive?
11. What kind of support would you like to have more of? Explain why.

Chapter 16
Ready to Engage?
Urban Middle School Teachers' Responsiveness to Virtual Engagement Interventions on Their Instructional Practices

Svetlana Nikic
Busch Middle School of Character, USA

ABSTRACT

This chapter examined teachers' responsiveness to targeted engagement interventions in their instructional practices in an urban middle school during virtual learning. These interventions were addressed through action research and consisted of professional development, coaching, and instructional feedback. Data collected in this eight-week study contained observational field notes, coaching plans, frequency charts, coaching questions, professional development constructs, surveys, artifacts, and interviews with six participant teachers. Findings show 1) positive responsiveness to teachers' engagement interventions, 2) increase in teachers' perceptions about instructional feedback and professional development, 3) coaching surfaced as most impactful intervention, 4) socio-emotional and behavioral engagement practices were least responsive to change, and 5) teachers' beliefs and growth mindset drove the need in practice change. Future recommendations consist of exploration into virtual practices.

INTRODUCTION

At the start of virtual learning, due to the 2019 COVID-19 pandemic, observations of teachers' instructional practices evidenced engagement in the 20 percentiles. This data was collaborated with teachers' interviews: "Simply students did not do any work and I could not tell if they were learning" (Teacher A, Interview). In addition, the transition to virtual learning required new instructional strategies to sustain student engagement. Consequently, compiled student and teacher data led to the necessity of change in teachers' practices to make learning more engaging for students.

DOI: 10.4018/978-1-7998-6922-1.ch016

The main purposes of this study were: a) to investigate how urban middle school teachers' instructional practices respond to targeted engagement interventions in a virtual environment; b) to find how a specific intervention such as coaching cycles, instructional feedback, and professional development (PD) associate with improvement in teachers' engagement practices; and c) to find specific features of teachers' instructional practices that are responsive to interventions.

The premise of the study was that change in an instructional practice might vary in specific aspects and differ by various approaches relevant to the features of the intervention. Therefore, identifying these specifics as well as effective approaches to teacher professional learning were additional goals of this study. This study took a systematic approach using current research to address interventions in teachers' engagement practices by aligning professional development, coaching and instructional feedback with the aim to improve teachers' engagement practices.

BACKGROUND

This study builds on prior research in interventions that were geared towards increasing teachers' effectiveness and outcomes in their instructional practices. Thus the following sections examine research associated with teachers' mindset, professional development, coaching, instructional feedback and engagement.

Teacher Effectiveness and Outcomes

Findings from earlier studies provide strong empirical support for improving teachers' practices through interventions such as professional development and advocate continuous inquiry that provides effective insights in linking changes in classroom practice with changes in student outcomes (Garret et al., 2019). Educational research has continuously recognized the importance of teacher quality for student achievement besides other school indicators (Garret et al., 2019, p 106). Studies show that classrooms are responsive to interventions. On average, there is a correlation between professional development interventions and meaningful positive impacts on classroom practice; however, there is a substantial variation in their effects and ability to improve classroom practice (Garret et al., 2019). There are several research reviews on the outcomes of interventions on teachers' instructional practice in K-12 schools. While most of these reviews investigate the relationship between professional learning strategies and student outcomes, they fail to examine the "degree to which they affect immediate outcomes like classroom practice" (Garret et al., 2019, p.109).

For positive educational outcomes relevant to interventions in teachers' practices, building a school culture in which all staff members are involved in the decision-making process is crucial because, according to Okantey (2012), buy-in happens when leadership involves members of its organization in creating a vision and mission. This can be achieved with continuous input from staff using surveys and evaluations for professional development sessions. Okantey (2012) points out the necessity of a convincing purpose for change by stating that "the vision for change must be compelling to draw even the most skeptical individual on board with the change process" (p.45). Use of various data points can be a powerful indicator for the necessity of change in teacher practices. Kanter (2013) points out that for successful outcomes, leaders need to explain the purpose for change. Therefore, PD and coaching sessions need a clear purpose and specified outcome. In a video interview, Senge (2015) underlines the importance of collaboration for learning processes stating that "learning organization is one in which people are working together at their best" and "is a continuous learning process" (p.35). As result, it is important to include teacher collaboration in the design of every PD. Change agents who repair relationships are less likely to encounter resistance (Ford, et al., 2008). Investing in teacher relationships can lead to positive outcomes and teacher buy-in.

Ultimately, studies continuously show positive impacts of instructional interventions; however, their effects and ability to improve instructional practices vary. This is important, because instructional practices relate to student outcomes. Even though some studies investigate the relationship between professional learning strategies and student outcomes, they fail to examine the degree to which these interventions affect teachers' instructional practices. In this transformational process, school culture plays a key role in teachers' effectiveness. Thus, a leadership that fosters an environment of collaboration, reflective practices, clear vision and support creates conditions for change. In order to examine conditions for change in teachers' practices an understanding of teacher mindset is necessary.

Teacher Mindset

Teachers' success in their professional development depends, in part, on whether they approach goals with fixed or growth mindset and not solely on their instructional abilities and talent. Dweck (2006) points out that a change in mindset is not about learning more on random topics but is about seeing the same in new ways. This also means intentional commitment to growth over a period of time to transition from a "judge-and be judged framework" to a "learn-and-help-learn" framework (Dweck, 2006, p. 244). This is based on the belief that although we all differ in talents, aptitudes, or temperament, we all can change through application and experience by cultivating qualities through effort, strategies, and help from others (Dweck, 2006). Teachers with a growth mindset are continuously monitoring instructional processes by conducting an "internal monologue" that is not about "judging themselves and others" (Dweck, 2006, p. 225); instead, they are receptive and sensitive to positive and negative information in terms of constructive actions and its implications for learning (Dweck, 2006). They constantly question their learning, improvement and opportunities to help others become more successful (Dweck, 2006).

It is crucial to have growth-minded teachers who help students close the achievement gap (Dweck, 2006). These teachers set high standards for all their students, not just the ones who are already achieving (Dweck, 2006). Contrary, individuals with fixed mindset thrive when things are "safely within their grasp" and lose interest when "things get too challenging" (Dweck, 2006, p. 22). Therefore, the key to success for a school and an academic coach is to cultivate a culture in which "teachers believe in the growth of the intellect and talent" and one where they are fascinated with the process of learning (Dweck, 2006, p. 194).

In sum, a schools' culture can have many barriers to change that relate to individuals' beliefs, school's systems and methods. Teachers' approach to goals with fixed or growth mindset can lead to success or deter a school's progress. In the next sections, the practitioner identifies three interventions: professional development, coaching, and instructional feedback as features that are linked to teachers' growth and ultimately to students' educational outcomes.

Professional Development

Research on what constitutes high-quality professional development (PD) for teacher has been mixed, although there is general consensus about its typical components (Hill et al., 2013). Desimone (2009) describes this consensus on effective professional development as consisting of a robust content, featuring active learning, consisting of a collaborative format and aligned with curricula and policies, and one that provides enough learning time for participants.

For a professional development to be effective, its design must address how and what teachers learn. In their review of 35 methodologically rigorous studies, Darling-Hammond et al. (2017) have found positive links between teacher professional development, teaching practices, and student outcomes. Based on their methodology, they identified seven characteristics of effective professional development to be as follows:

1. Content focused;
2. Use active learning and adult learning theory;
3. Address collaborative, typically in job-embedded contexts;
4. Use modeling effective practices;
5. Focused on coaching and expert support;
6. Offer opportunities for feedback and reflection;
7. Have a sustained duration (Darling-Hammond, et al. (2017, p.4)

Darling-Hammond, Hyler, and Gardner (2017) state that this outlined framework helps explain why teacher professional development that addresses active learning is impactful in supporting student learning. "Active learning" moves from traditional lecture models toward models that engage teachers directly in the practices they are learning and, preferably, are connected to teachers' classrooms and students. These models engage teachers in using authentic artifacts, interactive activities, and other strategies to provide highly contextualized professional learning while incorporating the elements of collaboration, coaching, feedback, and reflection and the use of models and modeling (Darling-Hammond et al., 2017, p. 7). Aguilar (2013) too, connects coaching to professional development because of its potential to bring out the best in people by uncovering their strengths and skills and by building effective teams, cultivating compassion, and by building emotionally resilient educators.

Professional development design can be enhanced by incorporating various themes. Using several theories of learning and adult development, Trotter (2006) outlines themes that are relevant for designing teacher professional development as follows:

- Adults come to learning with experiences that should be utilized as resources for new learning.
- Adults should choose their learning opportunities based on interest and their own classroom experiences/needs.
- Reflection and inquiry should be central to learning and development (Trotter, 2006, p.8).

Snow-Renner and Lauer (2005) point out the importance of opportunities for "sense-making" (p.10) activities during professional learning experiences. Therefore, when designing PDs, it is important to integrate active learning opportunities for teachers with follow up reflections on students learning where they can experience same activities as students to build pedagogical knowledge. Darling-Hammond et al.(2017) add that such activities could involve modeling the new practices and creating opportunities for teachers to "analyze, try out, and reflect on the new strategies" and state that active learning experiences "allow teachers to transform their teaching and not simply layer new strategies on top of the old, a hallmark of adult learning theory" (p.7). Consequently, PDs need to incorporate opportunities for role- play to help teachers create a vision of a model instruction that is linked to their curriculum and builds their own learning (Darling-Hammond, et al.,2017).

Knight (2018) emphasizes the power of modeling a specific teaching strategy to frame it in action. It is not sufficient for teachers to hear about a strategy; they also need to see it implemented in a classroom. That is where modeling comes into place. A teacher can observe a coach or another teacher model the targeted strategy effectively. Pre-recorded videos are also a useful aid for demonstrating a practice. The ultimate goal of modeling is for teachers to learn the targeted strategy so that they can confidently implement it in a classroom.

In review, research on what constitutes a high-quality PD is mixed. There are some guidelines on components and characteristics of effective PD design that address how teachers learn. These characteristics pertain to teachers using authentic artifacts, interactive activities, and other strategies that provide contextualized learning. Researchers recommend the incorporation of collaboration, coaching, feedback, reflection, use of models and modeling for effective PD design. In this study, the practitioner incorporated the seven characteristics of effective professional development and coaching as recommended by Darling-Hammond, et al. (2017). Coaching served as one of the three interventions in teachers' engagement practices.

Coaching

From an instructional coach perspective, interventions relate to "transforming schools through improving teacher practices, addressing systematic issues, and improving outcomes for children" (Aguliar, 2013, p.3). Teachers need additional supports besides the traditional approach to improvement when dealing with the complexities of their profession. Coaching is considered "a critical strategy to improve practice and outcome of schools" (Rebora, 2019, p.9). The role of a coach is to help "build the capacity of others by facilitating their learning" (Aguilar, 2013, p.19). Gawanade (2011) states that "Coaching done well may be the most effective intervention designed for human performance" (p.9) while reaffirming the crucial role of a coach in the transformative process of development.

In a meta-analysis of research, Kraft and Blazar (2018) found coaching to have significant positive effects on both teachers' instructional practice and students' achievement that is comparable to the "difference in performance between a novice teacher and an experienced veteran" (p.69). They state that what makes coaching so impactful is "specific attention to teachers' core classroom practices" in their day-to-day instructions. The authors also found coaching to be more effective with a smaller number of teachers and less effective with larger ones. They suggest that components of effective coaching such as coaching quality, teacher engagement, and programmatic flexibility decline as the numbers increases.

A coach can use various models of coaching such as *directive, facilitative*, and *transformative* in dependence of teachers' individual needs and level of expertise in specific instructional practices. According to Aguilar (2013), directive coaching generally focuses on changing behaviors and the coach is the "expert in a content or strategy and shares her expertise" (p.21). A facilitative coach "does not share expert knowledge" instead "builds on existing skills, knowledge, and beliefs" towards "constructing new skills, knowledge and beliefs" geared to improve an instructional practice (p. 23). Specifically, a facili-

Ready to Engage?

tative coach operates in the zone of proximal development, developed by psychologist Lev Vygotsky, by creating necessary scaffolding of a range of abilities that enable the teacher to accomplish necessary tasks. This scaffolding process is also known as "gradual release model" (p.23). Transformative coaching is grounded in system thinking and explores the interrelationship of patterns of change rather than isolated events in behaviors, beliefs and being while "incorporating strategies from directive and facilitative coaching, as well as cognitive and ontological coaching" (p.25).

Knight (2014) points out that "video captures the rich complexity of the classroom" and suggests that coaches use video as a solution to "unique challenges and opportunities" in teachers' experiences (p.60). The author further proposes the use of classroom videos in conjunction with coaching plans. Specifically, the coach enrolls the teacher in the coaching process by collaboratively developing a plan that consists of a focus area and measurable goal, which is tied to an instructional strategy that will help the teacher achieve the goal.

In order to identify a change the teacher wants to see based on the pre-set goal, the coach asks the teacher a set of questions. Knight (2014) suggests some of the following guiding questions that would lead the teacher closer to the goal: "On a scale of 1 to 10, how close was the lesson to your ideal, what would have to change to make the class closer to a 10, what would that look like, how would you measure that?" (Knight, 2014, p. 48).

In sum, research is linking coaching to schools' outcomes by pointing out significant positive effects on both, teachers' instructional practice and students' achievement. While there are various coaching models, transformative coaching is grounded in system thinking and overarches some of these models. In any coaching model, a coach's role is to serve as a system thinker by exploring root causes in a teacher's practice and by addressing these with high leverage actions that lead to transformational change. Some researchers suggest video recording lessons for coaching, while others recommend the use of videos as an instrument to measure change towards a pre-set coaching goal. Besides coaching, instructional feedback is also one of the three interventions in teachers' engagement practices.

Instructional Feedback

Educational research supports the idea that by teaching less and providing more feedback, we can produce greater learning (Bransford, et al., 2000; Hattie, 2008; Marzano, et al., 2001). This specific research supports students' as learners. Moreover, coaches and administrators, provide feedback to teachers after instructional observations with the aim to learn and improve their practices. Hattie's (2008) research revealed that feedback was among the most powerful influences on achievement, acknowledges that he has "struggled to understand the concept" (p. 173).

Buckingham and Goodall (2019) use compelling research to argue that there is often a misunderstanding about feedback in terms of evaluative versus improvement focused, stating that: "telling people what we think of their performance and how they should do better" stating that this "doesn't help them thrive and excel" (p.92). In addition, the authors point out that telling those individuals how we think they should improve actually "hinders learning" (Buckingham & Goodall, 2019, p. 92). They further explain:

Since excellence is idiosyncratic and cannot be learned by studying failure, we can never help another person succeed by holding her up performance against prefabricated model of excellence, giving her feedback on where she misses the model, and telling her to plug the gaps (Buckingham & Goodall, 2019, p. 94).

Knight (2019) advocates for coaching feedback that is in a form of dialogue to honor teachers' autonomy as a path to improve a practice. Moreover, Knight promotes the necessity for a structured conversation with teachers as dialogue "where both members are heard and where both parties' opinion count" (p.19). The use of various instructional data or "third points" such as examining student's work or video recordings of lessons is suggested for conducting effective dialogue where the focus is taken off the coach and teacher. This process empowers the teacher in the feedback process (Knight, 2019, p. 19). The author does not exclude the importance of coaches sharing their thoughts, but he suggests that these need to be "non-judgmental" and with the "humility appropriate for any conversation about what happens in a classroom" (Knight, 2019, p.19).

In sum, researchers emphasize the major impact of instructional feedback on student achievement. For this process, researchers again recommend the use of video recordings for the teacher and coach to describe a practice. Consequently, this claim confirms the benefits of using video recordings in this action research. In the process of providing feedback, researchers also recommend the use of dialogue as an effective way to empower teachers and give them autonomy in changing their practice. In this study, the practitioner used this dialogical approach based on confirmed research practices. Professional development, coaching and instructional feedback were focused on engagement practices.

Engagement Practices

Research has recognized the importance of effective teachers in classrooms and their effect on student achievement. On their part, teachers know that engagement is crucial in connecting students to school and learning, thus leading to a school's success (Davis et al., 2012).

Engagement occurs in multiple domains. Addressing each level can increase a teacher's chance to sustain students' engagement. There has been some disagreement on the number of theoretical dimensions of engagement. Some scholars argue for two dimensions: behavioral and emotional (Finn & Voelk, 1993; Skinner & Belmont, 1993 as cited in Davis et al., 2012), while others for three: behavioral, emotional and cognitive (Fredricks, et al., 2004 as cited in Davis et al., 2012). Davis et al. (2012) emphasize the need of three interconnected dimensions: behavioral engagement, cognitive engagement, and relational engagement. See Figure 1 below.

According to Davis et al. (2012), behavioral engagement relates to the quality of students' participation in the classroom and school community while integrating "effort, persistence, participation, and compliance with school structures" (p.23). On the other hand, cognitive engagement encompasses "the quality of students' psychological engagement in the academic tasks, including their interests, ownership and strategies of learning" (p. 22). Lastly, relational engagement, according to the same authors, relates to "the quality of students' interactions in the classroom and school community" (p.22). It is important to note that students can have one dimension of engagement present but not the others. For instance, a student may be behaviorally engaged, yet struggling with learning due to absence of cognitive engagement. Both, cognitive and behavioral engagement addresses effort in their definitions. This further builds on the notion that "cognitive engagement refers to the quality of students' engagement whereas sheer effort refers to the quantity of engagement" (Pintrich, 2003, p. 105).

Figure 1. Three interconnected dimensions: behavioral, cognitive and relational engagement (Davis et al., 2012, p.22)

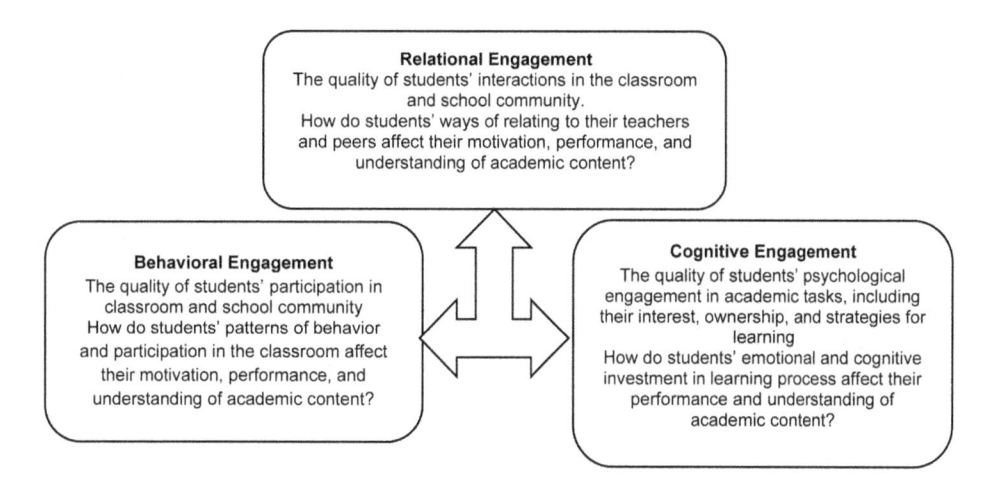

Relational Engagement
The quality of students' interactions in the classroom and school community.
How do students' ways of relating to their teachers and peers affect their motivation, performance, and understanding of academic content?

Behavioral Engagement
The quality of students' participation in classroom and school community
How do students' patterns of behavior and participation in the classroom affect their motivation, performance, and understanding of academic content?

Cognitive Engagement
The quality of students' psychological engagement in academic tasks, including their interest, ownership, and strategies for learning
How do students' emotional and cognitive investment in learning process affect their performance and understanding of academic content?

Relational engagement encompasses "students' reports of perceived teacher supports, perceived press for understanding and their sense of belonging" (Davis et al., 2012, p.24). Researchers relate to this notion as emotional engagement to students' interest, happiness, anxiety, and anger during educational activities (Skinner & Belmont, 1993). In contrast, other researchers describe emotional engagement as the extent of students' sense of belonging and degree to which they care about their school (Sciarra & Seirup, 2008). Theories of relational engagement address this type of engagement thru the motivational system and self-determination theory. The first theory is also known as competence and is defined as "attainment of personally or socially valued goals" (Davis et al., 2012, p.25). The second theory is also referred to as relatedness and autonomy and is explained as social-contextual conditions that provide individuals with prospects to satisfy their basic needs and leads to intensified motivation, favorable functioning, and psychological well-being (Deci & Ryan, 2000).

In a school setting, this means that students' self-determination is dependent on the level in which teachers and the classroom satisfy their basic needs and their need to relate to others (Davis et al., 2012). Davis et al. (2012) make a reference to Skinner to suggest that more research is needed to understand how students achieve relatedness with their peers and how schools can promote this practice.

Marzano and Pickering (2011) examined research on engagement and motivation, and found an abundance of strategies in which teachers can increase engagement in their classrooms. The authors encompassed engagement through four elements: emotions, interest, perceived importance, and perceptions of efficacy. Furthermore, the authors supplement these engagement elements with corresponding questions: 'How do I feel? Am I interested?, Is this important?, Can I do this?' The first two questions address short-term perceptions of engagement, specifically, a student's attention during the range of a few seconds to a few minutes. The following two questions deal with long-term perceptions of engagement, specifically, the extent to which class activities relate to students' goals and help them develop self-efficacy.

Hattie (2009), in a synthesis of over 800 meta-analysis studies, found that teacher-student relationships have an effect size of 0.72, and yet, according to Fisher et al. (2018), only 52% of students report that teachers make an effort to know them. Therefore, teachers can purposefully foster stronger relationships for student growth. According to Hattie (2009) providing an appropriately challenging task has an effect size of 0.57 yet Fisher et al., (2018) state that 43% of students find school boring. Therefore, according to Hattie (2009) instituting appropriate high expectations from students can positively impact their outcomes. Fisher et al. (2018) recommend a balance in task difficulty and complexity to increase the task challenge. The same authors define difficulty as the amount of time, work or effort the learner has to employ on a task, while complexity as a type of thinking, the number of steps, or background knowledge required to complete the task. The authors illustrate these two concepts on different axes, resulting in four distinct tasks to increase challenge: fluency, stamina, strategic thinking, and struggle. The graph in Figure 2 indicates each task with corresponding complexity and difficulty level.

Figure 2. Difficulty and complexity chart (Fisher et al., 2018, p.94)

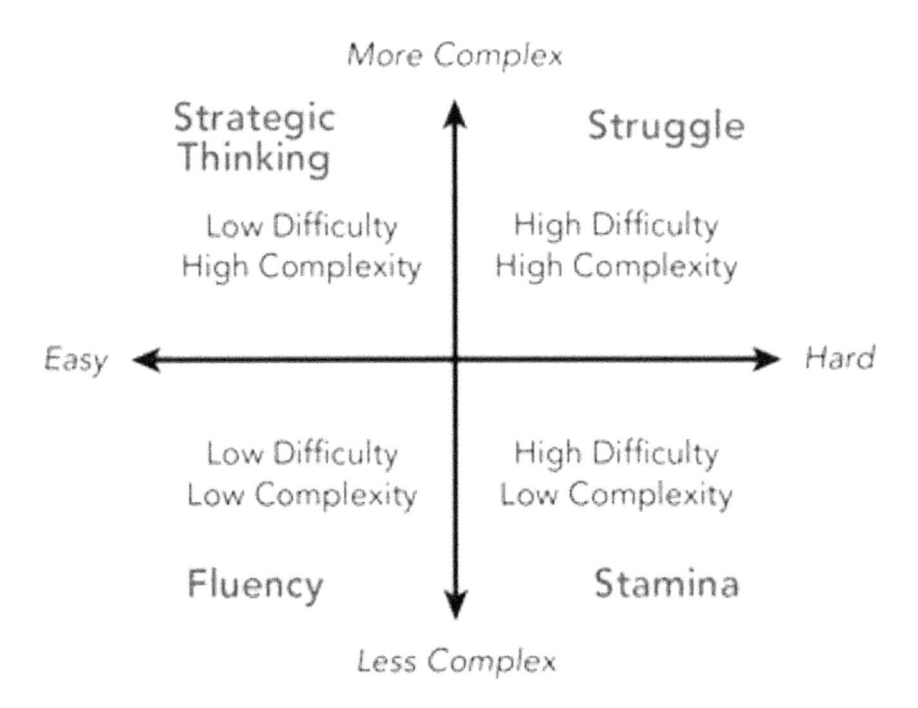

	More Complex	
Strategic Thinking Low Difficulty High Complexity		**Struggle** High Difficulty High Complexity
Easy ←		→ Hard
Fluency Low Difficulty Low Complexity		**Stamina** High Difficulty Low Complexity
	Less Complex	

Fundamentally, engagement by design, instructs teachers to intentionally tend to behavioral, cognitive and emotional needs of their students through the planning for the following:

- Academic behaviors and actions.
- Psychological effort put into learning and mastering content.
- Feelings and attitudes about school and students' relationships in school.

Teachers can stimulate engagement by encouraging students' self-worth, purpose, and voice while investing in relationships and curriculum choices that ensure that students remain at the center of engagement driven by teachers' practice design (Fisher et al., 2018).

Himmele and Himmele (2011) explain that total participation techniques are teaching techniques that allow teachers to get evidence of active participation and cognitive engagement from all students at the same time. Figure 3 illustrates the Cognitive Engagement Model and shows the relationship between total participation and higher-order thinking that can take place in a classroom. Even though learning happens in all four quadrants, activities that occur in Quadrant 4 bring evidence of high cognition and high participation.

Figure 3. Cognitive engagement model (Himmele & Himmele, 2011, p.15)

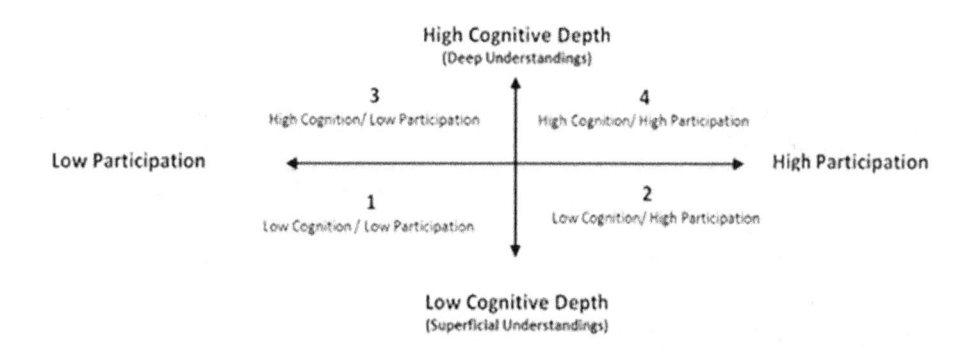

This model can guide coaching conversations. For instance: In which quadrants did you aim to linger? Can you develop questions through the lens of total participation to ensure the engagement of all students rather than just few? (Himmele & Himmele, 2011). The study used this model in conjunction with Webb's Depth of Knowledge (DOK) to measure instructional rigor. Webb's DOK levels pertain to knowledge acquisition (DOK1), knowledge application (DOK2), knowledge analysis (DOK3), and knowledge augmentation (DOK4) (Francis, 2017). Specifically, during instructional observations and coaching, these two models served as reference points when analyzing trends in students learning and teachers' engagement practices.

Lemov (2010) used Jim Collin's observations from *Built to Last* and *Good to Great* to study teaching techniques that distinguished good teachers from great ones and compiled those as a toolkit to help teachers improve their craft. Some of these techniques are aimed towards engaging students in learning, such as cold call, wait time, call and response, everybody writes and others. Lemov (2010) found that great teachers share some common elements, a tool box, for closing the achievement gap. He describes the techniques of a "champion teacher" in "concrete, specific, and actionable way, that allows them easy application in teachers' daily practices" (p.9).

Consequently, researchers disagree on the number of theoretical dimensions of engagement. Some argue for two dimensions: behavioral and emotional, while others argue for three by adding the cognitive domain. Engagement by design guides teachers to intentionally plan instructions based on the three domains to meet the needs of their students.

Researchers claim that engagement is one of the major contributors to student achievement and found an abundance of strategies in which teachers can increase engagement in their classrooms. Some researchers recommend a balance in task difficulty and complexity to increase the task challenge when addressing the cognitive domain. Others recommend an enhanced approach with total participation techniques that allow teachers to achieve active participation and cognitive engagement from all students at the same time. Some teachers at the school study were trained in these techniques, and DOK levels, yet they showed inconsistency in fidelity of implementation. The outcomes of engagement interventions in teachers' practices in this study were linked to the research purpose, context and participants.

MAIN FOCUS OF THE CHAPTER

Purpose of the Study

In this study, I used an action research process with qualitative and quantitative data sources. The study involved six participant teachers at an urban middle school. I was a collaborative participant due to my responsibilities as school's instructional coach.

The purpose of this study was to answer the following research questions (RQ):

1. How do urban middle school teachers' instructional practices respond to targeted engagement interventions?
2. How does a specific intervention such as coaching cycles, instructional feedback, and PD associate with improvement in instructional practices?
3. Which specific features of teacher's instructional practice are more or less responsive to interventions?

In order to answer the three research questions, observational, inquiry and artifact data was collected based on interventions in the three engagement domains. Participant teachers' expressed their needs for interventions in their instructional practices in a PD, after analyzing students' participation during virtual learning.

Research Context and Participants

This action research was conducted at an urban Saint Louis City public middle school where I have been employed as an academic instructional coach for the past 14 of 20 total years in education. The school has approximately 420 culturally diverse students enrolled (60% Black, 39% White, <1%Hispanic, and <1%Asian) with 40 staff members, and is situated in a middle class neighborhood. The school serves 6th, 7th and 8th grade students of whom over 90% are from low income communities, receiving free or reduced-price meals. Character education is part of the school's mission and it is integrated in all aspects of school's processes. The school's character education practices, besides strong emphasis on building relationships with students and creating a sense of belonging, also attempts to address the social emotional needs of students.

Six out of the 40 teachers employed in the school, three mathematics and three science, each teaching one of the corresponding sixth, seventh and eighth grade level, were purposely invited as participants in the study to ensure grade and content diversity. Participants' age ranged from early 30-ies to mid-40-ies with more than 80% having a master's degree or beyond. Study participants' teaching experience ranges from two to 15 years mostly in urban school districts serving medium to low-income student population.

Although in the past few years interventions in teachers' engagement practices were part of professional development, other mandates set by the district were prioritized and created a shift in school's focus.

This study took place in the fall semester of the 2020-2021 school year. The study was eight weeks wherein instruction was exclusively virtual (hybrid) learning, with both synchronous and asynchronous formats due to Corona virus pandemic that has started in spring 2020 and continued during the fall semester of the 2020-2021 school year. The entire student and staff population received iPads and in case of need, Internet hotspots. Microsoft TEAMs platform was used as the main unified communication and collaboration platform with access by all students and staff. This platform combines chat, video meetings, file storage (including collaboration on files), and application integration. In addition, the platform features extensions that can integrate with non-Microsoft products. This and additional platforms in which teachers received PD as part of interventions were used for instructional delivery.

Practitioner's Role

My role in this action research can be classified as a collaborative participant. I conducted this action research by collaborating with teachers and by participating in the implementation of engagement interventions with the aim to change teachers' instructional practices.

I have 14 years of experience as an academic instructional coach at the school of study, and have established personal and professional relationship with the majority of the faculty members. My duties include academic coaching, leading the math and science team, facilitating weekly professional learning communities (PLCs) and professional development (PD).

I am also part of the school's leadership team, a role that can lead teachers to perceive me as an outsider and limit their responses to teaching challenges they encounter. However, during previous coaching sessions I established a position of an insider by developing trusting relationships with teachers where they openly shared their instructional challenges. Therefore, in this study, I identify myself primarily as an insider and collaborative participant.

The Action Research Framework

The interventions in this study were based on the methodology of an action research process consisting of continuous actions, reflections and evaluations, all aiming to refine teachers' engagement practices. An action research concentrates on "investigating whether actions result in desired outcomes" using mixed methods, both quantitative and qualitative data analysis (Hendricks, 2013, p.2). This action research consisted of the three engagement interventions in teachers' practices: coaching, instructional feedback and professional development. The practitioner's goal in an action research is to study self and others while taking an action to "investigate and improve" a specific educational practice (Hendricks, 2013, p.3).

In the first week of this study, teachers received interventions in PD and coaching. Specifically, each teacher chose an engagement coaching goal that was registered in their coaching plan. These plans were revisited and revised during upcoming coaching sessions. Also, during the first week of the study, teachers participated in a PD relevant to engagement strategies and technology platforms.

Later, during the next five weeks of the study, each teacher was observed five times (45- minute synchronous observations per each teacher), participated in three coaching sessions and additional five PD session. After each observation, instructional feedback was shared with teachers and was later used in coaching sessions as a reference point. Instructional feedback was coded based on engagement type, frequency of student interactions, length of this interactions and DOK levels. The frequency in teachers' engagement practices during the first observation served as baseline data.

Coaching was based on Knight's Impact cycle and reflective questioning while fluctuating between the three models: directive, facilitative and transformative. During coaching, teachers were also asked to reflect on the cognitive engagement model and difficulty and complexity charts described in literature review. Coaching was grounded in engagement data collected during observations and referenced during coaching as measure of progress in instructional practice.

Professional development was virtual and used collaboration, participation and modeling of engagement strategies and technology platforms such as virtual ClassNotebook, Forms, Nearpod, Flipgrid, Canva, Padlets and Legends of Learning. See Figure 4 for the study's framework.

Figure 4. Action research methodology

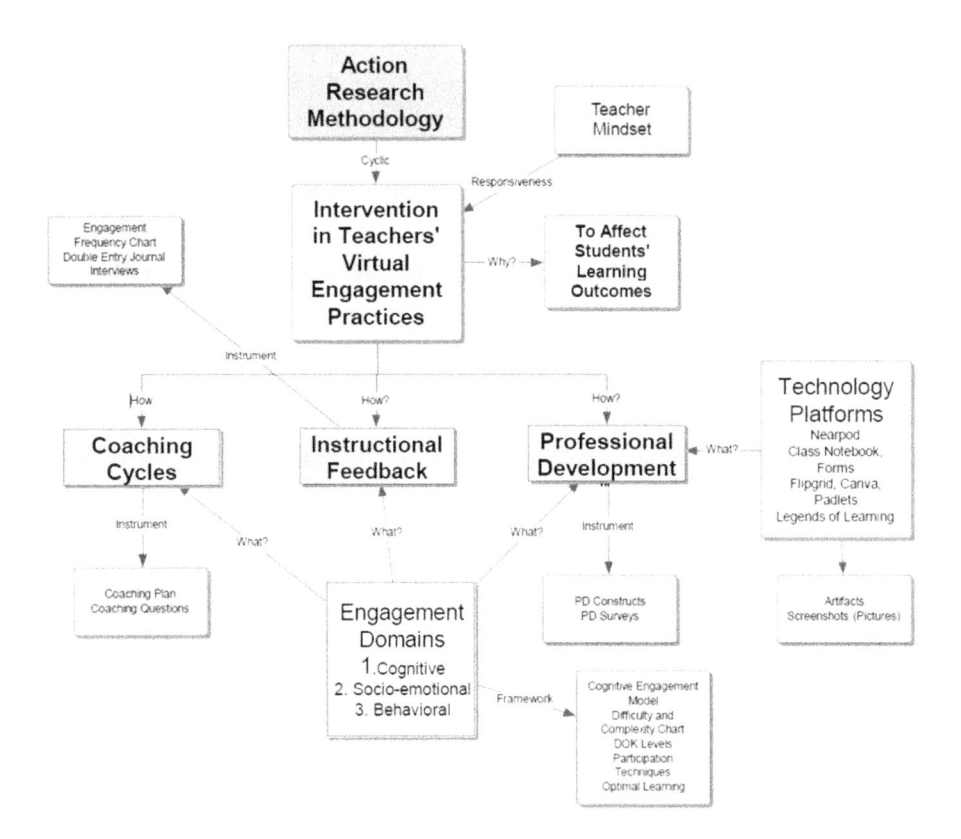

The first step in this action research consisted of reflection on teachers' engagement practices using data from synchronous observations as baseline data (Table 6, observation 1).

The next step consisted of an intervention. Specifically, professional development was facilitated to participant teachers in the three engagement domains as well as in the TEAMs technology platform consisting of virtual applications: Class Notebook, Collaborative Board and Forms. Professional development (PD) was based on the characteristics of effective PD design (Darling-Hammond et al., 2017)

Following this action step, the effectiveness of the implemented PD was evaluated based on instructional observations and a follow- up PD survey. Feedback was provided for each observation based

Ready to Engage?

field notes relevant to engagement practices. These notes were documented in double entry journals. In addition, I met with each teacher and collaboratively developed a coaching plan with an individual goal for his or her engagement practice based on Aguilar's (2013) coaching plan framework.

Next, I reflected by analyzing all data sources (Coaching Plan, PD survey, and instructional feedback) for change in engagement practices and for measuring the effectiveness of PD design. Then, I documented the reflections in the same double entry journals and coaching plans.

The next action was linked to the analysis of the previous data sources as reference point for additional interventions. These interventions consisted coaching cycles (one per teacher), an additional engagement PD, instructional feedback (one per teacher), and revisions in coaching plans in function of teachers' individual goals.

Later, in the next step, collected data from PD surveys and reflections was used to evaluate the effectiveness of coaching, instructional feedback and of the ongoing PD. This action research process was spiraled for the entire duration of the study as evidenced in Figure 5.

Figure 5. First cycle of the action research process adapted from Hendricks (2013, p.11)

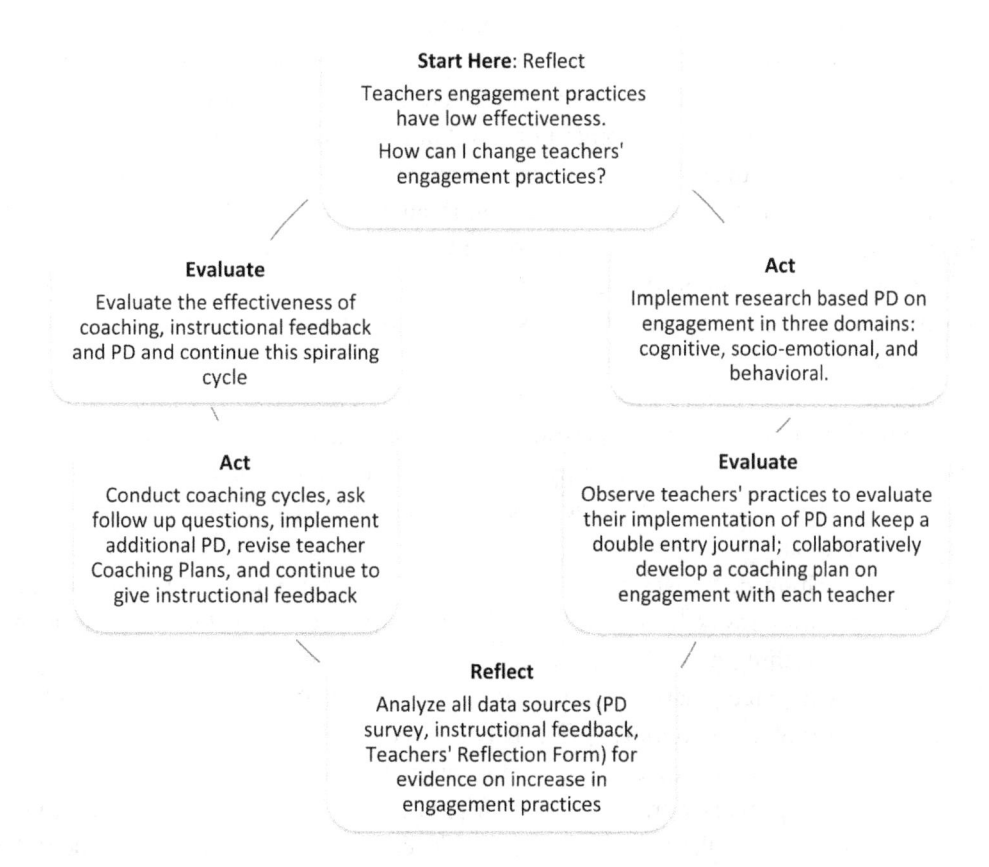

Start Here: Reflect
Teachers engagement practices have low effectiveness.
How can I change teachers' engagement practices?

Act
Implement research based PD on engagement in three domains: cognitive, socio-emotional, and behavioral.

Evaluate
Observe teachers' practices to evaluate their implementation of PD and keep a double entry journal; collaboratively develop a coaching plan on engagement with each teacher

Reflect
Analyze all data sources (PD survey, instructional feedback, Teachers' Reflection Form) for evidence on increase in engagement practices

Act
Conduct coaching cycles, ask follow up questions, implement additional PD, revise teacher Coaching Plans, and continue to give instructional feedback

Evaluate
Evaluate the effectiveness of coaching, instructional feedback and PD and continue this spiraling cycle

Interviews with teachers and post surveys were conducted in the last two weeks of the study.

Sampling, Data Sources and Analysis

According to Hendricks (2013), the types of data collected in an action research vary and can consist of observations, interviews, video records, work samples and journal entries. In order to answer the guiding questions of this study and determine the responsiveness to targeted engagement interventions in teachers' instructional practices, I collected artifacts, observational and inquiry data in various ways. Table 1, 3 and 4 illustrate the data sources and data types with corresponding research questions.

Observational Data

Observational data consisted of double entry journals, instructional feedback, coaching plans, videos files, and professional development constructs. The purpose of double entry journals is linked to answering research questions 1 and 3 (Table 1). Specifically, double entry journals enabled the practitioner to describe teachers' enacted engagement practices, patterns in behaviors and their attitudes towards change.

A double entry journal consisted of recorded field notes of teachers' instructional observations and my reflections to these notes. These notes were organized in a double entry journal consisting of two columns, observations and reflections. The "Observations" column depicted patterns in teachers' behaviors and their attitudes relevant to engagement interventions. Specifically, it contained logs of what was seen and heard during the observations relevant to the targeted interventions. The second column was labeled "Reflections" and contained practitioner's thoughts and responses to the field notes. This journal forced the practitioner to be reflective of own instructional feedback. Reflections were based on an engagement implementation rubric and on a common language established by teachers and coach (Table 2). In this study, observations were conducted from the standpoint of a passive observer, gathering and recording information in an unobtrusive way with an outsider's perspective. Merriam (1998) refers to this perspective as *etic* since the researcher tries to gain understanding of the phenomenon from the participant's perspective.

Instructional feedback was part of the action research cycle. The purpose of instructional feedback was linked to answering all three research questions. Specifically, data from instructional feedback was used to measure the increase or decrease in supports and intensity as well as intervention context of the targeted classroom interventions. The feedback was electronically shared with teachers, giving them option to respond or reflect.

The purpose of coaching plans was linked to answering research question 1 and 2. Specifically, a coaching plan set the framework for coaching cycles, and was used to surface factors of impact on teachers' practices. A coaching plan allowed the practitioner to compare the dimension gap between teacher's baseline in the targeted practice and progress towards an established goal. The development of a coaching plan consisted of a collaborative effort between the teacher and coach (myself)on establishing clear guidelines, measures and expectations for coaching cycles relevant to an engagement practice. Reflections of the coaching plans were used for both practitioner (myself) and teachers, to evidence teachers' transformation towards their established goal. Coaching plans offered a lens in adult learning and served as an indicator in teacher's mindset towards change. These coaching plans were updated during the three coaching sessions.

The purpose of video files served as a reflective tool into teachers' perceptions of practice implementation. Video files of targeted engagement practices were recorded by the teacher. These files were used in conjunction with a Teacher Reflection form to help the practitioner answer research question 1 and

3. The form was completed by the teacher at the beginning of each coaching session after the teacher watched the video file or viewed the observation logs. These reflection forms helped teachers rate the implementation context (learning structures), fidelity, and effectiveness of practice implementation.

Table 1. Observational data collection and analysis

Observational Data					
Type of Data	**Quantity**	**Instructional Data Sources**	**Purpose**	**Research Question**	**Data Analysis**
Double Entry Journal with Field Notes and Reflections	Five per teacher (Total of 30 Observations)	Hybrid: Observational notes on teacher practices based on synchronous and/or pre-recorded lessons in TEAMs	To describe teacher enacted engagement practices (patterns in teachers' behaviors and their attitudes).	RQ1 RQ3	Content Analysis
Instructional Feedback	Five per teacher (Total of 30 Instructional Feedbacks)	Hybrid: Descriptive feedback with action steps based on synchronous and/or pre-recorded lessons in TEAMs	To describe the effectiveness of engagement practices (increase and decrease in supports and intervention context).	RQ1 RQ2 RQ3	Content Analysis
Coaching Plans	One per teacher (Total of six Coaching Plans)	Hybrid: Collaboratively with teachers complete Coaching Plan Form on Microsoft TEAMs Teacher and coach reflect on the Coaching Plan	To surface factors of impact on teachers' practices (compare dimension gap between where the teacher is in the targeted practice and his progress towards goal).	RQ1 RQ2	Content Analysis
Video Files	Five per teacher (Total of 30 Video Files)	Hybrid: Teachers complete the Reflection Form based on synchronous and/or pre-recorded video lesson in TEAMs	To describe teachers' perception of practice implementation.	RQ1 RQ3	Content Analysis
Professional Development Constructs (Frameworks)	One per PD session (Total of six PD Constructs)	Hybrid: Collaboratively facilitate PD to teachers in Microsoft TEAMs	To measure the effectiveness of the PD design.	RQ2	Content Analysis

Inquiry Data

Inquiry data consisted of interviews, surveys, coaching cycle questions, and Engagement Rubric and Frequency Chart (Table 3). One semi-structured interview per teacher was conducted in the last two weeks of the study. Interview questions focused on teachers' implementation of engagement practices in the three domains and on the effectiveness of interventions. The purpose of these interviews was to depict specific features of instructional practices that were more or less responsive to interventions as well as teachers' roadblocks to progress. Some interviews were conducted in person at the school site while others were facilitated on TEAMs using the chat and recording option of this platform. Interviews varied in time and lasted up to 30 minutes.

A school's teacher Culture and Climate Pre-survey, based on the Panorama provider's framework, was administered prior to interventions and served as baseline data on teachers' perspectives on coaching, quality of professional development, instructional feedback and their perspectives on students' enthusiasm towards school. This data was compared to the post- surveys administered after the interventions.

The Engagement Rubric and Frequency Chart (Table 2) was one of the instruments used in the data collection process. Reports pertaining to engagement generated by platforms such as Nearpod and Legends of Learning were included in this rubric. Data illustrated the ratio, frequency and duration of class interactions, question- type and their corresponding DOK levels as means to measure teachers' progress towards change in practice.

Table 2. Engagement rubric and frequency chart

Observation 4 Teacher C	Cognitive	Frequency (Minutes)	Behavioral	Frequency (Minutes)	Social Emotion.	Frequency (Minutes)
Implementation with fidelity most of the time 60% and above class time minutes	21/32stud =65% 3DOK2 and 1DOK3				32/32 students=100%	
Implementation of some elements-for a short time <60%-20% of class time minutes		18min/45min =40%of class time				18min/45min =40%of class time
Inconsistent Implementation <20% of class time minutes						

The purpose of the Engagement Rubric and Frequency Chart was to measure the fidelity and frequency of implemented interventions in instructional delivery. This chart was populated by quantitative data based on the three engagement domains. Data was coded based on depth of knowledge (DOK level questioning frequency), student participation (number of students engaged per minute and duration of engagement) and frequency of socio-emotional practices by teacher (positive reinforcement, praise, participation points and duration of these practices). Behavioral engagement practices were attempted but not fully implemented to have significance for the study.

Coaching cycles aligned with coaching plans were analyzed based on teachers' responses to coaching questions (Knight, 2018). Coaching questions pertained to teachers' implementation of engagement practices and necessary changes and supports needed to improve these practices. These questions drove change in teachers' practice based on measurable goals in teachers' coaching plans. Teachers' answers to the coaching questions and their reflections established indicators of progress between coach (practitioner) and teachers as measures towards achieving an identified goal relevant to engagement interventions.

The professional development constructs were analyzed based on data from teachers' PD survey administered after each of the six PDs. This survey was created by the practitioner based on Darling-Hammond et. al. (2017)'s characteristics of effective professional development design. Surveys served as a measure of the effectiveness of PD design and implementation. The PD survey was based on rating

Ready to Engage?

scales from 1 to 10 as measures of effectiveness, learning style, opportunities for teachers to express their voice and choice, teacher collaboration and learning context. Survey from each PD was used to refine the next PD construct to attain optimal learning for teachers.

Table 3. Inquiry data collection and analysis

Inquiry Data					
Type of Data	**Quantity**	**Instructional Data Sources**	**Purpose**	**Research Question Addressed**	**Data Analysis**
Surveys	One Pre and Post survey Six PD surveys (Total of eight Surveys)	Hybrid: • Pre and Post Teacher Culture and Climate Survey using Microsoft Forms • PD surveys	To compare outcome of interventions. To evaluate the effectiveness of professional development design and implementation.	RQ1 RQ2	Content Analysis
Interviews	One per teacher (Total of six Interviews)	Hybrid: Teacher semi-structured interviews conducted over Microsoft TEAMs and in person	To depict teachers response to interventions and roadblocks to change.	RQ1 RQ2 RQ3	Thematic Analysis
Engagement Rubric and Frequency Charts	One per observation (Total pf 30 Engagement Rubrics and Frequency Charts)	Hybrid: Rubric on practice frequency based on synchronous and/or pre-recorded lessons in TEAMs	To measure the fidelity and frequency of practice implementation.	RQ1	Rubric Analysis
Coaching Cycle Questions	Twelve questions per coaching cycle	Hybrid: Questioning Protocol using Microsoft TEAMs	To describe indicators of progress between coach and teachers as measures towards achieving an identified goal.	RQ1 RQ2 RQ3	Content Analysis

Artifact Data

Teachers' instructional activities and screenshots (pictures) of synchronous and/or pre-recorded learning served as artifacts in assessing teachers' planning for interventions as well as their fidelity in implementing engagement practices that were addressed in professional development.

Specifically, screenshots (pictures) of instructions, forms, class notebooks, and class reports relevant to engagement served as points of reference for illustrating the intervention strategy through task or activity (see Table 4). Screenshots were compared before, during and after the interventions to show evidence of change over time.

Table 4. Artifact data collection and analysis

Artifact Data					
Type of Data	**Quantity**	**Instructional Data Sources**	**Purpose**	**Research Question**	**Data Analysis**
Instructional Activities	One per observation	Hybrid: Conduct task analysis of activities posted in Microsoft TEAMs based on engagement interventions.	To describe how certain tasks change over time as result of interventions.	RQ1 RQ3	Content Analysis
Screenshots (Photos)	One per observation	Hybrid: Digital pictures of online classroom resources posted in Microsoft TEAMs.	To compare how context changes before, during and after the interventions.	RQ3	Content Analysis

Data Analysis

Per the three Tables above (Table1, 3 & 4), I used content data analysis to analyze the following data: double entry journal, instructional feedback, coaching plans, video files, PD constructs (observational data) surveys, interviews, engagement rubric, coaching questions (inquiry data), and activities and screenshots (artifact data). Specifically, analysis through microscopic examination of data was used to determine teachers' responsiveness to engagement interventions within their instructional context. This type of analysis was used for in-depth observations, interviews and artifacts in order to discover relationships among concepts. My purpose as an instructional coach was to develop an in-depth understanding of factors that affected teachers' responsiveness to interventions as result of their involvement in targeted PD, coaching and observational feedback by examining multiple forms of data (observational, inquiry and artifacts).

To begin the data analysis process, all data sources were compiled and organized to infer meaning (Table 5). Data in this study were analyzed using content analysis as described by Merriam (1998). The content of interviews, observations (field notes) and documents produced during instructional activities (Nearpod, Forms, and Legends of Learning) were analyzed qualitatively for recurring patterns and meaning. The process involved the coding of raw data and the construction of categories that captured relevant characteristics of the data content.

The action research questions guided the initial search for meaning of events that seemed otherwise ambiguous. Additional sensitizing questions (Who, What, Where, How), theoretical questions (process and connection), structural questions (practical) and guiding questions (evolving, open-ended) helped me develop and define concepts and definition of categories. Categories were further defined in terms of properties (general or specific attributes of a category) and dimensions (range on which a property can be located) in search for communicating meaning (Straus & Corbin, 1998). Therefore, there was an ongoing comparison and contrast of meaningful details in data sources in order to identify recurrent patterns, themes, or categories under which they fitted best.

In this study, I aimed towards the development of themes and categories that emerged from analysis that were grounded in data. Coding procedures were used to help build the categories in a systematic and creative way by identifying, developing, and inter-relating concepts (Table 5).

Table 5. Emerged themes and categories

Categories and Themes/ Data	Teachers' Outcomes of Interventions	Organization and Implementation of PD	Structure and Interaction Relevant to Change in Practice	Perceived Outcomes	Implications of Context to Change	Teacher Mindset
Double Entry Journal Instructional Feedback Video Files Engagement Rubric and Frequency Charts	Cognitive engagement was most responsive and socio-emotional was least.	Data collected in in double entry journals showed evidence of teachers' implementation of practices modeled in PD sessions.	Teachers were mostly responsive to feedback when grounded in data.	Feedback was effective when backed by data and coaching.	Feedback was least responsive to socio-emotional and behavioral engagement domains.	Data from teachers' self-reflection showed a variance in perceptions of instructional practices as compared to collected data in double entry journals and reports.
Coaching Plans	All teachers met coaching goals in at least one domain. Goals were met at a range of 72% to 92%.	Coaching data (teachers' reflections to coaching questions) showed evidence of teachers' progression towards change in practice.	Coaching plans served as an effective framework for leading change in practice.	Baseline goals in engagement ranged from 40% to 80%.	Coaching was least responsive to socio-emotional and behavioral engagement domains.	Coaching goals impacted teachers' motivation and focus as response to change in practice.
PD Construct	Teachers implemented new technology platforms and learned about research based engagement strategies.	Teachers were responsive to elements of effective PD design based on modeling and collaboration.	Teacher had awareness of low engagement and low student interest.	Teachers expressed a positive perspective on PD that takes place over sustained amount of time and when it contributes to individual growth.	Teachers' response to PD was impacted by students' initial high learning curve in technology and school's transition to iPad during COVID-19 Pandemic.	Teachers sought PD in engagement and collaborative platforms as response to their beliefs about students' learning.
Coaching Cycles Questions	Coaching grounded in data was most responsive to interventions.	PD was aligned with coaching and focused on the three engagement domains and technology platforms.	The impact of coaching cycles was achieved through use of collaborative dialogue, transformative and facilitative was coaching models.	Coaching cycles were most responsive to cognitive engagement domain and technology platforms.	Coaching was most impactful for change in practice.	Teachers perceived coaching grounded in data and feedback as most responsive to their practices.
Surveys	Pre and Post Culture and Climate surveys showed average growth of 0.47 in teachers perceptions of feedback and ultimately coaching.	Pre and Post Culture and Climate survey showed average growth of 0.65. Highest change in individualized PD and learning.	Surveys compared outcome of interventions (Pre and Post).	Highest ratings on Culture and Climate Pre and Post survey (3.3) on value of colleagues' ideas in improving teaching.	No change in usefulness of feedback –still rated high on Pre and Post compared to initial ratings of other two questions.	Culture and Climate survey on PD showed highest growth (0.7) in school's support in teacher's growth.
Interviews	Teacher practices were responsive to implementation of cognitive and some socio-emotional engagement strategies facilitated in PD and supported by coaching.	Interviews confirmed teachers' responsiveness to modeling, input and collaboration.	Focus on one instructional practice over sustained period of time was evidenced as impactful.	Teachers perceived coaching as most responsive interventions. Technology platforms that helped monitor student learning and engagement.	Responsiveness to feedback driven by data.	Confirmed that teachers' beliefs were the driving force in change of practice.
Instructional Activities Screenshots	Showed evidence in interventions outcome.	Showed evidence of PD implementation.	Showed evidence of coaching and feedback.	Showed evidence in response to interventions.	Evidence of engagement context was in activities and reports.	Evidence in intervention responsiveness.

Analysis of quantitative data in this study was done through reporting, comparing and displaying (Hendricks, 2013). Although the double entry journal consisted of responses that were not quantitative, the data was reported by counting the numbers of student responses initiated by teachers for the corresponding engagement domain. These were then analyzed through the DOK levels and counted as numeric data points. These numeric data points were represented as ratios of the number of students who participated to the total number of students in attendance. Time logs from double entry journals were counted based on duration of student participation and reported as the ratio of the duration of student participation to total instructional time. The resulting percentages of these ratios were organized in the engagement frequency chart based on corresponding rubric (rubric analysis) and later displayed as bar graphs using mean scores for comparing teachers' outcomes of implemented engagement practices. Likewise, survey data was displayed in bar graphs using mean scores of responses to analyze the outcome and impact of interventions.

Findings

Findings in this study were based on the data that was selected in response to the research questions. This data showed: 1) positive responsiveness to teachers' engagement interventions evidenced by increase in engagement practices during the six weeks of interventions, 2) increase in teachers' perceptions about instructional feedback, PD and teachers' own personal growth, 3) coaching grounded in data surfaced as most impactful intervention in this study, and 4) engagement practices relevant to the socio-emotional and behavioral domain were least responsive to interventions.

Teachers' Response to Engagement Interventions (RQ1)

Compiled data showed positive responsiveness to teachers' engagement interventions evidenced by increase in engagement practices during the duration of interventions. Multi-layered data in Table 6 illustrates a teacher's responsiveness to targeted engagement interventions, spanning from 24% to 79% in student engagement during this study, surpassing the initial coaching goal of 40%. Data also shows low socio-emotional engagement and low implementation of DOK 3 levels.

Table 6. Engagement frequency chart

Observation	Cognitive	Frequency	Socio Emotional	Frequency	Behavioral	DOK1	DOK2	DOK3	Coaching	Engagement Practice	Feedback	Artifacts
			Engagement Teacher A Initial Coaching Goal 40% Highest Reached 79%							CFU=Check for Understanding SE-Socio-emotional Domain BE-Behavioral Domain		
1	24%	33%	0%	0%	0%	4	5	0	Yes	Class Notebook/ Teams Whiteboard	CFU, DOK, SE	Class Notebook Screenshot
2	38%	76%	4%	2%	0%	7	14	3	Yes	Microsoft Forms	Use of Forms, DOK	Microsoft Form Report
3	14%	29%	3%	2%	0%	6	6	0	Yes	Nearpod	SE, BE	Nearpod Report
4	72%	42%	17%	11%	0%	4	12	0		Nearpod	SE	Nearpod Report
5	79%	22%	0%	0%	0%	16	8	0		Nearpod	SE, BE, DOK Nearpod	Nearpod Report
M	45.4%	40.4%	4.8%	3%	0%	7.4	9	0.6				

In addition, data in Table 6 shows high use of cognitive and much lower use of socio-emotional engagement practices. Behavioral engagement was not evidenced. In addition, the frequency chart shows that the teacher engaged students by asking mostly questions at DOK2 with a compiled mean M=9 followed by DOK1 at M= 7.4, and DOK3 at M= 0.6.

Ready to Engage?

Despite the numerous technology challenges in virtual learning, teachers' responsiveness to interventions had a positive impact on their engagement practices, especially the ones related to the cognitive domain as evidenced by the graph below (Figure 6).

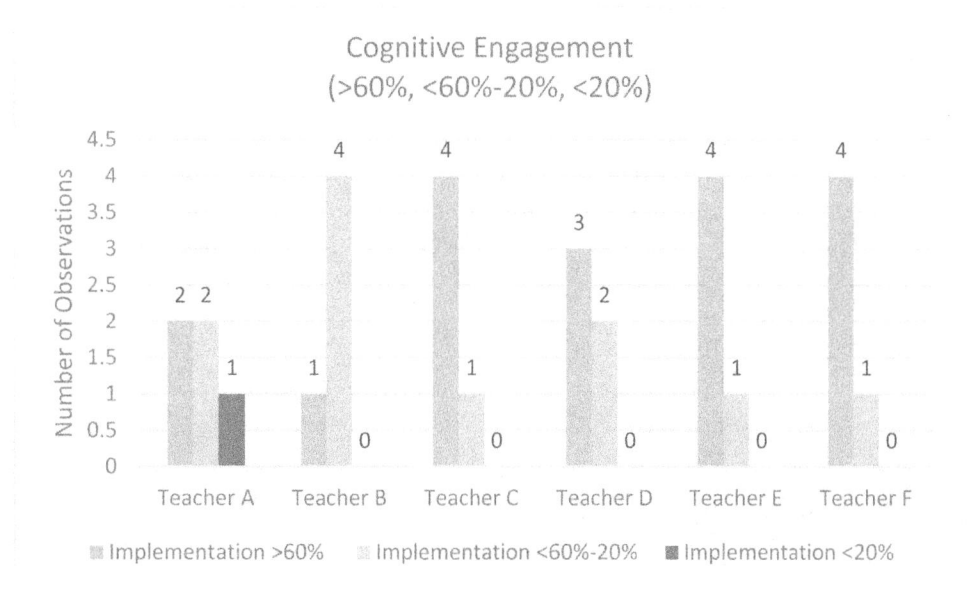

Figure 6. Cognitive engagement

Overall, out of thirty lessons observed, eighteen showed evidence of student engagement at over 60% of students eleven between 60% and 20%. Just one observed lesson had student engagement under 20%.

Teachers valued mostly platforms that allowed them to monitor students' activities in real time (such as, Nearpod, Legends of Learning, and Padlets). They regarded these as most impactful in implementing engagement strategies since they could check for students' understanding, keep them accountable and provide instant feedback.

Although the number of cognitively engaged students surpassed 60%, in more than half of the total lessons observed, the duration of engagement was rather short. In just six of the thirty lessons students' engagement lasted more than 60% of the total time (teacher A, C, D, and E). Specifically, this means that the engagement time surpassed 27 minutes out of the 45 minutes planned for synchronous instructional time. Likewise, in six lessons out of the total observed, students were less than 20% of the time engaged. This means that engagement practices lasted less than nine minutes of total instructional time. Eighteen lessons involved engagement practices lasted between 60% to 20% of the total instructional time. This means that in most of the lessons engagement practices had a duration between nine and 27 minutes (See Figure 7).

Figure 7. Total cognitive engagement time

Duration of Cognitive Engagement
(>60%, <60%-20%, <20%)

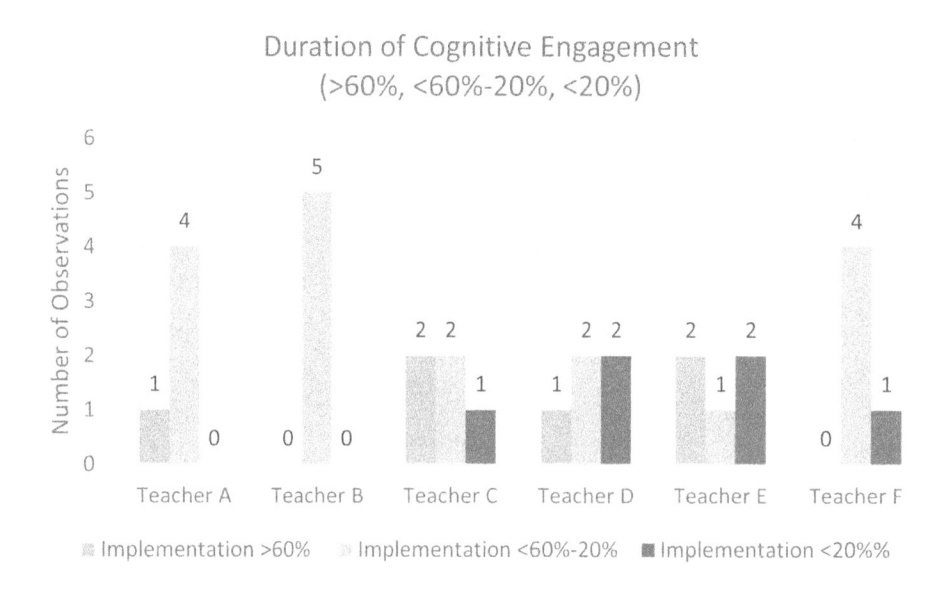

Teacher	Implementation >60%	Implementation <60%-20%	Implementation <20%%
Teacher A	1	4	0
Teacher B	0	5	0
Teacher C	2	2	1
Teacher D	1	2	2
Teacher E	2	1	2
Teacher F	0	4	1

Figure 8. Average DOK levels during 30 observation

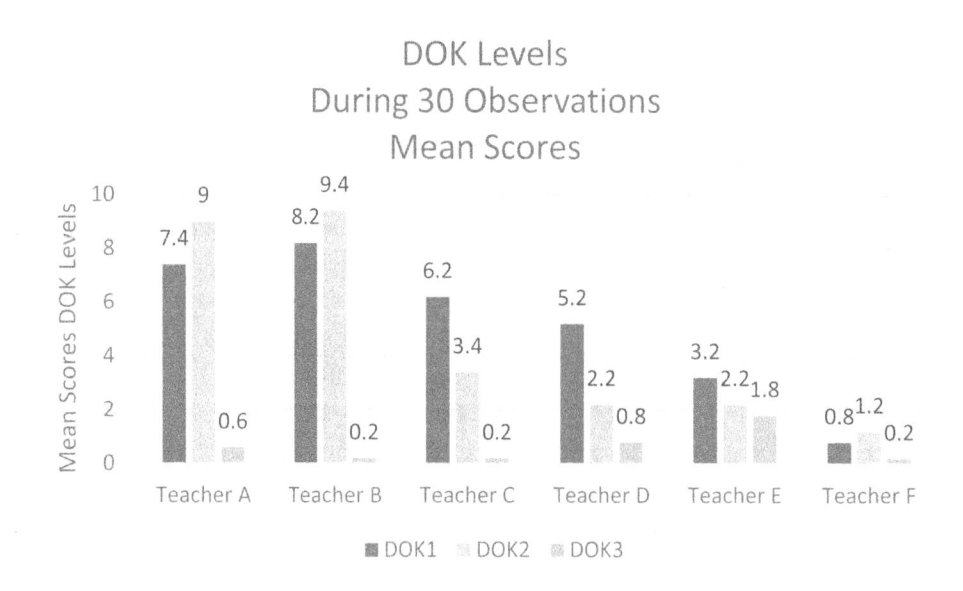

DOK Levels During 30 Observations Mean Scores

Teacher	DOK1	DOK2	DOK3
Teacher A	7.4	9	0.6
Teacher B	8.2	9.4	0.2
Teacher C	6.2	3.4	0.2
Teacher D	5.2	2.2	0.8
Teacher E	3.2	2.2	1.8
Teacher F	0.8	1.2	0.2

Level one Depth of Knowledge (DOK 1) questioning had a compiled M=5.2, followed by level two M= 4.8 and level three by and M=0.6. The frequency of questioning was higher in math than science classes and was more efficiently achieved with software platforms such as Google Forms or scaffolding during problem-solving using a whiteboard in TEAMs. However, questions in science had a higher average in DOK3 level with the implementation of Legends of Learning, digital textbook resources in

Ready to Engage?

TEAMs and simulations using Nearpod applications (Figure 8). The highest average of DOK levels during the five observation cycles was DOK2 at M= 9.4 followed by DOK1at M=8.2 and DOK3 at M=1.8.

Teachers' Responsiveness of Coaching, Instructional Feedback and PD (RQ2)

Coaching grounded in data surfaced as most impactful intervention in this study. The use of transformative, facilitative and cognitive coaching grounded in data and system thinking contributed to the exploration of interrelated patterns in teachers' practices (Aguliar, 2013). As result of coaching, teachers' became more reflective and aware of their engagement practices. This led to change in their instructions as evidenced by the statements below.

Coaching gives me awareness of things I should be doing and looking for –so I can focus on those areas. (Teacher D, Interview)

When you shared with me the numbers (I am very analytical) it made me think of how I can make things better. When I heard the feedback it made me think of opportunities that I can add to lessons. (Teacher B, Interview)

This first quarter it was very frustrating. What I got out of coaching is to see the positives through a more objective eye. You helped me look at things through multiple angles. (Teacher F, Interview)

Coaching grounded in data surfaced as the most impactful intervention in this study. Coaching plans with measurable goals and identified engagement strategies constituted the framework towards teacher growth. The impact of coaching is collaborated with teachers' statements:

Coaching was the most powerful. The statistical breakdown that you gave me made me picture of what you saw and what was in my mind (Teacher B, Interview)

Coaching helped most –because we discussed everything together on how I can implement certain criteria in lessons. It encompasses everything else feedback, socio-emotional and behavioral engagement. (Teacher D, Interview)

Coaching and looking at data was most impactful-also the talking about the lesson during coaching. (Teacher E, Interview)

You challenged me to set higher goals for myself and you made mi think of implemented various strategies on how to make kids participate-you gave me a lot of ideas –then it was up to me to see what works best for my students (Teacher C, Interview)

Much better to receive feedback through coaching than written-because I can follow up with questions. Or if I need examples –you can give them right away. It feels also less informal.(Teacher B, Interview)

Teachers' statements bring evidence of positive impact of dialogue use during coaching as advocated by Knight (2019). The use of collaborative dialogue during structured coaching was intended to honor teacher's autonomy and set a path to improve practice. In addition, during coaching, high leverage actions were triggered by data and analyzed through the Cognitive Engagement Model (Himmele & Himmele, 2011).

Survey data shows an increase in teachers' perceptions about instructional feedback, PD and teachers' own personal growth. The Culture and Climate Pre and Post-survey on PD (Figure 9) shows significant growth in teachers' perceptions of PD. Highest growth was in both teachers' perceptions of input in individualized PD (from M=1.3 to M=2.3); and amount of learning (from M=1.8 to M=2.8), followed by the value of PD (from M=1.8 to M=2.3), strategies learned (from M=2.3 to M=2.8) and growth (from M=3 to M=3.7).

Figure 9. Culture and climate pre and post survey

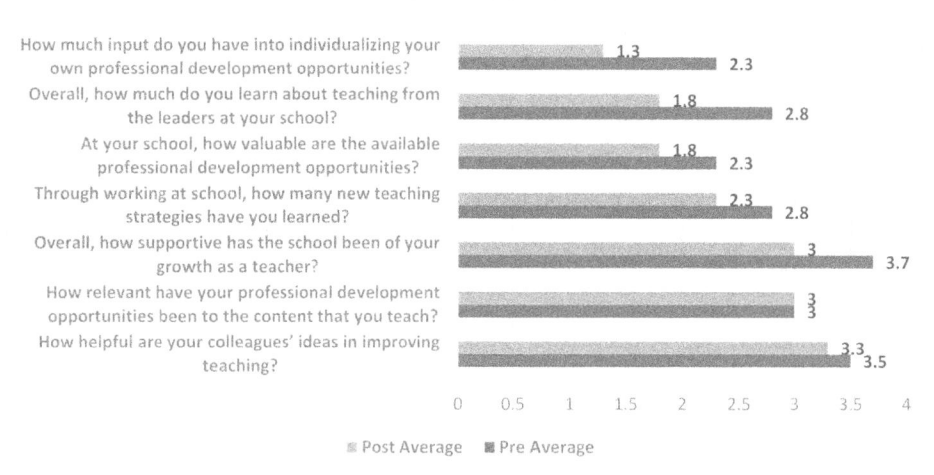

Culture and Climate Pre and Post Survey Professional Development Mean Scores

Question	Pre Average	Post Average
How much input do you have into individualizing your own professional development opportunities?	1.3	2.3
Overall, how much do you learn about teaching from the leaders at your school?	1.8	2.8
At your school, how valuable are the available professional development opportunities?	1.8	2.3
Through working at school, how many new teaching strategies have you learned?	2.3	2.8
Overall, how supportive has the school been of your growth as a teacher?	3	3.7
How relevant have your professional development opportunities been to the content that you teach?	3	3
How helpful are your colleagues' ideas in improving teaching?	3.3	3.5

PD data was collaborated with teachers' statements regarding interventions' impact: "PD was most impactful because it was collaborative and I love collaborating- I was able to see how other teachers do in their classrooms and I loved to share my stuff that worked." (Teacher F, Interview). Research by Senge (2015) and Darling-Hammond, et al. (2017) confirms the importance of collaboration in adult learning processes and effective PD design.

Responsiveness of Features of Instructional Practice to Interventions (RQ3)

Engagement practices relevant to the socio-emotional and behavioral domain were least responsive to interventions. Socio-emotional engaged practices that involved over 60% of the students in attendance were addressed in just eight of the thirty lessons observed. Most of the socio-emotional engagement was below 20%. Specifically, this type of engagement was in sixteen out of the thirty lessons observed while in six lessons the range was greater than 20% and less than 60% (Figure 10).

Ready to Engage?

Figure 10. Frequency of socio-emotional engagement

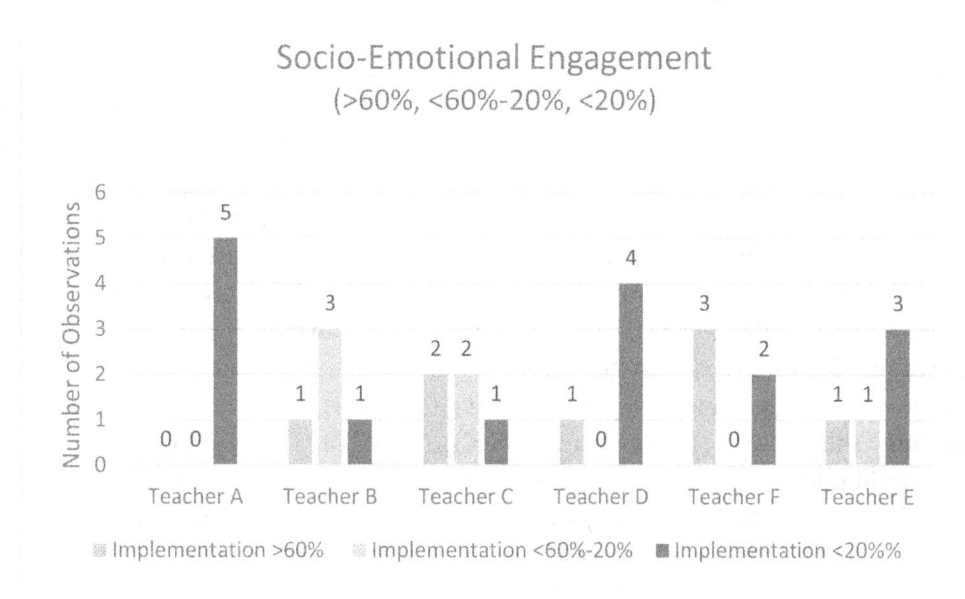

Socio-Emotional Engagement
(>60%, <60%-20%, <20%)

Teacher	Implementation >60%	Implementation <60%-20%	Implementation <20%
Teacher A	0	0	5
Teacher B	1	3	1
Teacher C	2	2	1
Teacher D	1	0	4
Teacher F	3	0	2
Teacher E	1	1	3

Most of the socio-emotional engagement practices observed during the thirty lessons lasted less than 20% of the total instructional time, while just in four of these were more than 20% and less than 60% of total time (Figure 11).

Figure 11. Duration of socio-emotional engagement

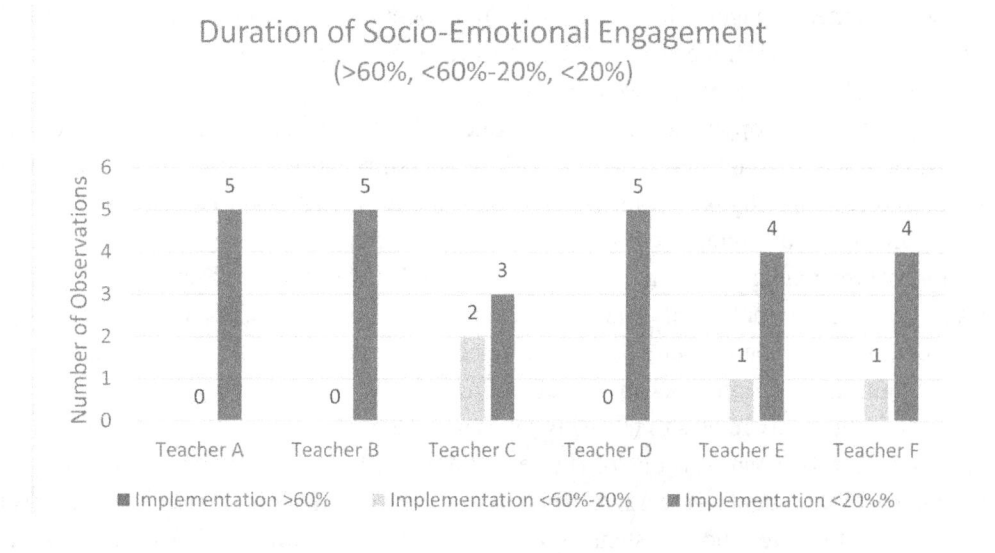

Duration of Socio-Emotional Engagement
(>60%, <60%-20%, <20%)

Teacher	Implementation >60%	Implementation <60%-20%	Implementation <20%
Teacher A		0	5
Teacher B		0	5
Teacher C		2	3
Teacher D		0	5
Teacher E		1	4
Teacher F		1	4

391

IMPLICATIONS AND RECOMMENDATIONS

Teachers' response to interventions was driven by their beliefs and growth mindset. They were eager to learn new practices since they believed that engagement is connected to students' learning outcomes. When asked what mostly impacted the implementation of engagement practices, the teacher's response was: "Realization that kids learn if engaged" (Teacher E, Interview).

From my perspective as the action researcher and instructional coach, the importance of alignment in intervention design, long- term focus and most importantly, the value of pre-existing positive relationships with participant teachers were pivotal conditions for teachers' response to interventions. In addition, involving teachers in the decision making process helped with their buy-in. The value of modeling during PD was confirmed in teachers' interviews. In addition, survey data showed teachers' positive perspectives to collaboration in learning processes and to focused sustained professional development. Data in this study shows that most tasks were at DOK1 (M=5.2) and DOK2 (M= 4.6). DOK3 was very low (M< 1). In addition, most of these tasks took place in the stamina quadrant of high difficulty (amount of time and effort to complete a task) and low complexity (number of steps and background knowledge).

My recommendations for teachers consist of further exploration of socio-emotional and behavioral engagement practices in virtual learning environments with emphasis on DOK3 and DOK4 levels. Likewise, I recommend that teachers take advantage of coaching, instructional feedback and PD as means to improve their practices and impact students learning outcomes.

FUTURE RESEARCH DIRECTIONS

This study added evidence that conditions for change are tied to teachers' mindset. This was evident during coaching sessions when teachers used reflective monologue to explain how their practices affected student engagement. They approached interventions with a growth mindset while taking risks in implementing more difficult practices especially relevant to technology platforms. Some even challenged themselves with higher engagement goals. Still, implementation of socio-emotional and behavioral engagement in a virtual environment surfaced as least responsive to interventions. Therefore, the future research should explore further these two domains.

During PD, teachers had opportunities to investigate their practices and reflect on their course content in the context of students' interests, academic task, ownership and relevance. Future research should also in focus on understanding how students achieve relatedness and how to promote this practice in a virtual environment. I had limited success in addressing this practice during coaching. In addition, the implementation of the four engagement elements examined by Marzano and Pickering (2011) presented challenges for teachers to implement. These elements are relevant to students' emotions, perceived importance of content, and students' perceptions of efficacy. Therefore, another recommendation for future research is to examine this framework in virtual environments.

A limitation of this study relates to fostering teacher-student relationships in virtual settings. Fostering teacher –student relationships is one of Hattie's (2009) evidences of impact on students' outcomes. During virtual learning students were not required to turn on their cameras and therefore the visual clues in building relationships were non-existent. In addition, breakout rooms in TEAMs were not activated during the study. This limited students from working in pairs or groups.

Even though engagement was increased, it was mostly linked to low cognition (superficial understanding) and high participation when analyzed through Himmele (20011) Cognitive Engagement Model and DOK levels. Himmele's framework was used during coaching as reference point when analyzing trends in teachers' engagement practices and as a coaching tool. Even after additional training in this model, teachers' practices mostly changed just in frequency of participation using cold call, wait time and call and response (Lemov, 2010). Future research is recommended to further examine engagement practices through the lens of this model with the aim to find best virtual engagement practices that lead to deep understanding and high participation.

CONCLUSION

This action research found positive teacher responsiveness to coaching driven by feedback that is grounded in engagement data. Interventions showed immediate outcome in teachers' practices due to alignment of intervention, intense approach and consistent follow-up. Coaching resulted to be more effective with smaller number of teachers than larger ones that I experienced in the past. This added evidence to the study done by Kraft and Bazar (2018). Smaller number of teachers led to a higher engagement in PDs and allowed the practitioner to build on teachers' existing skills, knowledge and beliefs as suggested by Aguilar (2013).

The use of this action research methodology can help teachers reflect and act in order to continually improve their practice. The outcomes of this study builds knowledge in the area of effective teaching practices during virtual learning. Understanding the impact of these interventions adds in-depth information to implementation context. The design of this methodology can be replicated in similar contexts with the aim to change teachers' practices.

ACKNOWLEDGMENT

I would like to thank my dissertation committee (Dr. Alina Slapac, Chair, and Drs. Natalie Bolton, Amber Candela, and Nancy Singer) for their constant support, mentorship and valuable feedback on my dissertation study from which this chapter evolved. Special thanks to this book co-editors, Drs. Alina Slapac, Phyllis Balcerzak, and Kate O'Brien for their support, edits, and guidance throughout the chapter process. Their valuable insights and continuous contribution to advance my chapter have been immeasurable. The participant teachers deserve a very special mention, as they have given me the opportunity to implement my action research. It was an honor to observe their instructions and collaborate during coaching and professional development. Thank you to the school's Principal for accepting my research idea, and allowing me to move forward with this project. Sincere thank you to my dear friends who have stood by my side throughout this research.

REFERENCES

Aguilar, E. (2013). *The art of coaching: Effective strategies for school transformation.* John Wiley & Sons.

Bransford, J. D., Brown, A. L., & Cocking, R. R. (Eds.). (2000). *How people learn: Brain, mind, experience, and school*. National Academy Press.

Darling-Hammond, L., Hyler, E. M., & Gardner, M. (Eds.). (2017, June). *Effective Teacher Professional Development*. Learning Policy Institute. Retrieved from https://learningpolicyinstitute.org/sites/default/files/product-files/Effective_Teacher_Professional_Development_REPORT.pdf

Deci, E. L., & Ryan, R. M. (2000). The "what" and "why" of goal pursuits: Human needs and the self determination of behavior. *Psychological Inquiry*, *11*(4), 227–268. doi:10.1207/S15327965PLI1104_01

Desimone, L. M. (2009). Improving impact studies of teachers' professional development: Toward better conceptualizations and measures. *Educational Researcher*, *38*(3), 181–199. doi:10.3102/0013189X08331140

Dweck, C. S. (2006). *Mindset: The new psychology of success*. Random House.

Fisher, D., Frey, N., Quaglia, R. J., Smith, D., & Lande, L. L. (2018). *Engagement by design: Creating learning environments where students thrive*. Corwin Literacy.

Ford, J. D., Ford, L. W., & D'Amelio, A. (2008). Resistance to change: The rest of the story. *Academy of Management Review*, *33*(2), 362–377. doi:10.5465/amr.2008.31193235

Francis, E. (2017). *What is depth of knowledge?* https://inservice.ascd.org/what-exactly-is-depth-of-knowledge-hint-its-not-a-wheel/

Garret, R., Citkowicz, M., & Williams, R. (2019). How responsive is a teacher's classroom practice to intervention? A meta-analysis of randomized field studies. *Review of Research in Education*, *43*(1), 106–109. doi:10.3102/0091732X19830634

Gawande, A. (2010). *The checklist manifesto: How to get things right*. Profile Books.

Hattie, J. (2009). *Visible learning: A synthesis of over 800 meta-analyses relating to achievement*. Routledge.

Hendricks, C. (2013). *Improving schools through action research: A reflective practice approach*. Pearson.

Hill, H. C., Beisiegel, M., & Jacob, R. (2013). Professional development research: Consensus, crossroads, and challenges. *Educational Researcher*, *42*(9), 476–487. doi:10.3102/0013189X13512674

Himmele, P., & Himmele, W. (2011). *Total participation techniques: Making every student an active learner*. ASCD.

Kanter, R. M. (2013, January 7). *Six keys to leading positive change* [Video file]. YouTube. https://www.youtube.com/watch?time_continue=8&v=owU5aTNPJbs

Knight, J. (2014). *Focus on teaching: Using video for high-impact instruction*. CORWIN.

Knight, J. (2018). *The impact cycle: what instructional coaches should do to foster powerful improvements in teaching*. CORWIN.

Knight, J. (2019). Why teacher autonomy is central to coaching success. *Educational Leadership*, *77*(3), 14–20. http://www.ascd.org/publications/educational-leadership/nov19/vol77/num03/Why-Teacher-Autonomy-Is-Central-to-Coaching-Success.aspx

Kraft, M. A., & Blazar, D. (2018). Taking teacher coaching to scale. *Education Next*, *18*(4), 69–74. https://www.educationnext.org/taking-teacher-coaching-to-scale-can-personalized-training-become-standard-practice/

Kraft, M. A., Blazar, D., & Hogan, D. (2018). The effect of teacher coaching on instruction and achievement: A meta-analysis of the causal evidence. *Review of Educational Research*, *88*(4), 547–588. doi:10.3102/0034654318759268

Lemov, D. (2015). *Teach like a champion 2.0: 62 techniques that put students on the path to college.* Jossey-Bass.

Marzano, R. J., Pickering, D., & Heflebower, T. (2011). *The highly engaged classroom.* Marzano Research.

Merriam, S. B. (1998). *Qualitative research study applications in education.* Jossey-Bass.

Okantey, P. C. (2012). Leading Change: When everything else is falling. *Leadership Review*, *2*(3), 42–46.

Pintrich, P. R. (2003). Motivation and classroom learning. *Educational Psychology, 7, 103–124.* doi:10.1002/0471264385.wei0706

Rebora, A. (2019). Expanding on coaching's potential. *Educational Leadership*, *77*(3), 9–9.

Sciarra, D., & Seirup, H. (2008). The multidimensionality of school engagement and math achievement among racial groups. *Professional School Counseling*, *11*(4), 218–228. doi:10.5330/PSC.n.2010-11.218

Senge, P. (2015, Jun 4). *How do you define a learning organization?* [Video file]. YouTube. https://www.youtube.com/watch?time_continue=2&v=vc2ruCErTok

Skinner, E. A., & Belmont, M. J. (1993). Motivation in the classroom: Reciprocal effects of teacher behavior and student engagement across the school year. *Journal of Educational Psychology*, *85*(4), 571–581. doi:10.1037/0022-0663.85.4.571

Snow-Renner, R., & Lauer, P. (2005). *Professional development analysis.* Mid-Content Research for Education and Learning. Retrieved from https://files.eric.ed.gov/fulltext/ED491305.pdf

Trotter, Y. D. (2006). Adult learning theories: Impacting professional development programs. *Delta Kappa Gamma Bulletin*, *72*(2), 8–13.

ADDITIONAL READING

Aguilar, E. (2020). *Coaching for equity: Conversations that change practice.* John Wiley & Sons.

Burgess, D. (2012). *Teach like a pirate: Increase student engagement, boost your creativity, and transform your life as an educator.* Dave Burgess Consulting, Inc.

DuFour, R., & Reason, C. (2015). *Professional Learning Communities at Work and Virtual Collaboration: On the Tipping Point of Transformation (Foster a Learner-Focused Culture with Technology) (Essentials for Principals).* Solution Tree.

Fisher, D., Frey, N., & Hattie, J. (2020). *The Distance Learning Playbook, Grades K-12: Teaching for Engagement and Impact in Any Setting* (1st ed.). Corwin.

Johnson, A. P. (2012). *A short guide to action research*. Addison-Wesley Longman.

Knight, J. (2014). *Focus on Teaching: Using Video for High-Impact Instruction* (1st ed.). CORWIN.

Rebora, A. (2019, November). Expanding on Coaching's Potential. *Educational Leadership, 77*(3), 9–9.

Slapac, A., & Navarro, V. (2011). Shaping action researchers through a Master's capstone experience. *Teacher Education and Practice, 24*(4), 405–426.

KEY TERMS AND DEFINITIONS

Academic Instructional Coach: A professional responsibility to collaborate with teachers on improving instructional practices using evidence-based strategies.

Asynchronous Learning: Online instructions that don't occur in real time and usually pertain pre-recorded lessons or modules.

Coaching: Act of analyzing current instructional reality, setting goals, identifying, and explaining teaching strategies to hit the goals, and provide support until the goals are met.

Hybrid Instructions: A mix of in-person and online instructions.

Instructional Feedback: Information about how we are doing in our efforts to reach a goal.

Professional Development: Information about the effects of teaching practices as related to a goal followed by high leverage action steps on how to fill in gaps to reach mastery in practice.

Synchronous Learning: Instructions that occur online in real time on various platforms such as Microsoft TEAMs, Blackboard, Google Classroom.

Virtual Instructions: Solely online instructions or components of face-to-face instruction taught online.

Chapter 17
Action Research Is Cyclical:
A Study in 9th Grade Conceptual Physics

Tiffany Cunningham
University of San Diego, USA

ABSTRACT

Due to the global pandemic, teachers have had to find and implement effective instructional strategies through distance learning. Current research surrounding "flipped learning" indicates this may be a viable option during distance learning. This study takes place in a 9th grade conceptual physics course taught entirely online. It focuses upon the cyclical nature of action research using four curricular units, concluding that the process of continual reflection, modifications, and improvements made as a result of data analysis contributes to student engagement and academic achievement. Finally, it brings to light the importance in guiding students to understand that teachers are always learning, modifying, and adapting, and that learning is a lifelong process. This transparency is crucial when developing rapport with students, especially during a global pandemic that we are all working through together.

INTRODUCTION

Action research within education is simply the scientific term to describe what educators do every day: teach a lesson, collect and analyze students' work as data, determine which instructional methods and strategies were most effective, and revise and prepare for the next lesson (Pine, 2009). Teachers continually use assessments to guide instruction (Tomlinson & Moon, 2013) and provide the most accessible and engaging lessons to students. Action research is clarifying the steps that teachers use to complete this process and formalizing it into a report to be shared with others.

More than the daily process of educators, action research is the system by which researchers work directly with participants to engage in change that will benefit all involved (Bhattacharya, 2017; Bradbury-Huang, 2015). It is a paradigm centered around social justice and activism, working to provide immediate relief and lasting change to the participants (Leavy, 2017). Action research, especially in education, can be viewed through a variety of theoretical frameworks, however Critical Theory may be at the forefront. This framework draws attention to the fact that there are racial, social, systemic and

DOI: 10.4018/978-1-7998-6922-1.ch017

institutional inequities across the United States, and they have existed and been solidified repeatedly over the course of this country's history (Anyon, 2009; Crenshaw, 1994; Ladson-Billings & Tate, 1995; Paris, 2012). These inequities hold by controlling the narrative and keeping the focus on what is considered the norm. However, Critical Theory seeks to take control of that narrative, to share that power with others, and to promote diversity and celebrate differences through engaging and sustainable methods (Ladson-Billings & Tate, 1995; Paris, 2012). Action research allows, and truly encourages, the many voices of participants to come together as one with the researcher (Tuck, 2009), highlighting the vulnerability necessary for research studies to truly be successful (Bhattacharya, 2017; Kuntz, 2016). The power of this narrative is insurmountable and can build upon current literature in nearly every field while also amplifying voices that are often hushed.

With so many voices working together, action research can ultimately take on a life of its own and the primary researcher is responsible for writing the narrative that explains the process: documenting each step taken and the effects of those steps, then sharing that information and the learning process with the educational research community (Bradbury-Huang, 2015). With a strong foundation in the current literature and an awareness of the social barriers affecting participants, the primary researcher can work as a guide or mentor, encouraging the participants to lead the charge and validating their experiences throughout this process (Bhattacharya, 2017; Kuntz, 2016; Slapac & Navarro, 2011). Even when participants do not take an active role, there is a continual awareness of the participants' explicit influence throughout the research process, allowing for more opportunities for growth and change, but also hindering the predictability of the research (Tuck, 2009). In doing so, this type of research can grow to be so much larger than what was imagined, leading to real and lasting change brought on or inspired by the participants. What may start as a small and simple research project in one classroom may grow to positively impact hundreds more students, families, and communities. Therefore, it is also important to note that action research is not a linear process. In particular, educators have shown the cyclical nature of action research by continually assessing and recalibrating lessons each and every day in accordance with data from students or participants, including informal feedback and formal assessments (Tomlinson & Moon, 2013).

As a science teacher, I found action research to be incredibly similar to the scientific method: on paper, these processes both appear very linear, with a clear problem to solve, experimentation, data analysis, and conclusions. And yet, in life, these processes are anything but linear with continual methodological modifications, repeating experimentation and observations with changes, and reanalysis of the data leading to new conclusions to be shared with the community - and the process repeats (Carey & Smith, 1993; Lombrozo, Thanukos, & Weisberg, 2008). Science done in the real-world involves the many, many routes that experimentation takes, from observations and exploring the literature to weighing the benefits and costs of the outcomes to sharing with the community and engaging with the feedback. Any one of those steps may require further experimentation, more data collected, and further analyses, setting off additional observations, literature reviews, and community engagement - further modification that leads to a renewed cycle of experimentation and the process repeats itself once more (Carey & Smith, 1993; Thanukos, et al., 2010; University of California Museum of Paleontology, 2021). Action research follows the scientific method and in doing so, it is also no longer simply identifying a problem, assessing needs and moving forward to experimentation. Instead, action research is also rather a continuous back and forth movement in an attempt to find the best solution for unique and specific circumstances in a specific classroom for specific students. Additional research must be done, following the same cyclical processes, when faced with a new course, new students, or a new community. The process of action research, like the scientific method, is truly never-ending as the participants and variables unceasingly change and grow.

Again, educators complete a very simplified version of action research on a daily basis - even if their individual research is not documented and published. Memes and stories are shared daily online demonstrating the perseverance and dedication teachers have to provide the best lessons possible for their specific classrooms and students. They are continually gathering and interpreting data from students, determining next steps based upon the outcomes of that data and community feedback. It is a constant ebb and flow, moving forward and back, reviewing literature and engaging with the community, attempting new methods and strategies with students, collecting and analyzing additional data from informal and formal assessments of students' work, and around again (Slapac & Navarro, 2011; Thanukos, et al., 2010; University of California Museum of Paleontology, 2021). It is a continuous cycle to ensure students' needs are met and academic success is attainable for all. Students are at the forefront of action research in education and as such, their contributions and feedback help to guide this process to create more equitable classrooms and accessible curriculum.

This chapter focuses upon the very cyclical nature of action research and the continual reflection, modifications, and improvements that are made as a result of analysis of student data. The study detailed uses action research while implementing "flipped classroom" methods and techniques during distance learning as a result of the global health pandemic to demonstrate the many cycles that teachers implement in order to find the most effective instructional strategies to engage students and support them toward their academic success. Feedback and assessment data from students play a pivotal role throughout this entire process as students' involvement and influence dictates which methods and practices are best. Finally, it brings to light the importance in guiding students to understand that teachers are always learning, modifying, and adapting and that learning is not only done in school, but continues for the rest of their lives. This transparency is crucial when developing rapport with students, especially during a global pandemic that we are all working through together.

BACKGROUND

With the emergence of the novel coronavirus, COVID-19, in early 2020, schools moved quickly to ensure students' safety. By March 13, 2020, nearly all schools across the United States had shifted to some kind of distance, online, or virtual learning, in which students attended class through video chat and classrooms moved to online learning management systems. Teachers and parents waited together for district administrators and school board members to decide on the best course of action for the 2020-2021 school year and most waited until just before the start of the new school year to decide on distance learning, in-person learning, or a hybrid option of both. Teachers in districts who chose distance or hybrid learning were faced with the monumental task of changing their lessons to an entirely new way of teaching, with an extremely limited "toolkit" to pull from. Activities, lectures, and projects that encourage engagement and participation, leading to students' academic success, during in-person learning do not always translate to distance learning - more often than not, these plans must be significantly modified or abandoned entirely.

This action research study took place during the fall semester of 2020 in a district that mandated distance learning for the entire semester. Significant changes to teachers' "toolkits" were required before the semester began, providing one week of preparation for new classroom routines and practices for the online learning management system. This action research focuses upon the new methods and strategies that were most favorable in increasing student engagement and academic success during this time, with particular focus on including "flipped classroom" techniques and practices.

Objectives

This study is focused upon developing effective, accessible, and relevant teaching methods and strategies that best used the extremely limited instructional time available. With only minimal knowledge of "flipped classroom" techniques and methods and its uses during limited instructional times, this study focused upon learning how to best incorporate these strategies in a distance learning format. The research questions were:

- Which "flipped classroom" methods, if any, best utilize the very limited instructional time?
- Which, if any, "flipped classroom" strategies engage students most and which, if any, strategies are students most comfortable with?
- Which, if any, "flipped classroom" teaching practices led to greater student success?

Literature Review

The ideas surrounding a "flipped classroom" have been around for over two decades and began to gain traction with King's (1993) saying of teachers shifting from "the sage on the stage to the guide on the side" (p. 30). This is in reference to the idea that in a "flipped classroom," the teacher is no longer simply in the front of the room, lecturing for the entire class time - instead they are moving around the classroom to assist students in a more personal manner of engaging with the instructional material, learning the individual concepts, and mastering the ideas at hand (Bergmann & Sams, 2015).

The movement of the "flipped classroom" really took off with Bergmann and Sams (2015): two high school chemistry teachers based in Colorado, who began recording their lectures, posting them to their class websites, and assigning those lectures as homework. In doing so, students were exposed to the foundational material before coming to class (Talbert, 2017), which allowed them to begin learning, identify areas of confusion, and come prepared to discuss the lessons of the day. The teachers were then free to use class time to focus on student understanding, student-centered activities, and guiding students toward understanding of difficult scientific concepts (Bergmann & Sams, 2015). As access to the internet has spread, so too has this idea of switching traditional classwork activities, including lectures and note-taking, to homework in order to use class time to focus entirely upon students' understanding and knowledge growth through lab experiments, mathematical practice problems, and group discussions (Bergmann & Sams, 2015; Talbert, 2017).

This switch of traditional classwork activities to homework often includes teachers creating their own lecture videos and posting them online for their students to access (Bergmann, & Sams, 2015). Some teachers find screen-recording their own PowerPoint presentations or recording themselves doing a full lecture in their classroom, complete with notes on their whiteboard, is the best option for their students (Fulton, 2012; Jeong, et al.,, 2016; Putri, et al., 2018). Others have discovered remarkable videos online through Khan Academy, Crash Course, and countless others that address the concepts their students need in clear, concise, and captivating ways (Subramaniam & Muniandy, 2019). Regardless of which videos are selected, students strongly benefit from the ability to pause and re-watch videos as many times as necessary to glean the necessary information (Jdaitawi, 2019). In doing so, they are able to take control of their education and learn at their own pace, developing the intrinsic motivation that will continue to benefit them in the future (Jeschofnig & Jeschofnig, 2011).

Additionally, by requiring students to engage with the lectures before participating in class (Fulton, 2012; Jdaitawi, 2019; Putri, et al., 2018; Tucker, 2012), teachers assist students in independently building the foundational knowledge that is necessary to be active learners during student-centered activities in class. The limited time together can then be dedicated to students' questions, student-led discussions, and practice working with concepts and ideas presented in the lectures. It is the movement of passive learning to the home and only allowing active learning in the classroom (Jeong, et al.,, 2018; Leo & Puzio, 2016; Tucker, 2012)

However, not all activities are created equal: not all activities should be flipped from class to home, or home to class (Lawson, et al., 2019). Some discussions are better as individual writing assignments, some practice worksheets are better when done in groups in class, and some lab activities can be done successfully, and more creatively, at home. Teachers must individually decide which activities work best for their students in class or at home - a process that may require practice in both settings or may change depending on the class and year (Bergmann & Sams, 2015; Lawson, et al., 2019).

With the ongoing global pandemic and the understanding that this action research study would be done entirely through distance learning, there are very clear caveats to seamlessly integrating "flipped classroom" techniques. Notably, online science courses have drawn attention to the facts that teachers in distance learning classes cannot rely on visual cues, that there is a greater weight on developing rapport with students while teaching from a distance, and that students must be taught to advocate for themselves online (Jeschofnig & Jeschofnig, 2011; Miller, 2008). In order to earn credit, students must engage with the material in some capacity rather than listen passively in class (Miller, 2008), which strongly plays into the active learning described by "flipped classroom" techniques. Therefore, preparing for a semester of distance learning by studying "flipped classroom" techniques and methods should yield effective and efficient strategies that lead to student engagement and academic success.

MAIN FOCUS OF THE CHAPTER

Context and Participants

This action research study took place in a 9th grade conceptual physics class at a mid-sized Title 1 high school (approximately 3,000 students) on the central coast of California. The class was made up of four sections, for a total of 72 students, with a nearly even split between males and females (males = 37, females = 35). Most students (67.6%, n = 48) are bilingual in Spanish and English and four students immigrated to the United States within the last two years.

All students were in distance learning for the entire semester and being 9th graders, these students were new to the high school and the online learning management system. Therefore, they needed assistance in navigating the school websites, accessing coursework online, and managing their online grade information system. The researcher used the first three weeks of the fall 2020 semester to assist students in becoming more comfortable in using each of these websites and building a rapport with students to encourage more frequent and meaningful communication outside of class time, including through email and phone calls.

Additionally, the majority of these students were enrolled in Algebra 1 (55%, n = 39) while the remainder were enrolled in pre-algebra (45%, n = 32). As such, these students did not have a strong mathematical foundation and the use of basic algebraic practices in this conceptual physics course was entirely new to them. This required the limited instructional time to be split between building the mathematical basis needed for this course and teaching the content and theories within conceptual physics.

Students attended class through video chat (Zoom) once each week, for 80 synchronous instructional minutes on either Tuesday or Wednesday, depending on assigned times. Each class period was made up of fifteen to nineteen students, for a total of four class periods in this study. Students also had the opportunity to attend office hours once each week, for 40 minutes, however this was optional. Finally, according to district mandates, students were to be assigned 120 asynchronous instructional minutes' worth of activities, for a total of 200 instructional minutes each week. This weekly work was made available to students by 8:00 in the morning each Monday and was due by 11:59 in the evening the following Sunday, as directed by district mandates.

Researcher Positionality

I am a fifth-year educator with experience teaching advanced placement biology, general biology, general chemistry, forensic science, integrated science, and conceptual physics. I earned my bachelor's degree and master's degree through online programs, with class sessions held through video chat prior to such methods becoming commonplace during the current global pandemic. With this background in a variety of science courses and online learning, I was able to approach the sudden shift to distance learning with more skills in my toolkit than most. However, professional development and training on how to effectively teach through distance learning were incredibly scarce: only two days were designated entirely to training teachers before the school year started. Both days were focused primarily upon how to use the learning management system (Canvas) and video chat (Zoom), with hour-long sessions on how to use various websites and applications that could be helpful (CK-12 Flexbooks, Gizmos, PhET simulations, Pivot Interactives, and Nearpod). Opportunities to learn best practices for teaching online or at a distance were not made available.

I chose to use "flipped learning" of my own volition because Bergmann and Sams' (2015) work demonstrated success in using extremely limited time in class to focus on interactive activities and working alongside students, centering students' experiences and educational progress. Additionally, I found personal success from a student perspective when practices similar to "flipped learning" were used: lecture and reading materials were provided before synchronous class times and students who came prepared had very effective and successful discussions together. I believed implementing similar techniques with my own students would allow us to maximize our very limited time together by focusing upon topics and concepts that students needed further assistance with, thereby building rapport and developing an inclusive classroom online and through virtual means. I sought out material on this methodology on my own time with personal resources and I was the only teacher at my school site using these teaching methods and practices and did not receive any formal training in how to do so. Because I was so new to this teaching methodology, I felt it necessary to use action research to ensure best practices were derived from current literature, my own students' data and testimony collected from my students throughout the unit.

Interventions: Instructional Strategies

This action research study focused on student engagement and academic success during the first curricular unit of the year, weeks four to twelve of the semester in a conceptual physics course for 9th grade students. This unit was on kinematics, from displacement and velocity to an introduction of Newton's laws and momentum. The study was divided into four cycles, each ending with a short assessment on the algebraic formula taught for that cycle. The formulas maintained some consistency in that each formula was made up of only three variables: velocity = distance ÷ time, acceleration = velocity ÷ time, force = mass × acceleration (or acceleration = force ÷ mass), and momentum = mass ÷ velocity.

The assessments at the end of each cycle were ten questions each and emphasized understanding of the connection between the variables and were made up almost entirely of calculations (7 to 8 out of 10 questions). The remaining questions discussed the conceptual understanding of the terms and ideas associated with each of the formulas above. Each assessment was multiple choice and students took the assessments during the synchronous class time.

The entire unit began with the immediate integration of "flipped classroom" techniques and strategies (Bergmann & Sams, 2015), including: virtual lab simulations available in and out of class time; practice problem worksheets and discussions to be completed in class; and recorded lectures with accompanying PowerPoints, Khan Academy videos, and assigned reading material available out of class. Lab activities were assigned through Gizmos lab simulations (ExploreLearning.com), Google Forms from Kesler Science, Pivot Interactives, and PhET simulations, all of which are available online. Gizmos lab simulations are based on traditional lab experiments that are typically done during in-person learning, including fan carts, graphing distance over time and velocity over time. Students have access to very detailed lab procedures to follow and they are able to manipulate a variety of factors within the lab simulation. Google Forms from Kesler Science are interactive documents with hyperlinks to videos, articles, and interactive activities online. They are designed to support students' engagement and exploration within a particular topic. Pivot Interactives are made up of videos of traditional lab activities with the ability to place rulers, timers, and protractors directly on the screen to record data as the video plays. Students are also able to record their data in tables and graphs on this website and teachers can personalize the activities, creating analysis or concluding questions for students to answer. Finally, PhET simulations were developed by the University of Colorado Boulder and have a variety of lab simulations, with the ability to change details about the independent variables. All practice problem worksheets were made available to students through their workbooks, discussed below. Additionally, all recorded lectures and assigned reading materials were made available on the learning management system or through CK-12's online flexbooks. CK-12 is a website of free online textbooks, renamed flexbooks because they include text, videos, and interactive activities within each chapter. All four of the cycles in the study used each of these instructional activities to varying degrees. Students were also informally surveyed at the end of each cycle to determine which activities they believed they were most engaged with and how to modify the activities they struggled with. This information was used to guide and modify instruction for each subsequent cycle.

Additionally, students did not have an assigned textbook, but rather a workbook that I specifically designed for this conceptual physics class in August of 2020. All students enrolled in this course in the high school received this workbook. It included all lab procedures, all practice problem worksheets, a glossary for students to progressively fill in each week, and specific areas for students to take notes on the lectures and assigned readings. Students showed completed pages of the workbook during class time in video chat or took pictures of their work and uploaded them to the online learning management system to show completion. Students used this workbook throughout the entire semester and received a second workbook, specifically designed for the spring semester of this course, in January of 2021.

Data Collection and Analysis

The research took place in four cycles, with modifications to instructional strategies and methods based upon students' data made between each cycle. Continuous conversation and discussions with students were used to determine engagement while a short assessment, given at the end of each cycle, was used in combination with discussion questions to determine students' academic success. Students' overall grades for the course were balanced between these assessments at the end of cycles, lab activities, discussion questions, practice problems, and engagement during and between classes.

Cycle 1

The first cycle focused on an introduction to kinematics and the velocity equation (velocity = distance ÷ time). During the synchronous class time, students worked through the practice problems and lab simulations in their workbook, asking questions almost entirely through the chat function in the Zoom session rather than un-muting their microphones and speaking aloud. It was very difficult to ensure that all students were engaged throughout the entire 80 minutes of instructional time as students' ability to keep cameras and microphones turned off is within their legal rights regarding privacy. However, it became clear within two class periods that there was a small group of three to four students in each class who were not at all engaged and likely logged into the video class link and then left their computers.

The emphasis on this subsection of the unit was identifying variables based upon contextual clues and the units of measure provided. Recorded lectures and the assigned reading material helped students to become familiar with the terms in the velocity equation as well as the units of measure associated with each variable before attending synchronous class. Practice problems gave students many opportunities to become more comfortable with the mathematical component during synchronous class, allowing students to ask questions of each other and the teacher while working. Virtual lab activities provided real-life scenarios in which the velocity equation could be used and were assigned during asynchronous time after class.

At the close of this subsection, students took a short assessment made mostly of calculations (8 out of 10 questions) on the velocity equation with the remainder of questions about the relationships between the variables. Their scores ranged from 0 to 9 out of 10, with an average of 6.4 (SD = 3.22).

Cycle 2

Based on the scores from the assessment and conversations with students during the first cycle, several changes were made during the second cycle, as shown in Table 1. First, it became clear that not all students were watching the recorded lectures or reading the assigned material before attending class. Therefore, it became part of the synchronous class time routine to survey students and learn who had not yet reviewed the lecture and reading material. These students were given time to do so before rejoining the class to participate in the activity for the day.

Action Research Is Cyclical

Second, to ensure engagement from all students, they were assigned to small groups for more individualized assistance during synchronous class time for 25 to 35 minutes per group. These small groups were made up of four to six students and their participation was much more visible during this time, leading to greater engagement and more discussions. Students who were off-task were easily identified and prescribed to the additional office hours available later in the week. Unfortunately, very few students (five out of 71 at most; two out of 71 on average) took advantage of this additional time.

Finally, after several discussions with students regarding virtual labs, it became clear that they were struggling with the websites themselves. To further emphasize the focus on the concepts, rather than the technology, screen-recorded videos of the virtual labs, following the lab procedure detailed in students' workbooks, were created to walk students through the lab activities. Students were still required to engage with material, record and analyze the data, and write their own conclusions while watching these videos, but the videos alleviated the struggle with the technology itself and provided scaffolding for those who needed it. The websites remained accessible for those students who preferred to work through the lab activities themselves.

Again, at the close of this subsection, students took a short assessment. This subsection was focused on the acceleration equation: acceleration = velocity ÷ time. The assessment was arranged in the same manner as the assessment in the first cycle, with the majority of questions (seven out of ten) being calculations and the remainder focused on the concepts and relationships between the variables. Students' range of scores was 0 to 8 out of 10, with a mean of 4.6 (SD = 2.11).

Cycle 3

With such low scores at the close of the second cycle, immediate changes were needed. First, the small groups were disbanded in favor of whole class meetings for the entire 80 instructional minutes. Although this cut down on participation rates, it allowed students to have more time interacting with the instructor and to see and hear peers' questions. Thankfully at this point in the semester, the students were very comfortable using the chat function in the Zoom sessions and would often ask questions both privately and publicly, allowing for greater discussion out loud for all to hear.

Second, to ensure that all students were engaging with the recorded lectures and assigned reading material before attending class, these assignments were made available through the interactive program Nearpod. This program records when students open the assignments as well as if, and for how long, they watch the videos embedded in those assignments. Using this data, it was possible to determine which students needed more guidance in engaging with the material prior to attending class and could make arrangements to do so without interrupting the limited synchronous class time.

Third, students were asked through a Google Forms poll to select which types of activities they enjoyed most this semester, if any. The top three selections were Pivot Interactives lab activities, screen-recorded videos walking students through the Gizmo lab activities, and Kesler Science Exploration Station lab activities. Using this information, the activities for this and the following cycles were shifted to include more lab activities during the synchronous class time.

Finally, the synchronous class time was shortened by 15 to 20 minutes each week to allow for more informal discussions and conversations with students. Students used this time to ask questions about any of the work done during class as well as any of the work assigned for the week. Students were encouraged to un-mute their microphones to ask questions and also use the chat function in the Zoom session, with consistent reminders that there is very likely another student with the same or similar question to their own who needs them to ask it.

This subsection was focused upon introducing Newton's Laws, most notably the second law associated with the equation force = mass × acceleration. Again, the assessment given at the end of the cycle was 10 questions, with the majority (7) being calculations and the remainder focused on relationships between the variables and the concepts of this law. Students' scores ranged from 0 to 10, with an average of 5.8 (SD = 2.39).

Table 1. Summary of progress through cycles

	Cycle 1	Cycle 2	Cycle 3
Successful Practices and Techniques	● Students' use of chat function in synchronous sessions ● Pre-recorded lectures made available before synchronous sessions	● More student engagement in smaller groups (chat function and verbal conversations) ● Accountability measures (survey at start of class) to ensure student engage before synchronous sessions	● Students' increased use of chat function in synchronous sessions ● Reserved 15-20 minutes at the end of class for questions and informal conversations ● Use of Nearpod to determine which students watched pre-recorded lectures
Challenges	● Ensuring students prepare for synchronous sessions with the pre-recorded lectures ● Maintaining student engagement during synchronous sessions	● Students' struggled with websites for lab simulations ● Limited synchronous time was limited further with small groups ● Continued struggles with ensuring students prepare before synchronous sessions	● Limited interaction with individual students in whole group setting
Modifications made for Next Cycle	● Developed surveys for students at start of synchronous session to ensure preparedness ● Assigned students to small groups for synchronous sessions	● Resumed whole group synchronous sessions ● Recorded lab procedures to assist students in working through online lab simulations ● Students surveyed to determine which activities were most engaging and accessible	● Increased use of interactive activities that students found most accessible and engaging

Cycle 4

At the start of the fourth and final cycle of this study, each of the classes had gotten into very smooth rhythm: students engaged with the material before class through recorded lectures and assigned reading material accessible through Nearpod; they participated during the synchronous class time by working through practice problems together or discussing virtual lab simulations from Pivot Interactives and Gizmos; and they finished the week's work by completing discussion questions or other conclusive writing based upon the virtual lab simulations and activities. However, this rhythm was cut short due to changes in scheduling from district mandates. Students were then required to attend class for the entire assigned 200 instructional minutes each week: 40 minutes on Mondays, 80 minutes on Tuesdays, and 80 minutes on Wednesdays. Additionally, with this change in class times, class sizes also changed as they were merged together and grew from 15 to 19 students to 35 and 36 students in the two classes.

With such massive changes to the schedule and class sizes, variables were no longer kept constant in this action research study. In order to maintain integrity in the current study, the data from this fourth and final cycle were excluded and were instead used as the needs assessment for the second curricular unit of the fall 2020 semester. Doing so led this cycle to be part of a second, informal action research study of distance learning in a very large conceptual physics class during a global pandemic.

Findings

Through the use of repeated cycles of action research, the most effective instructional methods and strategies were found and focused upon, leading to greater student engagement. Using "flipped classroom" ideas and techniques of assigning traditional lecture and reading materials during asynchronous times (Bergmann & Sams, 2015; Talbert, 2017), the study focused on how to best use the very limited synchronous instructional times as not all activities should necessarily be moved from traditional homework to be done during class times (Lawson, Davis, & Son, 2019). There were various lab simulations and mathematical practice to choose from to determine which activities were the best use of time each week with students, including Pivot Interactive virtual labs, Gizmos (virtual lab simulations), Kesler Science Exploration Station labs, and practice with calculations and basic algebraic functions.

Lecture and reading materials were the clearest demonstration of a "flipped classroom" (Bergmann & Sams, 2015), as these are traditionally assigned during class time and were instead assigned during asynchronous times. Building this foundational knowledge is especially helpful for students as it encourages them to become comfortable with new ideas and concepts at their own pace, with the ability to review the material as many times as they would like and as quickly or slowly as they would like. With such limited synchronous time, it was crucial that students completed this work before coming to class. However, it quickly became clear in this study that students needed to be held accountable for this work, which was a challenge in the virtual setting. The challenge of holding students' accountable to the foundational work before class is not new to "flipped learning" and has been documented in previous studies (Marshall & Kostka, 2020; Talbert, 2017). However, because this was an entirely new methodology to the researcher, this challenge was surprising and required immediate further review of the literature to determine effective ways to hold students accountable (Bergmann & Sams, 2015; Leo & Puzio, 2016; Marshall & Kostka, 2020; Talbert, 2017). Both student input and digital tracking were used to determine which students were completing this foundational work before class; it was found that the digital tracking through the program Nearpod was more effective: when assigning a lecture video for students to watch, short questions were added in the middle of the videos that checked for students' understanding before they could continue and finish the video. These scores were automatically recorded and the researcher was able to review this data before meeting with students for the synchronous sessions, thereby using formative assessments to guide instruction (Tomlinson & Moon, 2013).

Throughout the cycles of this study, students repeatedly noted that Pivot Interactive labs and screen-recordings of Gizmo lab activities were most engaging and helpful. These activities included real-life scenarios of the physics concepts at work while also remaining accessible and engaging to students. Additionally, taking a step back after the first cycle to recognize that students were struggling with the technology allowed for the development of scaffolding for those who needed it: some students watched a video of the lab activity worked out virtually, akin to a demonstration in class, while others felt fully capable of completing the lab activity on their own and were able to do so. Although the use of videos greatly impacted students' abilities to perform their own inquiry-based lab activities, these videos provided opportunities for students to familiarize themselves with classic physics experiments, including sliding a puck down a ramp and swinging a pendulum. Additionally, completing these experiments virtually allowed for fewer user errors and more precise measurements because students could stop the video and take as many measurements as they liked as many times as they liked. It, of course, was not the same experience as doing the experiments themselves, but students continued to greatly benefit from the use of lab activities.

Finally, it was found that if given the time to discuss the coursework and provide input on what is and is not working, students would rise to the occasion and participate. I was very open about creating this conceptual physics course from scratch, learning how to teach in a distance learning format, and using student data and feedback to guide instruction. I created an open space that allowed for vulnerability by sharing my own struggles with technology and curriculum development as well as how I was working to overcome these challenges by continually trying new methods, practices, and techniques. Students increasingly voiced their opinions and shared their concerns and challenges with the content and the technology in use as the semester wore on. Their responses and contributions were incredibly valuable in developing the pacing of the curricular unit in addition to determining which lab activities to implement for maximum efficacy and engagement.

SOLUTIONS AND RECOMMENDATIONS

The findings from this action research study have provided a strong foundation to build upon in preparation for the spring of 2021 semester. Moving forward, digital tracking through Nearpod will support preparation and differentiation during the limited synchronous time: students with strong foundational knowledge of the topic for the day will be able to immediately begin working on the lab activities or practice problems while those who are struggling will have access to more personalized support throughout that time. Virtual lab activities through Pivot Interactives, Gizmos, and PhET simulations have proven to be incredibly valuable to students' engagement and understanding of real-life scenarios of these rather abstract concepts. Additionally, screen-recording the lab activities while following the procedures already available to students allows for the scaffolding that some students need and would have used during in-person learning. Finally, students' input will continue to play a large role in determining pacing and effectiveness of new activities and simulations. Each of these findings are extremely useful in preparing for a second semester of distance learning with high school students.

FUTURE RESEARCH DIRECTIONS

The global pandemic that kick-started this action research study continues to rage on. In its wake, it is highlighting the growing educational inequities that have always been present (Dorn, et al., 2020; Fox, 2020; Goldstein, 2020a), but were more easily swept under the rug. It is a common myth that education levels the playing field, that it is the venue for those less fortunate to rise above, raise themselves up by their bootstraps. This global pandemic has shown that education is simply the band-aid covering the institutional wounds from systemic, social, and racial barriers (Ladson-Billings & Tate, 1995; Paris, 2012). This may very well be the best opportunity for educators to bring about lasting and sustainable changes to curriculum and to their teaching practices by including students in the discussion.

Action Research Is Cyclical

With so many other changes to education, this is the prime time to incorporate action research into every teacher's toolkit and assist teachers in understanding education research and how to embrace the role of an education researcher. Action research is the cyclical methodology that puts educators in the role of researchers, making decisions based upon current literature and ongoing data collection and analysis (Bradbury-Huang, 2015; Pine, 2009). It is a constantly changing process with experimentation, analysis, sharing with the community and making adjustments based upon feedback and participants' contributions before the next cycle. Action research is the scientific method come to life (Bradbury-Huang, 2015; Pine, 2009). But like the real nature of science (Carey & Smith, 1993; Thanukos, et al., 2010): action research is anything but linear.

Through action research, students become part of the research process: they are active participants, guiding the research to focus upon topics and methods they find most interesting and effective (Caraballo, et al., 2017). And they deserve this position as these instructional strategies and techniques directly affect them and their learning experiences. Their voices matter and should be included in the discussion of changes to education. They are experiencing this global pandemic right along with everyone else in this world and their education is impacted by this, just as educators' jobs are impacted (Goldstein, 2020b). Action research that includes students in the decision-making processes demonstrate that this is about more than education; it is about re-writing the narrative to include students, their families, and their communities (Anyon, 2009).

However, inviting students into these conversations can be incredibly difficult, as it requires students to be vulnerable, to admit that change is needed, and to suggest ways to change. One particularly effective way to bring about this vulnerability is for educators to also be vulnerable and to admit that they do not have all of the answers, that they are novices in distance learning as well, and that they are always trying to do better. It is crucial to demonstrate that teachers are lifelong learners and that it is okay to not know the answer and to ask for help. Voicing these themes of continuous learning, explaining the processes aloud, and exemplifying the grit and perseverance that teachers wish to see in their students makes room for students to also try, to make mistakes, and try again. Conversations that recognize the struggles everyone is facing during this pandemic and that actively find ways to work through them create a classroom, digital or not, that encourages students to be vulnerable and open. The focus continues to be upon creating a connection with students, opening the door to discussions about what works and what does not work, and moving forward together to enact successful instructional strategies and techniques.

Further research should focus upon identifying best practices in both "flipped learning" and distance learning. Additional studies using different "flipped learning" methods and practices can add to the literature surrounding its efficacy and strength in engaging students during limited class time. Also, studies on distance learning practices and strategies are incredibly useful during this ongoing global pandemic, when teachers and students are moving back and forth between in-person and distance learning. In particular, studies are needed that focus upon the cyclical nature of action research, the adjustments made with explanations for doing so, and recommendations on continuing the work forward. Together, more action research studies on both "flipped learning" and distance learning, from teachers currently working with students, will help to elevate students' voices and center the focus upon students' learning experience and academic achievement and engagement, providing a venue for these students to enact tangible change (Carabello, et al, 2017; Tuck, 2009).

CONCLUSION

This action research study focused upon identifying which instructional methods and techniques would 1) best utilize the very limited synchronous time, 2) engage students most and encourage them to be most comfortable, and 3) lead to the greatest student success. Based upon the findings, having open discussions with students led to the best use of time with the most engagement and greater student success. One of the key aspects to success during in-person learning is also extremely successful during distance learning: building a rapport with students and developing a mentor relationship.

Through informal discussions with students, changes were made to further encourage communication and collaboration between teacher and students. Using students' feedback, scaffolding was developed for the virtual lab activities, work on practice problems using the algebraic formulas was done through a more personally tutoring approach, and discussion board questions were completed through conversations during synchronous class time. Students were part of the decision-making process and their input helped direct the flow of class and which activities took precedence over others. Those students who remained engaged through the entire class period, every class period, had the greatest academic success, clearly demonstrating the need for relationships to be built between teachers and students.

However, there are serious limitations to this action research study as well: it is a case study with a researcher who never had formal training in "flipped learning" or teaching through a distance learning format. Without formal training, an action research study was extremely necessary to ensure that "flipped learning" was implemented to the best of my ability. Continually using students' feedback and data from assessments to guide instruction secured the focus upon students' and their experiences in distance learning. This study should be replicated to fully determine best practices for distance learning and "flipped learning" after formal training in either of these settings is available. This study showed that the teaching methodology that works best for in-person learning does not always work in distance learning and yet, the mentor relationships and rapport that are developed during in-person learning are just as sorely needed throughout distance learning.

As noted in the literature, it is incredibly difficult to get to know students through distance learning (Miller, 2008): the casual conversations that popped up between classes are missing, the visual cues and spontaneous jokes during class time are gone, the very human aspect of teaching has disappeared into the little black squares of video chat. Finding common ground to develop a connection with students is next to impossible and yet so desperately needed throughout this global pandemic that is affecting each and every person in some capacity. Performing action research throughout this very difficult time actually helped in developing this needed connection with students as open and honest dialogue allowed them a glimpse into the vulnerability that many teachers felt when faced with completely upending their teaching practices at the start of distance learning.

Conversations began with simply admitting that distance learning was entirely new to teachers and that students' input and feedback was needed to ensure effective strategies would be used. The stage was set from the beginning of the semester that teachers and students are a team who must work together to ensure students' success. I shared the intent to use action research throughout the course to improve teaching practices and techniques: I explained that the first unit would be broken down into sections and each section would end with a short assessment and survey, that students' feedback would guide which activities and assignments would be used as the unit progressed, and that the course would be focused upon using data to improve. I continually stressed that I wanted to assist students in their conceptual understanding of physics and their open and honest feedback helped me develop a clearer picture of how to do that. In doing so, I worked to create an online classroom built around students' experiences and ensured that students felt responsibility and ownership over their learning processes. Students knew they were active participants in their own education and their feedback led to a more personalized experience, designed for their individual success. Students understood that their voices would help to guide the course throughout the entire semester, that they would play a pivotal role in writing this narrative and they became active participants in this action research study.

By inviting students into the conversation regarding this action research study, it fully embodied the social justice and action-oriented paradigm it is known for (Bradbury-Huang, 2015; Caraballo, et al., 2017; Leavy, 2017). These students saw the immediate results of their feedback and input as changes were made and the curriculum shifted to better meet them where they were. Activities and websites they found engaging were used more often, methods they struggled with were discarded, and discussions were shifted to be more student-centric, moving at a pace they kept up with and geared around topics they were interested in. Students became active participants in the action research study and saw the power they hold in sharing their voices, their experiences, and their narratives (Kuntz, 2016; Leavy, 2017; Tuck, 2009). Action research provided an opportunity for teacher and students to work together and create an online classroom that encouraged inclusivity, vulnerability, and camaraderie.

ACKNOWLEDGMENT

Special thanks to Maya, Marlie, and Mikey Cunningham and Jacob Cooper for their incredible support throughout this study.

REFERENCES

Anyon, J. (Ed.). (2009). *Theory and educational research: Toward critical social explanation*. Routledge.

Bergmann, J., & Sams, A. (2015). *Flipped learning for science instruction*. International Society for Technology in Education.

Bhattacharya, K. (2017). *Fundamentals of qualitative research: A practical guide*. Routledge. doi:10.4324/9781315231747

Bradbury-Huang, H. (Ed.). (2015). *The SAGE handbook of action research*. ProQuest Ebook Central. https://ebookcentral.proquest.com

Caraballo, L., Lozenski, B. D., Lyiscott, J. J., & Morrell, E. (2017). YPAR and critical epistemologies: Rethinking education research. *Review of Research in Education*, *41*(1), 311–336. doi:10.3102/0091732X16686948

Carey, S., & Smith, C. (1993). On understanding the nature of scientific knowledge. *Educational Psychologist*, *28*(3), 235–251. doi:10.120715326985ep2803_4

Crenshaw, K. W. (1994). Mapping the margins: Intersectionality, identity politics, and violence against women of color. In M. Albertson Fineman & R. Mykitiuk (Eds.), *The public nature of private violence* (pp. 93–118). Routledge.

Dorn, E., Hancock, B., Sarakatsannis, J., & Viruleg, E. (2020, December 8). *COVID-19 and learning loss: Disparities grow and students need help*. McKinsey & Company. https://www.mckinsey.com/industries/public-and-social-sector/our-insights/covid-19-and-learning-loss-disparities-grow-and-students-need-help#

Fox, M. (2020, August 8). *Coronavirus has upended school plans*. CNBC. https://www.cnbc.com/2020/08/12/impact-of-covid-19-on-schools-will-worsen-racial-inequity-experts-say.html

Fulton, K. (2012). Upside down and inside out: Flip your classroom to improve student learning. *Learning and Leading with Technology*, *39*(8), 12–17. https://files.eric.ed.gov/fulltext/EJ982840.pdf

Goldstein, D. (2020a, June 5). The class divide:Remote learning at 2 schools, private and public. *New York Times*. https://www.nytimes.com/2020/05/09/us/coronavirus-public-private-school.html

Goldstein, D. (2020b, June 10). Research shows students falling months behind during virus disruptions. *New York Times*. https://www.nytimes.com/2020/06/05/us/coronavirus-education-lost-learning.html

Jdaitawi, M. (2019). The effect of flipped classroom strategy on students learning outcomes. *International Journal of Instruction*, *12*(3), 665–680. doi:10.29333/iji.2019.12340a

Jeong, J. S., Cañada-Cañada, F., & González-Gómez, D. (2018). The study of flipped-classroom for pre-service science teachers. *Education Sciences*, *8*(4), 163–174. doi:10.3390/educsci8040163

Jeong, J. S., González-Gómez, D., & Cañada-Cañada, F. (2016). Students' perceptions and emotions toward learning in a flipped general science classroom. *Journal of Science Education and Technology*, *25*(5), 747–758. doi:10.100710956-016-9630-8

Jeschofnig, L., & Jeschofnig, P. (2011). *Teaching lab science courses online: Resources for best practices*. Jossey-Bass, an Imprint of Wiley. http://www.josseybass.com/WileyCDA/WileyTitle/productCd-0470607041.html

King, A. (1993). From sage on the state to guide on the side. *College Teaching*, *41*(1), 30–35. doi:10.1080/87567555.1993.9926781

Kuntz, A. M. (2016). *The responsible methodologist: Inquiry, truth-telling, and social justice*. Routledge. doi:10.4324/9781315417332

Ladson-Billings, G., & Tate, W. F. (1995). Towards a critical race theory of education. *Teachers College Record*, *97*, 47–68.

Lawson, A. P., Davis, C. R., & Son, J. Y. (2019). Not all flipped classes are the same: Using learning science to design flipped classrooms. *The Journal of Scholarship of Teaching and Learning*, *19*(5), 77–104. doi:10.14434/josotl.v19i5.25856

Leavy, P. (2017). *Research design: Quantitative, qualitative, mixed methods, arts-based, and community-based participatory research approaches*. Guilford Publications.

Leo, J., & Puzio, K. (2016). Flipped instruction in a high school science classroom. *Journal of Science Education and Technology*, *25*(5), 775–781. doi:10.100710956-016-9634-4

Lombrozo, E., Thanukos, A., & Weisberg, M. (2008). The importance of understanding the nature of science for evolution. *Evolution (New York)*, *1*(3), 290–298. doi:10.100712052-008-0061-8

Marshall, H. W., & Kostka, I. (2020). Fostering teaching presence through the synchronous online flipped learning approach. *Teaching English as a Second or Foreign Language, 24*(2). https://files.eric.ed.gov/fulltext/EJ1268565.pdf

Miller, K. W. (2008). Teaching science methods online: Myths about inquiry-based online learning. *Science Educator*, *17*(2).

Paris, D. (2012). Culturally sustaining pedagogy: A needed change in stance, terminology, and practice. *Educational Researcher*, *41*(3), 93–97. doi:10.3102/0013189X12441244

Putri, M. D., Rusdiana, D., & Rochintaniawati, D. (2018). Students' conceptual understanding in modified flipped classroom approach: An experimental study in junior high school science learning. *Journal of Physics: Conference Series*, *1157*(2), 022046. Advance online publication. doi:10.1088/1742-6596/1157/2/022046

Slapac, A., & Navarro, V. (2011). Shaping action researchers through a Master's capstone experience. *Teacher Education and Practice*, *24*(4), 405–426.

Subramaniam, S. R., & Muniandy, B. (2019). The effect of flipped classroom on students' engagement. *Technology. Learning and Knowledge*, *24*(3), 355–372. doi:10.100710758-017-9343-y

Talbert, R. (2017). *Flipped learning: A guide for higher education faculty*. Stylus Publishing, LLC.

Thanukos, A., Scotchmoor, J., Caldwell, R., & Lindberg, D. R. (2010). Science 101: Building the foundation for real understanding. *Science*, *330*(6012), 1764–1765. doi:10.1126cience.1186994 PMID:21127217

Tomlinson, C. A., & Moon, T. R. (2013). *Assessment and student success in a differentiated classroom*. ASCD.

Tuck, E. (2009). Theorizing back: An approach to participatory policy analysis. In J. Anyon (Ed.), *Theory and educational research: Toward critical social explanation* (pp. 111–130). Routledge.

Tucker, B. (2012). The flipped classroom: Online instruction at home frees class time for learning. *Education Next*, *12*(1). https://www.educationnext.org/the-flipped-classroom/

University of California Museum of Paleontology. (2021). Real process of science [Illustration]. *Understanding How Science Really Works*. https://undsci.berkeley.edu/search/imagedetail.php?id=19&topic_id=&keywords=

KEY TERMS AND DEFINITIONS

CK-12 Flexbooks: An online, interactive textbook that teachers are able to customize to best fit their students (See https://ck12.org for more information).

Gizmos: Online virtual lab activities that simulate traditional in-person lab activities, including fan carts for physics activities and growing elodea in biology activities (See https://www.explorelearning.com for more information).

Google Forms From Kesler Science: Interactive activities developed by Chris Kesler in which students are presented with a Google Form (like a survey or quiz) that has hyperlinks to videos, interactive activities on other websites, and PDF articles for students to engage with prior to responding to multiple-choice or short-response questions (See https://www.keslerscience.com for more information).

Khan Academy: Founded by Sal Khan, this is library full of short (5- to 15-minute) videos by educators and professors explaining complex ideas and concepts in clear and concise manners; this website has grown to also include interactive activities and quizzes to assess students on their understanding of the concepts after watching a short video (See https://www.khanacademy.org for more information).

Nearpod: A program through which teachers can present PowerPoint presentations and Google Slides in a more interactive format as students are required to log into the program in order to gain access to the presentations; a record is automatically generated to show who logs in, at what time, and for how long; teachers may include videos as well as short formative assessments for students to engage with through this program (See https://www.nearpod.com for more information).

PhET Simulations: Free online interactive science and math simulations developed by students and educators at the University of Colorado - Boulder; teachers with accounts on the website may upload and download worksheets and lab procedures for each simulation as well (See https://phet.colorado.edu for more information).

Pivot Interactives: Interactive videos, rather than animated simulations, that are recorded live events in traditional laboratories; students are able to make measurements directly on the videos and record their own observations within a profile on the website; teachers are able to curate the lab activities by uploading their own videos and writing their own questions in addition to the mass library housed on the website (See https://www.pivotinteractives.com for more information).

Compilation of References

A trauma-informed approach to teaching through coronavirus (2020). *Teaching Tolerance.* https://www.tolerance.org/magazine/a-trauma-informed-approach-to-teaching-through-coronavirus

Adam, T. (2020, April 22). The privilege of #pivotonline: A South African perspective. *Open Development & Education.* https://opendeved.net/2020/04/22/the-privilege-of-pivotonline/

Adnan, M. (2018). Professional development in the transition to online teaching: The voice of entrant online instructors. *ReCALL, 30*(1), 88–111. doi:10.1017/S0958344017000106

Adnan, M., Kalelioglu, F., & Gulbahar, Y. (2017). Assessment of a multinational online faculty development program on online teaching: Reflections of candidate e-tutors. *Turkish Online Journal of Distance Education, 18*(1), 22–22. doi:10.17718/tojde.285708

Aguilar, E. (2013). *The art of coaching: Effective strategies for school transformation.* John Wiley & Sons.

Ahn, S., & Song, N. K. (2017). Unemployment, recurrent unemployment, and material hardships among older workers since the Great Recession. *Social Work Research, 41*(4), 249–260. doi:10.1093wrvx020

Ahumada, M., Antón, B. M., & Peccinetti, M. V. (2012). El desarrollo de la investigación acción participativa en psicología. *Enfoques, 24*(2), 23–52.

Ainsworth, S., & Oldfield, J. (2019). Quantifying teacher resilience: Context matters. *Teaching and Teacher Education, 82,* 117–128. doi:10.1016/j.tate.2019.03.012

Akyol, Z., & Garrison, D. R. (2008). The development of a community of inquiry over time in an online course: Understanding the progression and integration of social, cognitive and teaching presence. *Journal of Asynchronous Learning Networks, 12*(3), 3–23. doi:10.24059/olj.v12i3.66

Akyol, Z., & Garrison, D. R. (2013). *Educational communities of inquiry: Theoretical framework, research and practice.* IGI Global. doi:10.4018/978-1-4666-2110-7

Albion, P., & Redmond, P. (2008, September). Teaching by example? Integrating ICT in teacher education. In *Proceedings of the 2008 Australian Computers in Education Conference.* Australian Council for Computers in Education.

Alessandri, G., Truxillo, D., Tisak, J., Fagnani, C., & Borgnoni, L. (2019). Within-individual age-related trends, cycles, and event-driven changes in job performance: A career-span perspective. *Journal of Business and Psychology, 35*(5), 643–662. doi:10.100710869-019-09645-8

Alfaro, C., & Quezada, R. L. (2010). International teacher professional development: Teacher reflections of authentic teaching and learning experiences. *Teaching Education, 21*(1), 47–59. doi:10.1080/10476210903466943

Algozzine, B., Gretes, J., Queen, A. J., & Cowan-Hathcock, M. (2007). Beginning teachers' perceptions of their induction program experiences. *The Clearing House: A Journal of Educational Strategies, Issues and Ideas, 80*(3), 137–143. doi:10.3200/TCHS.80.3.137-143

Allen, I. E., & Seaman, J. (2015). Grade level: Tracking online education in the United States. *Babson Survey Research Group*. https://eric.ed.gov/?id=ED572778

Allport, G. W. (1937). *Personality: A psychological interpretation*. Holt.

Aloni, M., & Harrington, C. (2018). Research based practices for improving the effectiveness of asynchronous online discussion boards. *Scholarship of Teaching and Learning in Psychology, 4*(4), 271–289. doi:10.1037tl0000121

Alto comisionado para la Paz. (2016). *Acuerdo final para la terminación del conflicto y la construcción deuna paz estable y duradera*. http://www.altocomisionadoparalapaz.gov.co/Paginas/inicio.aspx

American Association of Colleges and Universities. (2018). *Fulfilling the American dream: Liberal education and the future of work*. https://www.aacu.org/research/2018-future-of-work

Andreotti, V. (2011). Towards decoloniality and diversity in global citizenship education in globalisation. *Social Education, 9*(3-4), 3–4. doi:10.1080/14767724.2011.605323

Angdhiri, R. P. (2020). Challenges of home learning during a pandemic through the eyes of a student. *The Jakarta Post*. https://www.thejakartapost.com/life/2020/04/11/challenges-of-home-learning-during-a-pandemic-through-the-eyes-of-a-student.html

Annamama, S. A. (2015). Whiteness as property: Innocence and ability in teacher education. *The Urban Review, 47*(2), 293–316. doi:10.100711256-014-0293-6

Antrop-Gonzales, R., & de Jesus, A. (2006). Toward a theory of critical care in urban small school reform: Examining structures and pedagogies of caring in two Latino community-based schools. *International Journal of Qualitative Studies in Education: QSE, 19*(4), 409–433. doi:10.1080/09518390600773148

Anwar, N. (2016). Action research a tool to build capacity of teacher educators. *The Journal of Educational Research, 19*(2), 105–116.

Anyon, J. (Ed.). (2009). *Theory and educational research: Toward critical social explanation*. Routledge.

Arbeláez, M. C., & Onrubia, J. (2014). Análisis bibliométrico y de contenido. Dos metodologías complementarias para el análisis de la revista colombiana Educación y Cultura. *Revista de Investigaciones UCM, 14*(23), 14–31. https://bit.ly/31A2xbH

Asia Society & OECD. (2018). *Teaching for global competence in a rapidly changing world*. https://asiasociety.org/education/teaching-global-competence-rapidly-changing-world

Asrifan, A., Zita, C. T., Vargheese, K. J., Syamsu, T., & Amir, M. (2020). The effects of CALL (Computer Assisted Language Learning) toward the students' English achievement and attitude. *Journal of Advanced English Studies, 3*(2), 94–106. https://bit.ly/3qjlmtg

Assunção Flores, M., & Gago, M. (2020). Teacher education in times of COVID-19 pandemic in Portugal: National, institutional and pedagogical responses. *Journal of Education for Teaching, 46*(4), 1–10. doi:10.1080/02607476.2020.1799709

Augusto-Navarro, E. H. (2015). The design of teaching materials as a tool in EFL teacher education: Experiences of a Brazilian teacher education program. *Ilha do Desterro, 68*(1), 121–137. doi:10.5007/2175-8026.2015v68n1p121

Compilation of References

Austin, J. L. (1975). *How to do things with words*. Harvard University Press. doi:10.1093/acprof:oso/9780198245537.001.0001

Aveling, E. L., & Jovchelovitch, S. (2014). Partnerships as knowledge encounters: A psychosocial theory of partnerships for health and community development. *Journal of Health Psychology*, *19*(1), 34–45. doi:10.1177/1359105313509733 PMID:24195915

Babić, S., Križan Sučić, S., & Sinković, G. (2020). Understanding the factors that influence secondary school teachers' intention to use e-learning technologies for Teaching After the COVID-19 Pandemic. In *MIPRO International Convention 2020*. Croatian Society for Information, Communication and Electronic Technology.

Badia, A., Garcia, C., & Meneses, J. (2017). Approaches to teaching online: Exploring factors influencing teachers in a fully online university: Factors influencing approaches to teaching online. *British Journal of Educational Technology*, *48*(6), 1193–1207. doi:10.1111/bjet.12475

Bakhtin, M. M. (1981). *The dialogic imagination* (C. Emerson & M. Holquist, Trans.). University of Texas Press., doi:10.2307/1770763

Bakhtin, M. M. (2010). *Speech genres & other late essays*. University of Texas Press.

Bakker, A., & Wagner, D. (2020). Pandemic: Lessons for today and tomorrow? *Educational Studies in Mathematics*, *104*(1), 1–4. doi:10.100710649-020-09946-3

Balazadeh, N. (1996, October 10-13). *Service-learning and the sociological imagination: Approach and assessment*. Presentation at the National Historically Black Colleges and Universities Faculty Development Symposium, Memphis, TN. https://files.eric.ed.gov/fulltext/ED402854.pdf

Bandura, A. (1986). *Social foundations of thought and action: A social cognitive theory*. Prentice-Hall, Inc.

Banegas, D. L., & Consoli, S. (2020). Action research in language education. In J. McKinley & H. Rose (Eds.), *The Routledge handbook of research methods in applied linguistics* (pp. 176–187). Routledge. https://bit.ly/342YhB6

Baran, E., & Alzoubi, D. (2020). Human-centered design as a frame for transition to remote teaching during the COVID-19 Pandemic. *Journal of Technology and Teacher Education*, *28*(2), 365–372. https://eric.ed.gov/?id=EJ1257151

Baran, E., Correia, A. P., & Thompson, A. (2011). Transforming online teaching practice: Critical analysis of the literature on the roles and competencies of online teachers. *Distance Education*, *32*(3), 421–439. doi:10.1080/01587919.2011.610293

Baran, E., & Correia, A.-P. (2014). A professional development framework for online teaching. *TechTrends*, *58*(5), 95–101. doi:10.100711528-014-0791-0

Barr, B., & Miller, S. (2013). *Higher education: The online teaching and learning experience*. files.eric.ed.gov/fulltext/ED543912.pdf

Basilaia, G., Dgebuadze, M., Kantaria, M., & Chokhonelidze, G. (2020). Replacing the classic learning form at universities as an immediate response to the COVID-19 virus infection in Georgia. *International Journal for Research in Applied Science and Engineering Technology*, *8*(3), 101–108. doi:10.22214/ijraset.2020.3021

Batchelor, K. E., & Cassidy, R. (2019). The lost art of the book talk: What students want. *The Reading Teacher*, *73*(2), 230–234. doi:10.1002/trtr.1817

Batson, C., Early, S., & Salvarani, G. (1997). Perspective taking: Imagining how another feels versus imagining how you would feel. *Personality and Social Psychology Bulletin*, *23*(7), 751–758. doi:10.1177/0146167297237008

Baylen, D. M., & Zhu, E. (2009). Challenges and issues of teaching online. In P. L. Rogers, G. Berg, J. Boettcher, C. Howard, L. Justice, & K. Schenk (Eds.), *Encyclopedia of distance learning* (2nd ed., pp. 241–246). Information Science Reference. doi:10.4018/978-1-60566-198-8.ch034

Beatty, K. (2010). *Teaching and researching Computer-Assisted Language Learning* (2nd ed.). Pearson.

Bell, A., & Morris, G. (2009). Engaging professional learning in online environments. *Australasian Journal of Educational Technology*, 25(5), 700–713. doi:10.14742/ajet.1116

Bell-Rose, S., & Desai, V. (2005). *Educating leaders for a global society*. Retrieved from: http://www.internationaled.org/publications/GSF_EducatingLeaders.pdf

Bembenutty, H., & Karabenick, S. A. (2004). Inherent association between academic delay of gratification, future time perspective, and self-regulated learning. *Educational Psychology Review*, 16(1), 35–57. doi:10.1023/B:EDPR.0000012344.34008.5c

Bender, L. (2020). *Key messages and actions for COVID-19 prevention and control in schools*. Unicef Romania. https://www.unicef.org/romania/documents/key-messages-and-actions-covid-19-prevention-and-control-schools

Berge, Z. L., Muilenburg, L. Y., & Van Haneghan, J. (2002). Barriers to distance education and training: Survey results. *Quarterly Review of Distance Education*, 3(4), 408–418. http://citeseerx.ist.psu.edu/viewdoc/download?doi=10.1.1.462.6499&rep=rep1&type=pdf

Bergmann, J., & Sams, A. (2015). *Flipped learning for science instruction*. International Society for Technology in Education.

Bhattacharya, K. (2017). *Fundamentals of qualitative research: A practical guide*. Routledge. doi:10.4324/9781315231747

Bielska, J. (2011). The experimental method in action research. In W: D. Gabryś-Barker (Ed.), *Action research in teacher development: an overview of research methodology* (pp. 85-119). Wydawnictwo Uniwersytetu Śląskiego. https://core.ac.uk/download/pdf/197740124.pdf

Biraimah, K. L., & Jotia, A. L. (2012). The longitudinal effects of study abroad programs on teachers' content knowledge & perspectives: Fulbright-Hays in Botswana and SE Asia. *Journal of Studies in International Education*, 17(4), 433–454. doi:10.1177/1028315312464378

Birgbauer, E. (2016). Student assisted course design. *Journal of Undergraduate Neuroscience Education*, 15(1), E3–E5.

Blackboard. (2021). *Blackboard Learn*. Blackboard. https://www.blackboard.com/Learn

Boettcher, J. V., & Conrad, R. M. (2016). *The online teaching survival guide: simple and practical pedagogical tips* (2nd ed.). John Wiley & Sons, Inc. https://ebookcentral.proquest.com/lib/open/detail.action?docID=4659728

Bogdan, R. C., & Biklen, S. K. (1992). *Qualitative research for education: An introduction to theory and methods* (2nd ed.). Allyn & Bacon.

Bogdan, R., & Taylor, S. J. (1975). *Introduction to qualitative research methods*. John Wiley & Sons.

Bond, M., Marín, V. I., Dolch, C., Bedenlier, S., & Zawacki-Richter, O. (2018). Digital transformation in German higher education: Student and teacher perceptions and usage of digital media. *International Journal of Educational Technology in Higher Education*, 15(1), 48. doi:10.118641239-018-0130-1

Borba, R., & Ostermann, A. C. (2007). Do bodies matter? Travestis' embodiment of (trans)gender identity through the manipulation of the Brazilian Portuguese grammatical gender system. *Gender and Language*, 1(1), 131–147. doi:10.1558/genl.2007.1.1.131

Borko, H. (2004). Professional development and teacher learning: Mapping the terrain. *Educational Researcher*, *33*(8), 3–15. doi:10.3102/0013189X033008003

Borko, H., & Putnam, R. T. (1995). Expanding a teachers' knowledge base: A cognitive psychological perspective on professional development. In T. R. Guskey & M. Huberman (Eds.), *Professional development in education: New paradigms and practices* (pp. 35–66). Teachers College Press.

Borup, J., & Evmenova, A. (2019). The effectiveness of professional development in overcoming obstacles to effective online instruction in a College of Education. *Online Learning*, *23*(2), 1–20. doi:10.24059/olj.v23i2.1468

Boston, M. D., & Smith, M. S. (2009). Transforming secondary mathematics teaching: Increasing the cognitive demands of instructional tasks used in mathematics classrooms. *Journal for Research in Mathematics Education*, *40*(2), 119–156. doi:10.2307/40539329

Boston, W., Diaz, S. R., Gibson, A. M., Ice, P., Richardson, K., & Swan, K. (2009). An exploration of the relationship between indicators of the community of inquiry framework and retention in online programs. *Journal of Asynchronous Learning Networks*, *14*(1), 3–19. https://www.researchgate.net/publication/330985126

Bozkurt, A., & Sharma, R. C. (2020). Emergency remote teaching in a time of global crisis due to the Coronavirus pandemic. *Asian Journal of Distance Education*, *15*(1), i–vi. doi:10.5281/zenodo.3778083

Bradbury, H., Lewis, R., & Embury, D. C. (2019). Education action research. In C. A. Mertler (Ed.), *The Wiley handbook of action research in education* (pp. 7–28). John Wiley & Sons. doi:10.1002/9781119399490.ch1

Bradbury-Huang, H. (Ed.). (2015). *The SAGE handbook of action research*. ProQuest Ebook Central. https://ebookcentral.proquest.com

Bransford, J. D., Brown, A. L., & Cocking, R. R. (Eds.). (2000). *How people learn: Brain, mind, experience, and school*. National Academy Press.

Braun, V., & Clarke, V. (2012). Thematic analysis. In H. Cooper, P. M. Camic, D. L. Long, A. T. Panter, D. Rindskopf, & K. J. Sher (Eds.), APA handbooks in psychology®. APA handbook of research methods in psychology, Vol. 2. Research designs: Quantitative, qualitative, neuropsychological, and biological (p. 57–71). American Psychological Association. doi:10.1037/13620-004

Braun, V., & Clarke, V. (2006). Using thematic *analysis in psychology. Qualitative Research in Psychology*, *3*(2), 77–101. doi:10.1191/1478088706qp063oa

Brinkley-Etzkorn, K. E. (2018). Learning to teach online: Measuring the influence of faculty development training on teaching effectiveness through a TPACK lens. *The Internet and Higher Education*, *38*, 28–35. doi:10.1016/j.iheduc.2018.04.004

Broere, M., & Kerkhoff, S. N. (2020). Discussing the word and the world: Discussion prompts for critical global literacies. *Voices from the Middle*, *27*(3), 50–53. https://library.ncte.org/journals/vm/issues/v27-3

Bronfenbrenner, U. (1979). *The ecology of human development: Experiments by nature and design*. Harvard University Press.

Bronfenbrenner, U. (1994). Ecological models of human development. In T. Husen & T. N. Postlethwaite (Eds.), *International encyclopedia of education* (2nd ed., Vol. 3, pp. 1643–1647). Elsevier.

Brooks, S. K., Webster, R. K., Smith, L. E., Woodland, L., Wessely, S., Greenberg, N., & Rubin, G. J. (2020). The psychological impact of quarantine and how to reduce it: Rapid review of the evidence. *Lancet*, *395*(10227), 912–920. doi:10.1016/S0140-6736(20)30460-8 PMID:32112714

Brouwer, N., & Korthagen, F. (2005). Can teacher education make a difference? *American Educational Research Journal*, *42*(1), 153–244. doi:10.3102/00028312042001153

Brown, E. C., Freedle, A., Hurless, N. L., Miller, R. D., Martin, C., & Paul, Z. A. (2020). Preparing teacher candidates for trauma-informed practices. *Urban Education*, 1–24.

Bullough, R. V. Jr, & Pinnegar, S. (2001). Guidelines for quality in autobiographical forms of self-study research. *Educational Researcher*, *30*(3), 13–21. doi:10.3102/0013189X030003013

Burd, B. A., & Buchanan, L. E. (2004). Teaching the teachers: Teaching and learning online. *RSR. Reference Services Review*, *32*(4), 404–412. doi:10.1108/00907320410569761

Burke, K., & Larmar, S. (2020). Acknowledging another face in the virtual crowd: Reimagining the online experience in higher education through an online pedagogy of care. *Journal of Further and Higher Education*, 1–15. Advance online publication. doi:10.1080/0309877X.2020.1804536

Burnouf, L. (2004). Global awareness and perspectives in global education. *Canadian Social Studies*, *38*(3), 1–12.

Burns, B. A., & Hamm, E. M. (2011). A comparison of concrete and virtual manipulative use in third- and fourth-grade mathematics. *School Science and Mathematics*, *111*(6), 256–261. doi:10.1111/j.1949-8594.2011.00086.x

Byker, E. J. (2016). Developing global citizenship consciousness: Case studies of critical cosmopolitan theory. *Journal of Research in Curriculum and Instruction*, *20*(3), 264–275. doi:10.24231/rici.2016.20.3.264

Calhoun, E. F. (2019). Action research for systemic change in education. In C. A. Mertler (Ed.), *The Wiley handbook of action research* (pp. 415–438). John Wiley & Sons. doi:10.1002/9781119399490.ch19

Caneva, C. (2020). Do pre-service teachers feel ready to teach with digital technologies? A study in two teacher training institutions in Costa Rica. *Research. Social Development*, *10*(1), 1–14. doi:10.33448/rsd-v10i1.11436

Cangelosi, J. S. (2014). Dealing with nondisruptive off-task behaviors. In *Classroom management strategies: Gaining and maintaining students' cooperation* (7th ed., pp. 330–355). John Wiley & Sons.

Caraballo, L., Lozenski, B. D., Lyiscott, J. J., & Morrell, E. (2017). YPAR and critical epistemologies: Rethinking education research. *Review of Research in Education*, *41*(1), 311–336. doi:10.3102/0091732X16686948

Carello, J. (2019). Trauma-informed teaching and learning online: Principles & practices during a global health crisis. *Examples of trauma-informed teaching and learning in college classrooms*. https://traumainformedteaching.blog/resources

Carey, S., & Smith, C. (1993). On understanding the nature of scientific knowledge. *Educational Psychologist*, *28*(3), 235–251. doi:10.120715326985ep2803_4

Carpenter, J., Weiss, S., & Justice, J. (2018). Opportunities and Challenges of Using Technology to Teach for Global Readiness in the Global Read Aloud. In *Society for Information Technology & Teacher Education International Conference* (pp. 822-831). Association for the Advancement of Computing in Education.

Carpenter, J. P., & Justice, J. E. (2017a). Can technology support teaching for global readiness? The case of the Global Read Aloud. *LEARNing Landscapes*, *11*(1), 65–85. doi:10.36510/learnland.v11i1.923

Carpenter, J. P., & Justice, J. E. (2017b). Evaluating the roles of technology in the Global Read Aloud project. *Computers in the Schools*, *34*(4), 284–303. doi:10.1080/07380569.2017.1387464

Carpenter, T. P., Franke, M. L., & Levi, L. (2003). *Thinking mathematically: Integrating arithmetic and algebra in elementary school*. Heinemann.

Compilation of References

Carr, W., & Kemmis, S. (1986). *Becoming critical: Education, knowledge and action research*. Falmer.

Carril, P. C. M., Gonzalez Sanmamed, M., & Hernandez Selles, N. (2013). Pedagogical roles and competencies of university teachers practicing in the E-learning environment. *International Review of Research in Open and Distributed Learning*, *14*(3), 462–487. doi:10.19173/irrodl.v14i3.1477

Carr, N. (2016). Pre-service teachers teaching about and across cultures using digital environments: The case of eTutor. *Educational Media International*, *53*(2), 103–117. doi:10.1080/09523987.2016.1211336

Carr, S. (2000). As distance education comes of age, the challenge is keeping the students. *The Chronicle of Higher Education*, *46*(23), A39–A41.

Cartledge, G., Singh, A., & Gibson, L. (2008). Practical behavior management techniques to close the accessibility gap for students who are culturally and linguistically diverse. *Preventing School Failure*, *52*(3), 29–38. doi:10.3200/PSFL.52.3.29-38

Casamassa (2014). *Action research: Models, methods, and examples*. Information Age Publishing.

Casey, A. (2012). A self-study using action research: Changing site expectations and practice stereotypes. *Educational Action Research*, *20*(2), 219–232. doi:10.1080/09650792.2012.676287

Casselman, P. (2019). The experience of students and faculty when elements of Bloom's mastery learning are used in an online statistics course: A participatory action research study. In C. A. Mertler (Ed.), *The Wiley handbook of action research* (pp. 463–480). John Wiley & Sons. doi:10.1002/9781119399490.ch21

CAST. (2018). *Universal Design for Learning Guidelines version 2.2*. http://udlguidelines.cast.org

Castellanos-Reyes, D. (2020). 20 Years of the Community of Inquiry Framework. *TechTrends*, *1–4*(4), 557–560. Advance online publication. doi:10.100711528-020-00491-7

Castells, M. (2010). *The rise of the network society* (2nd ed.). Wiley-Blackwell.

Cavanagh, S. (1997). Content analysis: Concepts, methods and applications. *Nurse Researcher*, *4*(3), 5–16. doi:10.7748/nr.4.3.5.s2 PMID:27285770

Celio, C. I., Durlak, J., & Dymnicki, A. (2011). A meta-analysis of the impact of service-learning on students. *Journal of Experiential Education*, *34*(2), 164–181. doi:10.1177/105382591103400205

Centro Nacional de Memoria Histórica. (2018). *Sujetos victimizados y daños causados. Balance de la contribución del CNMH al esclarecimiento histórico*. Centro Nacional de Memoria Histórica.

Chang, G.-C., & Yano, S. (2020). *How are countries addressing the Covid-19 challenges in education? A snapshot of policy measures*. https://bit.ly/2wgK6LO

Chang, C., Shen, H.-Y., & Liu, E. Z.-F. (2014). University faculty's perspectives on the roles of E-instructors and their online instruction practice. *The International Review of Research in Open and Distributed Learning*, *15*(3), 72–92. doi:10.19173/irrodl.v15i3.1654

Charles, C. M. (2005a). Fred Jones's positive classroom discipline. In *Building classroom discipline* (8th ed., pp. 55–72). Pearson.

Charles, C. M. (2005b). William Glasser's noncoercive discipline. In *Building classroom discipline* (8th ed., pp. 73–92). Pearson.

Charmaz, K. (2006). *Constructing grounded theory*. SAGE Publications.

Chen, C. C., & Yang, S. C. (2006). The efficacy of online cooperative learning systems, the perspective of task-technology fit. *Campus-Wide Information Systems, 23*(3), 112–127. doi:10.1108/10650740610674139

Chen, J., & McCray, J. (2012). A conceptual framework for teacher professional development: The whole teacher approach. *NHSA Dialog, 15*(1), 8–23. doi:10.1080/15240754.2011.636491

Choi, H. J., & Park, J. (2006). Difficulties that a novice online instructor faced: A case study. *Quarterly Review of Distance Education, 7*, 317–322. https://www.learntechlib.org/p/106761/

Choi, I., & Lee, K. (2009). Designing and implementing a case-based learning environment for enhancing ill-structured problem solving: Classroom management problems for prospective teachers. *Educational Technology Research and Development, 57*(1), 99–129. doi:10.100711423-008-9089-2

Ciocca, D. R., & Delgado, G. (2017). The reality of scientific research in Latin America; an insider's perspective. *Cell Stress & Chaperones, 22*(6), 847–852. doi:10.100712192-017-0815-8 PMID:28584930

Clark, J. (2001). Stimulating collaboration and discussion in online learning environments. *The Internet and Higher Education, 4*(2), 119–124. doi:10.1016/S1096-7516(01)00054-9

Clark, J. T. (2020). Distance education. In E. Iadanza (Ed.), *Clinical engineering handbook* (2nd ed., pp. 410–415). Elsevier. doi:10.1016/B978-0-12-813467-2.00063-8

Cochran-Smith, M., Barnatt, J., Friedman, A., & Pine, G. (2009). Inquiry on Inquiry: Practitioner Research and Student Learning. *Action in Teacher Education, 31*(2), 17–32. doi:10.1080/01626620.2009.10463515

Cochran-Smith, M., & Lytle, S. L. (2001). Beyond certainty: taking an inquiry stance on practice. In A. Lieberman & L. Miller (Eds.), *Teachers caught in the action: Professional development that matters* (pp. 45–58). Teachers College Press.

Cochran-Smith, M., & Lytle, S. L. (2015). *Inquiry as stance: Practitioner research for the next generation.* Teachers College Press.

Cochran-Smith, M., & Villegas, A. M. (2016). Research on teacher preparation: Charting the landscape of a sprawling field. In D. Gitomer & C. Bell (Eds.), *Handbook of research on teaching* (5th ed., pp. 439–547). American Educational Research Association. doi:10.3102/978-0-935302-48-6_7

Collier, V. P. (1995). *Promoting academic success for ESL students: Understanding second language acquisition for school.* New Jersey Teachers of English to Speakers of Other Languages.

Collins, K., Grroff, S., Mathena, C., & Kupczynski, L. (2019). Asynchronous video and the development of instructor social presence and student engagement. *Turkish Journal of Distance Education, 20*(1), 53–70. doi:10.17718/tojde.522378

Colmenares, E. A. M. (2012). Investigación-acción participativa: Una metodología integradora del conocimiento y la acción. *Voces y Silencios. Revista Latinoamericana de Educación, 3*(1), 102–115.

Cook, R. (2009). *The effects of a short-term teacher abroad program on teachers' perceptions of themselves and their responsibilities as global educators* (Doctoral dissertation). Retrieved from https://digitalcommons.usu.edu/etd/375

Coppola, N. W., Hiltz, S. R., & Rotter, N. (2001). Becoming a virtual professor: Pedagogical roles and ALN. *Proceedings of the 34th Annual Hawaii International Conference on System Sciences.* 10.1109/HICSS.2001.926183

Corbin, J., & Strauss, A. (2008). *Basics of qualitative research* (3rd ed.). Sage Publications.

Cornelius, S., & Macdonald, J. (2008). Online informal professional development for distance tutors: Experiences from The Open University in Scotland. *Open Learning, 23*(1), 43–55. doi:10.1080/02680510701815319

Costley. (2010). *Doing work based research. Approaches to enquiry for insider-researchers.* Sage Publications. doi:10.4135/9781446287880

Council for the Accreditation of Educator Preparation (CAEP). (2020). *CAEP consolidated handbook.* CAEP. http://www.caepnet.org

Cranton, P., & King, K. P. (2003). Transformative learning as a professional development goal. *New Directions for Adult and Continuing Education, 98*(1), 31–37. doi:10.1002/ace.97

Crawford, E. O., & Kirby, M. M. (2008). Fostering students' global awareness: Technology applications in social studies teaching and learning. *Journal of Curriculum and Instruction, 2*(1), 56–73.

Crenshaw, K. W. (1994). Mapping the margins: Intersectionality, identity politics, and violence against women of color. In M. Albertson Fineman & R. Mykitiuk (Eds.), *The public nature of private violence* (pp. 93–118). Routledge.

Crossman, A. (2020). *Pilot study in research.* https://www. thoughtco. com/pilot-study-3026449

Dance, L. J. (2002). *Tough fronts: The impact of street culture on schooling.* Routledge.

Darling-Hammond, L., Hyler, E. M., & Gardner, M. (Eds.). (2017, June). *Effective Teacher Professional Development.* Learning Policy Institute. Retrieved from https://learningpolicyinstitute.org/sites/default/files/product-files/Effective_Teacher_Professional_Development_REPORT.pdf

Darling-Hammond, L., & Hyler, M. E. (2020). Preparing educators for the time of COVID… and beyond. *European Journal of Teacher Education, 43*(4), 457–465. doi:10.1080/02619768.2020.1816961

Darling-Hammond, L., Hyler, M. E., & Gardner, M. (2017). *Effective teacher professional development.* Learning Policy Institute.

Davidson, N., & Major, C. H. (2014). Boundary crossings: Cooperative learning, and problem-based learning. *Journal on Excellence in College Teaching, 25*(3–4), 7–55.

Davies, B., & Harré, R. (2014). Positioning: The discursive production of selves. In M. Wetherell, S. Taylor, & S. J. Yates (Eds.), *Discourse theory and practice: A reader* (pp. 261–271). Sage Publications.

Davis, M. H. (2006). Empathy. In J. E. Stets & J. H. Turner (Eds.), *Handbook of the sociology of emotions* (pp. 443–466). Springer. doi:10.1007/978-0-387-30715-2_20

Day, S. L., & Connor, C. M. (2017). Examining the relations between self-regulation and achievement in third grade students. *Assessment for Effective Intervention, 42*(2), 97–109. doi:10.1177/1534508416670367 PMID:28439211

De La Rosa, S. (2020). Ed experts fear rise in dropouts as remote learning continues. *K12 Dive.* https://www.k12dive.com/news/ed-experts-fear-rise-in-dropouts-as-remote-learning-continues/585558/

De Metz, N., & Bezuidenhout, A. (2018). An importance–competence analysis of the roles and competencies of e-tutors at an open distance learning institution. *Australasian Journal of Educational Technology, 34*(5), 27–42. doi:10.14742/ajet.3364

de Oliveira Figueiredo, G. (2015). Investigación Acción Participativa: Una alternativa para la epistemología social en Latinoamérica. *Revista de Investigacion, 39*(86), 271–290.

Decety, J., & Lamm, C. (2006). Human empathy through the lens of social neuroscience. *TheScientificWorldJournal, 6,* 1146–1163. doi:10.1100/tsw.2006.221 PMID:16998603

Deci, E. L., & Ryan, R. M. (2000). The "what" and "why" of goal pursuits: Human needs and the self determination of behavior. *Psychological Inquiry*, *11*(4), 227–268. doi:10.1207/S15327965PLI1104_01

Dei, G. (2014). Global education from an 'indigenist' anti-colonial perspective. *Journal of Contemporary Issues in Education*, *9*(2), 4–23.

Delacruz, S. (2014). Using Nearpod in elementary guided reading groups. *TechTrends*, *58*(5), 62–69. doi:10.100711528-014-0787-9

Dempsey, H. (2007). Keller's personalized system of instruction: Was it a fleeting fancy or is there a revival on the horizon? *The Behavior Analyst Today*, *8*(3), 317–324. doi:10.1037/h0100623

Denzin, N. K., & Lincoln, Y. S. (2013). *The landscape of qualitative research*. Sage Publications.

Denzin, N. K., & Lincoln, Y. S. (Eds.). (2017). *The SAGE handbook of qualitative research* (5th ed.). SAGE Publications.

Dervin, F., Chen, N., Yuan, M., & Jacobson, A. (2020). COVID-19 and interculturality: First lessons for teacher educators. *Education and Society*, *38*(1), 89–106. doi:10.7459/es/38.1.06

Desimone, L. M. (2009). Improving impact studies of teachers' professional development: Toward better conceptualizations and measures. *Educational Researcher*, *38*(3), 181–199. doi:10.3102/0013189X08331140

Dewey, J. (1986). Experience and education. *The Educational Forum*, *50*(3), 241–252. doi:10.1080/00131728609335764

Dhawan, S. (2020). Online learning: A panacea in the time of COVID-19 crisis. *Journal of Educational Technology Systems*, *49*(1), 5–22. doi:10.1177/0047239520934018

Díaz-Larenas, C., Alarcón-Hernandez, P., & Ortiz-Navarrete, M. (2015). A case study on EFL teachers' beliefs about the teaching and learning of English in public education. *Porta Linguarum*, *23*, 171–186. https://bit.ly/35ywOZK

Dietrich, T., & Balli, S. J. (2014). Digital natives: Fifth-grade students' authentic and ritualistic engagement with technology. *International Journal of Instruction*, *7*(2), 21–34.

Dina, A., & Ciornei, S.-I. (2013). The advantages and disadvantages of Computer Assisted Language Learning and Teaching for foreign languages. *Procedia: Social and Behavioral Sciences*, *76*, 248–252. doi:10.1016/j.sbspro.2013.04.107

Domingo-Coscollola, M., Bosco, A., Segovia, S. C., & Valero, J. A. S. (2020). Fostering teacher's digital competence at university: The perception of students and teachers. *Revista de Investigación Educacional*, *38*(1), 167–182. doi:10.6018/rie.340551

Donahue, N., & Glodstein, S. (2013). Mentoring the needs of nontraditional students. *Teaching and Learning in Nursing*, *8*(1), 2–3. doi:10.1016/j.teln.2012.07.003

Donitsa-Schmidt, S., & Ramot, R. (2020). Opportunities and challenges: Teacher education in Israel in the Covid-19 pandemic. *Journal of Education for Teaching*, *46*(4), 1–10. doi:10.1080/02607476.2020.1799708

Doppen, F. H. (2010). Overseas student teaching and national identity: Why go somewhere you feel completely comfortable? *Journal of International Social Studies*, *1*(1), 3–19.

Dorn, E., Hancock, B., Sarakatsannis, J., & Viruleg, E. (2020, December 8). *COVID-19 and learning loss: Disparities grow and students need help*. McKinsey & Company. https://www.mckinsey.com/industries/public-and-social-sector/our-insights/covid-19-and-learning-loss-disparities-grow-and-students-need-help#

Dudzinski, M., Roszmann-Millican, M., & Shank, K. (2000). Continuing professional development for special educators: Reforms and implications for university programs. *Teacher Education and Special Education*, *23*(2), 109–124. doi:10.1177/088840640002300205

Dufour, R., & Fullan, M. (2012). *Cultures built to last: Systemic PLCs at Work*. Solution Tree.

Dugartsyrenova, V. A., & Sardegna, V. G. (2019). Raising intercultural awareness through voice-based telecollaboration: Perceptions, uses, and recommendations. *Innovation in Language Learning and Teaching*, *13*(3), 205–220. doi:10.1080/17501229.2018.1533017

Duncan, A. (2020, December 21). Pandemic has highlighted America's educational gaps: Connectivity has yet to catch up with demand for online, in-home learning. *St. Louis Post Dispatch*, p. A11.

Dweck, C. S. (2006). *Mindset: The new psychology of success*. Random House.

Educause. (2017). *2017 Horizon Report: K-12 Edition*. Retrieved from: https://library.educause.edu/~/media/files/library/2017/11/2017hrk12EN.pdf

Edwards, M., Perry, B., & Janzen, K. (2011). The making of an exemplary online educator. *Distance Education*, *32*(1), 101–118. doi:10.1080/01587919.2011.565499

Eiland, L. S., & Todd, J. D. (2019). Considerations when incorporating technology into classroom and experiential teaching. *The Journal of Pediatric Pharmacology and Therapeutics: JPPT: the Official Journal of PPAG*, *24*(4), 270–275. doi:10.5863/1551-6776-24.4.270 PMID:31337989

Eilers, L. H. (2006). Action research: The ultimate 'mirror test'. *The Delta Kappa Gamma Bulletin*, *72*(3), 14-29. http://web.b.ebscohost.com.ezproxy.umsl.edu/ehost/pdfviewer/pdfviewer?vid=1&sid=a9d60907-a62e-4c75-9d3e-c56de96bd50a%40sessionmgr101

Eliot, T. S. (1968). *Four quartets*. Mariner Books.

Ellis, A., O'Reilly, M., & Debreceny, R. (1998). *Staff development responses to the demand for online teaching and learning*. Southern Cross University. http://epubs.scu.edu.au/tlc_pubs/39/

Ellis, R. (2005). Principles of instructed language learning. *System*, *33*(2), 209–224. doi:10.1016/j.system.2004.12.006

Ellis, R., & Shintani, N. (2014). *Exploring language pedagogy through second language acquisition research*. Routledge.

Elo, S., & Kyngäs, H. (2008). The qualitative content analysis process. *Journal of Advanced Nursing*, *62*(1), 107–115. doi:10.1111/j.1365-2648.2007.04569.x PMID:18352969

Embury, D. C., Parenti, M., & Childers-McKee, C. (2020). Editorial: A charge to educational action researchers. *Action Research*, *18*(2), 127–135. doi:10.1177/1476750320919189

Emmer, E. T., & Evertson, C. M. (2009a). Organizing your classroom and materials. In *Classroom management for middle and high school teachers* (8th ed., pp. 1–16). Pearson.

Emmer, E. T., & Evertson, C. M. (2009b). Choosing rules and procedures. In *Classroom management for middle and high school teachers* (8th ed., pp. 17–41). Pearson.

Enerio, A. T. Jr. (2020). Master teachers' challenges in doing action research: A case study. *Universal Journal of Educational Research*, *8*(7), 2990–2995. doi:10.13189/ujer.2020.080727

Erduran, S. (2020). Science education in the era of a pandemic: How can history, philosophy and sociology of science contribute to education for understanding and solving the Covid-19 crisis? *Science and Education, 29*(2), 233–235. doi:10.100711191-020-00122-w PMID:32292244

European Commission. (1995). *White paper on education and training – Teaching and learning – Towards the learning society*. Commission of the European Communities.

Evans, C., O'Connor, C. J., Graves, T., Kemp, F., Kennedy, A., Allen, P., Bonnar, G., Reza, A., & Aya, U. (2020). Teaching under lockdown: The experiences of London English teachers. *Changing English, 27*(3), 244–254. doi:10.1080/1358684X.2020.1779030

Eyler, J., & Giles, D. E. Jr. (1999). *Where's the learning in service-learning?* Jossey-Bass.

Eyler, J., Giles, D. E. Jr, Stenson, C. M., & Gray, C. J. (2001). *At a glance: What we know about the effects of service-learning on college students, faculty, institutions and communities, 1993–2000* (3rd ed.). Vanderbilt University.

Ezzy, D. (2002). *Qualitative analysis. Practice and innovation*. Routledge.

Fairclough, N. (2011). Discourse and social change. *Polity*.

Farina, M. A. (2018, January 24-25). *E-service-learning and teacher education: A case study of experimental education*. International Congress of Creative Cities, Orlando, FL. 10.7195/piccc.00011

Farrell, O., & Brunton, J. (2020). A balancing act: A window into online student engagement experiences. *International Journal of Educational Technology in High Education, 17*(1), 25. doi:10.118641239-020-00199-x

Fasanella, K. P. (2020, October-December). 180 Days of Self-Care for Busy Educators. *Kappa Delta Pi Record, 56*(4), 191. doi:10.1080/00228958.2020.1813523

Feiman-Nemser, S. (2001). From preparation to practice: Designing a continuum to strengthen and sustain teaching. *Teachers College Record, 103*(6), 1013–1055. doi:10.1111/0161-4681.00141

Fernandez, M, Sturts, J., Duffy, L. N., Larson, L. R., Gray, J., & Powell, G.M (2019) Surviving and thriving in graduate school. *A Journal of Leisure Studies and Recreation Education, 34*(1), 3-15. doi:10.1080/1937156X.2019.1589791

Ferrance, E. (2000). *Action research*. Northeast and Islands Regional Educational Laboratory, Brown University. https://www.brown.edu/academics/education-alliance/sites/brown.edu.academics.education-alliance/files/publications/act_research.pdf

Ferreira-Barcelos, A. M., & Kalaja, P. (2012). Beliefs in second language acquisition: Teacher. In *The Encyclopedia of Applied Linguistics*. Wiley Online Library. doi:10.1002/9781405198431.wbeal0083

Feuer, W. (2020). *At least 24 million students could drop out of school due to the Coronavirus pandemic, U.N. says*. https://www.cnbc.com/2020/09/15/at-least-24-million-students-could-drop-out-of-school-due-to-the-coronavirus-un-says.html

Figuccio, M. J. (2020). Examining the efficacy of e-service-learning. *Frontiers in Education, 5*, 606451. Advance online publication. doi:10.3389/feduc.2020.606451

Fisher, D., Frey, N., Quaglia, R. J., Smith, D., & Lande, L. L. (2018). *Engagement by design: Creating learning environments where students thrive*. Corwin Literacy.

Flock, H. (2020). Designing a community of inquiry in online courses. *The International Review of Research in Open and Distributed Learning, 21*(1), 134–152. doi:10.19173/irrodl.v20i5.3985

Compilation of References

Foley, D. (2006a). Handling common problems. In *Ultimate classroom control handbook: A veteran teacher's on-the-spot techniques for solving adolescent student misbehavior* (pp. 43–66). JIST Publishing.

Foley, D. (2006b). Dealing with disruption. In *Ultimate classroom control handbook: A veteran teacher's on-the-spot techniques for solving adolescent student misbehavior* (pp. 67–90). JIST Publishing.

Folley, D. (2010). The lecture is dead long live the e-lecture. *Electronic Journal of e-Learning, 8*(2), 93-100.

Fonseca, L. & Trigos-Carrillo, L. (in press). Critical Service-Learning amidst conflict: Tensions and opportunities for peacebuilding in divided societies. In *Pursuit of liberation: Critical service-learning as capacity building for historicized, humanizing, and embodied action*. Academic Press.

Fonseca, L., & Reinoso, N. (2020). *Punto de encuentro: Reflexiones sobre la construcción de paz en el Centro Poblado Héctor Ramírez*. Universidad de La Sabana. doi:10.5294/978-958-12-0561-5

Ford, J. D., Ford, L. W., & D'Amelio, A. (2008). Resistance to change: The rest of the story. *Academy of Management Review, 33*(2), 362–377. doi:10.5465/amr.2008.31193235

Foulger, T. S., Graziano, K. J., Schmidt-Crawford, D., & Slykhuis, D. A. (2017). Teacher educator technology competencies. *Journal of Technology and Teacher Education, 25*(4), 413–448.

Fox, M. (2020, August 8). *Coronavirus has upended school plans*. CNBC. https://www.cnbc.com/2020/08/12/impact-of-covid-19-on-schools-will-worsen-racial-inequity-experts-say.html

Francis, E. (2017). *What is depth of knowledge?* https://inservice.ascd.org/what-exactly-is-depth-of-knowledge-hint-its-not-a-wheel/

Freeman, D., & Freeman, Y. (1988, September 30). *Sheltered English Instruction*. ERIC Digest. https://eric.ed.gov/?id=ED301070

Freire, P. (1972). *Pedagogy of the oppressed*. Herder & Herder.

Fulton, K. (2012). Upside down and inside out: Flip your classroom to improve student learning. *Learning and Leading with Technology, 39*(8), 12–17. https://files.eric.ed.gov/fulltext/EJ982840.pdf

Furco, A. (2002). *Self-assessment rubric for the institutionalization of service-learning in higher education* (Unpublished manuscript). University of California, Berkley, CA.

Furco, A. (2003). *Service-learning: A balanced approach to experiential learning. Introduction to service learning toolkit* (2nd ed.). Campus Compact.

Fuson, K., Kalchman, M., & Bransford, J. (2005). Mathematical understanding: An introduction. In M. S. Donovan & J. D. Bransford (Eds.), *How students learn: History, mathematics, and science in the classroom* (pp. 217–256). National Academies Press.

Ganser, T. (2000). An ambitious vision of professional development for teachers. *NASSP Bulletin, 84*(618), 6–12. doi:10.1177/019263650008461802

García, E., & Weiss, E. (2020). Covid-19 and student performance, equity, and U.S. education policy: Lessons from pre-pandemic research to inform relief, recovery, and rebuilding. *Economic Policy Institute*. https://www.epi.org/publication/the-consequences-of-the-covid-19-pandemic-for-education-performance-and-equity-in-the-united-states-what-can-we-learn-from-pre-pandemic-research-to-inform-relief-recovery-and-rebuilding/

Gardner, H. E. (2000). Intelligence reframed: Multiple intelligences for the 21st century. Hachette UK.

Garet, M. S., Porter, A. C., Desimone, L., Birman, B. F., & Yoon, K. S. (2001). What makes professional development effective? Results from a national sample of teachers. *American Educational Research Journal, 38*(4), 915–945. doi:10.3102/00028312038004915

Garret, R., Citkowicz, M., & Williams, R. (2019). How responsive is a teacher's classroom practice to intervention? A meta-analysis of randomized field studies. *Review of Research in Education, 43*(1), 106–109. doi:10.3102/0091732X19830634

Garrison, D. R., Anderson, T., & Archer, W. (2000). Critical inquiry in a text-based environment: Computer conferencing in higher education model. *The Internet and Higher Education, 2*(2-3), 87–105. doi:10.1016/S1096-7516(00)00016-6

Garrison, D. R., Anderson, T., & Archer, W. (2001). Critical thinking, cognitive presence, and computer conferencing in distance education. *American Journal of Distance Education, 15*(1), 7–23. doi:10.1080/08923640109527071

Garrison, D. R., Anderson, T., & Archer, W. (2010). The first decade of the community of inquiry framework: A retrospective. *The Internet and Higher Education, 13*(1–2), 5–9. doi:10.1016/j.iheduc.2009.10.003

Garrison, D. R., & Arbaugh, J. B. (2007). Researching the community of inquiry framework: Review, issues, and future directions. *The Internet and Higher Education, 10*(3), 157–172. doi:10.1016/j.iheduc.2007.04.001

Garrison, R., & Kanuka, H. (2004). Blended learning: Uncovering its transformative potential in higher education. *The Internet and Higher Education, 7*(2), 95–105. doi:10.1016/j.iheduc.2004.02.001

Gaudelli, W. (2006). Convergence of technology and diversity: Experiences of two beginning teachers in a web-based distance learning for global/multicultural education. *Teacher Education Quarterly, 33*(1), 97–116.

Gawande, A. (2010). *The checklist manifesto: How to get things right*. Profile Books.

Gay, G. (2011). Connection between classroom management and culturally responsive teaching. In C. M. Evertson & C. S. Weinstein (Eds.), *Handbook of classroom management: Research, practice, and contemporary issues* (pp. 343–370). Routledge.

Gee, J. P. (2011a). *An introduction to discourse analysis: Theory and method*. Routledge.

Gee, J. P. (2011b). *How to do discourse analysis: A toolkit*. Routledge.

Gehlbach, H., & Brinkworth, M. E. (2012). The social perspective taking process: Strategies and sources of evidence in taking another's perspective. *Teachers College Record, 114*(1), 1–29.

Geller, J. D., Zuckerman, N., & Seidel, A. (2016). Service-learning as a catalyst for community development: How do community partners benefit from service-learning? *Education and Urban Society, 48*(2), 151–175. doi:10.1177/0013124513514773

Gergen, K. J. (1994). Self-narration in social life. In M. Wetherell, S. Taylor, & S.J. Yates (Eds.), Discourse theory and practice: A reader (pp. 247-260). Sage Publications.

Ghanizadeh, A., Razavi, A., & Hosseini, A. (2018). TELL (Technology-Enhanced Language Learning) in Iranian high schools: A Panacea for emotional and motivational detriments. *International Journal of Applied Linguistics and English Literature, 7*(4), 92–100. doi:10.7575/aiac.ijalel.v.7n.4p.92

Ghiso, M. P., Campano, G., Player, G., & Rusoja, A. (2016). Dialogic teaching and multilingual Counterpublics. *International Perspectives on Dialogic Theory and Practice, 16*(Dial. Ped.), 1–26. doi:10.17239/L1ESLL-2016.16.02.05

Giamatti, A. B. (1988). *A free and ordered space: The real world of the university*. W.W. Norton.

Giannini, S. (2020,). *Three ways to plan for equity during the coronavirus school closures*. https://bit.ly/2XboNGv

Glaser, B., & Strauss, A. (1967). *The discovery of grounded theory. Strategies for qualitative research*. Aldine Press.

Glisczinski, D. J. (2007). Transformative higher education: A meaningful degree of understanding. *Journal of Transformative Education*, *5*(4), 317–328. doi:10.1177/1541344607312838

Goldman, D. (2009, January 9). *Worst year for jobs since '45*. CNNMoney.com. https://money.cnn.com/2009/01/09/news/economy/jobs_december/

Goldstein, D. (2020a, June 5). The class divide:Remote learning at 2 schools, private and public. *New York Times*. https://www.nytimes.com/2020/05/09/us/coronavirus-public-private-school.html

Goldstein, D. (2020b, June 10). Research shows students falling months behind during virus disruptions. *New York Times*. https://www.nytimes.com/2020/06/05/us/coronavirus-education-lost-learning.html

Gómez-Rey, P., Barbera, E., & Fernández-Navarro, F. (2018). Students' perceptions about online teaching effectiveness: A bottom-up approach for identifying online instructors' roles. *Australasian Journal of Educational Technology*, *34*(1), 116–130. doi:10.14742/ajet.3437

González-Sanmamed, M., Muñoz-Carril, P.-C., & Sangra, A. (2014). Level of proficiency and professional development needs in peripheral online teaching roles. *The International Review of Research in Open and Distributed Learning*, *15*(6), 162–187. doi:10.19173/irrodl.v15i6.1771

Goodwin, A. L. (2020). Globalization, global mindsets and teacher education. *Action in Teacher Education*, *42*(1), 6–18. doi:10.1080/01626620.2019.1700848

Grant, S. G. (2013). From inquiry arc to instructional practice: The potential of the C3 Framework. *Social Education*, *77*(6), 322–326, 351.

Gravett, S. (2004). Action research and transformative learning in teaching development. *Educational Action Research*, *12*(2), 259–272. doi:10.1080/09650790400200248

Gray, J. A., & DiLoreto, M. (2016). The effects of student engagement, student satisfaction, and perceived learning in online learning environments. *International Journal of Educational Leadership Preparation*, *11*(1).

Grushka, K., McLeod, J., & Reynolds, R. (2005). Reflecting upon reflection: Theory and practice in one Australian university teacher education program. *Reflective Practice*, *6*(2), 239–246. doi:10.1080/14623940500106187

Gunawardena, C. N., & Zittle, F. J. (1997). Social presence as a predictor of satisfaction within a computer-mediated conferencing environment. *American Journal of Distance Education*, *11*(3), 8–26. doi:10.1080/08923649709526970

Guskey, T. R. (1995). Professional development in education: In search of the optimal mix. In T. R. Guskey & M. Huberman (Eds.), Professional development in education: New paradigms and practices (pp. 1–35). Teachers College Press.

Guskey, T. R. (2002). Professional development and teacher change. *Teachers and Teaching: Theory and Practice*, *8*(3/4), 381-390. doi:10.1080/135406002100000512

Guskey, T. R. (2003). What makes professional development effective? *Phi Delta Kappan*, *84*(10), 748–750. doi:10.1177/003172170308401007

Gustafson, P., & Gibbs, D. (2000). Guiding or hiding? The role of the facilitator in online teaching and learning. *Teaching Education*, *11*(2), 195–210. doi:10.1080/713698967

Guy, B., Feldman, T., Cain, C., Leesman, L., & Hood, C. (2020). Defining and navigating 'action' in a participatory action research project. *Educational Action Research*, *28*(1), 142–153. doi:10.1080/09650792.2019.1675524

Hadar, L. L., Ergas, O., Alpert, B., & Ariav, T. (2020). Rethinking teacher education in a VUCA world: Student teachers' social-emotional competencies during the Covid-19 crisis. *European Journal of Teacher Education*, *43*(4), 573–586. doi:10.1080/02619768.2020.1807513

Hagenbuch, D. J. (2006). Service-learning inputs and outcomes in a personal selling course. *Journal of Marketing Education*, *28*(1), 26–34. doi:10.1177/0273475305280882

Hakim, B. (2020). Technology integrated online classrooms and the challenges faced by the EFL teachers in Saudi Arabia during the COVID-19 pandemic. *International Journal of Applied Linguistics and English Literature*, *9*(5), 33–39. doi:10.7575/aiac.ijalel.v.9n.5p.33

Hamann, K., Glazier, R. A., Wilson, B. M., & Pollock, P. H. (2020). Online teaching, student success, and retention in political science courses. *European Political Science*. Advance online publication. doi:10.105741304-020-00282-x

Hannafin, M. J. (2009). Interaction strategies and emerging instructional technologies: Psychological perspectives. *Canadian Journal of Educational Communication*, *18*(3), 167–179. doi:10.21432/T2GK6G

Harbecke, D. (2012, October 8). *Following Mezirow: A roadmap through transformative learning*. RU Training @ Roosevelt University in Chicago. https://rutraining.org/2012/10/08/following-mezirow-a-roadmap-through-transformative-learning/?blogsub=pending

Hardaker, G., & Singh, G. (2011). The adoption and diffusion of e-learning in UK universities: A comparative case study using Giddens's theory of structuration. *Campus-Wide Information Systems*, *28*(4), 221–233. doi:10.1108/10650741111162707

Hardin, C. J. (2008a). Assertive discipline. In *Effective classroom management: Models and strategies for today's classrooms* (2nd ed., pp. 43–61). Pearson.

Hardin, C. J. (2008b). Discipline with dignity. In *Effective classroom management: Models and strategies for today's classrooms* (2nd ed., pp. 101–118). Pearson.

Harrington, H. L. (1995). Fostering reasoned decisions: Case-based pedagogy and the professional development of teachers. *Teaching and Teacher Education*, *11*(3), 203–214. doi:10.1016/0742-051X(94)00027-4

Hart, A., & Northmore, S. (2011). Auditing and evaluating university–community engagement: Lessons from a UK case study. *Higher Education Quarterly*, *65*(1), 34–58. doi:10.1111/j.1468-2273.2010.00466.x

Hart, C. (2012). Factors associated with student persistence in an online program of study: A review of the literature. *Journal of Interactive Online Learning*, *11*(1), 19–42.

Hattie, J. (2009). *Visible learning: A synthesis of over 800 meta-analyses relating to achievement*. Routledge.

Hebert-Beirne, J., Felner, J. K., Kennelly, J., Eldeirawi, K., Mayer, A., Alexander, S., Castañeda, Y. D., Castañeda, D., Persky, V. W., Chávez, N., & Birman, D. (2018). Partner development praxis: The use of transformative communication spaces in a community-academic participatory action research effort in a Mexican ethnic enclave in Chicago. *Action Research*, *16*(4), 414–436. doi:10.1177/1476750317695413

Heffernan, K. (2001). *Fundamentals of service-learning course construction*. Campus Compact.

Hemphill, M. A., Richards, K. A. R., Gaudreault, K. L., & Templin, T. J. (2015). Pre-service teacher perspectives of case-based learning in physical education teacher education. *European Physical Education Review*, *21*(4), 432–450. doi:10.1177/1356336X15579402

Hendricks, C. (2009). Using modeling and creating a research discourse community to teach a doctoral action research course. *International Journal for the Scholarship of Teaching and Learning*, *3*(1), 1–14. doi:10.20429/ijsotl.2009.030125

Hendricks, C. (2013). *Improving schools through action research: A reflective practice approach*. Pearson.

Hendricks, C. (2017). *Improving schools through action research. A reflective practice approach* (4th ed.). Pearson.

Hendricks, C. (2017). *Improving schools through action research: A comprehensive guide for educators* (4th ed.). Pearson.

Henriksen, D., Gretter, S., & Richardson, C. (2018). Design thinking and the practicing teacher: Addressing problems of practice in teacher education. *Teaching Education*, *1*(21), 209–229. doi:10.1080/10476210.2018.1531841

Heron, J. (1996). Quality as primacy of the practical. *Qualitative Inquiry*, *2*(1), 41–56. doi:10.1177/107780049600200107

Herr, K., & Anderson, G. (2004). *The action research dissertation: A guide for students and faculty*. SAGE. doi:10.4135/9781452226644

Herr, K., & Anderson, G. (2014). *The action research dissertation: A guide for students* (2nd ed.). Sage.

Herr, K., & Anderson, G. L. (2014). *The action research dissertation: A guide for students and faculty*. SAGE.

Hervani, A. A., Helms, M. M., Rutti, R. M., LaBonte, J., & Sarkarat, S. (2015). Service learning projects in online courses: Delivery strategies. *The Journal of Learning in Higher Education*, *11*(1), 35–41.

Hiebert, J., & Lefevre, P. (1986). Conceptual and procedural knowledge in mathematics: An introductory analysis. In J. Hiebert (Ed.), *Conceptual and Procedural Knowledge: The Case of Mathematics* (pp. 1–27). Erlbaum.

Hill, H. C. (2009). Fixing teacher professional development. *Phi Delta Kappan*, *90*(7), 470–477. doi:10.1177/003172170909000705

Hill, H. C., Beisiegel, M., & Jacob, R. (2013). Professional development research: Consensus, crossroads, and challenges. *Educational Researcher*, *42*(9), 476–487. doi:10.3102/0013189X13512674

Himmele, P., & Himmele, W. (2011). *Total participation techniques: Making every student an active learner*. ASCD.

Hirsh, S. (2012). The Common-Core contradiction. *Education Week*, *31*(19), 22–24.

Hodges, C., Moore, S., Lockee, B., Trust, T., & Bond, A. (2020, March 7). The difference between emergency remote teaching and online learning. *EDUCAUSE Review*. https://bit.ly/2DwKOYM

Hodges, C., Moore, S., Lockee, B., Trust, T., & Bond, A. (2020). The difference between emergency remote teaching and online learning. *EDUCAUSE Review*, *27*. https://er.educause.edu/articles/ 2020/3/the-difference-between-emergency-remote-teaching-and-online-learning

Holly, M. L., Arhar, J. M., & Kasten, W. C. (2009). *Action research for teachers: Traveling the yellow brick road* (3rd ed.). Pearson.

Howlett, M. (2021). Looking at the 'field' through a Zoom lens: Methodological reflections on conducting online research during a global pandemic. *Qualitative Research*, 1–16. doi:10.1177/1468794120985691

Huang, J. (2020). Successes and challenges: Online teaching and learning of chemistry in higher education in China in the time of COVID-19. *Journal of Chemical Education*, *97*(9), 2810–2814. doi:10.1021/acs.jchemed.0c00671

Hudson, P. (2012). How can schools support beginning teachers? A call for timely induction and mentoring for effective teaching. *The Australian Journal of Teacher Education*, *37*(7), 71–84. doi:10.14221/ajte.2012v37n7.1

Huertas-Abril, C. A. (2020b, December). *Telecollaboration in Emergency Remote Language Learning and Teaching* [Conference paper]. The Sixth International Conference on E-Learning (ECONF20), Sakhir, Bahrain.

Huertas-Abril, C. A. (2018). Inglés para fines sociales y de cooperación (IFSyC): Contextualización y justificación. In C. A. Huertas-Abril & M. E. Gómez-Parra (Eds.), *Inglés para fines sociales y de cooperación. Guía para la elaboración de materiales* (pp. 9–24). Graó.

Huertas-Abril, C. A. (2020a). Implementation of cooperative learning strategies to create 3D-videos in EFL teacher training. In L. N. Makewa (Ed.), *Theoretical and practical approaches to innovation in higher education* (pp. 17–41). IGI Global. doi:10.4018/978-1-7998-1662-1.ch002

Huertas-Abril, C. A., & Gómez-Parra, M. E. (2018). English for social purposes: A new approach to language learning. In M. I. Amor, M. Osuna, & E. Pérez (Eds.), *Fundamentos de enseñanza y aprendizaje para una educación universal, intercultural y bilingüe* (pp. 73–78). Octaedro.

Hunter, D. (2007). The virtual student/client experience. *The Journal of American Academy of Business, Cambridge*, *12*(1), 88–92.

Ingvarson, L., Meiers, M., & Beavis, A. (2005). Factors affecting the impact of professional development programs on teachers' knowledge, practice, student outcomes & efficacy. *Education Policy Analysis Archives*, *13*(10), 1–28. doi:10.14507/epaa.v13n10.2005

International, Q. S. R. (2021). *NVivo. Qualitative data analysis software*. https://bit.ly/38EqKAN

Islam, N., Beer, M., & Slack, F. (2015). E-learning challenges faced by academics in higher education. *Journal of Education and Training Studies*, *3*(5), 102–112. doi:10.11114/jets.v3i5.947

ISO. (2020). *Standards*. Retrieved January 16, 2021, from https://www.iso.org/standards.html

Israel, M., Ribuffo, C., & Smith, S. (2014). *Universal Design for Learning: Recommendations for teacher preparation and professional development* (Document No. IC-7). http://ceedar.education.efl.edu/tools/innovation-configurations

ISTE. (2017). *International Society for Technology in Education standards for educators*. Retrieved from: https://www.iste.org/standards/for-educators

Jacobs, V. R., Lamb, L. L. C., & Philipp, R. (2010). Professional noticing of children's mathematical thinking. *Journal for Research in Mathematics Education*, *41*(2), 169–202. doi:10.5951/jresematheduc.41.2.0169

Jacoby, B. (2015). *Service-learning essentials: questions, answers, and lessons learned*. Jossey-Bass.

Jaggars, S. S. (2012, April). *Beyond flexibility: Why students choose online and face-to-face courses in community college*. In American Educational Research Association Annual Meeting, Vancouver, Canada. https://ccrc.tc.columbia.edu/media/k2/attachments/online-outcomes-beyond-flexibility.pdf

Jaggars, S. S., Edgecombe, N., & Stacey, G. W. (2013). *Creating an Effective Online Instructor Presence*. Community College Research Center, Columbia University. https://files.eric.ed.gov/fulltext/ ED542146.pdf

James, F., & Augustin, D. S. (2018). Improving teachers' pedagogical and instructional practice through action research: Potential and problems. *Educational Action Research*, *26*(2), 333–348. doi:10.1080/09650792.2017.1332655

Jan, H. (2017). Teacher of 21st century: Characteristics and development. *Research on Humanities and Social Sciences*, *7*(9), 50–54. https://bit.ly/3qhhZm5

Jdaitawi, M. (2019). The effect of flipped classroom strategy on students learning outcomes. *International Journal of Instruction*, *12*(3), 665–680. doi:10.29333/iji.2019.12340a

Jeong, J. S., Cañada-Cañada, F., & González-Gómez, D. (2018). The study of flipped-classroom for pre-service science teachers. *Education Sciences*, *8*(4), 163–174. doi:10.3390/educsci8040163

Jeong, J. S., González-Gómez, D., & Cañada-Cañada, F. (2016). Students' perceptions and emotions toward learning in a flipped general science classroom. *Journal of Science Education and Technology*, *25*(5), 747–758. doi:10.100710956-016-9630-8

Jeschofnig, L., & Jeschofnig, P. (2011). *Teaching lab science courses online: Resources for best practices*. Jossey-Bass, an Imprint of Wiley. http://www.josseybass.com/WileyCDA/WileyTitle/productCd-0470607041.html

Jirojwong, S., & Wallin, M. (2002). Use of formal and informal methods to gain information among faculty at an Australian regional university. *Journal of Academic Librarianship*, *28*(1-2), 68–73. doi:10.1016/S0099-1333(01)00284-1

Johnson, B. (1993). *Teacher as researcher*. ERIC Clearinghouse on Teacher Education.

Johnson, D. W., & Johnson, R. T. (2004). Implementing the teaching students to be peacemakers program. *Theory into Practice*, *43*(1), 68–79. doi:10.120715430421tip4301_9

Johnson, D. W., & Johnson, R. T. (2011). Conflict resolution, peer mediation, and peacemaking. In C. M. Evertson & C. S. Weinstein (Eds.), *Handbook of classroom management: Research, practice, and contemporary issues* (pp. 803–831). Routledge.

Johnson, L., McHugh, S., Eagle, J. L., & Spires, H. A. (2019). Project-based inquiry (PBI) global in kindergarten classroom: Inquiring about the world. *Early Childhood Education Journal*, *47*(5), 607–613. doi:10.100710643-019-00946-4

Kaempf, R. C. (2018). *A Phenomenological Study of the Influence of a Virtual Learning Project on an Elementary Class in the USA* (Doctoral dissertation). Texas Wesleyan University.

Kaiser, T., Hennecke, M., & Luhmann, M. (2020). The interplay of domain-and life satisfaction in predicting life events. *PLoS One*, *15*(9), e0238992. doi:10.1371/journal.pone.0238992 PMID:32941489

Kanter, R. M. (2013, January 7). *Six keys to leading positive change* [Video file]. YouTube. https://www.youtube.com/watch?time_continue=8&v=owU5aTNPJbs

Kaplan, O., & Nussio, E. (2018). Explaining recidivism of ex-combatants in Colombia. *The Journal of Conflict Resolution*, *62*(1), 64–93. doi:10.1177/0022002716644326

Kapoulitsas, M., & Corcoran, T. (2015). Compassion fatigue and resilience: A qualitative analysis of social work practice. *Qualitative Social Work: Research and Practice*, *14*(1), 86–101. doi:10.1177/1473325014528526

Karademir, A., Yaman, F., & Saatçioğlu, O. (2020). Challenges of higher education institutions against COVID-19: The case of Turkey. *Journal of Pedagogical Research*, 1-22. doi:10.33902/JPR.2020063574

Karasik, R. J. (2020). Community partners' perspectives and the faculty role in community-based learning. *Journal of Experiential Education*, *43*(2), 113–135. doi:10.1177/1053825919892994

Katz, W. A. (1992). *The "invisible college," Introduction to reference work*. McGraw-Hill.

Kebritchy, M., Lipschuetz, A., & Santiague, L. (2017). Issues and challenges for teaching successful online courses in higher education: A literature review. *Journal of Educational Technology Systems*, *46*(1), 4–29. doi:10.1177/0047239516661713

Keller, F. S. (1968). Good-bye teacher. *Journal of Applied Behavior Analysis*, *1*(1), 79–89. doi:10.1901/jaba.1968.1-79 PMID:16795164

Kemmis, S., & McTaggart, R. (2005). Participatory action research: Communicative action and the public sphere. In N. Denzin & Y. Lincoln (Eds.), Handbook of qualitative research (3rd ed., pp. 559-604). Sage.

Kemmis, S., & McTaggart, R. (2007). Communicative action and the public sphere. In N. K. Denzin & Y. S. Lincoln (Eds.), *The SAGE handbook of qualitative research* (pp. 559–603). SAGE.

Kemmis, S., McTaggart, R., & Nixon, R. (2014). *The action research planner: Doing critical participatory action research*. Springer. doi:10.1007/978-981-4560-67-2

Kerkhoff, S. N. (2017). Designing global futures: A mixed methods study to develop and validate the teaching for global readiness scale. *Teaching and Teacher Education*, *65*, 91–106. doi:10.1016/j.tate.2017.03.011

Kerkhoff, S. N. (2018). Teaching for global readiness: A model for locally situated and globally connected literacy instruction. In E. Ortlieb & E. H. Cheek (Eds.), *Addressing diversity in literacy instruction* (pp. 193–205). Emerald. doi:10.1108/S2048-045820170000008009

Kerkhoff, S. N. (2020). Collaborative video case studies and online instruments for self-reflection in global teacher education. *Journal of Technology and Teacher Education*, *28*(2), 341–351. http://learntechlib.org/primary/p/216212/

Kerkhoff, S. N., & Cloud, M. (2020). Global teacher education: A mixed methods self-study. *International Journal of Educational Research*, *103*. Advance online publication. doi:10.1016/j.ijer.2020.101629 PMID:32834467

Kerkhoff, S. N., Dimitrieska, V., Woerner, J., & Alsup, J. (2019). Global teaching in Indiana: A quantitative case study of K-12 public school teachers. *Journal of Comparative Studies and International Education*, *1*(1), 5–31. https//www.jcsie.com/ojs/dir/index.php/JCSIE/article/view/14

Kilgour, P., Reynaud, D., Northcote, M., McLoughlin, C., & Gosselin, K. P. (2019). Threshold concepts about online pedagogy for novice online teachers in higher education. *Higher Education Research & Development*, *38*(7), 1417–1431. doi:10.1080/07294360.2018.1450360

Killeavy, M. (2006). Induction: A collective endeavor of learning, teaching, and leading. *Theory into Practice*, *45*(2), 168–176. doi:10.120715430421tip4502_9

Kim, H., & Hannafin, M. J. (2009). Web-enhanced case-based activity in teacher education: A case study. *Instructional Science*, *37*(2), 151–170. doi:10.100711251-007-9040-7

Kim, J., Wong, C. Y., & Lee, Y. (2018). Transformative learning through an online global class project in teacher education. *Teacher Educator*, *53*(2), 190–207. doi:10.1080/08878730.2017.1422577

Kim, K.-J., & Bonk, C. J. (2006). The future of online teaching and learning in higher education: The survey says. *EDUCAUSE Quarterly*, *29*(4), 22–30. http://faculty.weber.edu/eamsel/Research%20Groups/On-line%20Learning/Bonk%20(2006).pdf

Kim, S., Phillips, W. R., Pinsky, L., Brock, D., Phillips, K., & Keary, J. (2006). A conceptual framework for developing teaching cases: A review and synthesis of the literature across disciplines. *Medical Education*, *40*(9), 867–876. doi:10.1111/j.1365-2929.2006.02544.x PMID:16925637

Kim, S., & Slapac, A. (2015). Culturally responsive, transformative pedagogy in the transnational era: Critical perspectives. *Educational Studies*, *51*(1), 17–27. doi:10.1080/00131946.2014.983639

Kindle, K. J., & Schmidt, C. M. (2019). Developing preservice teachers: A self-study of instructor scaffolding. *Reading Improvement*, *56*(2), 70–88.

King, A. (1993). From sage on the state to guide on the side. *College Teaching*, *41*(1), 30–35. doi:10.1080/87567555.1993.9926781

Kinginger, C. (2009). *Language learning and study abroad: A critical reading of research*. Springer. doi:10.1057/9780230240766

King, K. P. (2005). *Bringing transformative learning to life*. Krieger.

King, K. P. (Ed.). (2009). *The handbook of the evolving research of transformative learning: Based on the Learning Activities survey*. IAP.

King, K. P., & Dunham, M. D. (2009). Anytime? Anywhere? What needs face us in teaching professional educators online? In K. P. King (Ed.), *The handbook of the evolving research of transformative learning: Based on the Learning Activities survey* (pp. 133–135). IAP.

Kissock, C., & Richardson, P. (2010). Calling for action within the teaching profession: It is time to internationalize teacher education. *Teaching Education*, *21*(1), 89–101. doi:10.1080/10476210903467008

Kitchenham, A. (2006). Teachers and technology: A transformative journey. *Journal of Transformative Education*, *4*(3), 202–225. doi:10.1177/1541344606290947

Kitchen, J., & Stevens, D. (2008). Two teacher-educators practice action research as they introduce action research to preservice teachers. *Action Research*, *6*(1), 7–28. doi:10.1177/1476750307083716

Knight, J. (2004). Internationalization remodeled: Definition, approaches, and rationales. *Journal of Studies in International Education*, *8*(1), 5–31. doi:10.1177/1028315303260832

Knight, J. (2014). *Focus on teaching: Using video for high-impact instruction*. CORWIN.

Knight, J. (2018). *The impact cycle: what instructional coaches should do to foster powerful improvements in teaching*. CORWIN.

Knight, J. (2019). Why teacher autonomy is central to coaching success. *Educational Leadership*, *77*(3), 14–20. http://www.ascd.org/publications/educational-leadership/nov19/vol77/num03/Why-Teacher-Autonomy-Is-Central-to-Coaching-Success.aspx

Knowles, M. S., Holton, E. F., & Swanson, R. A. (2011). *The adult learner: The definitive classic in adult education and human resource development* (7th ed.). Elsevier Inc.

Koehler, M., & Mishra, P. (2009). What is technological pedagogical content knowledge (TPACK)? *Contemporary Issues in Technology & Teacher Education*, *9*(1), 60–70.

Koellner, K., Jacobs, J., & Borko, H. (2011). Mathematics professional development: Critical features for developing leadership skills and building teachers' capacity. *Mathematics Teacher Education and Development*, *13*(1), 115–136.

Kopish, M. A., Shahri, B., & Amira, M. (2019). Developing globally competent teacher candidates through cross-cultural experiential learning. *Journal of International Social Studies*, *9*(2), 3–34.

Korthagen, F. (2010). Situated learning theory and the pedagogy of teacher education: Towards an integrative view of teacher behavior and teacher learning. *Teaching and Teacher Education*, *26*(1), 98–106. doi:10.1016/j.tate.2009.05.001

Koshy, V. (2005). Action research for improving practice: A practical guide. *Sage (Atlanta, Ga.)*.

Kraft, M. A., & Blazar, D. (2018). Taking teacher coaching to scale. *Education Next*, *18*(4), 69–74. https://www.educationnext.org/taking-teacher-coaching-to-scale-can-personalized-training-become-standard-practice/

Kraft, M. A., Blazar, D., & Hogan, D. (2018). The effect of teacher coaching on instruction and achievement: A meta-analysis of the causal evidence. *Review of Educational Research*, *88*(4), 547–588. doi:10.3102/0034654318759268

Krashen, S. D. (1981). *Second language acquisition and second language learning*. Pergamon Press.

Kreber, C., & Kanuka, H. (2006). The scholarship of teaching and learning and the online classroom. *Canadian Journal of University Continuing Education, 32*(2), 109–131. doi:10.21225/D5P30B

Kress, G. (2010). *Multimodality: A social semiotic approach to contemporary communication*. Routledge.

Krippendorff, K. (2004). *Content analysis: An introduction to its methodology* (2nd ed.). SAGE Publications. https://bit.ly/2NR0V5i

Kristeva, J. (1986). Revolution in poetic language. In T. Moi (Ed.), The Kristeva Reader (pp. 89-136). Blackwell Publishing.

Kroc Institute for International Peace Studies. (2020). *Tres años después de la firma del Acuerdo Final en Colombia: Hacia la transformación territorial. Diciembre 2018 a Noviembre 2019*. http://peaceaccords.nd.edu/wp-content/uploads/2020/06/200630-Informe-4-resumen-final.pdf

Krystalli, P., Panagiotidis, P., & Arvanitis, P. (2020). Criteria for motivational Technology-Enhanced Language Learning activities. In M. R. Freiermuth & N. Zarrinabadi (Eds.), *Technology and the psychology of second language learners and users* (pp. 571–593). Springer. doi:10.1007/978-3-030-34212-8_22

Kuhfeld, M., Soland, J., Tarasawa, B., Johnson, A., Ruzek, E., & Lewis, K. (2020). How is Covid-19 affecting student learning? Initial findings from fall 2020. *Brown Center Chalkboard*. https://www.brookings.edu/blog/brown-center-chalkboard/2020/12/03/how-is-covid-19-affecting-student-learning/

Kulik, C.-L., Kulik, J. A., & Bangert-Drowns, R. L. (1990). Effectiveness of mastery learning programs: A meta-analysis. *Review of Educational Research, 60*(2), 265–299. doi:10.3102/00346543060002265

Kuntz, A. M. (2016). *The responsible methodologist: Inquiry, truth-telling, and social justice*. Routledge. doi:10.4324/9781315417332

Ladson-Billings, G., & Tate, W. F. (1995). Towards a critical race theory of education. *Teachers College Record, 97*, 47–68.

Laframboise, K. L., & Griffith, P. L. (1997). Using literature cases to examine diversity issues with preservice teachers. *Teaching and Teacher Education, 13*(4), 369–382. doi:10.1016/S0742-051X(96)00034-0

Lan, Y.-J. (2020). Immersion, interaction, and experience-oriented learning: Bringing virtual reality into FL learning. *Language Learning & Technology, 24*(1), 1–15. https://bit.ly/3jTNyPp

Lari, P., Rose, A., Ernst, J. V., Clark, A. C., Kelly, D. P., & DeLuca, V. W. (2019). Action research. *Technology & Engineering Teacher, 79*(2), 23–27.

Lather, P. (1986). Research as praxis. *Harvard Educational Review, 56*(3), 257–277. doi:10.17763/haer.56.3.bj2h231877069482

Lather, P. (1991). *Getting smart: Feminist research and pedagogy with / in the postmodern*. Routledge. doi:10.4324/9780203451311

Lave, J., & Wenger, E. (1991). *Situated learning: Legitimate peripheral participation*. Cambridge University Press. doi:10.1017/CBO9780511815355

Lawler, P. A., King, K. P., & Wilhite, S. C. (2004). Living and learning with technology: faculty as reflective practitioners in the online classroom. *Leadership, Counseling, Adult, Career and Higher Education Faculty Publications, 239*, 328-332. https://scholarcommons.usf.edu/ehe_facpub/239

Compilation of References

Lawson, A. P., Davis, C. R., & Son, J. Y. (2019). Not all flipped classes are the same: Using learning science to design flipped classrooms. *The Journal of Scholarship of Teaching and Learning, 19*(5), 77–104. doi:10.14434/josotl.v19i5.25856

Lazar, J., & Preece, J. (1999, December 22-27). *Implementing service learning in an online communities course* (Paper Presentation). 14th Annual Conference, International Academy of Information Management, Charlotte, NC, United States.

Leask, B. (2004). Internationalisation outcomes for all students using information and communication technologies (ICTs). *Journal of Studies in International Education, 8*(4), 336–351. doi:10.1177/1028315303261778

Leavy, P. (2017). *Research design: Quantitative, qualitative, mixed methods, arts-based, and community-based participatory research approaches*. Guilford Publications.

LeCompte, M. D., & Schensul, J. J. (2012). *Analysis and interpretation of ethnographic data: A mixed methods approach*. Rowman Altamira.Lewin, K. (1946). Action research and minority problems. *The Journal of Social Issues, 2*(4), 34–46. doi:10.1111/j.1540-4560.1946.tb02295.x

Lederman, D. (2000, March). The shift to remote learning: The human element. *Inside Higher Ed.* https://www.insidehighered.com/digital-learning/article/2020/03/25/how-shift-remote-learning-might-affect-students-instructors-and

Lee, C., Yeung, A. S., & Ip, T. (2016). Use of computer technology for English language learning: Do learning styles, gender, and age matter? *Computer Assisted Language Learning, 29*(5), 1033–1049. doi:10.1080/09588221.2016.1140655

Lee, J. (2008). *Visualizing elementary social studies methods*. John Wiley & Sons, Inc.

Lee, K., & Brett, C. (2015). Dialogic understanding of teachers' online transformative learning: A qualitative case study of teacher discussions in a graduate-level online course. *Teaching and Teacher Education, 46*, 72–83. doi:10.1016/j.tate.2014.11.001

Lehman, R. M., & Conceição, S. C. O. (2013). *Motivating and retaining online students: Research-based strategies that work*. John Wiley & Sons.

Lemke, J. (2000). Across the scales of time: Artifacts, activities, and meanings in ecosocial systems. *Mind, Culture, and Activity, 7*(4), 273–290. doi:10.1207/S15327884MCA0704_03

Lemov, D. (2015). *Teach like a champion 2.0: 62 techniques that put students on the path to college*. Jossey-Bass.

Leo, J., & Puzio, K. (2016). Flipped instruction in a high school science classroom. *Journal of Science Education and Technology, 25*(5), 775–781. doi:10.100710956-016-9634-4

Levin, M., & Greenwood, D. (2013). Revitalizing universities by reinventing the social sciences: Bildung and action research. In N. K. Denzin & Y. S. Lincoln (Eds.), *Landscape of qualitative research* (pp. 55–88). Sage Publications.

Lieberman, M. D. (2013). *Social: Why our brains are wired to connect*. Oxford University Press.

Lincoln, Y. S., & Guba, E. G. (1986). But is it rigorous? Trustworthiness and authenticity in naturalistic evaluation. *New Directions for Program Evaluation, 30*(30), 73–84. doi:10.1002/ev.1427

Lips, M., Eppel, E., McRae, H., Starkey, L., Sylvester, A., Parore, P., & Barlow, L. (2017). *Understanding children's use and experience with digital technologies*. Final research report. https://www.victoria.ac.nz/__data/assets/pdf_file/0003/960177/

Lobe, B., Morgan, D., & Hoffman, K. A. (2020). Qualitative data collection in an era of social distancing. *International Journal of Qualitative Methods, 19*, 1–8. doi:10.1177/1609406920937875

Lock, J. V. (2006). A new image: Online communities to facilitate teacher professional development. *Journal of Technology and Teacher Education, 14*(4), 663–678. https://www.learntechlib.org/primary/p/21030/

Lock, R. H., & Cooper Swanson, T. (2005). Provide structure for children with learning and behavior problems. *Intervention in School and Clinic*, *40*(3), 182–187. doi:10.1177/10534512050400030801

Lombrozo, E., Thanukos, A., & Weisberg, M. (2008). The importance of understanding the nature of science for evolution. *Evolution (New York)*, *1*(3), 290–298. doi:10.100712052-008-0061-8

Longview Foundation. (2008). *Teacher preparation for the global age: The imperative for change*. Retrieved on 2 July 2019 from: https://longviewfdn.org/programs/internationalizing-teacher-prep

López-Noguero, F. (2002). El análisis de contenido como método de investigación. *Review of Education*, *4*, 167–179.

Loughran, J. (2002). Effective reflective practice: In search of meaning in learning about teaching. *Journal of Teacher Education*, *53*(1), 33–43. doi:10.1177/0022487102053001004

Loughran, J. (2014). Professionally developing as a teacher educator. *Journal of Teacher Education*, *65*(4), 271–283. doi:10.1177/0022487114533386

Lou, S.-J., Chen, N.-C., Tsai, H.-Y., Tseng, K.-H., & Shih, R.-C. (2012). Using blended creative teaching: Improving a teacher education course on designing materials for young children. *Australasian Journal of Educational Technology*, *28*(5), 776–792. https://bit.ly/2MZNUJw. doi:10.14742/ajet.816

Loveless, A. (2011). Technology, pedagogy and education: Reflections on the accomplishment of what teachers know, do and believe in a digital age. *Technology, Pedagogy and Education*, *20*(3), 301–316. doi:10.1080/1475939X.2011.610931

Ludick, M., & Figley, C. R. (2017). Toward a mechanism for secondary trauma induction and reduction: Reimagining a theory of secondary traumatic stress. *Traumatology*, *23*(1), 112–123. doi:10.1037/trm0000096

Luka, I. (2014). Design thinking in pedagogy. *The Journal of Education, Culture, and Society*, *1*(2), 63–74. doi:10.15503/jecs20142.63.74

Maazouzi, K. (2019). Impact of teacher's personality and behavior on students' achievement. *Global Journal of Human Social Science*, *19*(9), 2249–2460.

MacDonald, J. (2006). *Blended learning and online tutoring*. Gower. doi:10.1111/j.1467-8535.2007.00749_10.x

Macharia, J. K., & Pelser, T. G. (2012). Key factors that influence the diffusion and infusion of information and communication technologies in Kenyan higher education. *Studies in Higher Education*, *39*(4), 1–15. doi:10.1080/03075079.2012.729033

MacKinnon, G. (2017). Highlighting the importance of context in the TPACK model: Three cases of non-traditional settings. *Issues and Trends in Educational Technology*, *5*(1), 4–16. doi:10.2458/azu_itet_v5i1_mackinnon

Madani, S. (2017). Promoting multilingual communicative competence for the labor market. *European Scientific Journal*, *13*(7), 201–214. doi:10.19044/esj.2017.v13n7p201

Magda, A. J. (2019). Online learning at public universities: Recruiting, orienting, and supporting online faculty. *The Learning House*. https://www.learninghouse.com/knowledge-center/research-reports/online-learning-at-public-universities/

Mahan, K. (2020). The comprehending teacher: Scaffolding in content and language integrated learning (CLIL). *Language Learning Journal*, 1–15. Advance online publication. doi:10.1080/09571736.2019.1705879

Major, C. (2010). Do virtual professors dream of electric students? College faculty experiences with online distance education. *Teachers College Record*, *112*(8), 2154–2208. http://www.tcrecord.org

Compilation of References

Manfra, M. M. (2019). Action research and systematic change in teaching practice. *Review of Research in Education*, *43*(1), 163–196. doi:10.3102/0091732X18821132

Manfra, M. M. (2020). Action research for classrooms, schools, and communities. *Sage (Atlanta, Ga.)*.

Manning, M. L., & Bucher, K. T. (2007a). Exploring the theories of democratic teaching: Rudolph Dreikurs. In *Classroom management: Models, applications, and cases* (2nd ed., pp. 62–76). Pearson.

Manning, M. L., & Bucher, K. T. (2007b). Exploring the theories of congruent communication: Haim Ginott. In *Classroom management: Models, applications, and cases* (2nd ed., pp. 77–93). Pearson.

Manning, M. L., & Bucher, K. T. (2007c). Exploring the theories of instructional management: Jacob Kounin. In *Classroom management: Models, applications, and cases* (2nd ed., pp. 94–109). Pearson.

Mansilla, V. B. (2017). *Global thinking*. http://www.pz.harvard.edu/sites/default/files/Global%20Thinking%20for%20ISV%202017%2006%2023_CreativeCommonsLicense.pdf

Marshall, H. W., & Kostka, I. (2020). Fostering teaching presence through the synchronous online flipped learning approach. *Teaching English as a Second or Foreign Language*, *24*(2). https://files.eric.ed.gov/fulltext/EJ1268565.pdf

Martin, F., & Bolliger, D. U. (2018). Engagement matters: Student perceptions on the importance of engagement strategies in the online learning environment. *Online Learning*, *22*(1), 205–222. doi:10.24059/olj.v22i1.1092

Martirosyan, N. M., Saxon, D. P., & Wanjohi, R. (2014). Student satisfaction and academic performance in Armenian higher education. *American International Journal of Contemporary Research*, *4*(2), 1–5.

Marzano, R. J., Pickering, D., & Heflebower, T. (2011). *The highly engaged classroom*. Marzano Research.

Masters, J. (1995). *The history of action research*. Ian Hughes Action Research Electronic Reader, University of Sydney. http://www.aral.com.au/arow/rmasters.html

Matusov, E. (2011). Irreconcilable differences in Vygotsky's and Bakhtin's approaches to the social and the individual: An educational perspective. *Culture and Psychology*, *17*(1), 99–119. doi:10.1177/1354067X10388840

Mayes, R., Luebeck, J., Yu Ku, H., Akarasriworn, C., & Korkmaz, O. (2011). Themes and strategies for transformative online instruction. *Quarterly Review of Distance Education*, *12*(3), 51–166.

Mbuva, J. M. (2014). Online education: Progress and prospects. *Journal of Business and Educational Leadership*, *5*(1), 91–101.

McCormack, L., Abou-Hamdan, S., & Joseph, S. (2017). Career derailment: Burnout and bullying at the executive level. *International Coaching Psychology Review*, *12*(1), 24–36.

McLoughlin, C., & Northcote, M. (2017). What skills do I need to teach online? Researching experienced teacher views of essential knowledge and skills in online pedagogy as a foundation for developing professional development. In *Search and Research: Teacher Education for Contemporary Contexts, Proceedings of the 18th Biennial International Conference on Teachers and Teaching, 3-7 July, 18th Biennial International Study Association on Teachers and Teaching (ISATT) Conference 2017* (pp. 1119-1129). Ediciones Universidad de Salamanca.

McNiff, J. (2016). *You and your action research project* (4th ed.). Routledge. doi:10.4324/9781315693620

McQuiggan, C. A. (2012). Faculty development for online teaching as a catalyst for change. *Journal of Asynchronous Learning Networks*, *16*(2), 27–61. doi:10.24059/olj.v16i2.258

Meng, L., Hua, F., & Bian, Z. (2020). Coronavirus Disease 2019 (COVID-19): Emerging and future challenges for dental and oral medicine. *Journal of Dental Research*, *99*(5), 481–487. doi:10.1177/0022034520914246 PMID:32162995

Merriam, S. B. (1998). *Qualitative research study applications in education*. Jossey-Bass.

Merryfield, M. M. (2002). The difference a global educator can make. *Association for Supervision and Curriculum Development*, *60*(2), 18–21.

Mertler, C. A. (2014). *Action research: Improving schools and empowering educators* (4th ed.). Sage Publications.

Mertler, C. A. (2019). Action research: Improving schools and empowering educators. *Sage (Atlanta, Ga.)*.

Meyer, A., Rose, D. H., & Gordon, D. (2014). *Universal design for learning: Theory and practice*. CAST.

Meyer, K. A. (2013). An analysis of the research on faculty development for online teaching and identification of new directions. *Online Learning*, *17*(4), 93–122. doi:10.24059/olj.v17i4.320

Meyers, S., Rowell, K., Wells, M., & Smith, B. C. (2019). Teacher empathy: A model of empathy for teaching for student success. *College Teaching*, *67*(3), 160–168. doi:10.1080/87567555.2019.1579699

Mezirow, J. (1990). *Fostering critical reflection in adulthood: A guide to transformative and emancipatory learning* (1st ed.). Jossey-Bass Publishers.

Mezirow, J. (1997). Transformative learning: Theory to practice. *New Directions for Adult and Continuing Education*, *1*(74), 5–12. doi:10.1002/ace.7401

Mezirow, J. (2003). Transformative learning as discourse. *Journal of Transformative Education*, *1*(1), 58–63. doi:10.1177/1541344603252172

Mezirow, J. (2011). Transformative dimensions of adult learning. *International Journal of Adult Vocational Education and Technology*, *2*(4), 58–66. doi:10.4018/javet.2011100105

Mezirow, J., & Rose, A. (1978). *An evaluation guide for college women's re-entry programs*. Distributed by ERIC Clearinghouse.

Michaels, S., O'Connor, C., & Resnick, L. B. (2008). Deliberative discourse idealized and realized: Accountable talk in the classroom and in civic life. *Studies in Philosophy and Education*, *27*(4), 283–297. doi:10.100711217-007-9071-1

Miles, H., Huberman, A. M., & Saldaña. (2014). *Qualitative data analysis: A methods sourcebook* (3rd ed.). Sage.

Miles, M. B., Huberman, A. M., & Saldaña, J. (2019). Qualitative data analysis: A methods sourcebook. *Sage (Atlanta, Ga.)*.

Miller, K. W. (2008). Teaching science methods online: Myths about inquiry-based online learning. *Science Educator*, *17*(2).

Miller, R. L. (2020). Service learning: A review of best practices. In A. Schwartz & R. L. Miller (Eds.), *High impact educational practices: A review of best practices with illustrative examples* (pp. 570–583). http://teachpsych.org/ebooks/highimpacted

Miller, S. C., McIntyre, C. J., & Lindt, S. F. (2020). Engaging technology in elementary school: Flipgrid's potential. *Childhood Education*, *96*(3), 62–69. doi:10.1080/00094056.2020.1766677

Mills, G. E. (2014). *Action research: A guide for the teacher researcher* (6th ed.). Pearson.

Milman, N. B. (2015). Distance education. In J. D. Wright (Ed.), International encyclopedia of the social & behavioral sciences (2nd ed., pp. 567–570). Elsevier. doi:10.1016/B978-0-08-097086-8.92001-4

Compilation of References

Ministerio de Educación Nacional. (2018). *Plan Especial de Educación Rural hacia el desarrollo rural y la construcción de paz*. MinEducación.

Mirra, N. (2019). From connected learning to connected teaching: Reimagining digital literacy pedagogy in English teacher education. *English Education*, *51*(3), 261–291.

Mishra, P., & Koehler, M. J. (2006). Technological pedagogical content knowledge: A framework for teacher knowledge. *Teachers College Record*, *108*(6), 1017–1054. doi:10.1111/j.1467-9620.2006.00684.x

Mishra, S. K. J. (2016). English language teaching: A shift from chalk to digitalization. *Critical Space*, *4*(3), 45–50.

Mohebbi, M., Linders, A., & Chifos, C. (2018). Community immersion, trust-building, and recruitment among hard-to-reach populations: A case study of Muslim women in Detroit Metro area. *Qualitative Sociology Review*, *14*(3), 24–44. doi:10.18778/1733-8077.14.3.02

Molano, A. (2015). *50 años de conflicto armado*. El Espectador.

Mortari, L. (2015). Reflectivity in research practice: An overview of different perspectives. *International Journal of Qualitative Methods*, *14*(5), 1–9. doi:10.1177/1609406915618045

Moyer, P. S. (2001). Are we having fun yet? How teachers use manipulatives to teach mathematics. *Educational Studies in Mathematics*, *47*(2), 175–197. doi:10.1023/A:1014596316942

Nandi, D., Hamilton, M., Chang, S., & Balbo, S. (2012). Evaluating quality in online asynchronous interactions between students and discussion facilitators. *Australasian Journal of Educational Technology*, *28*(4), 684–702. doi:10.14742/ajet.835

National Center for O*NET Development. (n.d.a). *About O*NET*. O*NET Resource Center. https://www.onetcenter.org/overview.html

National Center for O*NET Development. (n.d.b). 11-1021.00 - General and Operations Managers. *O*NET OnLine*. https://www.onetonline.org/link/details/11-1021.00

National Center for O*NET Development. (n.d.c). 21-1014.00 - Mental Health Counselors. *O*NET OnLine*. https://www.onetonline.org/link/details/21-1014.00

National Center for O*NET Development. (n.d.d). 25-1081.00 - Education Teachers, Postsecondary. *O*NET OnLine*. https://www.onetonline.org/link/details/25-1081.00

National Council for the Social Studies. (2013). *The College, Career, and Civic Life (C3) framework for the social studies state standards: Guidance for enhancing the rigor of K-12 civics, economics, geography, and history*. NCSS.

National Council of Teachers of Mathematics. (2000). *Principles and standards for school mathematics*. National Council of Teachers of Mathematics.

National Council of Teachers of Mathematics. (2014). *Principles to actions: Ensuring mathematics success for all*. National Council of Teachers of Mathematics.

National Mathematics Advisory Panel. (2008). *Foundations for success: The final report of the national mathematics advisory panel*. U.S. Department of Education.

National Research Council. (2001). *Adding it up: Helping children learn mathematics*. The National Academies Press., doi:10.17226/9822

Negash, S., & Wilcox, M. V. (2008). E-Learning classifications: Differences and similarities. In S. Negash, M. E. Whitman, A. B. Woszczynski, K. Hoganson, & H. Mattord (Eds.), *Handbook of distance learning for real-time and asynchronous information technology education* (pp. 1–23). IGI Global., doi:10.4018/978-1-59904-964-9.ch001

Negrea, V. (2013). Education policy, applied language learning, and economic development. *The European Integration - Realities and Perspectives, 8*(1), 313–317.

Nieto, S. (2009). *Identity and belonging: Culture and Learning. In Language, culture, and teaching: Critical perspectives* (2nd ed.). Routledge. doi:10.4324/9780203872284

Noddings, N. (1984). *Caring: A feminine approach to ethics and moral education*. University of California Press.

Noddings, N. (1995). A morally defensible mission for schools in the 21st century. *Phi Delta Kappan, 76*, 365–369.

Noddings, N. (2002). *Starting at home: Caring and social policy*. University of California Press.

Noreen, S., Ali, A., & Munaw, U. (2019). The impact of teachers' personality on students' academic achievement in Pakistan. *Global Regional Review, 4*(3), 92–102. doi:10.31703/grr.2019(IV-III).11

Norris, S. (2004). *Analyzing multimodal interaction: A methodological framework*. Routledge. doi:10.4324/9780203379493

Northcote, M. T., Reynaud, D., Beamish, P., Martin, T., & Gosselin, K. P. (2011). Bumpy moments and joyful breakthroughs: The place of threshold concepts in academic staff development programs about online learning and teaching. *ACCESS: Critical Perspectives on Communication, Cultural &. Policy Studies, 30*(2), 75–89.

Nowell, L. S., Norris, J. M., White, D. E., & Moules, N. J. (2017). Thematic analysis: Striving to meet the trustworthiness criteria. *International Journal of Qualitative Methods, 16*(1), 1–13. doi:10.1177/1609406917733847

O'Brien, K. G. (2016a). *Teacher Action Research 1 Course Syllabus, Spring 2016*. Unpublished.

O'Brien, K. G. (2016b). *Teacher Action Research 1 Course Syllabus, Summer 2016*. Unpublished.

O'Donnell, L., Stueve, A., San Doval, A., Duran, R., Haber, D., Atnafou, R., & Piessens, P. (1999). The effectiveness of the "Reach for Health" community youth service learning program in reducing early and unprotected sex among urban middle school students. *American Journal of Public Health, 89*(2), 176–181. doi:10.2105/AJPH.89.2.176 PMID:9949745

OECD. (2020). The potential of online learning for adults: Early lessons from the COVID-19 crisis. In *OECD tackling coronavirus (COVID-19): Contributing to a global effort*. OECD Publishing. https://read.oecd-ilibrary.org/view/?ref=135_135358-ool6fsocqtitle=The-potential-of-Online-Learning-for-adults-Early-lessons-from-the-COVID-19-crisis

Okantey, P. C. (2012). Leading Change: When everything else is falling. *Leadership Review, 2*(3), 42–46.

Onwuegbuzie, A. J., Frels, R. K., & Hwang, E. (2016). Mapping Saldaña coding methods onto the literature review process. *Journal of Educational Issues, 2*(1), 130–149. doi:10.5296/jei.v2i1.8931

Orkwis, R. (2003). *Universally Designed Instruction*. Council for Exceptional Children. (ERIC number: ED475386). www.eric.ed.gov

Osika, E. R., Johnson, R. Y., & Buteau, R. (2009). Factors influencing faculty use of technology in online instructions: A case study. *Online Journal of Distance Learning Administration, 12*, •••. https://www.westga.edu/_distance/ojdla/spring121/osika121.html

Ostashewski, N., Moisey, S., & Reid, D. (2011). Applying constructionist principles to online teacher professional development. *International Review of Research in Open and Distance Learning, 12*(6), 143–156. doi:10.19173/irrodl.v12i6.976

Compilation of References

Pajak, E. (2001). Clinical supervision in a standards-based environment: Opportunities and challenges. *Journal of Teacher Education, 52*(3), 233–243. doi:10.1177/0022487101052003006

Palacios-Hidalgo, F. J., Gómez-Parra, M. E., & Huertas-Abril, C. A. (2020). Digital and media competences: Key competences for EFL teachers. *Teaching English with Technology, 20*(1), 43–59. https://bit.ly/2GHgDML

Palacios-Hidalgo, F. J. (2020). TELL, CALL, and MALL: Approaches to bridge the language gap. In C. A. Huertas-Abril & M. E. Gómez-Parra (Eds.), *International approaches to bridging the language gap* (pp. 118–134). IGI Global., doi:10.4018/978-1-7998-1219-7.ch008

Palacios-Hidalgo, F. J. (2020a). An approach for providing LGBTI+ education and bridging the language gap: Integrating ESoPC into EFL teacher training. In C. A. Huertas-Abril & M. E. Gómez-Parra (Eds.), *International approaches to bridging the language gap* (pp. 195–213). IGI Global., doi:10.4018/978-1-7998-1219-7.ch012

Palmer, P. J. (2007). *The courage to teach: Exploring the inner landscape of a teacher's life*. Jossey-Bass.

Paris, D. (2012). Culturally sustaining pedagogy: A needed change in stance, terminology, and practice. *Educational Researcher, 41*(3), 93–97. doi:10.3102/0013189X12441244

Park, C., & Kim, D. G. (2020). Perception of instructor presence and its effects on learning experience in online classes. *Journal of Information Technology Education, 19*, 475–488. doi:10.28945/4611

Parkhouse, H., Glazier, J., Tichnor-Wagner, A., & Montana Cain, J. (2015). From local to global: Making the leap in teacher education. *International Journal of Global Education, 4*(2), 10–29. http://www.ijtase.net/ojs/index.php/ijge/article/view/409/492

Parkhouse, H., Tichnor-Wagner, A., Glazier, J., & Cain, J. M. (2016). "You don't have to travel the world:" Accumulating experiences on the path toward globally competent teaching. *Teaching Education, 27*(3), 267–285. doi:10.1080/10476210.2015.1118032

Parra, A., Mateus, J., & Mora, Z. (2018). Educación rural en Colombia: El país olvidado, antecedentes y perspectivas en el marco del posconflicto. *Nodos y Nudos, 6*(45), 52–65.

Patel, D. S. (2017). Significance of Technology Enhanced Language Learning (TELL) in language classes. *Journal of Technology for ELT, 4*(2). https://bit.ly/2E7G4qk

Patterson, T. (2013). *Stories of self and other: Four in-service social studies teachers reflect on their international professional development* (Doctoral dissertation). Retrieved from https://digitalcommons.sacredheart.edu/ced_fac/112

Patton, M. Q. (2003). *Qualitative evaluation checklist. Evaluation checklists project.* https://bit.ly/2F2sYOv

Patton, M. Q. (2002). *Qualitative research and evaluation methods* (3rd ed.). SAGE.

Pear, J., & Kinsner, W. (1988). Computer aided personalized system of instruction: An effective and economical method for short- and long-distance education. *Machine-Mediated Learning, 2*(3), 213-37. https://www.researchgate.net/profile/Joseph-Pear/publication/234597931_Computer-Aided_Personalized_System_of_Instruction_An_Effective_and_Economical_Method_for_Short-_and_Long-Distance_Education/links/58864a3992851c21ff4d5991/Computer-Aided-Personalized-System-of-Instruction-An-Effective-and-Economical-Method-for-Short-and-Long-Distance-Education.pdf

Pedreira, K., & Pear, J. (2015). Motivation and attitude in a computer-aided personalized system of instruction course on discrete-trials teaching. *Journal on Developmental Disabilities, 28*(1), 45–51.

Pence, H. M., & Macgillivray, I. K. (2008). The impact of an international field experience on preservice teachers. *Teaching and Teacher Education, 24*(1), 14–25. doi:10.1016/j.tate.2007.01.003

Phipps, R., & Merisotis, J. (1999). What's the difference: A review of contemporary research on the effectiveness of distance learning in higher education. *Journal of Distance Education*, *14*(1), 102–114.

Pidgeon, N., & Henwood, K. (1997). Using grounded theory in psychological research. In N. Hayes (Ed.), *Doing Qualitative Analysis in Psychology* (pp. 245–273). Psychology Press.

Piggot-Irvine, E. (2002). *Rhetoric and practice in action research.* Paper presented at the annual conference of the British Educational Research Association, University of Exeter.

Pigza, J. M. (2010). Developing your ability to foster student learning and development through reflection. In B. Jacoby & P. Mutascio (Eds.), *Looking in, reaching out: A reflective guide for community service-learning professionals* (pp. 73–94). Campus Compact.

Pinnegar, S. (1995). (Re-)Experiencing beginning. *Teacher Education Quarterly*, *22*(3), 65–81. https://www.jstor.org/stable/23475835

Pintrich, P. R. (2000). The role of goal orientation in self-regulated learning. In *Handbook of self-regulation* (pp. 451–502). Academic Press., doi:10.1016/B978-012109890-2/50043-3

Pintrich, P. R. (2003). Motivation and classroom learning. *Educational Psychology, 7, 103–124.* doi:10.1002/0471264385.wei0706

Pitkänen, K., Iwata, M., & Laru, J. (2020). Exploring technology-oriented Fab Lab facilitators' role as educators in K-12 education: Focus on scaffolding novice students' learning in digital fabrication activities. *International Journal of Child-Computer Interaction*, *26*, 100207. Advance online publication. doi:10.1016/j.ijcci.2020.100207

Piwowar, V., Thiel, F., & Ophardt, D. (2013). Training inservice teachers' competencies in classroom management. A quasi-experimental study with teachers of secondary schools. *Teaching and Teacher Education*, *30*(30), 1–12. doi:10.1016/j.tate.2012.09.007

Polly, D. (2011). Teachers' learning while constructing technology-based instructional resources. *British Journal of Educational Technology*, *42*(6), 950–961. doi:10.1111/j.1467-8535.2010.01161.x

Polly, D. (2012). Supporting mathematics instruction with an expert coaching model. *Mathematics Teacher Education and Development*, *14*(1), 78–93.

Polly, D. (2016a). Exploring the relationship between the use of technology with enacted tasks and questions in elementary school mathematics. *The International Journal for Technology in Mathematics Education*, *23*(3), 111–118. doi:10.1564/tme_v23.3.03

Polly, D. (2016b). Examining elementary school teachers' enactment of mathematical tasks and questions. *Research in the Schools*, *23*(2), 61–71.

Polly, D., & Hannafin, M. J. (2010). Reexamining technology's role in learner-centered professional development. *Educational Technology Research and Development*, *58*(5), 557–571. doi:10.100711423-009-9146-5

Polly, D., McGee, J. R., & Martin, C. S. (2010). Employing technology-rich mathematical tasks to develop teachers' technological, pedagogical, and content knowledge (TPACK). *Journal of Computers in Mathematics and Science Teaching*, *29*(4), 455–472.

Polly, D., Neale, H., & Pugalee, D. K. (2014). How does ongoing task-focused mathematics professional development influence elementary school teacher's knowledge, beliefs and enacted pedagogies? *Early Childhood Education Journal*, *42*(1), 1–10. doi:10.100710643-013-0585-6

Ponte, P. (2002). How teachers become action researchers and how teacher educators become their facilitators. *Educational Action Research*, *10*(3), 399–421. doi:10.1080/09650790200200193

Pöysä, J., & Lowyck, J. (2009). Communities in technology-enhanced environments for learning. In P. L. Rogers, G. Berg, J. Boettcher, C. Howard, L. Justice, & K. Schenk (Eds.), *Encyclopedia of distance learning* (2nd ed., pp. 345–351). Information Science Reference. doi:10.4018/978-1-60566-198-8.ch051

Putman, S. M., & Rock, T. (2018). *Action research: Using strategic inquiry to improve teaching and learning. Sage (Atlanta, Ga.)*.

Putri, M. D., Rusdiana, D., & Rochintaniawati, D. (2018). Students' conceptual understanding in modified flipped classroom approach: An experimental study in junior high school science learning. *Journal of Physics: Conference Series*, *1157*(2), 022046. Advance online publication. doi:10.1088/1742-6596/1157/2/022046

Raghavendra, C. (2020). The impact of COVID-19 lockdown on English language teaching & learning in India. *Language in India*, *20*(8), 283–286.

Rajab, M. H., Gazal, A. M., & Alkattan, K. (2020). Challenges to online medical education during the COVID-19 pandemic. *Cureus*, *12*(7), 1–11. doi:10.7759/cureus.8966 PMID:32766008

Rapoport, A. (2010). We cannot teach what we do not know: Indiana teachers talk about global citizenship education. *Education, Citizenship and Social Justice*, *5*(3), 179–190. doi:10.1177/1746197910382256

Raymond, O. (2003). *Universally designed instruction*. ERIC/OSEP digest, (ED475386). ERIC. https://files.eric.ed.gov/fulltext/ED475386.pdf

Razzouk, R., & Shute, V. (2012). What is design thinking and why is it important? *Review of Educational Research*, *82*(3), 330–348. doi:10.3102/0034654312457429

Rebeor, S., Rosser-Majors, M., McMahon, C., Anderson, S., Harper, Y., & Sliwinski, L. (2020). *Applying instructor presence*. https://www.instructorpresence.com/

Rebeor, S. M., Rosser-Majors, M. L., McMahon, C. L., Anderson, S. L., Harper, Y., & Sliwinski, L. J. (2019b). Effective instruction in virtual higher education: Ensuring cognitive, social and teaching presence. *International Conference on Education and New Developments*, Porto, Portugal. 10.36315/2019v1end118

Rebeor, S., Rosser-Majors, M. L., McMahon, C. L., & Anderson, S. L. (2019a). Social, cognitive, & teaching presence: Impact on faculty and AU's diverse student body. *TCC Worldwide Online Conference*.

Rebora, A. (2019). Expanding on coaching's potential. *Educational Leadership*, *77*(3), 9–9.

Redecker, C., & Punie, Y. (2017). *Digital competence framework for educators (DigCompEdu)*. Publications Office of the European Union. doi:10.2760/178382

Reeder, K., Macfadyen, L. P., Chase, M., & Roche, J. (2004). Negotiating culture in cyberspace: Participation patterns and problematics. *Language Learning & Technology*, *8*(2), 88–105.

Reeve, J., & Lee, W. (2019). A neuroscientific perspective on basic psychological needs. *Journal of Personality*, *87*(1), 102–114. doi:10.1111/jopy.12390 PMID:29626342

Reimers, F. (2009). Leading for global competence. *Educational Leadership*, *67*(1). http://www.ascd.org/publications/educational-leadership/sept09/vol67/num01/Leading-for-Global-competence.aspx

Reinhardt, J. (2019). Social media in second and foreign language teaching and learning: Blogs, wikis, and social networking. *Language Teaching*, *52*(1), 1–39. doi:10.1017/S0261444818000356

Reinoso, N., & Fonseca, L. (2020). Introducción al Encuentro: enseñar psicología comunitaria para la construcción de paz en Colombia. In L. Fonseca & N. Reinoso (Eds.), Punto de encuentro: Reflexiones sobre la construcción de paz en el Centro Poblado Héctor Ramírez (pp. 17-29). Bogotá: Universidad de La Sabana.

Resnick, M. (2002). Rethinking learning in the digital age. In G. Kirkman (Ed.), *The Global Information Technology Report: Readiness for the Networked World* (pp. 32–37). Oxford University Press.

Revere, L., & Kovach, J. (2011). Online technologies for engaged learning: A meaningful synthesis for educators. *Quarterly Review of Distance Education*, *12*, 113–124.

Richards, M., & Guzman, I. R. (2016). Academic assessment of critical thinking in distance education information technology programs. In P. Ordóñez & R. D. Tennyson (Eds.), *Impact of economic crisis on education and the next-generation workforce* (pp. 101–119). IGI Global. doi:10.4018/978-1-4666-9455-2.ch005

Riding, R., & Cheema, I. (1991). Cognitive styles–an overview and integration. *Educational Psychology*, *11*(3–4), 193–215. doi:10.1080/0144341910110301

Ripp, P. (2021). *The Global Read Aloud*. https://theglobalreadaloud.com/

Rittle-Johnson, B., & Alibali, M. W. (1999). Conceptual and procedural knowledge of mathematics: Does one lead to the other? *Journal of Educational Psychology*, *91*(1), 175–189. doi:10.1037/0022-0663.91.1.175

Roberts, J., & Styron, R. (2010). Student satisfaction and persistence: Factors vital to student retention. *Research in Higher Education*, *6*, 1–18.

Rogers, R. (2007). *A critical discourse analysis of family literacy practices: Power in and out of print*. Routledge.

Rogoff, B., Matusov, E., & White, C. (1998). Models of teaching and learning: Participation in a Community of Learners. In D. R. Olson & N. Torrance (Eds.), The handbook of education and human development: New models of learning, teaching and schooling (pp. 388-414). Blackwell.

Roodin, P., Brown, L. H., & Shedlock, D. (2013). Intergenerational service-learning: A review of recent literature and directions for the future. *Gerontology & Geriatrics Education*, *34*(1), 3–25. doi:10.1080/02701960.2012.755624 PMID:23362852

Rose, E., & Adams, C. (2014). "Will I ever connect with the students?": Online teaching and the pedagogy of care. *Phenomenology & Practice*, *7*(2), 5–16.

Rose, R. (2012). What it takes to teach online: While some instructors think online teaching will be a breeze, the truth is that the best teachers work very hard to connect with students. here are seven tips from an online insider. *T.H.E. Journal*, *39*(5), 28–30.

Rosser-Majors, M., Rebeor, S., McMahon, C., & Anderson, S. (2020). *Instructor presence training: Sustainable practices supporting student retention and success*. Teaching and Learning Conference, University of Arizona Global Campus (virtual). https://www.youtube.com/watch?v=4zrFNOtp198

Ross, L. L., & McBean, D. (1995). A comparison of pacing contingencies in classes using a personalized system of instruction. *Journal of Applied Behavior Analysis*, *28*(1), 87–88. doi:10.1901/jaba.1995.28-87 PMID:16795855

Rubin, H. J., & Rubin, I. S. (2012). *Qualitative interviewing: The art of hearing data*. Sage Publications.

Russell, T. (2018). A teacher educator's lessons learned from reflective practice. *European Journal of Teacher Education*, *41*(1), 4–14. doi:10.1080/02619768.2017.1395852

Rutten, L. (2021). Toward a theory of action for practitioner inquiry as professional development in preservice teacher education. *Teaching and Teacher Education*, *97*, 103–194. doi:10.1016/j.tate.2020.103194

Ryan, G. W., & Bernard, H. R. (2003). Techniques to identify themes. *Field Methods*, *15*(1), 85–109. doi:10.1177/1525822X02239569

Sagar, R. (2000). *Guiding school improvement with action research*. Association for Supervision and Curriculum Development. http://www.ascd.org/publications/books/100047.aspx

Sagor, R. (2000). *Guiding school improvement with action research*. ASCD.

Saldaña, J. (2012). *The coding manual for qualitative researchers* (2nd ed.). SAGE.

Salerno Valdez, E., & Gubrium, A. (2020). Shifting to virtual CBPR protocols in the time of Corona Virus/COVID-19. *International Journal of Qualitative Methods*, *19*, 1–9.

Samuelowicz, K., & Bain, J. D. (2001). Revisiting academics' beliefs about teaching and learning. *Higher Education*, *41*(3), 299–325. doi:10.1023/A:1004130031247

Sánchez, L., & Ensor, T. (2020). "We want to live": Teaching globally through cosmopolitan belonging. *Research in the Teaching of English*, *54*(3), 254–280.

Sandkuhl, K., & Lehmann, H. (2017). Digital transformation in higher education – the role of enterprise architectures and portals. *Digital Enterprise Computing*. https://eprints.win.informatik.uni-rostock.de/516/1/Sandkuhl,%20Lehmann%202017.0%20-%20Digital%20Transformation%20in%20Higher%20Education.pdf

Sandy, M., & Holland, B. A. (2006). Different worlds and common ground: Community partner perspectives on campus-community partnerships. *Michigan Journal of Community Service Learning*, *13*(1), 30–43.

Schaffhauser, D. (2020). Educators feeling stressed, anxious, overwhelmed and capable. *THE Journal*. https://thejournal.com/articles/2020/06/02/survey-teachers-feeling-stressed-anxious-overwhelmed-and-capable.aspx

Schleicher, A. (2018). *The future of education and skills*. OECD.

Schön, D. A. (1987). *Educating the reflective practitioner: Toward a new design for teaching and learning in the professions*. Jossey-Bass.

Schukar, R. (1993). Controversy in global education: Lessons for teacher educators. *Theory into Practice*, *32*(1), 52–57. doi:10.1080/00405849309543573

Sciarra, D., & Seirup, H. (2008). The multidimensionality of school engagement and math achievement among racial groups. *Professional School Counseling*, *11*(4), 218–228. doi:10.5330/PSC.n.2010-11.218

Scollon. (2008). *Analyzing Public Discourse*. Routledge.

Seaman, J. E., Allen, I. E., & Seaman, J. (2018). *Grade increase: Tracking distance education in the United States*. Babson Survey Research Group. https://onlinelearningsurvey.com/reports/ gradeincrease.pdf

Seaman, J. E., Allen, I. E., & Seaman, J. (2018). *Grade increase: Tracking distance education in the United States*. Babson Survey Research Group. https://onlinelearningsurvey.com/reports/gradeincrease.pdf

Seifer, S. D., & Mihalynuk, T. V. (2005). *The use of technology in higher education service-learning*. http://www.servicelearning.org/ instant_info/fact_sheets/he_facts/use_of_tech/

Selwyn, N. (2013). Discourses of digital "disruption" in education: a critical analysis. In *Fifth International Roundtable on Discourse Analysis*, City University Hong Kong.

Senge, P. (2015, Jun 4). *How do you define a learning organization?* [Video file]. YouTube. https://www.youtube.com/watch?time_continue=2&v=vc2ruCErTok

Sert, O., & Li, L. (2017). A qualitative study on CALL knowledge and materials design: Insights from pre-service EFL teachers. *International Journal of Computer-Assisted Language Learning and Teaching, 7*(3), 73–87. doi:10.4018/IJCALLT.2017070105

Shepherd, T. L., & Linn, D. (2015). Legal issues of behavior and classroom management. In *Behavior and classroom management in the multicultural classroom: Proactive, active, and reactive strategies* (pp. 33–60). Sage Publications. doi:10.4135/9781483366647.n2

Sheridan, K., & Kelly, M. A. (2010). The indicators of instructor presence that are important to students in online courses. *Journal of Online Learning and Teaching, 6*(4), 767–779.

Shotwell, A., & Sangrey, T. (2009). Resisting definition: Gendering through interaction and relational selfhood. *Hypatia, 24*(3), 56–76. doi:10.1111/j.1527-2001.2009.01045.x

Shulman, L. S. (1986, February). Those who understand: Knowledge growth in teaching. *Educational Research, 15*(2), 4–14. doi:10.3102/0013189X015002004

Shulman, L. S. (1999). Course anatomy: The dissection and analysis of knowledge through teaching. In P. Hutchings (Ed.), *The Course Portfolio: How Faculty Can Examine Their Teaching to Advance Practice and Improve Student Learning* (pp. 5–12). American Association for Higher Education.

Siemens, G. (2005). Connectivism: A learning theory for the digital age. *International Journal of Instructional Technology and Distance Learning, 2*(1). http://www.itdl.org/Journal/Jan_05/article01.htm

Sigueza, T. (2020, March 4). *Using graphic organizers with ells.* Retrieved from https://www.colorincolorado.org/article/using-graphic-organizers-ells

Simonson, M., Zvacek, S. M., & Smaldino, S. (2019). *Teaching and learning at a distance: Foundations of distance education* (7th ed.). Information Age Publishing.

Singh, V., & Thurman, A. (2019). How many ways can we define online learning? A systematic literature review of definitions of online learning (1988-2018). *American Journal of Distance Education, 33*(4), 289–306. doi:10.1080/08923647.2019.1663082

Sipilä, K. (2014). Educational use of information and communications technology: Teachers' perspective. *Technology, Pedagogy and Education, 23*(2), 225–241. doi:10.1080/1475939X.2013.813407

Skinner, E. A., & Belmont, M. J. (1993). Motivation in the classroom: Reciprocal effects of teacher behavior and student engagement across the school year. *Journal of Educational Psychology, 85*(4), 571–581. doi:10.1037/0022-0663.85.4.571

Skovholt, T. M., & Trotter-Mathison, M. (2014). *The resilient practitioner: Burnout prevention and self-care strategies for counselors, therapists, teachers, and health professionals.* Routledge. doi:10.4324/9780203893326

Slapac, A., & Kim, S. (2020). Negotiating teaching cultures and developing cultural competency towards classroom communities in early childhood (K-2) language immersion schools. In International Perspectives on Modern Developments in Early Childhood Education (pp. 77-93). IGI Global.

Slapac, A. (2021). Advancing students' global competency through English language learning in Romania: An exploratory qualitative case study of four English language teachers. *Journal of Research in Childhood Education, 35*(2), 1–17. doi:10.1080/02568543.2021.1880993

Slapac, A., & Coppersmith, S. A. (Eds.). (2019). *Beyond language learning instruction: Transformative supports for emergent bilinguals and educators*. IGI Global. doi:10.4018/978-1-7998-1962-2

Slapac, A., Kim, S., & Coppersmith, S. A. (2019). Preparing and enriching linguistically and culturally responsive educators through professional development. In A. Slapac & S. Coppersmith (Eds.), *Beyond language learning instruction: Transformative supports for emergent bilinguals and educators* (pp. 282–304). IGI Global Disseminator of Knowledge.

Slapac, A., & Navarro, V. (2011). Shaping action researchers through a Master's capstone experience. *Teacher Education & Practice: The Journal of the Texas Association of Colleges for Teacher Education*, 24(4), 405–426.

Slapac, A., & Navarro, V. (2011). Shaping action researchers through a Master's capstone experience. *Teacher Education and Practice*, 24(4), 405–426.

Sliwinski, L., & Rosser-Majors, M. L. (2018). Faculty development and student learning: A deep dive into instructor presence. OLC Accelerate: Online Learning Consortium, Orlando, FL.

Smith, F. G. (2012). Analyzing a college course that adheres to the Universal Design for Learning framework. *The Journal of Scholarship of Teaching and Learning*, 12(3), 31–61.

Smith, M. S., & Stein, M. K. (1998). Selecting and creating mathematical tasks: From research to practice. *Mathematics Teaching in the Middle School*, 3(5), 344–350. doi:10.5951/MTMS.3.5.0344

Smith, M. S., & Stein, M. K. (2018). *5 practices for orchestrating productive mathematics discussions* (2nd ed.). National Council of Teachers of Mathematics.

Smylie, M. A., & Wenzel, S. A. (2003). *The Chicago Annenberg Challenge: Successes, failures, and lessons for the future* (Final Technical Report of the Chicago Annenberg Research Project). Consortium on Chicago School Research.

Snow-Renner, R., & Lauer, P. (2005). *Professional development analysis*. Mid-Content Research for Education and Learning. Retrieved from https://files.eric.ed.gov/fulltext/ED491305.pdf

Sodexo. (2018). *Global workplace trends*. https://www.sodexo.com/workreimagined/2018-global-workplace-trends

Song, L., Singleton, E. S., Hill, J. R., & Koh, M. H. (2004). Improving online learning: Student perceptions of useful and challenging characteristics. *The Internet and Higher Education*, 7(1), 59–70. doi:10.1016/j.iheduc.2003.11.003

Spinazzola, J., Ford, J. D., Zucker, M., van der Kolk, B. A., Silva, S., Smith, S. F., & Blaustein, M. (2005). Survey Evaluates Complex Trauma Exposure, Outcome and Intervention Among Children and Adolescents. *Psychiatric Annals*, 35(5), 433–439. doi:10.3928/00485713-20050501-09

Spires, Himes, M. P., Paul, C. M., & Kerkhoff, S. N. (2019). Going global with project-based inquiry: Cosmopolitan literacies in practice. *Journal of Adolescent & Adult Literacy*, 63(1), 51–64. doi:10.1002/jaal.947

Sprang, G., Ford, J., Kerig, P., & Bride, B. (2019). Defining secondary traumatic stress and developing targeted assessments and interventions: Lessons learned from research and leading experts. *Traumatology*, 25(2), 72–81. doi:10.1037/trm0000180

Stanton, C. R. (2014). Crossing methodological borders: Decolonizing community-based participatory research. *Qualitative Inquiry*, 20(5), 573–583. doi:10.1177/1077800413505541

Starkey, L. (2020). A review of research exploring teacher preparation for the digital age. *Cambridge Journal of Education*, 50(1), 37–56. doi:10.1080/0305764X.2019.1625867

Stein, M. K., Grover, B. W., & Henningsen, M. (1996). Building student capacity for mathematical thinking and reasoning: An analysis of mathematical tasks used in reform classrooms. *American Educational Research Journal*, *33*(2), 455-488. doi:10.2307/1163292

Stern, T. (2019). Participatory action research and the challenges of knowledge democracy. *Educational Action Research*, *27*(3), 435–451. doi:10.1080/09650792.2019.1618722

Stewart, H., Gapp, R., & Houghton, L. (2020). Large online first year learning and teaching: The lived experience of developing a student-centered continual learning practice. *Systemic Practice and Action Research*, *33*(4), 435–451. doi:10.100711213-019-09492-x

Strait, J., & Sauer, T. (2004). Constructing experiential learning for online courses: The birth of e-service. *EDUCAUSE Quarterly*, *27*(1), 62–65.

Strangeways, A., & Papatraianou, L. H. (2016). Case-based learning for classroom ready teachers: Addressing the theory practice disjunction through narrative pedagogy. *The Australian Journal of Teacher Education*, *41*(9), 117–134. doi:10.14221/ajte.2016v41n9.7

Stringer, E. (2007). *Action research in education* (3rd ed.). SAGE. http://repository.umpwr.ac.id:8080/bitstream/handle/123456789/3706/Action%20Research.pdf?sequence=1&isAllowed=y

Stringer, E. T., Christensen, L. M., & Baldwin, S. C. (2010). Action research in teaching and learning. In *Integrating teaching, learning, and action research: Enhancing instruction in the K–12 classroom* (pp. 1–14). Sage., doi:10.4135/9781452274775.n1

Subramaniam, S. R., & Muniandy, B. (2019). The effect of flipped classroom on students' engagement. *Technology. Learning and Knowledge*, *24*(3), 355–372. doi:10.100710758-017-9343-y

Svenningsen, L., & Pear, J. J. (2011). Effects of computer-aided personalized system of instruction in developing knowledge and critical thinking in blended learning courses. *The Behavior Analyst Today*, *12*(1), 34–40. doi:10.1037/h0100709

Swan, K., Lee, J., & Grant, S. G. (2018). Questions, tasks, sources: Focusing on the essence of inquiry. *National Council for Social Studies*, *82*(3), 133–137.

Swenson, P., & Taylor, N. A. (2012). Online Teaching in the Digital Age. *Sage (Atlanta, Ga.)*. Advance online publication. libezproxy.open.ac.uk/. doi:10.4135/9781452244174

Tabor, S. W. (2007). Narrowing the distance: Implementing a hybrid learning model for information security education. *Quarterly Review of Distance Education*, *8*(1), 47–57.

Tafazoli, D., & Golshan, N. (2014). Review of computer-assisted language learning: History, merits & barriers. International Journal of Language and Linguistics, 2(5–1), 32–38. doi:10.11648/j.ijll.s.2014020501.15

Tafazoli, D., Gómez-Parra, M. E., & Huertas-Abril, C. A. (2017). A cross-cultural study on the attitudes of English language students towards Computer-Assisted Language Learning. *Teaching English with Technology*, *18*(2), 34–68. https://bit.ly/2q9YNtB

Tafazoli, D., Huertas-Abril, C. A., & Gómez-Parra, M. E. (2019). Technology-based review on Computer-Assisted Language Learning: A chronological perspective. *Pixel-Bit. Revista de Medios y Educación*, *54*(54), 29–43. doi:10.12795/pixelbit.2019.i54.02

Talbert, R. (2017). *Flipped learning: A guide for higher education faculty*. Stylus Publishing, LLC.

Compilation of References

Tallent-Runnels, M. K., Thomas, J. A., Lan, W. Y., Cooper, S., Ahern, T. C., Shaw, S. M., & Liu, X. (2006). Teaching courses online: A review of the research. *Review of Educational Research*, *76*(1), 93–135. doi:10.3102/00346543076001093

Tam, M. (2000). Constructivism, instructional design, and technology: Implications for transforming distance learning. *Journal of Educational Technology & Society*, *3*(2), 50–60.

Tan, M. Y. (2021). Discourses and discursive identities of teachers working as university-based teacher educators in Singapore. *Journal of Teacher Education*, *72*(1), 100–112. doi:10.1177/0022487119896777

Tauber, R. T. (2007a). Bullying. In Classroom management: Sound theory and effective practice (4th ed., pp. 333–345 & 369–370). Praeger Publishers.

Tauber, R. T. (2007b). Violence in today's schools. In Classroom management: Sound theory and effective practice (4th ed., pp. 347–353 & 365–368). Praeger Publishers.

Taylor, E. W., & Cranton, P. A. A. (2012). *The handbook of transformative learning: Theory, research, and practice* (1st ed.). Jossey-Bass.

Teater, M., & Ludgate, J. (2014). *Overcoming compassion fatigue: A practical resilience workbook*. PESI Publishing and Media.

Teshale, S. M., & Lackman, M. E. (2016). Managing daily happiness: The relationship between selection, optimization, and compensation strategies and well-being in adulthood. *Psychology and Aging*, *31*(7), 687–692. doi:10.1037/pag0000132 PMID:27831710

Thanukos, A., Scotchmoor, J., Caldwell, R., & Lindberg, D. R. (2010). Science 101: Building the foundation for real understanding. *Science*, *330*(6012), 1764–1765. doi:10.1126cience.1186994 PMID:21127217

Tichnor-Wagner, A., Parkhouse, H., Glazier, J., & Cain, J. M. (2016). Expanding approaches to teaching for diversity and social justice in K-12 education: Fostering global citizenship across the content areas. *Education Policy Analysis Archives*, *24*(59), 1–31. doi:10.14507/epaa.24.2138

Tichnor-Wagner, A., Parkhouse, H., Glazier, J., & Cain, J. M. (2019). *Becoming a globally competent teacher*. ASCD.

Timperley, H. (2011). *Realizing the power of professional learning*. McGraw-Hill.

Todd, A. R., Bodenhausen, G. V., & Galinsky, A. D. (2012). Perspective taking combats the denial of intergroup discrimination. *Journal of Experimental Social Psychology*, *48*(3), 738–745. doi:10.1016/j.jesp.2011.12.011

TOEFL ITP Test Taker Handbook. (2016). Education Testing Service.

Tomlinson, C. A., & Moon, T. R. (2013). *Assessment and student success in a differentiated classroom*. ASCD.

Toquero, C. M. (2020). Challenges and opportunities for higher education amid the COVID-19 pandemic: The Philippine context. *Pedagogical Research*, *5*(4), em0063. Advance online publication. doi:10.29333/pr/7947

Trigos-Carrillo, L. (2019). Community cultural wealth and literacy capital in Latin American communities. *English Teaching*, *19*(1), 3–19. doi:10.1108/ETPC-05-2019-0071

Trigos-Carrillo, L., Fonseca, L., & Reinoso, N. (2020). Social impact of a transformative service-learning experience in a post-conflict setting. *Frontiers in Psychology*, *11*(47), 1–12. doi:10.3389/fpsyg.2020.00047 PMID:32038445

Trotter, Y. D. (2006). Adult learning theories: Impacting professional development programs. *Delta Kappa Gamma Bulletin*, *72*(2), 8–13.

Trout, M. (2012). *Making the moment matter: Care theory for teacher learning*. Sense Publishers. doi:10.1007/978-94-6209-110-8

Trout, M., & Basford, L. (2016). Preventing the shut-down: Embodied critical care in a teacher educator's practice. *Action in Teacher Education*, *38*(4), 358–370. doi:10.1080/01626620.2016.1226204

Trust, T. (2017). Motivation, empowerment, and innovation: Teachers' beliefs about how participating in the Edmodo math subject community shapes teaching and learning. *Journal of Research on Technology in Education*, *49*(1–2), 16–30. doi:10.1080/15391523.2017.1291317

Tuck, E. (2009). Theorizing back: An approach to participatory policy analysis. In J. Anyon (Ed.), *Theory and educational research: Toward critical social explanation* (pp. 111–130). Routledge.

Tucker, B. (2012). The flipped classroom: Online instruction at home frees class time for learning. *Education Next*, *12*(1). https://www.educationnext.org/the-flipped-classroom/

Turvey, K. (2008). Student teachers go online; the need for a focus on human agency and pedagogy in learning about 'e-learning' in initial teacher education (ITE). *Education and Information Technologies*, *13*(10), 317–327. doi:10.100710639-008-9072-x

Ulbrich, F., Jahnke, I., & Mårtensson, P. (2011). Special issue on knowledge development and the net generation. *International Journal of Sociotechnology and Knowledge Development*, *2*(4), i–ii.

UNESCO & IESALC. (2020). *COVID-19 and higher education: Today and tomorrow. Impact analysis, policy responses and recommendations*. https://bit.ly/34TOSvu

UNESCO. (2015). *Rethinking education: Towards a global common good*. UNESCO. https://unesdoc.unesco.org/images/0023/002325/232555e.pdf

UNESCO. (2020). *How to plan distance learning solutions during temporary schools closures*. https://en.unesco.org/news/covid-19-10-recommendations-plan-distance-learning-solutions

UNESCO. (n.d.). *UNESCO*. Obtenido de https://en.unesco.org/creative-cities/home

University of California Museum of Paleontology. (2021). Real process of science [Illustration]. *Understanding How Science Really Works*. https://undsci.berkeley.edu/search/imagedetail.php?id=19&topic_id=&keywords=

Urban, E. R., Navarro, M., & Borron, A. (2018). TPACK to GPACK? The examination of the technological pedagogical content knowledge framework as a model for global integration into college of agriculture classrooms. *Teaching and Teacher Education*, *73*, 81–89. doi:10.1016/j.tate.2018.03.013

UVA Center for Teaching Excellence. (2020). *Applying the community of inquiry framework*. https://cte.virginia.edu/resources/applying-community-inquiry-framework

Valdemoros-San-Emeterio, M. Á., Ponce-De-León-Elizondo, A., & Sanz-Arazuri, E. (2011). Fundamentos en el manejo del NVIVO 9 como herramienta al servicio de estudios cualitativos. *Contextos Educativos: Revista de Educación*, *14*, 11–29. https://bit.ly/3i503IA

Van de Walle, J. A., Karp, K. S., & Bay-Williams, J. M. (2019). *Elementary and middle school mathematics: Teaching developmentally* (10th ed.). Pearson.

Van Lancker, W., & Parolin, Z. (2020). COVID-19, school closures, and child poverty: A social crisis in the making. *The Lancet Public Health*, *5*(5), e243–e244.

Compilation of References

Van Manen, M. (1991). Reflectivity and the pedagogical moment: The normativity of pedagogical thinking and acting. *Journal of Curriculum Studies, 23*(6), 507–536. doi:10.1080/0022027910230602

Vanassche, E., & Kelchtermans, G. (2015). The state of the art in self-study of teacher education practices: A systematic literature review. *Journal of Curriculum Studies, 47*(4), 508–528. doi:10.1080/00220272.2014.995712

Vansteenkiste, M., Ryan, R. M., & Soenens, B. (2020). Basic psychological need theory: Advancements, critical themes, and future directions. *Motivation and Emotion, 44*(1), 1–31. doi:10.100711031-019-09818-1

Vaughan, M., & Burnaford, G. (2016). Action research in graduate teacher education: A review of the literature 2000-2015. *Educational Action Research, 24*(2), 280–299. doi:10.1080/09650792.2015.1062408

Vaughn, L. M., Jacquez, F., Zhen-Duan, J., Graham, C., Marschner, D., Peralta, J., García, H., Recino, M., Maya, M., Maya, E., Cabrera, M., & Ley, I. (2017). Latinos Unidos por la Salud: The process of developing an immigrant community research team. *Collaborations: A Journal of Community-Based Research and Practice, 1*(1). http://scholarlyrepository.miami.edu/ collaborations/vol1/iss1/2

Ventura, A. (2018). Action research to improve higher education. In J. Calder & J. Foletta (Eds.), *Participatory) action research: Principles, approaches, and applications* (pp. 197–213). Nova Science.

Videnovik, M., Kiønig, L. V., Vold, T., & Trajkovik, V. (2018). Kahooting and learning: A study from Macedonia and Norway. In *Proceedings of the European Conference on Games Based Learning*. Academic Conferences International Limited.

VIF. (2014). *Global-ready teaching indicators by grade level*. Partnership for 21st Century Learning.

Villegas-Reimers, E. (2003). *Teacher professional development; an international review of literature*. UNESCO: International Institute for Educational Planning. http://www.unesco.org/iiep

Viner, R. M., Russell, S. J., Croker, H., Packer, J., Ward, J., Stansfield, C., Mytton, O., Bonnell, C., & Booy, R. (2020). School closure and management practices during coronavirus outbreaks including COVID-19: A rapid systematic review. *The Lancet Child & Adolescent Health, 4*(5), 397–404.

Voss, H. C., Mathews, L. R., Fossen, T., Scott, G., & Schaefer, M. (2015). Community–academic partnerships: Developing a service–learning framework. *Journal of Professional Nursing, 31*(5), 395–401. doi:10.1016/j.profnurs.2015.03.008 PMID:26428344

Vygotsky, L. S. (1938/1978). *Mind in society: The development of higher psychological processes*. Harvard University Press.

Vygotsky, L. S. (1978). *Mind in society: The development of higher mental processes*. Harvard University Press.

Wadsworth, Y. (1998). What is participatory action research? *Action Research International*. Paper 2. http://www.aral.com.au/ari/p-ywadsworth98.html

Wahlstrom, K. L., & Louis, K. S. (2008). How teachers experience principal leadership: The roles of professional community, trust, efficacy, and shared responsibility. *Educational Administration Quarterly, 44*(4), 458–495. doi:10.1177/0013161X08321502

Waldner, L. S., & Hunter, D. (2008). Client-based courses: Variations in service learning. *Journal of Public Affairs Education, 14*(2), 219–239. doi:10.1080/15236803.2008.12001521

Waldner, L. S., McGorry, S. Y., & Widener, M. C. (2010). Extreme e-service learning (XE-SL): E-service learning in the 100% online course. *Journal of Online Learning and Teaching, 6*(4), 839–851.

Waldner, L. S., McGorry, S. Y., & Widener, M. C. (2012). E-service-learning: The evolution of service-learning to engage a growing online student population. *Journal of Higher Education Outreach & Engagement, 16*(2), 123–150. https://files.eric.ed.gov/fulltext/EJ975813.pdf

Walker-Floyd, L. K. (2014). Individual action research: The PARJ and self study. Academic Press.

Walshaw, M., & Anthony, G. (2008). The teacher's role in classroom discourse: A review of recent research into mathematics classrooms. *Review of Educational Research, 78*(3), 516–551. doi:10.3102/0034654308320292

Wang, C., Horby, P. W., Hayden, F. G., & Ga, G. F. (2020). A novel coronavirus outbreak of global health concern. *Lancet, 395*(10223), 470–473. doi:10.1016/S0140-6736(20)30185-9 PMID:31986257

Wang, C., Pan, R., Wan, X., Tan, Y., Xu, L., Ho, C. S., & Ho, R. C. (2020). Immediate psychological responses and associated factors during the initial stage of the 2019 coronavirus disease (COVID-19) epidemic among the general population in China. *International Journal of Environmental Research and Public Health, 17*(5), 1729. Advance online publication. doi:10.3390/ijerph17051729 PMID:32155789

Wang, C., Polly, D., LeHew, A. J., Pugalee, D. K., & Lambert, R. (2013). Supporting teachers' enactment of an elementary school student-centered mathematics pedagogies: The evaluation of a curriculum-focused professional development program. *New Waves- Educational. Research for Development, 16*(1), 76–91. PMID:23154410

Wang, G., Zhang, Y., Zhao, J., Zhang, J., & Jiang, F. (2020). Mitigate the effects of home confinement on children during the COVID-19 outbreak. *Lancet, 395*(10228), 945–947. doi:10.1016/S0140-6736(20)30547-X PMID:32145186

Wang, Q., & Lu, Z. (2012). A case study of using an online community of practice for teachers' professional development at a secondary school in China. *Learning, Media and Technology, 37*(4), 429–446. doi:10.1080/17439884.2012.685077

Wanstreet, C. E., & Stein, D. S. (2011). Presence over time in synchronous communities of inquiry. *American Journal of Distance Education, 25*(3), 1–16. doi:10.1080/08923647.2011.590062

Warren, C. A. (2014). Towards a pedagogy for the application of empathy in culturally diverse classrooms. *The Urban Review, 46*(3), 395–419. doi:10.100711256-013-0262-5

Warren, C. A. (2018). Empathy, teacher dispositions, and preparation for culturally responsive pedagogy. *Journal of Teacher Education, 69*(2), 169–183. doi:10.1177/0022487117712487

Warren, C. A., & Hotchkins, B. K. (2015). Teacher education and the enduring significance of "False empathy". *The Urban Review, 47*(2), 266–292. doi:10.100711256-014-0292-7

Wei, R. C., Darling-Hammond, L., & Adamson, F. (2010). Professional development in the United States: Trends and challenges (Technical report). Stanford Center for Opportunity Policy in Education.

Wei, R. C., Darling-Hammond, L., Andree, A., Richardson, N., & Orphanos, S. (2009). *Professional learning in the learning profession: A status report on teacher development in the United States and abroad.* National Staff Development Council. https://edpolicy.stanford.edu/

Wenger, E. (1998). *Communities of practice.* Cambridge University Press. doi:10.1017/CBO9780511803932

Wennergren, A., & Ronnerman, K. (2006). The relation between tools used in action research and the zone of proximal development. *Educational Action Research, 14*(4), 547–568. doi:10.1080/09650790600975791

Whiteside, A. L. (2015). Introducing the social presence model to explore online and blended learning experiences. *Online Learning, 19*(2), n2. doi:10.24059/olj.v19i2.453

Whitford, D. K., & Emerson, A. M. (2019). Empathy intervention to reduce implicit bias in pre-service teachers. *Psychological Reports*, *122*(2), 670–688. doi:10.1177/0033294118767435 PMID:29621945

Wiley, J., & Ash, I. K. (2005). Multimedia learning in history. In R. E. Mayer (Ed.), *The Cambridge handbook of multimedia learning* (pp. 375–392). Cambridge University Press. doi:10.1017/CBO9780511816819.025

Williamson, B., Eynon, R., & Potter, J. (2020). Pandemic politics, pedagogies and practices: Digital technologies and distance education during the Coronavirus Emergency. *Learning, Media and Technology*, *45*(2), 107–114. doi:10.1080/17439884.2020.1761641

Willis, J., & Edwards, C. (2014). Varieties of action research. Academic Press.

Willis, C. E., & Casamassa, M. (2014). *Action research: Models, methods, and examples*. Information Age Publishing.

Willis, J., & Edwards, C. (2014). *Theoretical foundations for the practice of action research*. Academic Press.

Wong, K. M., & Moorhouse, B. L. (2020). The impact of social uncertainty, protests, and COVID-19 on Hong Kong teachers. *Journal of Loss and Trauma*, *25*(3), 649–655. doi:10.1080/15325024.2020.1776523

Woo, Y., & Reeves, T. C. (2007). Meaningful interaction in web-based learning: A social constructivist interpretation. *The Internet and Higher Education*, *10*(1), 15–25. doi:10.1016/j.iheduc.2006.10.005

Xu, D., & Jaggars, S. S. (2014). Performance gaps between online and face-to-face courses: Differences across types of students and academic subject areas. *The Journal of Higher Education*, *85*(5), 633–659. doi:10.1353/jhe.2014.0028

Yadav, N., Gupta, K., & Khetrapal, V. (2018). Next education: Technology transforming education. *South Asian Journal of Business and Management Cases.*, *7*(1), 68–77. doi:10.1177/2277977918754443

Yandell, J. (2020). Learning under lockdown: English teaching in the time of Covid-19. *Changing English*, *27*(3), 262–269. doi:10.1080/1358684X.2020.1779029

Yang, D., Tu, C., & Dai, X. (2020). The effect of the 2019 novel coronavirus pandemic on college students in Wuhan. *Psychological Trauma: Theory, Research, Practice, and Policy*, *12*(S1), S6–S14. doi:10.1037/tra0000930 PMID:32551764

Yemini, M., Tibbitts, F., & Goren, H. (2019). Trends and caveats: Review of literature on global citizenship education in teacher training. *Teaching and Teacher Education*, *77*(1), 77–89. doi:10.1016/j.tate.2018.09.014

Yin, R. K. (2018). *Case study research: Design and methods* (6th ed.). Sage.

Zeichner, K. (2007). Accumulating knowledge across self-studies in teacher education. *Journal of Teacher Education*, *58*(1), 36–46. doi:10.1177/0022487106296219

Zeni, J. (2001). A guide to ethical decision making for insider research. In J. Zeni (Ed.), *Ethical issues in practitioner research* (pp. 153–165). Teachers College Press.

Zhang, W., Wang, Y., Yang, L., & Wang, C. (2020). Suspending classes without stopping learning: China's education emergency management policy in the COVID-19 outbreak. *Journal of Risk and Financial Management*, *13*(3), 55–61. doi:10.3390/jrfm13030055

Zhao, Y., Meyers, L., & Meyers, B. (2009). Cross-cultural immersion in China: Preparing pre-service elementary teachers to work with diverse student populations in the United States. *Asia-Pacific Journal of Teacher Education*, *37*(3), 295–317. doi:10.1080/13598660903058925

Zong, G. (2009). Developing preservice teachers' global understanding through computer-mediated communication technology. *Teaching and Teacher Education*, *25*(5), 617–625. doi:10.1016/j.tate.2008.09.016

About the Contributors

Phyllis Balcerzak is an Associate Teaching Professor in the College of Education, in the Department of Educator Preparation & Leadership at the University of Missouri, St. Louis (UMSL). She joined the UMSL-COE in 2015 after retiring from her career at Washington University where she was a clinical associate professor of teacher preparation (1996-2006) and director of professional development in science education (2006-2014). During 2015-2020 she served as Co-PI for a National Science Foundation Noyce Teacher Scholarship grant where she designed, implemented, and researched mentoring programs for STEM teachers during their induction years in high-need schools. Balcerzak's teaching interests include advancing the practice of preservice and inservice teachers, introduction to research methods, and project-based STEM instruction. Her research interests are focused on how K-20 educators transfer professional learning to classrooms and the use of action research to document the impact of changes in teaching and learning.

* * *

Stephanie L. Anderson is an Associate Professor in the College of Arts and Sciences. She earned both her MA and PhD in Social Psychology from the University of Kansas, where her research focused on the cultural grounding of personal relationships, specifically with regard to the importance of attraction. She also holds a Bachelor's degree in psychology and sociology (with a minor in Spanish) from University of Nebraska at Kearney (UNK). She says her favorite thing about teaching is seeing students get excited, and she encourages them to push themselves to actively explore, discover, and grow from what they're their learning in the coursework. Dr. Anderson is a faculty advisor for the UAGC Psych Club and the Honors Program, and she serves on the Student Community Standards Committee.

Elena Aydarova is an Assistant Professor of Social Foundations at Auburn University. Her interdisciplinary scholarship examines global neoliberal transformations in education through the lens of equity, diversity, and social justice. Aydarova's book "Teacher Education Reform as Political Theater: Russian Policy Dramas" (2019 with SUNY Press) examines the theatricality of educational policy and the reorientation of educational systems at the service of global corporate sector.

Diana-Elena Banu is an English teacher at Colegiul Național "Andrei Șaguna", a state school in Brașov, Romania. She has been teaching English language and literature at secondary and lower-secondary school, as well as optional courses on the history of the UK and the USA and the culture and civilization of the English-speaking world. She holds a BA in Romanian and English Language and Literature from

About the Contributors

"Transilvania" University of Brașov (Romania, 2004), an MA in Linguistic Studies for Intercultural Communication (Romania, 2006), and a PhD in Literature in English, Postcolonial Studies (Romania, 2010). She has also been an associate professor at the Faculty of Letters of "Transilvania" University of Brasov, where she taught courses on postcolonial discourse, gender discourse, post-war British literature, American Utopia and academic discourse. She has also been a mentor for the students at the Faculty of Letters for over six years. Her interests range from qualitative research (explored in her MA and PhD theses) to improving assessment or enhancing language learning through literature and pop culture.

Andreea-Roxana Bell is an English teacher at Colegiul Național "Andrei Șaguna", a state school in Brașov, Romania. Her experience of English teaching ranges from various educational settings, from university to secondary and lower-secondary school, both public and private. She currently teaches English language to lower-secondary and secondary students, as well as literature to a bilingual English - social science class. In the past she has also taught an optional course on the culture and civilisation of the English-speaking world. She holds a BA in English and French Language and Literature from "Transilvania" University of Brașov (Romania, 1997), an MA in British Cultural Studies from the University of Bucharest (Romania, 1998), and a Postgraduate Certificate in Professional Studies in Education (PGCPSE) – Addressing Inequality and Difference in Educational Practice from The Open University (UK). As a result of her PCPSE she has developed an interest in action research and inclusive practice in education.

Alpana Bhattacharya is an Associate Professor of Educational Psychology in the Secondary Education and Youth Services department at Queens College, the City University of New York (CUNY) and the Ph.D. Program in Educational Psychology at the Graduate Center, CUNY. Her research interest includes literacy acquisition, language development, reading and writing processes, metacognitive strategy instruction, learning disabilities, culturally and linguistically diverse learners, and teacher preparation. Her research contributions include journal articles, book chapters, and conference presentations in the area of learning disabilities, literacy education, and teacher preparation. As an active faculty at Queens College, CUNY and Graduate Center, CUNY, she teaches undergraduate, graduate, and doctoral courses in Educational Psychology including Cognition, Technology, and Instruction for Diverse Learners; Classroom Management; Educational Psychology: Foundations and Contemporary Issues; and Socio-Emotional and Cultural Factors in Development and Education. She also mentors doctoral dissertations in the area of literacy acquisition and language development from early childhood through adulthood.

Constanța Bordea is the Deputy Headteacher at Colegiul Național "Andrei Șaguna", a highly selective state school in Brașov, Romania. She has been an English teacher since 2000. She currently teaches English language to lower-secondary and secondary students. In the past she also taught an optional course on the culture and civilisation of the English-speaking world, as well as literature to bilingual English - social science classes. She has prepared teachers of other subjects to successfully pass Cambridge exams and she has trained teachers of English to evaluate olympiads and nationwide exams. She holds a BA in Romanian and English Language and Literature from "Transilvania" University of Brașov (Romania, 2000). She is a member of the English National Committee, teacher trainer and mentor. As a result of the recent pandemic, she has developed an interest in action research and online education.

Elena-Corina Bularca is an English teacher and currently Head of the English and German Department at Colegiul Național "Andrei Șaguna," a highly-selective state school in Brașov (Romania). Her professional experience includes teaching at all pre-university levels, ranging from primary to upper secondary since 2003. She teaches English language and literature as well as optional courses on debate skills and the culture and civilization of the English-speaking world. She holds a BA in English and Romanian Language and Literature and an MA in the Theory and Practice of Translation in the English Language from "Lucian Blaga" University in Sibiu (Romania). Her main motivation and fulfillment as a teacher is a genuine and engaging interaction with her students, an objective which she could hardly reach when teaching online. To this end she attended the Teaching English Online course on the Future Learn platform, which she found extremely comprehensive, and also became involved in action research in order to further explore and understand the shifts and changes that took place at a deeper level during the pandemic and to what extent they will become mainstream in the future.

Anne Carr teaches in International Studies in the Faculty of Law. She received a Teacher's Certificate from Goldsmith College, University of London, Advanced Teaching Certificate from the Institute of Education, University of London, M.A. from Simon Fraser University, British Columbia Canada and an Ed.D from University of British Columbia. Her research interests are critical internationalization and various sustainable development projects with rural and indigenous communities in southern Ecuador.

Svetlana Chesser is an Assistant Clinical Professor of Educational Psychology at Auburn University. Her primary research examines how early childhood experiences shape adolescents' cognition and behavior. The goal is to identify cognitive and behavioral adaptations to harsh environments in youth who have experienced adversity and design educational interventions that work with, instead of against, these adaptations.

Sarah A. Coppersmith, Ph.D., serves/d as Assistant Research Professor and Adjunct Assistant Professor, University of Missouri-St. Louis College of Education, and as Dissertation Chair, Higher Education Leadership at Maryville University. Serving in the fields of education and geography, she was Library of Congress Grant Coordinator/Adjunct Instructor of Geography at Lindenwood University. While teaching research methods, teacher education courses, and geography, she has been a Fellow in the UMSL Inquiry Circle Program on global competency, Longview Foundation and a classroom teacher. Recent research and publications include examining global competencies and student agency, linguistically and culturally responsive teaching; moral agency beliefs of undergraduates and professors in World Regional Geography, and transformative learning and ambiguity tolerance via geospatial technology and primary sources in K-16 geo-history learning.

Tiffany Cunningham was born and raised in Orcutt, California. She earned her B.S. in Human Development, with a minor in Psychology, from Arizona State University and her M.Ed., with an emphasis on STEAM and Special Populations, from the University of San Diego. She returned to her hometown to teach high school science and has taught a combination of classes, including advanced placement biology, general biology, chemistry, forensic science, integrated science, and conceptual physics. She is currently a doctoral student in the Education for Social Justice program at the University of San Diego, with research interests in the use of home languages in secondary science classrooms.

About the Contributors

Katelyn Durham is an Educational Psychology doctoral student at Auburn University.

Alejandra Enriquez Gates is originally from Sonora, Mexico. Alejandra has over 30 years of international experience in the field of bilingual and multicultural education, English as a Foreign Language (EFL), international partnerships, and intercultural communication. She is a Program Director in the Center for Advanced Studies in Global Education where she supports international initiatives and strategic partnerships. In Alejandra's current role she has directed the Fulbright Distinguished Awards in Teaching Program for International Teachers (Fulbright DAI), and managed a number of international programs such as the Building Leadership for Change through School Immersion Program- Saudi Arabia, Next Generation Leaders- (NGL) Palestine, the Argentina Teacher Exchange Program (AETP) and the USAID- India Support for Teacher Education Program (In-STEP). Alejandra holds a Bachelor's in Science from Tecnológico de Monterrey, a Master's in Bilingual Education from the University of Arizona, and a Master's in Education Technology from Northern Arizona University.

Laura Fonseca is a social and community psychologist. Master in Health, Community and Development from the London School of Economics and Political Science (LSE) and PhD candidate in Social Psychology from LSE. Her research interests are identity processes, reconciliation and peacebuilding in post-agreement Colombia from a critical perspective.

Rebecca Grijalva received her BAE in Elementary Education from Arizona State University in 1989, a Master's Degree in Elementary Education from Northern Arizona University, and a full English as a Second Language endorsement from New Mexico State University. In addition to her degrees, she is also certified in principal and supervisor administration. After 18 years as a classroom teacher, she was hired by ASU in the Mary Lou Fulton Teachers College. Currently, she is the Project Manager for the Building Leadership for Change through School Immersion Project working with a grant awarded in partnership with the Ministry of Education in Saudi Arabia. Part of her work involves working with multiple leadership structures overseeing, managing, and supervising project structures. She has been a teacher for over 30 years working with diverse, traditional, and non-traditional K-20 students. Her research interests include teacher leadership development, English as a Second Language, and professional development.

Shae Hammack is a Masters student of Counselor Education in the University of North Florida's Supporters of Academic Rigor (SOAR) program. She works as a graduate research assistant for the College of Education and Human Services. She received her Bachelor's degree in English Literature from Florida State University, where she earned a membership in Phi Beta Kappa. Her research interests lie in the achievement gap, literacy, social justice advocacy, gifted education, and girls' empowerment.

Kristin E. Harbour is an Assistant Professor of Mathematics Education at the University of South Carolina. Her research focuses on support systems for teachers to advance their inclusive mathematics teaching practices to provide high-quality learning opportunities to all students.

Sherri L. Horner received her doctorate in Educational Psychology from the City University of New York, Graduate Center in 1998. She previously was an Assistant Professor at University of Memphis and is currently an Associate Professor in the School of Educational Foundations, Leadership, and Policy at Bowling Green State University. She writes and presents on emergent literacy development and also teacher preparation for early childhood.

Cristina A. Huertas-Abril belongs to the University of Córdoba (Spain). Her research interests are bilingual education, language gap, CALL and EFL. She has participated in several national and international research projects and published numerous scientific articles in prestigious journals. She is a member of the Research Group 'Research in Bilingual and Intercultural Education' (HUM-1006). She is the co-founder of the Ibero-American Research Network on Bilingual and Intercultural Education (IBIE).

Shea Kerkhoff is an Assistant Professor of literacy and secondary education at the University of Missouri-St. Louis College of Education. She holds a Ph.D. from North Carolina State University in Curriculum and Instruction. Dr. Kerkhoff utilizes mixed methods to investigate critical, digital, and global literacies. In 2018 she was named a Longview Foundation Global Teacher Educator fellow. Her work has been published in Teaching and Teacher Education, Reading and Writing: An Interdisciplinary Journal, and Journal of Adolescent and Adult Literacy.

Ruhi Khan received her Ed.D from Grand Canyon University in Organizational Leadership with an emphasis in Instruction. She joined the Mary Lou Fulton Teachers College at Arizona State University as a Clinical Assistant Professor and Student Teacher Supervisor in the teacher preparation program. In Ruhi's current role as a Project Director for the Center for Advanced Studies in Global Education, she supports international projects in educator professional development and research and also assists with Mary Lou Fulton Teachers College initiatives at a local level. Her experience includes leading the Building Leadership for Change through School Immersion Project to support 105 educators from the Kingdom of Saudi Arabia to develop their teacher leadership skills in collaboration with local school districts. Ruhi is a 16-year veteran classroom teacher and additionally served as a master teacher for two years, conducting teacher evaluations and leading professional development trainings. During her career, she was recognized as Teacher of the Year and also represented the United States as a Delegate for the Chinese Bridge Program. In this capacity, she visited schools in China with 450 American Educational Leaders to exchange best practices with fellow Chinese educators.

Diana Elena Lazăr is an English teacher at Colegiul Național "Andrei Șaguna", a state school in Brașov, Romania. She graduated in 2001 from the University of Bucharest with a Bachelor's Degree in English and Geography. Throughout her career, she has worked with both secondary school and high school students. She has been teaching English language and literature, as well as optional courses on the history of the UK and the USA and on the culture and civilisation of the English-speaking world. Her professional interests include literature, language teaching and teacher development.

Meghan McGlinn Manfra is an Associate Professor in the Department of Teacher Education and Learning Sciences in the College of Education at North Carolina State University. She attended Elon College as a North Carolina Teaching Fellow and began her career as a high school history teacher. She completed a master's degree (MA) in history at the University of North Carolina -Greensboro and received her doctorate (PhD) in education at the University of North Carolina - Chapel Hill. Her research focuses on social studies teacher education, teacher professional learning, and the integration of digital

About the Contributors

technologies into instruction. She is the editor of the Handbook of Social Studies Research and author of Action Research for Classrooms, Schools, and Communities.

Fatemeh Mardi is an engineer and a Project Management Professional. Her passion for teacher education led her to a Master's in TESOL and teaching certificates in math and elementary education. She earned her Ph.D. in Teaching and Learning from the University of Missouri -St. Louis (UMSL), with a focus on instructional technology. At UMSL, she is a post-doctoral fellow writing STEM (science, technology, engineering, and math) grants. She teaches educational technology, math education, and curriculum & instruction. Her research is focused on enhancing student online learning experiences and providing support for teachers. She has experience in teacher education in Iran as well. Her transdisciplinary academic background and cultural competence positions her to facilitate professional learning in a variety of content areas. She is interested in finding ways to integrate skills needed to be a 'literate citizen' in this century (technology, writing, global awareness, growth mindset, and computational thinking) into course content.

Christie Martin is an Associate professor in the Instruction and Teacher Education Department of the University of South Carolina, Columbia. Dr. Martin teaches undergraduate and graduate courses in elementary education and research. Her research focuses on content area literacy in mathematics and science.

Monica Martinez-Sojos is a full time Professor at the Faculty of Law, School of International Studies at Universidad del Azuay, Cuenca-Ecuador. She currently serves as the Academic Coordinator of the School of International Studies. Her prior positions include serving as the Coordinator of Research and Community Service at the Law Faculty, as well as Chief Assistant in the English Department at UDA. She is currently a PhD candidate in Philosophy, Education and Arts at Universidad Nacional de Rosario, Argentina. Her research interests deal with identity, culture, decolonization, education and relations of power. Her ongoing doctoral research explores "New interpretive perspectives of English teaching: Decolonization of knowledge and cultural identity in Ecuador". She has a Master Degree in English Language and Applied Linguistics from Universidad de Cuenca, and her Master's Thesis investigated "Ecuadorian legends and Folktales: A Journey from Storytelling to Reading in the EFL Classroom". She has a degree in Social Communication from Universidad del Azuay, with her thesis "Proposal to create a children's magazine in Cuenca."

Christine McMahon is an Associate Professor and Faculty Lead of the Bachelor of Healthcare Administration, Health and Wellness Emphasis, & Public Health Emphasis at the University of Arizona Global Campus College of Arts and Sciences. She received a Doctorate in Health Education from AT Still University in Kirksville, MO, and a Master's Degree in Exercise Science as well as a Bachelor's Degree in Kinesiology and Sports Studies from Eastern Illinois University in Charleston, IL. She is also a Certified Health Education Specialist and Certified Athletic Trainer. Prior to joining UAGC, she spent 15 years working as the Coordinator of Cardiopulmonary Rehabilitation at Salem Township Hospital in Salem, IL.

Mariana Mereoiu received her doctorate in Special Education from the University of North Carolina at Greensboro in 2011. The same year she was hired as an Assistant Professor at Bowling Green

State University and is currently Associate Professor and co-coordinator of the Inclusive Early Childhood Program in the College of Education and Human Development. She writes and presents on issues focused on collaboration with families and co-educators, cultural and linguistic diversity, and inclusive education teacher preparation.

Alicia A. Mrachko received her doctorate in Special Education and Early Intervention from the University of Pittsburgh in 2015. The same year she was hired as an Assistant Professor at Bowling Green State University. She is currently teaching in the Inclusive Early Childhood undergraduate program and is program coordinator of the Applied Behavior Analysis Master's program. Her research and writing include work on Coaching and Teacher Behavior, Universal Design for Learning, and Program Development.

Ann Nielsen received her Ed.D. from Arizona State University in Educational Leadership and Supervision. Her interests in education and research have focused upon teacher professional subjectivities, teacher leadership, and school leadership using visual and qualitative methodologies. In Ann's current role as the Associate Director of the Center for Advanced Studies in Global Education, she has served as the principal investigator for multiple international initiatives such as the International Leaders in Education Program, the Argentina Teacher Exchange Program, the Exchange Program for Brazilian Awarded Public School Principals, the Fulbright Distinguished Awards in Teaching Program, Building Leadership for Change Through School Immersion -Saudi Arabia and YouLead Youth and Business Start Up Program--Sri Lanka. In addition to leading the implementation of multiple international initiatives, Ann has provided technical expertise and assistance in the West Bank Pre-Service Teacher Activity and the Strengthening Higher Education Access in Malawi Activity. Ann previously served in the role as the TAP Director in the Arizona Ready for Rigor Grant where she oversaw the implementation of the TAP System for Teacher and Student Advancement in 59 schools across the state of Arizona. Ann has trained and collaborated with educators at the pre-service and in-service levels of the profession across Arizona, the United States and internationally.

Svetlana Nikic recently received a Ph.D. in Teaching & Learning Process from the University of Missouri-St. Louis (UMSL, 2021). She also holds two Masters' degrees, one from Washington University in Saint Louis (2001) and the other in Education Administration from UMSL (2019). In addition to her degrees, she is also certified in Educational Administration, Mathematics, Gifted Education, Special Reading and Business. She worked for Saint Louis Public Schools for seven years as a classroom teacher. She also worked for nine years as part-time math and science specialist and taught technical mathematics classes at Southwestern Illinois College. For the past fourteen years, she has been working as an Academic Instructional Coach in Saint Louis Public Schools. She was involved in a global classroom project, a platform that she designed to connect students from Saint Louis Public Schools to students in Neustrelitz, Germany. This research project was presented at national and international conferences. For her many contributions to education, she was recognized as Saint Louis Public School Teacher of the Year and Emerson Electric Educator of the Year in 2006.

Patricia Ortega-Chasi is an Associate Professor in the Department of Computer Science at the Universidad del Azuay (UDA). She currently serves as the Director of the Technological Formation Unit at Universidad del Azuay. Her prior positions include serving as Director of the School of System

About the Contributors

Engineering and Telematics at Universidad del Azuay. She was a recipient of the Fulbright Faculty Development Program scholarship (2012-2014). Her research interests include computer science undergraduate education and the intersection between technology, education, and neuroscience, focusing on exploring ways computer technology can improve education. Dr. Ortega-Chasi earned her Bachelor of Science from Universidad del Azuay, her Master of Sciences in Computer Science and Engineering, and her PhD in Curriculum, Instruction and the Science of Learning (Science Education) from the State University of New York at Buffalo.

Francisco J. Palacios-Hidalgo belongs to the University of Córdoba (Spain). He has experience in TEFL and develops his PhD thesis on the results of Spanish bilingual programs. He is a member of the Ibero-American Network of Bilingual and Intercultural Education (IBIE) and the Research Group 'Research in Bilingual and Intercultural Education' (HUM-1006). His research focuses on second language teaching and learning, bilingual education and educational technologies.

Drew Polly is a professor in the Elementary Education program in the Cato College of Education at the University of North Carolina at Charlotte. His research interests include supporting teacher candidates' and in-service teachers' use of learner-centered pedagogical.

Sandra Rebeor is an Associate Professor and Faculty Lead for the Applied Behavioral Science program in the College of Arts and Sciences. She earned her BBA in Business Administration with a minor in Management at Campbell University and her Master of Science in Health Sciences - Emergency and Disaster Management at Touro College & University System. Dr. Rebeor earned her Psy.D. in Health and Wellness Psychology at the University of Arizona Global Campus (formerly Ashford University). She was born and raised in Germany before coming to the United States. Her professional experience ranges from working with the German government to academic and military environments. Dr. Rebeor enjoys volunteering in her community in varying capacities. Within the online classroom, she loves to connect the learned material to applicable, real-world content to enhance learning but also to aid in the retention of the learned material in the long term.

Han Rong is now an Ed.D. candidate in the College of Education in UMSL majoring in Inquiry, Practice, and Curriculum. Her dissertation is about online collaborative teaching and learning. She will also focus on online construction of courses and instructional design in her future research. As a lecturer, she worked in the Foreign Training Department in Tie Ling Vocational Health College in China from 2009 to 2019. She has published eight academic paper related to English teaching, as well as participated in and completed two scientific research projects. As a co-contributing editor, she published the Basic Course of Medical English in 2011, and as the second editor-in-chief, she published the Medical Literature Retrieval and Paper Writing in 2018.

Michelle L. Rosser-Majors is a full Professor in the College of Arts and Sciences. She currently serves as Lead Faculty of the Bachelor and Master of Arts in Psychology programs. She also serves as faculty advisor for the UAGC Psych Club. Dr. Rosser-Majors is also an author. Her books include Psychology applied: Diverse domains, ample opportunity (2020) (co-author), Theories of Learning: An Exploration (2017), Becoming an Integrated Educational Leader (2014), and Jacob's New School (2014). Book chapters include The Case of the Plagiarized Paragraph: A Practical Exercise to Develop

Academic Voice (in Integrating Writing into the College Classroom: Strategies for Promoting Student Skills). She has presented research at conferences in Portugal, Spain, Canada, Virginia, Louisiana, Florida, Pennsylvania, and New York. She has been an educator for 21 years and feels blessed to be in the profession that encourages students to meet their goals.

Lorena-Mirela Spuderca is an English teacher at Colegiul Național "Andrei Șaguna", a highly-selective school from Brașov, Romania. Her professional experience comprises a variety of educational roles, being a primary school teacher from 1991 to 1998 and teacher of English since 1998. She holds a BA in Romanian and English Language and Literature from "Transilvania" University of Brașov (Romania, 1997). She is a mentor and trainer. She teaches English language and literature, and optional courses on the culture and civilization of the English-speaking world and on geography of the UK and USA. Being particularly interested in methodology, she obtained a Socrates II Programme scholarship and attended the course "Materials, Language and Technology" at Norwich Institute for Learning Education. As a consequence of the current pandemic, she has channeled her efforts into identifying and implementing the most suitable educational strategies adapted to the online environment.

Madalina Tanase is an Associate Professor at the University of North Florida, in the Department of Teaching, Learning, and Curriculum. For the past thirteen years, Dr. Tanase has taught both graduate and undergraduate foundations classes such as classroom management, instructional strategies, and educational psychology. Her research interests include, among others, culturally responsive classroom management and pedagogy.

Lina Trigos-Carrillo is an Associate Professor in the Department of Psychology of Development and Education at Universidad de la Sabana in Chia, Colombia. Lina is a professor of literacy education, community education and qualitative research methods. Lina received a Ph.D. in Learning, Teaching and Curriculum from the University of Missouri and she participated as a research postdoctoral fellow in the Project Strengthening Equity and Effectiveness for Teachers of English Learners (SEE-TEL), a National Professional Development Grant from the U.S. Department of Education. Lina's research focuses on critical sociocultural perspectives to writing and community/family literacies of people of color and multilingual learners across the Americas. She has conducted qualitative research with multilingual families in the US and with diverse families and communities in Mexico, Costa Rica and Colombia. She designs culturally sustaining professional development based on her research experiences in global contexts.

Nada Zaki Wafa is a doctoral student in the Department of Teacher Education and Learning Sciences in the College of Education at North Carolina State University. She completed a master's degree (MS) in New Literacies and Global Learning at North Carolina State University. Prior to starting her master's degree, she was teaching at an International School in Jordan. She completed her bachelors and earned her teaching licensure from North Carolina State University before moving abroad. Her research focuses on the integration of global education in schools, inquiry-based instruction, and infusing digital technologies into teaching and learning. She lives in Raleigh with her husband and three children and enjoys traveling and exploring the world together.

Index

A

academic instructional coach 376-377, 396
action research 1-2, 18-21, 23-32, 37-50, 52, 60-61, 63-68, 70, 72, 74-75, 82-85, 87, 89-94, 96-100, 105-107, 109-113, 121, 127-128, 137-138, 140-147, 150-154, 157, 161, 164, 166, 171, 174, 192, 194, 197, 199-200, 203, 215-217, 219-221, 224-226, 229, 231, 234, 236-242, 245-247, 249-251, 256, 258-261, 264, 266, 269, 282, 284, 286, 288-293, 295-298, 301-309, 311-312, 316-317, 319-322, 338-340, 344, 347, 359, 361-362, 366, 372, 376-380, 384, 393-394, 396-403, 407-411
adult learning 21, 145, 149, 152, 167, 169, 306, 313-314, 369-370, 380, 390, 395
advocacy 147
Assessment Rubric 113
Asynchronous Learning 66, 167, 193-194, 300, 306, 323, 334, 396
Asynchronous Online Classes 317, 341
asynchronous teaching 126, 316, 327, 334
avatar 183, 198, 352

B

breakout sessions 130-131, 135, 137, 143
Building Leadership for Change (BLC) team 290, 309, 314

C

C3 Framework 248-249, 253, 256-257, 259, 261
call 2, 34, 46, 68, 70-73, 85, 88, 94, 99, 130, 158, 332, 375, 393
Canvas 3, 12, 17, 53, 126, 130, 132-135, 137, 143, 356, 402
Capstone Action Research course 23, 27
Care Theory 1, 6, 20-21
caring 1-3, 6-8, 10-19, 21, 25, 92, 94, 126, 312
Caring Relation 6, 21
case analysis 91, 94, 97, 103-104, 158
case-based instruction 91-94, 96-97, 104, 107-109, 113
cast.org 1, 18
challenges 4, 14, 16, 19-20, 23-25, 30-33, 35, 38, 40-44, 48-49, 51-52, 59, 62, 69-70, 76, 78-79, 81-83, 86, 92-93, 116, 121-124, 126, 128-131, 134-141, 146, 157, 159, 171, 187, 189, 193, 199-200, 204, 206, 209, 211, 214, 224, 226, 243, 245-246, 248, 264, 270, 273, 277, 283, 290, 292, 300-301, 303, 307-308, 313, 316-322, 326, 328, 330, 332, 334, 338-339, 353-354, 357-358, 371, 377, 387, 392, 394, 408
Cisgender 226, 243
CK-12 Flexbooks 402, 414
Classroom Action Research 48
classroom management 33, 91-94, 96-101, 103-105, 107-114, 116, 126-127, 154, 159
coaching 62, 94, 241, 290-292, 314, 358, 362, 366-372, 375-382, 384, 386, 389-390, 392-396
coaching strategies 366
cognitive presence 171-173, 175, 177-180, 183-184, 187-189, 192, 195, 198
collaboration 4, 7, 25, 27, 30, 40-41, 47, 60, 83, 96-97, 99, 125, 139, 146, 151, 157-158, 162, 172, 183, 205-206, 246, 250, 256, 258, 265-267, 279, 301, 304, 316, 322, 328-329, 335-338, 341, 349, 356-359, 368-370, 377-378, 383, 390, 392, 395, 410
collaborative learning 48, 91, 107, 150, 270, 319, 359
Colombia 164, 199-202, 205, 208-209, 215-218
community 6, 19, 23, 26-28, 30, 35, 37, 40-41, 43-44, 46, 48-67, 69, 96-97, 125, 131, 134-135, 137, 146-149, 151-152, 156-158, 161, 163-164, 168, 170-174, 178, 181, 183, 192-196, 198-201, 203-216, 238-239, 247, 250-251, 255, 257, 265-267, 276, 279, 282, 288, 300, 303, 313, 316, 318-319, 329, 331, 335, 337-338, 341, 346, 352, 363, 372, 398-399, 409
Community of Inquiry (CoI) Model 171, 173, 198

community of learners 23, 27-28, 40, 43, 46, 48, 125, 134-135, 137, 157, 164, 181
community partner 51-62, 65, 67
community partners 49, 51, 57, 60, 62-64
community work 199-200, 203, 214
Community-Based Participation 49, 67
compelling question 252-256, 261
Conceptual Fluency 364
conceptual framework 53, 90, 93, 95, 111, 142, 268, 289-293, 297, 301, 304, 308-310, 314, 316
conceptual learning 343, 351
connectivity 24, 45, 130, 144, 164
content analysis 68, 70, 76, 78, 87, 128, 139, 229, 347, 384
course measures 100, 106, 113
COVID-19 pandemic 2-4, 7, 16, 24, 26-28, 31-32, 50, 52, 62, 68, 70-72, 74, 80, 83-84, 89-90, 121, 138-139, 141, 150, 168, 199-200, 204, 211, 214, 219, 239, 245, 258, 282, 290, 303, 307, 310, 316-317, 338-339, 344, 346-348, 357, 365-366
CPAR 199-200, 203-214, 217
crisis 1, 3-4, 23-26, 43-45, 47-48, 68, 72-73, 84, 87-90, 139, 171, 199-200, 204, 211, 214, 217, 246, 300, 310, 312, 318, 329, 333, 338-339, 363
critical action research 219, 221, 224, 226, 238-239
critical discourse 219, 221, 242-243
Critical Literacy 146, 169
critical participatory action research 199-200, 203, 217, 219, 225, 241, 284
critical thinking 27, 88, 91, 170, 178-179, 195, 228, 313, 318
cross-cultural learning 264

D

delivery method 292-293, 301, 314
dialogue 4, 26, 41, 97, 144, 152, 154, 158-159, 178, 183, 204, 206, 209, 212, 214, 236, 239, 247, 261, 293-294, 297, 319, 346, 372, 389, 410
digital learning 80, 257, 261-262, 301
digital literacy 48, 269, 285, 288
Digital Skills Training 24, 48
discourse 19, 167, 178, 184, 219, 221-223, 225, 240, 242-243, 344, 346, 349, 351-354, 358, 361, 363-364
discussion board 14, 23, 29-30, 48, 93, 133, 230, 272, 277, 296, 410
distance learning 28, 31, 44, 51, 69, 88, 121, 126, 134, 141-143, 165, 167-168, 198, 259, 331, 339-340, 396-397, 399-402, 407-410

E

Education Experts 314
Emergency Remote Language Teaching 68, 70, 72, 90
emergency remote teaching 68, 72-73, 87, 89-90, 168, 195, 310
empathy 1-3, 5, 7-12, 15-21, 150, 224, 257, 267, 301, 303, 336
engagement 1, 6-8, 15-16, 18, 22-23, 28, 30-33, 35, 38-39, 44, 48, 51, 60, 62, 64, 66, 100-101, 104, 121, 124, 126, 130, 145, 163, 170-172, 176, 178, 180-182, 184, 187-188, 191-192, 194-196, 198, 220-221, 225, 237-238, 248-249, 278, 290, 297, 301, 305, 353-355, 360, 366-367, 370-401, 403-405, 407-410, 413
English for Social Purposes and Cooperation 68-69, 72, 89-90
Epistemic Technologies 169
epistemology 144, 204
ERLT 68, 70-71, 73-84, 90
e-service learning 49, 52-53, 56-57, 59, 61, 66-67
ESoPC 19, 68-85, 90
ETCR 199-201, 217
Experiential Education 50, 64, 67

F

face-to-face instruction 84, 126, 143, 300, 349, 351, 354, 358, 396
Face-to-Face Teaching 336, 341
faculty development 63, 145, 165, 167-168, 170, 197, 318
flipped classroom 328, 333, 341, 354, 397, 399-401, 403, 407, 412-413
formative assessment 9, 152, 159-160, 261, 351-352, 354

G

General and Operations Manager 243
Gizmos 402-403, 406-408, 414
global awareness 259, 266, 277
global citizenship education 146, 165, 169, 265, 267, 281, 286-287
global competence 258, 264-270, 273-274, 277-279, 282-283, 286, 288
global education teacher 245-247, 250, 253, 258-259
global learning 248, 264, 266-268, 270, 273, 277-280, 282, 288
global readiness 264, 267-268, 270, 283-284, 288
Globally Competent Learning Continuum 288

Index

globally competent teaching 264, 266, 268, 270-271, 273, 276-278, 282-283, 286, 288
Google Forms From Kesler Science 403, 414
graduate students 3, 23-25, 27-29, 31-33, 35, 37-39, 41, 45, 113, 127, 130, 203, 220, 237
grammarly 186, 198
Grounded Theory 45, 68, 76-77, 86, 88, 90, 250
guerrilla member 204, 206, 217

H

Hermeneutic 146, 169
horizontal relationships 200, 206, 212, 214
Hybrid Instructions 396
hybrid teaching 48, 316-317, 320, 322, 324-325, 328, 331, 334, 337-338, 342

I

identity 9, 51, 148, 154, 219-226, 234, 238-240, 242-243, 282, 284, 295, 312, 411
IEP (Individualized Educational Plan) 48
Imagine Other (IO) 5, 21
Imagine Self (IS) 5, 21
in 1-101, 103-116, 121-176, 178-189, 191-231, 234-243, 245-262, 264-274, 276-288, 290-298, 300-314, 316-414
inquiry-based 245-250, 252, 255-258, 261, 270, 407, 413
in-service teachers 90, 93-94, 97-101, 103-109, 113, 266, 276
instructional feedback 366-368, 371-372, 376-377, 379-380, 382, 384, 386, 389-390, 392, 396
Instructor Presence (IP) 170-172, 198

K

Kesler Science 403, 405, 407, 414
Khan Academy 400, 403, 414

L

language acquisition 86, 276, 289-290, 292, 295-296, 305, 307-308, 310, 312, 314

M

Managerialism in Education 169
manipulatives 347-350, 355, 357-359, 361, 364
mathematical discourse 343-344, 346, 351-352, 364
mathematical representations 347-348, 359, 364

mathematical tasks 343, 345-346, 352, 362-363
mathematics 98, 138, 270, 283, 320, 332, 343-354, 356-365, 376
Mental Health Counselor 227, 243
Mixed-Methods Analysis 68
multilingualism 282

N

National Council of Teachers of Mathematics (NCTM) 343, 364
Nearpod 351-352, 360, 378, 382, 384, 387, 389, 402, 405-408, 414
Needs of Educators 314
Nel Noddings 1

O

older women and career change 239
online learning 24-26, 48-51, 66-67, 87, 121-125, 128-133, 138-139, 143, 148, 165, 167-168, 170-171, 182, 191-193, 195-198, 245, 264, 289-291, 300-301, 303, 305, 312, 314, 318, 325-326, 330, 332, 334-335, 337-341, 358, 399-402, 404, 413
online presence 6, 60, 121, 134, 136
online teaching 20, 50, 52, 72, 84, 90, 122-123, 125-126, 128-129, 134-140, 142, 144-147, 159, 163-168, 173, 195, 197, 280, 316-320, 322-327, 329-333, 335-342, 355, 358

P

participatory action research 18, 47, 140-141, 144, 146, 150, 152-153, 161, 164, 199-200, 203, 215-217, 219, 224-225, 241, 284
peace agreement 199, 201-202, 206, 218
Peace Studies 199, 216
peacebuilding 199-200, 204, 212-213, 215, 217
personalized system of instruction 289-290, 292, 296, 305, 308, 310, 312-314
perspective taking 1, 5-6, 15-16, 18-20, 22, 257
PhET simulations 402-403, 408, 414
Pivot Interactives 397, 402-403, 405-406, 408, 414
post-conflict 200, 203-204, 216
Postsecondary Teacher 243
practitioner inquiry 91, 112
preservice teachers 49, 51, 55, 57, 60, 63, 95, 101, 108, 111, 126, 241, 266, 286-287
privilege 3, 206, 219, 226, 238-240, 243, 310
problem solving 43, 91, 93, 95, 97, 105, 107-108, 110, 158, 187, 229, 236-237, 248, 296, 320, 346

procedural fluency 345-346, 352, 364
procedural learning 343
professional development 19, 24, 92, 101, 110, 112, 125, 139, 144-149, 152, 161, 163-168, 173, 192, 237, 256, 283, 286, 289-292, 297, 300-302, 305, 308-311, 313-314, 322, 325-326, 333, 338, 341, 344, 347, 352, 356-363, 366-370, 372, 377-378, 380, 382-383, 392-396, 402
professional identity 219-221, 226, 234, 238, 243
Professional Learning Communities 125, 355-356, 359, 364, 377, 395
Programmatic Adjustments 309, 314

Q

Qualitative data 53, 87, 174, 216, 285, 361, 377
qualitative study 51, 88, 128, 267, 351, 355

R

reflection 6, 27, 39, 53-55, 57-58, 60-62, 65, 67, 70, 72, 74, 80, 83, 92-97, 99-100, 105, 107, 113, 126, 138, 146, 149-152, 156-157, 160-161, 163, 178-179, 185, 219, 225, 236, 239, 276-280, 290, 293-294, 296, 308, 312, 317, 319, 339, 348, 369-370, 378, 380-381, 397, 399
reflection journal 53, 55, 57
reflection-in-action 316, 319, 337-338
reflective practice 43, 87, 91-94, 96, 111, 113, 238, 242, 289, 316, 319, 339, 342, 347, 394
reincorporation process 201, 208, 217-218
Remote Instruction 49, 121, 126, 134, 143
resilience 23, 25-26, 30, 35-37, 43-48, 359
Resilient Teaching Techniques 48
retention 170-173, 176, 181, 187-188, 192, 194-195, 197
rubric 64, 104, 113, 156-157, 169, 175, 179, 185, 198, 288, 380-382, 384, 386
rurality 218

S

satisfaction 26, 51-52, 56-58, 62, 137, 170-172, 175-176, 187, 191-192, 195-197, 213, 224, 241
Science Education 52, 139, 397, 412
scientific method 397-399, 409
self-reflexivity 164, 169, 225, 238
self-study 91-93, 96-97, 110, 112-113, 219, 221, 224-226, 239-241, 243, 285, 316-317, 320
semantic analysis 77
service-learning 49-54, 60-67, 204, 215-216

simulation 107, 255, 280, 403, 414
Situated learning 26, 46, 48, 147, 149, 166, 243
social goods 222, 226, 243
social presence 175, 181-184, 187-188, 194-195, 198
strength 13-14, 17, 25, 37, 39, 43, 187, 273, 276, 290, 409
stress 4, 13, 23-24, 26, 28, 30-32, 34-35, 39, 41-42, 44, 46, 48, 71, 81, 123, 137, 215, 301, 303, 344, 348
student engagement 1, 6-8, 16, 18, 22, 32-33, 38, 44, 48, 51, 121, 126, 145, 172, 178, 194-195, 248, 353, 366, 386-387, 392, 395, 397, 400-401, 403, 407
success 12, 14, 17, 19, 35, 38, 56, 60-62, 122, 124, 126, 170-174, 179, 181, 184, 186-189, 192-193, 195, 197-198, 246, 265, 273, 277, 291, 296, 303-304, 308, 310, 361, 368, 372, 392, 394, 399-404, 410-411, 413
summative assessment 160, 163, 261, 352
supporting questions 248-249, 252-254, 256, 261
synchronous learning 323, 334, 396
Synchronous Online Classes 317, 342
synchronous teaching 316, 327
Systemic Racism 243

T

teacher candidates 26, 45, 91-92, 95-97, 107-109, 113, 126, 266-267, 285, 344, 359
teacher education 1-2, 20-21, 25-26, 43-46, 49, 52, 64, 67-68, 74-76, 84-85, 87-90, 92, 96, 98, 101, 108, 110-113, 138-139, 141-142, 166-167, 225-226, 240, 242-243, 259, 264, 266, 280, 282-287, 310-311, 339-341, 344, 347, 358-362, 396, 413
Teacher Effectiveness 366-367
teacher preparation 5, 19, 49-50, 67, 91-94, 96, 98, 100-101, 107-110, 113, 285-286, 344
teacher-researchers 23-25, 31-34, 40, 43, 85
Teaching for Global Readiness Scale 284, 288
teaching presence 175, 184-188, 193, 197-198, 413
technology 24, 31-34, 36, 62, 65, 70-72, 74, 82-84, 87-90, 110, 123-126, 131-132, 140-143, 145, 147-148, 156-157, 165-168, 172, 194, 196, 198, 217, 245-250, 253-259, 265-268, 279-281, 283-285, 287, 290, 296-297, 300-301, 303, 305, 310, 316-319, 322, 324-325, 328, 331-333, 335-336, 338-341, 343, 348-349, 354-365, 377-378, 387, 392, 395, 405, 407-408, 411-413
TELL 5, 7, 36, 68, 70-73, 86, 88, 239, 330, 366
TPACK 147-148, 165, 264, 267-268, 280-281, 285, 287-288, 362
transformation 84, 144-146, 194, 197, 214, 217, 225, 292-295, 304, 307, 380, 393, 395

Index

transformative learning 146, 149, 159, 163-164, 166-169, 266, 285, 289, 292-294, 296, 304, 308, 310-314, 341
transformative learning theory 164, 289, 292-294, 296, 308, 314
trauma 23-26, 28, 43, 46-48, 301, 303
Trauma-Informed Teaching Approach 48

U

UDL 1-2, 5-8, 10-13, 15-17, 22
Universal Design for Learning (UDL) 1, 6, 22
university-based researcher 245-246, 249, 256, 258

V

Valediction 183, 198
Virtual Instructions 396

virtual learning environment 267, 351, 365
virtual manipulatives 350, 358-359, 364
Vocative Case 183, 198
VoiceThread 29, 48

W

white privilege 219, 226
Whole Teacher approach 289-292, 301, 304-305, 307-310

Z

Zoom 3, 9, 14-17, 29, 31, 33, 41, 48, 53, 57, 61-62, 74, 81, 130-132, 143, 157-159, 162, 164, 209, 215, 236-237, 280, 296, 300-301, 325, 333, 351, 357, 402, 404-405

Recommended Reference Books

IGI Global's reference books are available in three unique pricing formats:
Print Only, E-Book Only, or Print + E-Book.

Shipping fees may apply.

www.igi-global.com

Learning and Performance Assessment
ISBN: 978-1-7998-0420-8
EISBN: 978-1-7998-0421-5
© 2020; 1,757 pp.
List Price: US$ **1,975**

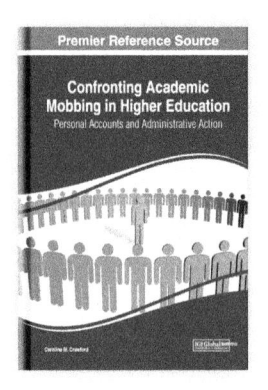

Confronting Academic Mobbing in Higher Education
ISBN: 978-1-5225-9485-7
EISBN: 978-1-5225-9487-1
© 2020; 301 pp.
List Price: US$ **195**

Cases on Models and Methods for STEAM Education
ISBN: 978-1-5225-9631-8
EISBN: 978-1-5225-9637-0
© 2020; 379 pp.
List Price: US$ **195**

Teaching, Learning, and Leading With Computer Simulations
ISBN: 978-1-7998-0004-0
EISBN: 978-1-7998-0006-4
© 2020; 337 pp.
List Price: US$ **195**

Form, Function, and Style in Instructional Design
ISBN: 978-1-5225-9833-6
EISBN: 978-1-5225-9835-0
© 2020; 203 pp.
List Price: US$ **155**

Emerging Methods and Paradigms in Scholarship and Education Research
ISBN: 978-1-7998-1001-8
EISBN: 978-1-7998-1003-2
© 2020; 330 pp.
List Price: US$ **195**

Do you want to stay current on the latest research trends, product announcements, news, and special offers?
Join IGI Global's mailing list to receive customized recommendations, exclusive discounts, and more.
Sign up at: **www.igi-global.com/newsletters.**

Publisher of Peer-Reviewed, Timely, and Innovative Academic Research

IGI Global
PUBLISHER of TIMELY KNOWLEDGE

www.igi-global.com | Sign up at www.igi-global.com/newsletters | facebook.com/igiglobal | twitter.com/igiglobal | linkedin.com/igiglobal

Ensure Quality Research is Introduced to the Academic Community

Become an Evaluator for IGI Global Authored Book Projects

The overall success of an authored book project is dependent on quality and timely manuscript evaluations.

Applications and Inquiries may be sent to:
development@igi-global.com

Applicants must have a doctorate (or equivalent degree) as well as publishing, research, and reviewing experience. Authored Book Evaluators are appointed for one-year terms and are expected to complete at least three evaluations per term. Upon successful completion of this term, evaluators can be considered for an additional term.

If you have a colleague that may be interested in this opportunity, we encourage you to share this information with them.

IGI Global Author Services

Providing a high-quality, affordable, and expeditious service, IGI Global's Author Services enable authors to streamline their publishing process, increase chance of acceptance, and adhere to IGI Global's publication standards.

Benefits of Author Services:

- **Professional Service:** All our editors, designers, and translators are experts in their field with years of experience and professional certifications.
- **Quality Guarantee & Certificate:** Each order is returned with a quality guarantee and certificate of professional completion.
- **Timeliness:** All editorial orders have a guaranteed return timeframe of 3-5 business days and translation orders are guaranteed in 7-10 business days.
- **Affordable Pricing:** IGI Global Author Services are competitively priced compared to other industry service providers.
- **APC Reimbursement:** IGI Global authors publishing Open Access (OA) will be able to deduct the cost of editing and other IGI Global author services from their OA APC publishing fee.

Author Services Offered:

English Language Copy Editing
Professional, native English language copy editors improve your manuscript's grammar, spelling, punctuation, terminology, semantics, consistency, flow, formatting, and more.

Scientific & Scholarly Editing
A Ph.D. level review for qualities such as originality and significance, interest to researchers, level of methodology and analysis, coverage of literature, organization, quality of writing, and strengths and weaknesses.

Figure, Table, Chart & Equation Conversions
Work with IGI Global's graphic designers before submission to enhance and design all figures and charts to IGI Global's specific standards for clarity.

Translation
Providing 70 language options, including Simplified and Traditional Chinese, Spanish, Arabic, German, French, and more.

Hear What the Experts Are Saying About IGI Global's Author Services

"Publishing with IGI Global has been **an amazing experience** for me for sharing my research. The **strong academic production** support ensures quality and timely completion." – **Prof. Margaret Niess, Oregon State University, USA**

"The service was **very fast, very thorough, and very helpful** in ensuring our chapter meets the criteria and requirements of the book's editors. I was **quite impressed and happy** with your service." – **Prof. Tom Brinthaupt, Middle Tennessee State University, USA**

Learn More or Get Started Here:

For Questions, Contact IGI Global's Customer Service Team at cust@igi-global.com or 717-533-8845

IGI Global
PUBLISHER of TIMELY KNOWLEDGE
www.igi-global.com

InfoSci®-Books

Celebrating Over 30 Years of Scholarly Knowledge Creation & Dissemination

www.igi-global.com

InfoSci®-Books

A Database of Nearly 6,000 Reference Books Containing Over 105,000+ Chapters Focusing on Emerging Research

GAIN ACCESS TO **THOUSANDS** OF REFERENCE BOOKS AT **A FRACTION** OF THEIR INDIVIDUAL LIST **PRICE**.

InfoSci®-Books Database

The **InfoSci®-Books** is a database of nearly 6,000 IGI Global single and multi-volume reference books, handbooks of research, and encyclopedias, encompassing groundbreaking research from prominent experts worldwide that spans over 350+ topics in 11 core subject areas including business, computer science, education, science and engineering, social sciences, and more.

Open Access Fee Waiver (Read & Publish) Initiative

For any library that invests in IGI Global's InfoSci-Books and/or InfoSci-Journals (175+ scholarly journals) databases, IGI Global will match the library's investment with a fund of equal value to go toward **subsidizing the OA article processing charges (APCs) for their students, faculty, and staff** at that institution when their work is submitted and accepted under OA into an IGI Global journal.*

INFOSCI® PLATFORM FEATURES

- Unlimited Simultaneous Access
- No DRM
- No Set-Up or Maintenance Fees
- A Guarantee of No More Than a 5% Annual Increase for Subscriptions
- Full-Text HTML and PDF Viewing Options
- Downloadable MARC Records
- COUNTER 5 Compliant Reports
- Formatted Citations With Ability to Export to RefWorks and EasyBib
- No Embargo of Content (Research is Available Months in Advance of the Print Release)

*The fund will be offered on an annual basis and expire at the end of the subscription period. The fund would renew as the subscription is renewed for each year thereafter. The open access fees will be waived after the student, faculty, or staff's paper has been vetted and accepted into an IGI Global journal and the fund can only be used toward publishing OA in an IGI Global journal. Libraries in developing countries will have the match on their investment doubled.

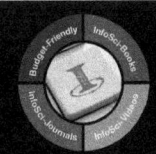

To Recommend or Request a Free Trial:
www.igi-global.com/infosci-books

eresources@igi-global.com • Toll Free: 1-866-342-6657 ext. 100 • Phone: 717-533-8845 x100

IGI Global
PUBLISHER of TIMELY KNOWLEDGE
www.igi-global.com

IGI Global
PUBLISHER of TIMELY KNOWLEDGE
www.igi-global.com

Publisher of Peer-Reviewed, Timely, and Innovative Academic Research Since 1988

IGI Global's Transformative Open Access (OA) Model:
How to Turn Your University Library's Database Acquisitions Into a Source of OA Funding

Well in advance of Plan S, IGI Global unveiled their OA Fee Waiver (Read & Publish) Initiative. Under this initiative, librarians who invest in IGI Global's InfoSci-Books and/or InfoSci-Journals databases will be able to subsidize their patrons' OA article processing charges (APCs) when their work is submitted and accepted (after the peer review process) into an IGI Global journal.

How Does it Work?

Step 1: Library Invests in the InfoSci-Databases: A library perpetually purchases or subscribes to the InfoSci-Books, InfoSci-Journals, or discipline/subject databases.

Step 2: IGI Global Matches the Library Investment with OA Subsidies Fund: IGI Global provides a fund to go towards subsidizing the OA APCs for the library's patrons.

Step 3: Patron of the Library is Accepted into IGI Global Journal (After Peer Review): When a patron's paper is accepted into an IGI Global journal, they option to have their paper published under a traditional publishing model or as OA.

Step 4: IGI Global Will Deduct APC Cost from OA Subsidies Fund: If the author decides to publish under OA, the OA APC fee will be deducted from the OA subsidies fund.

Step 5: Author's Work Becomes Freely Available: The patron's work will be freely available under CC BY copyright license, enabling them to share it freely with the academic community.

Note: This fund will be offered on an annual basis and will renew as the subscription is renewed for each year thereafter. IGI Global will manage the fund and award the APC waivers unless the librarian has a preference as to how the funds should be managed.

Hear From the Experts on This Initiative:

"I'm very happy to have been able to make one of my recent research contributions *freely available* along with having access to the *valuable resources* found within IGI Global's InfoSci-Journals database."

– **Prof. Stuart Palmer**, Deakin University, Australia

"Receiving the support from IGI Global's OA Fee Waiver Initiative *encourages me to continue my research work without any hesitation*."

– **Prof. Wenlong Liu**, College of Economics and Management at Nanjing University of Aeronautics & Astronautics, China

For More Information, Scan the QR Code or Contact: IGI Global's Digital Resources Team at eresources@igi-global.com.

Are You Ready to Publish Your Research?

IGI Global
PUBLISHER of TIMELY KNOWLEDGE

IGI Global offers book authorship and editorship opportunities across 11 subject areas, including business, computer science, education, science and engineering, social sciences, and more!

Benefits of Publishing with IGI Global:

- Free one-on-one editorial and promotional support.
- Expedited publishing timelines that can take your book from start to finish in less than one (1) year.
- Choose from a variety of formats, including: Edited and Authored References, Handbooks of Research, Encyclopedias, and Research Insights.
- Utilize IGI Global's eEditorial Discovery® submission system in support of conducting the submission and double-blind peer review process.
- IGI Global maintains a strict adherence to ethical practices due in part to our full membership with the Committee on Publication Ethics (COPE).
- Indexing potential in prestigious indices such as Scopus®, Web of Science™, PsycINFO®, and ERIC – Education Resources Information Center.
- Ability to connect your ORCID iD to your IGI Global publications.
- Earn honorariums and royalties on your full book publications as well as complimentary copies and exclusive discounts.

Join Your Colleagues from Prestigious Institutions, Including:

- Australian National University
- Massachusetts Institute of Technology
- Johns Hopkins University
- Tsinghua University
- Harvard University
- Columbia University in the City of New York

Learn More at: www.igi-global.com/publish
or Contact IGI Global's Aquisitions Team at: acquisition@igi-global.com

CPSIA information can be obtained
at www.ICGtesting.com
Printed in the USA
BVHW011824310821
615710BV00003B/132